LITERACY
IN GRADES 4-8
SECOND EDITION

Best Practices for a Comprehensive Program

Nancy Lee Cecil

CALIFORNIA STATE UNIVERSITY, SACRAMENTO

Joan P. Gipe

CALIFORNIA STATE UNIVERSITY, SACRAMENTO, EMERITUS
WALDEN UNIVERSITY, MINNEAPOLIS

Holcomb Hathaway, Publishers
Scottsdale, Arizona

Library of Congress Cataloging-in-Publication Data

Cecil, Nancy Lee.
  Literacy in grades 4-8 : best practices for a comprehensive program /
Nancy Lee Cecil, Joan P. Gipe. -- 2nd ed.
    p. cm.
  Rev. ed. of: Literacy in the intermediate grades. c2003.
  ISBN 978-1-890871-85-7
1. Reading (Elementary)   2. Reading (Middle school)   3. Literacy programs.
I. Gipe, Joan P.   II. Cecil, Nancy Lee. Literacy in the intermediate grades.
III. Title.   IV. Title: Literacy in grades four to eight.
  LB1573.C4334 2009
  372.4—dc22

                                                    2008018293

To my daughter, Chrissy—
my most powerful literacy teacher   —NC

To my new helper,
and reading dog, Cocoa   —JPG

Holcomb Hathaway, Publishers, Inc.
6207 North Cattletrack Rd.
Scottsdale, Arizona 85250
480-991-7881
www.hh-pub.com

10   9   8   7   6   5   4   3   2   1

ISBN 978-1-890871-85-7

Printed in the United States of America.

CONTENTS

Preface   *ix*
About the Authors   *xiv*

One

A COMPREHENSIVE LITERACY PROGRAM FOR GRADES 4–8   1

FOCUS QUESTIONS   1

IN THE CLASSROOM   3

WHAT IS LITERACY?   3

LITERACY INSTRUCTION AND THE CONSTRUCTIVIST MODEL   3

WHAT IS READING?   4

CHARACTERISTICS OF THE READING PROCESS   5

Reading Is a Holistic Process   5

Reading Is a Constructive Process   7

Reading Is a Strategic Process   7

Reading Is an Interactive Process   7

THE RELATIONSHIP OF READING TO THE LANGUAGE ARTS   7

Listening   8

Speaking   8

Writing   9

Viewing   10

Visually Representing   11

WHAT IS A BALANCED AND COMPREHENSIVE APPROACH TO LITERACY IN GRADES 4–8?   11

Teacher and Student Roles   12

Affective and Cognitive Components   14

A NATIONAL FOCUS ON LITERACY   19

CHARACTERISTICS OF LEARNERS IN GRADES 4–8   20

SUMMARY   21

QUESTIONS *for Journal Writing and Discussion*   *22*

SUGGESTIONS *for Projects and Field Activities*   *22*

References   *23*

Two

ASSESSMENT OF PROGRESS IN LITERACY   25

FOCUS QUESTIONS   25

IN THE CLASSROOM   27

CURRENT VIEWS OF ASSESSMENT   27

Defining Assessment   28

Standards and Assessment   28

PRINCIPLES OF ASSESSMENT   29

The Core of Assessment Should Be Daily Observation   29

Assessment Should Take Many Different Forms   30

Assessment Must Avoid Cultural Bias   30

Students Should Be Actively Engaged in the Assessment Process   30

Assessment Should Focus on Students' Abilities   30

ASSESSMENT OPTIONS   31

Standardized Testing   33

Curriculum-Based Assessment   35

Standards-Based Performance Assessment   35

Process-Oriented Assessment   38

STANDARDIZED, OR INDIRECT, ASSESSMENT PROCEDURES   39

Achievement Tests and Their Application by Teachers   39

Interpretation of Standardized Test Scores   39

INFORMAL, OR DIRECT, ASSESSMENT PROCEDURES   43

Informal Reading Inventory   43

Running Records   46

Anecdotal Notes   51

Checklists   52

Scoring Rubrics   54

Cloze Tests   55

Writing Folders   59

Word Lists   59

Interest and Attitude Inventories   61

USING PORTFOLIOS FOR MANAGING ASSESSMENT DATA   61

SUMMARY   63

QUESTIONS *for Journal Writing and Discussion*   64

SUGGESTIONS *for Projects and Field Activities*   65

References   66

Three

WORD STUDY AND FLUENCY   67

FOCUS QUESTIONS   67

IN THE CLASSROOM   69

DEFINING WORD STUDY   70

A REVIEW OF SPELLING AND READING STAGES   70

EARLY WORD STUDY INSTRUCTION   71

ADVANCED WORD STUDY INSTRUCTION   72

Syllabication   72

Morphology   73

ACTIVITY The Class Dictionary   75

Etymology   76

ADDITIONAL INSTRUCTIONAL PRACTICES FOR ADVANCED WORD STUDY   77

Word Walls   77

ACTIVITY Roots and Branches   78

ACTIVITY The Word Family Tree   79

Word Play/Word Formation   81

INCREASING FLUENCY   81

Skimming and Scanning   83

Readers Theatre   84

ACTIVITY Readers Theatre   84

Use of Phrase Markings   86

ACTIVITY Use of Phrase Markings to Increase Fluency   87

Fluency-Oriented Reading Instruction   87

ACTIVITY Using Fluency-Oriented Reading Instruction   88

Oral Recitation Lesson   88

ACTIVITY Initiating an Oral Recitation Lesson   89

TROUBLESHOOTING   89

No Decoding Strategy   90

Mispronounces Words   91

ACTIVITY Sylla-search   91

ACTIVITY CT-RA   92

SUMMARY   92

QUESTIONS *for Journal Writing and Discussion*   93

SUGGESTIONS *for Projects and Field Activities*   93

References   93

Four

VOCABULARY INSTRUCTION   95

FOCUS QUESTIONS   95

IN THE CLASSROOM   97

INTRODUCTION   97

TYPES OF VOCABULARY   98

SELECTING VOCABULARY WORDS TO TEACH   99

LEVELS OF WORD KNOWLEDGE   100

PRINCIPLES OF VOCABULARY INSTRUCTION   101

TEACHING INDIVIDUAL WORD MEANINGS   104

Incidental Learning   104

Explicit Instruction   105

EFFECTIVE STRATEGIES FOR A COMPREHENSIVE VOCABULARY PROGRAM   107

Relate New Words to Known Words   107

ACTIVITY Semantic Map   108

ACTIVITY Constructing and Using a Clarifying Table   110

ACTIVITY Creating a Semantic Feature Analysis   110

Use the Context   111

ACTIVITY C(2)QU   113

Consult Resources to Discover the Meaning of Words   114

ACTIVITY VIT Word Book   115

Learn to Determine the Meanings of Polysemantic Words   118

ACTIVITY How Is It Used?   118

ACTIVITY Possible Sentences   119

Infuse New Vocabulary into Writing and Speaking   120

ACTIVITY Camouflage   120

ACTIVITY Semantic Gradient   121

Commit to Learning New Words   122

ACTIVITY Hinky Pinkies   122

ACTIVITY Paraphrastics   123

TROUBLESHOOTING   124

Limited Interest/Experience in Independent Reading   124

Limited Schema for Remember New Vocabulary   126

ACTIVITY Virtual Field Trips   127

SUMMARY   128

QUESTIONS *for Journal Writing and Discussion*   *129*
SUGGESTIONS *for Projects and Field Activities*   *129*
References   130

Five

READING COMPREHENSION   133

FOCUS QUESTIONS   133

IN THE CLASSROOM   135

DEFINING COMPREHENSION   135

FACTORS AFFECTING READING COMPREHENSION   136

Factors External to Readers   136

Characteristics Within Readers   136

COMPREHENSION STRATEGIES FOR READERS TO USE   139

Predicting   139

Generating Questions   139

Checking Back   140

Imagery/Visualizing   140

Summarizing   140

EFFECTIVE DIRECT INSTRUCTIONAL PRACTICES   141

Collaborative Strategic Reading (CSR)   141

Think-Aloud   142

ACTIVITY Think-Aloud (FOCUS ON PROCESS)   **142**

Guided Reading   143

Directed Reading–Thinking Activity   144

ACTIVITY DRTA (FOCUS ON CONTENT AND PROCESS)   **144**

GIST   144

ACTIVITY GIST (FOCUS ON CONTENT)   **147**

Reciprocal Teaching   148

ACTIVITY Reciprocal Teaching (FOCUS ON CONTENT AND PROCESS)   **148**

Dyad Reading   149

ACTIVITY Dyad Reading (FOCUS ON CONTENT)   **149**

Question–Answer Relationships   149

ACTIVITY QAR (FOCUS ON CONTENT AND PROCESS)   **150**

Novel Study   151

IMPLICIT INSTRUCTION   154

Independent Reading   154

ACTIVITY Literature Circles/Book Clubs   **157**

ACTIVITY Jigsaw: Read a Book in an Hour   **160**

Reader Response Activities   161

ACTIVITY Sketch to Stretch   **164**

ACTIVITY Going Beyond Visualizing   **165**

READING COMPREHENSION AND THE INTERNET   167

TROUBLESHOOTING   169

Difficulty Making Connections During Prereading   169

Difficulty Making Connections During Reading   170

Difficulty Making Connections After Reading   172

SUMMARY   174

QUESTIONS *for Journal Writing and Discussion*   *174*

SUGGESTIONS *for Projects and Field Activities*   *174*

References   175

Six

READING AND WRITING CONNECTIONS   179

FOCUS QUESTIONS   179

IN THE CLASSROOM   181

HOW INSTRUCTION IN WRITING HAS CHANGED   181

THE WRITING PROCESS   182

Planning/Prewriting   183

Composing/Drafting   186

Revising   186

Editing   188

Publishing   189

WRITER'S WORKSHOP   189

Minilessons   189

State-of-the-Class Conference   190

Writing and Conferencing   190

Group Sharing   192

USING TECHNOLOGY IN CLASSROOM WRITING   192

TEACHING THE 6 + 1 TRAITS OF EFFECTIVE WRITING   193

Ideas   193

Organization   195

Voice   195

Word Choice   196

Sentence Fluency   197

Conventions   198

Presentation   199

FOSTERING WRITING FLUENCY   199

Speed   199

ACTIVITY Speed Writing   **199**

Automaticity   200

INSPIRING STUDENTS TO WRITE   201

Dialogue Journals   201

Extended Narrative Text   204

Poetry   206

ACTIVITY   Writing Poetry Using a Literacy
Scaffold   206

Informational Text   209

ACTIVITY   I-Search Process   210

TROUBLESHOOTING   212

No Confidence   213

No Ideas   213

Too Many Ideas   213

Unfamiliar Organizational Patterns   214

No Interest in Writing   215

SUMMARY   215

QUESTIONS   for Journal Writing and Discussion   216
SUGGESTIONS   for Projects and Field Activities   216
References   217

Organizational Techniques that Assist Expository
Writing   238

Scaffolds for Content Area Writing   240

ACTIVITY   Probable Passages   244

RESEARCHING IN THE CONTENT AREAS   246

Brainstorming   246

Locating Information   246

Online Search Skills   247

Data Charts   249

ACTIVITY   Internet Search   250

TROUBLESHOOTING   252

Lack of Familiarity with Expository Text Structures   253

ACTIVITY   Dictoglos   253

SUMMARY   254

QUESTIONS   for Journal Writing and Discussion   254
SUGGESTIONS   for Projects and Field Activities   255
References   255

Seven

LITERACY IN THE CONTENT AREAS:
LEARNING FROM INFORMATIONAL TEXT   219

FOCUS QUESTIONS   219

IN THE CLASSROOM   221

WHAT IS CONTENT AREA LITERACY?   221

LITERACY STANDARDS AND CONTENT AREA STANDARDS
OVERLAP   223

READING IN THE CONTENT AREAS   223

Content-Area Materials   224

ACTIVITY   The FLIP Strategy   224

Content-Area Strategies   227

ACTIVITY   Study Strategy Try-Out   230

ACTIVITY   Find Someone Who . . .   230

ACTIVITY   Important Words—The Top Five   232

WRITING IN THE CONTENT AREAS   232

Text-based Collaborative Learning   232

ACTIVITY   Text-Based Collaborative
Learning   232

Using Expository Text Structures   233

ACTIVITY   Read/Organize/Write (ROW)   233

Writing Summaries   233

ACTIVITY   Writing a Summary   234

Proposition/Support Writing   235

ACTIVITY   Proposition/Support Outline   236

Eight

FOSTERING ORAL LANGUAGE
IN THE CLASSROOM   257

FOCUS QUESTIONS   257

IN THE CLASSROOM   259

INTRODUCTION   260

INFORMAL SPEAKING   261

Conversations   261

ACTIVITY   Just Suppose   263

ACTIVITY   Campfire   263

Directed Group Discussions   263

Discussions About Literature   265

Informal Debates   266

FORMAL SPEAKING   267

Oral Reports   267

Interviews   268

ACTIVITY   Getting to Know You   270

Oral Histories   270

Panel Discussions   272

ACTIVITY   Controlled Participation (CONPAR)   272

Announcements   273

Impromptu Speeches   273

DRAMA   274

Role Plays   274

ACTIVITY Role Play   276

Simulations   278

ACTIVITY Haves and Have Nots   279

ACTIVITY Prejudice   280

Dramatic Productions   280

LISTENING INSTRUCTION   282

Designing Listening Instruction   282

ACTIVITY Listening Comprehension   284

TROUBLESHOOTING   285

Dominating a Discussion   285

Lack of Verbal Skills in English   285

Limited Knowledge of Academic Language   285

Lack of Participation   286

Limited Voice Projection   287

SUMMARY   287

QUESTIONS *for Journal Writing and Discussion*   *288*

SUGGESTIONS *for Projects and Field Activities*   *288*

References   289

Nine

DIFFERENTIATING INSTRUCTION FOR STUDENTS WITH SPECIAL NEEDS   291

FOCUS QUESTIONS   291

IN THE CLASSROOM   293

WHY DIFFERENTIATE INSTRUCTION?   293

DIVERSE LEARNER GROUPS   294

Students Who Are Linguistically Diverse (English Learners)   294

Students Who Are Gifted and Talented   299

Students Who Are Learning Disabled   301

Students Who Have Communication Disorders   304

Students Who Are Physically Challenged   306

Students Who Have Behavioral Disorders   307

THE CONCEPT OF DIFFERENTIATED INSTRUCTION   310

Planning and Implementing a Differentiated Lesson   312

Achieving Differentiation Through Tiered Activities   313

Sixth Grade Science: The Biosphere   313

SUMMARY   316

QUESTIONS *for Journal Writing and Discussion*   *317*

SUGGESTIONS *for Projects and Field Activities*   *317*

References   318

Ten

FOSTERING LITERACY BEYOND THE CLASSROOM   319

FOCUS QUESTIONS   319

IN THE CLASSROOM   321

EXPANDED GOALS FOR LITERACY INSTRUCTION   322

Developing Motivated Literacy Learners   323

Establishing Lifelong Literacy Habits   326

ACTIVITY Media Portrayals of People and Cultures   330

SERVICE LEARNING: TAKING LITERACY BEYOND THE CLASSROOM   333

REAL-WORLD CLASSROOM ACTIVITIES   335

ACTIVITY Bike Repair   335

ACTIVITY Job Market   335

ACTIVITY Developing Discriminating Consumers of Mass Media   336

ACTIVITY Reading Can Save You Money   336

ACTIVITY The World When You Were Born   337

GUIDELINES FOR CREATING AUTHENTIC LEARNING EXPERIENCES   338

INTO THE REAL WORLD: INFORMATION LITERACY   340

SUMMARY   342

QUESTIONS *for Journal Writing and Discussion*   *342*

SUGGESTIONS *for Projects and Field Activities*   *342*

References   343

Eleven

CONNECTING PARENTS, TEACHERS, AND STUDENTS   345

FOCUS QUESTIONS   345

IN THE CLASSROOM   347

LITERACY GROWTH AT HOME   347

UNDERSTANDING DIFFERENCES IN HOME PRACTICES   348

COMMUNICATING WITH PARENTS   351

What Parents Should Know About Literacy in Grades 4–8   351

Parent/Teacher Conferences   352

Helping Parents Help Their Children   354

Other Communication with Parents   356

WHAT IS FAMILY LITERACY?   356

Family Literacy Programs   357

TROUBLESHOOTING   359

Interfering Work Schedules   359

Reluctance to Attend School Functions   359

Lack of a Common Language   360

SUMMARY   360

QUESTIONS *for Journal Writing and Discussion*   *361*
SUGGESTIONS *for Projects and Field Activities*   *361*
References   *361*

Twelve

LITERACY IN GRADES 4–8: ORCHESTRATING A BALANCED AND COMPREHENSIVE PROGRAM   363

FOCUS QUESTIONS   363

IN THE CLASSROOM   365

INTRODUCTION   365

A CLASSROOM CLIMATE CONDUCIVE TO LITERACY   367

Setting Objectives   367

Providing for Differentiated Instruction   368

Implementing Powerful Activities and Assignments   369

Teaching for Depth and Connections   369

ORGANIZING THE CLASSROOM FOR INSTRUCTION   370

Materials and Equipment   370

Centers   371

DEVELOPING AN INSTRUCTIONAL PLAN   372

9:00-9:30 Journal Writing/Silent Reading/
Computer Buddies   374

9:30-10:15 DRTA   374

10:15-11:15 Language Arts/Social Studies/
Writer's Workshop   374

11:15-12:00 Math   375

12:00-12:40 Lunch and Recess   375

12:40-1:20 Library/Physical Education   375

1:20-2:30 Integrated Curriculum Block   375

2:30-2:45 Homeroom/Debriefing Session   376

SUMMARY   376

QUESTIONS *for Journal Writing and Discussion*   *377*
SUGGESTIONS *for Projects and Field Activities*   *377*
References   *378*

Appendices

A   **CHILDREN'S AND ADOLESCENT LITERATURE REFERENCES**   379

B   **LITERACY WEBSITES**   383

C   **COMMERCIAL ASSESSMENT TOOLS**   385

D   **INFORMAL CHECKLISTS AND ASSESSMENT DEVICES**   387

E   **FRY READABILITY GRAPH**   419

F   **WORD LISTS**   421

G   **A TYPICAL WEEK'S WORD STUDY PLAN**   423

Glossary   *425*
Author Index   *435*
Subject Index   *438*

Intermediate- and middle-grade teachers in today's schools face many critical issues. Among the most pressing are the following: What strategies should teachers use to help all of their students make sense of printed text? How do teachers help all students become capable, fluent readers who choose to read—and read often—far beyond the classroom doors? What practices and instructional materials has research found to be the most effective? How can assessment inform instruction? In what ways do family and community influence a student's success in reading? And how can state and district standards be used as a road map to guide effective instruction?

The need for answers to such questions resulted in the writing of *Literacy in Grades 4–8: Best Practices for a Comprehensive Program.* Clearly, the answers to these and similar questions profoundly affect what teachers do in the classroom. For example, if research findings, coupled with objective observations, identify certain strategies or materials as significantly more effective than others, teachers can make more intelligent decisions about day-to-day classroom activities. They are better able to distinguish potentially effective practices from professional folklore, yesterday's hit-or-miss traditions, and unexamined opinions about "what works."

Our challenge in writing *Literacy in Grades 4–8* was to show preservice and practicing teachers how to teach the language arts in a skillful yet motivational way; how to create a classroom climate where the joy of language, literacy, and learning thrives; and most important, how to inspire the heterogeneous garden of learners in today's grades 4–8 classrooms to want to engage in literate behaviors, while believing they can.

Because of the extent of recent media coverage, it is probably clear to all that literacy instruction has been undergoing major changes and shifts in emphasis. Our research and recent experiences in schools have confirmed that the change is as profound as it is reported to be. As educators, we ask ourselves this question: Is this dramatic shift in practice a positive spiraling of knowledge or simply the educational pendulum swinging back yet again from opposite extremes, as many would have us believe?

If we behave as reflective professionals, then every time the model shifts, we learn much from where we have been. The most recent shift is a case in point. Many of the resultant instructional changes we see are causes for guarded optimism; in some classrooms, something akin to a literacy Renaissance is occurring. This positive turnabout has been spurred by a wealth of evidence from literacy and other educational researchers suggesting that a comprehensive and balanced, language-based, interactive program of direct instruction in the skills of literacy, combined with an abundant exposure to quality children's and young adult literature, create a program that has an extraordinary chance of developing learners who can read and write, and choose to do so. Instead of emphasizing bits and pieces of fragmented reading and writing skills, a comprehensive, balanced program focuses more on reading, writing, listening, speaking, viewing, visually representing, and thinking as interrelated communication processes—processes that are pivotal to all learning.

Readers of this book will be given strategies and procedures that suggest how to implement a balanced, comprehensive literacy program by integrating direct and indirect instruction in word study, vocabulary, comprehension strategies and speaking, listening, and writing skills within the context of rich and varied language arts experiences. *Literacy in Grades 4–8* addresses such issues as teaching to standards, differentiating instruction for readers of all levels, motivating students to want to read, using assessment to inform instruction, integrating technology, working with English learners and struggling readers, and connecting with parents.

The book presents many topics of particular interest to intermediate and middle grade teachers, including content area literacy, developing motivated, lifelong readers and writers, listening to learn, formal and informal speaking instruction, planning and implementing a differentiated lesson, and developing authentic learning experiences.

Countless programs, procedures, and strategies are available for literacy instruction in grades 4–8 today, and choosing among them can be challenging to the seasoned teacher and overwhelming to the beginning one. Therefore, we have selected prototypes that seem to represent the most effective practices according to current research and the reinforcing testimonies of a host of outstanding teachers who were observed and interviewed for the writing of this book.

The order of the chapters contained in this text represents only one possible approach to teaching this material—the final order of presentation will be determined by you as you teach your course. For example, we feel the placement of the assessment chapter early in the text supports efforts to differentiate instruction, as assessment needs to occur prior to effective planning for differentiation. We recognize, however, that others might prefer to teach assessment later in the term. Therefore, with the possible exception of Chapter 1, the order in which the chapters are studied can be determined by the unique needs of your students.

New to This Edition

We have added and expanded coverage of many topics. You will find:

- An expanded discussion of fluency to help teachers better understand this vital literacy skill and how to teach it while keeping comprehension as the main focus, and a new section on writing fluency

- A new section on academic language and how to promote it

- An expanded discussion of the relationship of reading to the other five language arts of writing, listening, speaking, viewing, and visually representing

- A new section on oral histories explored through the use of interviews and technology

- An expanded discussion of direct vocabulary instruction with information on how to select words to teach

- A new framework for identifying the focus of direct instructional practices for reading comprehension
- Updates to content area literacy instruction, including Internet search activities
- A new section on comprehension and the Internet, with expanded coverage of media literacy and how it relates to reading

Other highlights of this edition include:

- Coverage expanded to include students who are in the intermediate and middle grades, typically grades 4–8. (The first edition of this text focused on grades 3–6.)
- An updated classroom orchestration chapter featuring a middle school classroom that uses an innovative Integrated Curriculum Block program.
- Additional websites for all aspects of literacy instruction
- Enhanced resources for children's and adolescent literature to integrate into every aspect of literacy instruction

The Book's Special Features

Some of the special features of *Literacy in Grades 4–8* aid readers in understanding new concepts and vocabulary. Other features are designed to foster reflection and mastery of the material and to encourage readers to try out ideas in the classroom. The following features are particularly noteworthy:

- **Chapter Maps.** These graphic features provide a visual map of the chapter's content, allowing readers to anticipate and connect text discussions. See page 2 for an example of this feature.
- **In the Classroom.** Each chapter begins with a vignette in which readers observe an authentic classroom setting and see how a practicing teacher deals with the subject addressed in the chapter. These small glimpses of literacy instruction build vicarious background and trigger readers' prior knowledge about the chapter's topic. Throughout the chapter and in some of the activities we refer to the vignette, helping readers make the connection between new concepts and classroom instruction. (See page 3 for an example of this feature.)
- **Activities.** More than 50 activities designed for use in classrooms are included in selected chapters. These specific, step-by-step procedures allow readers to put into practice in their field placement, practicum, or school the ideas and strategies they encounter in the chapter.
- **Concept Guides.** To help readers follow extended discussions of a topic, we've used special numbered headings that correspond to an introductory list; thus, readers will know, for example, when they've reached item 2 of 4 total discussion points. See page 5 for an example of this feature.
- **Questions for Journal Writing and Discussion.** Questions at the end of each chapter help readers reflect on and internalize key ideas. These questions are suitable for response in journal form or for stimulating lively discussion.
- **Suggestions for Projects and Field-Based Activities.** This special section makes the connection from research and theory to real classroom practice.

At the end of each chapter, readers find several suggestions for surveying, interviewing, or observing local teachers to compare strategies presented in the chapter with actual practice. Other activities ask readers to try out a strategy or activity in the chapter with a small group of learners.

- **Troubleshooting sections.** Many chapters end with a brief section intended to help teachers consider alternative suggestions and activities appropriate for students for whom the literacy focus discussed in the chapter is a particular challenge. Ideas for corrective instruction are offered.

- **Chapter on literacy and the family.** Understanding the vast array of literacy practices in students' homes can lead to a partnership between home and school that will greatly enhance the literacy program at school. In exploring this connection, we look at the best ways to communicate with diverse families and foster their active involvement in helping their children become truly literate beings.

- **Glossary.** An extensive book-end glossary is included, allowing readers to review critical terms and concepts highlighted throughout the text.

- **Appendices.** Book appendices include references for children's and adolescent literature; current websites for literacy suitable for teachers, parents, or students; a variety of literacy checklists and assessment tools for classroom use; and a list of widely used commercial evaluation instruments.

- **Student Website.** This interactive, web-based student resource (http://Lit4-8.hh-pub.com) and study guide includes chapter objectives, key concepts, questions and projects, relevant websites, teaching activities, and classroom videos with discussion questions.

- **Ancillaries.** A PowerPoint presentation and Instructor's Manual are available to adopters of this text. The Instructor's Manual provides several valuable tools for each chapter: a summary of key concepts, a list of key vocabulary, suggestions for in-class discussions and activities, and a range of assessment devices, including objective and subjective questions.

Our goal is to offer a text that facilitates the development of reflective teachers who are empowered to think through the miasma of political debates that often focus solely on simplistic answers to the complicated task of teaching students to become literate. This text provides readers with the most consistent research of the last 30 years and translates it into practice. We present evidenced-based perspectives in literacy education, describe a comprehensive range of instructional practices, and show preservice and practicing teachers how to select practices that conform to the individual needs of their students. A caring teacher, armed with the knowledge of how to carry out the most effective practices in literacy, is what is most needed to develop eager and proficient young readers and writers.

Note: We have made every effort to verify the website addresses that appear in this book. Such information changes frequently, however, so readers are likely to encounter some URLs that are no longer active. We regret any inconvenience this may cause.

ACKNOWLEDGMENTS

We wish to extend sincere thanks to the reviewers of our manuscript in its various stages. Their comments were insightful and helpful, and the book is better as a result of their efforts. They include: Patricia Becker, University of Texas at El Paso; Susan K. Bischel, University of San Francisco; Laurel Borgia, Western Illinois University; Jeanne Clidas, Roberts Wesleyan University; Betty J. Conway, Baylor University; Angela M. Ferree, Western Illinois University; Paige Furgerson, Texas Tech University; Sandra Gallagher, Ashland University; Donna Copsey Haydey, University of Winnipeg; Christina J. Keck, University of Findley; Leah Kinniburgh, Lynn University; Meryl K. Lazar, University of Pittsburgh; Claudia M. McVicker, Southern Illinois University; Alana Mosley, Franklin Pierce College; Edwardsville; Maryann Mraz, University of North Carolina, Charlotte; Pat Sharp, Baylor University; Carol Talbot, Marymount University; Sandra White, Mary Washington College; Kathleen Shoop, University of Pittsburgh; Susan Wiosinski, Canisius College; Janet Young, Brigham Young University; and Martha E. Zacharias, University of Alberta.

Special thanks to Colette Kelly and Gay Pauley of Holcomb Hathaway for their expertise, gentle pushing, and careful attention to detail. These two women are a delight to work with. Thanks, too, to Sally Scott of Holcomb Hathaway for her work in constructing the PowerPoint presentation for this book, and to John and Rhonda Wincek, who designed and typeset the book.

Finally, hugs and high fives to our husbands, Gary and Charlie, who were ever patient and supportive as we took precious time away from family life to bring this book to fruition. Heartfelt thanks to you both.

Dr. Nancy Lee Cecil has had a rich and varied background in education, as an elementary school teacher and a literacy specialist in New York, urban Savannah, Georgia, and in the public schools in the U.S. Virgin Islands. She is especially attuned to the needs of linguistically and culturally diverse children.

Dr. Cecil received her doctorate from the University of Buffalo and currently teaches in the Department of Teacher Education at California State University in Sacramento, where she recently won the prestigious Outstanding Educator Award. She has written seventeen books on literacy, most recently *Focus on Fluency: A Meaning-based Approach,* and received the Teacher's Choice award for an earlier book, *For the Love of Language: Poetry for All Learners.* Dr. Cecil has published articles in many literacy journals, including *The Reading Teacher.* She often speaks about literacy to groups of educators on the local, national, and international levels. She lives with her husband, Gary, in Carmichael, California with two cats and a dog, where she enjoys reading, traveling, hiking, and is involved in the issues of foster care youth.

Dr. Joan P. Gipe has spent many years working with learners of all ages, as a reading specialist in Kentucky, a grade 5 teacher in Indiana, a supervisor in a university reading clinic, and instructor for undergraduate, graduate, and doctoral students in several university contexts. She has also been a supervisor of student teachers, coordinator for teaching enhancement, university liaison for professional development schools, and department chairperson of Curriculum and Instruction.

Dr. Gipe received her doctorate from Purdue University in West Lafayette, Indiana, as well as a Distinguished Education Alumna Award. She is Research Professor Emeritus from the University of New Orleans, Department of Curriculum and Instruction, where she was a recipient of several teaching awards and a Career Service Award. She is also Lecturer Emeritus from the Department of Teacher Education at California State University in Sacramento, and is currently engaged in online mentoring of doctoral students for Walden University's Ed. D. Program in Teacher Leadership. Her textbook, *Multiple Paths to Literacy: Assessment and Differentiated Instruction for Diverse Learners, K-12,* is in its seventh edition. Dr. Gipe has published articles in many literacy journals, including *Reading Research Quarterly* and *Journal of Adolescent and Adult Literacy.* She lives in Healdsburg, California with her husband, Charlie, where she enjoys romping with her dog, Cocoa.

A Comprehensive Literacy Program for Grades 4–8

CHAPTER One

- What is literacy?
- What are the major characteristics of the reading process?
- What are the major building blocks for development of literacy knowledge and enjoyment in grades 4–8?
- How does a balanced and comprehensive literacy program for grades 4–8 differ from a more traditional program?
- What are some of the characteristics of learners in grades 4–8?

COMPREHENSIVE LITERACY PROGRAM FOR GRADES 4-8

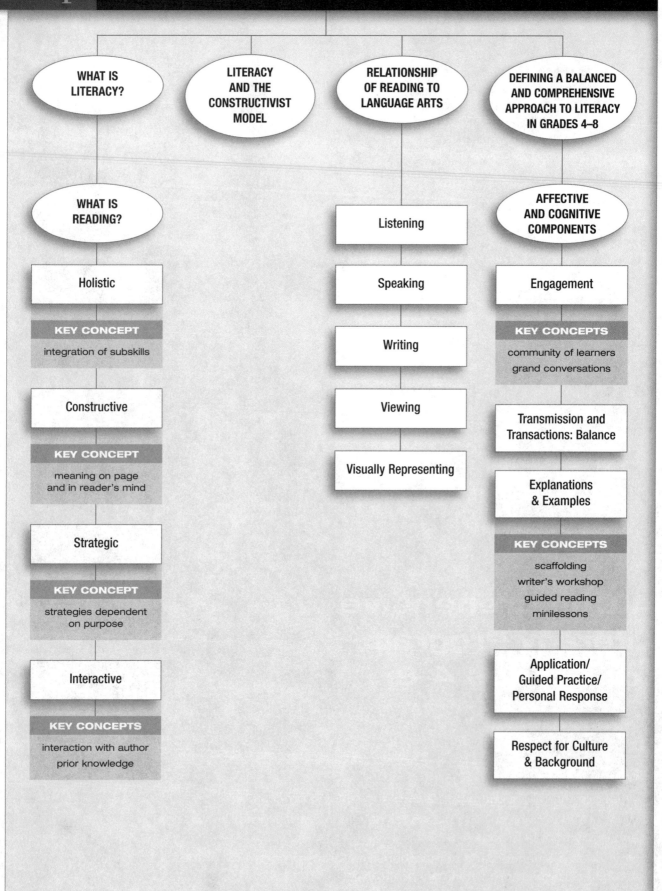

WHAT IS LITERACY?

LITERACY AND THE CONSTRUCTIVIST MODEL

RELATIONSHIP OF READING TO LANGUAGE ARTS

DEFINING A BALANCED AND COMPREHENSIVE APPROACH TO LITERACY IN GRADES 4–8

WHAT IS READING?

Listening

AFFECTIVE AND COGNITIVE COMPONENTS

Holistic

KEY CONCEPT

integration of subskills

Speaking

Engagement

KEY CONCEPTS

community of learners
grand conversations

Constructive

KEY CONCEPT

meaning on page and in reader's mind

Writing

Transmission and Transactions: Balance

Viewing

Explanations & Examples

Strategic

KEY CONCEPT

strategies dependent on purpose

Visually Representing

KEY CONCEPTS

scaffolding
writer's workshop
guided reading
minilessons

Interactive

KEY CONCEPTS

interaction with author
prior knowledge

Application/ Guided Practice/ Personal Response

Respect for Culture & Background

Mr. Piper's fifth-grade class is learning about the desert. He uses a globe to show his students the many deserts that exist in diverse parts of the world. He then asks them to share what they already know about deserts. He writes their answers on the board under a column labeled "What We Know." Next, Mr. Piper asks them to think about anything they would like to know about the desert and desert life. Students respond enthusiastically and he writes their questions, such as "Does it ever get cold there?" and "Do they ever run out of water?" on the board under a column labeled "What We Want to Know."

Mr. Piper then invites the students to close their eyes as he takes them on a guided imagery of a trek across the arid desert of Israel's Negev region in the blazing noonday heat. They ride camels for several long, uncomfortable miles and finally stop to rest when the stubborn animals will go no farther. They encounter an angry scorpion behind a bush and, as the sun is at its brightest in the cloudless blue sky, they realize (oh no!) that their water canteens . . . are empty.

As they open their eyes, the teacher tells the students they will be reading a true story about a 10-year-old boy who gets lost in the harsh desert and must save himself from dehydration by drinking the juice of a giant cactus. He asks them to read silently, and to be thinking about what they would do in the same situation. After everyone has finished reading, a lively discussion ensues, inspired by Mr. Piper's provocative question, "What would you have done to survive if you had been lost in the desert?" Mr. Piper waits until all the students have had a chance to respond to this question in their journals, and then he calls on them, one at a time, until all who wish to respond have had a chance. All answers are validated and written on the board. Later, in writers workshop, the students, divided into small groups, create their own desert survivor manuals using information gleaned from the Internet. Finally, the students revisit the chart on the board and share all that they have learned about desert life, while Mr. Piper records their responses under a column labeled "What We Learned." Any answers not revealed in the reading of the passage lead to a discussion of where answers can be found and, ultimately, self-directed research using the Internet and media center resources.

WHAT IS LITERACY?

Literacy is not something we do in school during English, reading, or language arts class. The term *literacy* has come to describe competence in a special field, such as computer literacy, and to include many types or multiple literacies, such as visual, media, cultural, emergent, family, and workplace, to name a few. While there can never be one definition of literacy that encompasses all that needs to be included in such a definition, the following description is useful to consider for this book. **Literacy** is a continuum of skills, including reading, writing, speaking, listening, viewing, visually representing, and critical thinking, applied in a social context to enable a person to function effectively in his or her group and community (Harris & Hodges, 1995).

● literacy

LITERACY INSTRUCTION AND THE CONSTRUCTIVIST MODEL

The definition of literacy instruction to be used in the remainder of this book draws upon research on the nature of literacy and literacy learning best understood through the ideas of Vygotsky. This forerunner of current understandings of students and how they learn to read and write defined *instruction* as "helping the student to become interested and involved in a meaningful activity, then providing the student with the support needed to complete the activity successfully" (Vygotsky, 1978, p. 68).

constructivist model
of learning ●

At the heart of the **constructivist model of learning** is the belief that students must actively build their own understandings of all literacy activities. Vygotsky further asserted that all learning is basically a social and psychological process that takes place through interactions between students and others in their environment. Over time, students begin to internalize the skills and knowledge acquired through these social interactions. Bauer (2003, p. 19) underscores the complexity of this task: "To tackle a course of reading successfully, we have to retrain our minds to grasp new ideas by first understanding them, then evaluating them, and finally forming our own opinions."

Teachers whose teaching proceeds from a constructivist model generally include many discussions of literature, either in small, teacher-led groups or in literature circles (see Chapter 5). While teachers generally help students to begin the group's meetings and may sometimes influence the course of the discussions, students are encouraged to share their own responses to the literature. Students often keep response journals in which they write their reactions to selections they have read. Finally, students may decide upon a multimedia project to share their reading with classmates, such as a PowerPoint presentation, a book poster, or a skit based on a scene from the story.

WHAT IS READING?

At first glance, it would hardly seem worth the trouble to answer the basic question, What is reading? because, in a sense, everybody knows perfectly well what it is: most people do it, in one form or another, every single day. But definitions underlie all intellectual endeavors. Definitions are assumptions that determine future educational activities. In other words, what teachers will do to teach reading will be determined, in large part, by what they believe reading is.

To define reading we must know exactly what is involved in this activity that sets it apart from other, similar activities. It is not enough, for example, to define reading as "a thought-getting process" because we can get thoughts just as easily from listening to a lecture or conversation, or from watching a film. There are, to put it another way, many similarities between reading a page of difficult text and hearing the same text read to us by another person. The problem of comprehension is paramount for both reader and listener.

No one would deny that a major purpose of reading is to get information or enjoyment of some sort from the printed page. But since we get information in the same way from spoken language, this purpose does not define reading in a way that distinguishes it from engaging in conversation. As soon as we understand this point, the problem of definition begins to resolve itself. If we see that meaning resides in the relationship between the language and the receiver, we might then ask how writing (which we read) is related to language (which we hear).

If language, which is composed of sounds, carries the meanings, then what is writing? Writing is a device, or a code, for representing the sounds of a language in a visual form. The written words of a language are, in fact, just symbols of the spoken words, which are sounds.

So reading, then, becomes the process of turning these printed symbols back into sounds again. The moment we say this, however, some reasonable soul is bound to ask, anxiously, But what about meaning? Can we propose to define reading as just deciphering the words without regard to the meaning?

The answer is yes, but only partly. **Reading** is, first of all, the mechanical skill of turning the printed symbols into the sounds of our language. Of course, the reason we turn the print into sound—in other words, the reason we *read*—is to get at the meaning. We decode the printed symbols to get what the author is attempting to *say* and then, more important, we make some meaning connection to the world as we know it (Pearson, 1993).

But there is even more to it than that. Reading entails both reconstructing an author's message and constructing one's own meaning using the print on the page as a stimulus. We can think of it as a transaction, or an exchange, among the reader, the text, and the purposes and context of the reading situation. A reader's reconstruction of the ideas and information intended by the author is somewhat like a listener's reconstruction of ideas from the combination of sounds the speaker makes. An artist creates a masterpiece that means one thing to him or her and a host of different things to different admirers of his or her piece. Likewise, the reader, like the listener, may create meanings that are different from those intended by the author. What readers understand from the reconstructed and constructed meanings depends on the readers' prior knowledge, prior experiences, and their maturity and proficiency in using language in differing social contexts.

CHARACTERISTICS OF THE READING PROCESS

A comprehensive approach to literacy instruction starts with the assumption that the purpose of reading is to create meaning from print. Early readers focus a great deal of attention on acquiring fluency as they learn to decode print, whereas more proficient decoders have more energy with which to address more subtle facets of critical reading and responding. In either case, the reading process consists of similar fundamental characteristics whether the reader in question has just recently learned to "crack the code" or is decoding fluently and "reading to learn."

The four essential underlying characteristics comprising the meaning-making process are the assumptions that

1. reading is a *holistic* process,
2. reading is a *constructive* process,
3. reading is a *strategic* process, and
4. reading is an *interactive* process.

The students in the opening classroom scenario were engaged in a literacy lesson that incorporated all these underlying characteristics.

In the following sections, we will explore these characteristics to provide a better understanding of the complex nature of the reading process (Hyde & Bizar, 1989).

1 READING IS A HOLISTIC PROCESS

The students in Mr. Piper's class were using reading as a *holistic* process: they put all their global decoding and comprehension skills together to think about the story. Observing such advanced readers as they read leads us to the realization that reading is not simply the sum total of the discrete skills that we have students practice in order to teach them how to read; rather, reading is a holistic process whereby the various subskills, such as decoding, finding the main idea, and using imagery, must be integrated to form a smooth, coherent whole (Baumann et al., 1998). The subskills, though crucial, must be applied to the act of reading by a competent reader who puts all the pieces together through constant practice. These subskills, and how they relate to each other, are outlined in Figure 1.1. As you can see from the figure, the subskills lead to recognizing and understanding words and ideas.

FIGURE   1.1   The reading subskills: an overview.

I. EMERGENT LITERACY FACTORS

Concepts about print (orthographic knowledge)

Experiential background

Language development

Visual acuity and discrimination

Auditory acuity and discrimination

Phonemic awareness

II. RECOGNIZING AND UNDERSTANDING WORDS

Sight Words

Word Study Skills

- Context clues
- Phonic analysis (single consonants, blends, vowels, digraphs, diphthongs, accents)
- Structural analysis (root words, inflectional endings, compound words, contractions, prefixes, suffixes, syllables, morphemes)

Vocabulary Development

- Context clues
- Multiple meanings
- Synonyms and antonyms
- Shades of meaning
- Word origins (etymology)

Dictionary Skills

- Locating words
- Using pronunciation key
- Finding appropriate definition

Oral Reading Skills

- Phrasing and punctuation
- Fluency (accuracy, rate, and expression)
- Pronunciation and enunciation
- Eye–voice span

III. RECOGNIZING AND UNDERSTANDING IDEAS

Comprehension Skills

- Receptive (nonoral) reading
  - Literal meanings (details, main ideas, sequence, directions)
  - Implied meanings (fact or fiction, characterization and setting, relationships, predicting outcomes, author's tone, mood and intent, comparisons and contrasts, conclusions and generalizations)
- Critical reading
  - Fact or opinion
  - Appraisal of author
  - Biased statements
  - Propaganda techniques
  - Cause and effect
  - Comparisons and contrasts
  - Figures of speech
  - Drawing conclusions
- Creative reading
  - Convergent (read to solve a problem)
  - Divergent (go beyond author to new ideas)

Study Skills

- Locating information
- Selecting and evaluating sources
- Organizing
- Interpreting maps, graphs, etc.
- Using SQ3R procedure

Rate of Comprehension Skills

- Flexibility
- Skimming
- Silent reading habits

② READING IS A CONSTRUCTIVE PROCESS

The students in Mr. Piper's class were seeing reading as a *constructive* process: they read to discover how the boy survived in the desert and compared it with what they might do under the same circumstances. As proficient readers engage in reading text while predicting what may happen next, meaning is constructed in their minds (Rumelhart, 1977; Stanovich, 1980). That meaning lies not only on the page, but it is also negotiated with the imagination and experience of the reader. Readers need to use what is already in their minds and combine it with what they find on the printed page in order to construct a meaning based upon a kind of reconciliation of these two sets of input.

③ READING IS A STRATEGIC PROCESS

The students in Mr. Piper's class were using reading as a *strategic* process: they used mental imagery to "see" the desert in their mind's eye. Proficient readers use different strategies depending upon the purpose for reading and the difficulty and genre of the material. The purpose for reading may be to determine who stole the wallet, to appreciate the beauty of certain images, to memorize a poem, or to put together a model airplane. Having in mind the exact purpose for which they are reading helps students to utilize the appropriate strategies for the nature of the literacy task at hand.

④ READING IS AN INTERACTIVE PROCESS

Finally, the students in Mr. Piper's class used reading as an *interactive* process: they compared their own knowledge of the desert with the new information provided by the author. We have come to think of reading as a process in which the reader must actually interact, or negotiate meaning, with the author and text in order for true comprehension to occur (Buehl, 2001; Rosenblatt, 1983). What the reader brings to the text in terms of prior knowledge of content, writing style, and vocabulary determines how well he or she will be able to derive a rich meaning from the text. We have all had the experience of reading something about which we had little or no background knowledge, or **schema**. When this happens, we soon realize that although we may know many of the words, we cannot make sense of the material. We do not have the background we need to construct a rich meaning to take away from reading.

● schema

THE RELATIONSHIP OF READING TO THE OTHER LANGUAGE ARTS

Literacy is more than just reading, for it encompasses all the various ways in which we can communicate. Learning to communicate through language is at the heart of how we relate to others and, therefore, who we are. We learn language naturally early in our lives by listening to and imitating the language of others and then, gradually, by using that language to express our needs and wants. Through constant modeling and feedback, family members, teachers, and caretakers help us understand how to interpret and construct language for our own purposes.

In the field of literacy we call the set of language processes that form literacy the *language arts*. The six language arts, as designated by the National Council of Teachers of English (NCTE) and the International Reading Association (IRA), are listening, speaking, reading, writing, viewing, and visually representing (*Standards for the English Language Arts*, 1996). The first

Reading entails both reconstructing an author's message and constructing one's own meaning.

four arts in the list have historically been considered the language arts, but the burgeoning Internet and other visual media have changed the way we obtain our information; hence, viewing and visually representing have come to be accepted as valid means of communication and comprise the last two entries in the list (Eagleton & Dobler, 2006). Three of the processes, speaking, writing, and visually representing, are ways of actively conveying information; reading, listening, and viewing, by contrast, are ways of receiving information (Roe & Ross, 2006).

Students do not develop their reading proficiency in isolation; they are busy developing all of the language skills needed to communicate simultaneously. Research and practical classroom experience indicate clearly how each of the language arts depends upon the others for successful communication. Let us now look at the importance of the other five language arts, which are reciprocal and supportive processes for reading development.

Listening

Listening has been called the "neglected" language art because it is so seldom taught in the literacy curriculum from kindergarten through middle school (Pinnell & Jaggar, 2003). We have all encountered children—and adults, for that matter—who having heard every word of a direction take no action, for the instructions have simply not registered in the person's mind. We also know how a simple fact can be distorted by a gossip. Good listening, therefore, consists of the ability to understand what is said: that is, to interpret the usage of words, phrases, and intonation so that both content and intent of what is related are appreciated. Listening ability is also important in learning to differentiate various speech sounds and to associate sounds and meaning with particular letter shapes and word forms. Listening helps the student relate the sound and the visual symbol by which it is represented in print; listening is, therefore, an aid to word recognition. It directs attention to words that have common sounds and helps students, especially those for whom English is a second language, to appreciate the unique cadences of the English language.

Listening is every bit as important to a successful discussion or conversation as is speaking, and though we want to encourage students to learn to speak freely, it is equally valuable that they be taught to listen carefully and critically. In their school career as a whole, students probably spend about 50 percent of their time simply listening; in their leisure time, this percentage is undoubtedly even greater, with the dominance of television. Concentration in listening is often enhanced when the content is accompanied by some type of visual presentation, so the use of visual media is reciprocal here. Moreover, highly developed listening comprehension skills, not surprisingly, are strongly correlated with increased reading comprehension skills (Pinnell & Jaggar, 2003).

Speaking

Speaking, or oral language facility, is directly related to the ability to read, for in oral language the symbols are spoken, while in reading the same symbols have been written. Reading instruction builds especially on oral language. If this foundation is weak, progress in reading can be slow and uncertain (Pinnell & Jaggar, 2003). Students must have at least a basic store of words, a reasonable knowledge about the world around them, and the ability to talk about their knowledge. These abilities form the basis for comprehending text. In addition to social or conversational language used at home or with friends, students learn more formal academic English, the language of instruction, at school. Academic language is also the language used on standardized assessments. Teachers are responsible for teaching academic English—the complex concepts, technical vocabulary and jargon, and sophisticated sentence structures for expressing abstract ideas—through literacy and content-area study. One way teachers do this is through talk. They move beyond asking literal questions to creating not only grand conversations that stimulate and support higher-level thinking about literature (see Chapter 8) but also instructional conversations that help in the study and analysis of content-area topics.

It is very difficult for students to be successful if they do not understand academic language. While all students need to learn academic language to be successful in school, it is especially challenging for students in the early stages of learning English. Lenders (2004/2005) reviewed the research associated with reading instruction for second-language learners and concluded that much attention must be put upon exposing students to oral language in a wide variety of contexts in order for them to reach the academic proficiency of their native English–speaking peers. Decreasing the achievement gap among ethnic, social, and linguistic groups has become a national concern, and an increased focus on speaking in the classroom is one way to address the problem.

Writing

The relationship between reading and writing, although highlighted in the past, has received much attention of late because of recent research (Farnan & Dahl, 2003; Wagner, 2003). Reading involves learning to communicate through written symbols using a background of experiences. Writing involves encoding those symbols in order to communicate ideas—based upon experience or research—to others. Another similarity between reading and writing is that they both require interpretation of meaning. Writing entails conveying messages to readers through the creation of text, while reading entails interpreting the meaning of text already formulated.

Writers participate in several reading activities. They read other authors' works for ideas and to learn about the structure of stories and informational pieces, but they also read and reread their own work to problem-solve and to discover, monitor, and clarify their thinking. Readers, too, are involved in many of the same activities that writers perform. In response to text, they generate ideas, organize their thoughts, problem-solve, and readjust their thinking as they encounter new information.

There are practical benefits to connecting reading and writing. Reading contributes to students' writing development, and writing contributes to students' reading development. Reading influences writing skills because readers unconsciously begin to "read like writers" (Gambrell, 2005). To read like a writer a student must engage with the author and what that author is thinking and feeling. A proficient reader anticipates what the author will say so that the author seems to be writing on the reader's behalf, not showing *how* it is done but doing it *with* the reader. Reading like a writer also involves an awareness of the writer's craft—a conscious or subconscious awareness of the author's decisions as a writer. Then, over time, a student learns, through reading like a writer, to write like a writer.

Viewing

visual literacy ●

Visual Literacy
http://academic.marist.edu/
pennings/vislit2.htm

viewing ●

Today's teachers need to recognize the importance of **visual literacy** for the children of the technology generation. Visual literacy involves being able to interpret the meaning of visual images as well as being able to construct effective visuals in order to convey ideas to others. The union of reading and technology on the Internet is causing educators to take a new look at what it means to be literate in today's world (Leu, 2002; Leu & Kinzer, 2000). These new forms of literacy call upon students to know how to read in both the print world *and* the digital world (Schmar-Dobler, 2003).

Viewing refers to the interpretation and analysis of visual media. These media include photographs, illustrations, graphs, maps, and diagrams found in books, as well as video presentations seen on television, CD-ROMs, DVD-ROMs, and Internet sites. Until recently, this skill was largely ignored. Students often were given textbooks and asked to read chapters without any real discussion of how to "read" the illustrations, diagrams, and so forth. Videos were shown without instruction explaining how to make inferences, evaluations, and creative responses that go beyond the material (Roe & Ross, 2006).

The computer, in particular, has become an integral tool in U.S. classrooms and culture (Gambrell, 2005), and visual media are suddenly in the forefront in students' lives. As the focus has shifted away from an almost exclusive use of story-type reading to more informational text delivered in a variety of ways for readers, there has been a decided change in the way most people in this country read and obtain their information.

Students today are inundated with visual media that are attempting to convey information to them, persuade them to do or believe something, or entertain them. An online publication entitled *A Nation Online: How Americans Are Expanding Their Use of the Internet* reported that 90 percent of school-aged children use computers (U. S. Department of Commerce, 2002), and virtually all schools now have Internet access. Students are using the Internet more than ever before as a source of information for their school reports. The messages received from all of these media must be comprehended using the same thinking processes used for comprehending printed material.

A survey entitled "Reading at Risk" decries a decline in the number of books that adults are reading in their leisure time (National Endowment for the Arts, 2004). According to this report, fewer than half the people surveyed reported that they read any literary works at all for pleasure in a year's time. Vogt (2004) implores teachers to think more broadly about the possible implications of the findings of this report. Does reading only entail reading so-called "great literature"? With personal computers in most homes, schools, and businesses, much time is now spent—by children and adults—viewing vast amounts of information on the Internet. Also, using the Internet and its inherent links often leads readers to read the original article they were seeking and then surf through related articles, blogs, chat responses, and so forth. Reading on the original topic, therefore, can be enhanced by the very nature of the Internet, exposing the reader to multiple versions, reactions to, and interpretations of the original article. It is quite possible that the Internet and its new literacy requirements may lead to a populace whose comprehension of any topic they are exploring becomes decidedly richer and deeper than it would have been without the Internet.

Visually Representing

Visual representing has recently become more prominent as the technological media have become more available for use by students. **Visually representing** refers to communicating through visual images that can be as varied as photographs, pictures, cartoons, drawings, video presentations, and other image types. Much as students become readers by writing, they become more astute at, and open to, viewing media critically if they have been given plenty of opportunities to enhance written reports and narratives by creating their own multimedia presentations.

● visually representing

The results of integrating visually representing into the language arts curriculum can be very powerful. As an example, Goetze and Walker (2004) invited at-risk intermediate-grade students to respond to narrative picture books with thought-provoking themes by creating Hyperstudio slides with original drawings and sentences explaining the main ideas or describing the main characters. They then used their slides to retell the stories and discuss the themes of the books they had read. They also used Inspiration software to create visual graphic organizers to show how the themes ran through all the books. They were able to use both words and graphics successfully to represent the similarities among the books. The researchers were amazed at how well these at-risk youngsters were able to tie their responses to the books together, demonstrating sophisticated intertextual understandings through the use of visual representations.

WHAT IS A BALANCED AND COMPREHENSIVE APPROACH TO LITERACY IN GRADES 4–8?

In the past few years, teachers of grades 4–8 have begun to reconcile their differences in terms of their perspectives on early literacy. Most teachers now agree that reading is a complex process incorporating the four characteristics (holistic, constructive, strategic, and interactive) discussed previously and evident in the opening scenario. Moreover, research has provided abundant support for the notion that a committed teacher who can integrate a program of explicit, systematic phonics instruction into a curriculum rich with quality literature, easily decodable text, and a variety of meaningful writing experiences will have the best chance of teaching students who will not only learn how to read but do so willingly—far beyond the classroom door (Larsen-Blair & Williams, 1999; Stahl, 1992).

Most reading educators have long agreed that a certain amount of direct instruction in phonics is vital in learning how to decode automatically, but most have also maintained a belief that incorporating the basic elements of a holistic, meaning-based program with such instruction will increase the instruction's positive influence on students' later attitudes toward reading as a chosen activity (Wink, 1996). To one degree or another, it seems, most competent teachers of literacy are now trying to incorporate the best of both perspectives in a balanced and comprehensive approach to teaching literacy. They are seeing results, too, measured by rising test scores and their own observations, which have been brought about by infusing many meaning-based strategies with a structured, skills-based program, or by supplementing a holistic, literature-based program with a systematic phonics program (Cecil, 2007).

Attention has begun to focus not only on early reading instruction, with its major focus on teaching students *how to read,* but on another, equally important phase: when readers have mastered the basic foundational skills of the reading act, they then need help learning *how to read to learn.* As students enter grades 4–8, when most are armed with a compendium of automatic decoding skills, they require a program of literacy that is both balanced in instruction and comprehensive in breadth.

Unfortunately, such a rich, comprehensive program often proves elusive. Dillon (2006) reports on a survey conducted by the Center on Education Policy that a majority of the nation's school districts have reduced the amount of time spent on the content areas to make more time for basic reading and math, thus narrowing the curriculum. Pearson (2006b) expresses a concern that reducing the amount of time spent reading in the content areas is harmful for reading proficiency. He offers that "Reading and writing must always be about something, and the something comes from subject matter pedagogy—not from more practice of reading skills. Reading skills are important, but without knowledge, they are pretty useless" (p. 22).

The Alliance for Excellent Education agrees, reporting in *Reading Today* (2005) that middle school youngsters need a "more balanced approach to literacy education that builds on what was taught in the earlier grades" (p. 23). Their report delineates the elements that must be contained in a comprehensive and exemplary literacy curriculum. Their suggestions are:

- direct, explicit comprehension instruction
- instructional principles embedded in content reading
- self-directed learning
- collaborative learning
- tutoring
- a rich diversity of texts
- much writing
- instruction in technology
- ongoing assessment
- a large block of time for reading

We would enlarge upon this list somewhat and suggest that a comprehensive program include:

- quality literature with personal response and analysis
- the use of multiple measures for assessment
- instruction in word identification and vocabulary strategies, such as the morphology and etymology of words
- instruction in reading comprehension strategies
- fostering of independent reading
- development of oral and written language and visual learning

Teacher and Student Roles

One basic difference between a balanced and comprehensive literacy program and a more traditional/skills-based view is the relative roles of the teacher and the students in such classrooms. In a balanced and comprehensive literacy program, the teacher's role is one of facilitator, offering students prompts and questions to focus their attention on strategies that will help them independently overcome challenges in present and future texts; in more traditional approaches, the teacher's role is directive, supplying short-term help by telling students exactly what to do as they need help. The aim of a balanced and comprehensive literacy program is to develop enthusiastic readers and writers who question, consider alternatives, and make informed choices as they seek meaning or to express meaning; the aim of the more traditional approach to literacy is often to draw students through a predetermined teaching sequence to ensure that all the basic skills of literacy are covered. Finally, as Figure 1.2 shows, a balanced, comprehensive literacy program is based on

Comparison of two approaches to teaching reading/literacy.   **FIGURE** **1.2**

BALANCED AND COMPREHENSIVE LITERACY PROGRAM	TRADITIONAL/SKILLS-BASED LITERACY PROGRAM
The teacher's role is to empower by providing instruction and questions that focus students' attention on: • strategies that will help them to decode and understand text; • becoming aware of textual cues that help students decode and comprehend. Readers are taught directly how to overcome challenges in present and future text.	The teacher's role is to supply short-term help by: • focusing students' attention on specific textual details; • explaining the meaning of a word if they don't know it; • explaining the meaning of text. Readers become dependent upon the teacher to tell them exactly what to do in each reading situation.
The goals of a balanced and comprehensive literacy program are to: • create independent readers who question, consider alternatives, and make informed inferences as they search for meaning; • entitle students to become independent problem solvers who can become long-term learners; • show students how and why to choose and employ strategies to ensure that meaning is gained and maintained; • use assessment to inform instruction.	The goals of a traditional, skills-based literacy program are to: • lead students through a predetermined teaching sequence using a specific book to teach a particular skill; • see that every student receives all the skills in a predetermined hierarchy, whether they are needed or not; • frequently administer formalized assessment devices that provide information about progress in the specific program.
A balanced and comprehensive literacy program is based upon the understanding that: • students are the readers; • students are the ones who must bring meaning to, and gain meaning from, the text they read. The teacher is aware of the constant need for comprehension to be considered as the act of the reader engaging with, and responding to, the text during reading.	A traditional, skills-based literacy program is based upon the understanding that: • connections between the reader and the author depend upon the teacher as interpreter; • the teacher is responsible for determining whether students understand. The teacher oversees comprehension for students and alerts them to mismatches between the errors and the text, hoping the students will use this behavior in the future.

the understanding that it is the students themselves who are the readers, and it is they who must bring meaning to and gain meaning from text as they read; in more traditional literacy programs the teacher more commonly adopts the role of interpreter, who makes the connections between the author and the readers and is responsible for checking that students have derived the correct meaning from text (Mooney, 1990).

Affective and Cognitive Components

A balanced and comprehensive literacy program in grades 4–8 also consists of five major affective and cognitive components. All of these components, offered separately, are crucial building blocks for literacy knowledge and enjoyment; when they come together as a whole entity, they are the essence of a strong literacy program for youngsters in grades 4–8. These five components are as follows:

1. engagement
2. transmission and transaction
3. explanations and examples
4. application, guided practice, and personal response
5. respect for each student's culture and background

1 ENGAGEMENT

That a student must be engaged in the subject to learn most effectively is not a new concept, nor one espoused only by literacy experts. Many years ago Jerome Bruner expounded on the importance of getting the student interested and involved in learning (Bruner, 1966), and a plethora of motivational educational programs and learning theories have emanated from his early postulations. Educators are now convinced that when students are highly engaged in what they are doing and their experiences are meaningful and purposeful to them, learning is optimal (Guthrie & Wigfield, 1997).

Engagement with reading material, in fact, may be considered the key to learning in a balanced and comprehensive literacy program; however, it often seems apparent that as students go through school, their motivation for school—and reading—too often decreases. The less they like to do it, the less they will do of it, and a downward cycle is set in motion. Practice in literacy, as in anything else, results in greater proficiency. And, indeed, how much students read is, in fact, one of the best predictors of how well they read and write. Therefore, if we want all our students to read and write as well as they possibly can, we must find ways to combat the problem of decreasing motivation leading to the inevitability of *aliteracy*—a state of being able to read but choosing not to—especially as students move into the middle grades (Cunningham & Allington, 1999).

engagement ● The answer to the question of engagement, however, lies not only in the method used, but also in the effectiveness and enthusiasm of the teacher. **Engagement** involves a complex set of ongoing attitudes and activities that occur in the classroom environment. These attitudes and activities lead to the creation of a community of learners, including the teacher, who is excited about all aspects of the literacy process. Such a teacher is thoughtfully eclectic, modifying methods and programs to fit the students' needs. Teachers with the ability to engage learners do not rely on a single method or program for all students in their charge, because they know that good teaching requires "doing the right thing the right way and at the right time in response to problems posed by particular [students] on particular occasions" (Garrison, 1997, p. 132; Nelson-Levitt, 2000).

The learning community conducive to engagement is an active, literate environment where reading, writing, speaking, listening, viewing, and visually representing are used as tools for almost all of the learning and problem solving that occurs in the classroom. Although the teacher thoughtfully creates the literacy curriculum to reflect the learners' needs and the dictates of the standards of the state in which they reside, there are also plenty of opportunities in such a program for students to choose their own reading materials and write connected text. In addition, students often collaborate as they work on reading and writing projects, and cooperative interactions among students are valued as critical to language learning and development, especially for English language learners (Slavin, 1989/1990).

Engagement also involves asking the kinds of questions that are provocative to students, or those that allow them to reflect on what they have read (Cecil, 1995). Such questions form the gateway to **grand conversations.** These kinds of open-ended questions and resultant discussions require students to come up with their own ideas about literature, as opposed to the more widespread "gentle inquisitions," which are mostly factually based questions used merely to determine whether students did, indeed, read the text and are able to recall verbatim the facts contained in it (Peterson & Eeds, 1990). To become proficient readers, students must be taught to solve problems actively with text; to respond to text critically and creatively in oral, visual, or written form; and to feel good about their ability to interact with the author's message (Tower, 2000). Such skills are acquired mainly through forming and responding to critical questions modeled by an effective teacher, or through grand conversations about text conducted by the teacher and, ideally, with their peers.

● grand conversations

② TRANSMISSION AND TRANSACTION

In grades 4–8, there must be a balance between the teacher directly imparting information through explicit instruction and systematic teaching—the **transmission model**—and a focus on negotiating with students about their individual thoughts and ideas about what they are reading and writing—the **transactional model** (Rosenblatt, 1978). A balanced and comprehensive approach to literacy uses both a transmission model and a transactional model at different times, for different purposes. These two models have similarities and differences in how they are used in the early grades. The latter approach is a more collaborative model that also integrates the four language modes of reading, writing, listening, and speaking and considers reading a transaction, or intellectual negotiation, between the reader and the author, where both parties bring their own experience to the text. In the transactional model, the teacher is not the only possessor of knowledge but takes on the role of facilitator in the literacy development process.

● transmission model

● transactional model

Using the transmission model in early literacy, the teacher assumes the responsibility of directly "transmitting" new information about letter sounds and symbols to students through explicit instruction and systematic teaching of the code that is the foundation of the English language. Other transmission responsibilities include rote instruction of **sight vocabulary,** or words immediately recognized, and the memorization of lists of **word families,** such as those

● sight vocabulary
● word families

words containing *oi*: voice, noise, moist, and so forth. By contrast, in the upper grades, when most decoding of new words has become automatic, the teacher must then show students how to gain information from text by explicit, systematic teaching of such comprehension strategies as summarizing, generalizing, using the context, making predictions, and visualizing (see Chapter 5). Additionally, the teacher must directly teach advanced decoding and morphological skills, such as the meaning and derivation of word parts, that can help students figure out the meanings of unknown words (see Chapters 3 and 4).

In a balanced and comprehensive approach to literacy in the primary grades, the process of transaction, or learning to negotiate meaning with the author of the text, begins in early literacy instruction even before children themselves are able to read. As they are sharing reading with a teacher, individual predictions and opinions are solicited, and children learn to bring their own set of experiences to all language-related situations. In grades 4–8, these negotiations are continued but refined, as students collaborate with the teacher and each other not only to think about the meaning of the text as the author intended it but also to consider how it appears to them, with all the personal experiences and background information that they now are able to bring to it.

③ EXPLANATIONS AND EXAMPLES

In a balanced and comprehensive literacy program in grades 4–8, students need to be explicitly taught how proficient readers construct text in order to comprehend written material. Explicit teaching still occurs at this level and involves making clear to learners what the particular skill is that they are learning, how they can best learn it, when and under what conditions to utilize the skill, and how they will know when they have been successful at employing it. They must be shown how effective comprehension strategies work, and then they must be given examples of how each strategy can help them as they read to make meaning from the written page. As basic a truth as this may appear to be, such explicit teaching has not always occurred in U.S. schools. Too often in classrooms, many students have been left alone to figure out how to go about understanding text and exactly what they have to do to become successful readers and writers (Hancock, 1999).

Delores Durkin, in a landmark study of comprehension instruction in American schools, found that little, if any, explanation of how to use comprehension strategies was offered in elementary schools; instead, much time was devoted to assessing how well students comprehended, using reams of basal workbook pages to do so (Durkin, 1990). In other words, students seem to have been expected to "intuit" comprehension strategies without anyone ever having taught them, directly, how to employ them! The results of this study caused a flurry of reform, dedicated to teaching comprehension strategies to students directly in a systematic, step-by-step fashion.

Lectures, definitions, general descriptions, and overviews rarely give students the complete raw material they need to construct meaning. Students deduction ● need both **deduction**—going from the general to the particular, through explainduction ● nation—and **induction**—going from the particular to the general, with the help of examples (Hyde & Bizar, 1989). Both explanations and examples are useful and necessary in a balanced and comprehensive literacy program to foster construction of text, and most teachers are now aware of the need to teach strategies directly to students. However, there is usually tremendous pressure on teachers to hurry through certain packaged literacy programs, perhaps causing teachers to provide to students minimal explanations of how, when, and under what conditions to use comprehension strategies and to offer few, if any, examples of what the strategies look like in actual practice. This time crunch is a significant hindrance to teaching students to construct text in a thoughtful way. Creating examples that will have meaning for students takes more time and effort than merely memorizing linear explanations of strategies. If a teacher does not take the time, students often lose a true grasp of the concepts behind the strategy. Additionally, students have fewer opportunities to think about and internalize such strategies.

Several examples of how comprehension strategies are used can be offered most effectively through teacher modeling, or **scaffolding,** as most human behaviors are acquired in this way (Bandura, 1986; Vygotsky, 1978) (see Chapter 5). Modeling, or showing students exactly how to perform a specific reading behavior, can be done at various times within a balanced and comprehensive literacy program. First, implicit—or indirect—modeling can occur many times during the day as students are engaged in reading and writing activities and the teacher takes the opportunity to share pertinent information. Second, modeling can occur during **writers workshop,** as the teacher directly demonstrates the various steps needed to publish a piece of written work. Third, using the vehicle of the **guided reading procedure,** the teacher has the opportunity to introduce literature, think aloud through a compendium of decoding and comprehension strategies, and demonstrate his own response to the text. Finally, **minilessons,** developed on the basis of the individual needs of students, are ideal opportunities for the teacher to model the exact literacy strategies that are needed for the literacy context (Cooper, 2000). All of these strategies will be discussed throughout the remaining chapters of this text.

- scaffolding
- writers workshop
- guided reading procedure
- minilessons

4 APPLICATION, GUIDED PRACTICE, AND PERSONAL RESPONSE

A review of the important research on successful literacy programs in the past few years offers teachers surprisingly consistent findings about what factors are critical in setting the stage for a successful balanced and comprehensive literacy program that enables students to construct meaning. Fielding and Pearson (1994), synthesizing the findings of research on reading comprehension, offer three critical findings to teachers. This important summary of research makes the following suggestions:

1. Teachers must provide a large block of time for application of newly acquired literacy skills. The amount of time devoted to actual reading and writing practice, according to Fielding and Pearson (1994), should be greater than the sum total of all specific skill instruction. In other words, after a skill or comprehension strategy has been introduced, there should be ample time immediately after these sessions for students to internalize their new understandings; the students should be actively adding them to their burgeoning literacy understandings through extensive teacher-guided practice. To ensure that such practice actually translates into enhanced comprehension, however, students should sometimes be given some choices about what they read. Additionally, the material used should be appropriate in difficulty, that is, not so difficult as to be frustrating, yet not so easy that nothing challenging is encountered.

2. Teachers must provide opportunities for students to practice literacy skills in a social setting. The absolutely quiet, teacher-directed classrooms, proudly heralded in some traditional schools, should be a thing of the past, according to these researchers—at least for certain times in the school day. Students, especially English learners, learn best when they are able to talk about what they are reading and writing. Besides enhancing their learning by adding sensory input and vocabulary development afforded by oral discussion, reading, when it becomes a social activity, is more enjoyable for most students. Therefore, in a balanced and comprehensive literacy program, a continuum of literacy instructional configurations should be offered in most classrooms. While **shared reading** and guided reading, where the teacher is prominent and working with small groups, are ideal formats for direct transmission of skills, other more collaborative approaches, such as **dyad reading** or simple **partner reading, literature response groups,** and **interest groups** should also be instituted (see Chapter 5 for discussion of these concepts).

shared reading ●
dyad reading ●
partner reading ●
literature response groups ●
interest groups ●

3. Teachers must ensure that students are given myriad opportunities to respond personally to text. To act on this suggestion, teachers must ensure that they do not limit themselves to factual-type questions that require only a monosyllabic answer. They must allow time for the type of critical and creative questions for which there is no one "correct" answer, and for which every student has an opportunity to voice an opinion emanating from her own life (e.g., "What would *you* have done if the boy treated you that way?"). It is also helpful for teachers to sometimes pose provocative questions about text for which they themselves do not have an answer, not seeking a response they have in mind or one provided by the basal teacher's manual. Moreover, in a truly balanced and comprehensive program for grades 4–8, adequate time should be set aside for sharing journal reactions to literature, or original writing, in small groups, where the climate is risk free and conducive to personal conversations about text.

Students in a balanced and comprehensive literacy program can also use modern technology to share their responses about books they are reading using electronic dialogues. Using a computer, students can write their thoughts and feelings about books and e-mail them to students reading the same material in other classrooms, older students in the same school, or even preservice education students at a university. The "computer pal," if chosen wisely, can encourage students to elaborate on their entries, make personal connections with text, and reflect more deeply on their reading (Moore, 1991).

 RESPECT FOR EACH STUDENT'S CULTURE AND BACKGROUND

Finally, perhaps the most pressing issue in a balanced and comprehensive approach to literacy in grades 4–8 is for each teacher to possess a deep sensitivity and appreciation for learners of all diverse backgrounds. Diversity must never be merely tolerated, but must be actively celebrated by the teacher as well as the students. We simply cannot hope to be successful with all learners in today's heterogeneous classrooms without first understanding each student's reasons for becoming literate. Without that knowledge, we may fail in our attempts to fully engage the learner as an equal partner in his own pursuit of knowledge. As teachers, we must somehow lead students to fall in love with books and, as Lucy Calkins (1994, p. 111) suggests, we must get them to "write from the heart about their own unique experiences with the world." Then they will be able to see the purpose of concomitant skill instruction and, consequently, become actual co-conspirators in the quest for literacy.

Instruction in literacy for students in grades 4–8, in order to be successful, must take into account each student's culture and understand each student's particular way of learning. All human beings learn according to their existing understandings and cultural backgrounds in socially constructed settings, particularly through conversations with family and loved ones. Therefore, any instructional plans in literacy must be developed with great care, using observation, home visits, and formal and informal assessment, along with all other available background information about each student's language, culture, values, knowledge, and interests.

A NATIONAL FOCUS ON LITERACY

This is an exciting time to be a teacher of literacy. We now have more conclusive evidence about what can be considered "effective literacy instruction" than at any other time in history (Block, 2004). Within the past decade, national panels in the United States have completed a greater number of reports about best practices in reading than have been produced in any prior decade (National Institute of Child Health and Human Development, 2000a, 2000b; Sweet & Snow, 2002).

All educators of grades 4–8 have known that the teaching of literacy is one of the most important tasks—if not *the* most important task—that every teacher faces. For years teachers often taught literacy using mainly the instructor's manual of the basal reader but always seeking ways to reach every student, to find out what would work best. They often supplemented the literacy curriculum with activities taken from *Instructor* magazine or with ideas borrowed from other teachers or gleaned from a summer workshop, trying every new commercial program that promised to make all students successful readers (Kronowitz, 2008).

Instruction in literacy must take into account each student's culture and particular way of learning.

Now, literacy is very much on the minds of politicians, the public, and the media. U.S. teachers have witnessed unprecedented political insistence on the use of research-based, scientifically proven assessments and instructional techniques (Invernezzi et al., 2005). Science offers compelling reasons explaining why so many students have failed to read using traditional reading methods. The National Institute of Child Health and Development (NICHD) has studied normal reading development and reading difficulties in children for 35 years. NICHD-supported researchers have studied more than 10,000 children, published more than 2,500 articles, and written more than 50 books that present the results of 20 large-scale longitudinal studies and more than 1,500 smaller-scale experimental and cross-sectional studies. Some children were studied for 15 years, others for at least five years (Fletcher & Lyon, 2002).

In 2000, the National Reading Panel (NRP) added yet another scientific voice to the discussion. They issued a report in response to a congressional mandate to help parents, teachers, and policy-makers identify key skills and methods critical to reading achievement. NRP was charged with reviewing research in reading instruction, such as the research just described. A carefully developed screening procedure was designed to bring balance to a field in which decisions about literacy instruction were, in the past, often made on the basis of ideology (or even intuition) rather than on any clear evidence. In addition to discovering effective practices, the panel identified five areas essential to reading success: phonemic awareness, phonics, fluency, vocabulary, and comprehension.

Influenced by NRP's report, the No Child Left Behind (NCLB) Act of 2001 mandated higher standards and greater accountability throughout the nation's school systems. The bill also contained a program called Reading First, designed to help every child become a successful reader.

The report of the National Reading Panel and resultant legislation have changed the way teachers regard instruction. A more informed profession now demands materials that are based upon sound scientific evidence. This can only be good; however, other aspects of literacy besides the five skills identified by the NRP are also important. These aspects provide richness and motivation in students and create a broad-based literacy program that ensures that students learn to read, read to learn, and enjoy the process. This text takes a wider focus, providing the reader with the tools for what can be called a balanced, comprehensive approach to literacy.

CHARACTERISTICS OF LEARNERS IN GRADES 4–8

Teaching literacy in grades 4–8 offers a wide range of exciting instructional possibilities, as well as the academic satisfaction that comes from sharing the spectrum of literacy activities with a community of young learners who have curious, challenging, and highly creative minds. Also, students in this age group often possess a fascinating combination of tremendous amounts of enthusiasm and an increased ability to examine ideas critically. Both the challenges and the rewards of teaching students in this age group are, arguably, greater than for any other (Atwell, 1987).

Ages 9 to 14, the traditional age span of students in grades 4–8, are times of major transitions. Students in the turbulent period of pre- and early adolescence universally experience challenging physical, intellectual, and emotional characteristics. These characteristics are critical for teachers to consider, as they have a direct bearing on the responses of students in this age group to the literacy curriculum.

Students in this age group can manifest pronounced behavior that often baffles new teachers. Their attitudes and behavior can change from one moment to the next, seemingly without a reason. The unexpected becomes the norm. A student who one day exhibits all the traits of an extremely engaged reader and writer may the next day be difficult and unresponsive. This inconsistent behavior in pre- and early adolescence is due in part to the tremendous physical and hormonal changes taking place at a rapid and irregular pace. During these years physical maturity is reached—and seemingly at an increasingly earlier age.

Literacy teachers of students in this age range learn to build a degree of flexibility into their programs and lessons to capitalize on students' boundless energy and to accommodate the shifting patterns of their youthful behavior. Any successful intermediate and middle school literacy curriculum must consider the unique attributes of students of this age. Goals and objectives may be accomplished through a variety of literacy activities and experiences that can become helpful outlets for the students' volatile—and confusing—feelings. Writing, speaking, creating presentations, reading informational texts and fiction about matters that interest them, and researching and learning interactively on the Internet, among other literacy forums, can provide outlets for students' energies, as long as students are given choices and opportunities to use their burgeoning social skills to collaborate with their peers. Finally, although students of all ages need verbal reinforcement and praise to develop positive self-perceptions and the confidence to attempt new challenges, it is especially true of students in grades 4–8. The ultimate goal for literacy teachers is to help these students become consumers and producers of all facets of literacy.

SUMMARY

The past decade has seen a major emphasis on creating a balanced and comprehensive literacy program designed to teach young children how to read. Now, the focus is also on older students, most of whom have mastered the early skills necessary for automatic decoding and are now ready to turn their attention to reading to learn. For either developmental level, the fundamental characteristics of the process are basically the same. Reading is a holistic process, not just a sum of all its parts. It is a constructive process whereby the reader predicts the meaning. Additionally, reading is a strategic process, in which the reader must choose which strategies in her repertoire are appropriate to the task. Reading is also an interactive process, with the reader and the author together negotiating the meaning of the text.

A balanced and comprehensive approach parts company from a more traditional approach to literacy mainly in its view of who holds responsibility for meaning-making from text. In a balanced and comprehensive approach, the teacher accepts the role of facilitator—prompting, advising, questioning, and providing direct instruction on reading strategies, yet allowing students the freedom to interpret text according to their own experiences.

A balanced and comprehensive approach to literacy in grades 4–8 differs from a similar approach used for early readers in that the focus is now less on decoding and more on making sense of the world through print. Many of the underlying beliefs remain the same, but the focus shifts slightly in subtle ways. While there must continue to be a transmission of strategies—in this case more related to comprehension than decoding—there must also be an emphasis on transaction, or a personal meaning-making with text. In addition, engagement is crucial in grades 4–8 to ensure that students, now able to read, do so willingly as a chosen recreational activity. Clear explanations and examples are critical in these grades to make sure students know exactly how to apply the comprehension strategies that proficient readers use. Abundant guided practice and opportunities to apply the skills that have been taught will help to solidify understandings and increase students' confidence as well as enjoyment. Whole texts and authentic literature, both fiction and nonfiction, can be utilized for these purposes. Finally, a clear respect and appreciation for the culture and background of each learner will enable the teacher to understand what each learner needs to become a literate individual.

In the following chapters we explore the specific components needed in a balanced and comprehensive literacy program for grades 4–8 that will help to develop readers and writers who have the tools to read, write, and incorporate technology—and joyfully do so—to explore their worlds.

Questions
FOR JOURNAL WRITING AND DISCUSSION

1. Reflect upon your own experience with reading and writing in grades 4–8. Do you believe you received a balanced and comprehensive or a more traditional model of instruction? Give examples. In retrospect, can you think of any measures your teachers might have employed to make your literacy instruction more meaningful?

2. Think about your own definition of what it means to be a literate person. How do you think your definition will influence how you teach reading, writing, listening, speaking, viewing, and visually representing?

3. Discuss with a classmate what you consider to be the three most striking differences between literacy instruction today and literacy instruction in the recent past. What do you think caused these changes?

Suggestions
FOR PROJECTS AND FIELD ACTIVITIES

1. Make notes while observing a literacy lesson in a grade 4–8 classroom. Analyze the lesson in terms of the components of a balanced and comprehensive literacy program proposed in this chapter.

2. Ask a group of intermediate or middle-school students to discuss the characteristics they feel a good teacher of literacy should possess. Then ask them how they feel when they are allowed to select their own books or topics to read, write, discuss, or analyze. Do they seem to find it easier or more difficult to create without first being given an idea and/or a direction?

3. Try to recall the most significant literacy development activity you experienced in these grades. With your instructor or a classmate, discuss how a similar experience could be designed into a lesson for you to teach to a small group of intermediate or middle-school students.

4. List the six components of the language arts delineated in this chapter. Ask a middle-school teacher to describe how he addresses each of them when planning the year's literacy curriculum.

REFERENCES

Atwell, N. (1987). *In the middle: Writing, reading, and learning with adolescents.* Portsmouth, NH: Boynton/Cook.

Bandura, A. (1986). *Psychological modeling: Conflicting theories.* Chicago: Aldine-Atherton.

Barone, D., Hardman, D., & Taylor, J. (2006). *Reading first in the classroom.* Boston: Allyn & Bacon.

Bauer, S. W. (2003). *The well-educated mind: A guide to the classical education you never had.* New York: W.W. Norton.

Baumann, J. F., Hoffman, J. V., Moon, J., & Duffy-Hester, A. M. (1998). Where are the teachers' voices in the phonics/whole language debate? Results from a survey of U.S. elementary teachers. *The Reading Teacher, 51,* 636–650.

Berliner, D., & Biddle, B. (1996). *The manufactured crisis.* White Plains, NY: Longman.

Block, C. C. (2004). *Teaching comprehension: The comprehension process approach.* Boston: Allyn & Bacon.

Bruner, J. (1966). *Toward a theory of instruction.* Cambridge, MA: Harvard University Press.

Buehl, D. (2001). *Literacy-building strategies for content teachers.* Newark, DE: International Reading Association.

Calkins, L. M. (1994). *The art of teaching writing.* Portsmouth, NH: Heinemann.

Cecil, N. L. (1995). *The art of inquiry: Questioning strategies for k–6 classrooms.* Winnipeg, Manitoba: Peguis.

Cecil, N. L. (2007). *Striking a balance: Positive practices for early literacy* (3rd ed). Scottsdale, AZ: Holcomb Hathaway.

Cooper, J. D. (2000). *Literacy: Helping children construct meaning.* Boston: Houghton Mifflin.

Cummins, C. (2006). *Understanding and implementing reading first initiatives: The changing role of administrators.* Newark, DE: International Reading Association.

Cunningham, P. M., & Allington, R. L. (1999). *Classrooms that work: They can all read and write* (2nd ed.). New York: Longman.

Darling-Hammond, L. (1997). *Doing what matters most: Investing in quality teaching.* New York: National Commission on Teaching and America's Future.

Dillon, S. (2006). Schools cut back subjects to push math and reading. *New York Times* (March 26): 1, 16.

Durkin, D. (1990). Delores Durkin speaks on instruction. *The Reading Teacher, 43,* 472–476.

Eagleton, M. B., & Dobler, E. (2006). *Reading the web: Strategies for Internet inquiry.* New York: Guilford Press.

Farnan, N., & Dahl, K. (2003). Children's writing: Research and practice. In J. Flood, D. Lapp, J. R. Squire, & J. Jensen (Eds.), *Handbook of research on teaching the English language arts* (2nd ed), pp. 993–1007. Mahwah, NJ: Lawrence Erlbaum.

Fielding, L. G., & Pearson, P. D. (1994). Reading comprehension: What works. *Educational Leadership, 2,* 62–68.

Fletcher, J. M., & Lyon, G. R. (2002). *Reading: A research-based approach.* Palo Alto, CA: Hoover Institute.

Gambrell, L. B. (2005). Reading literature, reading text, reading the Internet: The times they are a' changing. *The Reading Teacher, 58,* 588–591.

Garrison, J. (1997). *Dewey and Eros: Wisdom and desire in the art of teaching.* New York: Teachers College Press.

Goetze, S., & Walker, B. J. (2004). At-risk readers can construct complex meanings: Technology can help. *The Reading Teacher, 57,* 146–153.

Guthrie, J. T., & Wigfield, A. (Eds.). (1997). *Reading engagement: Motivating readers through integrated instruction.* Newark, DE: International Reading Association.

Hancock, J. (Ed.). (1999). *The explicit teaching of reading.* Newark, DE: International Reading Association.

Harris, T. L., & Hodges, R. E. (Eds.). (1995). *The literacy dictionary: The vocabulary of reading and writing.* Newark, DE: International Reading Association.

Hyde, A. A., & Bizar, M. (1989). *Thinking in context: Teaching cognitive processes across the elementary curriculum.* White Plains, NY: Longman.

Invernezzi, M. A., Landrum, T. J., Howell, J. L., & Warley, H. P. (2005). Toward the peaceful coexistence of test developers, policy-makers, and teachers in an era of accountability. *The Reading Teacher, 58,* 610–618.

Kronowitz, E. L. (2008). *The teacher's guide to success.* Boston: Pearson Education.

Larsen-Blair, S. M., & Williams, K. A. (1999). *The balanced reading program: Helping all students achieve success.* Newark, DE: International Reading Association.

Lenders, K. (December 2004/January 2005). No half measures: Reading instruction for your second-language learners. *The Reading Teacher, 58,* 328–336.

Leu, D. J. (2002). The new literacies: Research on reading instruction with the Internet. In A. E. Farstrup & S. J. Samuels (Eds.), *What research has to say about reading instruction* (3rd ed.), pp. 310–336. Newark, DE: International Reading Association.

Leu, D. J., & Kinzer, C. K. (2000). The convergence of literacy instruction with networked technologies for information and communication. *Reading Research Quarterly, 35,* 108–127.

Mitchell, J., & Reutzel, D. R. (2007). Looking in the rear-view mirror: The best of the worst times or the worst of the best times? *The Reading Teacher, 60,* 714–717.

Mooney, M. E. (1990). *Reading to, with, and by children.* Katonah, NY: Richard C. Owens.

Moore, M. A. (1991). Electronic dialoguing: An avenue to literacy. *The Reading Teacher, 45,* 280–286.

National Center for Education Statistics. (2000). Digest of Education Statistics. Retrieved June 5, 2007, from http://nces.ed.gov/pubs 2001/digest.

National Endowment for the Arts (2004). Reading at risk: A survey of literary reading in America (Rep. no. 46). Washington, DC: Author.

National Institute of Child Health and Human Development (2000a). *Report of the National Reading Panel. Teaching children to read: An evidence-based assessment of the scientific literature on reading and its implications for reading instruction.* (NICHD Publication no. 00-4769). Washington, DC: U.S. Government Printing Office.

National Institute of Child Health and Human Development (2000b). *Teaching children to read—Summary report of the National Reading Panel.* Washington, DC: U.S. Government Printing Office.

Nelson-Levitt, J. (2000). *Why Jeannie can't teach: Reflections of a first-grade mentor teacher.* Unpublished master's thesis, California State University, Sacramento.

Pearson, J. D. (2006a). Foreword. In K. S. Goodman (Ed.), *The truth about DIBELS: What it is, what it does,* pp. v–xix. Portsmouth, NH: Heinemann.

Pearson, J. D. (2006b). Reading, rehashing, 'rithmatic: To the editor. *New York Times* (March 28): A22.

Pearson, P. D. (1993). Teaching and learning reading: A research perspective. *Language Arts, 70,* 502–511.

Peterson, R., & Eeds, M. (1990). *Grand conversations: Literature groups in action.* New York: Scholastic.

Pinnell, G. S., & Jaggar, A. M. (2003). Oral language: Speaking and listening in the classroom. In J. Flood, D. Lapp, J. R. Squire, & J. M. Jensen (Eds.), *Handbook of research on the teaching of the English language arts* (2nd ed.), pp. 881–913. Mahwah, NJ: Erlbaum.

Reading Today. (2005). Report targets reading in middle school and high school. *Reading Today* (February–March), 22, 23.

Roe, B. D., & Ross, E. P. (2006). *Integrating language arts through literature & thematic units.* Boston: Pearson.

Rosenblatt, L. (1978). *The reader, the text, the poem: The transactional theory of the literary work.* Carbondale: Southern Illinois University Press.

Rosenblatt, L. (1983). *Literature as exploration* (4th ed.). New York: Modern Language Association.

Rumelhart, D. E. (1977). Toward an interactive model of reading. In S. Dornic (Ed.), *Attention and performance* (vol. 6). Hillsdale, NJ: Erlbaum.

Samovar, L. A., & Porter, R. E. (2001). *Communication between cultures.* Belmont, CA: Wadsworth.

Schmar-Dobler, E. (2003). Reading on the Internet: The link between literacy and technology. *Journal of Adolescent & Adult Literacy, 47,* 80–85.

Slavin, R. E. (December 1989/January 1990). Research on cooperative learning: Consensus and controversy. *Educational Leadership, 47*(4), 52–55.

Squire, J. R. (1983). Composing and comprehending: Two sides of the same basic process. *Language Arts, 60*(5), 581–589.

Stahl, S. A. (1992). Saying the "P" word: Nine guidelines for exemplary phonics instruction. *The Reading Teacher, 15,* 33–50.

Standards for the English Language Arts (1996). Urbana, IL: National Council of Teachers of English and the International Reading Association.

Stanovich, K. (1980). Toward an interactive-compensatory model of individual differences in the development of reading fluency. *Reading Research Quarterly, 16,* 22–71.

Sweet, A., & Snow, C. (2002). *Understanding comprehension: RAND report on comprehension.* Washington, DC: RAND.

Tower, C. (2000). Questions that matter: Preparing elementary students for the inquiry process. *The Reading Teacher, 53*(7), 550–557.

U.S. Department of Commerce. (2002). A nation online: How Americans are expanding their use of the Internet. Retrieved May 31, 2007, from http://www.ntia.doc.gov/ntiahome/dn/anationonline2.pdf.

U.S. Congress. (2001). No Child Left Behind Act. Retrieved October 5, 2006, from http://www.ed.gov/policy/elsec/leg/esea02/index.html.

Vogt, M. E. (2004). Book reading drops, says new survey. *Reading Today* (August/September), 22.

Vygotsky, L. S. (1962, 1979). *Thought and language.* Cambridge, MA: MIT Press.

Vygotsky, L. S. (1978). *Mind in society.* In M. Cole, V. John-Steiner, S. Scribner, & E. Souberman (Eds.), pp. 128–173. Cambridge, MA: Harvard University Press.

Wagner, B. J. (2003). Imaginative expression. In J. Flood, D. Lapp, J. R. Squire, & J. M. Jensen (Eds.), *Handbook of research on the teaching of the English language arts* (2nd ed.), pp. 1008–1025. Mahwah, NJ: Erlbaum.

Wink, J. (1996). Jonathan: Linking critical pedagogy and literacy. *Clip: A Journal of the California Literacy Project, 2*(4), 27–30.

Assessment of Progress in Literacy

FOCUS QUESTIONS

- How is assessment different from evaluation?
- What are the types of literacy assessment possible for use in grades 4–8?
- In what ways can literacy assessment inform instruction?

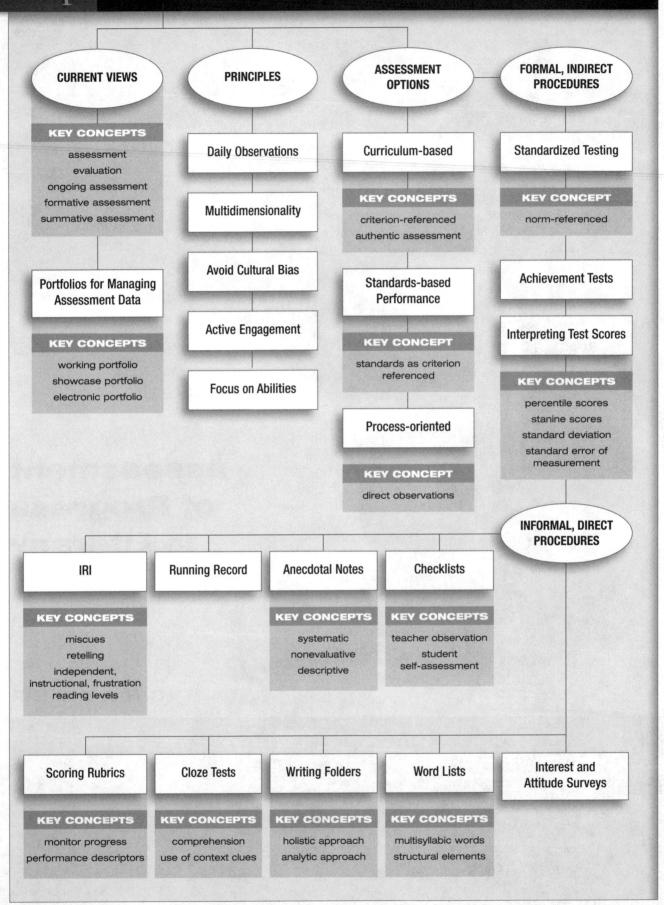

CURRENT VIEWS

KEY CONCEPTS

assessment
evaluation
ongoing assessment
formative assessment
summative assessment

Portfolios for Managing
Assessment Data

KEY CONCEPTS

working portfolio
showcase portfolio
electronic portfolio

PRINCIPLES

Daily Observations

Multidimensionality

Avoid Cultural Bias

Active Engagement

Focus on Abilities

ASSESSMENT OPTIONS

Curriculum-based

KEY CONCEPTS

criterion-referenced
authentic assessment

Standards-based
Performance

KEY CONCEPT

standards as criterion
referenced

Process-oriented

KEY CONCEPT

direct observations

FORMAL, INDIRECT PROCEDURES

Standardized Testing

KEY CONCEPT

norm-referenced

Achievement Tests

Interpreting Test Scores

KEY CONCEPTS

percentile scores
stanine scores
standard deviation
standard error of
measurement

INFORMAL, DIRECT PROCEDURES

IRI

KEY CONCEPTS

miscues
retelling
independent,
instructional, frustration
reading levels

Running Record

Anecdotal Notes

KEY CONCEPTS

systematic
nonevaluative
descriptive

Checklists

KEY CONCEPTS

teacher observation
student
self-assessment

Scoring Rubrics

KEY CONCEPTS

monitor progress
performance descriptors

Cloze Tests

KEY CONCEPTS

comprehension
use of context clues

Writing Folders

KEY CONCEPTS

holistic approach
analytic approach

Word Lists

KEY CONCEPTS

multisyllabic words
structural elements

Interest and
Attitude Surveys

Small groups of four or five students arrange their desks in circles around Ms. West's fourth-grade classroom. Within each group one student will present his language arts portfolio to the others. Ms. West scheduled this sharing of portfolios as a kind of dress rehearsal in preparation for student-led conferences with parents later in the week. Let's eavesdrop on one student, Artis, and listen to his portfolio introduction.

My name is Artis. I hope I will be going to the fifth grade next year. I created this language arts portfolio during fourth grade. My teacher's name is Ms. West.

I began working on things and saving things for my portfolio on September 15 and put my portfolio together on May 20. I began deciding what to include in my portfolio in April and May.

I picked items that were important to me to include in this portfolio. I wanted to show what I had learned and I put all of my favorite projects in the portfolio. I also wanted to show that I am a hard worker.

The way I decided which things would go first in my portfolio was easy—I picked my favorite thing first. I had a list of everything I wanted in my portfolio and I just put it in order starting with my favorite item.

This portfolio shows that I kept a book list for my readings. It also shows that I have a prediction log that I use when I am reading stories. My portfolio shows what I learned through read-

ing. I learned about hurricanes and sand dollars. It also shows that there are some things about my reading that I still have to work on.

My portfolio shows the different types of writing I can do. I included a book that I wrote and illustrated. I also included some comic strips that I wrote the story for as well as a story that uses new vocabulary.

I think that my best items are the comic strips, my hurricane book, and my movie review. These activities were all fun and I learned a lot from completing each of these.

My portfolio shows the improvements I have made this year. It shows what I can do. I can write a book if I use my imagination! It shows I can improve with practice and it shows that I am a hard worker.

Artis proceeds to share individual items from his portfolio with his group members. He tells why each item is special to him and what he has learned from that item. Later, he will also be asked to share with his parents those areas for which he feels he needs to learn more. By the end of this day, all Ms. West's students will have an idea of what their classmates have accomplished and will see each one at his or her best. The students are proud of their efforts and it is truly a literacy celebration. Following the sharing, students are invited to have pizza and cold drinks in the cafeteria, compliments of Ms. West.

CURRENT VIEWS OF ASSESSMENT

Many in the field of education today are dismayed by what appears to be a testing frenzy within our school systems (O'Sullivan & Jiang, 2002). Each day it seems students at all levels face more and more testing. Teachers are now familiar with the influence of testing as mandated by the No Child Left Behind Act of 2001 (NLCB; U.S. Department of Education, 2002). Schools must show Adequate Yearly Progress (AYP), with annual testing now required in grades 3–8 in mathematics and reading or language arts. Annual testing, as of 2007–2008, extends to science and to grades 10–12 and must occur once during each of the following grade breakdowns: 3–5, 6–9, and 10–12. States are being given some latitude in the tests they use, so teachers need to check the NCLB requirements for their own states. In addition to AYP scores, achievement test scores for area schools are also published in the local newspaper; real estate agents even use them to market homes.

The commonsense thinking is that if we want our students to perform better we need to test them more. Everyone wants students to perform at their best, but is testing the way to achieve this? According to Daniels and Bizar

www

No Child Left Behind
www.ed.gov/nclb

(1998), "since most standardized test scores correlate highly with socioeconomic status, any new round of testing will usually reconfirm the unworthiness of the underclasses and comfort the privileged" (p. 205). Testing is about **evaluation,** or placing a value on a performance. Evaluation is not, however, synonymous with assessment.

evaluation

Defining Assessment

assessment

Assessment is the process of gathering information (data) about students' abilities that will help teachers, parents, and other caregivers know more about a learner's strengths and weaknesses so they may provide appropriate instruction or assistance for the learner. As such, assessment certainly can include tests, since they provide one piece of data, but assessment is about more than just testing. It is about looking at instruction in terms of how it impacts student learning. It is about self-evaluation, much like what Artis did in preparing his portfolio. (See the accompanying vignette.) It is about performing to a set of identified criteria. Thus, assessment is a much broader and richer concept than testing. But, as Neill (2000) states, "Assessment is at a crisis point: the old model is incapable of meeting real needs, and a new approach is not yet clear. . . . Whatever forms of exams are eventually used, they cannot provide much help for teachers in learning to integrate assessment with instruction in a continuous flow—and that is the heart of assessment in the service of learning" (p. 145).

Ongoing assessment of literacy development refers to the use of multiple instruments, daily observation, and many work samples to measure progress. It also refers to the ongoing analysis of the data from these instruments and observations concerning individuals, small groups, and the entire class so that the teacher can customize instruction and, when necessary, plan appropriate interventions. This type of ongoing assessment is also referred to as *formative assessment;* it helps us know how we are progressing. *Summative assessment* is a compilation of formative assessment data, or summary data provided at program endings, units of study, or other intervals (e.g., midterm, final, every eight weeks) to report progress (e.g., report cards).

The assessment in Ms. West's classroom is ongoing and dynamic; it is the basis on which she makes all of her instructional decisions. In effective grade 4–8 classrooms, instruction is based on information acquired through valid assessment procedures. Moreover, students in the class are also involved in their own assessment and, like Artis, are able to recognize their own strengths and limitations and are encouraged to use strategies designed to increase their literacy competence. Finally, in a classroom like Ms. West's, the teacher is able to use and interpret the results from a variety of curriculum-based and standardized assessment tools and effectively communicate those results to students, their parents or caretakers, and relevant school personnel. Artis knows how well he is doing, and so does everyone who cares about his learning process.

Standards and Assessment

professional teaching standards

Teachers today are being held accountable for meeting a wide array of standards. These standards are of two basic types: **professional teaching standards** (i.e., related to how well the teacher performs) and *curriculum* or *content standards* (i.e., related to what the teacher must teach). In addition to national standards for both teachers and content, individual states have developed their own sets of standards. In California, for example, professional standards for teachers are referred to as the "California Standards for the Teaching Profession," while the content standards are addressed within two documents: (1) "Content Standards" and (2) "Curriculum Frameworks," which are blueprints for implementing the content standards. Content standards for any state can be found online at that state's Department of Education website. Individual school districts usually adopt the state content standards or include a few additional standards. When standards are referred to in this chapter, it is content standards that are the focus.

The assessment tools discussed in this chapter can coordinate easily with state-mandated content standards. English language arts standards need not be viewed as something above and apart from the practices of actual classroom teachers. Rather, well-designed standards represent what "teachers and the many others involved in English language arts education agree is the best and most productive current thinking about teaching and learning" (Smith, 1996, p. v). Hill, Ruptic, and Norwick (1998) provide an appropriate analogy: "Classroom based assessments provide sign posts to document growth. The [standards] provide the roadmap to show where we are going" (p. 175).

Standards also give students performance goals and provide teachers with an impetus for assessing and guidance for giving students feedback (Guskey, 2005). Wiggins (as cited in Wilcox, 2006) argues that providing good feedback, not just praise or advice, is perhaps the most important skill a teacher needs and one that is often neglected. Wiggins states, "We get fixated on the inputs, the content, and not enough on the desired output: resultant quality performance. The result is superficial. To get quality performance, you need feedback. . . . Feedback tells you what you just did. Feedback is information you can use. It's descriptive and useful information about what you did and didn't do in light of a goal" (pp. 2, 6). In order for teachers to know what feedback to provide students, they need to do more *assessing*, not testing, but *information gathering* about student learning while the learning is still happening.

WWW

National Standards
www.nbpts.org
www.ncte.org/about/over/ standards

State Standards Example
www.cde.ca.gov
www.cde.ca.gov/be/st/ss
www.cde.ca.gov/be/st/fr
www.cde.ca.gov/pd/ps

PRINCIPLES OF ASSESSMENT

As a result of reflective practice, lesson observations, checklists, and other measures, teachers perform assessments; in turn, these assessments inform teachers as to what needs to be taught, or retaught, and the kinds of feedback to provide students. The following five principles of assessment reveal this reciprocal, synergistic relationship between assessment and teaching: assessment should ❶ involve daily observation, ❷ take many different forms, ❸ avoid cultural bias, ❹ actively involve students, and ❺ focus on students' abilities. Careful study of these assessment principles can help teachers determine whether their assessment plan will be complementary to instruction (adapted from Cooper, 1997).

 ### THE CORE OF ASSESSMENT SHOULD BE DAILY OBSERVATION

Teachers, who frequently observe and take notes on each aspect of literacy development, know much more about the status of their students than can be obtained from any standardized testing, no matter how reliable the testing is purported to be. It is imperative that assessment be a daily event, occurring as the student reads and writes. Through observing patterns of growth over time, the teacher is in the ideal position to get a clear picture of how students are progressing. By observing several students each day, the teacher can easily observe all students at least once each week.

 ## ASSESSMENT SHOULD TAKE MANY DIFFERENT FORMS

Different types of assessment tools should be used for different purposes to ensure that the most accurate measure of each learner's literacy progress is obtained. For example, writing samples, teacher-developed checklists about summaries of text, and anecdotal notes give insights that are not scientific but based solely upon the teacher's judgment. Although these data are critical to effective planning and decision making, the teacher also needs standardized test results that have accepted statistical *reliability* (i.e., dependability and consistency) and *validity* (i.e., soundness); in other words, the tests consistently measure what they claim to be measuring. To get a truly multidimensional overview of a student's performance in any aspect of literacy, teachers need to look at the data from all available sources.

 ## ASSESSMENT MUST AVOID CULTURAL BIAS

Learners from different cultures, linguistic groups, and backgrounds may have different language issues as well as varied experiences and styles of learning. When planning assessment procedures, and particularly when interpreting and reporting them to others, these factors should be judiciously considered (Schellenberg, 2004).

The importance of considering cultural bias can be illustrated by a situation encountered by a teacher who had a student in her class from the Virgin Islands. It had been determined that the student had a severe reading disability. However, upon examining the test items and the test results, the teacher realized the student was certainly not reading disabled: she had scored poorly because she had not known many vocabulary words, such as *chimney* and *caboose*—words that have little meaning for residents of a tiny tropical island!

 ## STUDENTS SHOULD BE ACTIVELY ENGAGED IN THE ASSESSMENT PROCESS

Although students cannot be involved in every aspect of literacy assessment, sometimes asking for input when evaluating their work can be a key factor in encouraging students to take charge of their own learning, and it invites ownership of their successes. Since teaching and learning are ideally collaborative processes, we do not want students to view assessment as an uncomfortable practice that the teacher does *to* them. Therefore, when students and teachers are allowed to work and think together, assessment becomes a shared responsibility, with learners participating enthusiastically as team players in their own learning (Stiggins et al., 2004).

ASSESSMENT SHOULD FOCUS ON STUDENTS' ABILITIES

Assessment should focus on determining what learners *can* do, not what they *cannot* do. When teachers really understand the reading and writing abilities of their students, it becomes much easier to decide which new literacy experiences should be offered to help them develop further and to provide them with useful feedback. Not only is this a more constructive way of looking at learning, but students benefit in other crucial ways. They are able to progress more readily when the atmosphere is one where mistakes are viewed as building blocks rather than failures that must be avoided (Cousin, Weekly, & Gerard, 1993).

ASSESSMENT OPTIONS

Teachers have at their disposal an almost overwhelming array of instruments to use as part of the assessment process. Many of these instruments blend naturally into instruction; others provide a separate means to assess literacy progress, in either more or less direct ways as related to actual classroom instruction. Think of assessment as a continuum. As shown in Figure 2.1, teacher observation is the most direct form and standardized tests are the least direct form of assessment (Johnston, 1992). Traditionally, these distinctions in assessment have been referred to as informal and formal, respectively.

Distinctions in assessment can also be thought of as formative and summative. As briefly described earlier, **formative assessment** refers to the process of ongoing data gathering during instruction that both informs and guides teachers as they make instructional decisions. It also guides students as they recognize gaps in their learning and then proceed to fill those gaps. Formative assessment is closely related to the ongoing direct assessment measures used by teachers; it is also referred to as classroom assessment (although not all forms of classroom assessment are formative). Information from formative assessments helps teachers provide the level of quality feedback students need about their learning. **Summative assessment** refers to evaluative assessments, or tests, resulting in a grade or a ranking, as from a final unit test, end of chapter test, weekly spelling test, or standardized achievement test. Large-scale, high-stakes testing is an example of summative assessment. Summative assessments are more comprehensive in nature and provide for some degree of accountability. Brookhart (1999) shares the following analogy to describe the difference between formative and summative assessment: "When the cook tastes the soup, that's formative assessment; when the customer tastes the soup, that's summative assessment" (Formative and Summative, para 1).

Because so many assessment tools are available, it is impossible to discuss each one in this chapter. Therefore, we explore a sampling of some of the most

● formative assessment

● summative assessment

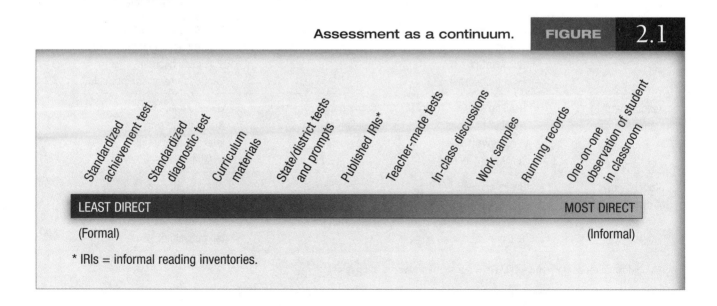

Assessment as a continuum. FIGURE 2.1

Standardized achievement test • Standardized diagnostic test • Curriculum materials • State/district tests and prompts • Published IRIs* • Teacher-made tests • In-class discussions • Work samples • Running records • One-on-one observation of student in classroom

LEAST DIRECT   MOST DIRECT

(Formal)   (Informal)

* IRIs = informal reading inventories.

pervasive assessment devices that are compatible with a balanced and comprehensive literacy program. An example of a balanced and comprehensive framework for guiding the assessment process is presented in Figure 2.2. Here, the assessment process is guided by two questions: What kind of information do I need? and How am I going to gather this information? The options for gathering information are (1) *direct*, which refers to teacher-developed or one-on-one observations of what the student can do; (2) *ongoing*, which refers to a set of direct data collected over time; and (3) *indirect*, which refers to data

| FIGURE | 2.2 | A framework for guiding the literacy assessment process. |

What kind of information do I need?   How am I going to gather this information?

	DIRECT	ONGOING	INDIRECT
Structural analysis/ word analysis	One-on-one observation Word games	Anecdotal notes Running records	Stanford Diagnostic Subtest Woodcock Reading Mastery Test
Vocabulary	Observation Pretest Free writing Class presentations	Daily discussions Anecdotal notes Weekly tests Writing samples	Stanford Achievement Test Language Assessment Scales Carver Vocabulary Test PPVT III
Fluency	One-on-one observation Paired reading	Anecdotal notes Running records Tape recordings IRI/miscue analysis	State/district-developed instruments
Spelling	Free writing Pretests Dictations	Writing samples Journals Weekly tests	Standardized tests
Reading comprehension	Retellings QARs Discussions Cloze tests	Paraphrases Summaries Class contributions Sketchings	Standardized tests (Stanford Achievement, Metropolitan Achievement, California Achievement)

Writing	Free writing
	Journals
	Quickwrites
	Editing checklist
		Writing samples
		Daily work
			Rubrics that accompany
			   curriculum materials
			   (scaled scores)
			Language Assessment Scales

Reading/writing attitudes	Reading logs
	Number of books
	   read/written
	Teacher interviews
		Conferences
		Reading response
		   journals
			Questionnaires
			Attitude surveys
			Interest inventories
			   (all published)

Student views of own literacy	Books chosen Self-evaluations Response journals Teacher interviews	Portfolio choices Dialogue journals Reflection log	Attitude surveys Reading surveys Questionnaires (all published)

IRI = informal reading inventory; QARs = question–answer relationships.

that come from standardized instruments or instruments devised by someone outside the classroom setting. Once the teacher has determined the area for which he needs information, the framework provides several alternatives for obtaining that assessment data.

Most of the techniques discussed in the remainder of this chapter can be used easily on the basis of the information given; others require reviewing an examiner's handbook. Appropriate references are given for those that require more detailed study, and samples of others are presented in Appendix C.

Common classifications for the assessments used in grades 4–8 are: standardized testing, curriculum-based assessment, standards-based performance assessment, and process-oriented assessment. These classifications are not always mutually exclusive. For example, criterion-referenced tests (often curriculum-based) can also be standardized, and the use of checklists can occur across classifications. It may be helpful to think of these classifications as related to the purpose for

Different types of assessment tools should be used for various purposes to ensure the most accurate measure of each learner's literacy progress.

assessment. In other words, is an assessment needed for screening purposes, diagnostic purposes, or to monitor progress, or is the purpose to measure the outcome of instruction? As discussed in the following sections, each classification offers a unique perspective for a balanced and comprehensive literacy program, providing information for both formative and summative purposes.

Standardized Testing

Standardized testing focuses on the use of norm-referenced tests to measure reading and writing skills as well as the subskills of these areas. (See "Standardized, or Indirect, Assessment Procedures" later in this chapter for specific, technical information about tests that fall under this category.) These tests are administered by the teacher or reading specialist and usually provide numerical scores that represent a student's rank compared to the performance of other learners at the same age or grade. The data obtained from these tests can be, but are not always, related to the content of instruction. Because they are **norm-referenced tests**—that is, administered to a large group of students to establish the reference scores to which subsequent scores are compared (refer to Figure 2.3)—they have not been developed to assess a specific curriculum. Therefore, some items may address material a teacher has taught, but there might also be items about topics not taught. Or, the test might measure the content of the curriculum, but in ways different from the instructional format used by the teacher. For instance, synonyms might be taught by the teacher within the context of sentences, whereas the standardized test might assess knowledge of synonyms through word matching.

Since the passage of the NCLB Act, many states have developed their own standardized tests (e.g., Illinois State Assessments) for measuring adequate yearly progress (AYP). For a closer look at what your state might require, visit your state's Department of Education website. While most teachers are familiar with

● standardized testing

● norm-referenced tests

NORM-REFERENCED ASSESSMENTS	CRITERION-REFERENCED ASSESSMENTS
1. Assess student's knowledge of particular subject matter.	1. Assess student's ability to perform a specific task.
2. Compare performance with that of a **norm group** (large number of students representative of the students for whom the test was designed in order to establish scoring values for the test).	2. Determine whether the student has the skill needed to progress to the next level of learning.
	3. Are used as often as needed to determine skills to be taught and skills that have been mastered.
3. Are used annually as pretests/posttests to determine student gain and compare gains with those of the norm group.	4. Contain items that determine whether the student is able to use a learned skill in a variety of situations.
4. Contain items considered to be precise, valid, and reliable for the purpose of selecting and sorting low-achieving and high-achieving students.	5. Have high **content validity** (items assess the ability needed to perform the behaviors expected in the course or in the curriculum).
5. Have high **construct validity** (items assess the skills, knowledge, and understandings that most experts agree comprise the area being tested).	6. Are not concerned with reliability; students are not expected to show the *same* behavior, but *improved* behavior.
6. Have high **reliability** (consistently measure the same behavior with each administration of the test).	7. Are interpreted by noting whether the student is able to perform a specific task, and to what degree.
7. Are interpreted by comparing student's scores with those obtained by the norm group.	8. Yield analytical data regarding specific objectives.
8. Yield global measurements of general abilities.	9. Provide a score that is considered acceptable by the teacher (e.g., 80 percent accuracy); incorrect items can be further examined.
9. Provide scores that are statistically compared with those of a norm group (e.g., percentiles).	10. Are designed to assess ability to perform a specific task as stated by a specific objective or curriculum content standard.
10. Are written to create variability among individual scores in a group for the purpose of sorting students.	

Source: Adapted from Eddie Kennedy, *Classroom Approaches to Remedial Reading,* 1977. Itaska, FL: F.E. Peacock Publishers.

FIGURE 2.3 **Comparison of norm- and criterion-referenced assessments.**

administering standardized achievement tests, including the Stanford Achievement Test (SAT) and Iowa Test of Basic Skills (ITBS), standardized tests are also available for diagnostic purposes. Examples include such tests as the Woodcock Reading Mastery Test, Pearson Assessments, and Stanford Diagnostic Reading Test (SDRT). The forms of these instruments appropriate for grades 4–8 offer subtests that provide a systematic appraisal of a student's ability to recognize meaningful word parts (roots, affixes, and compounds), to determine main ideas and supporting details, and to correct sentences that are poorly written, as well as an accounting of vocabulary words the student knows compared with age-matched peers. For instance, the Green (grades 3.5–4.5), Purple (grades 4.5–6.5), and Brown (grades 6.5–8.9) levels of the SDRT cover the range of intermediate and middle grades.

The results of standardized tests are most appropriately used to get an overall sense of how well a group (school, class) is performing and what general academic areas might need more focus in the classroom. These indirect assessments are often viewed by teachers before they have had an opportunity to get to know their students' strengths and needs better. As a result, they are used to make initial placements in instructional groups *until more direct information can be obtained with the actual materials the students will be using in the classroom.* It would be unfortunate if these initial placements were left unexamined once the teacher learns more about her students!

Curriculum-Based Assessment

Curriculum-based assessment uses school district–adopted curriculum materials to provide information about students' abilities. This category of assessment relates directly to the teacher's literacy curriculum to identify instructional needs and to determine what is required for learners to "master" a concept. Such assessment also may include **criterion-referenced tests**—tests that compare a student's performance to standards (the criteria) deemed appropriate for mastery in a particular area. Scores from such tools typically offer a number, or percentage, for the amount of material each student has mastered. These scores are then compared with the criterion score required; usually 80 percent accuracy determines "mastery." See Figure 2.3 for a comparison of norm-referenced and criterion-referenced assessments.

- curriculum-based assessment

- criterion-referenced tests

Curriculum-based assessments are usually administered in the classroom using items and materials derived from the curriculum. Examples of curriculum-based assessments include asking a student to read a passage aloud from a text and counting the number of words read correctly per minute, or culminating a thematic unit on exploration by asking students to write down as many words related to the study of exploration as they can in a limited time. The first example represents a criterion-referenced test in that students are expected to be able to read a certain number of words correctly per minute at particular grade levels (refer to Figure 3.7). The teacher is evaluating whether this criterion has been met. The second example is more direct, as the results will inform the teacher how effectively the thematic unit increased students' vocabulary for a particular area of instruction. The teacher might have certain expectations for a minimum number of words that each student should list, but these expectations can also vary according to the student. An English learner might be expected to list at least 5 words, whereas a native English speaker might be expected to list 10.

Standards-Based Performance Assessment

Relatively new to classrooms, **standards-based performance assessment,** a type of criterion-referenced assessment, describes assessment that views standards as the criteria on which performance is evaluated. These standards are most often devised by state curriculum committees, and several states have addressed the national standards for the English Language Arts (NCTE/IRA, 1996) within their own sets of standards. Standards can be met in a variety of ways, or performances (e.g., essays, exhibitions, performance by a group, short story writing), and students can reflect on their progress toward achieving the standards (Wilhelm, 1996). In other words, *using standards-based performance assessment does not dictate the type of tools that might be used for assessment.* Any of the tools found in Figure 2.2 could be used; each standard provides only the criterion for the assessment. Rather than ask what students know and can do in relation to other students (norm-referencing), standards-based performance assessment asks what students know and can do in relation to a set of standards (see Figure 2.4).

- standards-based performance assessment

WWW

National Standards
www.ncte.org/about/over/standards

Aligning Assessments to Standards
www.aera.net/uploadedFiles/Journals_and_Publications/Research_Points/RP_Spring03.pdf

Performance Assessment
www.performanceassessment.org

FIGURE 2.4   Checklist for observations of progress toward standards.*

NAME: _Luke_   GRADE: _6_

Standards	Context	Date Observed	Context	Date Observed	Context	Date Observed
1. Reads a wide range of print and nonprint texts	Reading book of poetry before writing own poem	9/5	Internet material	10/4		
2. Reads a wide range of literature (many time periods, many genres)	Read Whitman's "Song of Myself"	9/5	Read daily newspaper	9/7		
3. Applies a wide range of strategies to comprehend, interpret, evaluate, and appreciate texts	Reading journal	9/12	Peer conferences	9/23		
4. Adjusts use of spoken, written, and visual language to communicate effectively	Presented culture report using photos and drama	10/4	Listens to radio shows—said "I want to get ideas for my readers theatre. Other people will be listening and I want to get it right."	10/20	Readers theatre	11/6
5. Employs a wide range of strategies for writing and different writing process elements to communicate effectively	Used galley sheet to formulate a creative story	9/15	Using word processing and desktop publishing and time lines	10/21		
6. Applies knowledge of language structure, conventions, media techniques, figurative language, and genre to create, critique, and discuss print/nonprint texts	Used punctuation in effective ways—added to the punctuation chart in the writing area	9/28	Engaged in PQP⁺ with a partner	10/12		

Standards	Context	Date Observed	Context	Date Observed	Context	Date Observed
7. Conducts research by generating ideas and questions, and by posing problems	Began research KWH† chart about whales	10/3	Wrote a business letter to request more information on whales	10/10		
8. Uses a variety of technological and informational resources to gather/synthesize information and create/communicate knowledge	Visited WWW museum sites	10/4	Worked on hypermedia stack	10/22		
9. Understands and respects diversity in language use, dialects, cultures	Contributed a question related to family life in culture study	9/3	Helped team collect artifacts (maps, clothing) related to culture study	9/4		
10. If English learner, makes use of native language to develop English competency	n/a	/	/	/		
11. Participates in a variety of literacy communities	Small group & whole class	9/13	Book Club	10/3	Pen pal	10/24
12. Uses spoken, written, and visual language to accomplish own purposes	Requested information from Kay	10/6	Shared information with Kay that helped her answer one of her research questions	10/7	Used free time to read article about Keiko the whale	10/15

*The standards used in this checklist are the NCTE/IRA Standards for the English Language Arts. Any state standards could be used, and the checklist can be made grade-level specific as well.

† PQP = Praise, Question, Polish; KWH = Know, Want to know, How to find out.

Beverly Falk (2000) provides a clear statement of the purposes and benefits of standards-based performance assessments:

> Standards-based performance assessments support teaching by providing teachers with a guide for their teaching and with information about *what* students can do as well as *how* they do it. They support student learning by offering students opportunities to demonstrate their understandings in a variety of ways and, because of their open and clear expectations, by giving students a fair shot at demonstrating what they know. At the same time, standards-based performance assessments are useful accountability measures because they allow the public to see student and school progress in relation to valued goals. (p. 83)

Teachers using standards-based performance assessment are continually thinking of how they can organize a set of experiences that will help their students meet the standards. They try to use what they know about their students' interests, abilities, and competencies. The term *authentic assessment* has some relevance here. **Authentic assessment** is often understood to mean assessment that represents literacy behavior found in the community and in the workplace. Instruction focuses on learning that has direct application in the real world. For example, students concerned about the environment may engage in service-learning projects centered around recycling. (See Chapter 10 for more about service learning.) In this example, authentic assessment would focus on how successful their recycling projects were in the eyes of the community.

authentic assessment

Teachers involved in such projects, just as those using standards-based performance assessment, often rely on anecdotal records, checklists, and scoring rubrics to help them determine how well their students have met the standards. The checklist in Figure 2.4 is one way a teacher can record evidence that students are working toward each of the standards.

WWW

Authentic Assessment
*http://suse-step.stanford.edu/resources/
LanguageSite/Authentic_Assessment.html*

Process-Oriented Assessment

process-oriented assessment

Process-oriented assessment refers to a teacher's direct observations of students' actual reading and writing abilities for the purpose of noting which specific behaviors or strategies students use. In process-oriented assessment, the literacy behavior being examined is documented in the learning context in which it normally occurs. For example, a process-oriented assessment could consist of anecdotal notes or a checklist designed by the teacher that asks such questions as, "Is the learner able to separate affixes from root words to assist decoding?" or "Is the learner able to use word parts to determine word meaning?" The assessment then might take place when the student reads one-on-one with the teacher from a content area text, such as a social studies text.

The key to making observation systematic lies in creating a tool for note taking and record keeping that reduces the amount of writing required. Figures 2.4, 2.10, and 2.11 are examples of such tools. Computer-based systems are also available for teachers to maintain observational records. Pearson Education's Work Sampling Online is one example. For a demonstration tour of this computer-based observation system, visit the website listed in the margin. In addition to anecdotal notes and checklists, the use of *running records* or an *informal reading inventory* (IRI) (both discussed later in this chapter), with follow-up miscue analyses, also falls under

WWW

Designing Assessments
http://edrev.asu.edu/reviews/rev50.htm

Observation Tools
*www.colorincolorado.org/webcasts/middleWebcast%20
1003%20-%20Teacher%20checklist.pdf*

Computer-Based Observational Systems
www.worksamplingonline.com/School/Home/Tour/

this category. Such assessments are quite compatible with standards-based performance assessment.

STANDARDIZED, OR INDIRECT, ASSESSMENT PROCEDURES

There are advantages and disadvantages to using standardized assessment devices in the classroom. Although standardized group tests can be used, in a very broad way, to compare student performance with that of a cross-section of students in other areas of the country, such tests provide little or no usable information about the specific needs of individual students in a particular classroom context. As with any assessment device, teachers must first determine what information they are seeking and then decide whether the standardized instrument is appropriate to those goals. As Cunningham and Allington (1999) so wisely remind us, "Tests that do not help us teach better are generally a waste of time and resources" (p. 263).

Achievement Tests and Their Application by Teachers

In most schools, reading achievement is evaluated by a standardized, or norm-referenced, test. These tests have been administered to a large group of students, representative of those for whom the test is intended, in order to establish the norm, or reference, group. This, then, is the group to which the scores of other students taking the test are compared. Standardized tests also have a standardized set of directions that must be followed for valid comparisons to be made.

Achievement tests are generally administered in a group and offer the teacher a "ballpark" estimate of the students' reading performance. The results are more helpful for comparing groups than for making judgments about how to meet the specific needs of individual students. As mentioned earlier, teachers often use the results of these tests to help with *initial* placement of students into instructional groups. Scores can be charted and decisions for planning general areas for instructional focus can be made (see Figure 2.5). A diagnostic test, however, such as the SDRT, would need to be administered in order to obtain more specific information from a standardized test. Teachers also use standardized test scores as confirmation of the results from their own direct assessments. Nevertheless, standardized tests present the teacher with a variety of types of scores that must be interpreted cautiously.

Interpretation of Standardized Test Scores

The most commonly reported score from a standardized test is the percentile score. **Percentile scores** range from 1 to 99, with an average score of 50, but they do *not* represent the percentage of items answered correctly on the test. They are scores that have been converted from the raw scores to allow comparisons among students of the same age or grade in the norm group, or in the same classroom or school. Each test's technical manual explains the manner in which this conversion was done. For example, students receiving a percentile score of 76 did not answer 76 percent of the items correctly. This score means that these students have done as well as or better than 76 percent of students in the norm group and in their own classroom on this test. An individual's subtest scores can be compared, but not averaged. In other words, a comprehension subtest score of 65 and a vocabulary subtest score of 43 mean the

● percentile scores

FIGURE 2.5 **Graphic profile for examining class standardized test scores.***

TEACHER: Ms. G   GRADE LEVEL: 4   DATE: September

NAME OF TEST: CAT/6   DATE TEST ADMINISTERED: April

Pupil's Name	Word Analysis		Vocabulary		Comprehension		Comments
Carolyn B.	39	4	37	4	35	4	steady progress
Artis C.	34	4	53	5	36	4	good progress
Mary D.	49	5	23	(3)	23	(3)	vocabulary & comprehension
Isaac D.	63	6	83	8	74	7	could peer tutor?
Doug F.	18	(2)	29	(3)	18	(2)	use vocab. to build skills
Raul H.	38	4	38	4	6	(1)	focus on comprehension
Brandon L.	53	5	18	(2)	40	4	verify vocabulary
Cory M.	56	5	39	4	9	(1)	twins—but very different
Kerri M.	29	(3)	56	5	54	5	could Cory lean too much on Kerri?
Kalisha P.	36	4	26	(3)	3	(1)	focus on comprehension
Darlene P.	30	4	24	(3)	27	(3)	some comp. & vocab. work
Marcus R.	10	(2)	57	5	58	5	verify word analysis skills
Brenda R.	99	9	98	9	85	8	could peer tutor?
Sara R.	6	(1)	8	(1)	5	(1)	English learner
Carmen T.	12	(2)	14	(2)	11	(2)	English learner
Luis T.	37	4	31	4	14	(2)	comprehension strategies
Patricia W.	8	(1)	34	4	25	(3)	verify with an IRI
Mark W.	38	4	26	(3)	21	(3)	some comp. & vocab. help
Greg W.	57	5	38	4	37	4	good, steady progress
Linda Y.	36	4	35	4	16	(2)	comprehension strategies
	% ile	stanine	% ile	stanine	% ile	stanine	

*Below-average stanine scores are circled. Twelve of 20 students, more than half, are below average in comprehension. The instructional focus needs to be on comprehension.

An Assessment Program

Ms. West, the teacher we met at the beginning of this chapter, has created an assessment program that incorporates data from a wide variety of assessment tools to evaluate the literacy growth of Artis and the other students in her class. The tools listed here are discussed elsewhere in this chapter.

- Once a year, usually during spring, the students take a norm-referenced *achievement test* called The Stanford Achievement Test (The Psychological Corporation). Reviewing these results at the beginning of the school year allows Ms. West to obtain general literacy information about her new class and an indication of how well the students in her school are doing in comparison with other students of the same age and grade across the nation (standardized testing).

- At the beginning of the year Ms. West first gives students a *group cloze* test developed from the material they will be expected to read to evaluate their ability to handle the content area texts (curriculum-based).

- For students who score below 30 percent accuracy on the group cloze test, Ms. West administers an *informal reading inventory* to more carefully evaluate their reading strategies, determine their reading levels, and identify specific strengths and needs in comprehension and word analysis. Eventually, Ms. West will administer an informal reading inventory to all her students (process-oriented).

- Twice a month Ms. West listens to each student alternately read from either narrative or expository material and takes *running records* to check their comparative reading fluency (curriculum-based, standards-based).

- Every day Ms. West observes her students and takes *anecdotal notes* monitoring anything she considers significant in their struggles, their successes, and their attitudes; she sometimes uses checklists to make these observations more structured when determining their knowledge of multisyllabic words, ability to answer a range of comprehension questions, or progress toward state standards (process-oriented, standards-based).

- At the end of each content area unit, Ms. West gives students an oral or a written *cloze test* to determine their comprehension and their understanding of grammatical structures and content vocabulary (curriculum-based, standards-based).

- Once a week Ms. West listens as students *summarize* and *paraphrase* both narrative and expository material to evaluate their English language fluency, knowledge of story structure and organizational patterns, and comprehension skills (process-oriented, standards-based).

- Once or twice a week Ms. West and her students examine and briefly discuss the work in their *writing portfolios* (process-oriented, standards-based).

- Every six to eight weeks Ms. West administers a *structural analysis word list test* to those students who need it to measure growth in structural elements; she also gives a quick survey of *specialized vocabulary words* to determine which words students still need to master (standards-based, curriculum-based).

student performed better in comprehension than in vocabulary and may benefit from enhanced instruction in vocabulary, which, in turn, might help both scores. However, we *cannot* say the student's average reading score is the 54th percentile (the average of 65 and 43).

Another type of reported standardized test score is **stanine scores.** These are scores that have been converted into nine equally spaced units, with 1 being the lowest and 9 the highest. A stanine of 5 is considered the mean (average) score, so stanines 1, 2, and 3 represent below-average performance; 4, 5, and 6 represent average performance; and 7, 8, and 9 represent above-average performance (see Figure 2.6).

- stanine scores

When interpreting test scores it is important to know the reported standard deviation for the test. The **standard deviation** (SD) is the number used to

- standard deviation

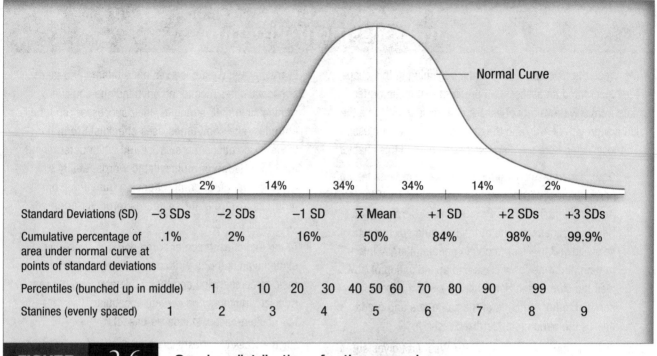

				Normal Curve		
	2%	14%	34%	34%	14%	2%
Standard Deviations (SD)	−3 SDs	−2 SDs	−1 SD	x̄ Mean	+1 SD	+2 SDs	+3 SDs
Cumulative percentage of area under normal curve at points of standard deviations	.1%	2%	16%	50%	84%	98%	99.9%
Percentiles (bunched up in middle)	1	10	20 30	40 50 60 70	80	90	99
Stanines (evenly spaced)	1	2	3	4 5 6	7	8	9

FIGURE **2.6**   Scoring distributions for the normal curve.

describe the variability in a set of scores as indicated by their distance—plus or minus 1, 2, or 3—from the mean (average) score. Think of the mean as the center of the distribution of scores. The higher the SD, the more spread out the scores are in a distribution. For example, consider means and standard deviations for scores on intelligence tests. The Wechsler Intelligence Scale has a mean (average) score of 100 and an SD of 15; thus, an IQ score of 100 is average. A score of 115 is one standard deviation above the average, or +1 SD; a score of 85 is −1 SD below the mean. Approximately 70 percent of all the scores in a normal distribution fall between +1 SD and −1 SD from the mean, or between 85 and 115 in the case of the Wechsler (see Figure 2.6 for cumulative percentages within a normal curve). Therefore, any score between 85 and 115 would not be considered exceptional, but within the average range. Similarly, about 95 percent of all scores are within two standard deviations; a score of 130 is 2 SD above the average (+2 SD) and a score of 70 is 2 SD below the average (−2 SD). However, a score of 145 is 3 SDs above the average (the criterion score for joining Mensa)—an extremely high score, while a score falling 3 SDs or more below the mean would be exceptionally low. If we consider the distribution of percentile scores, those that are between approximately the 30th and 70th percentiles fall within an average range, as shown in Figure 2.6. Likewise, stanine scores of 4, 5, and 6, also shown in Figure 2.6, are considered average scores.

It is important for interpreting test results to know not only what the mean and SD are, but also to know how much error is associated with the test. All tests have some error, and that error is represented by a number known as the **standard error of measurement** (SEM). Using this number provides a range of scores that a student's "true" score will likely fall within. For example, let's say the standardized test score for a student is the 77th percentile, but the SEM for this test is 12. This means that the student's "true" score falls somewhere between the 65th (77 − 12) and the 89th (77 + 12) percentile. This is quite a range. With so much room for error, we might wonder why so much empha-

standard error of measurement ●

sis is placed on standardized test scores. Of course, the SEM may be lower, but this example indicates why it is important for those reporting test results to report this information to aid in interpretation. Information about the mean, SD, and SEM is available in the test's technical manual.

INFORMAL, OR DIRECT, ASSESSMENT PROCEDURES

Literacy assessment devices that provide a teacher with information *directly* applicable to instructional planning are numerous and include IRIs; running records; interest and attitude surveys; interviews; teacher-made activities such as cloze tests; curriculum material placement tests; retelling tasks; word list and spelling tests; and written teacher observation procedures such as checklists, anecdotal notes, and scoring rubrics. Instructional lessons themselves are inextricably intertwined with direct assessment, as teaching and assessing continually inform one another. A discussion of all the assessment devices available is beyond the scope of this chapter, and it is not necessary or possible for a teacher to use every device contained in this chapter. Because a teacher has limited instructional time, the choice of which tools to use should be based on the specific literacy needs of the class and the type of information the assessment tool provides. For example, teachers who wish to use interest groups when studying particular content area units would administer an interest inventory developed to help identify potential groupings (see Appendix D). The descriptions that follow should help teachers decide what tools would be best to use for their particular purposes.

Informal Reading Inventory

An **informal reading inventory,** or IRI, is one of the most valuable diagnostic tools for assessing the reading progress of each student in the class as well as diagnosing specific reading strengths and needs. These inventories are referred to as "informal" because they are not norm-referenced. The IRI is an individual diagnostic reading test composed of lists of leveled sight words or sentences and a set of graded reading passages (both narrative and expository) from preprimer through grade 8 or even grade 12, with accompanying comprehension questions for each passage. Most basal reader series include their own IRI (sometimes called a *student placement test*) as part of their evaluation program, but devices such as the *Analytical Reading Inventory* (Merrill/Prentice Hall), the *Basic Reading Inventory, Preprimer–12* (Kendall/Hunt), the *Flynt–Cooter Reading Inventory for the Classroom* (Merrill/Prentice Hall), and the *Qualitative Reading Inventory* (HarperCollins) are also available (see Appendix C for a list of these and other assessment tools). Teachers can also design their own IRI by compiling a series of graded passages from their own curriculum materials by using readability formulas and taxonomies (tools that provide a classification of types of knowledge, such as Bloom's Taxonomy) for developing appropriate questions. Because they actually listen to the student reading aloud, observant teachers are offered a kind of "window into the learner's brain" to see what strategies for word analysis and construction of meaning are used. The IRI is an invaluable tool because it enables the teacher to:

- estimate a student's independent, instructional, frustration, and listening comprehension levels;
- determine strengths and needs in word analysis and comprehension abilities;

● informal reading inventory

- understand how a student is using syntactic (structure), graphophonic (visual–sound), and semantic (meaning) cues to make sense of reading;
- compare how a student decodes words in isolation with how that student decodes words in the context of meaningful sentences; and
- assess oral reading fluency if the oral reading is timed. The reading rate in words per minute can then be computed, and a determination made about fluency as related to reading rate (see Figure 3.7 on page 82).

Procedures for administering published IRIs vary, so teachers should follow the instructions for the particular IRI chosen. In general, the following guidelines, while not universal, are representative of the recommended procedures for administering IRIs.

The IRI takes about 20 to 30 minutes to administer and is often taped; the **miscues** ● student reads aloud while the teacher records the reader's **miscues**—deviations from the actual text—by using a kind of shorthand. After the oral reading, the teacher asks for a retelling and then poses a series of comprehension questions. **retelling** ● The **retelling**, which asks the reader to describe what she just read, gives insight into the reader's general ability to recall, interpret, and draw conclusions from the text. The follow-up comprehension questions assess specific aspects of the reader's understanding of the material read. Because comprehension of text is a critical issue beyond the early grades, it is also helpful for teachers to ask for retellings and follow-up questions after students have read passages silently. These results can then be compared with results following an oral reading, especially when the oral reading reveals a low comprehension score. Oral performance can interrupt students' comprehension as they focus on a flawless performance. Additionally, since most reading in grades 4–8 and beyond is done silently, the results are important data for the classroom teacher. In addition to providing both narrative and expository passages, published IRIs provide several forms, so it is an easy task to use one form for oral reading and another for silent reading. The following questions, modified as appropriate, can be asked to elicit a thorough retelling for both narrative (stories) and expository (informational) material.

- What can you tell me about [topic of passage or story]?
- What else was this passage/story about besides [the topic student mentioned already]?
- What happened after [event mentioned in retelling]?
- What do you think the author(s) is (are) trying to tell us [in the part mentioned in retelling]?
- How was [event or fact mentioned in retelling] important to this passage/story?
- How do you think you might use this information?
- How is this reading like anything you have read about before?

Retellings should be done prior to asking the comprehension questions provided in a published inventory. If a retelling is complete enough and time constraints are an issue, very few comprehension questions may need to be asked because they would essentially have been answered already. Whenever possible, however, all the comprehension questions should be asked directly. In reviewing published IRIs it is important to look for 8 to 10 questions per passage and a balance of the following question types:

- *Literal*—The student recalls or recognizes information directly stated in the text.

- *Inferential*—The student recognizes or discovers relationships in the text that are not directly stated.

- *Critical/evaluative*—The student uses original and logical thought and previous knowledge or experiences to solve a problem or make a value judgment.

Analysis of results might indicate strengths in literal comprehension but weaknesses in inferential or critical/evaluative thinking. Such information certainly helps a teacher plan appropriate instruction.

After beginning the IRI with an easy passage, the student continues to read progressively more difficult passages. When the student falls below about 90 percent in word recognition accuracy for oral reading, or achieves less than 60 percent accuracy in comprehension, or appears frustrated, the test is terminated; the passage level at which this occurs is called the **frustration level.** After   • frustration level
the student reaches the frustration level, the teacher reads aloud passages at successively higher grade levels until the student is unable to answer correctly at least 75 percent of the comprehension questions (this percentage may vary depending on the IRI being used). The purpose of this last step is to determine the learner's reading capacity level, also called *listening comprehension level.*
A **reading capacity level** is the highest level of material a student can under-   • reading capacity level
stand when the passage is read to him.

Material is at the student's **independent level,** appropriate for recreational   • independent level
reading, when that student can read the passage without stress, correctly pronounce 97 percent of the words, and correctly answer at least 90 percent of the comprehension questions. The passage at which the student can correctly pronounce between 91 and 96 percent of the words and correctly answer at least 60 percent of the comprehension questions is the student's **instructional level,** the   • instructional level
appropriate level of difficulty for classroom instruction in reading (see Figure 2.7).

After analyzing decoding and comprehension errors to establish what instruction is needed in these skill areas, the teacher conducts a *miscue analysis* to determine how the learner is using language clues (i.e., syntactic, semantic, graphophonic) to think about reading. The teacher looks for patterns

Summary of informal reading inventory percentages.*   FIGURE **2.7**

	WORD RECOGNITION	COMPREHENSION
Independent level	97% or above	90% or above
Instructional level	91–96%	60–89%
Frustration level	90% or below	Below 60%
Listening comprehension level		75% or above

*Percentages may vary among inventories and for grade levels. These percentages of accuracy are suggested for grades 4–8 (Cooper, 1952; Klesius & Homan, 1985; Powell & Dunkeld, 1971).

of miscues, such as those that retain the meaning (e.g., *Dad* for *father*), those that retain the syntactic pattern (e.g., *being* for *begging*), or those that simply retain the visual/sound similarities (e.g., *father* for *feather*). Miscues such as repetitions of words or phrases usually do not signify errors but indicate that the student may be rereading to try to rework a word or passage that did not seem to make sense.

Teachers should choose a commercial IRI that corresponds as closely as possible to the instructional materials used in the classroom and should agree with what the inventory considers a text deviation (e.g., a *repetition* is usually considered a positive second search for meaning). Additionally, by noting the types of comprehension questions, the number asked, and how scoring is handled, teachers can examine how the inventory evaluates comprehension. Teachers should also look at the clarity of instructions for administration, scoring, and interpretation and select an IRI with which they feel comfortable. See Figure 2.8 for an example of a completed IRI protocol demonstrating coding, scoring, retelling, comprehension, and miscue analysis for one student (Woods & Moe, 1999).

Running Records

running records ● Another method for analyzing a reader's miscues is **running records** (Clay, 1985, 2000). Running record assessments use a system of checks and other marking conventions to represent what a reader says and does while reading text aloud. Analysis of running records reveals whether the reader uses the language cue systems (V = visual, or graphophonic; S = syntactic; M = meaning, or semantic) and engages in self-correction of errors. Running records may appear easier to administer than IRIs and more expedient because no special materials are needed other than paper and pencil. The IRI, however, is a more thorough assessment, because it generally requires the student to read more than one passage and allows for comparisons of the student's oral reading with the silent reading of both narrative and expository material. It is important to keep in mind that multiple samples will always offer a clearer picture of any student's "true" reading ability, but at times the expediency of the running record makes it more appealing, especially as a means of tracking reading fluency or measuring reading rate if the reading of the passage is timed.

WWW

Norms for Oral Reading Fluency
www.readnaturally.com/pdf/oralreadingfluency.pdf
http://brt.uoregon.edu/techreports/TR_33_
NCORF_DescStats.pdf

Words read correctly per minute has been shown to be an accurate indicator of overall reading performance (Fuchs et al., 2001). National performance norms for oral reading fluency are available and can be found in Hasbrouck and Tindal (2006) or at the websites provided here.

With the running record, students orally read text passages ranging from easy to difficult. Because the focus of running records is the word level, they may be more appropriate for use with students in grades 4–8 who struggle. Although comprehension is not assessed with comprehension questions, teachers often ask readers to do a retelling after the passage is read to check for understanding. Teachers are able to examine students' strengths and limitations in the use of various decoding strategies by making a check mark on a piece of paper as the student reads each word correctly, and by writing the word diacritically to denote substitutions, repetitions, mispronunciations, or unknown words. Refer to Figure 2.9 for an illustrative example of the coding conventions used for running records. Again, a check mark indicates the word was read correctly. *R* indicates repetition. The arrow shows what was repeated. Words in the original text are written below the horizontal lines and what

Example of a completed IRI protocol.   **FIGURE**   2.8

FORM C, LEVEL 4	READER'S PASSAGES PAGE 31

Prior Knowledge/Prediction

☐ Read the title and predict what the story is about. A sick pony.

    Q: What do you know about a sick pony?

    SR: I don't know. I've never been on a pony.

	Prior Knowledge
	☐ a lot
	☐ some
	☑ none

☐ Read the first two sentences and add more to your prediction.

    A boy is really worried about his pony. The pony's sick.

A Sick Pony*	O	I	S	A	Rp	Rv
1 Jody was so/worried that he didn't even want to eat. He had stayed						
2 in the barn all day/to take care of his sick pony, ~~Gabilan~~. The pony's/condition *(Gab / Gabil above Gabilan; cold above condition)*		/	/		/	
3 was growing worse as/his/breathing grew louder and harder. *(breath above breathing)*			/		/	
4 At nightfall, Jody/brought a blanket from the house so he could sleep/ *(night; horse SC)*			/		/	
5 near/Gabilan. In the middle of the night/the wind whipped around the barn *(wind SC)*					/	
6 and blew the door open.						
7 At dawn Jody awakened to the banging of the barn door. Gabilan						
8 was gone! In (alarm) he ran from the barn following the pony's tracks. *(follow above following)*	/		/			
9 Looking upward he saw buzzards, the birds of/death, flying overhead. *(up; buzz SC)*			/			
10 Jody stood still, then ran to the top of a small hill. In a clearing below, he *(clear above clearing)*			/			
11 saw something that filled his heart with anger and hate. A/buzzard/was *(anjer above anger)*			/		/	
12 perched on his (dying) pony's head. *(pointed above perched)*	/		/			
TOTALS Number of miscues __16__ Number of self-corrections __3__						

O = omission   S = substitution   Rp = repetition

I = insertion   A = aided by teacher   Rv = reversal

*This passage is a retelling from the novel *Tuned Out*, by Maia Wojciechowska.   *(continued)*

FIGURE   2.8   Continued.

FLUENCY: Does the reader . . .

- ☐ read smoothly?   ☑ word-by-word?   ☐ read words in meaningful phrases?
- ☐ use pitch, stress, and intonation to convey the meaning of a text?
- ☑ repeat words and phrases because he or she is monitoring the meaning (self-correcting)?   *some*
- ☑ repeat words and phrases because he or she is just trying to sound out the words?
- ☑ use punctuation to divide the text into units of meaning?   *Some WR difficulties are beginning to interfere.*
- ☐ ignore the punctuation?

RATING SCALE

1 = clearly labored, disfluent reading, very slow pace   3 = poor phrasing/intonation/reasonable pace
2 = slow and choppy reading/slow pace   *2.5*   4 = fairly fluent reading/good pace

Cueing Systems		Graphophonically Similar Initial Medial Final (word level)	Syntactically Acceptable Unacceptable (sentence level)	Semantic Change in Meaning (CM) No Change in Meaning (NCM) (sentence level)
LINE #	Miscue			
2	cold	I	A	CM
3	breath*	IM	A	*slight* CM
4	night*	IM	A	*slight* CM
8	follow*	IM	A	*slight* CM
9	up*	I	A	NCM
10	clear*	IM	U	CM
11	anjer	IF	U	CM
12	pointed	IF	A	CM
	* Note the omissions of word endings.			

SUMMARY

- ☑ Most, ☐ few, ☐ no   miscues were graphophonically similar to the
  some   word in the passage.
- ☐ Most, ☐ few, ☐ no   miscues were syntactically matched.
- ☐ Most, ☑ few, ☐ no   miscues maintained the author's meaning.
- ☑ The self-corrections demonstrate that the reader monitors the meaning.

RETELLING

It's about a pony. Jody is really worried about the pony. It's sick. And the barn door started banging.
Q: Can you tell any more?
SR: That night Jody stayed with the horse. He saw something buzz around. The pony was gone.
Q: Can you tell more?
SR: No

RETELLING SUMMARY: ☐ many details, logical order ☐ some details, some order ☑ few details, disorder

Note: Indicate any probing with a "P"

Story Elements	All	Some	None
Main Character(s)	✓		
Time and Place		✓	
Problem		✓	
Plot Details in Sequence			✓
Turning Point			✓
Resolution			✓
Reader's Thumbnail Summary:	A pony is sick.		

COMPREHENSION QUESTIONS AND POSSIBLE ANSWERS

(RIF = Retells in fact; PIT = Puts information together; CAR = Combines author and reader;
EAS = Evaluates and substantiates)

_+_ (RIF) 1. Who are the two main characters in this story? (Jody and his sick pony, Gabilan)

_+_ (RIF) 2. Where does this story take place? (in a barn, in the country)

_½_ (PIT) 3. What is the problem in this story? (the pony is sick and getting worse)

_−_ (CAR) 4. What do you know about the phrase the **pony's condition**? (state of health, Gabilan is sick, his health was poor) He has a cold.
What does the phrase **pony's condition** have to do with this story? (the pony's condition was growing worse as his breathing grew louder and harder) He's sick.

_+_ (RIF) 5. Why did Jody take a blanket from the house? (so he could sleep near Gabilan) with his pony

_−_ (CAR) 6. What do you know about the word **dawn**? (sunrise, the start of the day)
What does the word **dawn** have to do with this story? (Jody woke up at dawn) I don't know.

_−_ (PIT) 7. Why was the barn door banging? (in the middle of the night a wind whipped around the barn and blew the door open; at dawn some wind was still blowing) It's loose.

_−_ (EAS) 8. Do you think Jody's pony was dying? You think this because . . . (yes, he was really sick; it didn't say that the veterinarian had been to treat the pony; his breathing was loud; when Jody found Gabilan he saw a buzzard perched on his head) No. It ran out of the barn.

READER TEXT RELATIONSHIP (RTR): From the Text ☐ adequate ☑ not adequate
From Head to Text ☐ adequate ☑ not adequate

Scoring Guide Summary		
Word Recognition	Comprehension	Emotional Status:
Independent 2	Independent 0–1	Uncertain, signs of stress
Instructional 7 −16	Instructional 2 −4½	and tension
Frustration 14+	Frustration 4+	

FIGURE 2.9 Example of a coded and analyzed running record.

CLAIRE'S READING

Claire made a number of errors on this text but she often self-corrected without any assistance. (Only a portion of the record is shown.)

CLAIRE'S RECORD

Analysis of errors and self-corrections

Information used

Page of Text	Running Record	E M S V	SC M S V
"Because I'm years older," Hannah smirked.	✓ ✓ ✓ ✓ R ✓ ✓.		
He gave up arguing and stomped off towards his	✓ ✓ ✓ ✓ ✓ ✓ ✓ ✓		
room. "See you in the morning," he said to	bedroom. She | SC ✓ ✓ ✓ ✓ ✓ ✓ room. See |	Ⓜ Ⓢ Ⓥ Ⓜ Ⓢ Ⓥ	M S Ⓥ
his mother to emphasize that he was ignoring	✓ ✓ and | SC emphases ✓ R ✓ ✓ ✓ to | emphasize	Ⓜ Ⓢ V M S Ⓥ	M S Ⓥ
Hannah.	Anna | SC Hannah |	Ⓜ Ⓢ Ⓥ	M S Ⓥ
He posed in front of his bedroom mirror. If	✓ possed ✓ ✓ ✓ ✓ ✓. ✓ posed	M S Ⓥ	
Hannah was a damsel in distress, she couldn't	✓ ✓ ✓ ✓ ✓ district | SC ✓ ✓ distress |	M S Ⓥ	Ⓜ Ⓢ Ⓥ
expect him to come galloping to her rescue.	✓ ✓ ✓ ✓ ✓ ✓ ✓ ✓.		
She could stay tied to the stake. He would	✓ ✓ ✓ died | SC ✓ ✓ ✓. ✓ ✓ tied |	M S Ⓥ	Ⓜ Ⓢ Ⓥ
charge in cutting this way and that with his	✓ ✓ ✓ the ✓ ✓ ✓ ✓ this	M Ⓢ Ⓥ	
fearsome sword. All would fall before him and	✓ sWord | SC ✓ ✓ ✓ ✓ ✓ sword. |	M S Ⓥ	Ⓜ Ⓢ V
he would fight his way to where she was tied	✓ ✓ ✓ ✓ ✓ ✓ ✓ ✓ ✓		
and then . . .	✓ ✓ . . .		

Her teacher summarized the analysis of the reading like this:

Claire uses meaning, structure, and visual information, repeats words occasionally, self-corrects most of her errors, picking up more visual information, and attempts all words.

Claire needs to take more responsibility for making all the information match. She needs to be encouraged to recognize when meaning is lost, and self-correct.

the reader said is written above the lines. *SC* means self-correct, and these mis-cues are analyzed under a separate column because they give important information, but they will not count as words read incorrectly for scoring pur-poses. *E* means error. Alternatively, teachers can duplicate the pages the student will read and record errors next to or on top of the text copy.

After identifying the words that the student read incorrectly, the teacher cal-culates the percentage of words read correctly. For the example in Figure 2.9, this would be 92/96, or 96 percent accuracy. Teachers use the percentage of words read correctly to determine whether the material is too easy, too difficult, or at the appropriate instructional level for the student at that time using the same percentages discussed for the IRI estimation of reading levels.

As with the IRI, the teacher can then do a miscue analysis, categorizing the student's miscues according to the semantic, syntactic, and graphophonic cue-ing systems, in order to examine what word identification strategies are being used. The letters *M* (for meaning cues), *S* (for syntactic cues), and *V* (for visu-al cues) are used. Errors can then be classified and charted and instructional decisions made accordingly.

Anecdotal Notes

Many teachers incorrectly assume that their own observations about a stu-dent's literacy status are not as important as the results of standardized tests. Researchers strongly dispute this belief (Cambourne & Turbill, 1990). One of the most powerful and reliable parts of any teacher's assessment and evalua-tion process, researchers claim, is teachers' daily, systematic observation of their students, using either a clipboard or a tape recorder. Ideally, some obser-vation time should be scheduled every day to focus on particular students and take brief logs, or **anecdotal notes,** about the students' involvement in literacy events (Rhodes & Nathenson-Mejia, 1992). Teachers should observe students in every possible language context: one-on-one interactions, small group dis-cussions, and large class settings. The focus should always be on what learners *do* as they read and write. The most useful notes

● anecdotal notes

- describe specific events.
- report rather than evaluate.
- relate the events to other information about the student.

Teachers can make observations about learners' attempts to use word parts, their success with daily reading and writing activities, the questions they ask, the books they are reading, what they seem to like and dislike in reading, and whether they use strategies and skills fluently or indicate some level of confusion.

These anecdotal records provide truly dynamic documentation of students' growth over time while also directing the teacher's attention to problem areas needing direct instruction for individuals and possible minilesson topics for small groups. Based on the anecdotal notes provided in Figure 2.10, Luke's teacher concluded that he

- is learning to use his prior knowledge and the context of the passage to determine new words' meanings.
- is developing positive reading habits.
- still needs to expand his vocabulary but is developing more confidence in using background knowledge, context, and word parts.

DATE	NOTES
12/4/08	During independent reading, Luke attempted a guess at a new word's meaning, <u>spectacles</u>. He said he remembered his brother talking about his glasses as his "specs."
1/6/09	Luke asked to return to the library to find a different book after starting one that he said was not interesting.
1/14/09	During guided reading, Luke came across the word <u>tireless</u>. He immediately recognized the <u>-less</u> ending and said "without tire." After a brief time, he said, "Oh, they wanted to make enough money to get a gift for their mother and they were working as if they were not tired."
1/27/09	Luke assembled a set of nonfiction literature and located several websites on the topic of planets. He has chosen drawings, charts, and diagrams as the activities he will use to show what he has learned.
2/17/09	Luke created an attractive and accurate mobile of the sun and the planets to share with the class as a visual for his oral report.

FIGURE 2.10   **Example of anecdotal notes for Luke.**

- has an interest in the topic of planets.
- has a well-developed spatial intelligence.

This information helps Luke's teacher provide appropriate instruction for him that might include the use of literature circles, which allow students to choose the books they wish to read and discuss with their peers (see Chapter 5) and provide opportunities to create artistic responses to what they have read.

Checklists

Often teachers use checklists as a starting point for documenting their observations. These checklists can be developed by school districts to reflect district criteria, teacher developed, or located in other professional references. A checklist is especially helpful in providing guidance to novices for what to observe. Checklists should provide for multiple observations and use in a variety of contexts so that conclusions are more accurate. They can be used quite effectively to gather large amounts of data that are easily compiled and reviewed. For example, the teacher can use school district content standards to develop a checklist of strategies that students are being taught. The checklist includes columns for marks (e.g., checks, plus signs, minus signs) and space for comments. Checklists can be used while observing individuals or groups, with dates or students' names inserted as column headings. Such checklists can be used periodically to monitor students' progress. Figure 2.11 is an example of a checklist for observing literacy behaviors in grades 4–8 for either individuals over time or for groups of students.

Literacy observation checklist for grades 4–8.   FIGURE 2.11

GRADE LEVEL: 4   TEACHER: Mrs. B

CONTENT STANDARDS	Brad	Sasha	Jen	Mark	Raul	Jack	COMMENTS
Reads narrative text with fluency		9/8	9/8	9/11	9/11		partner Jack & Raul
Reads expository text with fluency			9/20		9/20		
Identifies main events of the plot		9/8	9/8	9/11	9/11	9/11	
Makes inferences using text		9/8		9/11			
Makes inferences using illustrations			9/8			9/11	work with Brad 1-on-1
Identifies structural patterns in expository text:							Do more in next grading period
—compare and contrast							
—cause and effect							
—order (enumeration or sequential)			10/4	10/4			
Asks questions				9/16			
Makes predictions	9/16	9/16	9/16	9/16	9/16	9/16	
Monitors own understanding			9/20				
Applies appropriate fix-up strategies			9/20				
Creates mental images while reading							
Retells to include salient points		10/12	10/12	10/12	10/12		focus more on this
Makes text-to-self connections	10/4						
Uses clues to determine word meanings:							
—word clues							work on affixes
—sentence or paragraph clues			9/16	9/16			
—background knowledge				9/16			

NAME: _Mark_

TITLE(S) OF WORK ASSESSED: _The Solar System_

Did I . . . ?

☑ have a plan before I started writing?

☑ write complete sentences that are not run-on sentences?

☑ write some compound sentences that are connected with *and, or, but?*

☑ write a good topic sentence for each paragraph?

☑ write supporting sentences that help support the topic sentence in each paragraph?

☑ write accurate nonfiction that is also interesting?

☑ provide good transitions between paragraphs?

NA write a story that has a beginning, a middle, and an end?

NA write a story with a problem and a solution?

NA describe the main character well?

NA include dialogue in my story?

NA use correct punctuation in any dialogue?

☑ use interesting and vivid words?

☑ confer with others to revise?

☑ edit my drafts?

FIGURE 2.12 Student self-assessment checklist for effective writing.

Checklists can also be constructed for students to use for self-assessment. Such checklists help students recognize the specific elements of performance that are expected of them. They also provide a kind of road map for completing their work. Figure 2.12 is an example of a checklist used with students in grades 4–8 for effective writing.

Scoring Rubrics

scoring rubric ●

performance descriptors ●

A **scoring rubric** describes the levels of performance that a student must demonstrate related to a particular achievement goal, whether it be written, oral, or multimedia. These criteria, or **performance descriptors,** help communicate to both teachers and students the standards that will be used to evaluate students' work. Scoring rubrics help provide consistency in evaluating student work. Appendix D offers examples for evaluating written work, oral performance, and multimedia presentations. Scoring rubrics represent a more analytical assessment of student work in that specific areas of strength and weakness can be readily identified.

The use of scoring rubrics also provides opportunities for involving students in self-assessment and in the formative assessment process. Effective rubrics help provide descriptive feedback to students, and as such model the kind of metacognitive thinking we want students to do as self-assessors. For example, using a rubric like the one in Figure 2.13 engages learners in reflecting on their own learning and in goal-setting behaviors for meeting a specific learning target. As students engage in self-assessments, they become capable of designing their own rubrics. The result of including students in self-assessment and goal setting may be more purposeful learning and more motivated students (Locke & Latham, 2002; Shepard, 2005). Many websites provide effective rubrics. Others describe the process of designing, refining, and implementing rubrics in a variety of subject areas, for both teacher- and student-generated rubrics.

Cloze Tests

A **cloze test** is an easy-to-use assessment device that consists of a representative 250–300 word passage from any relevant reading material, making it a useful tool across the curriculum, as Figure 2.14 illustrates. To construct a cloze passage, the first sentence is left intact, followed by an every *n*th word (*n* = 5, 7, or 10) deletion pattern to achieve 25–50 blanks to be filled in. Cloze tests are used to determine a student's ability to comprehend the ideas in the sentences as well as in the entire passage (Taylor, 1953). Students must read the passage and supply the missing words. Besides establishing whether or not the text is at the appropriate instructional level (or *suitability*) for a student, this procedure may be used to assess the student's ability to use context clues in reading (see Chapter 4). By examining each incorrect response made by the student, the teacher can determine whether the response makes sense syntactically or semantically. Often, a response may be both semantically and syntactically correct without being the exact keyed response (e.g., for "The boy *stroked* the dog" the reader substitutes "The boy *petted* the dog"), which would be considered acceptable as evidence of using these two cueing systems. However, for determining appropriateness of the material in terms of reading level, only the exact keyed response can be accepted as correct. A score of 30 to 50 percent accuracy is considered instructional level, quite a lenient score as a result of only accepting exact keyed responses. A score above 50 percent is considered independent level, and a score below 30 percent is considered frustration level. The cloze material can be designed in written form or orally, on tape, for struggling readers. A variation on cloze, called maze, provides three word choices for deleted words instead of a blank. Students must choose the best word that fits the passage. The same deletion patterns that are used with cloze can be used with maze, but word choices are very specific (the correct word, a word of the same part of speech, a word of a different part of speech), and the scoring changes to 85 percent for independent level, 60 to 75 percent for instructional level, and below 50 percent for frustration level (Guthrie et al., 1974).

● cloze test

FIGURE   2.13   Example of a self-assessment scoring rubric for a specific learning target.

RUBRIC: _Creatures of the Sea From A to Z_   STUDENT: _Luke_

Requirements	FANTASTIC 4	NICE JOB! 3	OKAY 2	NEEDS IMPROVEMENT 1	SELF-ASSESSMENT	TEACHER'S ASSESSMENT
Cover Page	Includes title, author, and an appropriate illustration.	Includes two of the three required elements.	Includes one of the three required elements.	Does not include any of the three required elements, or is missing.	3 _I forgot to put my name on the cover page._	3 _No name on cover page_
Alphabet Pages	Each of the 26 pages includes all required elements: (1) target word (2) word used in context (3) three facts about word (4) illustration for the word	Most pages include at least three required elements, and frequently four elements.	Many pages include two required elements, with several including three or four elements.	Many pages include only one or two required elements, or some pages are missing.	4 _I did pages for all the letters._	3 _Sometimes the three required facts were left out._
Author Page	Includes author name, background information, an illustration or photo.	Includes two of the three required elements.	Includes one of the three required elements.	Does not include any of the three elements, or is missing.	1 _I forgot to do the author page._	1 _The author page is missing._

My strengths are: _My illustrations are really first-rate. I am skilled at drawing._

What I need to work on: _I need to read the directions for my assignments carefully._

Example of group cloze test for eighth grade social studies material about Joseph Cinque.*   FIGURE   2.14

Directions: In the numbered space preceding each line of text, write one word that you think best fits the blank. Read through the entire selection before you begin. This will give you clues for filling in the missing words.

MISSING WORDS	TEXT
	Human bondage has always been part of civilization.
1. _____	The ancient Egyptians enslaved the people _____
2. _____	conquered. So did the ancient Romans _____ Greeks.
3. _____	Moslem traders of the eleventh _____ exported
4. _____	their North African captives to _____ Moslem
5. _____	countries. Long before Europeans came _____ the
6. _____	scene, a small percentage of _____ Africans
7. _____	enslaved fellow black Africans. But _____
8. _____	was a difference between ancient and _____
9. _____	slavery. In ancient times, slavery was _____
10. _____	about race. Most victims were convicted _____
11. _____	or captives in wars and religious _____. They
12. _____	usually remained in the same_____ area or at
13. _____	least on the _____ continent.
14. _____	The global economy did not _____ the
15. _____	African slave trade until Spain _____ Portugal
16. _____	discovered the New World. Even _____, the
17. _____	Spanish first tried to enslave _____. They failed
18. _____	because Indians were nomadic _____, not laborers or
19. _____	farmers, and fiercely _____. As forced laborers, they
20. _____	tended to _____ and die. In fact, so many
21. _____	_____ that in 1517 a missionary named

*To be used to determine the suitability of the text for the students. *Source:* Adapted from K. Abdul-Jabbar and A. Steinberg, "Resistance," in *Black Profiles in Courage*, pp. 40–45. Copyright © 1996 by William Morrow & Co.

(continued)

FIGURE 2.14 **Continued.**

22. _____ _____ Bartolome de las Casas suggested substituting

23. _____ _____ blacks instead. And that's what happened.

24. _____ _____ blacks were better suited. Most lived

25. _____ _____ settled villages, towns, and cities. They

26. _____ _____ expert farmers who grew permanent crops,

27. _____ _____ the men were used to laboring

28. _____ _____ the fields. Also, Africans understood that

29. _____ _____ could become a slave at any

30. _____ _____. And once enslaved, especially in a

31. _____ _____ culture, they knew they could not

32. _____ _____ and hide in the crowd. In

33. _____ _____ Caucasian society, where could a black

34. _____ _____ hide? . . . So African blacks quickly became the

slaves of choice. (A minimum of 25 blanks are scored.)

ANSWER KEY:

1. they	13. same	25. in
2. and	14. impact	26. were
3. century	15. and	27. and
4. other	16. then	28. in
5. on	17. Indians	29. anyone
6. black	18. hunters	30. time
7. there	19. independent	31. different
8. modern	20. sicken	32. escape
9. not	21. died	33. a
10. criminals	22. Bishop	34. person
11. feuds	23. African	
12. geographic	24. African	

Writing Folders

The **writing folder** is a folder where students keep all their rough drafts in various stages of the writing process and other daily compositions or reports, topics for future pieces they might like to write, and notes from minilessons. Students also include their own assessments and reflections about any piece they have completed. Pieces can be assessed using an analytic approach (see the earlier section titled "Scoring Rubrics") or a holistic approach. In a **holistic approach** to writing assessment, the whole piece is judged, whereas in an **analytic approach,** its individual parts are assessed. Important characteristics of good writing are considered, such as the impact of the piece (does the paper engage the reader in a clear, imaginative, convincing way?), its inventiveness (does it surprise or is it clever?), and its individuality (does it have a voice?) (Kirby, Liner, & Vinz, 1988). Material from writing folders is the basis for teacher–student conferences on individual instructional needs, and minilesson topics are chosen from observations during these sessions.

For special displays, publications, or parent–teacher meetings, the teacher often meets with each student to make collaborative decisions on what piece(s) should be selected to put in a special "showcase portfolio" (see "Using Portfolios for Managing Assessment Data" later in this chapter) that will be shown to parents. Writing folders are often proudly decorated and personalized by students and kept in a special place in the classroom where they are easily accessible. Anecdotal notes, checklists, or scoring rubrics regarding the contents of these folders provide important assessment data on students' writing progress.

- writing folder

- holistic approach
- analytic approach

www

Writing Folders

www.sasked.gov.sk.ca/docs/xla/ela15c3.html

www.cesa12k12.wi.us/teach/write/process.html

www.powa.org

www.ipl.org/div/aplus

Word Lists

Periodically, teachers in grades 4–8 may wish to conduct an informal assessment of their students' recognition of particular words and especially their use of structural elements often found in multisyllabic words. To keep an account of known structural elements for each student, 3×5 index cards can be numbered and arranged in the same order as the words on a list of polysyllabic words such as *The Nifty-Thrifty-Fifty* (Cunningham & Hall, 1998). While holding the cards for a student to respond to, the teacher uses an accompanying checklist to note which words the student recognizes and reads successfully. (Appendix F lists the Nifty-Thrifty-Fifty; Figure 2.15 shows a partial checklist; Appendix D includes the full checklist.) The student must say the entire word quickly, with no hesitation or sounding out, in order to receive a check for knowing that particular word. For each correct response, the teacher makes a check next to the corresponding word. If the student cannot say the entire word correctly, but does say any of the transferable chunks, these recognized parts should be checked, but the word will not be considered correct in the final scoring. The teacher can also write above the word any attempts, parts recognized, mispronunciations, or substitutions for later analysis. The student's score is the total number of words, not chunks, checked. This raw score can then be converted easily to a percentage since there are 50 words in the list. Lists of academic words (see Chapter 4) can also be used for this purpose.

NIFTY-THRIFTY-FIFTY*		TRANSFERABLE CHUNKS		
1. ✓ antifreeze	1. ✓ anti			
2. ____ beautiful *beauty-ful*			2. ✓ ful (y - i)	
3. ____ classify *class - class - classy*			3. ____ ify	
4. ____ communities *com - tees*	4. ✓ com		4. ✓ es (y - i)	
5. ____ community *com - ty*	5. ✓ com		5. ✓ y	
6. ____ composer *composition*	6. ✓ com		6. ____ er	
7. ____ continuous *continent*	7. ✓ con		7. ____ ous (drop e)	
8. ✓ conversation	8. ✓ con		8. ✓ tion	
9. ____ deodorize *deodorant*	9. ✓ de		9. ____ ize	
10. ✓ different			10. ✓ ent	
11. ✓ discovery	11. ✓ dis		11. ✓ y	
12. ✓ dishonest	12. ✓ dis			
13. ✓ electricity	13. ✓ e		13. ✓ ity	
14. ✓ employee	14. ✓ em		14. ✓ ee	
15. ____ encouragement *encourage*	15. ✓ en		15. ____ ment	
16. ____ expensive *expense*	16. ✓ ex		16. ____ ive	
17. ✓ forecast	17. ✓ fore			
18. ✓ forgotten			18. ✓ en (double t)	
19. ____ governor *government*			19. ____ or	
20. ✓ happiness			20. ✓ ness (y - i)	

Cards:

2. beautiful

1. antifreeze

3. classify

4. communities

Interest and Attitude Inventories

The interests and attitudes of students about reading, writing, and school in general have been found to be highly correlated with success in literacy. **Interest and attitude inventories** provide information about these factors and should therefore be included in any comprehensive assessment program. Given the importance of these factors, they should be monitored incidentally, using anecdotal notes, and deliberately through an interview or questionnaire, administered orally or in writing, to the whole class or to individuals. A sample reading interest inventory and an attitude survey are found in Appendix D. Teachers can design their own inventories appropriate to the age and developmental level of their learners, but the questions should be designed to solicit at least the following critical information:

- the subject areas that are motivating to the student
- the student's favorite book
- what the student does in his or her spare time
- what sports or hobbies the student enjoys
- the student's favorite television program
- the student's preferred instructional arrangements; for example, teacher directed or working alone, with a small group, or with one other student
- the student's attitudes toward reading and writing
- what reading materials and experiences the student has been exposed to

• interest and attitude inventories

Teachers then use these data to form interest groups or establish "partners" for reading, or to provide appropriate book selections for students to choose from for participation in book clubs (see Chapter 5).

USING PORTFOLIOS FOR MANAGING ASSESSMENT DATA

Teachers and students work together toward literacy development, so they each have responsibilities for managing assessment data that document that development. Teachers engaged in data-driven decision making welcome suggestions for organizing and managing assessment data (Harp, 2006). In Ms. West's classroom, portfolios offer a management system for classroom work. They also provide a way for students to take on some responsibility for organizing and self-evaluating their work.

Portfolios are defined here as a collection of selected products accompanied by evidence of reflection and self-evaluation; that is, each artifact, or selected product, within the portfolio is explained by a caption. The caption provides a brief description of the artifact and why it has been included. This latter part of the caption is referred to as a *reflective statement* because it requires the portfolio-maker to reflect on why the artifact is important to include, and to self-evaluate his or her growth in the area represented by the artifact. Use of checklists, such as in Figure 2.12, will help students prepare their reflective statements. The process of constructing a portfolio helps students understand what they know and what they still need to learn. And the process of explaining what they have learned and what they still need to learn, as Artis did in the opening scenario, helps students gain insight into themselves as learners (Chappuis, 2005).

WWW

Managing Assessment Data
*www.microsoft.com/education/
ThoughtLeadersDDDM.mspx*
www.3d2know.org/FAQ.html

• portfolios

WWW

Portfolio Assessment

http://school.discoveryeducation.com/
schrockguide/assess.html#portfolios

www.teachervision.fen.com/teaching-methods/
experimental-education/4528.html?detoured=1

With defined categories, a portfolio keeps products systematically sorted and can guide the daily work schedule. For example, one portfolio system could define categories that match the curriculum framework or state standards. Thus, portfolios from students in grades 4–8 might use comprehension, composition, vocabulary and word study, and independence as defined categories (Glazer, 1998). This kind of system enables both the teacher and the students to maintain an organized daily schedule, and it provides a point of entry for regular student–teacher conferencing. Selected artifacts are generally items the teacher designates for the portfolio (e.g., an attitude survey administered at the beginning of a school year to be compared with end-of-school-year attitudes) and those the student self-selects for particular reasons that are explained by the student. An example of a seventh-grade student's table of contents is provided in Figure 2.16.

working portfolio ●   Usually, students develop and maintain two types of portfolios: working and showcase. The **working portfolio** contains completed work samples or works in progress. It is the holding place for artifacts that may eventually be

FIGURE 2.16   Table of contents for a seventh-grade student's portfolio.

TABLE OF CONTENTS

Introduction to the Portfolio

Comprehension
- Written analysis for *Long Gone Daddy*
- Science project drawing of the plant cells compared to animal cells and summary report
- Tape recording of Book Club discussion

Composition
- Original story: "How the Red Cabbage Became Red"
- Persuasive letter to school principal for change in PE time
- Research report
- PowerPoint presentation

Vocabulary and Word Study
- Word sort sheets for contractions, prefixes, and suffixes
- Idiomatic expressions and what they really mean
- Roots and branches (Greek and Latin roots)
- New terms for math
- New terms for social studies
- New terms for science

Independence
- Self-assessment of writing checklist
- List of books read and time sheet initialed by parent

selected for placement in a showcase portfolio. The **showcase portfolio** is a collection of artifacts chosen to demonstrate excellence in achievement. Selected from the working portfolio, these artifacts are few but represent a student's best efforts, and each is accompanied by a reflective statement that explains the importance or value of the artifact to the portfolio owner. Both types can be developed as electronic portfolios; that is, technology-based portfolios. Using the power of digital technology, **electronic portfolios** provide students with the option of storing a great deal of information on a computer hard drive, jump/flash drive, CD, or DVD. Items such as work samples, pictures, art, and even oral reading samples that would be cumbersome to store and difficult to present to others using binders or files are easily stored, accessed, and presented through digital technology. The ability to connect sections of a portfolio through hyperlinks, allowing access to a variety of artifacts that might show how specific goals have been met, is also a benefit of the electronic portfolio. Sound, music, and video clips can also be included to enhance the electronic portfolio. Electronic portfolios would be a very attractive assessment option for students in grades 4–8 as they have grown up with computer technology and have little difficulty manipulating current technological devices. Such programs as PowerPoint and Hyperstudio can easily be used by students in these grades to create their portfolios.

The portfolios Ms. West's students shared, described at the beginning of this chapter, are examples of showcase portfolios. These portfolios were prepared and finalized for presentation to parents and guardians as a way of demonstrating to significant people each student's achievements for the school year.

Many excellent resources provide information on how to start portfolios, what they might include, how they can be organized, and student examples. Some of these are as follows:

- showcase portfolio

- electronic portfolio

WWW

Electronic Portfolios
*www.educationworld.com/
a_tech/tech/tech111.shtml*

Clemmons, J., Laase, L., Cooper, D., Areglado, N., & Dill, M. (1993). *Portfolios in the classroom: A teacher's sourcebook.* New York: Scholastic Professional Books.

Danielson, C., & Abrutyn, L. (1997). *An introduction to using portfolios in the classroom.* Alexandria, VA: Association for Supervision and Curriculum Development.

DeFina, A. A. (1992). *Portfolio assessment: Getting started.* New York: Scholastic Professional Books.

Fiderer, A. (1995). *Practical assessments for literature-based reading classrooms.* New York: Scholastic Professional Books.

Jenkins, C. B. (1996). *Inside the writing portfolio: What we need to know to assess children's writing.* Portsmouth, NH: Heinemann.

Myers, M., & Spalding, E. (Eds.). (1997). *Exemplar series grades 6–8.* Urbana, IL: National Council of Teachers of English.

Myers, M., & Spalding, E. (Eds.). (1997). *Standards exemplar series: Assessing student performance grades K–5.* Urbana, IL: National Council of Teachers of English.

Sunstein, B. S., & Lovell, J. H. (2000). *The portfolio standard: How students can show us what they know and are able to do.* Portsmouth, NH: Heinemann.

SUMMARY

The major goal of literacy assessment is twofold: to determine how each student is progressing in particular areas at a given time and to make instructional adjustments that are focused on students' needs. The best way to achieve this assessment goal is to use a variety of direct and indirect assessment tools; that is, to take a multidimensional approach for examining students' strengths and needs.

Indirect measures, or standardized instruments, provide important comparative data that have been proven to be valid and reliable but that do not always provide accurate and specific information for individual students. Data from such measures should, therefore, be interpreted cautiously, especially when the test-takers are culturally or linguistically diverse learners.

Direct assessments such as observations, anecdotal notes, and checklist data can support or refute standardized test data. Data compiled frequently and interpreted carefully by means of direct assessments are excellent for continually informing instruction.

The value of the assessment tools presented in this chapter depends largely on reflective analysis and how the devices are used for communicating literacy progress and resultant instructional plans with the students and their caregivers. By recognizing the strengths and limitations of different types of assessment tools, teachers can maximize their value within a balanced and comprehensive literacy program.

Questions
FOR JOURNAL WRITING AND DISCUSSION

1. Interview a local grade 4–8 teacher to determine what assessment strategies he uses. What components of literacy does the teacher assess? How are these areas assessed? Does the teacher rely more on direct or indirect assessment, or is there a balance? Discuss your findings with your classmates to compare your findings to theirs.

2. Daniels and Bizar (1998, pp. 207–209) offer 12 ideas to keep in mind for making sure assessment methods enact the ideals of best practice. Using the content of this chapter and other readings or information you have, consider these ideas. In your journal, choose two or three of the 12 statements and indicate whether you agree with the statement, and why or why not. Then, in class with a partner or small group, discuss the statements you chose.

   a. Assessment should reflect, encourage, and become an integral part of good instruction.

   b. Powerful evaluation efforts focus on the major, whole outcomes valued in the curriculum (real things such as writing, researching, reading, experimenting, problem solving, creating, speaking).

   c. Most school assessment activities should be formative (to ensure students learn better and teachers teach more effectively).

   d. Traditional norm-referenced, competitive measures that rank students against each other provide little helpful formative assessment and tend to undermine progressive instruction (constructive programs rely more on self-referenced growth measures).

   e. A key trait of effective thinkers, writers, problem solvers, readers, researchers, and other learners is that they continually self-monitor and self-evaluate (self-assessment).

   f. Skillful and experienced evaluators take a developmental perspective (stages).

   g. Teachers need a rich repertoire of assessment techniques.

h. It is never enough to look at learning events from only one angle; rather, we now use multiple measures, examining students' growth from several different perspectives (for a "thick" picture of students' learning).

i. Teachers need to reallocate the considerable time that they already spend on assessment, evaluation, record keeping, testing, and grading activities (less time scoring, more time saving and documenting—new assessment procedures do not require any more time, nor any less).

j. Sound evaluation programs provide, where necessary, a database for deriving legitimate, defensible student grades (however, norm-referenced grading should be deemphasized).

k. It takes many different people working cooperatively to effectively evaluate student growth and learning (external test-makers, teachers, students, parents or guardians, school support personnel).

l. The currently available state and national standardized tests yield an exceedingly narrow and unreliable picture of student achievement, are poor indicators of school performance, and encourage archaic instructional practices (professional teachers avoid teaching to standardized tests).

3. It is no longer enough to provide students with opportunities to learn and develop their literacy skills; schools must now provide proof in the form of standardized test scores that learning has actually taken place. Discuss this pervasive approach to measuring learning. What implications does it have for other forms of literacy assessment?

Suggestions
FOR PROJECTS AND FIELD ACTIVITIES

1. Arrange to meet with a teacher and examine the report for one student's achievement test results (no need to see the student's name). Analyze the report with the teacher as if you were trying to use the data for planning instruction. What additional information do you feel might be helpful?

2. Administer a reading or writing attitude survey to a student from grades 4–8. Tabulate and analyze the responses. The following questions are provided to help you analyze the information. What are the implications for instruction?

   a. What are the student's perceptions about reading/writing?

   b. What does the student feel are important characteristics of good reading/writing?

   c. How insightful is this student in terms of how he or she perceives reading/writing?

   d. What other relevant information did you discover about the student?

   e. Do your data indicate that the student has a healthy attitude toward reading/writing?

3. Observe a classroom teacher as she administers a specific literacy assessment tool (e.g., running records, cloze test, word lists, spelling test, district writing prompts). Discuss the interpretation of the results with the teacher. Why was the assessment given? What was learned? How will the teacher adapt instruction as a result of the information gained?

REFERENCES

Brookhart, S. M. (1999). Review of the book Wiggins, Grant. (1998). *Educative assessment: Designing assessments to inform and improve student performance.* San Francisco: Jossey-Bass. Retrieved August 10, 2006, from http://www.coe.asu.edu/edrev/reviews/rev50.htm.

Cambourne, B., & Turbill, J. (1990). Assessment in whole language classrooms: Theory into practice. *Elementary School Journal, 90,* 337–349.

Chappuis, J. (2005). Helping students understand assessment. *Educational Leadership, 63*(3), 39–43.

Clay, M. (1985). *The early detection of reading difficulties* (3rd ed.). Auckland, New Zealand: Heinemann.

Clay, M. (2000). *Running records for classroom teachers.* Portsmouth, NH: Heinemann.

Cooper, J. D. (1997). *Literacy: Helping children construct meaning.* Boston: Houghton Mifflin.

Cooper, L. J. (1952). *The effect of adjustment of basal reading materials on achievement.* Unpublished doctoral dissertation, Boston University.

Cousin, P. T., Weekly, T., & Gerard, J. (1993). The functional uses of language and literacy by students with severe language and learning problems. *Language Arts, 70,* 548–556.

Cunningham, P. M., & Allington, R. L. (1999). *Classrooms that work: They can all read and write* (2nd ed.). New York: Longman.

Cunningham, P. M., & Hall, D. P. (1998). *Month-by-month phonics for upper grades: A second chance for struggling readers and students learning English.* Greensboro, NC: Carson-DeLosa.

Daniels, H., & Bizar, M. (1998). *Methods that matter: Six structures for best practice classrooms.* York, ME: Stenhouse.

Falk, B. (2000). *The heart of the matter: Using standards and assessment to learn.* Portsmouth, NH: Heinemann.

Fuchs, L. S., Fuchs, D., Hosp, M. K., & Jenkins, J. R. (2001). Oral reading fluency as an indicator of reading competence: A theoretical, empirical, and historical analysis. *Scientific Studies in Reading, 5,* 239–256.

Glazer, S. M. (1998). *Assessment IS instruction: Reading, writing, spelling, and phonics for ALL learners.* Norwood, MA: Christopher Gordon.

Guskey, T. R. (2005). Mapping the road to proficiency. *Educational Leadership, 63*(3), 32–38.

Guthrie, J. T., Siefert, M., Burnham, N. A., & Caplan, R. I. (1974). The maze technique to assess, monitor reading comprehension. *The Reading Teacher, 28,* 161–168.

Harp, B. (2006). *The handbook of literacy assessment and evaluation* (3rd ed.). Norwood, MA: Christopher-Gordon.

Hasbrouck, J., & Tindal, G. A. (2006). Oral reading fluency norms: A valuable assessment tool for reading teachers. *The Reading Teacher, 59,* 636–644.

Hill, B. C., Ruptic, C., & Norwick, L. (1998). *Classroom based assessment.* Norwood, MA: Christopher-Gordon.

Johnston, P. (1992). Nontechnical assessment. *The Reading Teacher, 46,* 60–62.

Karlsen, B., & Gardner, E. F. (1995). *Stanford diagnostic reading tests* (4th ed.). San Antonio, TX: Harcourt. (Also available online at: www.hemweb.com/trophy/readtest/sdrt4.htm)

Kirby, D., Liner, T., & Vinz, R. (1988). *Inside out: Developmental strategies for teaching writing.* Portsmouth, NH: Boynton/Cook.

Klesius, J. P., & Homan, S. P. (1985). A validity and reliability update on the informal reading inventory with suggestions for improvements. *Journal of Learning Disabilities, 18*(2), 71–76.

Locke, E. A., & Latham, G. P. (2002). Building a practically useful theory of goal setting and task motivation: A 35-year odyssey. *American Psychologist, 57*(9), 705–717.

National Council of Teachers of English. (1996). *Standards in practice* (series of 4 books: K–2, 3–5, 6–8, 9–12). Urbana, IL: National Council of Teachers of English.

Neill, D. M. (2000). Transforming student assessment. In R. D. Robinson, M. C. McKenna, and J. M. Wedman (Eds.). *Issues and trends in literacy education* (2nd ed., pp. 136–148). Boston: Allyn & Bacon.

O'Sullivan, S., & Jiang, Y. H. (2002, Summer). Determining the efficacy of the California reading instruction competence assessment (RICA). *Teacher Education Quarterly, 29*(3), 61–72.

Powell, W., & Dunkeld, C. (1971). Validity of the IRI reading levels. *Elementary English, 48,* 637–642.

Rhodes, L. K., & Nathenson-Mejia, S. (1992). Anecdotal records: A powerful tool for ongoing literacy assessment. *The Reading Teacher, 45,* 502–511.

Schellenberg, S. J. (2004, April). Test bias or cultural bias: Have we really learned anything? Paper presented at the Annual Meeting of the National Council for Measurement in Education. San Diego, CA. (Available at http://data center.spss.org/site/.)

Shepard, L. A. (2005). Linking formative assessment to scaffolding. *Educational Leadership, 63*(3), 66–70.

Smith, K. (1996). Foreword. In M. Sierra-Perry (Ed.), *NCTE standards in practice: Grades 3–5* (p. v). Urbana, IL: National Council of Teachers of English.

Stiggins, R. J., Arter, S., Chappuis, J., & Chappuis, S. (2004). *Classroom assessment for student learning: Doing it right—using it well.* Portland, OR: Assessment Training Institute.

Taylor, W. L. (1953). Cloze procedure: A new tool for measuring readability. *Journalism Quarterly, 30,* 415–433.

U.S. Department of Education. (2002). No Child Left Behind Act of 2001. Washington, DC: Author.

Wilcox, J. (2006, February). Less teaching, more assessing: Teacher feedback is key to student performance. *Education Update, 48*(2), 1–2, 6, 8.

Wilhelm, J. D. (1996). *Standards in practice: Grades 6–8.* Urbana, IL: National Council of Teachers of English.

Woods, M. L., & Moe, A. J. (1999). *Analytical Reading Inventory* (6th ed.). Upper Saddle River, NJ: Merrill/Prentice Hall.

Word Study and Fluency

FOCUS QUESTIONS

- What are the key components of word study at the primary, intermediate, and middle-grade levels?

- In what ways do elements of word study for intermediate and middle grades differ from the elements of primary-grade word study?

- How is word study related to fluency?

- Why does fluency decline around grade 4 and what can be done to improve it?

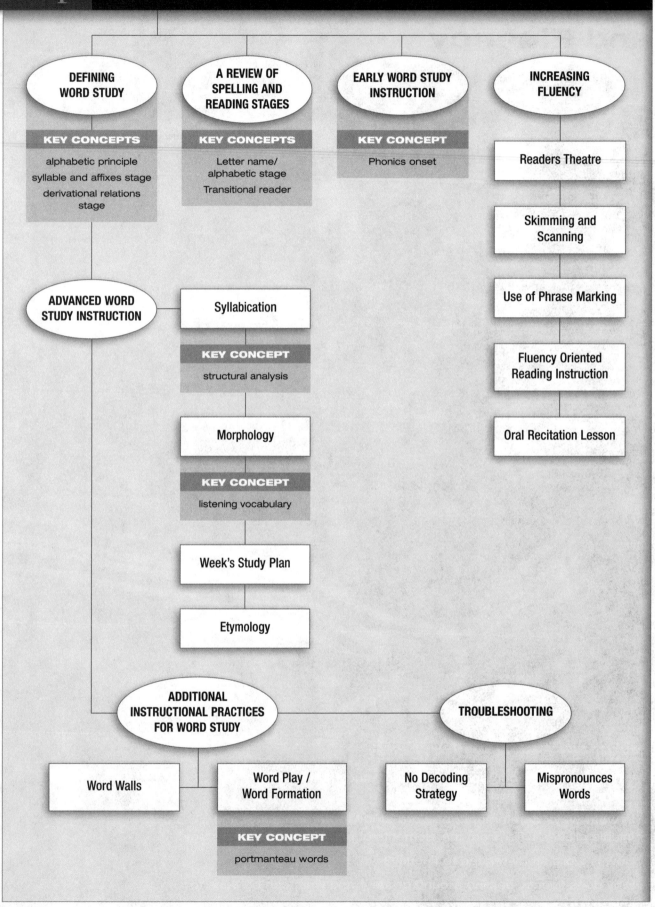

DEFINING
WORD STUDY

KEY CONCEPTS

alphabetic principle
syllable and affixes stage
derivational relations
stage

A REVIEW OF
SPELLING AND
READING STAGES

KEY CONCEPTS

Letter name/
alphabetic stage
Transitional reader

EARLY WORD STUDY
INSTRUCTION

KEY CONCEPT

Phonics onset

INCREASING
FLUENCY

Readers Theatre

Skimming and
Scanning

Use of Phrase Marking

Fluency Oriented
Reading Instruction

Oral Recitation Lesson

ADVANCED WORD
STUDY INSTRUCTION

Syllabication

KEY CONCEPT

structural analysis

Morphology

KEY CONCEPT

listening vocabulary

Week's Study Plan

Etymology

ADDITIONAL
INSTRUCTIONAL PRACTICES
FOR WORD STUDY

TROUBLESHOOTING

Word Walls

Word Play /
Word Formation

No Decoding
Strategy

Mispronounces
Words

KEY CONCEPT

portmanteau words

Mrs. Diaz's sixth-grade students come to school on Monday morning talking about seeing the movie *Jurassic Park III* over the weekend. The classroom reading center includes several magazines with articles about dinosaurs and the making of the Jurassic Park movies, as well as several copies of the book *Jurassic Park* (Crichton, 1990). The students are very interested in exotic animals and places. Knowing her students as well as she does, Mrs. Diaz recognizes an opportunity to teach her students about more advanced word parts, and something about the morphology, or internal structure, of words through the use of their interest in exotic animals. She has prepared an activity called "Create an Exotic Animal" that involves students putting meaningful parts of words together to form a new, exotic animal (Johnson & Pearson, 1984). By the time each student has created a new animal and shared the animal with classmates, most of the students will know what the word parts mean and be able to apply this new skill to unknown words they may meet in other texts. Mrs. Diaz's activity, with example animals, follows.

CREATE AN EXOTIC ANIMAL

Directions: You are a scientist in charge of creating exotic animals for a Jurassic-type adventure park. You must create names for your animals that are understood by scientists and people around the world. This means you must use the prefixes, suffixes, and roots that come from ancient Latin and Greek. For example, a unicorn is an animal that has one horn (uni = one + cornis = horn). Use the following chart of prefixes, suffixes, and roots to help you name your animal. You also need to draw the animal so we will know what it looks like.

Scientist's Vocabulary Chart

mono = one	macro = large, long	melano = black	uni = one	poly = many
leuco = white	bi = two	micro = small, short	erythro = red	tri = three
lineatus = lined	bruno = brown	quadro = four	punctata = dotted	ocu = eye
pento = five	pedi, pod = foot	dent, dont = tooth	dec = ten	cephalus = head
corp = body	-let = small	cornis = horn	cord, cardi = heart	-kin = small
-ling = small	-trix = female			

Once students finish sharing their exotic animals, Mrs. Diaz discusses other more commonly used words found in their readings that derive from the roots and affixes in the chart (e.g., *gosling, ocular, microcosm, dentist*). In this way students can see how they might use structural analysis (identification of meaningful word parts such as roots and affixes, and compounds) to figure out unknown words. Some of the students' creations were a *punctata tricephalopento-pod*, a *polymicroocutrix*, and a *bruno macrocorpmicroped*, seen here.

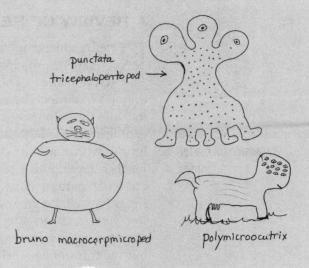

punctata
tricephalopentopod →

bruno macrocorpmicroped

polymicroocutrix

DEFINING WORD STUDY

word study ●

Word study is a systematic, conceptual learner-centered approach to instruction in spelling, word analysis (to include phonics), and vocabulary (Bear et al., 2000). Instruction of approximately 10 to 15 minutes daily links directly to the texts and other materials being used in the classroom and provides many opportunities for students to manipulate word parts. Word study teaches students how to look at words and should be approached developmentally. At the primary-grade level, word study is mainly about

alphabetic principle ●

1. developing an understanding of the **alphabetic principle** (knowing that each speech sound has a distinctive graphic representation).

2. helping students learn about and use phonics to decode words unknown in print.

At the intermediate- and middle-grade levels, word study is primarily about

syllables and affixes stage ●
derivational relations stage ●
affixes ●

1. developing spelling at the **syllables and affixes stage** and the **derivational relations stage** (stages of spelling development characterized by polysyllabic words that often contain **affixes** [prefixes and suffixes], and derive from Greek or Latin roots, respectively).

2. helping students determine word meanings using the meaningful parts of words (Henderson, 1990; Kemper & Brody, 2001).

Thus, word study is developmental. While we hope that students will be ready to study words at the syllables and affixes stage, this might not be the case. It is advisable for a teacher to assess students directly using a spelling inventory (see Appendix D) to look at the way each student spells words. By analyzing what the learner does when he spells, the teacher can determine that learner's conceptual understandings of our English word system and the level at which the student is able to study words.

Following is a brief review of reading and spelling stages. This information is provided to help teachers determine a student's readiness for word study based on her spelling/reading stage.

A REVIEW OF READING AND SPELLING STAGES

Briefly, emergent readers demonstrate a lack of understanding of the alphabetic principle, and they do not have a concept of letter–sound correspondences. Their "spelling" consists of scribbles, random marks, drawings, or mock letters (see Figure 3.1). As learners develop an understanding of the alphabetic principle and become beginning readers, they

letter name/alphabetic stage ●
transitional reader ●
rimes ●

demonstrate the **letter name/alphabetic stage.** They spell by using letters they hear in words, usually consonants, even if it might be only one letter per word. Further development produces the **transitional reader,** who understands there are letter pattern units, also called word families, and frequently occurring **rimes** (vowel[s] with any following consonants in a single syllable) such as *-at*, *-in*, *-and*, and *-ot*, and who spells words using these patterns, although not always correctly. For example, the letter name speller might spell boat as BOT, but the transitional speller will try to use a long *o* pattern and might produce BOTE, BOWT, BOOT, or BOAT. At the intermediate and advanced stages of reading development, students recognize single syllable patterns automatically

READING/SPELLING STAGE	AGES	GRADES	CHARACTERISTICS
Emergent	1–7	pre-K to mid-1	scribbles, random marks, drawings, mock letters
Beginning/Letter name	4–9	K to early 3	M or MN for *man;* L or LD or LED for *land;* B or BP or BOP or BUP or BOMP for *bump*
Transitional	6–12	1 to mid-4	MEET or METE for *meat;* NALE for *nail;* SOKE for *soak;* SMOAK for *smoke;* FOWT for *fought;* FODE for *food;* CAFE for *cough;* CLOKE for *clock*
Intermediate/Syllables and affixes	8–18	3 to 8	GRIPING for *gripping;* MIDLE for *middle;* CONFUSSHUN for *confusion;* PLESURE for *pleasure;* RUPSHUR for *rupture;* MONKY for *monkey;* BARBAR for *barber;* DISPOSUL for *disposal*
Advanced/Derivational relations	10+	5 to 12	SOLEM for *solemn;* ANAMAL for *animal;* OPISITION for *opposition;* CRITASIZE for *criticize;* BENAFIT for *benefit;* TELAGRAM for *telegram;* APPEARENCE for *appearance;* AMMUSEMENT for *amusement*

Stages of reading/spelling development.   **FIGURE** 3.1

and have already been reading and writing polysyllabic words, so they begin to apply this knowledge to spelling words containing syllables and affixes and word derivations—thus, the respective spelling stages.

In addition to this review of reading/spelling stages, a brief overview of primary-grade–level word study elements is in order because not all intermediate grade students will have reached an advanced word study stage.

EARLY WORD STUDY INSTRUCTION

Instruction in word study begins in the primary grades with activities that develop **phonemic awareness,** that is, the ability to attend to sounds in the context of the spoken word independent of the visual representation or meaning of the word. These activities usually focus on rhyming, blending, segmenting, and manipulating sounds in spoken language. From there students learn to recognize the relationships between the 44 sounds in the English language and the 26 graphic symbols (the letters of the alphabet) used to represent those sounds. This focus on learning letter–sound correspondences is called **phonics.**

Because there is not a one-to-one match between the sounds and letters in English orthography, some letters will represent more than one sound or combine with other letters to form a sound. For example, the letter *m* (as is true for most of the 21 consonant letters) has only one sound; however, the letters we call vowels (*a, e, i, o, u*) typically represent at least two sounds, referred to as long and short. The two letters *w* and *y* do double duty by sometimes act-

● phonemic awareness

● phonics

Word study instruction in the primary grades focuses on helping students learn phonics and apply it most often to single syllables or to one-syllable, decodable words

ing as consonants (for example, in the initial position in words such as *yes, you, yellow*) and sometimes acting as vowels (e.g., *day, buy, cow, sew, try*). The letter *c* does not have its own sound but represents the sound of either *s* or *k*. Certain letter combinations represent additional sounds, such as *ch, sh, th, wh, au, oi, oo, ou,* or contain silent letters, as in *know, lamb,* and *fight*. What adds to the confusion that some learners experience is that there are sounds that can be represented by more than one letter or letter combination. Take the long sound of /a/. It can be represented by *a, ai, a_e, ay, eigh,* or *ey*. There are many other examples like these, and young readers must begin to recognize these letter–sound patterns that make up the content of phonics.

Word study instruction, then, in the primary grades, focuses on helping students learn phonics and apply it most often to single syllables or to one-syllable, decodable words. For example, students are directed to remove the beginning consonant(s) (the **onset**) from the rest of a one-syllable word (e.g., h—at). They then say the sounds indicated by the rime, or /at/. They are directed to say, and finally add to the rime, the sound for the beginning consonant(s) (/h/ + /at/ = hat). At this point, they have pronounced the word and must cross-check it within the context of what they are reading to be sure it makes sense: *He wore a hat on his head.*

ADVANCED WORD STUDY INSTRUCTION

Students in the intermediate and middle grades must continue to learn to recognize increasingly complex words quickly and accurately. While some students still need instruction with phonics, or decoding (see "Troubleshooting"), a major focus of word study instruction in grades 4–8 is having students

onset ●

1. learn to syllabicate, or "chunk," multisyllable words.

roots ●
base words ●

2. study the internal structure of words, including (a) affixes and **roots** (**base words**) and the forms of various parts of speech (morphology; also structural analysis), and (b) the origins and derivations of words (**etymology**).

etymology ●

The focus on the internal structure of words will also enhance spelling development because these word parts will be learned and spelled as whole units. Additionally, much of this work will be helpful for learning new word meanings, so it can also be intertwined with instruction for **vocabulary** development (see Chapter 4).

vocabulary ●

Syllabication

The process of analyzing a polysyllabic word is the same as that for one-syllable words, except the process is applied more than once. Multiple applications are based on the total number of syllables in the word; that is, the process will be applied twice for a two-syllable word, three times for a three-syllable word, and so forth (Gipe, 2006). Basically, the learner must first divide the unknown word into individual syllables, then pronounce each syllable, and finally put the syllables back together. The steps are as follows:

1. To begin to locate syllables in a polysyllabic word, locate the vowels.
2. Try to make syllables by using the consonants just before and after the vowels.
3. Attempt to pronounce these trial syllables.
4. Try to blend the trial syllables together.
5. Cross-check the pronounced word within the context of what is being read to see whether it makes sense. If the resulting pronounced word does not seem right, try segmenting the syllables in another way (see Figure 3.2).

This strategy is not always precise, but if the word is part of the student's **listening vocabulary** (words understood in speech, but not recognized in print), it may provide a close enough approximation that the context will help identify the word. In the case of a totally new word, students will need to be told what the word is, and that word can become part of a personal dictionary for further vocabulary study and assistance with spelling if the word is later needed for writing purposes.

● listening vocabulary

Morphology

In addition to syllabication, students need instruction on morphology to help them recognize words (Carlisle & Stone, 2005). **Morphology** refers to the internal structure and forms of words. The structural features of words that need to be taught are *roots* (base words), *prefixes* (affixes that precede

● morphology

Analyzing a multisyllabic word.   **FIGURE** 3.2

STEP	WORD: HOSPITAL
1. Find the vowel(s).	o i a
2. Make syllables with the consonants just before and after the vowels.	"hos" "pit" "tal"
3. Try to say these syllables.	"hos" "pit" "tall"
4. Blend the syllables together.	"hospit" "tall" . . . "hospital"
5. Cross-check with the context.	"Oh yes, it makes sense. His father was sick so he went to the hospital."

inflections ●
compound words ●

root), *suffixes* (affixes that follow root), and **inflections** (plurals, past tense endings, possessive form); another structural form is **compound words** (two base words together, e.g., *sidewalk*). Roots, prefixes, and compound words are most directly tied to meaning so they provide the most helpful information related to vocabulary. Suffixes and inflections also carry meaning, but it is more general in nature (Ruddell, 1993). Consider the differences by examining the word *dentist*. If the reader recognizes the "ist" suffix and knows "ist" means "one who" but does not know that the meaning of the root "dent" is "tooth," then recognizing "ist" is not much help other than to know the word is a noun.

Students should be shown how to figure out the meaning of unknown multisyllabic words by recognizing the many meaning-bearing affixes that are added to the base, or root, of other words. Figure 3.3 presents some common meaning-bearing prefixes, roots, and suffixes that, if memorized, will go a long way toward helping students discover the meaning of hundreds of words (Bear et al., 2000). Activities that require students to use these word parts, such as the exotic animal naming activity mentioned at the beginning of this chapter and the class dictionary activity presented next, will assist in their memorization.

FIGURE 3.3   **Meaning-bearing affixes and roots.***

auto (self)	dic (say)
anti (against; opposite)	post (carry)
tele (far)	vit, viv (life)
bi (two; twice)	vert (turn)
dia (through)	sol (sun)
con (together)	mania (fondness for)
trans (across)	phobia (fear of)
re (back; again)	ist (one who)
in, im, in (not; within)	ic (pertaining to)
pre (before)	ism (condition of)
circum (around)	able, ible (able to)
graph (writing)	ment (state of)
phon (sound)	er (one who)
hydr (water)	tion, ion (act of)
therm (heat)	less (opposite of)
meter (measure)	

* A more detailed list of such word parts can be found in *The Reading Teacher's Book of Lists,* 4th ed. (Fry, Kress, & Fountoukidis, 2000).

The Class Dictionary

For this activity, students are involved in a science unit on ecology. They are engaged in service-learning projects related to the environment and cleaning up their surrounding community (see Chapter 10). Throughout the unit students keep a record of the words that they are learning and need to use when speaking and writing about ecology issues; they also create words that have potential meaning to gain practice using the word parts. Here are guidelines for creating a class dictionary on this or any topic:

1. Over several weeks, introduce each of the chosen word parts with example words for each. Extend this list as desired using additional meaning-bearing word parts; for example, *ology:* ecology; *ment:* environment; *aero:* aerate; *aqua:* aquifer; *cosm:* cosmos; *bio:* biosphere; *ics:* politics; *ish:* flourish; *off:* offshore; *bene:* beneficial; *re:* recycle.

2. Conduct a word hunt for words containing each part as they are introduced.

3. Put students in groups of three and ask them to create three original words by combining a prefix, a root, and a suffix from the list.

4. Instruct each group to define their new words creatively by considering the meaning of each of the parts. Explain that the definitions can be serious or humorous.

5. Have a spokesperson for each group share each of their new words with the rest of the class, encouraging the other class members to hypothesize what the meanings of the words might be based on their knowledge of the meaning of the individual components.

6. Invite each group to create an illustration to accompany each of their new words. For example, see the classroom scenario at the beginning of this chapter.

7. With the entire class working together, help students to alphabetize all the groups' words, decide on the part of speech for each entry, and enter them into an illustrated class dictionary.

A direct approach for teaching **structural analysis** (identification of meaningful word parts) is to identify a structural element found in a critical word from students' reading assignments. For example, in a social studies unit dealing with forms of government, the element "cracy" in the words *aristocracy* and *autocracy* might be chosen. Instruction proceeds by examining the more familiar word *democracy.* The important element "cracy" should be highlighted and students invited to provide a meaning for that part based on their understanding of the word *democracy.* Most students can define a democracy as majority rules, or a government of the people, by the people, and for the people; in short, rule by the people. Then students are told that "cracy" comes from the Greek *kratia* and means strength or power; in other words, who rules. Whatever is attached to "cracy" tells who does the ruling. The form of government, democracy, contains the roots "demo" and "cracy," so students can deduce that "demo" means people, and, in fact, "demo" is from the Greek *demos,* meaning people.

Other forms of government can now be examined in the same way (e.g., aristocracy, autocracy, theocracy, bureaucracy). Additionally, it would be useful

● structural analysis

for this example to introduce and discuss the membership structure for each of these forms of government, that is, aristocrat, autocrat, theocrat, and bureaucrat, respectively.

Related words should be introduced and discussed at this time. These might be posted on a word wall, or become part of a word study notebook that students maintain. Both of these methods will assist with spelling development because the words are written and a visual representation is also readily available. Some examples are *demography, demagogy, epidemic, aristocratic, autobiography, autonomy, automatic, bureau, bureaucratic, theology, theocentric,* and *atheism.*

Learning the words on a word list such as the Nifty-Thrifty-Fifty (Cunningham & Hall, 1998, discussed in Chapter 2 and Appendix F) will provide students with morphological patterns for figuring out many other words. These 50 words include common affixes (see Figure 3.3 for others) as well as reveal common spelling changes that occur when suffixes are added to root words. These words can be introduced in groups of five each week using daily activities (see Appendix G for a typical week's study plan). After 10 weeks all of the words will have been learned. Because these 50 words contain morphological patterns for so many other words, they should be overlearned. The various elements will then be recognized and recalled automatically when needed during reading and writing. The **transfer words**—words containing elements that are also found in many other words—in Appendix F contain parts of the Nifty-Thrifty-Fifty words. Many other words can also be used as transfer words. Students and teachers alike will find www.sentex.net/~mmcadams/spelling.html to be a useful website for word study.

Teachers can use this general pattern when teaching the morphology and etymology (see below) of words:

1. Begin with the known and move to the unknown.
2. Provide a means for making the transfer. Talk through the process. With practice and repetition, the process becomes internalized.
3. Discuss related words so that knowledge increases in an exponential way as opposed to just one word being studied at a time.
4. Value the content of particular disciplines by using the critical language in that discipline as a means of teaching a functional skill—word analysis.

The words chosen should also be taught within their authentic contexts so students will not only be able to recognize the words, but also know how they are used.

Bloodgood and Pacifici (2004) use a strategy for word study from meaningful word parts in which the teacher places a base word, or root, in the center of a web (for example, see the activity "Roots and Branches," later in this chapter). Students work in small groups recording the derived words from the web using one marker color. The students then use a dictionary to find the word meanings and record them in different colors.

Etymology

Exploring the histories or derivations of words (etymology) with students not only helps them with spelling (e.g., knowing that *ballet* and *buffet* are both French words helps them to understand the "et" making a long /a/ sound), but also provides interesting multicultural word walls and lessons. Many dictionaries, such as *The New Webster's Dictionary,* offer information about the

transfer words

language from which each word derives. Additionally, books on the history of words found in any school library can provide entertaining stories of words' origins. For example, the word *tank*, which is defined as a heavily armored vehicle, was originally used as a secret code word to keep the Axis powers from knowing about its existence during World War I. The sharing of such information adds a spark to the study of history, and it can also help students to remember the concept and meaning of the word (Rasinski & Padak, 2000). Many prefixes and suffixes in the English language are also derived from other languages, and understanding these word parts will often give students an idea as to their meaning in new words.

Greek and Latin are common ancient languages from which many of the words in our language derive; however, they are not the only languages of word origin. Students will be interested in studying the etymology of our words. One example is *lagoon*, which derives from the

Books on histories of words found in any school library can provide entertaining stories of words' origins.

French (*lagun*) and Italian (*laguna*) languages and means a shallow lake or pond. Another, from one of the author's experiences living in New Orleans, is the word *lagniappe*, whose origins are in the Creole French (*la*) and Spanish (*napa*) languages, and the combination results in a word meaning a small present given to a customer with a purchase, or, as the store owners would say, "a little something extra." English learners especially would be interested in identifying words originating from their native language.

ADDITIONAL INSTRUCTIONAL PRACTICES FOR ADVANCED WORD STUDY

The following practices were chosen because they are especially geared toward intermediate- and middle-grade students.

Word Walls

One way to emphasize new, essential, or troublesome words is to post them on word walls, as described earlier, so students will have ready access to these words. It is especially helpful in the intermediate grades for word walls to focus on particular syllabic elements. Word walls can be organized into the prefixes, suffixes, and roots most appropriate for a particular topic of study, by meaning, or as identified by grade-level curriculum groups. Another way to present word walls is to introduce a word part that has a large family of words associated with it and encourage students to add words to this group as they find them in their reading. They can place the word on a word card, share it with the class along with its meaning and where they found the word, and then place it on the word wall. These word groupings can also become the spelling words to be studied. For instance, "ology" is a good example of one such family. Many subjects will contain words that have "ology" in them. Science is the

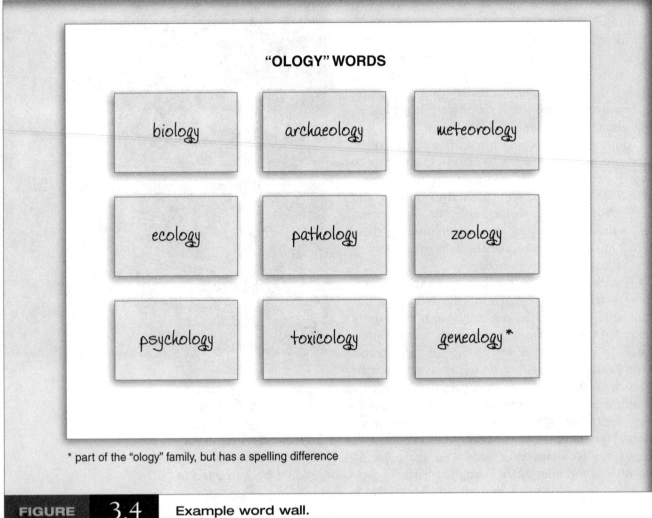

"OLOGY" WORDS

biology	archaeology	meteorology
ecology	pathology	zoology
psychology	toxicology	genealogy*

* part of the "ology" family, but has a spelling difference

FIGURE 3.4   **Example word wall.**

most obvious perhaps (e.g., *biology, dermatology, ecology, entomology, hydrology*), but there are other subjects as well (e.g., *sociology, theology, morphology, anthropology*). Students can be told that the suffix "ology" means "the study of" or "the science of" whatever it is preceded by (e.g., geo = earth + ology = the study of) (see Figure 3.4).

ACTIVITY   *Roots and Branches*   (Bloodgood & Pacifici, 2004)

This word study, a type of graphic organizer, is a technique that focuses on Greek and Latin roots, from which a preponderance of our words derive, to discover within-word patterns that will help with word recognition and meaning, as well as spelling.

1. Present a root written within a circle on a large piece of poster paper without revealing its meaning (e.g., *graph*).
2. Ask students to provide words they already know that contain that word part. Write these on the poster paper as branches off the central root (see Figure 3.5). This web uses the roots *tract, graph, dic/dict, spect,* and *ortho.*

Roots and branches.   FIGURE   3.5

3. As students discuss these words they can infer the meaning of the root (e.g., "graph means to write"); write that meaning within the circle.

Additional words can be added to the posters as they appear in material read over the course of time. Several of these "Roots and Branches" posters can be prepared and hung around the classroom for students to add to as they finish other assignments. As posters are added, the meaning of the root written within the circle is discussed, and as new words are added to these posters, the new words are discussed as to their relationship to the central root.

The Word Family Tree   (Buehl, 2001)   ACTIVITY

An excellent strategy for etymological exploration, the word family tree involves students connecting word origins, key terms from a unit of study, common roots, and other current meanings of the word. Using the analogy of a family tree, the teacher introduces the concept of the word family as listing the individual word's "ancestors," or origins, direct descendants, and related words, or "relatives," that contain the root. Words that have similar meanings to already known words can also be introduced.

1. Begin with a word that is found in students' text material; for instance, from a social studies selection the word *segregation* could be chosen.

2. Give students the original word forms: the Latin "se" (apart) + "greg" (herd), the Latin "com" or "con" (with), and the Latin "ag" (the "ad" becomes "ag" when followed by the letter *g*, and means *to*). Students will notice root forms and may be able to give related words (e.g., *congregate* and *segregate*).

3. Ask students to speculate about the word's connection to other words. A "What's the Word Connection?" activity establishes how the word's origin can help determine its current meaning:

What's the word connection . . .

. . . between a flock of sheep and a group of outcasts?

. . . between a crowd and a loner?

. . . between concrete and a group of people who attend the same church?

4. Introduce the word family tree (see Figure 3.6). Explain how the word is linked to a meaningful root to help students speculate about the

---

FIGURE 3.6   A word family tree for the word *segregation*.

Who would use this word, or a relative of it?

Judge: Segregation is against the law.

Minister: I am happy to see all of my congregation at church.

Sentence: Expecting Rosa Parks to sit at the back of the bus was a form of segregation.

Definition: noun. The isolation of a race, class, or ethnic group by forced or voluntary residence in a restricted area, by barriers, or by separate educational facilities or other discriminatory means.

Segregation

(Direct Descendant)

Pronunciation Key
seg-ri-gā-shen

Memory Clue
 - 4 syllables with accent on third syllable
 - isolation by discrimination

Ancestor (Root Word[s])
"greg" means gather or herd
"se" means apart

Relatives
congregation
aggregate
gregarious

kinds of contexts in which this word or its relatives will likely appear. It might help to think about who would use these words and what they might say (see "Who would use this word, or a relative of it?" in Figure 3.6).

5. Provide other target words that students can investigate (e.g., *concert, genetics, sonar, treaty*). Students can work with a partner or in small groups to complete word family trees for these words to share with the entire class.

Word Play/Word Formation

Students need to realize that the English language is a living, growing language. New words are continually added to our language. There are words in our dictionaries today that were not there a few short years ago. And the word parts students are learning in the intermediate and middle grades are generally how new words come into existence. Prefixes and suffixes are added to existing root words to form new words (e.g., *preview, Americanism*). Sometimes two words are combined to create a new word. These are called **portmanteau words,** or words that are blended together (e.g., *motel* from *motor* + *hotel*, or *smog* from *smoke* + *fog*). Students get excited about creating potential new words, and they enjoy sharing them and their definitions with classmates.

● portmanteau words

The following examples of "created" words were found, unclaimed, on the Internet (modified from Johnson, 2001, p. 162). They could be used as examples for challenging students to create their own words:

Aquadextrous (ak wa DEKS trus) adj. Having the ability to turn the bathtub faucet on and off with your toes. Susan was able to relax in her reclined position as she used her *aquadextrous* ability to warm up her cooling bathtub water.

Elevacelleration (el a VA cel er AY schun) n. The mistaken idea that the more you press the elevator button the faster it will arrive. The businessman tapped his foot impatiently as he demonstrated *elevacelleration.*

Elboatics (el bo AT iks) n. The physical maneuvering two people engage in for trying to use the one armrest between them at the movie theater. Because they were engaged in *elboatics,* the couple missed an important part of the movie.

Students can work in teams or alone to create the new words. Each new word should be presented like a dictionary entry with the pronunciation key, part of speech, a definition, and a sample sentence, as seen in the examples. If an illustration is appropriate, this can also be provided.

INCREASING FLUENCY

As students advance through the grades, the texts they are expected to read contain increasingly complex linguistic and syntactical features. A reader who up to now has been able to read with **fluency**—that is, speed, accuracy, and prosody (or appropriate pacing, intonation, expression)—may suddenly begin to read more slowly, or less accurately, and with less confidence. In fact, reading rate charts do show a drop-off at grade four, when reading requires more emphasis on expository text (see Figure 3.7).

● fluency

Reading rate is measured in words read correctly per minute. This rate is used to evaluate automaticity of word recognition. Words per minute (WPM) is determined by multiplying the number of words in the passage by 60 and then dividing by the number of seconds taken to read the passage. This measure can be used with both oral and silent reading; use of a stopwatch is recommended. For silent reading, direct the student to indicate when he or she is starting to read, and to look up when he or she has finished the selection. (See Chapter 2 for oral reading fluency norms.)

INSTRUCTIONAL LEVELS	ORAL RATE RANGE	SILENT RATE RANGE
Preprimer	13–35 WPM	NA*
Primer	28–68 WPM	NA
First	31–87 WPM	NA
Second	52–102 WPM	58–122 WPM
Third	85–139 WPM	96–168 WPM
Fourth, Fifth	78–124 WPM	107–175 WPM
Fifth, Sixth	113–165 WPM	135–241 WPM
Seventh, Eighth	128–177 WPM	180–290 WPM

*NA = not available.

FIGURE 3.7   Reading rate ranges for instructional-level reading.

The structure of the texts that students now encounter is often different from that of earlier text. Students need to learn new functions for some words. They need to learn what is preferred and what is to be avoided in inflection and syntax. The use of more varied punctuation will likely reduce fluency until those new patterns can be practiced. Teachers in grades 4–8 would do well to read aloud to students to model these new patterns (Richardson, 2000).

Students also need time reading so they can gain experience and practice with the more complex forms of written language. A minimum of 20 minutes per day of silent reading, more if possible, will go a long way toward providing the necessary practice for increasing fluency. In schools that have higher achievement levels, students spend more than 75 percent of the time scheduled for reading instruction actually reading. Thus, if instruction were scheduled for 100 minutes, then 75 minutes of that time students would actually be reading, not working with a group or with the teacher on skill lessons (Allington & Cunningham, 2002, p. 134).

No matter what grade level is involved, students' comprehension of text is improved when they are taught to read in meaningful chunks, phrasing well and using appropriate expression (Herrell & Jordan, 2006). Although this is easier for some students than others, almost all students can benefit from this instruction. Instruction in sentence-level "chunking" (breaking words into pronounceable chunks) is especially valuable for struggling readers and readers for whom English is a second language. Listening to teachers or students who are proficient readers model good phrasing and expression often helps students to better understand that good reading is not necessarily fast reading, but that it should be paced and phrased so that it sounds meaningful.

Providing opportunities for repeated readings of familiar text is a vital component to sound instruction in the fostering of reading fluency. The reading of poetry, readers theatre scripts, and texts of a variety of genres is critical in building the reader's confidence and reading rate. Observation and planned interventions by the teacher in the form of brief echo reading and modeling place value on fluency and encourage students to focus more deliberately on this important aspect of literacy that will allow them more energy to expend on the comprehension of written material (Kuhn & Stahl, 2003).

Skimming and Scanning

For most readers, fluency develops over time and through extensive reading. But fluency is *not* static, as novice readers mistakenly believe. A reader's level of fluency quite naturally varies, depending on the reader's familiarity with the words in the text, the subject matter of the material, and the purposes for reading. For example, one might read a mystery novel at a rapid pace, but studying a social studies chapter to prepare for a quiz would require much slower, more deliberate reading. Even very proficient adult readers may tend to read in a slow, laborious manner when confronted with material that contains highly technical vocabulary, or if the text addresses subjects of which they have little background knowledge. Students need direct instruction in knowing when to adjust their rate according to the text and their purposes for reading.

Two different kinds of in-class silent reading require a variation in normal fluency, as they are often done for purposes other than simple pleasure reading: skimming and scanning. **Skimming** is reading that is done rapidly, but purposefully, to get a general idea what a reading selection is about. Readers engaged in skimming will be expected to get the main idea of the selection as well as a few supporting details. **Scanning,** in contrast, is pursued when a reader is looking for some specific information, such as when one is looking at the blurb on the back of a book to decide if one wishes to read it.

- skimming

- scanning

Both skimming and scanning are critical skills to teach for increasing fluency because they show students that reading rate is not a constant but changes for the purposes for which one is reading. In addition, both skimming and scanning are discrete reading skills that encourage students to push themselves to read at a faster than normal rate while still attending to comprehension.

Practice in Skimming

An effective way to practice skimming with students is to incorporate it as a regular routine when introducing new chapters in content-area material, such as science or social studies, using the following procedure:

- Before beginning the chapter, ask students to look through or "skim" the chapter to get a general idea of what it might contain. Tell them to pay particular attention to boldfaced headings, section titles, the introduction, and the summary.

- Invite them to jot down their ideas about the possible content of the chapter and share those ideas with the rest of the class.
- When the students have completed the chapter, ask them to revisit their ideas to see if they were correct.
- This activity can eventually be timed to emphasize for students that skimming should be done more rapidly than normal reading.

A variation on this activity would be to have students skim sports articles to determine why their favorite sports team won or lost.

Practice in Scanning

Scanning abilities can be fostered by encouraging students to locate specific information from reference material, such as *TV Guide,* the telephone book, encyclopedia, or an almanac. For example, using the telephone directory, students can be asked to find the telephone number of a particular person or the number of the nearest pizza restaurant. Similarly, they can scan news articles to find out the what, why, where, and when of a recent event. To enhance student interest and increase speed, make the activity into a teamed competition, pairing an empathic but rapid reader with one who may need more assistance.

Readers Theatre

readers theatre ●

One effective strategy for improving fluency and oral reading that many students also find motivating is readers theatre. Sloyer (1982) defines **readers theatre** as "an interpretative reading activity for all the children in the classroom. Readers bring characters to life through their voices and gestures. . . . Readers Theatre becomes an integrated language event centering upon oral interpretation of literature" (p. 3). As such, readers practice oral reading and address all the areas of fluency (speed, accuracy, prosody) through "rehearsals" of the material to be read before an audience. To provide an appealing performance, the reader must not only comprehend the material and read it accurately, but also dramatize his interpretation through appropriate intonation and expression.

ACTIVITY *Readers Theatre*

In this type of group-reading activity, a narrator speaks directly to the audience, establishing the basic premise of the story and linking the various segments. The narration text is created with the help of the other students. The narrator also simplifies the language and abstract concepts. The other actors read the dialogue of the characters, and each actor may take the part of more than one character. The success of the readers theatre production depends on the oral aspects of the presentation rather than on acting skills or props. The actors will read their parts fluently. The actors use facial expressions and tone of voice to convey the emotions and moods of the characters. Action is merely suggested; the audience must visualize the activity in their mind's eye. Readers theatre usually omits stage properties, lights, and costumes, so that nothing distracts the audience's attention from the characterization.

Readers Theatre Resources for Grades 4–8

Readers theatre for building fluency: Strategies and scripts for making the most of this highly effective, motivating, and research-based approach to oral reading, by Jo Worthy, Scholastic, 2005. A fine introduction to readers theatre in the classroom, with detailed instructions, plus the theory behind how and why it works—all in a brief, lively, easy-to-read presentation. Grades 3–6.

Stories on stage: Children's plays for readers theatre, with 15 play scripts from 15 authors, including Roald Dahl's The Twits *and Louis Sachar's* Sideways Stories from Wayside School (2nd ed.), Shepard Publications, 2005. The premier collection of readers theater scripts, with adaptations of stories by a variety of authors. www.shepardpub.com

Folktales on stage: Children's plays for readers theatre, with 16 play scripts from world folk and fairy tales and legends, including African, Chinese, Southeast Asian, Indian, Middle Eastern, Russian, Scandinavian, and Native American, by Aaron Shepard, Shepard Publications, 2004. Scripts based on Shepard's own picture books and stories. www.shepardpub.com

Frantic frogs and other frankly fractured folktales for readers theatre, by Anthony D. Fredericks, Teacher Ideas Press, 1993. Fiercely funny flummery. Kids love this kind of stuff! One of many by this author. www.teacherideaspress.com

From the page to the stage: The educator's complete guide to readers theatre, by Shirlee Sloyer, Teacher Ideas Press, 2003. Just what the subtitle says, plus sample scripts. www.teacherideaspress.com

Institute book of readers theatre: A practical guide for school, theater, & community, by William Adams, Institute for Readers Theatre, 2003. A university-level textbook that can be used with middle school from a bastion and pioneer of readers theatre. The most comprehensive treatment of readers theatre available. Best ordering is direct from the publisher, at www.readerstheatreinstitute.com.

Playbooks for young readers by Aaron and *Playbooks for tween readers by Aaron,* adapted from tales told by Aaron Shepard, Playbooks, Laguna Hills, California, 2002. Each book includes adaptations of three of the author's scripts into Playbook format, which features illustrations, color-coding, and diverse reading levels for small groups of students or for families. For ages 5–10 and 8–13, respectively. Available in both printed and electronic formats. Best ordering is direct from the publisher, at www.eplaybooks.com.

Multicultural folktales for the feltboard and readers' theatre, by Judy Sierra, Oryx, 1996. Short and simple scripts by a popular children's author.

Great moments in science: Experiments and readers theatre, by Kendall Haven, Teacher Ideas Press, 1996. Combines scripts about famous scientists with experiments that demonstrate the principles they discovered. www.teacherideaspress.com

---

unique personalities. The language of such a story should be thought provoking, colorful, and rhythmic. The plot should have an element of conflict and/or suspense. The completed script may be made into a laminated booklet and placed in a learning center for students to enjoy as a free-time oral reading activity. The websites listed on the next page offer free readers theatre scripts. Also see the box above for more resources.

The development of a script requires two distinct steps: (1) selecting material with strong dramatic appeal, and (2) adapting the selection to bring about a positive audience response. Almost any piece of literature containing lots of dialogue will do, but folktales are especially well suited to the vehicle.

An adaptation of readers theatre is books on tape, which are recorded literature selections for an unseen audience. Using this method, small groups

WWW

SCRIPTS FOR READERS THEATRE

Aaron Shepard's RT Page
www.aaronshep.com/rt/RTE.html

Gander Academy Theatre
www.cdli.ca/CITE/langrt.htm

Readers Theater Scripts and Plays
http://teachingheart.net/readerstheater.htm

Storycart Press
www.storycart.com

of students select a piece of quality literature and practice reading it until it has become fluent and expressive, adding sound effects and including various voices for different characters. One teacher in Sowams School in Barrington, Rhode Island, asked businesses to contribute the literature as well as the blank tapes. The tapes, with the books and biographies of the different readers, were then sent to children's hospitals in the surrounding area as a class service-learning project.

Stories can also be adapted into more traditional plays portraying the physical actions of the characters for classes seeking more formal productions. The following seven steps briefly outline a more spontaneous process for creating an adaptation of readers theatre that allows students' own words to bring literature to life:

1. After setting a purpose for listening, read the story aloud for comprehension. Then have students reread the story aloud with all the dramatic intensity they can muster.

2. Have several students relate the story in sequence from memory with the aid of a story grammar or story frame.

3. Select a scribe to write down the story, section by section, in the students' own words. Distribute copies of this new version to each student, thus providing each with a "script." (In a traditional play, this script is memorized; in readers theatre, it is simply read.)

4. Have small groups of students act out, or "block," each section of the play as another student reads it.

5. As a group, discuss how different characters might talk, walk, look, and behave. The roles of all characters should be considered in this discussion—from narrator to those involved in crowd scenes.

6. While the play is in the rehearsal stage, tell the music teacher the theme of the upcoming performance and ask her to select several songs that might enhance the script. Also ask the art teacher if she would be willing to set aside some class time to help students create scenery to enhance the setting.

7. Encourage students to design invitations that reflect the theme of the performance and allow them to distribute the invitations to those who will be in the audience (e.g., parents, classmates, other classes within the school).

Use of Phrase Markings

Phrase marking (Fox, 2003) improves students' expression by helping them read in meaningful word groups. This is accomplished by having the teacher physically mark the phrase boundaries in text, through the use of colored highlighters or slashes, or by rewriting sentences using spaces between the phrases (see Figure 3.8). The student reads the text while adhering to the word groupings the teacher has identified.

> The wounded cowboy/ could not move. /He struggled for a while/ and then lost consciousness./ Rambo, his dog,/ licked the cowboy's face/ with his tongue./ He tried to get/ the unconscious man/ to answer him/ but the cowboy/ did not stir./ Rambo finally ran/ to the road/ and howled./ Every once in a while/ he would trot back/ to the wounded man/ and try to wake him.

A phrase-marked passage.   **FIGURE** 3.8

Using Phrase Markings to Increase Fluency   **ACTIVITY**

The student can be encouraged to mark the phrase boundaries in a new passage, thinking aloud through the appropriate phrasing with the assistance of the teacher. Specifically, the following steps can be followed to use phrase markings to increase fluency.

PROCEDURE

1. Preview the passage to be read. Discuss the title, make connections with the student's background, and have the student make predictions about the passage.

2. Read the first sentence to the student. Make slashes where the ends of groupings would be and then read the sentence again, showing the student how the slashes indicate where you pause in the reading. Do several more sentences in this fashion.

3. Ask the student to read the next sentence silently. Then invite him to make slashes where the word group should end. He then reads the sentence aloud, according to how the phrase has been marked.

4. Discuss where the student placed the slashes and if the sentence was indeed broken into meaningful units.

5. The teacher and student then take turns reading a sentence and marking the phrases using slashes or highlighting them using colored markers. The student may reread the passage several times to practice good phrasing.

6. Finally, ask the student, "What was that passage about?" and prompt her to summarize the passage, including components of narrative structure if fictional text is used, or relevant facts and details if nonfiction material is used.

Fluency-Oriented Reading Instruction

One group activity for assisted reading combines teacher-assisted reading with partner reading. This promising intervention program, *fluency-oriented reading instruction (FORI)*, connects the research-based practices of repeated readings with independent, silent reading within a three-part classroom program, set up and partially assisted by the teacher.

The three components of FORI are

- a reading lesson that includes teacher-led, repeated oral reading and partner reading
- a free reading period at school
- prescribed at-home reading

This fluency intervention program produced gains of almost two years in second-grade students (Stahl, 2002; Stahl, Heubach, & Cramond, 1996).

| ACTIVITY | *Using Fluency-Oriented Reading Instruction* |

The following are the steps in FORI.

PROCEDURE

1. The teacher initiates the activity by modeling the reading of a story or passage, modeling correct expression, phrasing, and attention to punctuation. Although the passage can be fiction or nonfiction, it should be highly motivational and on the students' independent reading level.

2. After the reading, the teacher solicits the students' responses to the selection, gauging their appreciation for the story and making sure that the students understand what has been read.

3. The teacher then reviews key vocabulary and concepts and has students engage in comprehension activities built around the reading. For example, the students might make a recording of themselves orally retelling the sequence of events in an expository piece about penguins in small share groups, or they might act out scenes from a story about a wounded knight, one group at a time.

4. The students then take the selection home and—with prior instructions to parents or other caregivers (e.g., "Simply listen to your child read this passage and provide positive feedback.")—read it aloud an additional time.

5. The following day, the students reread the selection in pairs. One student reads a page as the other student monitors the reading. Then the partners switch roles for another page. This continues until the text is finished.

6. After the partner reading, the teacher leads extension activities that can cross the curriculum, such as having the students research the continent of Antarctica after reading an expository piece on penguins.

7. In the independent reading phase of FORI, time is reserved later in the day for students to select their own reading material, at their independent reading level, to practice the skills leading to reading fluency in a nonstructured way. Optionally, they may do oral reading with partners during this time.

Oral Recitation Lesson

The *oral recitation lesson (ORL)* is another fluency instruction intervention that contains the key ingredients of effective fluency instruction and provides teacher assistance and modeling (Hoffman, 1987; Hoffman & Crone, 1985).

Like the other teacher-assisted techniques described earlier, it too has been reported to lead to increased gains in fluency, but it also has a major focus on comprehension and appears to improve scores in that component of literacy as well (Reutzel & Hollingsworth, 1993).

The ORL can be used in both whole-group and small-group situations, and contains both direct and indirect instruction.

Initiating an Oral Recitation Lesson   ACTIVITY

The following steps are recommended in initiating an ORL.

PROCEDURE

1. The teacher reads a story to the students and then guides them in discussing and analyzing it.

2. From the discussion, the teacher helps the students to create a story map or story grammar summarizing the key elements in the story.

3. Using the story map or story grammar, each student creates a written summary of the story.

4. The teacher selects certain segments of the story and models reading them aloud, calling attention to different features of fluent oral reading, such as effective oral expression.

5. The students imitate the teacher's reading, both individually and chorally.

6. Individual students "perform" the reading of self-selected parts of the story for small groups of students, while the impromptu audience offers praise and positive comments.

7. For ten minutes daily, the students practice reading portions of the story by themselves, using a kind of "whisper reading." The teacher listens to each student, checking progress using anecdotal notes.

TROUBLESHOOTING

It would be wonderful if we could assume that all students in grades 4–8 possessed the decoding ability needed to focus on comprehension strategies. Unfortunately, we cannot make this assumption. For students still having difficulty decoding, it is imperative that they continue to receive instruction that will enhance their decoding ability so they can increase their sight vocabulary, in turn permitting rapid access to word and text meaning. Generally, older students still having trouble with decoding will

- not pronounce the word at all.
- pronounce the word like some other word they know.
- pronounce the word differently each time they encounter it.

They are demonstrating that they do not have a decoding strategy or that they are not focusing on and/or recognizing the letters and letter clusters within the word. Techniques that directly address these decoding difficulties follow.

No Decoding Strategy

Students who demonstrate no use of a decoding strategy often benefit from using a structured approach for figuring out an unknown word in print. DIS-SECT is a decoding strategy that offers students step-by-step alternatives for learning unfamiliar words (Bryant et al., 1999; Lenz et al., 1984; Sadler, 2001). There are seven steps to the strategy, and after the teacher has modeled the steps, they can be printed on index cards, laminated, and used as book-marks for a ready reference during reading. Of course, if the student identifies a word without using all seven steps, it is not necessary to continue with the remaining steps. The seven steps are as follows:

D   Discover the word's context by using the clues in the text around the word.

I   Isolate the prefix, if there is one, and think of its meaning.

S   Separate the suffix, if there is one.

S   Say what is left. This is the root, or stem.

E   Examine the stem by separating the letters to make decoding easier. Try to look for a part you can say.

C   Check with someone if necessary.

T   Try the dictionary pronunciation key.

Assume that the word causing difficulty is *unsaturated*. The student is reading a section of a health or science text that deals with good eating habits. This word is being used to describe a type of fat. The student recognizes, or is told to remove, the prefix *un*. The teacher might ask, "What does the prefix *un* do to the word it is attached to?" The student may respond with "It means *not* or it changes the word to its opposite, like unfinished means *not* finished, or the opposite of finished is *not* finished." Next, the student separates the suffix. In this word the suffix is identified as *ed*. It might help the student to actually write down what is left after removing the prefix and the suffix. The word would now look like *saturat*. But it may need to be pointed out that sometimes when *ed* is added to a word, the original word already had an *e* (relate to a known word like fade/faded). In this case, when *ed* is added, the last *e* in the word is dropped, so it needs to be replaced when the *ed* is removed. Hence, the stem, or root, is actually written *saturate*. The teacher has now provided a mini spelling lesson as well as a decoding strategy. However, the word cannot yet be pronounced by the student, so further examination is needed. The student recognizes the syllables "sat" and "ate." The teacher might point out that what is left is "ur," and say that syllable. Now the student can put the three syllables together: "sat"—"ur"—"ate." If this word is unknown in terms of listening or meaning vocabulary, then this process will not trigger an "aha." The dictionary will be needed to check both pronunciation and meaning. It would be useful for the teacher to also relate the word to the context in which it has occurred: if *saturate* means to absorb or to soak, then *unsaturated* means something has *not* absorbed or become soaked. The meaning of the new word will be reviewed as a final step. The student can then list other words already known, or found during reading, that have some of these same syllables, such as *Saturday, satisfied, Saturn, create, mediate,* or *delegate.*

Mispronounces Words

Direct instruction in decoding the most consistent aspects of our written language, such as syllables, and then blending these syllables to form whole words and using these words in context should be provided for older students who consistently mispronounce words. The following activity, called Sylla-Search, is adapted from a phonics exercise used by classroom teacher Barbara Panza with second and third graders.

Sylla-Search   ACTIVITY

This activity uses multisyllabic words and focuses the learner on the syllables that are pronounced most consistently either in isolation or within other words.

1. Write the multisyllabic word *attendance* on the board. Then ask the following series of questions about the syllables in this word:

    What two letters make the /at/ sound?   A-T

    What three letters make the /ten/ sound?   T-E-N

    What five letters make the /dance/ sound?   D-A-N-C-E

    How would you say the syllable T-E-N?   /ten/

    How would you say the syllable A-T?   /at/

    How would you say the syllable D-A-N-C-E?   /dans/

    Is there another word you can think of that contains the syllable A-T or /at/? The syllable T-E-N or /ten/? (write these words on the board for students to see):

    cat bat mat sat fat . . . tend tens tense

    How about words with more than one syllable? (write these words on the board for students to see):

    attack matter attend tension

2. Ask students to look through some of their books for other words that contain these syllables.

3. Ask students to write these words in their personal dictionaries with a definition or sentence that will help them remember the word.

Another approach involves the use of creative thinking–reading activities (CT-RAs). CT-RAs are brief, small-group activities designed to generate many solutions to a problem and then to combine possible solutions into one "best" solution to be shared with the whole group (Ruddell, 1993). Standard starters such as "Think of all the ways . . ." or "What would happen if . . ." are used. Only about 10 to 15 minutes at the beginning or end of a class are needed to complete these activities. To focus on decoding, starters might include "Think of all the ways you can figure out an unknown word," "What would happen if the prefix *un* was added to this list of words?" "Think of as many words as you can that start with the syllable 'con'," or "Think of all the words you can find in the word *assignment.*"

ACTIVITY | *CT-RA*

A modification of the classroom activity that begins this chapter could serve as a CT-RA (Tierney, 1985).

1. Using copies of the pictures of the animals created by the students in the In the Classroom vignette, have students cut them out, cut off the head, and pass the head to the student sitting next to them.

2. Ask students to tape the new head onto the animal they are holding.

3. Using the scientist's vocabulary chart, ask each student to rename the animal they have now created.

4. Move the students into small groups and have them develop habitats and behaviors for their animals, finally sharing this information with the entire class.

This activity can help students with decoding and spelling difficulties to gain practice with useful and consistent Greek and Latin roots as well as demonstrate to them how manipulating word parts leads to the creation and pronunciation of other words.

SUMMARY

Word study is presented as a continuum of development in spelling, word analysis, and vocabulary abilities. The focus in grades 4–8 changes from attention to mapping sounds onto letters to recognizing units that make up whole words. Of most importance are units that hold meaning, such as prefixes, suffixes, roots, and endings. These units are also very consistent in their pronunciation and meaning, thus aiding both decoding and spelling. Because the nature of word study in grades 4–8 involves word parts that hold meaning, instruction is also closely tied to meaning vocabulary. It would be extremely difficult to avoid talking about the meanings of words when providing instruction in roots, prefixes, suffixes, compound words, and derivational words. While students in the primary grades learn to decode words that are for the most part in their speaking and listening vocabularies, students in grades 4–8 are learning to decode many words for which they have no conceptual knowledge. Instruction in word recognition, then, must be closely related to instruction in meaning vocabulary to be most effective and efficient. As students in grades 4–8 encounter text with structures different from the more familiar narrative structures of primary-grade materials, their fluency levels drop off. Teacher modeling of fluent reading for more complex materials is helpful, as is providing time for students to practice reading these more complex materials.

Questions
FOR JOURNAL WRITING AND DISCUSSION

1. Describe in your own words the stages of reading/spelling development. What characteristics might a student demonstrate in each of the stages? Explain how being aware of these stages might help a teacher plan appropriate spelling instruction for each learner.

2. Discuss how word study may be of particular value to English learners.

3. What is the value in teaching morphology to students? Use examples to support your response.

4. What is your understanding of the nature of fluency? Do you believe more fluent reading can lead to enhanced comprehension? Why or why not?

Suggestions
FOR PROJECTS AND FIELD ACTIVITIES

1. Administer a spelling inventory (see Appendix D) to three students in grades 4–8. Analyze their responses as to what reading/spelling stage is represented most often in their spelling. What are some instructional activities that would benefit these students?

2. Develop a list of 15 words based on similar or related roots, affixes, or derivations. Invite a small group of students to sort the words as they think they should be sorted. Then have these students make statements about their findings. Present your list and your findings to your classmates. What were the students able to learn from the sorting activity?

3. Observe a word study lesson taught to students. Through discussion with the teacher and your direct observation, answer the following questions:

   a. What strategies are students being taught about how to spell new words?

   b. How are students being taught about syllables, affixes, and derivations?

   c. How is word study applied in reading and writing situations in the classroom?

4. With a classroom teacher's help, identify a fluent reader and a disfluent reader in any grade 4–8. Observe each of the two students reading a passage. Describe the differences between their reading. What would you predict their relative comprehension abilities to be, based on their oral reading? Check your perceptions with the children's teacher.

REFERENCES

Allington, R. L., & Cunningham, P. M. (2002). *Schools that work: Where all children read and write* (2nd ed.). Boston: Allyn & Bacon.

Bear, D. R., Invernizzi, M., Templeton, S., & Johnston, F. (2000). *Words their way: Word study for phonics, vocabulary, and spelling instruction* (2nd ed.). Upper Saddle River, NJ: Merrill.

Bear, D., Templeton, S., Invernizzi, M., & Johnston, F. (Eds.) (2000). *Words their way: Word study for phonics, vocabulary, and spelling instruction* (2nd ed.). Upper Saddle River, NJ: Merrill/Prentice Hall.

Bloodgood, J. W., & Pacifici, L. C. (2004, November). Bringing word study to intermediate classrooms. *The Reading Teacher, 58,* 250–263.

Bloodgood, J. W., Pacifici, L. C., & Rullman, A. (2001, December). *Bringing word study to upper elementary and preservice teacher classrooms.* Alternative Session presented at the annual meeting of the National Reading Conference, San Antonio, TX.

Bryant, D. P., Ugel, N., Thompson, S., & Hamff, A. (1999). Instructional strategies for content-area reading instruction. *Intervention in School and Clinic, 34*(5), 293–302.

Buehl, D. (2001). *Classroom strategies for interactive learning* (2nd ed.). Newark, DE: International Reading Association.

Carlisle, J. F., & Stone, C. A. (2005). Exploring the role of morphemes in word reading. *Reading Research Quarterly, 40*, 428–449.

Cecil, N. L. (2007). *Focus on fluency: A meaning-based approach.* Scottsdale, AZ: Holcomb Hathaway.

Crichton, M. (1990). *Jurassic Park.* New York: Knopf.

Cunningham, P. M., & Allington, R. L. (1999). *Classrooms that work: They can all read and write* (2nd ed.). New York: Longman.

Cunningham, P. M., & Hall, D. P. (1998). *Month-by-month phonics for upper grades: A second chance for struggling readers and students learning English.* Greensboro, NC: Carson-DeLosa.

Fox, B. J. (2003). *Word recognition activities: Patterns and strategies for developing fluency.* Upper Saddle River, NJ: Merrill/Prentice Hall.

Fry, E. B., Kress, J. E., & Fountoukidis, D. L. (2000). *The reading teacher's book of lists* (4th ed.). Paramus, NJ: Prentice Hall.

Gipe, J. P. (2006). *Multiple paths to literacy: Assessment and differential instruction for diverse learners k–12* (6th ed.). Upper Saddle River, NJ: Merrill-Prentice Hall.

Henderson, E. (1990). *Teaching spelling* (2nd ed.). Boston: Houghton Mifflin.

Herrell, A. L., & Jordan, M. (2006). *50 strategies for improving vocabulary, comprehension, and fluency: An active learning approach.* Boston: Allyn & Bacon.

Hoffman, J. V. (1987). Rethinking the role of oral reading in basal instruction. *Elementary School Journal, 87*, 367–373.

Hoffman, J. V., & Crone, S. (1985). The oral recitation lesson: A research-derived strategy for reading basal texts. In J. A. Niles & R. A. Lalik (Eds.), *Issues in literacy: A research perspective. Thirty-fourth Yearbook of the National Reading Conference* (pp. 76–83). Rochester, NY: National Reading Conference.

Johnson, D. D. (2001). *Vocabulary in the elementary and middle school.* Boston: Allyn & Bacon.

Johnson, D. D., & Pearson, P. D. (1984). *Teaching reading vocabulary* (2nd ed.). New York: Holt, Rinehart and Winston.

Kemper, L. W., & Brody, F. (2001). Advanced decoding and fluency. In F. Brody (Ed.), *Teaching reading: Language, letters and thought* (2nd ed., pp. 144–167). Milford, NH: LARC.

Kuhn, M. R., & Stahl, S. A. (2003). Fluency: A review of developmental and remedial practices. *Journal of Educational Psychology, 95*, 3–21.

Lenz, B. K., Schumaker, J. G., Deshler, D. D., & Beals, V. L. (1984). *The word identification strategy.* Lawrence, KS: University of Kansas.

Rasinski, T., & Padak, N. (2000). *Effective reading strategies: Teaching children who find reading difficult* (2nd ed.). Upper Saddle River, NJ: Merrill-Prentice Hall.

Reutzel, D. R., & Hollingsworth, P. M. (1993). Effects of fluency training on second graders' reading comprehension. *Journal of Educational Research, 86*, 325–331.

Richardson, J. S. (2000). *Read it aloud!* Newark, DE: International Reading Association.

Ruddell, M. R. (1993). *Teaching content reading and writing.* Boston: Allyn & Bacon.

Sadler, C. R. (2001). *Comprehension strategies for middle grade learners: A handbook for content area teachers.* Newark, DE: International Reading Association.

Sloyer, S. (1982). *Readers theatre: Story dramatization in the classroom.* Urbana, IL: National Council of Teachers of English.

Stahl, S. A. (2002). Fluency: Instruction and assessment. PowerPoint presentation presented at A Focus on Fluency Forum, San Francisco, CA. Available at www.prel.org/programs/rel/fluency/Stahl.ppt.

Stahl, S. A., Heubach, K., & Cramond, B. (1996). *Fluency Oriented Reading Instruction* (NRRC Report no. 79). College Park, MD: National Reading Research Center.

Tierney, B. (1985). In the fifth grade, they all raise their hands. *Learning, 85*, 34.

Vocabulary
Instruction

CHAPTER

Four

- What are important factors to keep in mind when teaching vocabulary?

- What are some research-based instructional strategies to teach vocabulary directly to students?

- How can teachers assist students in learning how to figure out the meanings of new words on their own?

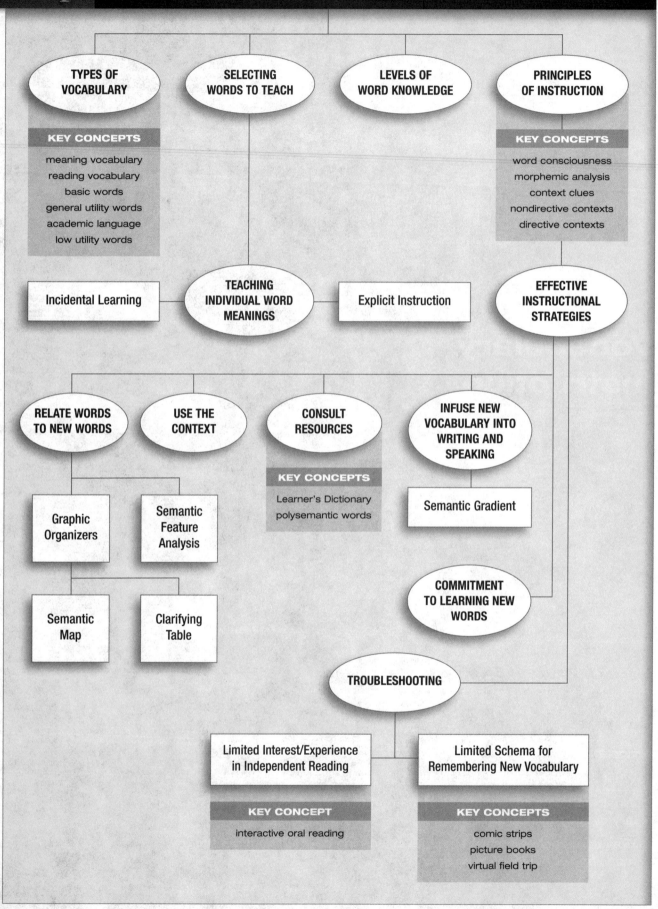

TYPES OF VOCABULARY

KEY CONCEPTS

meaning vocabulary
reading vocabulary
basic words
general utility words
academic language
low utility words

SELECTING WORDS TO TEACH

LEVELS OF WORD KNOWLEDGE

PRINCIPLES OF INSTRUCTION

KEY CONCEPTS

word consciousness
morphemic analysis
context clues
nondirective contexts
directive contexts

Incidental Learning

TEACHING INDIVIDUAL WORD MEANINGS

Explicit Instruction

EFFECTIVE INSTRUCTIONAL STRATEGIES

RELATE WORDS TO NEW WORDS

USE THE CONTEXT

CONSULT RESOURCES

INFUSE NEW VOCABULARY INTO WRITING AND SPEAKING

KEY CONCEPTS

Learner's Dictionary
polysemantic words

Semantic Gradient

Graphic Organizers

Semantic Feature Analysis

Semantic Map

Clarifying Table

COMMITMENT TO LEARNING NEW WORDS

TROUBLESHOOTING

Limited Interest/Experience in Independent Reading

Limited Schema for Remembering New Vocabulary

KEY CONCEPT

interactive oral reading

KEY CONCEPTS

comic strips
picture books
virtual field trip

Mrs. Chase briefly explains the term *eternal life* to her students and gives them a few seconds to imagine what it would be like to live forever. She then leads a lively discussion about what the students believe are the possible advantages and disadvantages of living forever, writing all their comments on the chalkboard. Jennifer believes that living forever would be a wonderful thing because "you wouldn't have to die and make people sad"; Ethan counters that all his friends would be gone and he might become "lonely and bored."

Following the discussion, Mrs. Chase's sixth-graders begin reading Natalie Babbitt's *Tuck Everlasting* (1975) in heterogeneous literature groups. During this time, Mrs. Chase uses a *clarifying table* to anchor the meaning of the term *eternity* within the context of the book. She writes the word *eternity* under the heading "Core Idea" and writes below it that this term means "an endless period of time." She then asks if someone can give an example of what eternity means from his own life experience. "When you're waiting for the mail to arrive because you are expecting a special birthday present from your aunt. It seems like an eternity! But it's not, really," exclaims Raul.

Next, Mrs. Chase asks the students for examples of another word with which the term might be easily confused. Rachel suggests, "Anything that has a life span that you can predict would not be a good example of eternity. Recess lasts for about 15 minutes, a fixed amount of time—not an eternity." After this, the teacher asks for "clarifiers," or phrases that will help the students to think more clearly about what the term does and does not mean. After the students brainstorm in small groups, the teacher writes down their responses:

- You don't know the beginning and you don't know the end.
- Some religions believe that we live on for an eternity after we die.
- Always and forever.
- Events that go on longer than you want them to seem to take an eternity, but that's an exaggeration.

At this point, Mrs. Chase asks the students to think about how the term *eternity* was used in the book. They offer that the Tuck family drank from a spring that gave them everlasting life so they would never grow older and would exist for "all the time that will ever exist in the world." Finally, the teacher asks the students to create a sentence using the term *eternity*. After thinking about the meaning of the word, all the students are able to quickly complete this task, providing sentences that reflect their own lives or the book they have just read.

Andy's contribution is typical: "An eternity is an amount of time that has no end, or just feels like it will never end."

Mrs. Chase's use of the clarifying table has solidified the students' understanding of the most critical concept discussed in this book. (See the activity "Constructing and Using a Clarifying Table," later in this chapter.)

INTRODUCTION

Our knowledge of words is an often overlooked, yet critical factor in the mosaic of our entire personalities. Indeed, the word knowledge we have stored somewhere in our minds determines how well we are able to take part in discussions; comprehend the books and other texts we read; share our most intimate thoughts; explain our ideas for others; and, in sum, form a cohesive worldview. A larger vocabulary means not only that we know more words but, more important, that we are able to express our thoughts and feelings in a more complex and satisfying way. We may use our storehouse of words to think and even to dream; therefore, it follows that the richer our vocabulary, the more potentially productive our inner life can be.

In a more specifically educational setting, vocabulary is absolutely integral to proficient reading. If students do not understand the meaning of the words in text, the process of reading is reduced to meaningless word calling, or "barking at print." No student should ever have to struggle along producing only a series of verbal nonsense. As teachers, we want students to understand a wide range of words. A fundamental part of critical thinking necessary for adequate reading comprehension is rapid access to the necessary word meanings (Anderson & Freebody, 1981; Baumann & Kame'enui, 2004; Baumann, Kame'enui, & Ash, 2003; Graves, 1986).

Proficient readers are able to connect new words with other words they know and to understand the connotations attached to them by virtue of their various uses. Because each proficient reader's particular background varies, for every passage a social history and context is created that continually attaches personal meaning to it. Encountering words over and over again, both through text and in conversation, builds a fabric of understanding that clarifies the meaning of familiar words and then makes it even easier to solve the meaning of new words, creating a snowballing spiral of vocabulary acquisition. Indeed, Nagy and Anderson (1984) estimated that by fifth grade, average readers read 10 times more than poor readers, and voracious readers read up to 50 times as many words! As a result, by merely encountering more words, good readers learn much more about language.

TYPES OF VOCABULARY

Two major types of vocabulary are relevant in grade 4–8 classrooms: meaning vocabulary and reading vocabulary. **Meaning vocabulary,** as the name implies, is the sum total of a person's understanding of the meaning of words. Some of these word meanings are understood when spoken or written by others (*receptive vocabulary*), and others are words we are able to use in our speech or writing (*productive* or *expressive vocabulary*) (Graves, 2006). Meaning vocabulary is extremely important, because readers need to draw from this store as they emerge into reading to learn. Meaning vocabulary can therefore be likened to a vast reservoir from which readers draw known meanings when figuring out new meanings as they read. **Reading vocabulary** refers to words both recognized and understood when reading (Harris & Hodges, 1995, p. 213). Reading vocabulary utilizes receptive vocabulary.

meaning vocabulary ●

reading vocabulary ●

Vocabulary can be further broken down into three subcategories, or tiers, that have major implications as to how the various words encountered could most effectively be introduced to students in the intermediate and middle grades (Beck, McKeown, & Kucan, 2002). These subcategories are

1. basic words
2. general-utility words
3. low-utility words

Our decision about which words to teach students directly is influenced by the occurrence of those words. How frequently the words will be seen in text and therefore afford opportunities for practice by students should be in direct proportion to the time we spend introducing the words (Beck, McKeown, & Omanson, 1987). Once we are aware of which words are the most instructionally significant, then we can consider a variety of methods for teaching those words, either directly or by assisting students in using strategies that aid in new vocabulary acquisition.

basic words ●

Basic words are the building blocks of everyday language. They are so commonplace and are used so often that their meanings do not require specific instruction except in the case of second language learners, who usually will have the concept but will require a new English label for the word. Often referred to as sight words, examples of such words are *am, boy, said,* and *from.*

General-utility words are more complex terms that proficient readers and speakers use often in speech, but these words are not specific to any one subject area and include words considered part of **academic language**. Thus, the words on the Academic Word List (AWL) (Coxhead, 2000) are considered general-utility words. This list consists of 570 word families that are divided into 10 sublists. When studying the sublists, students should also study the various derivations for the word families (i.e., the verb, noun, adjective, and adverb forms plus variants). The AWL represents Tier Two words (Beck, McKeown, & Kucan, 2002) because they appear with great frequency in a broad range of academic texts. Although intended for older students, teachers in grades 4–8 can readily identify words from the AWL that are appropriate and necessary for their students to learn. These words are best learned in context. Exercises such as fill-in-the-blank or matching would be appropriate ways to practice using these words. For some examples, 150 fill-in-the-blank, self-checking exercises are available online at http://web.uvic.ca/~gluton/awl/id17.htm. Instruction in common root words, prefixes, and suffixes can also help students to discover the meaning of words in this category. The majority of vocabulary study during a reading lesson would be directed at this second tier of words. Words such as *create, combine, examine,* and *transfer* are examples of this tier of vocabulary. For a downloadable version of the AWL, visit the second site listed at right.

Low-utility words, the third tier of vocabulary, are the words that are encountered less frequently, and they are usually found in particular content areas. Such words should be introduced before students engage in their content area texts and tasks and should be grouped according to the particular concept with which they are identified. Examples of such words include *tropism, solar, biped,* and *crater.*

- general-utility words
- academic language

WWW

Academic Word List
www.vuw.ac.nz/lals/research/awl.aspx
http://language.massey.ac.nz/staff/awl/index.shtml

- low-utility words

SELECTING VOCABULARY WORDS TO TEACH

Choosing which words to teach is a more complicated task than one might think. Graves (2006) estimates the reading materials students will encounter while in school include more than 180,000 different words. Because students need to learn so many words each year, it is critical for teachers to select "words that are most important for understanding a specific reading selection or [content area] concept, [and] words that are generally useful for students to know and are likely to encounter" frequently in their reading (Hiebert, Lehr, & Osborn, 2004, p. 10). Ellis and Farmer (2000) offer the following suggestions for selecting vocabulary:

1. *Teach words that are essential to the unit or theme of study.* Instead of teaching all words that appear in a list at the end of a text chapter, teach the ones that are so critical that it would be impossible to understand the chapter without knowing them.

2. *Go for depth and connections.* Do not try to teach a large quantity of words that students will probably not encounter again; instead, teach a few words in a manner that results in deep understandings by connecting to concepts with which students are already familiar.

3. *Teach only key concepts.* Although a chapter of study may contain 15 or more highlighted vocabulary terms, there may be only four or five that address crucial concepts in the chapter.

4. *Reinforce words that will be used often during the school year.* General-utility words that will be revisited often provide a foundation upon which much information will be built over time.

Beck, McKeown, and Kucan (2002) concur with these suggestions but emphasize the importance of teaching the words classified as general-utility words, which they refer to as Tier Two words, including:

1. words that are characteristic of mature language users and appear frequently across a variety of domains (i.e., importance and utility).

2. words that can be worked with in a variety of ways so that students can build deep knowledge of them and of their connections to other words and concepts (i.e., instructional potential).

3. words for which students understand the general concept but provide precision and specificity in describing the concept (i.e., conceptual understanding). (p. 19)

While the criteria for selecting words to teach can be useful, teachers still need to apply guidelines with the specific needs of their students in mind. The words finally selected for teaching are up to the judgment of each teacher but should reflect a decision made with thought and care.

LEVELS OF WORD KNOWLEDGE

Knowing a word is *not* an all-or-nothing proposition. Researchers (Dale, 1965; Beck et al., 1987) have created a continuum of word understanding ranging from being completely unfamiliar with a word to having a rich network of meaning attached to it. Words often have both a denotation and a connotation and can evoke a constellation of meanings and ideas to different people depending on their own experiences and cultural settings. Moreover, knowing a word in context is different from knowing a word in isolation, and being able to use a word in daily conversation is different from merely being able to understand the word in written format (see Figure 4.1).

Knowledge of a word, then, can best be viewed in terms of the extent or degree of understanding that a person has about it. Students can engage in

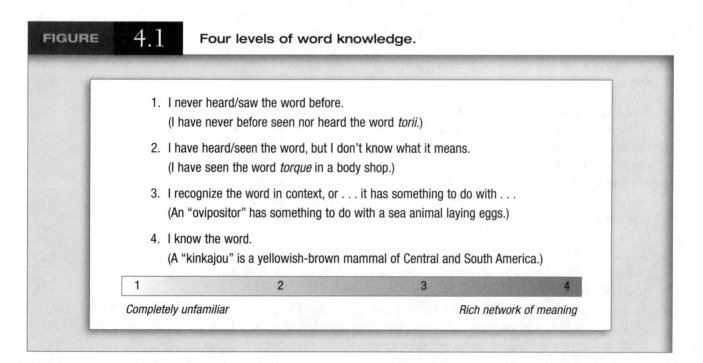

FIGURE 4.1 Four levels of word knowledge.

1. I never heard/saw the word before.
   (I have never before seen nor heard the word *torii*.)

2. I have heard/seen the word, but I don't know what it means.
   (I have seen the word *torque* in a body shop.)

3. I recognize the word in context, or . . . it has something to do with . . .
   (An "ovipositor" has something to do with a sea animal laying eggs.)

4. I know the word.
   (A "kinkajou" is a yellowish-brown mammal of Central and South America.)

| 1 | 2 | 3 | 4 |

Completely unfamiliar   *Rich network of meaning*

self-assessment by rating their knowledge of a word using the four levels seen in Figure 4.1. Pointing out to students the continuum of ways it is possible to be familiar with a word helps them begin to experience how working with words and reading widely support growth in meaning vocabulary. For example, a reader comes across an unfamiliar word (*extinction*) but can associate it with something with which she is familiar (preservation of animals). This partial recognition, supported by context, may let her continue to read without interrupting the "flow" of her understanding of the passage. In fact, encountering a partially known word in context and relating it to the meaning of a whole text is the kind of literacy event that will gradually enhance her knowledge of that word and help her to move it along the continuum toward a richly known word. As the student encounters the word again and again, recognition of the word's meaning will grow at a relatively constant rate, depending upon the helpfulness of the context (Schwanenflugel, Stahl, & McFalls, 1997). Finally, Beck et al. (2002) have suggested that when readers reach the stage where they feel they truly "know" a word, they are able to provide an original sentence containing the word, or a restatement of the definition in their own words.

PRINCIPLES OF VOCABULARY INSTRUCTION

Effective vocabulary instruction for intermediate- and middle-grade students begins with *explanations* as opposed to definitions (Feldman & Kinsella, 2003). These "explanations" should use (1) language familiar to students; (2) examples that exist in students' background knowledge or worldviews; and (3) images or metaphors known to students.

Such instruction is not accomplished through traditional vocabulary acquisition methods of having students copy the words, look them up in the dictionary, memorize definitions, and then use the words in contrived sentences. Rather, some guiding principles for effective vocabulary instruction, with examples, include the following (Blachowicz et al., 2006; Graves, 2006; NICHD, 2000):

New words should be integrated with familiar words and concepts. A major task in vocabulary instruction is to choose words for students that include known words as well as unfamiliar words so that personal connections can be made. Students can create knowledge connections between new words and their own background knowledge in a wide variety of ways. For example, teachers can help them to identify how the new words are related to previous subject matter they have learned (e.g., "a novel is like a long story"), to identify something from their personal life experiences that reminds them of a particular word (e.g., "filibuster reminds me of my talkative Uncle Buster"), to create metaphors or similes for a term (e.g., "a chrysanthemum is like a yellow mum"), or to discuss how some of the words might relate to solving a real-life problem they have had (e.g., "because I always procrastinated about feeding my hamster, I taped a sign on his cage to help me remember").

Students should experience multiple exposures to words in meaningful and varied contexts. Comprehension is greatly enhanced when students can quickly identify examples of the words or ways the new words can be appropriately applied in the context of a discussion of an already familiar concept.

Teacher Behaviors That Enhance Vocabulary Learning

LINK	Relate students' past experiences with present ones.
ELABORATE	Add more information about familiar content, or suggest a rewording of the content.
REINFORCE	Introduce new vocabulary and reinforce through constant use.
CONNECT	Tie new words to the activity or the activity to the new words.
CLARIFY	Add examples, illustrations, or descriptions.
QUESTION	Stimulate thinking about terms through questioning.
RELATE	Show how new words compare with those students know.
CATEGORIZE	Group new words, ideas, and concepts.
LABEL	Provide names for concepts, ideas, and objects.

When choosing words to be taught directly, teachers should focus not only on words important to understanding the material, but also on words their students will encounter often in their reading (Beck et al., 2002). These new words should be taught in the context of a meaningful subject-matter lesson, and discussion with students should then center on the use of the new words. For example, the word *phototropism* could best be taught after an experiment in which plants are observed growing toward the sun. Students should then be encouraged to use the new terms themselves in multiple contexts—through reading, writing, listening, and speaking. In short, they should frequently use the words in a variety of language experiences.

Also, increasing the amount of reading students complete will increase vocabulary (Anderson, 1996). Beginning in the intermediate grades, wide "reading becomes the principal language experience for enlarging students' vocabularies" (Cunningham & Stanovich, as cited in Graves, 2006, p. 5). Wide reading can provide the multiple encounters necessary for learning new vocabulary. Jenkins, Stein, and Wysocki (1984) found that between five and 10 encounters with a new word are needed to see results in vocabulary gains.

Students should be taught word-learning strategies they can independently apply to words they meet in other contexts. *Independent word-learning strategies* are procedures teachers can model and teach explicitly to show students how to determine the meanings of unknown words (Baker, Simmons, & Kame'enui, 1998). "While teaching word meanings is a major goal of vocabulary programs, helping students become independent word learners is another aspect of vocabulary development that cannot be ignored, especially for students who have developed meager strategies and weak views of themselves as word learners" (Harmon, 2000, p. 526). Three important word-learning strategies for vocabulary growth are (1) using context clues to infer word meanings; (2) using morphemic analysis (word parts) to decipher word meanings; and (3) using the dictionary (Baumann et al., 2003; National Reading Panel, 2000).

context clues ●   **Context clues** refer to other words, definitions, examples, or illustrations in text that provide clues to the meaning of the unknown word. Although students may have learned to identify and use context clues (Baumann et al.,

2003), not all texts provide helpful context clues for determining a word's meaning. For example, "Our *pod* swam with other pods in the center, where it was safe" demonstrates a context not helpful in determining the meaning of *pod*, other than to know it is a noun capable of swimming. Such contexts are referred to as **nondirective contexts,** while contexts that do provide helpful clues for figuring out unknown words are referred to as **directive contexts** (Beck, McKeown, & McCaslin, 1983; Beck et al., 2002, p. 5). Context clues will be discussed in more detail later in this chapter.

● nondirective contexts
● directive contexts

    Morphemic analysis (also known as structural analysis) focuses attention on word parts: root words, prefixes, derivational suffixes, and inflectional suffixes. A **morpheme** is the smallest element having meaning in a word. For example, words such as *skill* and *pod* are morphemes (i.e., root words), and so are word parts such as *-ful,* as in *skillful* (i.e., derivational suffix), and *-s,* as in *pods* (i.e., inflectional suffix). Knowing word parts plays an important role in learning word meanings as more than 60 percent of new words that students meet contain identifiable morphemes (Nagy, Anderson, Schommer, Scott, & Stallman, 1989). As noted in Chapter 3, morphological awareness is a crucial skill for students in grades 4–8, and effective instructional practices are described there.

● morphemic analysis

● morpheme

    Dictionaries can be valuable resources for learning word meanings. But instruction using dictionaries is seldom helpful if students are asked only to look up definitions and then use the word in a sentence (Gipe, 1978/1979; Scott & Nagy, 1997). Effective dictionary instruction includes teacher modeling of how to use a dictionary and how to select the most appropriate meaning for a word. Students should also have access to learner-friendly dictionaries, such as *Collins COBUILD Learner's Dictionary* (2003), that provide age-appropriate definitions and example sentences (Feldman & Kinsella, 2003). McKeown (1993) provides evidence that such dictionary definitions designed to reveal the essential characteristics of word meanings help students produce sentence constructions that are 50 percent accurate versus only 25 percent accurate when they use traditional dictionary entries. One example she offers is for the word *conspicuous,* with a traditional dictionary definition of "easily seen" and a revised definition of "describes something you notice right away because it stands out" (p. 23).

Vocabulary instruction should engage students in active processing of word meanings and in developing an interest in learning new words. Whereas some students can acquire new vocabulary through listening and discussion, many others, including English learners, need more active engagement in order to process the new words (Carlo et al., 2004). For example, the teacher could relate the word *propaganda* to a sales pitch with which students are familiar, such as a car salesperson's spiel, and then lead a discussion of other high-pressure, and often misleading, advertisements they have seen on television; the students could be asked to take notes on some of the most offensive ones they have seen. The teacher could then end the discussion with an informal survey about which propaganda techniques the students like the least and why.

    Recently, the impact of electronic text on vocabulary learning has been explored (Blachowicz et al., 2006). These authors conclude, "electronic texts can be both motivating and effective for word learning when they provide or couple their presentations with facilitation that calls on the students to actively engage with the words" (p. 533). The term *facilitation* in this context refers to some form of mediated instruction that emulates what a supportive adult might provide if the reading were not occurring through electronic text. For example, to facilitate vocabulary learning, illustrative sentences or pictures rich with information could be linked to difficult concepts to enhance their meaning. Using new terms in essays or creative writing affords students an even greater opportunity for reflection and thinking about how words are used. Other forms of active engagement include acting out the words, creating mnemonic devices, or drawing pictures that capture the essence of the word's meaning.

Developing a curiosity and interest in learning new words is also critical to vocabulary instruction. Researchers have referred to students' awareness of new words and their desire to learn and use them when speaking and writing as **word consciousness** (Graves & Watts-Taffe, 2002). Activities focused on raising the level of curiosity and interest in learning word meanings include (1) learning the history of some of our English words (e.g., *bayou, pecan, toboggan* from the American Indian tribes Choctaw, Illinois, and Micmac, respectively; *renegade, mosquito, tuna* from the Spanish language; *gingham, ketchup* from Malay); (2) learning figurative uses of words (e.g., idioms, puns, tongue twisters); (3) engaging in word play (e.g., Hinky Pinky and other word riddles such as, Riddle: How do you take a pig to a hospital? Answer: In a hambulance! Blachowicz & Fisher, 2004, p. 229); and (4) participating in word contests (e.g., Reader's Digest National Word Power Challenge).

word consciousness ●

WWW

Word Power Challenge
www.wordpowerchallenge.com

TEACHING INDIVIDUAL WORD MEANINGS

Teachers always seem to be looking for better ways to increase their students' vocabularies because they are aware that the old ways, for the most part, did not result in long-term retention of new words. Traditionally, students copied a list of words from the chalkboard, looked up their meaning in the dictionary, memorized a definition (usually a simple synonym), and then wrote sentences that were supposed to demonstrate an understanding of the word's essence. Here is an example of a product from such a method: "I was exhausted." This method of memorizing isolated vocabulary one word at a time is not only ineffective, as the example suggests, but it is also impractical. While students may remember approximately 200 words a year through this rote method, Anderson and Nagy (1992) advise that students must acquire more than 3,000 words a year to keep up with the demands of content area material! However, results of vocabulary intervention studies suggest that only about 8–10 words can be taught effectively per week, so only about 360 words (180 school days/5 = 36 weeks) can reasonably be learned through direct instruction (Stahl & Fairbanks, 1986). Clearly, teachers must offer a variety of approaches to vocabulary instruction to assist students in their substantial vocabulary needs and to enable them to acquire new vocabulary through incidental learning and from explicit instruction.

Incidental Learning

Although how it happens is not clear, most learning of word meanings occurs through incidental learning: listening and discussion, writing, and the act of reading widely (Graves, 2006; NICHD, 2000). Teachers concerned with enhancing their students' vocabularies make conscious decisions to include new and sometimes challenging words in their verbal interactions with students, sometimes stopping to explain the word's meaning but more often just using the words in appropriate contexts. For example, "Today we will *commence* our lesson by sharing what we know about whales."

Teachers can encourage wide reading not only by building a well-stocked classroom library, but also by providing time for students to read these books. Scheduling in-class independent reading using a structured silent reading program (e.g., DEAR, or, Drop Everything and Read; SSR, or, Sustained Silent Reading) with some sort of written follow-up in a vocabulary log or journal is strongly recommended (see the activity: "Very Important Term (VIT) Word Book" later in this chapter). Teachers can also encourage independent reading through **book talks** (reading aloud a brief, enticing selection from and/or sharing positive impressions about a book to arouse interest in it (see "Sample Interactive Book Talk" on p. 106).

Estimates indicate that students must learn more than 3,000 words a year to keep up with the demands of content area reading.

Explicit Instruction

Even if students are reading independently, they will still need to learn many word meanings in order to successfully comprehend content area materials. Explicit instruction for such individual word meanings needs to occur. Although there are many approaches to directly teaching students the meaning of a word, the approach a teacher should take depends on three discrete factors (Stahl, 1999):

● book talks

- the nature of the word—concrete or abstract?
- the possibility for grouping the word with others
- the possibility for graphically illustrating the word

Is the word concrete or abstract? First, the word itself should be considered. If the word requires little explanation (e.g., *mountainside*) or can be easily shown to students (e.g., *rutabaga*), then little extended elaboration is required. However, if the word is more abstract and difficult, such as *propaganda,* a lengthier explanation would be more appropriate. Additionally, an instructional strategy designed to help students focus on what the word is as well as what it is not, in relationship to words they already know, is often illuminating.

Can the word be grouped with others? Second, since teaching word meanings solely as single units is decidedly inefficient, teachers should look for ways to link words and ideas together so that students encounter a group of similar, or related, words at one time. For example, if students are studying the newspaper, it would make sense to introduce all the parts of the paper—obituaries, headlines, editorial, classified advertisements, and so forth—because all these

Sample Interactive Book Talk

I've got some paper cups right here. And I've got this bottle of water. And I've got a promise. If you drink a single sip of my magic water, you will remain at your present age forever. You will never die. Take a paper cup if you want some. [Pass out cups.] I see some of you refused my offer. Why? People have searched for centuries for the Fountain of Youth! [Your remarks will depend on the answers you get, but the following are possibilities.] Oh, you don't want to survive all the people you love? Take enough for them, too. You feel that you're too young right now? Ok, take some for later; it will retain its magic for several years. Don't worry, it doesn't stop you from growing, learning, experiencing new things. It merely prevents you from *aging*. [Allow for more discussion.]

As you may have guessed, I've lied to you. I got the water from the drinking fountain outside the door. But the book I have here, *Tuck Everlasting* by Natalie Babbitt (1975), has a spring with the property I've tried to tempt you with. The 11-year-old protagonist, Winnie Foster, finds the spring and a family who drank the water—87 years ago. Now, she has a decision to make. If you've ever wondered why things have to die, if you've ever pondered the mysteries of the life cycle, if you've ever thought about the concept of "forever," read this book to find out if and when Winnie drinks the water.

From S. Kane, *Literacy and Learning in the Content Areas,* 2nd ed. (2007), Scottsdale, AZ: Holcomb Hathaway.

elements are related to the same concept, or belong to the same "semantic field." Similarly, as mentioned in the previous chapter, skill in morphemic analysis makes it possible for students to determine the meanings of many words that share the same root. As Carlisle and Stone (2005) state, "combining instruction in morphemic units for purposes of both reading and vocabulary development inherently makes sense, as such instruction might provide the essential links between form and meaning that are the potential benefit of morphemic processing in the natural act of reading [i.e., incidental learning]" (p. 446). For example, a student reading a selection on medical professions might encounter *cardiologist* and mentally associate it with *ophthalmologist, psychologist,* and *optometrist* at the same time.

Can the word be graphically illustrated? Finally, a word should be acted out or in some other way made graphic to students when the word in question lends itself to such treatment. Such words as *meandered* or *exhausted* can be immediately made clear through pantomime or drawings; likewise, the word *chrysanthemum* is instantly accessible through a photo or through examining the live flower. Moreover, such multisensory approaches to vocabulary development, with their de-emphasis on oral language, help encourage English learners to be active participants in the learning and comprehension process.

Alber and Foil (2003) describe a procedure for introducing new vocabulary that includes physical action or dramatic movement to represent the word's meaning. Some examples of words with their corresponding actions follow:

Exalted: start at floor level and lift an imaginary object high into the air

Frigid: cross arms over chest and pretend to shiver with teeth chattering

Lugubrious: make a sad face and pretend to cry uncontrollably

Pirouette: spin around on the ball of one foot

Pixilated: stagger around and pretend to be confused or distracted

Studious: pretend to read a textbook with a serious expression on face

EFFECTIVE STRATEGIES FOR A
COMPREHENSIVE VOCABULARY PROGRAM

Through a well-planned vocabulary instructional program, students will add new words to their meaning vocabulary; in addition, the stress of an overwhelming number of new words and concepts encountered in instructional reading material will diminish. The end result is that by reducing the number of unfamiliar words with which readers must struggle, the teacher increases the chances of creating a positive literacy experience. In this section, we explore five student goals for an effective program in vocabulary instruction that ensures the maximum acquisition of new words throughout the school years. Students should strive to:

1 relate new words to what they already know.

2 use context to figure out partially known words.

3 consult a resource (e.g., a dictionary) when necessary.

4 learn to determine the meanings of polysemantic words

5 infuse new vocabulary words into their writing and speaking.

6 commit to learning new words.

In the remainder of this chapter, we also consider the assumptions about vocabulary knowledge that underlie practice. Through an understanding of the options involved in teaching vocabulary, preservice and practicing teachers will be able to make informed instructional choices in this critical area.

1 **RELATE NEW WORDS TO KNOWN WORDS**

Reliance on incidental learning opportunities in the classroom is not sufficient for students to acquire the number of words necessary for them to learn when that load appears to be roughly 3,000 words per year, or approximately 17 words per day (Baumann & Kame'enui, 1991; Beck & McKeown, 1991; Graves, 2006). In addition, English learners or learners who are linguistically disadvantaged largely due to growing up in poverty have a much larger vocabulary-learning task (Carlo et al., 2004; Coyne, Simmons, & Kame'enui, 2004). Therefore, as stated earlier, a combination of incidental learning and direct vocabulary instruction is needed. Recent studies have explored the benefits of alternative vocabulary-learning techniques, such as graphic organizers including semantic maps, which help students relate the meaning of new words to known words by activating their prior knowledge (Baumann, Kame'enui, & Ash, 2003).

Two major methods for clarifying and enriching the meanings of known words as related to new words are (1) graphic organizers, such as semantic maps, and (2) semantic feature analysis.

Graphic organizers

Graphic organizers, also referred to as visual organizers, graphic representations, and structural overviews, work well for meaning-related concepts. A graphic organizer visually represents a body of knowledge that includes the critical concepts, ideas, events, generalizations, and/or facts pertaining to the word, using a diagram, cluster, or other type of visual display. Examples of graphic organizers are semantic maps and clarifying tables.

Semantic maps (Johnson & Pearson, 1986) help students visualize related information and develop new words for the same concept (see the following activity and Figure 4.2). Semantic mapping can also be used as a valuable prewriting strategy. The steps outlined in the activity can be adapted for individual purposes.

ACTIVITY *Semantic Map*

Using the following instructions, help students create a semantic map:

1. Choose a key word or concept from a book, story, or passage that students will be reading soon.
2. Write the core idea at the center of a large sheet of chart paper, on an overhead transparency, or on the board.
3. Ask students to think of as many words as they can that are related to the word. As you list them, place them in broad categories (see Figure 4.2). You may wish to add related categories that have been overlooked.

FIGURE 4.2 A semantic map for "money."

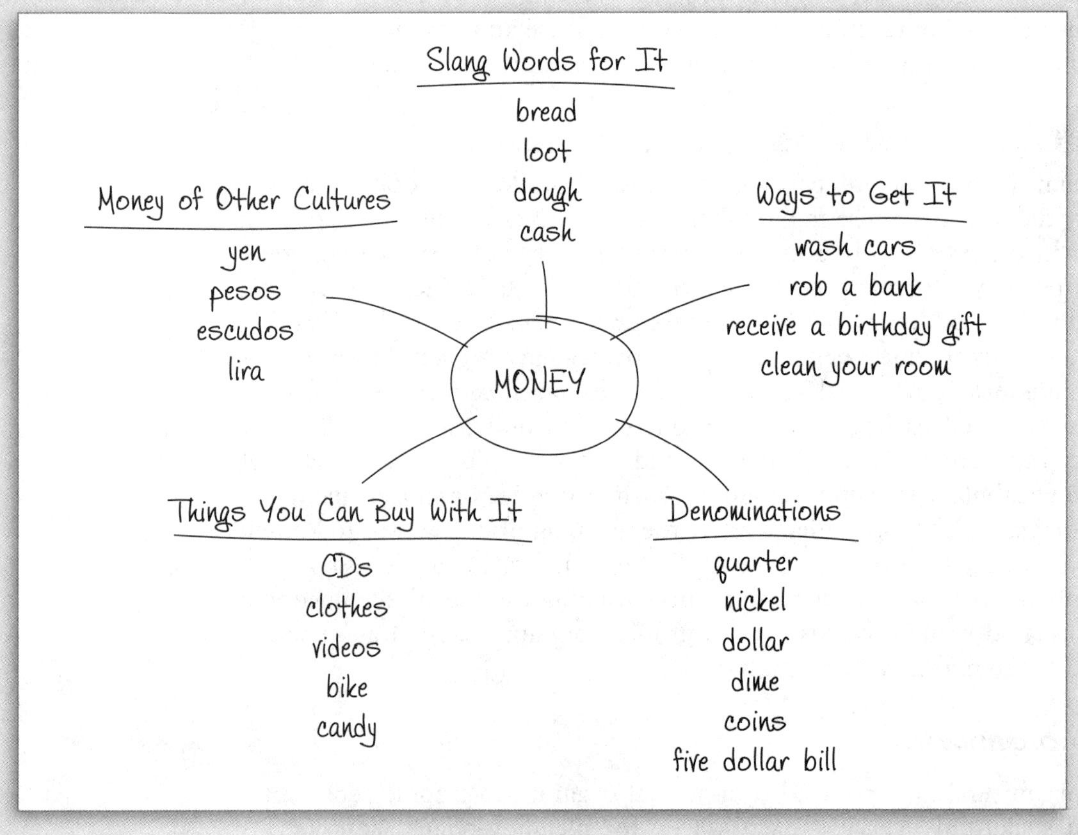

Slang Words for It
bread
loot
dough
cash

Money of Other Cultures
yen
pesos
escudos
lira

Ways to Get It
wash cars
rob a bank
receive a birthday gift
clean your room

MONEY

Things You Can Buy With It
CDs
clothes
videos
bike
candy

Denominations
quarter
nickel
dollar
dime
coins
five dollar bill

4. Lead students in a discussion of the broad categories and invite them to help you label these. Some words may fit into more than one category.

5. When the map is completed, discuss the categories and focus attention on those that will be highlighted in the passage to be read (e.g., students will be reading material about minting currency after completing the semantic map in Figure 4.2).

6. After reading the passage, revisit the map and augment it with new categories and words that were not mentioned in the original map-creating discussion.

A **clarifying table** is a graphic-organizing strategy teachers may use to preteach, or "clarify," vocabulary terms—usually low-utility words—students will encounter in an upcoming lesson, or to anchor the meanings of terms that have already been explored through content area lessons. As a rule, clarifying tables work best when the meanings of the new words are introduced at the beginning of the lesson and explored more thoroughly during the content area lesson, and then the terms that are most critical to the lesson are solidified using the clarifying table (see Figure 4.3). The following activity illustrates how to construct a clarifying table and the steps used to employ it.

● clarifying table

A clarifying table. **FIGURE** 4.3

TERM:	Propaganda
CORE IDEA:	"A plan to spread opinions or beliefs"
CLARIFIERS:	It's used by people who want you to think the way they do for some reason.
EXAMPLES:	Political candidates give lots of facts and figures of why you should vote for them. Advertisements tell you why you should buy their product.
CONFUSED WITH:	An opinion. Jennifer believes cats make better pets than dogs. However, she is not trying to make others believe this.
KNOWLEDGE CONNECTIONS:	Door-to-door salespeople offer propaganda. Salespeople on the telephone. Activists. Lobbyists.
EXAMPLE SENTENCE:	The senator used lots of propaganda—like telling us he had reduced crime in the state by 18 percent—to convince us we should reelect him.

Source: Adapted from Ellis & Farmer, 2000.

ACTIVITY   *Constructing and Using a Clarifying Table*

(Ellis & Farmer, 2000)

1. From the content area selection, identify several low-utility words that are particularly critical to the understanding of the selection.

2. Write one of those words on chart paper with its core idea, or simple definition. For example, propaganda's core idea would be "a plan to spread opinions or beliefs."

3. Under the core idea, label a row "Clarifiers." With students, brainstorm some descriptions of propaganda, such as "it's used by people who want you to think the way they do for some reason."

4. After discussing the word with students, brainstorm some examples of propaganda and write on the chart one or more that epitomize the essence of the concept most clearly. Example: "Political candidates give lots of facts and figures of why you should vote for them." List these under the heading "Examples."

5. With students, brainstorm some instances that might easily be confused with the term but are substantively different. Discuss how the instances differ. Example: "Jennifer believes cats make better pets than dogs. However, she is not trying to make others believe this." Use the heading "Confused with:" for these entries.

6. Brainstorm some everyday examples of how propaganda is used and list these under the heading "Knowledge connections." Examples from a student's background might be a door-to-door salesperson or members of an activist group.

7. Place students in small groups and have them create a sentence for the term *propaganda*, illustrating that they understand its meaning. With group consensus, select a sentence that captures the sense of the word to write on the chart and complete the clarifying table. Example: "The senator used lots of propaganda—like telling us he had reduced crime in the state by 18 percent—to convince us we should reelect him."

Semantic feature analysis

semantic feature analysis ●   **Semantic feature analysis** can be used when the concepts fall into one category (e.g., kinds of trees, breeds of dogs, past presidents). The procedure can also be used to compare two versions of the same story, or to compare a video to its source novel (Pittelman et al., 1991). Semantic feature analysis works best for words that form a group and are similar in meaning. The following activity outlines steps for creating a semantic feature analysis (Nagy, 1988).

ACTIVITY   *Creating a Semantic Feature Analysis*

1. Select words that form a semantically close group (e.g., words that represent precipitation: *rain, snow, sleet, hail, slush, fog*). At least some of the distinctions in meaning should be immediately understandable to students.

Precipitation

	rain	sleet	hail	fog	snow	slush	mist
solid	no	yes	yes	no	yes	sort of	no
liquid	yes	no	no	no	no	sort of	sort of
cold	sometimes	yes	sometimes	no	yes	yes	no
frozen	no	yes	yes	no	yes	yes	no
white	no	yes	sort of	sort of	yes	yes	sort of
clear	yes	no	yes	no	no	no	yes
wet	yes	yes	yes	yes	yes	yes	yes

Semantic feature analysis. **FIGURE** 4.4

2. On the board or overhead, use the selected words as column heads in a two-dimensional matrix (see Figure 4.4).

3. For the horizontal rows, decide on a number of words or phrases describing components of meaning shared by some of the words, or phrases that distinguish some words from others, such as solid, liquid, cold, frozen, and white.

4. One square, or cell, will represent the intersection of a given word and a semantic feature. One by one, ask students if the feature is shared by the given word. Discuss why or why not.

5. Record in the square whether or not, or to what extent, the feature applies to each word. Students may also suggest words to be added (e.g., mist), as well as descriptive terms (e.g., clear, wet).

2 USE CONTEXT

Proficient readers use many strategies to identify and pronounce words that might be unfamiliar to them in print. Often, such words are in a reader's speaking and listening vocabularies, but it may be the first time the student has encountered these words in written material. In such cases, readers try to use context clues to identify and pronounce the words. The syntactic (grammar) and semantic (meaning) information provided in the words, phrases, sentences, and paragraphs in a text are called *context clues*. Context clues occur in the surrounding information, including pictures, to help identify a word. They are very important to word analysis and, ultimately, comprehension. But context clues do not always offer enough information in a passage to help students actually learn the meaning of an unknown word. The clues may be obvious to someone who already knows the meaning of a word, but context clues often provide only limited information (i.e., nondirective contexts), which can be misleading, or no help at all. For example, consider the following two sentences: "Dyan looked over the members of her team. Each looked more hapless than the next." No real clue as to the meaning of the word *hapless* can be gleaned from the context of the sentences. However, researchers still recommend that students be taught how to use context clues because certain context clues can be helpful; moreover, context clues can be tools to help readers develop word-learning strategies they can use independently during incidental learning opportunities (Nagy, 1988).

As stated earlier, contexts that provide helpful clues for figuring out a word's meaning are referred to as "directive contexts" (Beck et al., 2002, p. 5). Directive context clues can sometimes help students find the meaning of an unfamiliar word in the following ways:

- by directly defining the word
- by providing an appositive or comparison of the word
- by contrasting the word with a known word

Readers are also using context clues when they:

- think logically through the rest of the sentence
- consider examples provided in the sentence

Sentences with one or more of these features should be used to directly show students how word meaning can be gleaned through context. Examples of each of these context clues are as follows:

> A <u>gendarme</u> is a police officer in France and several other European countries who has had military training. (definition)
>
> She was <u>exhausted</u>, or extremely tired, after being up half the night. (appositive)
>
> Rather than being famous in his homeland for defeating the enemy in the war, the man found he was <u>notorious</u>. (contrast)
>
> Sandra said <u>morosely</u>, "This town will be the death of us." (logic)
>
> Cats, dogs, and hamsters are all examples of <u>domestic</u> animals. (illustration or description)

Context clues can also be found in sentences other than the one in which the new word appears, so students should be encouraged to read surrounding sentences for clues to meaning. Sometimes an entire paragraph embodies the explanation of a word, as in the following example: "The climb took far longer than Sara and Michelle had expected. But when they arrived at the top, they were greeted by the most spectacular sight they had ever imagined. Their whole five-mile hike had been worth it. They were <u>exhilarated</u>!"

In a study on directive contexts and other methods for teaching vocabulary, Gipe (1978/1979) asked third- and fifth-graders to read new words in meaningful, or directive, contexts; she also had them apply these words to their own experiences. Her method required students to read a passage of three or four sentences in which each sentence used the target word in a progressively defining context. The sentences had a simple structure and contained common words to ensure that the context was familiar. Each student was asked to respond in writing to a question or instruction at the end of the passage with a response from his or her own personal background experiences. This written response further exemplified the target word as it connected to the student's own life. For example, the meaning of the word *wretched* was taught using the following passage.

> Walking to school, Mary got caught in the rain, and a car splashed mud on her clothes. She looked *wretched*. A *wretched* person looks very unhappy and miserable. *Wretched* means feeling terrible, very unhappy, and unlucky in life. Write about something that made you feel *wretched* or that you think would make you feel *wretched*.

She then compared this method with three other methods for teaching students the meaning of new words: having students pair an unknown word with a synonym, having students categorize words, and having them look up the new words in the dictionary and use them in sentences. She found that having students apply new words to their own experiences in a written response after deriving the meaning of the word from context was most effective.

A modification to the written response for English learners is to ask students to draw or identify pictures representing the word's meaning. For example, Morgan and Odom (2006) had their fourth- and sixth-graders draw cartoons for clarifying word meanings, increasing both vocabulary knowledge and motivation for learning new words. Some examples follow.

> To illustrate *fortune,* Alison drew a Magic 8 Ball showing the words "Better not tell you now."
>
> Jack drew an *echo* powerful enough to knock a man off the rim of the Grand Canyon. As the man fell—portrayed by a series of tumbling stick figures—he repeatedly bounced off ledges and rocks, shouting "Ouch!" each time.
>
> Meg's idea of a *labyrinth* was a hungry girl wandering through an endless maze, trying to reach the Pizza Palace.
>
> In Alexa's cartoon, *hypnosis* was the only way a frustrated mom could get her daughter to clean her room. (p. 41)

Research in using context clues to infer word meanings reveals that effective instruction takes time and must be well-planned. Ten 30- to 45-minute sessions devoted to teaching students to use context clues is not unreasonable (Graves, 2006, p. 94).

C(2)QU

(Blachowicz, 1993)

ACTIVITY

C(2)QU stands for context and two questions. This instructional activity can help teachers show students how to work through the use of context clues to discover the meaning of an unfamiliar word.

1. Provide a broad, meaningful context for an unfamiliar word using one of the five context types: definition, appositive, contrast, logic, illustration. Example: "When it was time to help clean up the house, the little girl <u>vanished</u>." Invite students to offer suggestions about the meaning of the word through the hints provided by the way it is used in the sentence(s).

2. Provide one or two sentences that offer more explicit contextual information for the word. Example: "Ramon watched as the horse grew smaller

and smaller and finally <u>vanished</u> from sight. Now it was really gone." Now ask students to reconsider their original hypotheses about the word.

3. Ask students direct questions that involve the meaning of the word. Example: "When something vanishes, do you expect to see it again? What kinds of things might vanish?"

4. Invite students to use the word appropriately in oral or written form. Example: "The puppy was so hungry that the food we put out for her <u>vanished</u> in an instant."

In addition to context clues, Graves (2006) also suggests students use word parts (structural analysis, as discussed in Chapter 3) to infer the meaning. Research conducted by Baumann, Edwards, et al. (2003) with fifth-graders in the context of learning content about social studies supports this suggestion. They found that combining context and morphological, or structural, analysis led to success at inferring the meanings of affixed words and contextually decipherable words on a delayed test.

To summarize what we know about using the context, there are four key points to keep in mind when teaching students to use this important skill:

1. Acknowledge that context may not always be enough.

2. Only select examples of text that allow students to discover the word.

3. Model for students a strategy for thinking through how to get the meaning from context, using a "Think Aloud" (see Chapter 5).

4. Encourage students to immediately apply the new word to their own experience in written form (e.g., have them write about a time they felt "rejected").

 ## CONSULT RESOURCES TO DISCOVER THE MEANINGS OF WORDS

Proficient readers use various strategies to discover the meanings of unknown words. For example, they might ask someone, read around the word, use the context, or look up the word in the glossary or a dictionary. Although the last option is one that directly leads to autonomy in acquiring vocabulary, if we ask students to look up every unknown word, they may lose the continuity of what they are reading and, eventually, lose interest in reading.

Allen (1999) offers 12 options students can consider as resources to figure out the meaning of unfamiliar words:

1. See how the word fits into the sentence (i.e., part of speech).

2. Use the dictionary to find the meaning of the word.

3. Say the word out loud to see if it can be recognized.

4. Read the sentence again to see if the meaning of the word becomes clearer.

5. Look at the beginning of the sentence again.

6. Think about what other word would make sense in the sentence.

7. Look for other words in the sentence that give clues.

8. Ask someone else to read the sentence out loud.

9. Look at the picture, if there is one.

10. Read around the word and then go back to it.

11. Skip the word if it is not needed.

12. Ask the teacher, another adult, or a classmate.

Before encouraging students to use dictionaries, a teacher should consider the appropriateness of the dictionaries that are available to them. For example, collegiate dictionaries are not the most appropriate for students in grades 4–8 or for English learners. Rather, learners' dictionaries that include fewer yet more high frequency words and definitions, written in accessible language with age-appropriate sample sentences, should be used. For example, *Collins COBUILD Learner's Dictionary* (2003) is an excellent choice for a classroom dictionary; it provides explanations rather than definitional phrases: "Something that is *sparse* is small in number or amount and spread out over an area." Students also need instruction in using online resources, such as dictionaries, glossaries, and the thesaurus.

Although we have come a long way since the days when we simply asked students to copy definitions of words or look up every unknown word, we still need to teach students the value of using the dictionary to learn about the meanings of words and the thesaurus to teach them how to locate synonyms and antonyms. Teachers can provide structured opportunities for students to use these important tools during minilessons and other word study activities. Additionally, students can be encouraged to use the dictionary through ongoing practice of the Very Important Term Word Book activity.

WWW

Online Resources
www.Factmonster.com
www.ldoceonline.com
http://nhd.heinle.com/home.aspx

Very Important Term Word Book Activity   **A C T I V I T Y**

1. Ask students to designate a binder or special folder as their Very Important Term (VIT) Word Book.

2. Select words from any number of sources that are appropriate for the grade level, and divide the total number of words into lists of ten words each. The words might come from the Academic Word List mentioned earlier, or from the curriculum materials used for any of the subject areas.

3. Each week, introduce ten words, five words on Day 1 and five words on Day 2, by first pronouncing each word, showing the syllabic breakdown or pronounceable parts, and having students guess at the meaning of the words (see Part A, Figure 4.5).

4. Develop and read aloud sentences for each word to provide a meaningful context, and have the students make additional predictions about the meaning of the words (see Part B, Figure 4.5).

5. Solicit student volunteers to offer their definitions, and write them on the board. Circle those that are accurate or partially accurate.

6. Have students go to their dictionaries, find the words, and write the page number on which the word is found, the part of speech, and the definition(s) (see Part C, Figure 4.5).

FIGURE 4.5 Very Important Term Word Book Activity, grade 7.

Name: Sam Walker Period: 7

Date: 2-20 Vocabulary List # 21 Total Points Earned:

PART A Day 2 Words: Copy each word from the board. Write what you think is the meaning of each.

1. Digit (dig-it) A single form in a number
2. Dismal (dis-mal) To become mad or bad
3. Enclose (en-close) To be put in an object
4. Garb (garb) Like a dog's bark
5. Portion (port-ion) An amount of something

PART B The teacher will read a sentence using each word; thereafter, the class will discuss the word and possible definitions. Write the word again & write what you now think the word means.

1. Fingers or toes
2. Bad or dreary
3. To be sealed in an object
4. Clothing
5. An amount of something

PART C Go to the dictionary. Look up each word and write its dictionary definition.

1. (p181)(n) A finger or toe
2. (p189)(adj) ~~Dark, gloomy~~ Dreary
3. (p215)(v,n) To shut in all around
4. (p269)(n) Clothing
5. (p512)(n) ~~Helping of food~~ Part of

Reprinted with permission.

PART D   For this section you need to work with one other person.

1. Write three different sentences (at least six words in length) for each of the five vocabulary words.

2. Each sentence must (if possible) be a different form of the word (plural, past tense, different part of speech, etc).

3. Identify the part of speech of each vocabulary word as it is being used in that sentence.

4. Underline each vocabulary word.

1a. One of my <u>digits</u> (pln) are shorter than the other.

1b. Barney picks his nose with his <u>digits</u> (n).

1c. The <u>digits</u> (poss n) length was truly unbelievable.

2a. It was a <u>dismal</u> (adj) day from the fog.

2b. His <u>dismalness</u> (n) made him look part Emo.

2c. This day is more <u>dismal</u> (com adj) than the other day.

3a. The toy was <u>enclosed</u> (ptv) in a very small box.

3b. I was born while <u>enclosing</u> (v) my brain in my head.

3c. She will <u>enclose</u> (ftv) a shell in her hands.

4a. My <u>garb</u> (n) costs way more than your's does.

4b. The <u>garb's</u> (poss n) beauty was barely stunning.

4c. All the <u>garbs</u> (pln) added up to 100 pounds of cloth.

5a. My <u>portion</u> (n) of food wasn't enough for me.

5b. The <u>portions</u> (pln) of crumbs filled the rat's stomach.

5c. The <u>portion's</u> (poss n) taste was like eating an eraser.

7. Direct students to use the words in their own sentences, including different forms of the word (e.g., different part of speech, past tense form, plural form) (see Part D, Figure 4.5).

8. On Day 3, go back to step 6 (Part C, Figure 4.5) and give the correct definition for each word. Students self-correct their work or confirm that a meaning they have predicted is acceptable. Then start again at step 3 with five new words.

9. On the fourth day ask students to write a paragraph using five of the new words and indicate the part of speech for each word. In order for students to check the appropriate use of the word, have them rewrite the same paragraph, but instead of the new word, write in the definition of that word where it would occur to see if the sentence/paragraph makes sense.

10. On the fifth day, administer a vocabulary test. For example, choose four of the ten words for students to use in sentences. Then ask them to write three more sentences using any additional three words of their choice.

LEARN TO DETERMINE THE MEANINGS OF POLYSEMANTIC WORDS

polysemantic ●

Many words in the English language are **polysemantic**: that is, they have multiple meanings. If we include shades of meaning or related meanings as multiple meanings, then nearly every word in the English language in some way has more than one meaning associated with it. It is often perplexing for readers to find a word they thought they knew used in a context that is unfamiliar to them.

The dictionary, while a potentially excellent source for discovering the meanings of unknown words, can be confusing when students are attempting to determine the appropriate meanings of words that have multiple meanings or specific, technical definitions. In some cases, the student may be familiar with several common meanings of a word but not with the specialized meaning found in content area subjects, such as science, social studies, and mathematics. For example, a student may understand the word *change* and be able to use it appropriately when discussing replacing school clothes with casual clothes after school, but he might be unaware that the word can also be used to discuss a process of metamorphosis in science, a financial transaction system in mathematics (making change), and a transition to a different political system in social studies (Burns, Roe, & Ross, 1999).

Because polysemantic words can have different meanings depending on the context in which they are used, such words can be extremely confusing. The following activity can help show students, especially English learners, how to determine the appropriate definition for a polysemantic word.

ACTIVITY *How Is It Used?*

1. Write the following sentences on the board:

The man had to pay room and board at the country inn.

She was on the Board of Education in her city.

The board was made of the finest redwood.

We got on board just as the train was departing.

The board member offered advice on the proposed idea.

2. Distribute student dictionaries to pairs of students.

3. Ask each pair of students to look up the word *board* in the dictionary and find the specific definition to fit each sentence.

4. With the whole class, discuss each meaning as it is located.

5. Have students create new sentences of their own that fit each definition.

6. Invite pairs of students to read other dictionary definitions for the word *board* and compose sentences for these meanings.

7. Use the same procedure for other multiple-meaning words as they are encountered.

If a variant meaning for a word does not represent a difficult concept, it can be taught simply by discussing with students their current understanding of the word's meaning, presenting the word's new meaning, and then noting the similarities and differences when the word is used in the variant way. However, if the new meaning is more complex, then the method outlined in the following activity, ideal for expository text, may be more helpful.

Possible Sentences   (Stahl & Kapinus, 1991)   **ACTIVITY**

1. From an upcoming reading assignment, choose several key terms that might be difficult because they are being used in a way that is unfamiliar to students (for example, *base, run, board*).

2. Provide short explanations for the words as they will be used in the upcoming assignment. For example:

    A character in literature can have *base,* or evil, motives for doing seemingly good deeds.

    A person decides to *run* for, or pursue, a political position, such as mayor.

    A *board* of directors is a group of people who get together to oversee a project.

3. Have the students form small groups and ask them to create *possible sentences,* using the words as they believe the words might be used in the passage they are about to read.

4. Write the suggested sentences on the board. Read and discuss them together.

5. After reading the assignment, revisit the possible sentences and discuss whether the sentences reflect the appropriate meaning of the specified word, based on the new information from the passage.

6. If students decide any of the sentences do not reflect the appropriate meaning of the word, help students revise them to make the meanings match. For example:

> The men will <u>run</u> for their life when they are chased by the lion. (would not be a meaning match)

> The woman was the first female to <u>run</u> for governor of Kentucky. (revised)

 ### INFUSE NEW VOCABULARY INTO WRITING AND SPEAKING

Teachers can encourage students to expand their speaking vocabularies, or the words they use in oral language, by actively recognizing and praising appropriate word usage in the classroom, as well as by allowing ample time for spontaneous word play, in which students experiment with words they discover and choose to share. Students often have words in their reading and listening vocabularies they have never used in speaking or writing. "Rich" instruction (i.e., "instruction that goes beyond definitional information to get students actively involved in using and thinking about word meanings and creating lots of associations among words" (Beck et al., 2002, p. 73) is important in getting students to use new words. For example, specific word games such as Camouflage can encourage students to stretch their speaking vocabularies by telling stories, deliberately selecting words for which they are just beginning to grasp the meaning. Semantic gradients, used with a dictionary or thesaurus, can help older students think about and discuss relationships among similar and different words (synonyms and antonyms) as well as discern slight shades of meaning between words.

The following activities will help expedite this process of moving words into students' speaking vocabularies.

ACTIVITY *Camouflage*   (Cecil, 1994)

1. Pass out to each student a 3 × 5 card with a word written on it that may be in the student's reading and listening vocabularies but that has not yet entered the student's speaking vocabulary.

2. Tell students they may look at their own card, but not at each other's. Also instruct them that they may use a dictionary or a thesaurus if they want to get a clearer understanding of the word and clues about its usage.

3. Have students take turns creating a story or personal anecdote that "hides" their word in it. For example (fifth-grader hiding the word *pallid*):

> My sister and I went into a haunted house last weekend. I was so apprehensive I could barely converse, and my sister's face was pallid when she heard eerie sounds coming from the upstairs. Eventually we spotted a diminutive feline and realized that that must have been what we heard!

4. When a student has finished telling his story, encourage the other students to try to guess the word the student has "camouflaged." If the number of incorrect guesses is greater than the number of correct guess-

es, the storyteller wins. (Hint: Advise students that the best strategy is to use the most sophisticated words they can think of to throw off the other students. Encourage them to use the dictionary or thesaurus.)

Semantic Gradient   **ACTIVITY**

1. Have students form small groups and encourage them to choose two known words with opposite meanings, such as *race/crawl, gigantic/ minuscule,* and *frigid/torrid.*

2. Have students write one of the words toward the top of a sheet of paper and the opposite word toward the bottom. The space in the middle will be used for placement of other words according to how closely they fit in terms of meaning.

3. With the help of a dictionary and/or thesaurus, invite students to discuss the meanings of the two words and then list other words in the continuum according to how closely they match the meaning of the first two words. Explain that each word on their paper must be the same part of speech as the original two words. (An easier version would be to supply a list of words for the students.) Also stress that there are no right or wrong answers but that they should be able to defend their placement of words. For example (for fifth-graders):

fly	walk
race	stroll
skedaddle	saunter
run	meander
jog	shuffle
power walk	crawl
trot	stand still

4. Invite students to share their lists and explain why they placed the words where they did by giving examples of how such words could be used in sentences. Greenwood and Flanigan (2007) provide examples of sentences for use with semantic gradients.

5. Place the lists on linear charts (see Figure 4.6) around the classroom so that they can be added to as students encounter other words that are related to the original two words. Optional: Have students act out words.

Example of a semantic gradient.   **FIGURE**   4.6

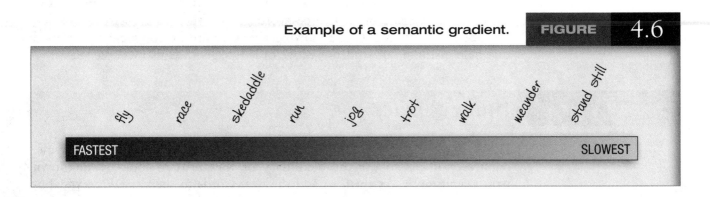

⑥ COMMIT TO LEARNING NEW WORDS

Because of the sheer number of words that students must acquire every year, as noted earlier in this chapter, perhaps the most proactive instructional approach teachers can take with vocabulary is to encourage students to commit themselves individually to building their word knowledge. Having such a personal commitment is, of course, especially critical for students who face the extraordinary task of learning English as a second language.

One way teachers can get students to commit to building their word knowledge is to discuss with the whole class a variety of ways that they can learn new words. During this discussion, teachers should not only offer their own ideas but also incorporate those that the students suggest. Some ideas to consider are the following:

- Have students make a commitment to learn one new word a day, from any source.

- Have students make a commitment to look up in the dictionary one word a day that has been heard in conversation or on the news.

- Have students "adopt" a certain prefix or suffix, or Greek or Latin root, and learn and use words containing these elements over a few weeks' duration.

- Have students agree to acquire at least two or three new words each week from their context and to record both the words and the context from which they were derived in a vocabulary notebook (e.g., VIT Word Book).

- Have students make a list of "tired" words, or words that are used too often in one's own writing and speaking (e.g., *nice*). Look these up in a thesaurus and commit to using newly discovered synonyms for these words, one a week.

- Each day, have a different student find one word that she believes will "stump the teacher." Allow the student to write this word on the board for you to try to define. Keep a running list of the new words—and your success at defining them.

Finally, we believe it is the teacher's own fascination with words—their history, sound, origin, and so forth—that can make all the difference in students' curiosity about and interest in acquiring them. Ultimately, a love for our language is "caught" rather than "taught." Consequently, a teacher who frequently stops reading a passage to dramatically repeat a phrase filled with imagery, or one who often shares favorite words, puns, riddles, and other word play with students, will help to create learners who notice words and remember them. Word play can be done incidentally during any literacy activity, or it can consist of structured word games, such as crossword puzzles, Scrabble, or Password. The following activities are prototypical of the kind that help instill in our students a love of language. (See also Chapter 3.)

ACTIVITY　*Hinky Pinkies*

Hinky Pinkies is a word play activity that fosters appreciation of rhyme, requires students to use the dictionary or thesaurus to look up unknown words, and motivates them to add the new words to their speaking vocabularies. Additionally, the game provides important practice in determining what is and is not an appropriate synonym. The activity proceeds as follows:

1. Explain to students that Hinky Pinkies are rhyming definitions for terms with either one syllable (*hink pinks*), two syllables (*hinky pinkies*), or three syllables (*hinkety pinketies*).

2. Have students form pairs and pass out a dictionary and a thesaurus to each pair.

3. Show the following example to students:

   a thicker arachnid

4. Explain to students that in order to find the answer, they must find synonyms for both the word *thicker* and the word *arachnid*. Advise them that they may use the dictionary or thesaurus if they do not know the meaning of a word and for help finding appropriate synonyms. Further, explain that the synonyms for the original words must rhyme and be the same number of syllables. In this example, each word will be two syllables—a hinky pinky.

5. Ask students to look up the word *arachnid* in the dictionary or thesaurus. Write the words they discover on the board (the most prominent definition will be *spider*).

6. Ask students to think of a two-syllable word that rhymes with spider and means the same thing, or is a synonym for, the word *thicker*. Write the answer on the board:

   a thicker arachnid = a wider spider

7. Do this exercise for several other examples, making sure to use one word that is unfamiliar to students in each definition:

   an evil pastor (sinister minister)

   an ebony slit (black crack)

   a mean gem (cruel jewel)

8. Create 20 of these word plays for students to do in pairs. Then ask each pair of students to create their own hink pinks, hinky pinkies, or hinkety pinketies with the help of the dictionary or thesaurus.

9. Have each pair of students read their examples to the class so that the other students can guess the answers. Make a class book of their contributions.

Paraphrastics

Learners are intrigued by adages in which synonyms have replaced the original words and phrases, although the original meaning has been kept intact. Additionally, understanding such adages often requires a dictionary and a thesaurus, thus making them excellent activities for increasing vocabulary and awareness of appropriate synonyms.

1. Place students into small groups and give each group a dictionary and a thesaurus.

2. Using the board or an overhead projector, show students several adages that they are likely to know but that have been modified by different words and phrases so that the adage sounds entirely different. For example:

> Members of an avian species of identical plumage congregate. (Birds of a feather flock together.)

> All articles that coruscate with resplendence are not necessarily auriferous. (All that glitters is not gold.)

> The stylus is more potent than the claymore. (The pen is mightier than the sword.)

> Male cadavers are incapable of yielding any falsehoods. (Dead men tell no lies.)

3. Ask students to try to figure out the original adage by looking up unfamiliar words in the dictionary. After they have come up with the solution, write the original adage under the paraphrased one.

4. Brainstorm some other adages that they have heard. Invite students, in their small groups, to paraphrase these adages using the thesaurus for synonyms.

5. When all groups have finished this exercise, have them read their revised adages to the rest of the class so that the other students can try to guess the original adage. Create a class book with the paraphrased adages. Encourage students to try to stump their parents and other family members with the paraphrased adages.

6. For an added challenge, encourage students to take the original adages and design new phrases that mean just the opposite of the originals. For example, "All that glitters is not gold" would become "None that tarnishes is silver."

TROUBLESHOOTING

Inadequate vocabulary is often the result of a limited background of experiences and intellectual stimulation, as well as a lack of habitual reading. Lack of oral stimulation, limited experiences with printed material, few books in the home for recreational reading, and an aversion to reading can all contribute to a vocabulary deficit. Speech defects or hearing difficulties may also be factors in slow or weak language development (Crawley & King, 2000). The following suggestions will not only be helpful for learners with inadequate vocabularies but will also enrich the vocabularies and intellectual lives of all students in a class. These suggestions will be especially valuable for English learners.

Limited Interest/Experience in Independent Reading

The importance of wide reading for its impact on vocabulary development cannot be overemphasized. Just reading a few minutes each day will make staggering differences in the number of words students encounter in the course of a school year (see Figure 4.7).

The chart in Figure 4.7 indicates that, on average, the student who is at the 90th percentile of minutes spent reading recreationally (a mere 21.1 minutes a day) reads almost 2 million words outside of school—or more than 200 times

INDEPENDENT READING		
Reading Minutes Percentile	Minutes Per Day	Words Read Per Year
98th	65.0	4,358,000
90th	21.1	1,823,000
80th	14.2	1,146,000
70th	9.6	622,000
60th	6.5	432,000
50th	4.6	282,000
40th	3.2	200,000
30th	1.3	106,000
20th	0.7	21,000
10th	0.1	8,000
2nd	0.0	0

Effect of time spent reading independently on number of words encountered.

FIGURE   4.7

more words than the student at the 10th percentile, who reads only 8,000 words per year on his own. Although all words encountered are not necessarily "learned," it has been suggested that readers acquire approximately 1 in 10 new words from reading (Cunningham & Stanovich, 1998).

Therefore, students who read widely will come across a plethora of new words and, with every subsequent encounter with each word, will begin to move the words through the four levels of word knowledge (refer back to Figure 4.1), from never having heard it before to knowing it well. Teachers can encourage students to read widely by continuing throughout grades 4–8 to read aloud to them, from books selected from a variety of genres and representing diverse ethnic groups.

The positive impact that reading aloud to students has on their vocabulary development is well documented (National Reading Panel, 2000). Using an **interactive oral reading** technique, in which the teacher reads aloud, stopping periodically to focus on and discuss individual words, as well as other aspects of what is being read, is a highly recommended strategy for developing the vocabulary of students who are linguistically disadvantaged and English learners (Carlo et al., 2004; Carlo, August, & Snow, 2005). In their research with young students, Coyne, Simmons, and Kame'enui (2004) found that "explicitly teaching word meanings within the context of shared storybook reading" is especially helpful to learners at risk of experiencing reading difficulties (pp. 49–50). Hickman, Pollard-Durodola, and Vaughn (2004) found read-alouds to be central to developing the academic language of English learners. Reading

● interactive oral reading

aloud by the teacher provides access to books that these learners in particular may not be able to experience on their own. In this way, students are introduced to a wide variety of genres and text structures, as well as vocabulary.

Guidelines follow for using read-alouds with English learners and students who are linguistically disadvantaged (Carlo et al., 2004; Carlo, August, & Snow, 2005; Harmon, 2002; Hickman et al., 2004; Ulanoff & Pucci, 1999):

1. Provide 20–30 minutes of read-aloud time daily.
2. Choose books thematically—e.g., for an immigration theme, read Will Hobbs' *Crossing the Wire* (2006) and Mike Lupica's *Heat* (2006)—and read each book over a period of five days; focus on three or four new words each day. An academic word list, such as the one mentioned earlier in this chapter, may be of help in choosing words (Coxhead, 2000).
3. Separate the text to be read into passages that fit the natural flow of the story.
4. Stop during each day's reading to check for understanding and to review the vocabulary words.
5. In addition to choosing three or four words to discuss, invite the students to identify words for which they do not know the meanings.
6. At the end of each day's reading, and again at the end of the book, provide opportunities to discuss the words further, reread certain passages for clarification, and engage students in "facilitated peer dialogue"—an activity for readers who struggle to focus on vocabulary and word-learning strategies (Harmon, 2002, p. 606).

Students who read widely come across a plethora of new words and, with every subsequent encounter with each word, begin to move the words through the four levels of word knowledge.

Providing a good selection of literature in the classroom (see Appendix A and Table 5.2) and allowing ample time during the school day for students to read self-selected material help foster an interest in reading (e.g., DEAR, SSR). Finally, students tend to encourage each other to read when time is set aside for them to share and respond to what they are reading in meaningful ways (e.g., literature circles, book clubs).

Limited Schema for Remembering New Vocabulary

The term *schema* refers to a person's organized knowledge of the world. This knowledge provides the basis for understanding and remembering new vocabulary words. If the learner already has some relevant background or word knowledge, or both, about the topic being introduced, new vocabulary can be enhanced by activating the existing schema or bringing it to the surface. The more actual, concrete experiences teachers provide for their students, especially those for whom English is a second language, the more teachers will be adding to this schema upon which students can attach new words and concepts. Words seldom exist in a vacuum, and offering such experiences helps students greatly expand their knowledge of the words associated with the topic under consideration in a relatively short amount of time.

Book talks, art in all its forms, cooking, experiments, and objects associated with reading and discussion are forms of realia that engage learners in questioning, discussing, and thinking about new words and incorporating them into their meaning vocabularies.

Sometimes a student has limited knowledge of or background about a certain subject being introduced. In that case, the teacher must actually construct a schema for that student. Since it is not always possible to offer either virtual reality or an opportunity to experience an event directly, sometimes vicarious (or "simulated") experiences can provide a context for new vocabulary. For example, a chapter on the Amazon would clearly be best enhanced by a field trip to show students the rain forest, the canopy, and the different flora and fauna; however, because such a journey is not generally feasible, activities involving video clips, television excerpts, websites, or pictures from books and magazines are usually more practical. With appropriate explanation and description from the teacher, these activities can result in almost as much new vocabulary acquisition as an actual field trip would provide.

Virtual Field Trip   (Adapted from Kane, 2007)   **A C T I V I T Y**

Although field trips to actual places are not always possible, virtual field trips can often provide students with a simulated experience to help them learn new vocabulary associated with a particular place or time.

1. Choose a place or location relevant to a content area lesson you are preparing, such as the Gobi Desert or the Amazon rain forest.

2. Select book(s), websites, photographs, videos, artifacts, or other materials relevant to the lesson.

3. Brainstorm what a student might expect to find at the chosen location.

4. Divide students into groups and have them prepare questions for their "tour guide."

5. Have the groups "tour" the location by reading.

6. Ask students to prepare a summary of the highlights of their tour, telling what they learned about the location and its related content area subject.

7. Have students plot their journeys on a map or timeline, or both.

8. Discuss where the students' inquiry can go from here and what other resources they might "tour" next to learn about the topic in more depth; answer any remaining or new questions.

Picture books can also be used to enhance schema and provide visual clues to the meanings of new words. For example, in *The Shell Book*, Lember (1997) presents stunning photographs of seashells commonly found along our shorelines and provides brief descriptions of the seashells. After sharing this picture book, the teacher could invite groups of students to generate seashore murals depicting the variety of shells associated with a particular coastline (e.g., limpets along the Pacific coast; cockles on the Atlantic coast). Not only will students learn many new shells, they will also learn the academic vocabulary associated with geography and the coastal United States.

WWW

Garfield
www.professorgarfield.org

Picture Book Abstracts
www.lib.muohio.edu/pictbks

Similarly, well-chosen comic strips can provide visual representations for help in learning word meanings (McVicker, 2007). For instance, the *Family Circus* cartoon often embeds visual clues to the meanings for words. One example is a cartoon showing Billy asking, "What does *meandering* mean?" as he winds through his neighborhood and a dotted line connects all the places he visits. Also, *Garfield* cartoonist Jim Davis hosts a website useful for vocabulary building (see the Reading Ring link at the website for the Word Wrestler game).

SUMMARY

Acquiring the meaning of many new words may not be all there is to reading, but because words can be considered the building blocks that comprise all written and spoken text, their importance in a balanced and comprehensive literacy program must not be underestimated. Students need to learn the meanings of approximately 3,000 new words a year—and more if those students are learning English as a second language—so a teacher needs to do more than simply have students memorize a list of vocabulary words and their meanings. Strive to provide effective meaning vocabulary development strategies, such as helping students appreciate words and their origins and make a personal commitment to find out about them. Furthermore, encourage wide reading and provide strategies for independently figuring out the meaning of unknown words. Above all, share your fascination with and curiosity about words. Ultimately, the goal of all vocabulary instruction should be to inspire students to become independent word collectors who actively enjoy learning new words. Such learners become the students who comprehend best and thus read the most, entering into a self-perpetuating cycle of success.

Actively learning the meanings of many new words, through a wide variety of means, is unquestionably an integral part of a balanced and comprehensive literacy program for grades 4–8. The more numerous the reading, writing, listening, and speaking experiences students of this age are offered, the more they will come into contact with intriguing new words. And it is through just such experiences that students' stores of vocabulary steadily grow, just as it is through the excitement of abundant reading and writing that they become proficient readers and writers.

Questions
FOR JOURNAL WRITING AND DISCUSSION

1. From a page in this chapter, create three columns of words: the first one entitled "Basic Words," the second, "General-Utility Words," and the third, "Low-Utility Words." With a partner from the class, arrange the words from this page in the three different categories. Defend your choices in a discussion with other classmates. Why do you think it is important to classify the words you would teach to your students in this manner?

2. Review the chart showing the relationship between the time spent on recreational reading and the number of words encountered in a year in Figure 4.7. Based on this evidence, how important would you consider efforts to motivate students to read for their own enjoyment? How would you make sure this occurs in your own classroom?

3. Consider the following selection from *Venus Among the Fishes* (Hall & O'Dell, 1995). The underlined words are those chosen for direct instruction with students in intermediate grades. The same criteria would apply to works used with readers in the middle grades. In this work of juvenile fiction, the narrator is Coral, a young female dolphin. Her story captures the drama of underwater life. Referring to the criteria for selecting words to teach (Ellis & Farmer, 2000; Beck et al., 2000) decide which underlined words you agree are important and useful words to teach and which are not.

My father was the largest male in our <u>herd</u> of white-sided <u>dolphins</u>. From his white face, a light <u>stripe</u> <u>curved</u> up over his head and along his <u>gleaming</u> black back to his white and black <u>dorsal fin</u>. His belly was a <u>pearly</u> white. Father was such a <u>skillful</u> swimmer that his skin had never been <u>scraped</u> or scarred, <u>despite</u> his many <u>encounters</u> with sharks, orcas, or angry dolphins.

    As I watched for orcas now, my father and the older males swam on the sides of the herd, looking for squid and herring. Our <u>pod</u> swam with other pods in the <u>center</u>, where it was safe.

    I could hear the herd call as it moved through the water. Again and again each dolphin <u>whistled</u> its name and <u>announced</u> that all was well. The <u>messages</u> told the rest of the herd that it was safe to <u>continue</u> the hunt. At the first <u>threatening</u> <u>echo</u> from behind, I would stop whistling my name and warn the herd with the loud crack of <u>sensor sound</u> that <u>signaled</u> danger. <u>Warnings</u> travel fast <u>beneath</u> the water. (pp. 2–3)

4. As you are reading for work or pleasure, make note of several words that are unfamiliar to you. What strategies would you use to determine the meaning of these new words? Are the strategies you would use always the same? What factors determine when you would resort to looking up the words in the dictionary? How are your own habits relevant to your future classroom teaching?

Suggestions FOR PROJECTS AND FIELD ACTIVITIES

1. With the other members of your class, list 10 words from a newspaper. From this chapter, consider the different instructional strategies you might use to teach these words to students. In an intermediate or middle-grade classroom, use one of the strategies to teach the selected words to a small group of students. How successful were you? Compare your experience with that of other classmates who chose to use a different instructional strategy.

2. Spend a day discovering the interesting words that students in grades 4–8 are naturally curious about. Can you categorize these words? How would you incorporate these concepts into the daily curriculum to encourage curiosity about words?

3. Prior to reading a short story to a group of students in grades 4–8, ask them to guess the meaning of three or four words that you deem to be especially difficult. During the reading, ask them to determine the meaning of each word after it occurs in the story. Are the responses enhanced with the additional contextual information? What does this experience teach you about the value of discussing words as they occur when reading aloud?

REFERENCES

Alber, S. R., & Foil, C. R. (2003). Drama activities that promote and extend your students' vocabulary proficiency. *Intervention in School & Clinic, 39*(1), 22–29.

Allen, J. (1999). *Words, words, words.* Portsmouth, NH: Heinemann.

Anderson, R. C. (1996). Research foundations to support wide reading. In V. Greaney (Ed.), *Promoting reading in developing countries* (pp. 55–77). Newark, DE: International Reading Association.

Anderson, R. C., & Freebody, P. (1981). Vocabulary knowledge. In J. T. Guthrie (Ed.), *Comprehension and teaching: Research reviews.* Newark, DE: International Reading Association.

Anderson, R. C., & Nagy, W. E. (1992). The vocabulary conundrum. *American Educator, 16*(4), 14–18, 44–47.

Baumann, J. F., Edwards, E. C., Boland, E., Olejnik, S., & Kame'enui, E. J. (2003). Vocabulary tricks: Effects of instruction in morphology and context on fifth-grade students' ability to derive and infer word meaning. *American Educational Research Journal, 40,* 447–494.

Baumann, J. F., & Kame'enui, E. J. (1991). Research on vocabulary instruction: Ode to Voltaire. In J. Flood, J. J. D. Lapp, & J. R. Squire (Eds.), *Handbook of research on teaching the English language arts.* New York: MacMillan.

Baumann, J. F., Kame'enui, E. J., & Ash, G. E. (2003). Research on vocabulary instructing: Voltaire redux. In J. Flood, D. Lapp, J. R. Squire, & J. M. Jensen (Eds.), *Handbook on research on teaching the English language arts* (2nd ed., pp. 752–785). Mahwah, NJ: Erlbaum.

Beck, I., & McKeown, M. (1991). Conditions of vocabulary acquisition. In R. Barr, M. Kamil, P. Mosenthal, & P. D. Pearson (Eds.), *Handbook of reading research* (vol. 2, 789–8l4). New York: Longman.

Beck, I. L., McKeown, M. G., & Kucan, L. (2002). *Bringing words to life: Robust vocabulary instruction.* New York: Guilford Press.

Beck, I. L., McKeown, M. G., & McCaslin, E. S. (1983). Vocabulary development: All contexts are not created equal. *The Elementary School Journal, 83*(3), 177–181.

Beck, I. L., McKeown, M. G., & Omanson, R. C. (1987). The effects and uses of diverse vocabulary instructional techniques. In M. G. McKeown & M. E. Curtis (Eds.), *The nature of vocabulary acquisition.* Hillsdale, NJ: Erlbaum.

Blachowicz, C. L. Z. (1993). C(2)QU: Modeling context use in the classroom. *The Reading Teacher, 47,* 268–269.

Blachowicz, C. L. Z., & Fisher, P. (2004). Keep the "fun" in fundamental. In J. F. Baumann and E. J. Kame'enui (Eds.), *Vocabulary instruction: Research to practice* (pp. 218–237). New York: The Guilford Press.

Blachowicz, C. L. Z., Fisher, P. J. L., Ogle, D., & Watts-Taffe, S. (2006). Vocabulary: Questions from the classroom. *Reading Research Quarterly, 41,* 524–539.

Burns, P. C., Roe, B. D., & Ross, E. P. (1999). *Word recognition and meaning vocabulary: A literacy skills primer.* Boston: Houghton Mifflin.

Carlisle, J. F., & Stone, C. A. (2005). Exploring the role of morphemes in word reading. *Reading Research Quarterly, 40,* 428–449.

Carlo, M. S., August, D., McGlaughlin, B., Snow, C. E., Dressler, C., Lippman, D. N., Lively, T. J., & White, C. E. (2004). Closing the gap: Addressing vocabulary needs of English-language learners in bilingual and mainstreamed classes. *Reading Research Quarterly, 39,* 188–215.

Carlo, M. S., August, D., & Snow, C. E. (2005). Sustained vocabulary-learning strategies for English language learners. In E. Hiebert & M. Kamil (Eds.), *Teaching and learning vocabulary: Bringing research to practice* (pp. 137–153). Mahwah, NJ: Erlbaum.

Cecil, N. L. (1994). *Freedom fighters: Affective teaching of the language arts.* Salem, WI: Sheffield.

Collins COBUILD Learner's Dictionary (2003). (2nd revised). London: HarperCollins.

Coxhead, A. (2000). A new academic word list. *TESOL Quarterly, 34,* 213–238.

Coyne, M. D., Simmons, D. C., & Kame'enui, E. J. (2004). Vocabulary instruction for young children at risk of experiencing reading difficulties: Teaching word meanings during shared storybook reading. In J. F. Baumann & E. J. Kame'enui (Eds.), *Vocabulary instruction: Research to practice* (pp. 41–58). New York: Guilford Press.

Crawley, S. J., & King, M. (2000). *Remediating reading difficulties* (3rd ed.). Boston: McGraw-Hill.

Cunningham, A. E., & Stanovich, K. E. (1998, Spring/Summer). What reading does for the mind. *American Federation of Teachers.*

Dale, E. (1965). Vocabulary measurement: Techniques and major findings. *Elementary English, 42*(8), 895–901.

Ellis, E., & Farmer, T. (2000). *The clarifying routine: Elaborating vocabulary instruction.* Kansas City, MO: Edge Enterprises.

Feldman, K., & Kinsella, K. (2003). Narrowing the language gap: Strategies for vocabulary development. Available at www.fcoe.net/ela/pdf/Narrowing%20Vocab%20Gap%20KK%20KF%201.pdf.

Fountas, I. C., & Pinnell, G. S. (1996). *Guided reading: Good first teaching for all children.* Portsmouth, NH: Heinemann.

Fry, E. B., Fountkidis, D. L., & Polk, J. K. (1985). *The new reading teacher's book of lists.* Upper Saddle River, NJ: Prentice Hall.

Gipe, J. P. (1978/1979). Investigating techniques for teaching word meanings. *Reading Research Quarterly, 14,* 624–644.

Graves, M. F. (1986). Vocabulary learning and instruction. In E. Z. Rothkopf (Ed.), *Review of research in education* (vol. 13). Washington, DC: American Educational Research Association.

Graves, M. F. (2006). *The vocabulary book: Learning and instruction.* Newark, DE: International Reading Association.

Graves, M. F., & Watts-Taffe, S. (2002). The place of word consciousness in a research-based vocabulary program. In

A. Farstrup and S. Samuels (Eds.), *What research has to say about reading instruction* (3rd ed., pp. 140–165). Newark, DE: International Reading Association.

Graves, M. F., Watts, S., & Graves, B. (1994). *Essentials of classroom teaching: Elementary reading*. Boston: Allyn & Bacon.

Greenwood, S. C., & Flanigan, K. (2007). Overlapping vocabulary and comprehension: Context clues complement semantic gradients. *The Reading Teacher, 61*(3), 249–254.

Harmon, J. M. (2000). Assessing and supporting independent word learning strategies of middle school students. *Journal of Adolescent and Adult Literacy, 43*, 518–528.

Harmon, J. M. (2002). Teaching independent word learning strategies to struggling readers. *Journal of Adolescent and Adult Literacy, 45*, 606–616.

Hickman, P., Pollard-Durodola, S., & Vaughn, S. (2004). Storybook reading: Improving vocabulary and comprehension for English-language learners. *The Reading Teacher, 57*, 720–730.

Hiebert, E. H., Lehr, F., & Osborn, J. (2004). A focus on vocabulary. Second in the Research-Based Practices in Early Reading Series published by the Regional Educational Laboratory at Pacific Resources for Education and Learning. Available at www.ppo.prel.org.

Jenkins, J. R., Stein, M. L., & Wysocki, K. (1984). Learning vocabulary through reading. *American Educational Research Journal, 21*, 767–787.

Johnson, D. D., & Pearson, P. D. (1986). *Teaching reading vocabulary* (3rd ed.). New York: Holt, Rinehart and Winston.

Juel, C., & Deffes, R. (2004). Vocabulary: The plot of the reading story. In J. F. Baumann & E. J. Kame'enui (Eds.). *Vocabulary instruction: Research to practice* (pp. 3–10). New York: Guilford Press.

Kane, S. (2007). *Literacy and learning in the content areas* (2nd ed.). Scottsdale, AZ: Holcomb Hathaway.

Lember, B. H. (1997). *The shell book*. Boston: Houghton Mifflin.

McKeown, M. G. (1993). Creating effective definitions for young word learners. *Reading Research Quarterly, 28*, 16–31.

McVicker, C. J. (2007). Comic strips as a text structure for learning to read. *The Reading Teacher, 61*(1), 85–88.

Morgan, B., & Odom, D. (2006). Stories from tween classrooms. *Educational Leadership, 63*(7), 38–41.

Nagy, W. E. (1988). *Teaching vocabulary to improve reading comprehension*. Newark, DE: International Reading Association.

Nagy, W. E., & Anderson, R. C. (1984). How many words are there in printed school English? *Reading Research Quarterly, 19*, 233–253.

National Reading Panel. (2000). *Report of the National Reading Panel: Teaching children to read*. Bethesda, MD: National Institute of Child Health and Human Development.

NICHD. (2000). Report of the National Reading Panel: Reports of the subgroups. Washington, DC: U.S. Government Printing Office.

Pittelman, S. D., Heimlich, J. E., Berglund, R. L., & French, M. P. (1991). *Semantic feature analysis: Classroom applications*. Newark, DE: International Reading Association.

Rasinski, T., & Padak, N. (2000). *Effective reading strategies: Teaching children who find reading difficult* (2nd ed.). Upper Saddle River, NJ: Merrill.

Schwanenflugel, P. J., Stahl, S. A., & McFalls, E. I. (1997). *Partial word knowledge and vocabulary growth during reading comprehension* (Research Report No. 76). Athens, GA: University of Georgia, National Reading Research Center.

Scott, J. A., & Nagy, W. E. (1997). Understanding the definitions of unfamiliar verbs. *Reading Research Quarterly, 32*, 184–200.

Stahl, S. A. (1999). Vocabulary development. *Reading research to practice: A series for teachers*. Cambridge, MA: Brookline.

Stahl, S. A., & Fairbanks, M. M. (1986). The effects of vocabulary instruction: A model-based meta-analysis. *Review of Educational Research, 56*, 72–110.

Stahl, S. A., & Kapinus, B. (1991). Possible sentences: Predicting word meanings to teach content area vocabulary. *The Reading Teacher, 45*, 36–43.

Ulanoff, S. H., & Pucci, S. L. (1999). Learning words from books: The effects of read-aloud on second language vocabulary acquisition. *The Bilingual Research Journal, 23*, 400–422.

Reading Comprehension

Five

FOCUS QUESTIONS

- What are the key factors that affect reading comprehension?
- What are the five most effective reading comprehension strategies?
- How can teachers use guided reading to help students learn comprehension strategies?
- What is a novel study?
- What skill areas are important for online reading comprehension?
- What strategies are appropriate for teaching online reading comprehension?

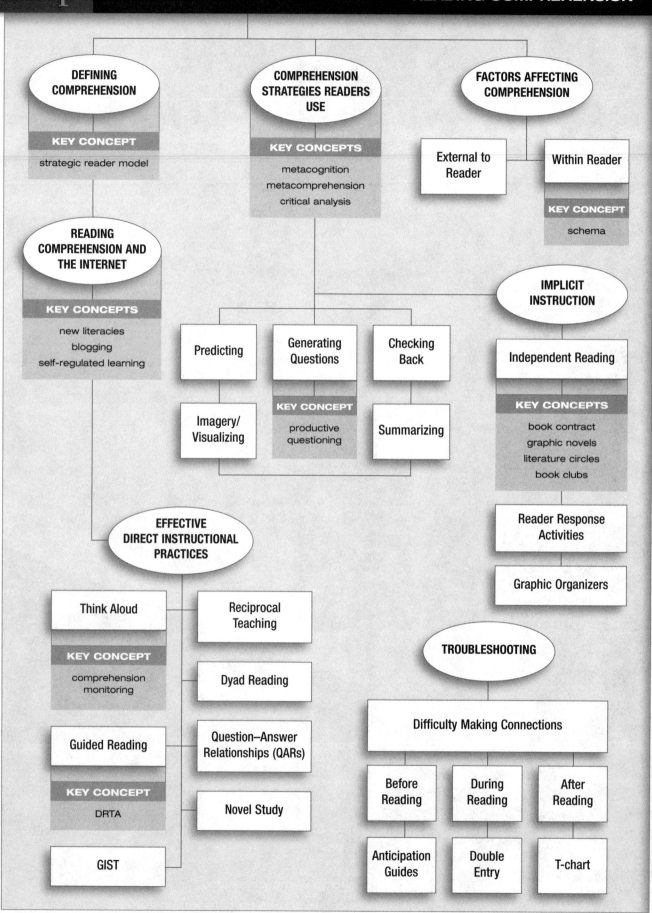

DEFINING COMPREHENSION

KEY CONCEPT

strategic reader model

READING COMPREHENSION AND THE INTERNET

KEY CONCEPTS

new literacies
blogging
self-regulated learning

COMPREHENSION STRATEGIES READERS USE

KEY CONCEPTS

metacognition
metacomprehension
critical analysis

Predicting

Generating Questions

KEY CONCEPT

productive questioning

Checking Back

Imagery/ Visualizing

Summarizing

FACTORS AFFECTING COMPREHENSION

External to Reader

Within Reader

KEY CONCEPT

schema

IMPLICIT INSTRUCTION

Independent Reading

KEY CONCEPTS

book contract
graphic novels
literature circles
book clubs

Reader Response Activities

Graphic Organizers

EFFECTIVE DIRECT INSTRUCTIONAL PRACTICES

Think Aloud

KEY CONCEPT

comprehension monitoring

Guided Reading

KEY CONCEPT

DRTA

GIST

Reciprocal Teaching

Dyad Reading

Question–Answer Relationships (QARs)

Novel Study

TROUBLESHOOTING

Difficulty Making Connections

Before Reading

During Reading

After Reading

Anticipation Guides

Double Entry

T-chart

Mr. Perez is preparing for Monday's science lesson and wants to use the technique of *questioning the author* (Beck et al., 1997) to better engage his fifth-grade students in their expository reading *while* they read material from a new unit on mammals. He believes that this technique will also help them focus on their understanding of the content. He reads the following paragraph from his science materials:

What are mammals?

The name "mammal" refers to the female's mammary glands, which provide milk for her young. This characteristic sets off mammals among the warm-blooded, back-boned animals. Mammals are hairy; young are born alive. Most have varied teeth, for cutting, tearing, or grinding. The mammal's skull is unique; the brain is more complex than in other animals.

Mr. Perez realizes that this paragraph contains the major characteristics of mammals. He decides he will first direct his students' attention to the essential characteristic of the mammary glands. Following this he will focus their attention on the other features found in mammals.

Mr. Perez then plans a set of queries. To begin discussion, he decides to ask at the end of the first paragraph, "What has the author told us about mammals?" If students do not mention the main characteristic, his follow-up query will be, "What does the author mean by saying that the word *mammal* refers to the female's mammary glands, and that this characteristic *sets off* mammals?" Next, Mr. Perez will use the query "What else does the author tell us about mammals?" to begin a discussion that compares mammals with other warm-blooded, back-boned animals, and with other animals in general. He will use a visual, probably a T-chart (see Figure 5.10 later in this chapter), to keep track of students' ideas for later use.

As Mr. Perez proceeds through his science material, he anticipates where he will need to assist his students in constructing their understanding of this material. He is aware that he may need to interpret what his students try to say (revoice), model how to arrive at meaning, or provide additional information not available in the text (annotate). He may also need to draw attention to particular students' ideas (marking) or to turn students back to the text for further thinking or clarifying. Once students indicate they have understood the essential meaning and are ready to move on, Mr. Perez will recap, or summarize, the major ideas, or he may ask another student to recap. With this lesson plan in mind, Mr. Perez now feels ready to begin the new science unit about mammals.

DEFINING COMPREHENSION

You might want to think first about what the term *comprehension* means to you. Is it the ability to recall text? Is it knowing the answers to questions asked about the text? Does it mean the ability to critique what has been read, or to summarize it, or to cull a theme or characters' motives? The No Child Left Behind Act describes the component of reading comprehension as "the ability to read for understanding, to remember what has been read, and to communicate what has been read" (Yell & Drasgow, 2005, p. 72). Certainly comprehension includes all of these abilities. **Comprehension** is currently thought of as the construction of meaning, and it is the ultimate goal of exemplary reading instruction.

● comprehension

The theoretical framework for reading comprehension instruction that we support in this chapter views comprehension instruction as an active process; that is, it encourages students

- to relate text to their own prior experiences, or make predictions about what might happen.
- to construct mental images during their reading.
- to question themselves about text ideas while they read.
- to summarize the big ideas in what they read. (Pressley, 2002)

Our framework also recognizes that meaning is socially constructed; in other words, students need to engage in conversations about what they read to help clarify and broaden their understandings of the text. We support a **strategic reader model** for comprehension instruction that implies you will demonstrate for your students strategies that help them actively process text (e.g., relate to prior experiences, question, form images, predict, clarify, summarize, make inferences). A combination of direct explanation and modeling, or "thinking out loud," can work well as a form of explicit teaching for comprehension strategies (Duffy, 2002). In addition, reading comprehension strategies need to be modeled and practiced, one strategy at a time, using a variety of text, in order to teach and practice the strategy at a deep level, while you gradually allow the student to take over use of the strategy (Pearson & Gallagher, 1983).

FACTORS AFFECTING READING COMPREHENSION

Fortunately, there is quite a bit of research on reading comprehension. This research finds that a number of factors affect comprehension, including factors external to the reader and characteristics within the reader.

Factors External to Readers

The factors external to readers that affect comprehension include (1) the reader-friendliness of the text and (2) the context in which the reading takes place.

Reader-friendliness of text. It seems logical to expect that text clearly written with a minimum level of abstractness would be easier to comprehend. In fact, research studies do support this notion. For example, a study by Jorm (1977) demonstrated that texts using high-frequency words and high-imagery words are easier for all students to comprehend. Englert and Thomas (1987) found that texts organized sequentially are easiest to comprehend, followed by those that are enumerated, descriptive, and comparative/contrasting, in that order (see Chapter 7 for descriptions of these text structures). We refer to text that is easy to comprehend as user- or reader-friendly.

Context. The context, or environment, in which reading takes place can also affect comprehension. Consider how your own reading differs when you read within a classroom setting compared with when you read at home or in a library. The classroom environment itself can affect comprehension (Gipe, 2006). Opportunities for reading practice, access to appropriate materials, availability of modeling and direct instruction, and a risk-free atmosphere are all factors that teachers can influence in a positive way.

Characteristics within Readers

The characteristics within readers that affect comprehension include (1) ability to construct a mental representation, (2) ability to make connections, (3) ability to attend to information in the text, (4) amount of background knowledge, (5) engagement with text, (6) knowledge of basic skills, and (7) knowledge of reading strategies and metacognition.

Ability to construct a mental representation. It has become more and more apparent that the reader's ability to construct a mental representation, or picture, of the information read and its interpretation is a major factor in comprehension. The research on mental representations of text indicates that such representations resemble a network of nodes (the individual text elements) and connections (the meaningful relations between the elements) (van den Broek, 1990; van den Broek et al., 1996). Two important types of connections are referential (e.g., pronouns) and causal/logical (e.g., if . . . then; this . . . because) (Britton & Graesser, 1996). That is, when events or statements have clear connections to other events or statements in the text, generally in the form of pronouns, direct references, or cause/effect relationships, they are more easily recalled. Readers proceed through text attempting to make sense of it by connecting explicitly stated information to two main sources of information: related concepts in their background knowledge (or **schema**), and a subset of concepts from the preceding text. As noted in the section "Factors External to Readers" above, a coherent, well-written text is reader-friendly and easy to comprehend. A coherent, well-written text also helps the reader make the necessary referential and causal/logical connections and facilitates a clear mental representation of the text. But, even with reader-friendly text, the reader still needs to develop the ability to actually make the connections.

● schema

Ability to make connections. A reader who can make meaningful connections between the text information and related background knowledge will better comprehend the text. Readers need to be able to relate what they read to their own lives (text-to-self connections). They also need to make connections between the text they are reading and other similar texts (text-to-text connections) or events and concerns that occur in the world at large (text-to-world connections) (Moravcsik & Kintsch, 1993; Harvey & Goudvis, 2000).

Ability to attend to information in the text. The general ability to attend to the information in the text is influenced by short-term memory, concentration, and motivation. In addition, the approach to the comprehension process will vary depending on how the reader interprets the level of attention necessary when reading for pleasure or for some educational, or informational, purpose. A reader might decide that the book he has chosen to read for pleasure does not need a high level of attention in order to understand it, especially when the reader is already very familiar with the author's writing style. In contrast, a reader may decide upon opening her statistics textbook the night before a test that a high level of attention is needed.

Amount of background knowledge. A reader who has background knowledge relevant to the text being read has a head start on comprehending the text. Such background knowledge may include, but is not limited to, knowledge of the text structure the author has used, familiarity with the literary genre, recognition of the vocabulary, and possession of information about the topic. This prior knowledge constitutes a schema for the topic. Try reading a topic about which you know very little (quantum physics?) and see how much you comprehend!

Engagement with the text. It is quite likely that the major issue in comprehension for students in grades 4–8 is engagement with the text (Wilhelm,

1997). To construct meaning, the learner needs to be purposefully and actively involved with the text. The use of multicultural literature (see Appendix A for some suggestions) provides "the textual features (recurring themes, linguistic patterns, and ethnic group practices)" that you may use as points of engagement for students of all ethnicities (Brooks, 2006, p. 390). Active engagement is also necessary for **critical analysis,** which requires the reader to interpret text and produce a cultural understanding of the text (Harris & Hodges, 1995). Activating relevant background knowledge, making real-life connections, collaborating with other students, and realizing when comprehension has occurred or has broken down are all important aspects of being involved with the text.

● critical analysis

Knowledge of basic skills.   Well-developed basic skills, such as letter/sound recognition, word decoding, and knowledge of grammar, will increase the amount of cognitive energy available for constructing coherent mental representations of the text. In general, for grade 4–8 students, word-decoding abilities are sufficient (see Chapter 3 for advanced word analysis skills). Ongoing vocabulary instruction (see Chapter 4) will enhance comprehension, especially in content areas that have specialized vocabulary.

Knowledge of reading strategies and metacognition (or metacomprehension).   Knowledge of reading comprehension strategies is a crucial factor (see next section), but one that also requires **metacognition** (understanding how one knows, or thinking about thinking) and **metacomprehension** (realizing when one has or has not understood) abilities to ensure that readers will recognize when and under what conditions a comprehension strategy needs to be used. Students who demonstrate good metacomprehension, or comprehension-monitoring ability, know when they do and do not understand what they have read. They use fix-up strategies to resolve their comprehension difficulties. They can identify where their difficulty lies—"I don't understand the last section on page 45"—and what the difficulty is—"I am confused by the phrase *cornhusk mattresses.* What kind of mattress is this?" They may try to use their own words to restate a difficult sentence or passage: "So the author meant the quiet forest became noisy with the sounds of crickets and a howling wolf when he said the stillness of the forest was broken." Students who use fix-up strategies do not hesitate to look back through the text for clues that might help them understand: "I think I remember something about how old Abe Lincoln was when he went to school, but by the time he was 16 he only had one year of school? I need to look back to see how old he was when he first went to school." And they also look ahead in the text for information that might help them: "This sentence says Abe Lincoln's first home was a one-room log cabin and that he was born in Kentucky. I thought he lived in Illinois? He must have moved. . . . Oh, I see the next section is called 'The Lincolns Move to Indiana.' That will tell me more about his later life and where else Lincoln may have lived."

● metacognition
● metacomprehension

Students who demonstrate good metacomprehension know when they do and do not understand what they have read.

COMPREHENSION STRATEGIES FOR READERS TO USE

According to the National Center for Education Statistics (2003), more than 66 percent of students in grades 4–12 struggle to read proficiently, largely due to problems with comprehension. In response to this finding, the Alliance for Excellent Education formed a panel to examine the research related to adolescent literacy. The resulting report, *Reading Next: A Vision for Action and Research in Middle and High School Literacy* (Biancarosa & Snow, 2006), identifies nine research-based instructional strategies and six structural supports for effective instruction in adolescent literacy. Comprehension instruction is one of the nine instructional areas of focus. Reviews of research in this area reveal a relatively small, but powerful, set of strategies that are recommended for comprehension instruction (Pressley, 2000):

1. Predicting
2. Generating questions
3. Checking back
4. Imagery/visualizing
5. Summarizing

These five strategies should be taught directly through considerable teacher explanation and modeling of their use (see the procedures described in the "Think-Aloud" activity, pg. 142). Then, extensive, long-term student practice within a print-rich context, across content areas, and with a variety of text types must be provided (see the websites listed here and Appendix A for literature resources).

1 PREDICTING

Proficient readers make mental predictions, or calculated hunches, about what might happen next in the text they are reading. Their hunches are based on what they already know about the topic, what they know about the literary structure the author is using (e.g., narrative, expository, fairy tale, historical fiction, or autobiographical), and what they have learned thus far in the text. As skilled readers continue to read, they tend to confirm or deny their previous hunches, according to new understandings that occur. With expository text, they often preview the text to get an overview of what information will be covered and look through the text to see if it matches their expectations. Skilled readers also ask themselves questions for which they hope to find answers as they read, thus setting their own purposes for reading the text. (See the DRTA and Jigsaw: Read a Book in an Hour activities for example lessons that encourage students to use predicting.)

2 GENERATING QUESTIONS

One of the most valuable ways proficient readers construct text meanings is by asking and answering important questions about text as they read. They are aware of the difference between "thinking-type" questions and "locating information–type" questions, and they are able to reflect later on the caliber of the questions they have asked themselves.

Students do not generate important questions automatically, but learn this skill when their teachers model questioning skills and use productive questioning as an instructional tool. **Productive questioning** focuses on the process of both

www

Reading Next
www.all4ed.org/publications/ ReadingNext/ReadingNext.pdf

www

Children's Literature Resources
www.carolhurst.com/index.html
www.ala.org/ala/yalsa/yalsa.cfm
www.reading.org/resources/tools/ choices.html

● productive questioning

thinking about and learning the content of the text (Dantonio & Beisenherz, 2001). Through carefully crafted questions that use open question stems, as well as thoughtful reactions (both verbal and nonverbal) to students' responses, you can guide the way your students think about their texts as they read. Open question stems (e.g., *what are, in what way, how, why*) allow for meaningful instructional conversations as opposed to closed question stems (e.g., *can you, will you, do you, are you, do you know*) that imply there is a correct answer. For example, changing the question, *Do you understand?* to *What do you understand?* gives students the opening they need to share their understandings. In the classroom vignette, Mr. Perez prepared questions that invite students to engage in the instructional conversation. (See the Reciprocal Reading, Dyad Reading, QAR, and Jigsaw: Read a Book in an Hour activities for example lessons that require students to recognize question types and generate questions.)

③ CHECKING BACK

Proficient readers are continually checking their own understanding as they read, making sure what they are confronting conforms to what they already know, as well as ensuring that they have not missed something. It is, therefore, quite normal for skilled readers to make frequent regressions, or to go back and reread a sentence or passage, to check that they initially "got it right." Such monitoring of understanding is very similar to the rereading that takes place when a skilled reader is reading an unstimulating text late at night and suddenly realizes that not a word has been understood—a phenomenon to which most readers can relate! (See the GIST and DRTA activities for examples that encourage the use of checking back.)

④ IMAGERY/VISUALIZING

Proficient readers tend to create pictures in their mind's eye as they read text, especially text containing elaborate descriptions or well-developed story characters. Placing themselves in the story's setting or time period and/or imagining themselves as the main character, facing the same trials and tribulations, helps them appreciate, remember, and internalize the story that is unfolding before them. The experience of mental vision is so personal and intense that readers skilled in this strategy are often disappointed when they see the film version of a story they have read, because it frequently pales in comparison to what occurs in their rich imaginations. (See the Sketch to Stretch and Going Beyond Visualizing activities for example lessons that use imagery.)

⑤ SUMMARIZING

Proficient readers tend to remember important ideas and information they discover throughout a text and formulate them into a "big picture" of the reading material. Such a strategy is the basis on which skilled readers are able to summarize what they have read, or to articulate the main idea in expository text and separate it from the supporting details. Summarizing also includes the ability to identify particular underlying themes in literature. In addition, summarizing can reveal personal opinions about the text. Proficient readers internalize the meanings certain works have held for them, review ideas frequently, and evaluate what they have read compared with other texts and what they had hoped to gain from the text. Summarizing text can thus be influenced by these previously internalized views. (See the GIST, Reciprocal Teaching, and Dyad Reading activities for example lessons that use summarizing.)

EFFECTIVE DIRECT INSTRUCTIONAL PRACTICES

The activities and instructional frameworks offered in this section incorporate and support the five comprehension strategies just discussed. Where appropriate, specific aspects of an activity are designated as before reading, during reading, or after reading. In addition, based on the work of Liang and Dole (2006), the activities described here are identified by the main focus of the comprehension instruction: that is, a focus on understanding the content of a text, on understanding the process of comprehending the text, or on understanding both the content and the process.

Collaborative Strategic Reading (CSR)

A framework for comprehension instruction that focuses on process is Collaborative Strategic Reading (CSR). Based on Klingner and Vaughn (1996), CSR has been adapted to include the following four comprehension strategies that students apply in small cooperative groups before, during, and after reading: (1) preview (before reading), (2) click and clunk (during reading), (3) get the gist (during reading), and (4) wrap-up (after reading).

WWW

Collaborative Strategic Reading
*www.ncset.org/publications/
researchtopractice/NCSET
ResearchBrief_1.2.pdf*

Preview (before reading). Preview activates students' prior knowledge, facilitates predictions about the text they will read, and generates interest. It includes two activities: (1) brainstorming and (2) making predictions. To teach the strategy, begin by asking students to think about movie previews they may have seen. Ask them about what they have learned from the previews; use questions such as, *What did you learn about the characters in the movie?* or *What did you learn about where and when the movie will take place?* Then ask students to preview the text they will read by skimming headings, looking at pictures, and examining the boldface terms to determine (a) what they know about the topic and (b) what they think they will learn by reading the text.

Click and clunk (during reading). Click and clunk encourages students to monitor their understanding and to use fix-up strategies when they fail to understand the material. To introduce the concepts of click and clunk, describe a click as something that "you really get" as in "you know it just clicks" and describe a clunk as when you feel you have run into a brick wall and do not understand a word the author is using. When students understand these concepts, read a short selection aloud and have them identify their clicks and clunks. Then, teach fix-up strategies for the clunks.

Get the gist (during reading). Get the gist helps students identify a text's main ideas by answering (1) Who or what is it about? and (2) What is most important about the who or what? In addition, students learn to limit their response to 10 words or less, so that their gist conveys the most important idea(s) and not unnecessary details. When teaching students to get the gist, begin by having them read a single paragraph and asking them to identify the most important person, place, or thing and what is most important about the person, place, or thing. Teach the students to state the information in a sentence containing 10 words or less. (See the section on GIST, p. 144, for an example activity.)

Wrap-up (after reading). Wrap-up includes the following two activities: (1) generating questions and (2) reviewing. To teach wrap-up, ask students to put themselves in the role of teacher and think of questions they would ask on a test based on the following question starters: who, what, when, where, why, and how. You should also encourage students to formulate some questions that require higher-level thinking skills rather than literal-level skills. Next, have students write the text's most important ideas in the form of a review.

The activities can be used with students of all abilities with some appropriate modifications. For instance, if written responses are called for, they can be included as soon as students have the required writing proficiency; in the meantime, oral responses are an acceptable option. Encourage oral discussions during the activities, accompanied by pictures, objects, or other visuals, for the added benefit of allowing English learners to listen to the way others are thinking and participate as they feel comfortable.

Think-Aloud

think-aloud ●

Think-aloud—the oral verbalizing of one's thinking—is one of the most effective ways you can model the comprehension strategies a reader uses to gain meaning from the printed page (Davey, 1983). Think-aloud activities also help learners, especially Intermediate (Level 3 according to the CELDT) English learners, develop their comprehension monitoring ability (McKeown & Gentilucci, 2007). **Comprehension monitoring** is the reader's awareness of whether what is being read makes sense and, when it does not, her ability to make adjustments to improve her comprehension. The following activity provides suggested steps for think-aloud.

comprehension monitoring ●

| ACTIVITY | *Think-Aloud* (FOCUS ON PROCESS) |

1. Ahead of time, make copies of the text passage that will be demonstrated or prepare the passage for an overhead projector.

BEFORE READING

2. After looking at the title on the cover and any illustrations in the passage, ruminate aloud about the passage. (Figure 5.1 represents an example of a teacher using think-aloud to model the strategy of visualizing.)

DURING READING

3. Read the passage aloud as the students track. Continually organize images by explaining the passage after every sentence or paragraph.

4. Answer aloud such questions as:

What am I reminded of here that I already know? (tapping prior knowledge)

What are some ways I can get help in understanding unfamiliar words and/or ideas? (monitoring understanding)

What does this remind me of in my own life? (making connections)

AFTER READING

5. After modeling the reading of several paragraphs in this fashion, invite students to add their own problem-solving tactics and personal impressions by reading succeeding passages in pairs.

Note: Text material is in bold; teacher think-aloud comments are in italics.

The title of the story is "The Desert Man." . . . *I have a pretty good picture in my mind of what the desert looks like. Miles and miles of sand, blazing hot, very little vegetation.*

The old man was hot and tired. His long white robe billowed in the dry desert wind.

My picture in my head is of a very old man. . . . *He is dressed in a long white robe, and the material must be light enough to be blown by the wind. I can see his robe blowing in the wind.*

He wiped his brow as he started to trudge up yet another of the endless dunes of the desert. He saw only a sea of sand surrounding him.

I can see in my own mind what the old man sees . . . *hills and hills of hot sand* . . . *he is wiping his forehead and is bent over because he is so tired and weary.*

The sun beat down on him mercilessly. He would not give up. He knew the camp was near.

The look on the old man's face is very clear to me now. He has a look of determination. He is very determined to make it to the camp. . . . .

The pictures I made in my head about this passage helped me understand the story, and they will help me remember what I have read. This is a comprehension strategy that good readers use to help them learn and remember. It is a strategy that you can use to improve your comprehension.

Source: Gambrell, L. B., & Bales, R. J. (1987). Visual imagery: A strategy for enhancing listening, reading and writing. *Australian Journal of Reading, 10*(3), 147–153.

FIGURE 5.1

Teacher modeling of the think-aloud procedure for the strategy of visualizing.

Guided Reading

Students need to be directly shown how to process text so that they can become independent readers. **Guided reading** is an instructional framework that provides direct teacher support for developing effective strategies for comprehending text independently at increasingly difficult levels. Generally you will work with a small group of students who are reading at a similar level of difficulty. A guided reading lesson involves three stages: before reading, during reading, and after reading. Before reading deals with building schemata for the reading selection. During reading is the core of the lesson in which important strategies are modeled and practiced. Students are encouraged to read silently during this stage and request help as needed. After reading is a time to check for understanding, invite personal response, check the accuracy of predictions, and generally interpret and clarify what was read. More information about guided reading can be found in *Guiding Readers and Writers in Grades 3–6* (Fountas & Pinnell, 2001).

● guided reading

Directed Reading-Thinking Activity

directed reading-thinking ● activity

As a type of guided reading (teacher-led, small-group reading instruction that focuses on questioning and predicting to aid comprehension), the **directed reading-thinking activity (DRTA)** is one of the most commonly used approaches for enhancing comprehension with both narrative and expository materials, and especially with literature-based instruction. The objective of the DRTA, developed by Stauffer (1975), is to improve comprehension by having students focus on a particular passage and make predictions about it based on its textual features.

ACTIVITY *DRTA* (FOCUS ON CONTENT AND PROCESS)

Although a DRTA lesson can be conducted in various ways, the steps include the following:

BEFORE READING

1. Direct students' attention to the title of the selection and ask them to predict its content. After students have volunteered their predictions and the reasons for their responses, ask a preselected group whether they agree or disagree and why.

DURING READING

2. Read aloud, or have students read silently, several sentences, and then ask students what they think the text is about based on this new information.

3. Direct the students' attention to particular vocabulary or phrases that are prominent to the meaning of the text. Ask them to use these words to hypothesize what the text will be about.

4. Ask students to look at pictures, graphs, and figures and make more predictions based on this new information.

AFTER READING

5. Ask students to reread or review the text to confirm or negate their predictions and hypotheses. Discuss their findings. See Figure 5.2 for an example of a teacher–student discourse that occurred during a DRTA conducted with social studies material.

GIST

GIST ●

The GIST procedure (generating interactions between schemata and text) is intended to improve students' comprehension and provide a tool for guiding student summary writing (Cunningham, 1982). **GIST** is a teacher-directed, small-group strategy that takes students from writing a summary of no more than 15 words for paragraphs to writing a summary of 20 or fewer words for short passages. Beginning with the paragraph version, students are asked to compose a summary sentence of no more than 15 words following the reading of each sentence in the paragraph. That is, after reading the first sentence they summarize what is said. Then, as each new sentence is read, students incorporate the additional information into a new summary statement of no more than 15 words. Paragraphs should have from three to five sentences.

Example discourse from a DRTA lesson for social studies.   FIGURE   5.2

Before Reading:

Ms. Clark: Based on the title of this chapter section, "Abe Lincoln Grows Up With America," what do you predict that you might learn in this section and why?

Brian: I predict this section will tell me where Abe Lincoln grew up because it says "grows up" in the title.

Jennifer: I think it will tell me where he was born and where he lived because in the picture it shows him sitting inside a house.

Ms. Clark (to other students): Do you agree with these predictions? Why or why not?

Students: Yes, agree. The title talks about growing up, so this section will talk about Abraham Lincoln when he was a young boy.

During Reading:

Ms. Clark: After reading the first page in this section (four paragraphs), what would you change about any of your predictions, or what new ones would you make?

Brian: Well, we now know where Abe Lincoln was born—Kentucky.

Timothy: And he lived in a one-room log cabin, so we know that is where he is sitting in the picture. Inside the log cabin.

Jennifer: And we found out he was born on February 12, 1809.

Ms. Clark: So it sounds like we need to make some new predictions.

Brian: The book talks about his mother and father and uses the word *children,* so I think Abe Lincoln had a brother or sister. I think we will find that out in the next part.

Ms. Clark: Timothy told us Abe Lincoln lived in a one-room log cabin. Look at that sentence in your text. It says, "His first home was a one-room log cabin." What does that tell you or make you think about?

Brian: It makes me think he moved into another home sometime. This was just his first home.

Jennifer: I think Abe Lincoln moves to Washington, D.C., and then he became president since Kentucky was where his first home was.

Ms. Clark: Look at that picture again. Where is Abe sitting, and why is he sitting there?

Brian: He is sitting by the fireplace. He might be cold. It might be winter.

Timothy: But he has a book in his hand. He looks like he is trying to use the glow of the fireplace to see the book.

Jennifer: Maybe the electricity went out!

Ms. Clark: What is there about the text or the picture that makes you think there was electricity in Abe's first house?

(continued)

FIGURE 5.2 **Continued.**

Brian: The book says the house had deerskin windows, a door with leather hinges, and the floor was hard-packed earth. I think Abe Lincoln's family was very poor.

Ms. Clark: What do you think we will learn on the next page?

Brian: If Abe Lincoln has a brother or sister.

Timothy: Where the family moved to.

Jennifer: How Abe Lincoln became president.

Ms. Clark: Let's read the next page.

After Reading:

Ms. Clark: Now that you have finished this section, were your predictions supported? What did you find out?

Brian: We learned more about Lincoln's family. His father's name was Thomas Lincoln, and his mother's name was Nancy Hanks Lincoln. His father was a farmer and they had a cow.

Timothy: Abe Lincoln went to school when he was seven.

Jennifer: The family was very poor.

Brian: It just kept saying "children." I still don't know if Abe Lincoln had a brother or sister!

Timothy: But it did tell us that the family moved to Indiana when Abe was still seven. And two years after they moved his mother died. So he was nine when his mother died.

Jennifer: His father married a woman who had three children, so we know Abe had either brothers or sisters, or both, but not what they were. His stepmother's name was Sarah Johnston Lincoln.

Brian: Abe Lincoln only had about one year of school! But the book said that many people never went to school at all! Wow!

Timothy: Abe grew up tall in Indiana. He was six feet, four inches by the time he was 16.

Ms. Clark: You learned quite a bit about the young Abe Lincoln. How do you think his early life may have helped him to become president of the United States?

Brian: Since he was poor, he would know what poor people need.

Jennifer: He had to work real hard when he was young, so he knew how to work hard to become a president.

Timothy: He read books and wrote things, so he was smart enough to be president.

GIST (FOCUS ON CONTENT)

Using a paragraph from the chapter section read for the DRTA lesson in Figure 5.2, GIST might proceed as follows:

1. Choose an appropriate paragraph. For example,

   Abe's father, Thomas Lincoln, worked hard to raise crops in the stony soil of his little farm. His mother, Nancy Hanks Lincoln, was a good housekeeper. When hunting was good, Thomas Lincoln could shoot deer, bear, rabbits, and turkeys in the woods. The family also had corn bread, greens from the garden, and potatoes.

2. Present only the first sentence to the students. The sentence should have 15 blanks underneath.

   Abe's father, Thomas Lincoln, worked hard to raise crops in the stony soil of his little farm.

   _____ _____ _____ _____ _____

   _____ _____ _____ _____ _____

   _____ _____ _____ _____ _____

3. Cover or remove the displayed sentence and have students, as a group, generate a summary from memory. After the summary statement has been created, reveal and reread the sentence. Students can decide at that time to revise their statement. Do not evaluate the statement or interfere with the group decision. Once the students are satisfied with their statement, go on to step 4. One summary statement for the first sentence might appear as

Abe's	hard-working	father	raised	crops
on	his	farm.		

4. Ask students to read the first two sentences and retell them using the same 15-word limit as they had for just the first sentence.

5. Have students create a summary statement for sentences one and two that is no longer than 15 words. Again have students revise until they are satisfied from memory of the text. Then allow them to look at the text before proceeding to the next step. The new summary statement might look like this:

Abe's	hard-working	father	raised	crops
on	his	farm	and	his
mother	kept	house.		

6. Continue in the same manner for the rest of the paragraph. Students will soon realize that they are using up their allotted 15 words too quickly and will need to think of new ways to combine information, as well as to decide what information is most important to keep. The summary statement for the next two sentences might become

Abe's	hard-working	parents	provided	a
well-kept	house	and	food	from
crops	raised	or	from	hunting.

7. Now that students are becoming adept at sentence-by-sentence summarizing, have them write paragraph summaries using short passages. Explain to students that the procedures are the same, except the number of words they can use is now 20.

This technique can be motivating for students if not overly used. Pretending to write telegraph messages is another way to create summary statements. When each word used costs money, it becomes more critical to focus on and choose only the most important ideas for a summary. (Also see "Writing in the Content Areas" in Chapter 7 for more information on writing summaries.)

Reciprocal Teaching

reciprocal teaching ●

Reciprocal teaching is an interactive procedure that fosters comprehension by helping students actively monitor their thinking (Rosenshine & Meister, 1994). Students are taught to summarize text, anticipate questions, clarify unclear text, and make predictions about upcoming text. During reciprocal teaching, you demonstrate how to monitor reading comprehension, how to observe the thinking process while reading, and how to determine when reading is successful and when it is not (Palincsar, 1987; Palincsar & Herrenkohl, 2002). Then you would ask the students to attempt the same activities on their own, offering them feedback on their performance. Your involvement remains high until students can summarize and ask main idea questions on their own.

WWW

Reciprocal Teaching General Information
www.ncrel.org/sdrs/areas/issues/students/ atrisk/at6lk38.htm

ACTIVITY *Reciprocal Teaching* (FOCUS ON CONTENT AND PROCESS)

This activity requires extensive modeling and guidance from the teacher and is initially conducted as follows:

DURING READING

1. Read a paragraph from a passage of text, usually expository, aloud. (*Note:* As students learn these procedures, they will work in small groups, with each student taking on the teacher role for each new paragraph; thus the term *reciprocal.* At that point, reading will be done silently, or with partners in the case of struggling readers.)

AFTER READING

2. Model how the paragraph might be summarized. Focus on the main ideas in the paragraph, include the topic sentence, and point out that a summary should be no more than one-third the length of the original paragraph.

3. Ask the group an important question about the paragraph, one that focuses on the key issue. Solicit other questions from the group.

4. Think aloud about any unclear concepts or new vocabulary. Attempt to determine meanings from context. Also think about the need for clarifying information that might help students to understand the paragraph more completely. (*Note:* This step is not always necessary for well-written

paragraphs that are appropriate for the reader's skill level.) Solicit other ideas about what information might be needed.

5. Predict aloud what might be expected to be in the next paragraph or in the remainder of the passage. Explain the reason for this prediction. Solicit other predictions from the group.

6. Proceed to the next paragraph. According to Palincsar and Brown (1984, 1986), these modeling sessions should last about 30 minutes.

Dyad Reading

Dyad reading is a form of paired oral reading (also called "buddy reading," "partner reading," or "say something") that has the added dimension of reinforcing the important comprehension strategies of summarizing and questioning (Cecil, 1995).

● dyad reading

Dyad Reading (FOCUS ON CONTENT)

ACTIVITY

This activity consists of the following format:

DURING READING

1. Select two students to demonstrate the activity. Have one read a sentence or a paragraph aloud.

2. As that student reads, have the other student listen carefully and then summarize (orally or in writing) what was in the sentence or paragraph. For variation, the second student may simply draw what was read and then describe the picture.

AFTER READING

3. Have the reader ask the listener critical comprehension questions.

4. Encourage the students to discuss the answers and, where there is disagreement, have them refer to the text selection to support their answers.

5. Have the students change roles with succeeding material.

Question–Answer Relationships

Question–answer relationships, or QARs (Raphael, 1982), help students enhance their comprehension by learning to answer a range of questions and understand each question's relationship to the text, to the author, and to themselves (i.e., in the book, in my head). With this strategy, students ask themselves, "Where would I find an answer to this question in the text?" Use the following hierarchy of questions and answers to help them decide.

● question–answer relationships

Literal question (right there). The answer is "right there." This tells the student that the answer to the question is easy to find in the text. In fact, the exact words in the question are contained within the text.

Inferential question (think and search). The answer can be found if you "think and search" or "put it together." This tells the student that the answer is in the text, but two ideas will have to be brought together; that is, the words used in the question may be a bit different from the words used in the text and span several paragraphs or chapters, so the answer will be slightly harder to find.

Critical question (author and you). The answer is in the mind of "the author and me." The answer is not directly stated in the text, but if students bring their own ideas to the text and combine them with the opinion the author seems to hold, they will be able to answer the question.

Creative question (on my own). The answer has to be determined "on my own." The student will not find a direct answer to the question in the text. There is a wide range of correct answers to the question; the answer must emanate from the student's imagination or from information he already has about the topic.

Raphael and Au (2005) describe the potential for QARs as a framework for comprehension instruction and an aid for helping students with test preparation. By delineating the comprehension strategies associated with each of the four types of QARs, Raphael and Au provide a guide for alerting students to the task demands of the questions they will face both in their daily work and in the high-stakes tests they must take.

ACTIVITY   *QARs* (FOCUS ON CONTENT AND PROCESS)

Following is an outline of how students can be guided to incorporate the use of these questions to boost their own comprehension:

BEFORE READING

1. Give students four passages with questions for which the question types have already been determined. (Figure 5.3 shows a sample QAR lesson using a passage from a well-known nursery rhyme to help students identify the question types.)
2. Using the first passage, model how the answers to each question might be found in the text by identifying the appropriate QAR.

DURING READING

3. Read the second passage aloud to students. Ask the questions aloud and have volunteers explain which kind of question is being asked and how they would find the answer in the text.

DURING/AFTER READING

4. Divide the class into small cooperative groups. Ask them to read the third passage and answer the questions, identifying the appropriate QARs.
5. Using the fourth passage, have students follow the same procedure individually, while going around the classroom offering assistance as needed.
6. Follow-up would consist of practicing with questions such as those found in Figure 5.3.

An introductory QAR lesson must first define all the question types. Using the familiar nursery rhyme "Jack and Jill," examine the following questions to note the characteristics of each type.

Jack and Jill went up the hill
to fetch a pail of water.
Jack fell down and broke his crown
and Jill came tumbling after.

1. Where did Jack and Jill go?
   Response: Up the hill to get some water
   QAR: Right there

2. Did Jill get the pail of water?
   Response: No, she fell down the hill too.
   QAR: Putting it together (or think and search)

3. What could have caused Jack's crown to break in his fall down the hill?
   Response: I bet the pail full of water hit him in the head.
   QAR: Author and me

   Or

   What happened to Jill?
   Response: She fell down the hill after Jack did and hurt herself too because when she fell, she rolled right into Jack.
   QAR: Author and me

4. Do you think Jack and Jill ever got the pail of water they went up the hill to get?
   Response: I think they got the water but it all spilled out when they fell down the hill. Then they were too badly hurt to go back up to get more water.
   QAR: On my own

QAR sample passage and question types.   **FIGURE** **5.3**

Novel Study

You can apply all of the previous strategies in the curricular framework of the novel study. **Novel study** refers to the in-depth reading and interpretation of a novel (or a group of stories by one author), addressing both efferent (reading for information) and aesthetic (reading for enjoyment) dimensions. Common goals of novel studies are (1) to introduce students to quality literature, (2) to teach students to interpret literature and see meaning and relevance in a variety of genres, and (3) to familiarize students with the various literary awards.

- novel study

For example, one middle school bases its reading instruction on novel studies, which the teachers term "anchor units" because the content is anchored in the grade level standards, benchmarks, and indicators from their state curriculum. Each anchor unit is designed to take four to five weeks to complete. The novels or stories are specifically chosen for grade-appropriate reading levels, high interest for students, and experiences with multiple genres in grades 6–8. Using novel studies geared more to a connection with a benchmark or indicator skill, rather than a retelling of the book, also allows the teachers to use additional texts, including informational books, on occasion to accommodate special needs students, or those whose parents may object on personal grounds to a particular author or text. The texts listed in Table 5.1 are currently used in the anchor units.

One teacher did a novel study after completing the Grade 8 unit on Edgar Allan Poe. The group read "Annabel Lee," "The Raven," "The Tell-Tale Heart," "The Pit and the Pendulum," "The Fall of the House of Usher," "The Murders at the Rue Morgue," "The Purloined Letter," and "The Masque of the Red Death." In each story the emphasis was on the setting, the mood, and the symbolism found or inferred in the text. Context clues to help determine meanings of unknown words addressed the grade level word study emphasis, and practice worksheets were given at seventh- and eighth-grade reading levels. The group also read a nonfiction article that summarized symptoms, causes, and treatments of clinical depression. Students wrote reading responses to each Poe work read, watched an A & E video on Poe's life while taking notes using different graphic organizers, and kept an ongoing chart that summarized story information about the setting, mood, symbolism, and theme of each story.

Following the novel study, students applied their understanding of mood, symbolism, theme, and context clues to a final assessment on "Goodbye, Grandma," by Ray Bradbury. Questions were written in multiple choice, short

WWW

Example for Grades 4–8 of _A Company of Fools_
www.fitzhenry.ca/Download/guides/Companyof
FoolsTG.pdf

Rainbow Horizons Publishing
(for one free unit of choice)
www.rainbowhorizons.com

Novel Studies Links
www.edselect.com/novel_studies.htm

TABLE 5.1 Texts used for anchor units in grades 4–8.

TEXT	AUTHOR	DATE	GENRE	THEME/TOPIC
Grade 4				
The Kid in the Red Jacket	Barbara Park	1987	Realistic Fiction	Moving/Household/Humor
Jackie Robinson Breaks the Color Line	Andrew Santella	1996	Nonfiction/ Biography	Discrimination in sports/Baseball
Sadako and the Thousand Paper Cranes	Eleanor Coerr	1977	Historical Fiction	Hiroshima/Atomic bomb/Bombardment 1945/Leukemia in children/Death/ Psychological effect
The Cricket in Times Square	George Selden	1960	Fiction/Fantasy	Times Square, New York/Friendship/ Adventure/Crickets

(continued)

TEXT	AUTHOR	DATE	GENRE	THEME/TOPIC
Grade 5				
Sign of the Beaver	Elizabeth George Speare	1983	Historical Fiction	Frontier/Pioneer life/Survival/North American Indians/Friendship
George Washington's Socks	Elvira Woodruff	1991	Historical Fiction	U.S. Revolution, 1775–1783/George Washington/Space and time
Endurance: Shackleton's Antarctic Expedition	Janice Marriott	1995	Nonfiction	Survival/Endurance/Discovery and exploration
Mrs. Frisby and the Rats of NIMH	Robert O'Brien	1971	Fiction/Fantasy	Heroism/Friendship/Mice/Rats
Grade 6				
Maniac Magee	Jerry Spinelli	1990	Realistic Fiction	Legends/Athletes/Orphans
The Acorn People	Ron Jones	1977	Nonfiction	Children with disabilities
Where the Red Fern Grows	Wilson Rawls	1998	Realistic Fiction	Dogs/Hunting/Ozark Mountains
The Devil's Arithmetic	Jane Yolen	1988	Fiction/Fantasy	Jews/Concentration camps/Time travel/Poland–occupation 1939–1945
Grade 7				
House of Dies Drear	Virginia Hamilton	1968	Historical Fiction/ Mystery	Underground Railroad/African Americans/Mystery
City of Light, City of Dark	Avi	1993	Science Fiction/ Fantasy	Graphic Novel
No Promises in the Wind	Irene Hunt	1970	Historical Fiction	Great Depression/Family life
The Titanic	Daniel Harmon/ Victoria Sherrow	2001/ 1999	Nonfiction	Shipwrecks/Disasters
Grade 8 (Poe's works)				
My Brother Sam Is Dead	James Lincoln Collier and Christopher Collier	1974	Historical Fiction	Revolutionary War, 1775–1783
Izzy Willy Nilly	Cynthia Voight	1986	Fiction	People with disabilities/Amputees
Tangerine	Edward Bloor	1997	Fiction	Physical handicaps/Brothers/Soccer
The Pigman and Me	Paul Zindel	1992	Fiction	Social life/Customs
Driver's Ed	Caroline Cooney	1994	Biography	Children and youth

answer, and extended response formats, which mirrors the format of the state achievement test. Students also completed an individual project about Poe independently. Students chose one of five design options, which were offered to accommodate multiple intelligences. Students

1. created a poster on Poe's life and works,
2. wrote a horror story in the style of Poe,
3. wrote three poems in the style of Poe,
4. created four illustrations for one of Poe's stories (since the texts are not illustrated), or
5. found three poems not read in class and prepared to read them aloud to the class with musical accompaniment, using instrumental music appropriate for the mood of the poem.

The final assignment was the writing of a five-paragraph essay about Poe's life and works, using the graphic organizers and discussion from the previous four weeks. Projects and essays were graded using rubrics that students received prior to the due date (M. Daniels, personal communication, October 29, 2007). For additional examples of novel studies, see the websites listed on page 152.

IMPLICIT INSTRUCTION

In addition to direct instruction in comprehension strategies, students learn to comprehend through more implicit types of instruction. Implicit instruction includes independent reading and activities that are often called *reader response activities* (Beach, 1993). There is much overlap between independent reading and reader response activities, as you will see in the section on literature circles and book clubs.

Independent Reading

Students need to be given time to read if we expect them to be able to practice using comprehension strategies and simply to enjoy reading. Independent reading is a central factor to developing lifelong enjoyment of reading. According to the landmark study *Becoming a Nation of Readers* (Anderson et al., 1985), "Children should spend more time in independent reading. Independent reading, whether in school or out of school, is associated with gains in reading achievement. By the time they are in third or fourth grade, children should read independently a minimum of two hours per week. Children's reading should include classic and modern works of fiction and nonfiction" (p. 119).

Graphic novels

graphic novels ●

For students reluctant to read traditional works of fiction or nonfiction, graphic novels may hold some appeal. **Graphic novels** are book-length (130 to 150 pages) comics usually published in softcover. The highly visual, action-oriented story lines of many graphic novels can serve to increase student interest. "A student *reads* the words, *sees* the action, *comprehends* the meaning, and is motivated to read more. It's an end that justifies the means" (McTaggert, 2006, p. 2). And as Kiefer (1995) states, "the visual art . . . can illuminate such devices as character development, elaboration, mood, point of view, irony, and satire" (p. 184). *Anime* and *manga* are words associated with the visual art of graphic novels. **Anime,** a Japanese word for animation, refers to an art form that makes inanimate objects look like they are moving (see Figure 5.4). **Manga** is a highly stylized and intricate Japanese art form that has become a label for the Japanese print comic that has become quite popular among girls. These Japanese comics are read from back to front and from left to right. Graphic novels can be the start some students need to engage in other forms of reading and to avoid becoming aliterates. See suggested websites for more information about graphic novels and Appendix A for suggested titles.

- anime
- manga

WWW

Graphic Novel Resources
*www.graphicnovels.brodart.com/
selection_criteria.htm*
www.noflyingnotights.com

Book contracts

Teachers who are held more accountable for how students spend their independent reading time and for encouraging reader response may wish to consider the concept of a book contract. A **book contract** is a packet of required and alternative activities, such as the following: journal writing; cross-curricular activities that involve art, science, math, and/or social studies projects; and author research, from which a student will choose in order to fulfill a contract with the teacher (see the Extension Activities in Figure 5.6).

- book contract

Anime and manga series, available by the thousands online, may stimulate interest in reading for some students resistant to more traditional print formats.   **FIGURE** 5.4

Source: www.animevenue.com

The student may be expected to complete 6 of 8 activities, but the student will choose the 6 that she wishes to complete. The required activities usually consist of a chart for documenting the pages read each day, a page for maintaining new vocabulary, and any other documentation that you may be responsible for collecting. The packet may include a cover page made from a photocopy of the book's cover for the student to personalize (N. L. Cecil, personal communication, July 26, 2002). Book contracts can be helpful to the teacher in individualizing instruction because there can be several different book contracts at different readability levels functioning at the same time.

Literature circles and book clubs

literature circles •

book clubs •

Daniels (2002) defines **literature circles** as "small, peer-led discussion groups whose members have chosen to read the same story, poem, article, or book. While reading each group-assigned portion, members make notes to help them contribute to the upcoming discussion, and everyone comes to the group with ideas to share" (p. 2). **Book clubs** are student-led groups whose members read literary selections, write reactions and questions in a reading response log, and engage in both small-group and whole-class discussions (McMahon & Raphael, 1997).

Though literature circles and book clubs are not exactly the same thing, they are more alike than different. They both recognize the social nature of learning and the transactional nature of the reading process. Their success depends on students being given a choice of material to read and discuss with peers. In this way, the text read is reentered and explored by a group of readers for a more thorough and complete understanding. The discussion group negotiates the meaning of the text, combines and connects ideas, and constructs meaning that one person reading alone might not ever achieve.

Literature circles and book clubs are especially beneficial for English learners, helping these students feel more a part of a community and the American culture and encouraging them to engage in comfortable talk about books. English learners hear natural oral language when native English speakers talk about the books and pay closer attention to the way their English-speaking classmates use English within the relaxed setting of the literature circle (Hadaway, Vardell, & Young, 2004). Feelings of anxiety about speaking before the whole class are diminished. Everyone in the literature circle has a turn to speak, so English learners gain much needed practice in using the language.

Literature circles and book clubs usually involve a written component—individual readers maintain written logs, also called reader response logs, that document special passages or issues, or they place stick-on notes with brief comments on particular pages that will be shared with group members. Readers also document interpretations of their reading with sketches, illustrations, and diagrams. Often teachers will initiate literature circles by using role sheets as a "getting started" tool for helping students understand how to participate in peer-led discussion groups (see Figure 5.5). The book club program has four components: daily reading in a book of one's choice, daily writing in a journal or log related to the reading, student-led discussion groups, and community share—the whole class component. This last component provides the opportunity for you to model for, or explicitly teach, your students how to lead and maintain good group discussions, as well as suggest ideas for what to write in a journal (Raphael, 2000).

DISCUSSION LEADER	CONNECTOR
Develop a set of questions that you will ask your group members to discuss in regard to the material you read for today. Think about what your own feelings are or areas that confused or concerned you. Ask questions about what was read, or try some general questions such as, How did you feel about what you read? Did it remind you of anything? Were you surprised by anything? What do you think were the most important ideas?	Make connections between what you read and your life experiences. You might make a connection to something you experienced as a student, or to something that has happened in the community, in another place or time, or to other people. You could also make a connection to something else that you have read. Sharing these connections with your group members may help to trigger other connections that they can share.

VOCABULARY MASTER	SUMMARIZER
Choose three or four words from the reading that you find especially important, interesting, unusual, confusing, or totally new. Try to learn as much as you can about these words. Learn what they mean, and then help your group members learn these words also.	In a one- or two-minute statement, summarize what today's reading was about. Focus only on the main points and give the essence of the reading assignment. You might wish to list the main points if there are several.

ARTIST	LITERARY LUMINARY
Draw a picture, sketch, diagram, or cartoon that is related to what you read. The drawing should be a representation of what the text was about. Show the drawing to your group members without telling them what it means to you. After they each have had a chance to say what they think it means, tell them what you intended.	Locate one or two special sections of today's reading. There might be a part of the reading that is especially interesting, funny, sad, confusing, controversial, thought-provoking, or important. Decide which parts are worth rereading or revisiting. Then think about how to share them again with your group members. You might wish to read them aloud, or have group members reread them silently and follow up with a discussion.

Source: Adapted from Daniels, 2002.

Role descriptions for book club discussions. FIGURE 5.5

Literature Circles/Book Clubs ACTIVITY

Literature circles and book clubs are powerful activities for readers in grades 4–8 because these "students find that peers provide important support for their comprehension and interpretation of text, and that the literate activities . . . help develop their ownership over literacy" (Raphael, 2000, p. 85). Steps for implementing literature circles and book clubs follow:

BEFORE READING

1. Provide students with a selection of books from which they can choose to read and discuss with classmates (see Table 5.2). This list can include informational books, ebooks, and graphic novels. Titles can be presented

WWW

Top Ten Young Adult Books
www.ala.org/ala/yalsa/yalsa.cfm

Annual IRA Children's Choices, Teachers' Choices, and Young Adults' Choices
http://reading.org/resources/tools/choices.html

Bookfinder (search by theme)
www.literatureplace.com/awards/book_finder_ by_subject.asp

Lesson example: "Give Them a Hand: Promoting Positive Interaction in Literature Circles"
www.readwritethink.org/lessons/lesson_view.asp? id=1078

in the form of a book talk (reading aloud a brief selection and/or sharing positive impressions from a book to arouse interest in reading the book). Students can freely choose a book, but sometimes a student will have to make a second choice if no one else chooses the same book. The optimum discussion group should have four or five members to ensure "a variety of perspectives on the text, a range of responses that enlivens discussion" (Daniels, 2002, p. 19).

Book selection is critical for ensuring vibrant and meaningful discussions. It is important that the books relate to students' lives and their interests, but the books offered for student choice must also encourage positive discussion strategies (Clarke & Holwadel, 2007). Table 5.2 presents a sample of books that inspire good discussions. For help in choosing quality literature, and for a lesson example, visit the suggested websites.

2. Have students choose their books and meet with others reading the same book to determine how much they will read for their first discussion meeting. Meetings are regularly scheduled, daily or weekly, and should allow at least 30 to 45 minutes for group discussion.

TABLE 5.2   **Short list of books recommended by and for students in grades 4–8.**

TITLE/DATE	GENRE/THEME	AUTHOR/PUBLISHER	NOTES
Double Dutch (2002)	Realistic fiction/Social acceptance/Friendship/Dyslexia	Sharon M. Draper/Atheneum	Text-to-self connections are readily made with the focus on the fear of not fitting in. Delia, Randy, and YoYo reveal their secrets as they prepare for a jump rope competition.
The Slave Dancer (2001, revised format)	Historical fiction/Slavery	Paula Fox/Atheneum	This Newbery Medal book provides information about the history of slavery and what it was like to be a slave through the experiences of 13-year-old Jessie.
Travels of Thelonious: The Fog Mound (2006)	Fiction/Adventure	Susan Schade and Jon Buller/Simon & Schuster	Thelonious Chipmunk, along with a bear, a porcupine, and a lizard, sets out to prove that humans once inhabited the earth. Alternating chapters of prose and graphic novel appeal to reluctant readers.
Crossing the Wire (2006)	Realistic fiction/Illegal immigrants/Survival/Mexicans/Friendship	Will Hobbs/HarperCollins	Fifteen-year-old Victor crosses the Arizona border to work in the United States in an effort to support his family.

(continued)

TITLE/DATE	GENRE/THEME	AUTHOR/PUBLISHER	NOTES
Sand Dollar Summer (2006)	Realistic fiction/ Coming of age/Family	Kimberly K. Jones/ Simon & Schuster	Twelve-year-old Lise's formerly safe world becomes complicated after her mother's accident and by other personal and environmental obstacles.
Hana's Suitcase (2002)	Biography/Holocaust	Karen Levine/Albert Whitman & Co.	After Fumiko Ishioka, the curator of a children's Holocaust museum, receives the suitcase of a Czech girl, he researches the history of the suitcase and tells the story of Hana through alternating chapters.
Peter and the Star Catchers (2004)	Fantasy/Friendship/ Good versus evil	David Berry and Ridley Pearson/ Hyperion	This seafaring adventure serves as a prequel to J. M. Barrie's *Peter Pan,* revealing a secret about a chest full of a substance that can make people fly.
Locomotion (2003)	Juvenile poetry/ Self-discovery/African American boys/Orphans	Jacqueline Woodson/ G. P. Putnam's Sons	Lonnie discovers his own poetic voice when he has to adjust to the death of his parents and separation from his sister.
The Curious Incident of the Dog in the Night (2004)	Realistic fiction/Autism/ Coping with loss	Mark Haddon/ Doubleday	Both a mystery and a comedy, this novel explores an autistic boy's reactions to emotional losses.
Al Capone Does My Shirts (2004)	Historical fiction/Family problems/Responsibility	Gennifer Choldenko/ G. P. Putnam's Sons	The story of 12-year-old Moose Flanagan and his life on Alcatraz during the 1930s.
The Time Hackers (2005)	Science fiction/Space and time/Computer games	Gary Paulsen/Wendy Lamb Books	Futuristic technology is used to play practical jokes on seventh grader Dorso Clayman. He and his good friend journey through space and time to stop the pranksters.
Hearts of Stone (2005)	Historical fiction/ U.S. Civil War/Family/ Personal cost of war/ Sacrifice	Kathleen Ernst/ Dutton Juvenile	Fourteen-year-old Hannah becomes head of her household when her mother dies in a raid and her father joins the Union forces. This is the story of Hannah and her siblings' 200-mile journey to a relative's house.
Something About America (2005)	Poetry/Immigrants/ National characteristics/ Children of immigrants	Maria Testa/ Candlewick	Told in simple verse, this is the tale of an eighth-grader who fled to the U.S. eight years earlier with her parents to escape Kosovo. It is a tale of fear, starting over again, hope, and challenge.

DURING READING

3. Have students read the agreed-upon pages of the text. For the written preparation, have students record their comments about the text, listing important page numbers, drawing pictures, noting difficult words or passages, making connections to their own lives, and developing questions to ask their group members. The nature of these comments is an individual one; however, they should help prepare the student for the upcoming group discussion.

AFTER READING

4. Have groups meet to discuss their reading. Students generally take turns leading the discussion, but all students must be involved. At the end of the discussion, have students decide on the amount of reading for the next discussion period. At this point, how well the groups are functioning and whether each member is participating fully should be apparent. The student-led discussions can indicate areas that need to be addressed during community share (book club) or whole-class sharing.

5. Have the whole class meet to listen to what the other groups have been discussing. This also provides an opportunity for you to offer explicit instruction or scaffolding.

6. If desired, ask students to complete self-assessments at the end of each discussion, or at the end of a complete book, to evaluate their own goals, roles, and performance as a group member.

ACTIVITY ## Jigsaw: Read a Book in an Hour

Teachers in grades 4–8 find it especially difficult to provide the depth of coverage necessary to achieve thorough understanding for the breadth of content knowledge expected. One approach that takes full advantage of collaborative working groups for the purpose of learning new material is jigsawing (Aronson & Patnoe, 1997). A specific jigsaw activity called Read a Book in an Hour (Cecil, 1990; Childrey, 1980) allows students to share responsibility for reading specific material. The material is divided into small portions and assigned to members of the class to read. Later, class members share the information to achieve the whole of the material. In other words, an individual student, or partnership, takes the responsibility of reading and learning a small amount of material well enough to summarize it for others, and as this information is shared, all members of the class learn the required material.

BEFORE READING

1. Identify a topic of study and its components along with books that correspond to the topic of study (see earlier discussion of novel studies). Then develop a sign-up list that identifies enough "portions" for all members of the class to be involved.

2. Have students sign up for, or assign them, one portion of the topic/material/novel.

DURING READING

3. Allow students ample time to read the material.

4. Students are responsible for understanding the material for which they are accountable. Instruct them to identify and learn new vocabulary and concepts. Ask them to formulate ideas for how to present this information to classmates. Also ask them to speculate about what may have happened or been discussed in the sections before or after their portion.

AFTER READING

5. Have "expert" groups (those who have read the same material) come together and prepare for their "teaching" of the new material. This might involve preparing visuals, as well as an oral presentation. Conferencing with the teacher is acceptable.

6. Have students present their material and answer questions.

While jigsawing is typically used with expository material, the modification, Read a Book in an Hour, can be used with narrative material for the express purpose of engaging students with a literary piece that they might not otherwise read on their own. Often students in upper grades are required to read particular works of literature as part of state content standards. Many students do not have either the confidence in themselves or the motivation to complete these required texts. Using this strategy, which adapts the jigsaw concept, enables these students to participate more fully in reading these texts. The anticipated benefit of this experience is that students will get a sense of the entire piece and thus have the schema necessary to read the book on their own, confident that they will be successful. And, much like book talk activities, by using high-quality literature, this technique will increase students' interest and desire to read the entire book on their own. A sample Read a Book in an Hour lesson with suggestions for integrating other areas of the curriculum is presented in Figure 5.6.

Reader Response Activities

Support for reader response activities as part of a comprehensive program for comprehension instruction is based on the work of Vygotsky (1978, 1986) and Rosenblatt (1938, 1969, 1978, 1983, 1994). Vygotsky's work views comprehension as socially constructed through negotiation among text, readers, teachers, and other members of the classroom community; Rosenblatt's work views comprehension as the result of the interaction, or transaction, between the reader and the text. Rosenblatt (1969) proposes a transactional theory in which the meaning of a text derives from the transaction between the text and the reader within a specific context. Rosenblatt (1938) eloquently described this concept many years prior to proposing the transactional theory:

> The special meaning, and more particularly, the submerged associations that these words and images have for the individual reader will largely determine what the work communicates to him. The reader brings to the work personality traits, memories of past events, present needs and preoccupations, a particular mood of the moment, and a particular physical condition. These and many other elements . . . determine his response to the peculiar contribution of the text. (pp. 30–31)

FIGURE 5.6   "Read a Book in an Hour": Example lesson and book contract activities.

Book: *The Summer of the Swans,* by Betsy Byars. Grade Level: 6th

Goals: To help students learn how to summarize and how to develop one key question from a passage; to encourage students to read *The Summer of the Swans* in its entirety on their own.

Content Standard(s): Reading-Language Arts Content Standard 2.4: Clarifying an understanding of texts by creating outlines, logical notes, summaries, or reports; and Standard 3.2: Analyzing the effect of the qualities of the character on the plot and the resolution of the conflict.

FACTORS TO BE CONSIDERED:

1. Motivation for the lesson cannot give away the story line.
2. Students should be grouped according to their reading abilities.
3. The number of chapters and the number of students should be compatible.
4. Books should have dramatic intensity and be of high literary quality; those that are very predictable are not good choices.

OTHER STORIES BY BETSY BYARS:

The Eighteenth Emergency and *Pinballs*

OTHER STORIES ABOUT DISABILITIES:

Take Wing, by Jean Little, and *A Racecourse for Andy,* by Patricia Wrightson

ANTICIPATORY SET/MOTIVATION:

Relate feelings of awkwardness, loneliness, or simply being different. "Is everyone the same? Is it wrong to be different? Are people always happy? Have you ever felt you weren't good enough? Or simply that you just can't fit in? I'd like to introduce you to a girl named Sara and let's see what problems she encounters and how she attacks and solves her problems."

THE PROCESS:

1. Pair students and assign chapters/sections.
2. Tell students that partners may move to another location while doing their paired reading but must return to their seats when the reading is completed.

3. Remind the class of the rules for partner reading, which include shoulder-to-shoulder reading and a *12-inch voice* (voice cannot be heard beyond 12 inches from mouth) maximum.
4. Read the first chapter to the entire group to establish setting.

SUMMARIZING:

5. Review the meaning of *to summarize.* Summaries should be no more than 2 minutes long.
6. Summarize the chapter and ask a prediction question for the upcoming section. Students are now ready to do their paired reading and prepare their summaries and a prediction question from their assigned section. *Note:* The prediction question is posed to the following group during the sharing phase.

THE PROCESS CONTINUES:

7. Once students have read their sections and prepared their summary and prediction question, allow the process to continue. This should take about 15 to 20 minutes depending on the reading abilities and the length of the chapters assigned.
8. Repeat the prediction question to the first group. The first group then addresses the question and answers, if possible, and summarizes their reading. (These summaries may be written down and read, read from a prepared outline, or merely recited from memory, depending on the grade level.) This group then asks their prediction question to the following pair.
9. Allow the process to continue until the last group has participated.
10. For the last chapter, either read it aloud or assign it to the students to read.

COMPREHENSION CHECK:

- Literal
   1. What made Charlie leave his home in the middle of the night?
   2. Why did Sara dislike Joe Melby?
   3. What did Charlie lose while he was lost?

4. Why was Aunt Willie nervous when Frank came to pick up Sara's sister, Wanda?

- Inferential

  1. Is Sara happy at the end of the story? Why do you think so?

  2. Why did Sara decide to accept Joe Melby's invitation to Benny Hoffman's party?

  3. Why do you think Sara knew that Charlie had gone out in the night to see the swans and that he had taken the one he had into the forest?

- Critical

  1. What does it mean to care more about someone else than you care about yourself?

  2. Often characteristics are revealed about a person when he or she reacts to a situation. When Gretchen called Charlie a "retard," Sara squirted water on her. When Sara believed Joe had stolen Charlie's watch, she became angry at Joe and would not believe him when he denied being the thief. What do these incidents tell you about Sara?

  3. On page 140, Betsy Byars writes that Sara "suddenly saw life as a series of huge, uneven steps." What do you think the author meant by this?

  4. Could Charlie really relate to the swans? Why or why not?

- Creative

  1. Charlie found the place where the swans were to be beautiful and serene. Create and describe a place that you think would be like this, a place where you might go at a time like this.

  2. Create a character who is in a situation that makes him or her feel awkward or out of place. Describe the situation and help the character cope with his or her feelings.

  3. Describe Aunt Willie's next ride on a motor scooter. Will she ever ride solo?

  4. What happened to Sara at the party? Did she enjoy herself?

ENRICHMENT ACTIVITIES:

1. Reread the entire novel on your own.

2. Keep a diary for Sara during the summer that Charlie is lost. Write entries for her dated at the beginning of the summer, during Charlie's absence, and at the end of the summer. Show her cares and concerns. Does she mature?

**EXTENSION ACTIVITIES TO CHOOSE
FROM FOR BOOK CONTRACT:**

- Art

  1. Using poster paints, mix the paints to create puce (brownish-purple) and then paint a picture using this new color.

  2. Create a mobile of scenes from *Summer of the Swans* (swans, lakes, puce tennis shoes, watch, Sara, Charlie, etc.)

- Science

  3. Prepare a research report on birds and swans.

  4. It became very cold the night Charlie was lost. Conduct a study of weather and why temperature drops at night. Record at least six daytime and six nighttime outdoor temperatures for a week, but try to use the same times of day.

- Math

  5. Graph the outdoor temperatures from their science work in choice #4.

  6. Solve math problems finding kilometers walked by Sara, Joe, and Charlie. (The problems use decimals and the directions north, south, east, and west.)

- Social Studies

  7. Author Betsy Byars used West Virginia for the location of her story. Conduct a study of the geography of West Virginia. Decide where in the state the story took place, and write a paper supporting this answer.

  8. Conduct research on disabilities. Then choose one and write a paper on that one disability.

The instructional frameworks and strategies that follow support the development of comprehension through independent reading.

Students can respond to what they read in an infinite number of ways. Many teachers and students are already familiar with written forms of responding, such as journals, paraphrases, and summaries. Students also write letters to authors, or to a character in a story that they have read. Some students write as if they were the character in the story. Personal essays, poems, scripts for a readers theatre, and short stories are additional forms of written response. There are spoken forms of response as well. In addition to readers theatre, students might be asked to teach the text, or discuss in small groups, retell the text, or role play. Engaging in panel discussions or in a student–teacher conference are also spoken ways of responding to text. Finally, there are visual ways to respond that involve artistic endeavor and the use of graphic organizers.

ACTIVITY   *Sketch to Stretch*

In Sketch to Stretch (Harste et al., 1988), students create a simple line drawing that depicts their interpretation of the material read. This sketch is then shared with a small group of peers who give their interpretations of each other's sketches. For an example lesson for students in grades 4–6, visit the suggested website. The guidelines are as follows:

1. Place students in groups of four or five. Ask them to think about the selection and draw a sketch of what the selection meant to them or what understanding they took from the selection.

2. When sketches are complete, have students in the group share their sketches with the other group members.

www

Lesson using Sketch to Stretch
*www.readwritethink.org/lessons/
lesson_view.asp?id=229*

3. Have the group members give their interpretations of the sketch before the artist tells his or hers. What is important about this activity is that it allows readers who struggle with verbally oriented procedures the opportunity to demonstrate understanding and alternative interpretations. Examples are presented in Figure 5.7.

FIGURE 5.7   **Example sketches for Sketch to Stretch.**

Sketch for *Fox Song*   Sketch for *The Bracelet*

Going Beyond Visualizing

This activity encourages the reader to use all the senses to comprehend and respond to text, not just visualizing. Direct readers to create mental images that involve all of the senses when they read. Using the sentence starters I see . . . , I hear . . . , I feel . . . , I smell . . . , and I taste . . . , ask the students to write, tell, or draw what they saw, heard, felt, smelled, and tasted as they were reading.

The sentences one fifth-grade student generated after reading a *National Geographic* article about sea turtles follow:

I see turtles trying to get to the water. Thousands.

I hear the sound of thumping against their flippers.

I can feel all of the sand kicking into my eyes.

Some turtles died so I can smell the rot.

I can taste other turtles' backs. I can taste sand flinging into my open mouth.

(Harvey & Goudvis, 2000, p. 104)

Graphic Organizers

Graphic organizers, defined in Chapter 4 as visual ways of representing a body of knowledge, can also be used to help students focus their thoughts for responding to text. In general, they help students

- categorize words, ideas, and characters.
- organize a sequence of events.
- compare what they read to something else.
- identify important elements in a text.
- examine the organizational pattern of the information or story read.

Graphic organizers can use only drawings or pictures, only written words, or some combination of both. Examples of a target organizer, so called because of its shape, and a conversational roundtable (Burke, 2000) are presented in Figure 5.8. Here, these graphic organizers compare two versions of the same story and demonstrate story features, respectively, in writing. Drawings could be used instead of words. Generally speaking, organizers are flexible enough to be used for a variety of purposes. For example, the target organizer could also be used for vocabulary development by placing a word such as *independence* in the center of the target and writing other words in the next level that represent varying aspects of this concept. In the outermost circle, synonyms, antonyms, definitions, explanations, or instances of use could be written. Likewise, the conversational roundtable could be used to explore essential and nonessential characteristics, with examples and nonexamples for the concept located in the center circle. Additional examples of graphic organizers can be found in Chapters 4 and 7.

FIGURE   5.8   Graphic organizers: Target organizer and conversational roundtable.

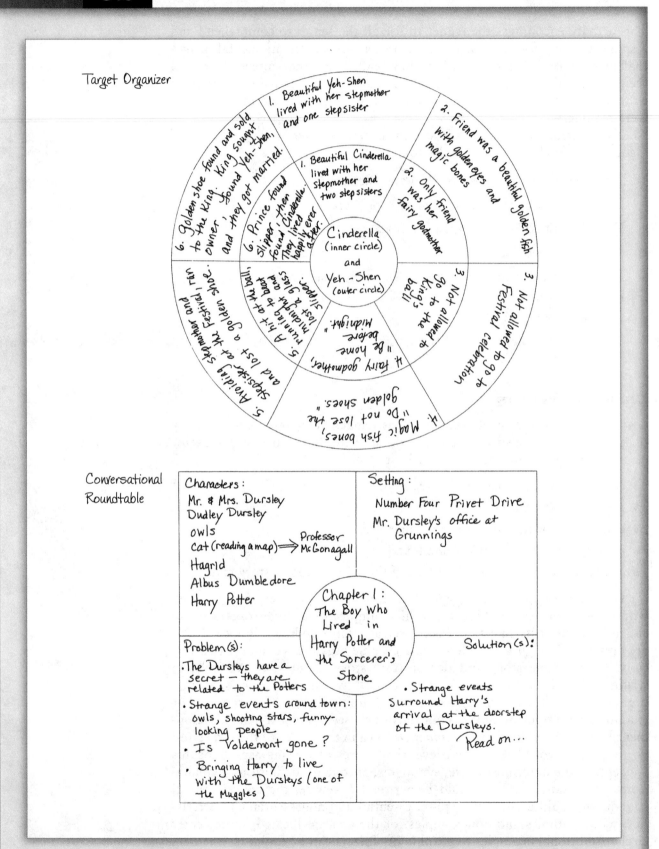

Target Organizer

Conversational Roundtable

READING COMPREHENSION AND THE INTERNET

Since almost 75 percent of young people 12 to 17 years old in the United States regularly use the Internet as a source of information (Lenhart, Madden, & Hitlin, 2005), you must address the topic of reading comprehension in the online environment. Helping students comprehend is a challenge made even more difficult because of the ever-increasing complexities brought about by *new literacies* (O'Brien & Bauer, 2005). According to Johnston and Costello (2005), the advent of "instant messaging, book tapes, cell phone text messaging, speech translation software, interactive hypertext, and the facility with which text and image (moving or still) are fused" (p. 257) has obliterated the boundaries between and the conventions for spoken and written words. As a result, these new technologies, which can be considered literacies, require new skill sets. How to analyze and teach these new skills is still being explored (RAND Reading Study Group, 2002). Furthermore, today's technological tools change so rapidly that you are also continuously confronted with the need to learn new digital literacy skills and new literacy practices.

Students might be challenged to remain motivated and engaged in school practices that have not evolved along with the opportunities afforded by the new literacies (i.e., *the digital disconnect*). An example of a new literacy is the practice of blogging. **Blogging** is the online publication of one's commentary on specific topics of interest (e.g., political, social, and so forth) or of one's personal diary. A key feature of a blog is that it allows readers to respond interactively to its content. Blogging can present opportunities for changing literacy practices in schools (Lankshear & Knobel, 2003). As Coiro (2003) summarizes,

● blogging

> reading on the Internet is different, and our definition of reading comprehension needs to reflect those differences. Our job now is to envision new constructs of reading comprehension that introduce students to strategies for interacting with these new literacies. We must help students appreciate the distinctions of each one and also be willing to explore digital information environments together in more thoughtful ways. (p. 464)

WWW

7th Grade Science Blog
http://newliteracies.typepad.com/science_exchange

RAND Study Group
www.rand.org/multi/achievementforall/reading/readreport.html

The RAND Reading Study Group (2002) suggests the following definition for reading comprehension: "the process of simultaneously extracting and constructing meaning through interaction and involvement with written language" (p. 11). Although this definition seems similar to the traditional notion of reading comprehension, the report goes on to recognize a broad description of text, including electronic text and multimedia documents as well as conventional print. "Electronic text can present particular challenges to comprehension, such as dealing with the nonlinear nature of hypertext, but it also offers the potential for supporting the comprehension of complex texts, for example, through hyperlinks to definitions or translations of difficult words or to paraphrasing of complex sentences" (p. 14). However, the use of electronic text requires skills and abilities different from those required for conventional, linear print (Coiro & Schmar-Dobler, 2005). Skill areas emerging as most important to online reading comprehension and the use of the Internet include (Leu, Kinzer, Coiro, & Cammack, 2004): "identify important questions, locate information, analyze the usefulness of that information, synthesize information to answer those questions, and then communicate the answers to others" (p. 1570). Additionally, a study by Azevedo and Cromley

(2004) provides evidence that instruction in comprehension monitoring (realizing when something read is understood or not, and making needed adjustments to ensure understanding) transfers well to learning in hypermedia.

Reciprocal teaching, a technique already presented in this chapter, is appropriate for reading comprehension instruction using the Internet because it helps develop a high level of self-regulated learning. **Self-regulated learning** (SRL) is a process that requires awareness and application of learning strategies and extensive reflection and self-awareness. Pintrich (1995) describes self-regulation as the "active, goal-directed self-control of behavior, motivation, and cognition for academic tasks by an individual student" (p. 5). Students who are self-regulated learners understand their strengths and weaknesses as learners. They are skilled at recognizing the demands of the specific academic tasks required of them, and they know when they have mastered the tasks or not (Isaacson & Fujita, 2006). For the academic task of reading comprehension, this ability is referred to as comprehension monitoring; thus, comprehension monitoring is closely related to SRL.

• self-regulated learning

A large body of research findings already exists supporting reciprocal teaching as effective for teaching reading comprehension strategies and improving reading comprehension, especially among adolescents (Palincsar & Herrenkohl, 2002; Rosenshine & Meister, 1994). But research by Leu, Castek, Hartman et al., (2005) clearly supports the use of intensive small group instruction especially when using reciprocal teaching for developing online reading comprehension skills. Their research also found that groups receiving special Internet instruction did not outperform groups receiving instruction without access to the Internet on traditional measures of reading comprehension, which perhaps indicates both the need for alternative measures for online reading comprehension and the fact that the skills used during online learning ae different.

Henry (2006) suggests that the most critical skill for online reading is the ability to search for and locate information. She goes on to present and discuss SEARCH, an instructional framework of the most essential skills for searching and locating information on the Internet. These skills are as follows:

Students who are self-regulated learners understand their strengths and weaknesses as learners.

1. Set a purpose for searching.
2. Employ effective search strategies.
3. Analyze search-engine results.
4. Read critically and synthesize information.
5. Cite your sources.
6. How successful was your search? (p. 618)

Current instructional techniques, such as I-Search and clustering (see Chapter 6), K-W-L charts (see Chapter 7), and certain software products (e.g., Inspiration) that help students activate prior knowledge and brainstorm terms and key words, will enhance your students' search strategies. Once material is located, students then need to evaluate the information. Again, traditional techniques, like Question the Author (see "In the Classroom" at the beginning of this chapter), lay the groundwork for evaluating Internet

WWW

Inspiration

www.inspiration.com/productinfo/inspiration/using_
insp/index.cfm?fuseaction=insp_archive

content. More information about the use of technology, specific strategies for locating information, and Internet search skills can be found in Chapter 7.

TROUBLESHOOTING

S tudents of all ages can have difficulty with comprehension for a variety of reasons. Comprehension will obviously be difficult if the reader cannot quickly and automatically pronounce many of the words that he is trying to read. In addition, the reader needs some prior knowledge of the topic being read to be able to adequately comprehend the material. Assuming the reader has access to material at an appropriate level of difficulty, he needs to be able to relate, or make connections, to the text for it to be meaningful. This is why the before-reading strategies are so important—to activate, build, or enhance background knowledge prior to beginning a lesson. Readers who have difficulty with comprehension often are not making meaningful connections to the text. The following recommendations are for those students who have a difficult time making connections to the text.

Difficulty Making Connections Before Reading

Students need to begin thinking about connections to the text even before they start to read. Used before reading, **anticipation guides** consist of a set of three to five statements that serve two basic purposes: (1) to activate the student's background knowledge for the topic by asking the student to either agree or disagree with the statement and be prepared to explain her position, and (2) to provide guidance for the upcoming reading. Anticipation guides are also intended to arouse curiosity about the topic by presenting statements that are potentially controversial or challenging. Students become motivated to read the material to prove their choice or to resolve conceptual conflicts or lack of understanding. The anticipation guide can thus also serve as an after-reading activity, to revisit the statements and allow for changes in viewpoints.

● anticipation guides

You prepare an anticipation guide by

- reading the text to identify the major concepts students should learn.
- considering students' current knowledge about these concepts.
- creating statements in a way that students have sufficient knowledge to understand what they say, but not enough to conceptually understand the statements or the rationale behind them.
- listing the statements in a particular order—one that follows the order presented in the text is usual, but not mandatory.

Once completed, the anticipation guide can be presented as an individual handout accompanied by a visual using an overhead transparency or multimedia. Read aloud the directions and the statements for the students, who should respond individually to each statement by agreeing or disagreeing, and explaining why. In order to do this, students must make connections to their own background knowledge related to the topic they are about to read. A group discussion follows after you tally the responses for agreement and disagreement with each statement. Discussion should include at least one explanation for each point of view. Following this discussion, students read the material, keeping the anticipation guide in mind. After the reading, the students may return to the guide and respond once more. This time they will have the actual text to

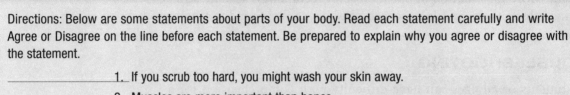

Directions: Below are some statements about parts of your body. Read each statement carefully and write Agree or Disagree on the line before each statement. Be prepared to explain why you agree or disagree with the statement.

_____ 1. If you scrub too hard, you might wash your skin away.

_____ 2. Muscles are more important than bones.

_____ 3. You don't really see with your eyes, but with your brain.

_____ 4. It would be best if you just drank liquids to nourish your body.

FIGURE   5.9   Anticipation guide for use with *Outside and Inside You.*

use to support or refute points expressed in the earlier discussion (Duffelmeyer, 1994; Readence et al., 1998). Figure 5.9 shows an anticipation guide for a book entitled *Outside and Inside You* (Markle, 1991), which is used with struggling readers to help them learn more about their bodies.

Difficulty Making Connections During Reading

Comprehension improves when students actively seek to connect the content of what they read with what they already have experienced or have learned (Brown, 2002). The strategy called "It reminds me of . . ." (Richards & Gipe, 1992) encourages students to make connections verbally between what they read and their background knowledge *while they are reading.* To be able to state what the passage "reminds me of . . ." the student has to make a connection between the material and his own background knowledge.

Model this strategy by reading a portion of a text selection, stopping, and saying aloud, "It reminds me of . . .". Modeling works best if realistic fiction, a memoir, or a version of a familiar tale is used because these will be more likely to provide situations that readers can recall or relate to in their own lives. For example, the story *Fox Song* (Bruchac, 1993) tells of a young girl who is experiencing the recent death of her beloved grandmother. As the girl walks around her community, she is constantly reminded of the things she did with her grandmother, and what she learned from her. After reading an early section of how sad the girl feels when she is told of her grandmother's death, you might say, "It reminds me of the time when I heard my mother on the phone with my grandmother. She had just learned that my grandfather, her father, had died. This sad, empty feeling just came over me." Then students are given the opportunity to respond to the same passage. You might also use just the cover of a book and ruminate about what it reminds you of as a way of modifying this activity for use during prereading. After a few examples, students will soon be able to identify parts in other content with which they connect.

Similarly, you might introduce students to the double entry journal with the specific purpose of making connections to the text being read. Bromley (1993) defines a **double entry journal** as "one in which students keep two separate entries related to the same topic, idea, or activity" (p. 71). The main purpose of the double entry journal is to encourage students to make connections between the material they are reading and their own lives, another text they have already read, or world issues and current events outside the school community. Introduce the double entry journal by first dividing a journal page

double entry journal ●

into two columns and then selecting a quote from an assigned reading. Write the quote in the left column and then model a personal response in the corresponding right column. Then ask your students to read a portion of the material until they find a sentence that causes them to recall a particular event in their own lives. Direct them to write the sentence in the left column and their personal connections in the right column.

It is easiest to introduce double entry journals using personal connections (i.e., text-to-self connections) as a way of responding to text. In addition, Herrell and Jordan (2002) suggest

> As students become more proficient in responding to text, they can be taught to connect other books they have read to the text currently being read. They can also learn to relate current events to reading materials in this same way. In the process they practice writing skills. The discussions that follow the journaling are equally important because they support the students in understanding the impact of life experiences in the way text is interpreted and valued. (p. 99)

See Figure 5.10 for an example of a page from a double entry journal demonstrating a format for making connections to self, to text, and to the world (also see the following section for more on text-to-text and text-to-world connections).

Example page from a double entry journal for making connections.   **FIGURE 5.10**

BOOK	CONNECTIONS
Title: The Giver (Lois Lowry)	Text-to-Me/Text-to-Another Text/Text-to-World
Date: 3/13 Page(s): 1—2 Then all the citizens had been ordered to go into the nearest building and stay there. IMMEDIATELY, the rasping voice through the speakers had said. LEAVE YOUR BICYCLES WHERE THEY ARE.	Me ✓ Another Text ___ World ___ I remember one time when there was a tornado warning while I was at school. We all had to drop everything and go down to the cafeteria because there were no windows there. I was scared because I did not know what would happen.
Date: 3/14 Page(s): 5—7 "I feel a little sorry for him," Jonas said, "even though I don't even know him. I feel sorry for anyone who is in a place where he feels strange and stupid."	Me ___ Another Text ___ World ✓ I bet all the people who come here from other countries feel strange and stupid when they first come. We should think of ways to help the Mexican immigrants who are coming to our town feel welcome.
Date: 3/15 Page(s): 8—10 "I know there's really nothing to worry about," Jonas explained, "and that every adult has been through it. . . . But it's the Ceremony that I'm apprehensive about."	Me ___ Another Text ✓ World ___ This reminds me of the Harry Potter books and the Sorting Hat Ceremony for finding out what house new students would live with while at Hogwarts School.
Date: 3/16 Page(s): 18—19 But her father had already gone to the shelf and taken down the stuffed elephant which was kept there. Many of the comfort objects, like Lily's, were soft, stuffed, imaginary creatures.	Me ✓ Another Text ___ World ___ I still like to hug my stuffed dog when I'm feeling sad, so it is my comfort object.

Difficulty Making Connections After Reading

The possibilities for making connections following the reading are many. The simplest connections are most likely to be to our own experiences. These text-to-self connections come more naturally and are similar to the "it reminds me of . . ." during-reading connections. But we also can make connections to other things we have read, or to events that happen in the world. Some common types of text-to-text connections, from easiest to more difficult, include

- comparing characters, their personalities, and their actions.
- comparing story events and plot lines.
- comparing lessons, themes, or messages in stories.
- finding common themes, writing style, or perspectives in the work of a single author.
- comparing the treatment of common themes by different authors.
- comparing different versions of familiar stories. (Harvey & Goudvis, 2000, p. 73)

You can model text-to-text connections by choosing to share books that have similar themes, or that are actually versions of the same story. It is best to model with the easier material first. For example, read the more familiar *Little Red Riding Hood* and then share *Lon Po Po*, a Chinese version of the same story (Young, 1989). These books would not be too difficult for struggling intermediate-grade students to grasp the connections. After practice with easy material, students will be better able to identify the similarities, and make connections, between more age-appropriate stories. A **T-chart** (a two-column chart for comparing information) can be used to list the connections, with you beginning the list and students contributing to it (see Figure 5.11).

T-chart ●

As students become comfortable making text-to-self and text-to-text connections, they may naturally begin to make connections to more global issues, or they can be encouraged to make these text-to-world connections through modeling. Additionally, as Harvey and Goudvis (2000) point out, "Encouraging students to make text-to-world connections supports our efforts to teach students about social studies and science concepts and topics" (p. 75). They share an example of a fourth/fifth-grade teacher who introduced *The Lotus Seed* (Garland, 1997) to his students. This book relates the story of a Vietnamese family fleeing their home for the United States during the Vietnam War. Most of the students had little knowledge about, or direct experience with, the content of this book, but there was one particular text-to-self connection that enabled the teacher to illustrate a text-to-world connection. As the class discussed the book, one student shared, "My uncle fought in Vietnam and he told me all about it." In response to this statement another student looked rather confused and then looked back to a picture in the book that showed bombs falling on a rice paddy. She exclaimed, "You mean *we* were the ones dropping the bombs on Vietnam?" At this point the teacher interjected with a text-to-world connection and some information about the war: "The rice paddy is probably in North Vietnam and U.S. planes may have been doing the bombing. The North Vietnamese were fighting for communism and the South Vietnamese were fighting for freedom."

It is important to note that these connections can often overlap. It is not that crucial for students to accurately distinguish among what is a text-to-self, text-to-text, or text-to-world connection, or to come up with a long list of

T-chart of text-to-text connections for *Hana's Suitcase* and *The Diary of a Young Girl*, two books about the Holocaust.   FIGURE   5.11

Hana's Suitcase (by Karen Levine)	*The Diary of a Young Girl* (by Anne Frank)
written about Hana by someone else (biography)	written as a diary by Anne herself—Anne received the diary on her 13th birthday, June 12, 1942 (autobiography)
Born Jewish on May 16, 1931, Hana Brady was 13 when she died on October 23, 1944.	Born Jewish on June 12, 1929, Anne Frank was 15 when her diary stopped on August 1, 1944.
Hana, her older brother George, and her parents lived in Nove Mesto, Moravia, Czechoslovakia.	Anne, her older sister Margot, and her parents lived in Amsterdam, Netherlands.
Hana's mother was arrested and sent to a women's concentration camp in Germany.	Fearing arrest, Anne's family made plans for a hiding place. They stored canned foods and books in the hiding place.
Soon after, Hana's father was arrested.	When Anne's father and sister received notices from the SS, it was time to hide.
Hana and George went to live with their aunt and uncle until ordered to report to a deportation center. Hana turned 11 while at the center.	On July 9, 1942, Anne's family went into hiding in the Secret Annex. They could no longer go outside. Friends helped them get food.
Hana and George were separated into housing for boys and for girls at a camp in Theresienstadt (or Terezin).	On July 13, 1942, another family of three, Mr. and Mrs. Van Daan and their son Peter, came to hide in the Secret Annex (their real name was Van Pels). Later, a dentist, Albert Dussel (Fritz Pfeffer) joined them to make eight people in the small annex.
Hana loved her mother very much and missed her terribly.	Anne's relationship with her mother was not very good, and it did not improve while they lived in their small space.
Hana spent her days in the camp attending art, music, and sewing classes. Art class was her favorite.	Anne spent her days in the annex doing schoolwork, reading, and being quiet.
Theresienstadt was becoming too crowded, and George was sent away.	Only days before they were found, Anna was hopeful about going back to school in October.
Four weeks after George went away, Hana was sent to Auschwitz, and the gas chamber.	Anne was taken to Bergen-Belsen at the end of October, 1944, where she died in late February or early March, 1945—about 3 months short of her 16th birthday.
George survived and returned to Nove Mesto to learn his parents and Hana were all dead. At least through 2003, George shared Hana's story with students and teachers in Tokyo.	Otto Frank, Anne's father, was the only member of her family to survive. He made sure his daughter's diary was published. Anne's diary was first published in 1947. Otto Frank died in 1980.

these connections. In the process of contemplating and making some connections, students begin to monitor their understanding, think about what they are reading, and thus enhance their comprehension. That is the purpose.

SUMMARY

Comprehension is the reason we read. But comprehension cannot occur without the simultaneous use of all the language cue systems (semantic, syntactic, graphophonemic). That is, the reader has to construct meaning from the words that have been decoded while simultaneously connecting what is read to prior knowledge as well as connecting new information to previously known information. It is a complex and arduous process best consummated through a program that offers guidance in specific comprehension strategies and many opportunities to apply them with quality literature as well as expository text. For a literacy program to be balanced and comprehensive, it must not only enable learners to decode text, but also offer them guidance in strategic reading and provide ample opportunities for independent reading using techniques such as those presented in this chapter.

Questions
FOR JOURNAL WRITING AND DISCUSSION

1. Think about what you do when you read. What comprehension strategies did you use while reading this chapter? Make a list of the strategies that you can identify. Then spend a few minutes reading a novel or other narrative material. Make a second list of the strategies you used with the narrative text. Compare the two lists. Are there major differences? Discuss the lists with your classmates.

2. Prepare an argument for why you allow students in your classroom the time to read self-selected material and discuss it in small groups. How would you change this argument for your administrator and for a parent?

3. How does your definition of reading impact the importance of comprehension instruction to your total reading program?

Suggestions
FOR PROJECTS AND FIELD ACTIVITIES

1. Select one of the comprehension strategies from this chapter. Locate a selection from a grade 4–8 classroom that would be appropriate material for teaching this strategy. Teach the strategy to a small group of classmates. Discuss their reactions. How would you modify your teaching for grade 4–8 students? What feedback helped you the most?

2. Teach a comprehension strategy to a small group of students or to an individual student. What problems did they have with the lesson? What problems did you have with the lesson? What did they like and dislike about the strategy? Discuss the results with your class.

3. Observe a classroom teacher during reading lessons for at least five days (try to observe a full week, or different days). Make a list of all the activities the teacher and students engage in during this time. Keep track of how much time is spent on each activity. How much time was spent on direct teaching of comprehension strategies? How much time was spent on the application of these strategies? How much time was spent on actual reading by the students?

REFERENCES

Anderson, R., Hiebert, E., Scott, J., & Wilkerson, I. (1985). *Becoming a nation of readers.* Washington, DC: National Institute of Education.

Aronson, E., & Patnoe, S. (1997). *The jigsaw classroom: Building cooperation in the classroom* (2nd ed.). New York: Longman.

Azevedo, R., & Cromley, J. G. (2004). Does training on self-regulated learning facilitate students' learning with hypermedia? *Journal of Educational Psychology, 96*(3), 523–535.

Beach, R. (1993). *A teacher's introduction to reader-response theories.* Urbana, IL: National Council of Teachers of English.

Beck, I. L., McKeown, M. G., Hamilton, R. L., & Kucan, L. (1997). *Questioning the author: An approach for enhancing student engagement with text.* Newark, DE: International Reading Association.

Biancarosa, G., & Snow, C. E. (2006). Reading next: A vision for action and research in middle and high school literacy: A report to Carnegie Corporation of New York (2nd ed.). Washington, DC: Alliance for Excellent Education. Available online at: www.all4ed.org/publications/ReadingNext/ReadingNext.pdf.

Block, C. C., & Pressley, M. (Eds.). (2002). *Comprehension instruction: Research-based best practices.* New York: Guilford.

Bremer, C. D., Vaughn, S., Clapper, A. T., & Kim, A. (2002). Collaborative strategic reading (CSR): Improving secondary students' reading comprehension skills. Research to Practice Brief: Improving Secondary Education and Transition Services through Research. July 2002, vol. 1, issue 2.

Britton, B. K., & Graesser, A. C. (Eds.). (1996). *Models of understanding text.* Mahwah, NJ: Erlbaum.

Bromley, K. (1993). *Journaling: Engagements in reading, writing and thinking.* New York: Scholastic.

Brooks, W. (2006). Reading representations of themselves: Urban youth use culture and African American textual features to develop literary understandings. *Reading Research Quarterly, 41,* 372–392.

Brown, R. (2002). Straddling two worlds: Self-directed comprehension instruction for middle schoolers. In C. C. Block & M. Pressley (Eds.), *Comprehension instruction: Research-based best practices* (pp. 337–350). New York: Guilford.

Bruchac, J. (1993). *Fox song.* (P. Morin, Illus.). New York: Putnam.

Burke, J. (2000). *Reading reminders: Tools, tips, and techniques.* Portsmouth, NH: Boynton/Cook.

Cecil, N. L. (1990). Read a book in an hour: A smooth transition to multi-chaptered texts. *Reading Improvement, 27*(3), 188–191.

Cecil, N. L. (1995). *The art of inquiry: Questioning strategies for K–6 classrooms.* Winnipeg, Manitoba: Peguis.

Childrey, J. (1980). Read a book in an hour. *Reading Horizons, 20,* 174–176.

Clarke, L. W., & Holwadel, J. (2007). "Help! What is wrong with these literature circles and how can we fix them?" *The Reading Teacher, 6*(1), 20–29.

Coiro, J. (2003). Reading comprehension on the Internet: Expanding our understanding of reading comprehension to encompass new literacies. *The Reading Teacher, 56,* 458–464.

Coiro, J., & Schmar-Dobler, B. (2005). Reading comprehension on the Internet: Exploring the comprehension strategies used by sixth-grade skilled readers as they search for and locate information on the Internet. Unpublished manuscript. Available online at: http://ctell1.uconn.edu/coiro/research.html.

Cunningham, J. W. (1982). Generating interactions between schemata and text. In J. A. Niles & L. A. Harris (Eds.), *New inquiries in reading research and instruction* (pp. 42–47). Thirty-first Yearbook of the National Reading Conference. Washington, DC: National Reading Conference.

Daniels, H. (2002). *Literature circles: Voice and choice in Book Clubs and reading groups* (2nd ed.). York, ME: Stenhouse.

Dantonio, M., & Beisenherz, P. C. (2001). *Learning to question, questioning to learn: Developing effective teacher questioning practices.* Boston: Allyn and Bacon.

Davey, B. (1983). Think aloud—Modeling the cognitive processes of reading comprehension. *The Reading Teacher, 27,* 44–47.

Duffelmeyer, F. A. (1994). Effective anticipation guide statements for learning from expository prose. *Journal of Reading, 37,* 452–457.

Duffy, G. G. (2002). The case for direct explanation of strategies. In C. C. Block & M. Pressley (Eds.), *Comprehension instruction: Research-based best practices* (pp. 28–41). New York: Guilford.

Englert, C. S., & Thomas, C. C. (1987). Sensitivity to text structure in reading and writing: A comparison between learning disabled and non-learning disabled students. *Learning Disabilities Quarterly, 10,* 93–105.

Fountas, I. C., & Pinnell, G. S. (2000). *Guiding readers and writers grades 3–6: Teaching comprehension, genre, and content literacy.* Portsmouth, NH: Heinemann.

Gambrell, L. B., & Bales, R. J. (1987). Visual imagery: A strategy for enhancing listening, reading and writing. *Australian Journal of Reading, 10*(3), 147–153.

Garland, S. (1997). *The lotus seed* (T. Kiuchi, Illus.). New York: Harcourt.

Gipe, J. P. (2006). *Multiple paths to literacy: Assessment and differentiated instruction for diverse learners, K–12* (6th ed.). Upper Saddle River, NJ: Merrill/Prentice Hall.

Hadaway, N., Vardell, S., & Young, T. (2004). *What every teacher should know about English learners.* Boston: Pearson.

Harris, T. L. & Hodges, R. E. (1995). *The literacy dictionary: The vocabulary of reading and writing.* Newark, DE: International Reading Association.

Harste, J., Short, C., & Burke, C. (1988). *Creating classrooms for authors.* Portsmouth, NH: Heinemann.

Harvey, S., & Goudvis, A. (2000). *Strategies that work: Teaching comprehension to enhance understanding.* York, ME: Stenhouse.

Henry, L. A. (2006). SEARCHing for an answer: The critical role of new literacies while reading on the Internet. *The Reading Teacher, 59,* 614–627.

Herrell, A., & Jordan, M. (2002). *50 active learning strategies for improving reading comprehension.* Upper Saddle River, NJ: Pearson Merrill Prentice Hall.

Hyman, T. S. (1986). *Little red riding hood.* New York: Holiday House.

Isaacson, R. M., & Fujita, F. (2006). Metacognitive knowledge monitoring and self-regulated learning: Academic success and reflections on learning. *Journal of the Scholarship of Teaching and Learning, 6*(1), 39–55.

Johnston, P., & Costello, P. (2005). Principles for literacy assessment. *Reading Research Quarterly, 40,* 256–267.

Jorm, A. (1977). Effect of word imagery on reading performance as a function of reader ability. *Journal of Educational Psychology, 69,* 46–54.

Kiefer, B. Z. (1995). *The potential of picture books: From visual literacy to aesthetic understanding.* Englewood Cliffs, NJ: Merrill Prentice Hall.

Klingner, J. K., & Vaughn, S. (1996). Reciprocal teaching of reading comprehension strategies for students with learning disabilities who use English as a second language. *Elementary School Journal, 96*(3), 275–293.

Lankshear, C., & Knobel, M. (2003). *New literacies: Changing knowledge and classroom learning.* Buckingham, UK: Open University Press.

Lenhart, A., Madden, M., & Hitlin, P. (2005). *Teens and technology: Youth are leading the transition to a fully wired and mobile nation.* Washington, DC: Pew Internet & American Life Project.

Leu, D. J. Jr., Castek., J., Hartman, D., Coiro, J., Henry, L. A., Kulikowich, J. M., & Lyver, S. (2005). *Evaluating the development of scientific knowledge and new forms of reading comprehension during online learning.* Final report submitted to the North Central Regional Educational Laboratory, a subsidiary of Learning Point Associates (LPA). Available online at: www.newliteracies.uconn.edu/ncrel.html.

Leu, D. J., Kinzer, C. K., Coiro, J., & Cammack, D. (2004). Toward a theory of new literacies emerging from the Internet and other information and communication technologies. In R. B. Ruddell & N. Unrau (Eds.), *Theoretical models and processes of reading* (5th ed., pp. 1568–1611). Newark, DE: International Reading Association.

Leu, D. J., Zawilinski, L., Castek, J., Banerjee, M., Housand, B., Liu, Y., & O'Neil, M. (in press). What is new about the new literacies of online reading comprehension? In A. Berger, L. Rush, & J. Eakle (Eds.), *Secondary school reading and writing: What research reveals for classroom practices.* National Council of Teachers of English/ National Conference of Research on Language and Literacy: Chicago, IL.

Liang, L. A., & Dole, J. A. (2006). Help with teaching reading comprehension: Comprehension instructional frameworks. *The Reading Teacher, 59,* 742–753.

Markle, S. (1991). *Outside and inside you.* New York: Scholastic.

McKeown, R. G., & Gentilucci, J. J. (2007). Think-aloud strategy: Metacognitive development and monitoring comprehension in the middle school second-language classroom. *Journal of Adolescent and Adult Literacy, 51*(2), 136–147.

McMahon, S. I., & Raphael, T. E. (1997). The book club program: Theoretical and research foundations. In S. I. McMahon & T. E. Raphael (Eds.), *The book club connection: Literacy learning and classroom talk* (pp. 3–25). New York: Teachers College Press.

McTaggert, J. (2006). *The graphic novel: Everything you ever wanted to know but were afraid to ask.* Unpublished ms. available from author at www.theteachersdesk.com.

Moravcsik, J. E., & Kintsch, W. (1993). Writing quality, reading skills, and domain knowledge as factors in text comprehension. *Canadian Journal of Experimental Psychology, 47,* 360–374.

National Center for Education Statistics. (2003). The Nation's Report Card: Reading. Washington, DC: U. S. Government Printing Office. Available online at: http://nces.ed.gov/nationsreportcard/reading/results2003/nat achieve-g8.asp.

O'Brien, D. G., & Bauer, E. B. (2005). New literacies and the institution of old learning. *Reading Research Quarterly, 40,* 120–131.

Palincsar, A. (1987, January). Reciprocal teaching: Can student discussions boost comprehension? *Instructor,* 56–60.

Palincsar, A. S., & Brown, A. L. (1984). Reciprocal teaching of comprehension-fostering and comprehension-monitoring activities. *Cognition and Instruction, 1*(2), 117–175.

Palincsar, A. S., & Brown, A. L. (1986). Interactive teaching to promote independent learning from text. *The Reading Teacher, 39,* 771–777.

Palincsar, A. S., & Herrenkohl, L. R. (2002). Designing collaborative learning contexts. *Theory Into Practice, 41*(1), 26–32.

Pearson, P. D., & Gallagher, M. (1983). The instruction of reading comprehension. *Contemporary Educational Psychology, 8,* 317–344.

Pintrich, P. R. (1995). Understanding self-regulated learning. In P. R. Pintrich (Ed.), *Understanding self-regulated learning* (pp. 3–12). San Francisco, CA: Jossey-Bass.

Pressley, M. (2000). Comprehension instruction in elementary school: A quarter-century of research progress. In B. Taylor, M. Graves, & P. van den Broek (Eds.), *Reading for meaning: Fostering comprehension in the middle grades* (pp. 32–51). New York: Teachers College Press.

Pressley, M. (2002). Comprehension strategies instruction: A turn-of-the-century status report. In C. C. Block & M. Pressley (Eds.), *Comprehension instruction: Research-based best practices* (pp. 11–27). New York: Guilford.

RAND Reading Study Group. (2002). Reading for understanding: Toward an R & D program in reading comprehension. Santa Monica, CA: RAND. Available online at: www.rand.org/multi/achievementforall/reading/read report.html.

Raphael, T. E. (1982). Question-answering strategies for children. *The Reading Teacher, 36,* 186–190.

Raphael, T. E. (2000). Balancing literature and instruction: Lessons from the Book Club Project. In B. Taylor, M. Graves, & P. van den Broek (Eds.), *Reading for meaning: Fostering comprehension in the middle grades* (pp. 70–94). New York: Teachers College Press.

Raphael, T. E., & Au, K. H. (2005). QAR: Enhancing comprehension and test taking across grades and content areas. *The Reading Teacher, 59,* 206–221.

Readence, J. E., Bean, T. W., & Baldwin, R. S. (1998). *Content area reading: An integrated approach* (6th ed.). Dubuque, IA: Kendall/Hunt.

Richards, J. C., & Gipe, J. P. (1992). Activating background knowledge: Strategies for beginning and poor readers. *The Reading Teacher, 45,* 474–476.

Rosenblatt, L. (1938). *Literature as exploration.* New York: Appleton-Century. Reprinted, 1995. New York: Modern Language Association.

Rosenblatt. L. (1969). Towards a transactional theory of reading. *Journal of Reading Behavior, 1*(1), 31–51.

Rosenblatt, L. M. (1978). *The reader, the text, the poem.* Carbondale: Southern Illinois University Press.

Rosenblatt, L. M. (1983). *Literature as exploration.* New York: The Modern Languages Association of America.

Rosenblatt, L. M. (1994). The transactional theory of reading and writing. In R. B. Ruddell, M. R. Ruddell, & H. Singer (Eds.), *Theoretical models and processes of reading* (4th ed., pp. 1057–1092). Newark, DE: International Reading Association.

Rosenshine, B., & Meister, C. (1994). Reciprocal teaching: A review of the research. *Review of Educational Research, 64,* 479–530.

Stauffer, R. G. (1975). *Directing the reading-thinking process.* New York: Harper & Row.

van den Broek, P. W. (1990). The causal inference maker: Towards a process model of inference generation in text comprehension. In D. A. Balota, G. B. Flores d'Arcais, & K. Rayner (Eds.), *Comprehension processes in reading* (pp. 423–445). Hillsdale, NJ: Erlbaum.

van den Broek, P. W., Risden, K., Fletcher, C. R., & Thurlow, R. (1996). A "landscape" view of reading: Fluctuating patterns of activation and the construction of a stable memory representation. In B. K. Britton & A. C. Graesser (Eds.), *Models of understanding text* (pp. 165–187). Mahwah, NJ: Erlbaum.

Vygotsky, L. S. (1978). *Mind in society.* Cambridge, MA: MIT Press.

Vygotsky, L. S. (1986). *Thought and language* (A. Kozulin, Trans.). Cambridge, MA: MIT Press.

Wilhelm, J. D. (1997). *"You gotta BE the book": Teaching engaged and reflective reading with adolescents.* New York: Teachers College Press.

Yell, M. L., & Drasgow, E. (2005). *No Child Left Behind: A guide for professionals.* Upper Saddle River, NJ: Pearson Merrill Prentice Hall.

Young, E. (1989). *Lon Po Po: A Red Riding Hood story from China.* Daly City, CA: Philomel.

Reading and Writing Connections

FOCUS QUESTIONS

- What are the components for an effective writing program in grades 4–8?

- What is writer's workshop and how can it help students become skilled and motivated writers?

- How can teaching the 6 + 1 traits of effective writing provide a common vocabulary for both narrative and expository writing?

- What are the main components of writing fluency?

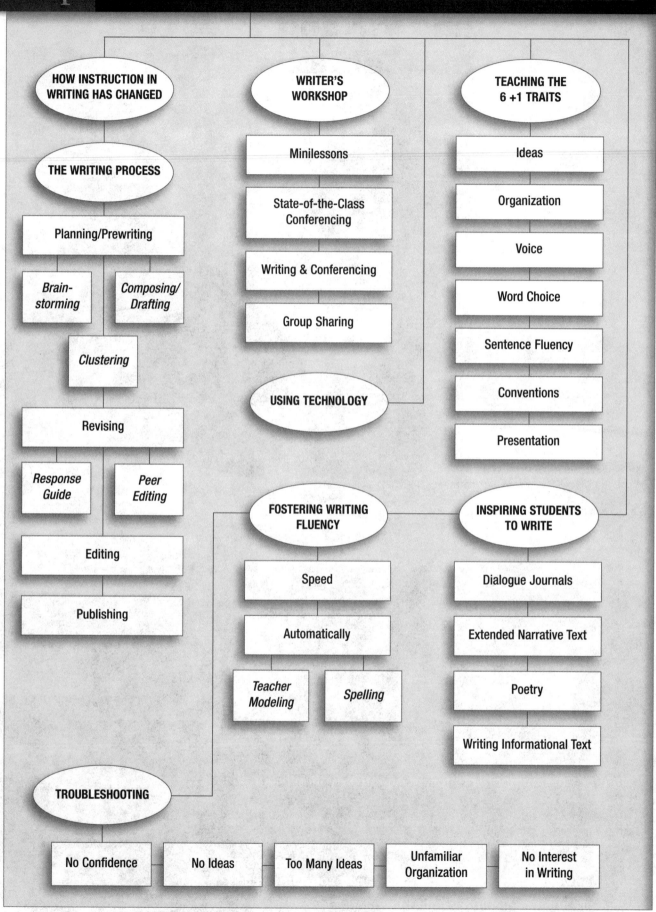

HOW INSTRUCTION IN WRITING HAS CHANGED

THE WRITING PROCESS

- Planning/Prewriting
  - *Brainstorming*
  - *Composing/Drafting*
  - *Clustering*
- Revising
  - *Response Guide*
  - *Peer Editing*
- Editing
- Publishing

WRITER'S WORKSHOP

- Minilessons
- State-of-the-Class Conferencing
- Writing & Conferencing
- Group Sharing

USING TECHNOLOGY

TEACHING THE 6 +1 TRAITS

- Ideas
- Organization
- Voice
- Word Choice
- Sentence Fluency
- Conventions
- Presentation

FOSTERING WRITING FLUENCY

- Speed
- Automatically
  - *Teacher Modeling*
  - *Spelling*

INSPIRING STUDENTS TO WRITE

- Dialogue Journals
- Extended Narrative Text
- Poetry
- Writing Informational Text

TROUBLESHOOTING

- No Confidence
- No Ideas
- Too Many Ideas
- Unfamiliar Organization
- No Interest in Writing

The students in Mrs. McCray's fifth-grade class have just returned from lunch. They eagerly head for the file full of individually decorated writing folders in the back of the classroom. Each student has her own folder in which papers are kept related to the writing projects she is working on. As the students retrieve their folders, they quickly sit down at their desks, arranged in small groups. Three students are sitting at computers, using a word-processing program to print out their final draft of pieces they have been working on all week. Some students are quietly discussing new writing ideas with a classmate. Other students are writing intently, while still others are sharing their drafts with their classmates—or "peer editors"—who offer suggestions about content or writing conventions, as requested by the author. Everyone is focused and clearly on task, yet working at his or her own pace.

At her desk, Mrs. McCray conferences briefly with several students: the rest of the students will be engaged in such encounters over the remainder of the week. During these one-to two-minute sessions, Mrs. McCray asks individual students to talk quietly about what they are writing, listens to them read a paragraph or two of their work, and questions them about what they are planning to do next. Hoa, for example, explains that yesterday she received valuable input from her peer editor, so she is now going to correct spelling mistakes and add a more exciting opening idea that will better "grab" her audience.

Other students are at the revising stage of writing. Jessie and Alyce sign up to meet with Mrs. McCray so that she can offer feedback about the strengths of the current work each is doing and ask questions about ideas that may be unclear. Sometimes Mrs. McCray also offers suggestions for improvement, and the two collaborators—the teacher and the author—decide if the suggestions are compatible with what the writer is trying to say.

After a half hour, Mrs. McCray calls the whole class together in a circle in a large section of the room. Brianne and Raúl, who have just finished the writing they have been working on, are ready to sit in the "author's chair" to read their finished pieces to the rest of the class. Although a couple of classmates propose specific suggestions to each student, the rest of the class offers mostly praise and celebratory comments for the two completed writing projects—a detailed description of Harriet Tubman's house that was visited recently on a field trip for Brianne, and an amusing autobiographical incident for Raúl.

When all who wish to have shared their writing with the whole class, the students return to their desks and Mrs. McCray conducts a 10-minute minilesson. She usually focuses such lessons on writing strategies and skills that, from her charted observation of students' writing, she feels most students will find helpful to allow them to move forward in their writing. Today, Mrs. McCray shows the students how to use quotation marks to express dialogue in conversation. She shows them a transparency of a student's writing on an overhead projector (examples are usually obtained from the preceding year's class to avoid embarrassment). The writing is a conversation that is told secondhand, without the benefit of direct quotes. She guides students to see how much richer and more personal the writing seems with the addition of dialogue and quotation marks. For similar lessons, Mrs. McCray often copies excerpts from books the students are reading to show how published authors use the writing skills and strategies she is trying to portray.

HOW INSTRUCTION IN WRITING HAS CHANGED

In the past 30 years, our attitude toward the teaching of writing has changed dramatically. Many older adults recall writing homework compositions that were essentially a "one-shot deal." In those days, students would write a draft; turn it in to the teacher; and receive a grade, usually based primarily on spelling, grammar, and handwriting. In the 1970s, researchers began to stop focusing solely on the writing product in such a simplistic manner and started to study how the entire process of writing can impact thinking. Among their most consistent findings was that students truly needed direct teaching at every stage of the writing process—to enable them to generate better ideas, to elaborate on those ideas, to organize their writing for a specific purpose or audience, to edit their work so that it was communicated effectively, and to develop their own style of writing (Block, 2000).

In the 1980s and 1990s, our knowledge expanded so that instruction went beyond assisting students to select topics, compose, and edit to eliminate errors. In that era students were instructed to adjust to new purposes and audiences and to revise their thoughts and ideas. Researchers of the time noted that "the problem with writing is not poor spelling, punctuation, grammar, and handwriting. The problem with students' writing is NO writing" (Stuart & Graves, 1987, p. 12).

In the current millennium, instruction continues to move toward increasing the student's abilities to generate thoughts and ideas and then, as a second but equally important concern, to strive to communicate these ideas in written form, and to do so often. Moreover, for the student, writing requires specific kinds of critical thinking: questioning, citing evidence, evaluating content, and using one's own personal schema (Langer & Applebee, 1987). Today's teachers, more than ever before, consider the thinking processes that go into forming a final product and use the writing process as a vehicle to help students to think through the problems that all writers encounter. As Laib (1989) stated,

> Good writing cannot be understood or taught effectively as an empty and unsystematic collection of rules . . . The real objective of a writing course is literacy in the highest sense: to be knowledgeable and observant, inventive in thought but careful in method, respectful of one's sources, impressive in reason and wit, appropriate in style, graceful in expression, and effective in result. (p. 22)

Mrs. McCray is informed about the current theories and research in the teaching of writing. She is also acquainted with the language arts framework and the standards set for grades 4–8 by the state where she teaches. But what makes her students passionate about the hard work of drafting, revising, and editing a piece of writing is simply this: Mrs. McCray has created a literacy-centered classroom where reading and writing are not only connected, but viewed as important life skills. This teacher allows plenty of opportunities for her students to experience what it is like to share a writing topic one is engrossed in with someone else. She is well aware that each student in her class will be engaged with writing if that student is allowed to explore a variety of topics in which he or she is interested. Above all, this teacher knows that it is all but impossible to resist the appreciation of a sincere and respectful audience (Cohle & Towle, 2001).

THE WRITING PROCESS

The writing process is a series of experiences that a writer engages in to solve certain problems unique to a certain stage of writing. It is exactly this problem-solving approach that makes the writing process more effective in creating thoughtful writers than more traditional approaches that focus solely on the finished product. In traditional writing programs, the finished product is usually a second draft that the student produces by copying the teacher's corrections made in red ink. Through the writing process, with continuous and scaffolded support from a competent teacher/facilitator, students go through the stages published authors do and, thus, begin to think of themselves as authors, a process that furthers their ability to construct meaning.

The writing process consists of five recursive stages, each of which should be explained and modeled for students (Gillet & Beverly, 2001). The stages are

  planning/prewriting

 composing/drafting

revising

An Effective Writing Program in Grades 4–8

Mrs. McCray and many other teachers across the country have found that it is possible to get students to become enthusiastic and capable writers with a writing program that is characterized by the following five elements, which we elaborate upon throughout the remainder of this chapter:

1. **Schedule plenty of time for writing.** Students need ample time to draft, share, and think about their writing. Donald Graves (1994) suggests that students write at least four days a week; less writing than that encourages poor habits, which often leads to the dislike of writing. Moreover, the time set aside should be predictable. When students know when they will be writing, they begin to anticipate and plan mentally for what they will write. They are able to "mull over the possibilities" when they are away from the task (Calkins, 1994).

2. **Teach the writing process as a way to write.** The focus on the writing process is what writers think and do as they write. The process consists of prewriting, drafting, editing, revising, and sharing as a series of recursive cycles as students think through a piece of writing. Strive to model this process often with your own writing.

3. **Use writer's workshop as a structure for writing.** Writer's workshop encourages students to become a community of writers who write and share. You become a facilitator in the process.

4. **Provide feedback on students' writing through peer and teacher conferences.** When students are taught to provide critical feedback on each other's work, they become better able to evaluate their own writing. When students write for peers, even those at a distant school through e-mail correspondence, the quality of their work has been shown to be significantly better than if they write solely for their teachers (Cohen & Riel, 1989). The teacher also provides information about each student's writing strengths and needs.

5. **Use the "6 + 1 Traits" to explain good writing in ways students can understand.** The important aspects of writing can be narrowed down to six essential traits—ideas, organization, voice, word choice, sentence fluency, and conventions—plus presentation, which can be taught to students so that they know exactly what good writing is and how to produce it themselves. Each trait can be discussed in minilessons and then practiced through authentic writing situations. Samples of students' writing or the writing of published authors can be used to point out how the samples exemplify or do not exemplify any one of the 6 + 1 traits.

④ editing

⑤ publishing

Although students will often follow the steps through to the final reward of publication, *all* writing need not progress through these steps. There will be times when students will not be making progress with a piece of writing or lose interest and decide to go in an entirely different direction with it. This may occur at any point in the writing process, and you may strive to make it clear that all writing does not have to be published. The student and you may make the decision after considering both the quality of the piece and how the student feels about it.

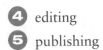

PLANNING/PREWRITING

The first stage of any writing effort is a "planning/prewriting" stage in which writers explore and then organize ideas that they feel passionate enough about to sustain all the hard work that will follow. This stage often includes a kind of mental rehearsal and often emanates from a **quick write,** a rapid writing down of ideas about a topic. In most writer's workshops, much time is spent allowing students in this stage to select their own topics. Although this

● quick write

may seem easy because it is so wide open, it often initially leaves many students wondering what to write about. Peha (1996) suggests having students take out a sheet of paper and divide it into two columns. In one column, students should make a list of all the things they really like; in the other, all the things they really detest. These topics can then lead to a whole-class discussion in which the teacher supports topic selection by making comments such as, "That sounds like a good topic to write about!" It is also a good idea for students to keep a list of topics (which can continue to grow) attached to the inside corner of their writing folder. Peha (1996) further suggests discussing with students exactly what makes an idea good enough to explore in written form. The idea is worth pursuing if it is:

- *something you have strong feelings about.* What do you feel about the subject? Can you communicate those feelings to readers? How?

- *something you know a lot about.* What can you share with readers that they would be interested in knowing? What is the most important part to tell readers?

- *something you are able to describe in great detail.* Why are these details important? Will they help readers see what you see and feel how you feel?

- *something your audience will be interested in.* Who is your audience? What could you tell them that will interest them most?

- *something your audience will feel was worth reading.* Will your audience learn something new from your piece? What will keep them reading all the way to the end?

Brainstorming

Another way to help students select ideas for writing is through brainstorming with a partner or with the larger group. This oral prewriting activity helps students, especially reluctant writers, to bounce their ideas off another person and gain confidence that their idea is worth pursuing. Similarly, oral discussions on a topic before a writer's workshop session can help students come up with their own intriguing ideas. For example, a teacher writes a provocative question on the board, such as, "What would it be like if everyone looked exactly the same?" Students then consider the pros and cons of such a scenario. Some muse that prejudice would disappear and people would be judged for their character rather than their looks; others suggest that such a world would be as boring as a garden with only one variety of flower. After such a discussion, students are able to write a three-paragraph persuasive piece, with the first paragraph containing advantages of such a situation; the second, negatives; and the third, their own personal opinion.

Clustering

Students may sketch a map of their ideas, or "cluster" them, to form a kind of graphic outline that can then be filled in with details that flesh it out. Using the clustering technique, students start with their idea, which forms the nucleus of the cluster. Then, using a process akin to free association, they write down everything they can think of that relates to their topic. Many teachers report that this technique is very helpful in assisting second language learners and reluctant writers to plan their compositions effectively (Martinez, 1986). Figure 6.1 shows a cluster created by a seventh-grader, as she prepared to write her

Cluster for "My Sister" and the resultant essay.   FIGURE   6.1

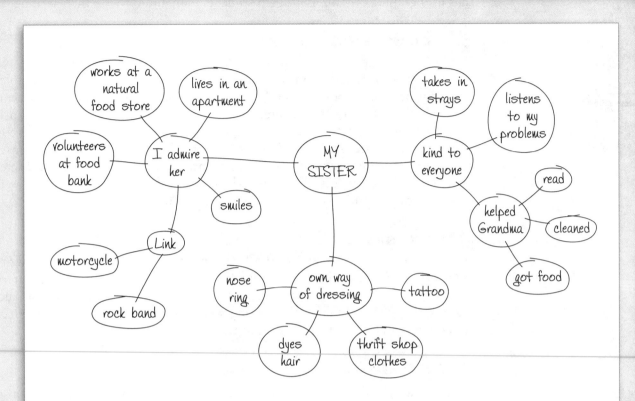

My Sister

The person I most admire in my family is my sister. My oldest sister, Jenna, is 20 years old and lives in an apartment with two other girls. She works at a natural food store and helps out at the food bank on weekends. She has a boyfriend named Link who rides a motorcycle and is in a rock band. When Jenna smiles, she lights up the room.

Jenna is always kind to everyone. When my grandma was sick, Jenna took time off from work to help her get groceries and clean her house. She read to her every single night. Also, Jenna takes in every stray animal that comes around and has always listened to my problems when I ask her to. Everyone is drawn to Jenna like a magnet.

My oldest sister has her own way of dressing. Some people say she looks like a punk, but I think she looks more like a rocker. She has a nose ring and a little wrist tattoo that looks like poison ivy. Even though she has a job, she wears old clothes that she buys at thrift shops. She changes her hair color about every month. It has been red, blue, and black. This month it is brown with red streaks. Jenna dresses for herself, not others.

When people first meet my sister they sometimes think she is weird. At times, they even call her names because she looks so different. Just because she looks different they should not judge her; they should take the time to get to know her. Her outside appearance may be strange, but inside she has a heart of gold. To know my oldest sister Jenna is to love her. If you met her you would see what I mean.

first draft of a four-paragraph essay on her sister, and the resultant essay. The same strategy can be used on the computer, using Inspiration software, a tool that uses graphic organizers to help students plan and develop their writing.

② COMPOSING/DRAFTING

Composing, or drafting, is the stage where writers develop their topic and actually translate their ideas into written form. If computers are available, a word-processing program is perfect for this stage, because later revisions can be accomplished easily. If computers are not available, it is often helpful to ask students to write drafts on lined paper, using every other line, so that there is ample room for later revisions. Students should also be instructed not to erase, but to draw one line through words or sentences they wish to change or delete; many times, in retrospect, their original ideas seem better than later ones, so it is important for students to have access to those ideas.

③ REVISING

Revising, in short, entails the "big changes." This is the step in the writing process that may require the most difficult work and generally encounters the most resistance. Revision requires reexamining content, word choice, and organization and rethinking the writing style with an emphasis on how effectively it communicates its intention to the audience.

Response guides

response guide ● Revision can be initially introduced by showing students how to use a response guide to examine pieces of writing. A **response guide** offers specific compliments to and asks specific questions of the writer concerning the effectiveness of the writing. A sample response guide is shown in Figure 6.2.

FIGURE 6.2   Response guide.

COMPLIMENTS	QUESTIONS
I liked the part where . . .	Could you write an opening sentence to "grab" the reader?
You used some great words like . . .	
The imagery was effective in the sentence(s) . . .	Could you throw away these tired words . . . ?
I like the way you explained . . .	Is this paragraph all on one topic?
Your writing made me feel . . .	Do you need an ending that summarizes better?
I like the order you used in the piece because . . .	Are your paragraphs in the right order?
	Could you add more details to this part?
The dialogue was realistic when [the character] said . . .	I got confused in the part where . . .
	Could you combine these sentences?
Your writing made me more interested in this topic because . . .	Can you make this part clearer?
	Can you tell me more about . . . ?
	Could you leave this part out because . . . ?

Using this or a similar response guide, you can show students examples of bland or ineffective writing (decodable text is perfect for this purpose) on the overhead projector and have students practice commenting on the writing by selecting phrases appropriate to the piece from the response guide. To extend this activity further, you can invite small groups of students to rewrite the piece and discuss with the class exactly how the writing has been made more effective.

Peer editing

When students are adept at offering suggestions that are both helpful to the writer and appropriate to the piece of writing, they are ready to become peer editors. **Peer editors** are selected by a writer who has written a draft and is seeking constructive feedback in order to make the piece communicate its intent more effectively. By taking on the role of author as well as peer editor, students not only get the benefit of an audience with whom to share their work, but also begin to learn how to evaluate a piece of writing objectively.

• peer editors

Cecil (2007a) suggests that peer editors give their feedback to the authors in written form using a format known as *PQP*, which stands for praise, question, and polish. Multiple copies can be available for students so that when they are ready to share a draft and get revision suggestions from a peer editor, this template makes the work easier. An example of a PQP form is in Figure 6.3.

PQP form for peer editing.   FIGURE 6.3

Author   Rachel   Title of Piece   Grandfather's watch

Peer Editor   John   Date   3/12

PRAISE: I particularly like these things about your piece of writing.

The beginning sentence made me really want to read on. I could really relate to what Nellie was feeling when she lost her watch. That happened to me once. I was actually worried she would get into trouble. By leaving the outcome until the end, you had me dying to find out what kind of punishment she would get.

QUESTION: These things were unclear to me.

Why didn't she just go back to the park and look for the watch? Wouldn't she have tried to do something about it? I also don't understand who Martin is. Is he her brother or just a friend?

POLISH: I have these suggestions to help make your piece even better.

Your dialogue is realistic but could you use another word besides said all the time. Maybe a word that explains more how Nellie is feeling. It might be helpful, also, to describe what Nellie looks like. You described other things about her so well that I care about her and would like to know if my mental image is correct.

4 EDITING

The editing stage of the writing process is where the writer "cleans up" the spelling, punctuation, and other mechanics of the language that make the writing more accessible to the reader. This step should only take place after the writer has made all the content changes he feels are necessary. During a mini-lesson, you and your students should make a list of age-appropriate factors to look for in the editing stage, and the list should be prominently displayed in the classroom so that students can refer to it as they write and edit their work.

An example of a generic checklist is provided in Figure 6.4. Such a checklist can be used by the writer to edit her own writing as well as by the peer editor, who may be specifically requested to look for problems with the conventions of the language. The items on the checklist can be adjusted as needed to meet students' levels of writing sophistication.

FIGURE 6.4 Editing checklist.

Author: _____   Peer Editor: _____

Author	Peer Editor	
☐	☐	1. Did I read the piece backwards, one sentence at a time, to check for spelling errors, sentence fragments, and run-on sentences?
☐	☐	2. Did I use a dictionary, friend, spell checker, or other resource to find spelling errors?
☐	☐	3. Did I check to make sure all proper nouns and the first word of each sentence are capitalized?
☐	☐	4. Did I indent each paragraph?
☐	☐	5. Did I make sure each sentence has the appropriate ending punctuation?
☐	☐	6. Did I use commas appropriately? Are they used only for compound sentences, a list of items, an introductory word or phrase, to set off interruptions, to separate adjectives, or in dates?
☐	☐	7. Do I need to add commas? Have I made sure commas are not separating complete sentences?
☐	☐	8. Have I used apostrophes only for contractions or to show ownership?
☐	☐	9. Have I used more complex punctuation (dashes, semicolons, hyphens, parentheses, etc.) correctly?
☐	☐	10. Have I used common homonyms correctly, for example they're/their/there; your/you're; its/it's; too/two/to?
☐	☐	11. Was I consistent in the use of either present or past tense in the entire piece?
☐	☐	12. Was I consistent in my use of either first person or third person throughout the entire piece?

5 PUBLISHING

Publishing is the celebratory step in the writing process where you help students find many ways to share and disseminate their writing. This public phase of the writing process creates a sense of the real purpose of writing and allows students to feel genuine pride in their completed product. The more students publish their writing, the more they will develop a true sense of themselves as "authors," and the cycle begins to perpetuate itself. Soon, even reluctant writers become prolific.

Allowing students to illustrate their efforts and provide attractive covers is part of the reward for the writer's accomplishment. Though the format may vary according to the type of piece written, book form is the most common way for students to publish their work. A laminated or cloth cover is appealing and sturdy enough to allow the book to be read many times by classmates. Commercially made hard-cover blank books can be decorated by students.

Besides sharing their final product with the class, there are other avenues for publication that make students feel that all the hard work was worthwhile. Work can be displayed on classroom home pages or bulletin boards and in special showcases around the school. Class or school newspapers are another way to highlight the work of individual students. In addition, there are several magazines, such as *Merlyn's Pen* and *Young World,* that solicit the creative work of students. Additionally, students can share their writing online at the Kids Online Magazine, Frodo's Notebook, or White Barn Press.

WWW

Kids Writing Online
www.kidsonlinemagazine.com
www.frodosnotebook.com
www.whitebarnpress.com

WRITER'S WORKSHOP

Writer's workshop has been recommended by numerous researchers and practicing writing teachers (Atwell, 1998; Calkins, 1994; Hansen, 1987). Descriptions of writer's workshops appear in several full-length books (see, e.g., Calkins, 1991; Calkins & Huron, 1987; Stuart & Graves, 1987). The workshop itself is a very flexible plan that places students and teacher in a partnership for learning. Managing writer's workshop cannot be reduced to a simple how-to formula; it is an ongoing, complex set of tasks that develop differently within the context of different classrooms (Peha, 1996).

Writer's workshops that buzz with the activity of students working on a variety of tasks may, to an outsider, appear to be disorganized and chaotic. However, most of these classrooms are built on a firm, underlying structure (Muschla, 1998a). In most classrooms, writer's workshop takes place two or three times a week, often alternating with reader's workshop or literature circles. The writer's workshop approach to organizing a writing program can be conducted in three or four centers, or writing stations, through which students rotate to complete the writing stages discussed in the previous section. In smaller classrooms, as in the opening vignette, students can be completing all stages of writing at their desks. The writer's workshop consists of four basic parts: ❶ minilessons, ❷ state-of-the-class conferences, ❸ writing and conferencing, and ❹ group sharing.

1 MINILESSONS

The minilesson is a focused lesson done with the whole class that usually lasts no more than 5 to 10 minutes. The content of this brief lesson is determined by what you have observed to be a mutual writing need of most members of the class. To model the topic being addressed, prepare a good example of the skill and/or a poor example of the skill procured from literature with which the students are familiar or from writing saved from former students. Such lessons do not focus exclusively on isolated skills but on a range of topics based on student needs. The only absolute topics addressed in these sessions are the six traits of effective writing, discussed later in this chapter. Although there is no end to the possible topics for minilessons, following are some common topics that can be addressed:

- appropriate vocabulary and strategies for finding words
- how to determine when a paragraph is needed
- how to select specific mood words to convey fear or sadness
- the conventions for a business letter
- procedures for writer's workshop
- how to select a topic that has relevance to the writer
- examples of imagery from familiar literature

2 STATE-OF-THE-CLASS CONFERENCES

For means of assessment and accountability, you may choose to build in a five-minute "state-of-the-class conference" once or twice a week to make sure you know exactly what each student is going to be doing during writer's workshop. By examining a chart such as the one in Figure 6.5, determine who is at what stage in the writing process and who might benefit from a teacher conference, or a discussion about how to become "unstuck" from a certain stage, such as getting an idea. Additionally, although the stages in the writer's workshop are not necessarily linear but recursive, you may feel a student is leaving out a certain step that would be beneficial with a particularly problematic piece.

3 WRITING AND CONFERENCING

The majority of students' time in writer's workshop—30 to 40 minutes, depending on grade level—is spent in actual writing and talking about that writing in peer-editing conferences and/or teacher conferences.

Students may select a peer editor and schedule a peer conference with an individual or a small group at any time when informal feedback is needed about formulating and planning an idea or the need for revisions, or for specific proofreading for the purpose of editing.

The teacher in a writer's workshop is not the "authority," but a co-collaborator who also writes and shares pieces of work as well as ideas. During the writing time, the teacher may be holding individual or small group conferences that have been scheduled by previous sign-ups on a special place on the bulletin board. Writing conferences should be brief (usually between one and four minutes) and concentrate on a piece the writer is doing or finishing. During the conference, you can answer questions and help solve writing problems. In addition, you might do the following:

1. Ask for more information about the content of the piece.
2. Restate or mirror the student's ideas.
3. Share similar writing experiences you have had.

NAMES:	MON.	TUES.	WED.	THURS.	FRI.
José	1stD	S	R	2ndD	(3)
Brianne	1stD	S	2ndD	(2)	T
Jennifer	P	1stD	(2)	P	2ndD
Hoa	T	R	2ndD	S	(1)
Svetlana	(1)	(1)	1stD	P	2ndD
Garrett	P	2ndD	R	(3)	S

	CODE		CODE
Prewriting	(1)	Drafting	D
Peer editing	P	Proofreading	(2)
Sharing with group	S	Revising	R
Teacher conference	T	Illustrating	(3)

State-of-the-class chart.   **FIGURE** 6.5

Comments during the conferences should take a positive, encouraging tone, focusing on particularly effective writing and pointing out to the student what has made it effective (Graves, 1983). When there are significant problems, concentrate on only one or two concerns in any one session, making a note to check on progress in those areas in the next conference. Finally, students should take an active role in the conference by asking their own questions about the pieces they are working on.

If no conferences are scheduled, walk around the room, engaging in "writer's talk" (e.g., "What an interesting observation" or "The way you described the avatar made me just shudder!"), prompting, encouraging, and lending support. Carry a notebook to jot down anecdotal records (see Chapter 2) on the progress of students, which will provide information about what to address in future minilessons.

There is no one correct organizational scenario for writer's workshop, because each day tends to be different from the day before. Some days most students will be conferencing with each other or with the teacher in an attempt to bounce their ideas off others; other days students will be at work drafting or revising their ideas and the teacher will be busy talking to individual students at their desks. The key concepts to remember are flexibility and decision making based not on curriculum but on the demonstrated needs of the students.

4 GROUP SHARING

Group sharing is an oral activity, as compared with publishing, and is usually done in front of the whole class (often in a special "author's chair"). The purpose is not to obtain feedback to create a better piece, but to get group appreciation, suggestions for future pieces, and celebratory comments for the completed piece and all the hard work that it necessarily entailed. Though the time allotted for this sharing is ordinarily brief—five minutes or so—it is incredibly important and should never be omitted because

- sharing their work gives students a real reason to write—to impress an audience.
- sharing work allows peer editors to see how their ideas had an effect on a piece.
- sharing work in a safe environment builds a sense of community.
- sharing work makes literacy public.
- reading one's own writing shows the interconnectedness between the two processes. (Graves, 1983)

USING TECHNOLOGY IN CLASSROOM WRITING

The writing process is a valuable approach for teaching students how to write, but often students who lack the skills of good handwriting and appropriate spelling can allow these conventions to interfere with bringing their thoughts and ideas to publication. Technology can help in each stage of the writing process.

In the planning stage, students can use the Internet to further their understanding of the topic. Then, through the use of the word processor, they can generate ideas and explore the topic they are writing about. They can prewrite, web, brainstorm, or do free association without worrying about hurriedly producing pages so rough they are unreadable even to the author.

Word-processing programs can help students avoid frustration by allowing them to explore their ideas while composing without fear of mistakes, which lead to extra effort. Students can easily make deletions and move sentences and paragraphs without erasing or starting all over again.

Revising, perhaps the hardest stage to "sell" to any student, is far more manageable when students can easily incorporate suggested word changes, add or delete paragraphs, or even do more extensive rewriting of certain parts of the piece. Because revising is more easily done with a word-processing program, students are more open to the constructive feedback of the teacher and peer editors.

Editing also becomes easier with a word-processing program. The spellchecker and thesaurus built in to most word-processing programs can be valuable tools to students, helping them to find misspellings as well as choose among many synonyms to express their ideas in more powerful ways. In addition, some programs contain a grammar check that can help students, especially English learners, structure their sentences more effectively.

Finally, the wide variety of fonts available on most word-processing programs allows all students—even those with the poorest handwriting—to produce neat, professional-looking pieces of writing. This writing can be further enhanced with clip-art from the Internet or provided by the word-processing program.

TEACHING THE 6 + 1 TRAITS OF EFFECTIVE WRITING

● 6 + 1 Trait Writing

The **6 + 1 Trait Writing** framework was developed in the Northwest Regional Educational Laboratory (1998/1999) to create an easy-to-understand language that helps teachers describe to students just what it is that makes good writing effective. 6 + 1 Trait Writing is not a program but, rather, a common vocabulary for describing quality in writing, both narrative and expository. As discussed earlier, the traditional approaches to writing instruction tended to focus solely on the teaching of isolated subskills of writing, such as grammar, spelling, and punctuation. The "rules" taught in such programs often amounted to little more than dutifully memorized tricks for achieving the correct mechanics of writing. Such instruction tends to spend too much time and effort on having students write "correctly," without really addressing what they are attempting to say; moreover, such instruction rarely motivates students to want to write beyond their minimum classroom assignments.

With 6 + 1 Trait Writing, students do not simply learn tricks; they learn the traits that make quality writing work. They come to know exactly what good writing is and how to produce it themselves. They do this by comparing their own efforts as writers with those set forth in the high standards of the 6 + 1 Trait Writing criteria. Thus, they are encouraged to become steeped in the real purpose of writing as a medium for communication, rather than the various subskills that have no purpose at all if not used in the context of written communication. Moreover, since virtually every state now has some criteria-based writing standards, the 6 + 1 Trait Writing framework more than covers what is required in the sets of standards the authors have surveyed.

6 + 1 Trait Writing represents the most basic knowledge we need to impart to students about what good writing—in all genres—is and how they may go about producing it. The traits are as follows:

1 ideas   **4** organization   **+1** presentation

2 voice   **5** word choice

3 sentence fluency   **6** conventions

See Figure 6.6 for a 6 + 1 Trait guide to revision.

WWW

6 + 1 Trait™ Writing
www.nwrel.org

1 IDEAS

In order to be effective writers, students need to understand that the *ideas* they come up with are the most important element of their writing. The ideas are the fundamental core of the writer's message, the content of the piece, or the theme that, together with the supporting details and images, enriches and develops the writing by building new insight in a way that holds the reader's attention.

Evidence of the writer's ideas can be found dispersed throughout the piece. However, the general "idea" is more than simply the main idea or topic sentence; it also consists of the careful fleshing out, or elaboration of the topic; the quality and quantity of the details; and how these supporting sentences help convey and clarify the writer's message.

The best ideas come from our own lives, from the unusual as well as the mundane aspects of our lives. But just writing about our lives does not guarantee an effective piece of writing. There also has to be a specific purpose for the writing that makes readers so aware of its significance that they want to continue reading.

IDEAS

☐ Does my paper have a clear, focused idea?

☐ Did I use details to elaborate?

ORGANIZATION

☐ Does my piece have a clear introduction, middle, and conclusion?

VOICE

☐ Does my piece have a spark, a mood, a personality, a specific tone—
formal or informal—that expresses what I want the reader to feel?

WORD CHOICE

☐ Did I use a variety of interesting words?

SENTENCE FLUENCY

☐ Do my sentences sound smooth? When I read the piece to myself, does
it flow?

CONVENTIONS

☐ Did I check my capitals, periods, and spelling (editing for conventions)?

PRESENTATION

☐ Does my writing look neat and professional?

Based on the 6 + 1 Trait writing assessment model from the Northwest Regional Educational Laboratory. Copyright © 1998 Christopher-Gordon Publishers.

FIGURE 6.6   6 + 1 Trait Writing guide to revision.

You can facilitate the free flow of ideas by holding brainstorming sessions with students or by offering provocative prompts, such as "What is one thing you have done that you will never regret?" or "What would the world be like if everyone looked exactly alike?" (See the section "The Writing Process" for additional suggestions.) You may also help students grasp the importance of ideas and what they should look like by posting the following questions, which will help them analyze their own ideas as well as others':

- Does the writing make sense?
- Do I know the topic well?
- Have I included interesting details?
- Does the writing have a clear purpose?
- Does the writing make you want to continue reading?

② ORGANIZATION

Students need to understand that good writing constitutes much more than just an endless flow of freely associated thoughts. For writing to be truly effective, it must demonstrate strong organization, or a logical sequence of ideas, which means that it begins with a purposeful, enticing lead sentence and terminates with a satisfying, thought-provoking ending. In between, the writer carefully links each new detail or development with the larger picture, building to a turning point or key revelation. Strong transitions are provided, so that the reader never feels lost.

Some adults may remember being given a writing assignment in which they were instructed to produce a specified number of words. This preconceived way to write promotes form over function, the opposite of how real authors write. In other words, a piece should be as long as it takes to express the author's ideas in such a way that the reader is not left with questions at the end. Similarly, a section or paragraph of the piece should only exist if it has a specific function to perform, such as stating the theme, advancing the plot, or providing more information about a character.

You can introduce the idea of structure by initially introducing expository frames for expository writing (see Chapter 7) and story grammars for narrative writing. To help your students see how the internal structure of a piece is important, post the following questions, which will help them analyze the organizational structure of their own and others' work:

- Will my beginning grab the reader's attention?
- Do all of the sections or paragraphs hang together?
- Does the writing build up to a key part?
- Is the writing in a logical sequence that is easy to follow?
- Does the piece feel finished at the end?
- Will it make the reader think?

③ VOICE

Students need to understand that the heart and soul of a piece of writing is its voice. That **"voice,"** or life force, is the writer's personality emerging through words. When a writer has especially strong feelings for the chosen topic, the result is a piece that explodes with energy, and the reader feels close to not only the writing but the writer.

● voice

All writing has voice. Even a dreary encyclopedia entry has voice, in that the person who wrote it had to determine what facts to include and those to overlook. What determines a person's likelihood of including certain facts over others is a person's unique personality, or voice.

Voice is perhaps the most fundamental element of 6 + 1 Trait Writing because all the others flow from it. From the writer's own voice come the ideas that are chosen and a unique way of organizing those ideas. Word choice flows from voice, for the words we select are part of who we are. Sentence fluency, especially, emanates from a complex interaction of the words and phrases we choose. And even conventions, such as the way a writer decides to use an exclamation point to show emphasis, are part of the exclusivity that is voice.

If students never find their voice, they will never really discover who they are as writers. Without this trait, they will be forever guessing when it comes to selecting topics, organizing ideas, choosing words, and revising for clarity

When a writer has especially strong feelings for the chosen topic, the result is a piece that explodes with energy and the reader feels close to not only the writing but the writer.

and style. Confusion will lead to frustration and frustration will lead to fear. When students fear writing—because they think they have nothing to say or they are afraid to say what they think in a way that makes them feel comfortable—they do less of it and decrease their chances of ever becoming good at writing.

Students can find their voice when a teacher values their unique perspective and urges them to tell their own stories—stories that all students have to tell. For students to find their voice, the teacher must expect, and actually require, a diversity of opinions within the class. Students must hear that even if they start with the same topic, no two pieces of writing should be the same because no two writers are exactly the same. A strong voice, however, usually develops over time with much practice, reflection, and feedback from a knowledgeable writing coach. A strong voice can be demonstrated to students by examining the voice of familiar authors, such as Gary Paulsen or Cynthia Rylant.

You can introduce the idea of voice by closely examining each student's writing to find the part that is unique and personal to the student who wrote it and holding that up as an example of "voice." Students can be invited to reflect on why the writing works and what was done to make it sound just like the person who wrote it. To help students use their own voice in a piece of writing, post the following questions, which will help them analyze the use of voice in their own writing as well as others':

- Does this writing sound like me?
- Is this what I really think and feel?
- Could a reader feel my commitment to the topic?
- Do I know why I am writing and who my audience is?
- Do I want to share this writing with someone?

④ WORD CHOICE

word choice ●

Appropriate **word choice** is the artistic element of writing that involves using fresh and colorful language to fascinate the reader and make certain passages memorable and worthy of reading aloud. Word choice emanates from a true love of language and a desire to select words to express the exact image, impression, or mood in the reader's mind's eye.

Word choice becomes apparent to the reader when a writer's language describes an event or feeling in such a manner that the reader feels he or she has received new insights into the mundane; with such writing, it seems clear that no other words or phrases would have worked as perfectly. Word choice is much more than simply effective adjectives or phrases; it entails many factors, such as unusually vivid descriptions and sensory impressions ("a white carpet of fresh snow"), strong and specific verbs ("enveloped by the gloom"), effective use of colloquial language ("He hogtied the critter and threw him into the truck"), and even the occasional use of invented words ("He went shrooming down the slide") when they add to the image needed.

Effective use of words is often confused with using large, grandiose-sounding words. When introduced to the thesaurus, students often delight in finding unfamiliar words because they sound, to them, astute and therefore better. Instead, they need to be shown that clarity is the goal and that this often entails using fewer words to get the reader to see clearly what is in the writer's head. For example: "There were multitudinous tomes creating a dis-array underneath the man's bed" versus "The books littered the carpet under Joe's bed."

Perhaps the most effective way to help students become aware of sub-tleties in language choice is to give them plenty of experiences with good literature. While conducting a guided reading lesson or reading aloud to students, point out excellent word choice as it is encountered: "Oh, I can really see that sunset!" or "Wow! I feel as though I were there, don't you?" or "Gosh, I never thought of it that way!" Help students practice word choice by having them transform simple sentences, orally or in written form, into ones that vividly depict a situation. For example, they could transform the simple sentence "The boy ran" into "The tiny, freckle-faced boy ran swiftly through the field, fearing the angry bull would make a meal of him." You may also help students choose appropriate words and phrases by posting the following questions, which will help them analyze their own word choices as well as others':

- Is this the best way I can say this?
- Do my words and phrases create mind pictures?
- Have I tried new ways to say everyday things?
- Are my verbs powerful?
- Do any of my words and phrases linger in my mind?
- Would any of my phrases be interesting to read aloud?

5 SENTENCE FLUENCY

Writing fluency is that intangible essence that separates excellent writing from the ordinary. It is the careful crafting of sentence structures into graceful sentences so that paragraphs flow smoothly and effortlessly. While effective word choice is part of this trait, **sentence fluency** is more than just the individual words chosen. It is the entire effect of the way the sentences sound when read aloud, including such features as parallel construction, easy transitions between paragraphs, alliteration, and the variety of lengths and constructions of the sentences—all of which provide a sense of aesthetic satisfaction to the reader.

- sentence fluency

Sentence fluency takes time and practice for students to develop because, more than any of the other traits, it depends heavily on their ability to hear the difference between awkward writing that is hard to understand and follow, and crisp, smooth writing that communicates the writer's intent with an efficiency of words.

As with attuning students' ears to effective word choice, sentence fluency can best be fostered by reading aloud often to them with expression and gusto, and pointing out examples of excellent writing when they appear. Point out the use of alliteration ("pink poppies"), conversational style ("Aaaahhh, I wish I weren't so tired!"), and similes ("as brown as the tired desert"), as well as pleasing and consistent rhythm in pieces of writing. Teachers can also demonstrate how *they* write, modeling how they think through the process. In addition, with the overhead projector, students can practice rewriting awkward sentences so they more clearly and concisely convey intended ideas. Finally, teachers can help students write fluent sentences by posting the following questions, which will help them analyze their sentence fluency and that of others:

- Are my sentences a variety of lengths?
- Do my sentences "flow" as I read them aloud?
- Do I use alliteration and/or similes to make my sentences interesting?
- Does the writing flow easily from sentence to sentence?
- Do the sentences begin in different ways?
- Are the sentences powerful and memorable?

⑥ CONVENTIONS

The most important traits of writing are, arguably, the ones just covered because they concern the core of what the writer has to say. They all concern the composing part of writing. Conventional correctness, however, should not be overlooked, because it constitutes the tools of the trade that help bring the writing to others in a uniform manner that readers expect.

conventions ●

Conventions include grammar, spelling, paragraphing, capitalization, punctuation, and all the mechanics of the language that are often corrected in the editing process.

Conventions are more than the window dressing used to make our writing correct, or a list of simple rules to be obeyed. They should be presented as "tools," not "rules." Combined, they are a systematic set of symbols to facilitate communication between writer and reader. Conventions have meaning just as words do, and it is a skillful writer who takes advantage of a full range of these meaning-making tools and situations to communicate most effectively with the reader.

While more materials exist for the teaching of conventions than for all the other traits combined, there is much evidence that assigning worksheet after worksheet on grammar usage, punctuation, and the like out of context is ineffective in teaching students to write; such undue focus often interferes with what the writer has to say (Weaver, 1996). Individual conventions, such as the proper use of capital letters, should be taught in short minilessons but be reinforced continually by showing writers how important it is for their writing to be readable and telling them how much we appreciate being able to clearly understand what they have written. Appropriate use of conventions should be pointed out as they occur, rather than negative ones. Students also need to hear that the more they read and write, the more proficient they will become at using conventions appropriately. Teachers can help students use conventions properly by posting the following questions, which will help them proofread their writing and that of others:

- Have I used capital letters correctly?
- Is all the punctuation in the right place?
- Are all the words spelled correctly?
- Have I used a resource to help spell unfamiliar words?
- Did I indent each paragraph?
- Are my sentences logical and grammatically correct?

+1 PRESENTATION

For years teachers and readers alike have indicated that the format of a piece of writing—the spacing, handwriting, layout, graphics, and so forth—were influencing their ability to read and fairly assess for the traits. Now, instead of not treating those issues as part of the criteria, teachers discuss them and integrate them into the 6 + 1 Trait Writing model. Teachers can use this feature or ignore it, but it is an option that many educators are finding useful as students use many different formats to practice and develop their writing skills.

FOSTERING WRITING FLUENCY

Fluency in writing, as well as in reading, should be a fundamental goal of every literacy program. All writers, through their thinking and problem-solving, learn about both writing and reading and how they are connected (Shanahan, 1988). Early writers, through their rich experimentation, learn about the conventions of print. Writers in grades 4–8 learn how to think like authors, which helps them as they read and evaluate what other authors have written. Moreover, older writers learn the importance of using exactly the right word or sentence to communicate their intended meaning. This way of thinking about words and sentences also applies to reading. Thus a strong focus on writing is an important component in literacy programs—especially for children who are struggling with reading (Rasinski & Padak, 2000).

Two main components comprise **writing fluency:** The speed with which   ● writing fluency
students write, and the automaticity of the conventions of writing—spelling in particular—that allow them independence and confidence when drafting their ideas (Cecil, 2007b).

Speed

Writing speed can be increased with an approach known as "speed writing." Speed writing, also known as free writing and a form of quickwrites, is designed to alleviate writers' anxieties about penmanship and the correctness of language conventions in drafts (Norton, 1993).

Speed Writing   ACTIVITY

- Tell students that they will be writing nonstop for a specified amount of time (e.g., two to five minutes).

- Instruct them that they should not be concerned with erasing, crossing out, or requesting help with spelling. Explain that the idea is that they should be relaxed when writing and allow their ideas to flow.

- At the end of the designated writing time, ask individual students to share their writing with the group.

- Invite the listeners to ask questions and offer comments and suggestions that may help the authors clarify or further develop their work.

- As an extension to speed writing, listeners may be invited to respond to the authors' messages in written form; for example, in one speed writing session, a fifth-grade girl shared her personal narrative about her grandmother, who had recently undergone an operation and died. The other children, after hearing the sad tale, immediately responded by writing sympathy cards to the bereaved child (Gipe, 2006).

Speedwriting techniques can be used to respond to stories that have been read, but they may also be used to have students write about what they have been learning in science, social studies, or other content areas. The teacher reads and responds to the writing and writes the correct form of misspelled words at the bottom of the page so that students will notice the correct spelling. Sometimes, the teacher may encourage students to revise and edit their speedwriting and make a final, published copy, but the major goal is to develop writing fluency rather than to create polished compositions.

Automaticity

To become "automatic" in their writing, students must have a command of the conventions of writing so that they can spend more energy with their ideas than the actual formulation of text. They must also be aware of strategies that help them think through problems and concerns that all writers encounter as they are composing a piece of writing. To help students develop automaticity in their writing, consider the following sections, which show how to model fluent writing behavior for students and provide strategies that students can use when they possess limited spelling prowess.

Teacher Modeling

A comprehensive program of writing instruction should provide daily demonstrations and minilessons, modeling how writers use the conventions of language and think through many different kinds of writing strategies. As a teacher you can then offer (1) guided practice sessions in which students will use the new skills with the assistance of a proficient writer and (2) independent writing sessions in which students have the opportunity to practice their newly acquired skills. Such sessions show students how fluent writers think through the host of writing decisions that authors must make, and what they do when they discover problems. After each such session, allow students to gain valuable practice in implementing these writing tools until they become second nature. Students can then be said to have reached the stage of automaticity in writing.

Spelling

Of all the conventions necessary for writing fluency and automaticity, spelling problems, especially, tend to slow down and "inhibit many students who would otherwise be imaginative, intelligent writers" (Silva & Yarborough, 1990, p. 48). To become fluent writers, students must be able to spell words automatically and, if handwriting a document, must be able to rapidly form letters. Just as disfluent readers read word by word and decode many words, disfluent writers write slowly, word by word, and have to stop and sound out the spelling of many words. In fact, some disfluent writers write so slowly that by the time they get to the end of a sentence, they have forgotten what it is they were writing!

Using the spell-check feature of a word-processing program offers students a way to ensure that spelling is correct and will help to develop a spelling conscience within the students. Although students do need to practice automatically forming their letters quickly and legibly when handwriting, a balance of students' using a word-processing program and writing longhand helps to diminish the frustration associated with a lack of fine motor skills.

Fluent writers seem to have a continuous flow of ideas. With such a built-in writing agenda, these writers quickly get to work on assigned writing tasks and therefore have considerably more practice than their less fluent counterparts, who may spend endless time struggling to think of topics about which they can write. Fortunately, this problem can be remedied by engaging students in writing for authentic purposes, as we shall explore in the next section.

INSPIRING STUDENTS TO WRITE

Writer's workshop and 6 + 1 Trait Writing are highly effective tools to help students become proficient writers; however, writing, like any other skill, requires continual practice to hone and refine its many nuances. The crafting necessary for good writing can be developed through daily writing for real purposes, with continual feedback from caring peers and adult coaches. The following sections concern four practices that can help students become engaged writers who write for authentic purposes.

1 The use of dialogue journals, offering a vehicle through which students can use writing in much the same way as they use conversation with friends.

2 The opportunity to write a narrative piece that is both longer and more in-depth than the ordinary story writing assignment.

3 Writing poetry through the use of literacy scaffolds, which offers students the opportunity to express their creative thoughts and ideas.

4 Writing informational text, which allows students to explain ideas, objects, or processes to a reader in an understandable way while at the same time improving their own knowledge and understanding of the topic.

1 DIALOGUE JOURNALS

Of the variety of journal-writing formats used in grades 4–8, the one that provides students with the most helpful feedback about their writing is the **dialogue journal,** also known as the interactive journal (Cecil, 1994a). The "dialogue" part simply means that in this journal, a running dialogue is carried on between the teacher and each individual student. The student begins the dialogue by writing down anything that is of interest to him, and the teacher simply responds, in the margins, to what the student has expressed. The teacher may comment on the student's ideas, use thoughtful questions to ask for elaboration, or paraphrase what the student has said to validate and affirm the student's ideas. The teacher and no one else (unless the student initiates sharing with someone else) reads what the student has written.

To launch the idea of dialogue journals in the classroom, it is often helpful to write two or three questions on the board to inspire students, such as, *What are your favorite things to do on a Saturday morning?* or *Who is one famous sports figure you admire and why?* Advising students that these topics are only possibilities for writing and not mandates frees those who already

● dialogue journal

have their own diary-like writing agenda, which can include problems, goals, fears, or just a recording of the things they have recently been doing.

Gradually in the course of dialogue journal writing, a writing stimulus becomes less and less important as the written conversation, or dialogue, between the teacher and student follows its own natural path. Most teachers find that, while the first dialogue topics are cautiously neutral to begin with, their positive feedback leads to a more trusting and caring relationship. At that point, the student will look forward to the writing as a chance to complain, share successes, express undying love for the teacher, confess to wrongdoing, or reveal many other personal feelings that make the writing rewarding. Ideally, students should have some time set aside for journal writing every day, beginning with a few minutes and graduating to 15 or 20 as they find more and more to say in their dialogue.

Justification for adding dialogue journal writing to an already overcrowded literacy curriculum is compelling, and in this age of teacher accountability, it is worth examining. First, students who participate in such a program develop a much more positive attitude toward writing. If sessions are frequent; endure for most of the school year; and include caring, nonjudgmental feedback from the teacher, even reluctant writers will be more favorably inclined toward writing and will write much more (Cecil, 2007b).

Second, students become more confident as they begin to believe in the power of their writing ability and look forward to the teacher's comments, rather than dreading the proverbial "sea of red marks" common in traditional writing programs. As they realize their thoughts and ideas have merit, their self-perception as writers will increase. In addition, the nonthreatening nature of dialogue journals makes them particularly appropriate for students for whom English is a second language. They can write in their home language or "code switch," by using words from their native language and their newly acquired language. Such learners are too often fearful of being publicly ridiculed for their lack of oral and written fluency (Peyton & Reed, 1990).

Students become more confident as they begin to believe in the power of their writing ability.

Third, students receive important writing practice through journal writing and, as a result, they become more fluent writers. As in any activity—skiing, typing, riding a bicycle—writing improves with continual practice. Moreover, through the teacher's modeling and questioning (see Figure 6.7), students begin to recognize just what details to include to make their writing more effective. Additionally, through modeling, student's use of conventions such as spelling, grammar, and punctuation improves markedly (Cecil, 1994a). The teacher is able to be there for certain "teachable moments" when students need to use an unaccustomed grammatical construct or to spell an unfamiliar word, as with the word *Hawaii* in Figure 6.7.

Finally, students begin to see an authentic use for writing for their own purposes rather than to fulfill a teacher-directed assignment. In the informal venue of their own private journals, many students find that writing can be a most cathartic experience—especially when they are using it to vent strong

Dialogue journal entry (fourth grade).   FIGURE   6.7

No, I have never been to Hawaii, Kim, but I have always wanted to go there. Did you get to do any snorkeling? Yes, I noticed your lovely tan!

We had such a fun time in ~~Hawiiy~~ Hawie Mrs. Cecil. Were you ever thare? I got sun bruned like a ~~lob~~ lobstor. Did you notis Mrs. Cecil. I can't wait to go back thare.

Snorkeling is fun, isn't it, Kim? How did you learn? Did your mother teach you? Was it difficult? What else did you do in Hawaii?

Yes we got to ~~sn~~ snorkel when we were in Hawaii. It was so neat! There were so many fish with all difrint colors. I never saw anything like that befor.

I'm sorry you are being bothered, Kim. I will change your seat and speak with Meg. No, I am not angry with you!   ☺

You know, Mrs. Cecil. You were telling me to stop talking today in math class. but it wasn't me. Meg was talking. Meg keeps bothing me. Please move her seat. Dont be mad at me please, Mrs. Cecil??

I have one daughter, Kim. Like you, I am sure she thinks I am mean sometimes. It is hard being a Mommy!

Mrs. Cecil, do you have any children? I wish I was your child. Instead of your student. My mother is to mene. I think you are probly never mene to your children?

Kim, the important thing is that you have now told the truth. Sometimes it's hard to tell the truth. No, I am not angry, but please don't do it again, okay?   ☺

Now I want to tell you something o.k. Last weak when I was absint I was'nt sick. I ~~wu~~ just made that up becuase I wanted to stay home and watch Scuby Do. Im sorry, Mrs. Cecil. Are you angry now???? Do'nt be.

feelings and emotions. As students get older, they find, too, that writing can be a positive outlet to defuse potentially explosive situations ahead of time because they can examine their written feelings before they act on them. In this age of school violence, the importance of such a constructive outlet should not be underestimated.

❷ EXTENDED NARRATIVE TEXT

Students who have had the experience of writing an extended form of narrative text, such as an original episodic novel or a multichaptered novelette, come away with a tremendous feeling of accomplishment and a sense of pride at having produced a complex set of characters who have evolved with time and effort. These characters actually become real to them in much the same way as any characters do to adults who have just finished reading a satisfying novel. Indeed, students who write novelettes are understandably quite impressed that their creation more closely resembles an adult novel in scope and size than the typical shorter pieces they traditionally pen (Cecil, 1994a).

To initiate the writing of a novelette, it is often helpful to provide an extensive outline of what possible chapters could look like. Outlines might focus on themes related to a certain emotion, such as greed, jealousy, love, or hope. Or, after reading with students a variety of Greek and Roman myths, teachers can create an outline of the adventures of a similar hero or heroine. After reviewing the basic elements of narrative structure, the teacher can invite students to write chapters telling about their main character and his or her struggles and resolutions, or use the longer format to explain a natural phenomenon, such as tornadoes or hurricanes.

After distributing guidelines to students, such as the ones offered in Figure 6.8, have them brainstorm a list of possible ideas for the first chapter. For example, in the first chapter in Figure 6.8, the characters brainstormed may range from a telepathic Martian to a young woman living out on the prairie with eight children. Students will thus be inspired to select an idea to work up for their own chapter, or choose another that comes to their mind. It is crucial for the teacher to remind students that there are no right or wrong characters, only many ideas, each of which can be an interesting beginning for a novel.

After the class brainstorming session, each student selects a character and then fleshes out the chapter with class ideas as well as his own. Students can then be paired with a peer editor during writer's workshop to share their chapter and receive praise, questions, and suggestions for improvement. New chapters are usually written weekly or biweekly, with revisions and teacher and peer editor conferences occurring in between. However, by the second or third chapter, the class brainstorming, and even the outline, become less and less important as students become very close to their characters and look forward to expanding them wherever the characters decide to go.

By the fourth or fifth chapter, the characters in most novelettes have usually evolved to the point where they seem to have minds of their own. Therefore, as the teacher presents the next chapter in the outline, she can encourage students to deviate from the outline if they feel their character is heading in other directions. As more and more chapters are written, the outline lessens in importance and the excitement of the deepening development of the character and plot becomes a unique source of motivation.

When the last chapter is completed, through the joint efforts of the author, the teacher, and the author's editorial partners, which can take anywhere from a few weeks to several months, students are eager to do the final editing and illustrating. A minilesson can address the fact that a title should be chosen with great care, not only to catch the reader's attention but also to capture the essence of the novelette. Completed novelettes can then be word processed and professionally bound. Finally, the authors can read them aloud to the entire class and receive appreciative comments, and the teacher can explore other venues to share students' accomplishments, such as reading the

1. Invent and describe a character; physical characteristics, habits, likes, dislikes, traits. (characterization)

2. Provide your character with a history: What has his or her life been like up to now? Who were his or her parents? What sort of childhood did he or she have? What were his or her friends like? (background)

3. Describe where your character lives. (setting)

4. Describe a typical day in the life of your character.

5. Your character is going to leave town; describe what led to this decision.

6. Just before leaving town, your character receives advice from someone; re-create this scene in dialogue.

7. The first day out of town your character meets someone strange; describe this person and what makes him or her strange.

8. This person asks your character to do something, but your character is not sure if he or she should. What was your character asked to do and what goes through his or her mind?

9. Your character decides to do what has been asked; describe the decision and its consequences.

10. Some time later, your character turns up in a large city with very little money. Your character decides to find a job. Describe the search for a job and the job he or she finally secures.

11. Describe a typical day on the job.

12. Despite the fact that your character likes the job, he or she is fired. Describe this scene, making clear why he or she was fired.

13. Your character is depressed and inattentive. As a result, he or she has an accident. Describe it.

14. Your character is taken to a hospital and learns that he or she is not expected to live. Describe this scene and your character's feelings about the imminence of death.

15. Despite the doctor's predictions, your character recovers and decides the city is not for him or her. Your character moves to a small town where he or she lives for a year. Describe this period.

16. While living in this small town, your character sees a number of things he or she believes ought to be changed. What are they?

17. In order to bring about changes in the town, your character decides to run for mayor. Describe the campaign.

18. Your character wins the campaign and begins to inaugurate changes; however, he or she encounters difficulties. What are they? How are they resolved? How will you end the novelette? (Cecil, 1994a)

Writing a novelette.   FIGURE   6.8

novelettes to another class or taking a field trip to a convalescent home to read to the residents.

High-quality literature for children and adolescents can be the inspiration for writing these novelettes in particular styles and genres. Teachers can foster this inspiration by calling attention to interesting phrases, word choice, dialogue, character development, and foreshadowing in books that are read aloud to students or those that are read by students in their literature circles (see Chapter 5). If the books are wisely chosen, students will have excellent models from which to draw for their own writing. Some high-quality novels for children and adolescents can be found through recommendations from the school librarian, or from professional organizations such as the International Reading Association or the American Library Association. An additional source is a list of Newbery Medal books. The Newbery Medal is awarded each year by the American Library Association to the author of the most distinguished contribution to literature for children published during the preceding year.

Some titles that we have found to be particularly useful for modeling the traits of a well-crafted novelette are listed in the box on page 206.

Models for the Well-Crafted Novelette

Balliett, B. (2004). *Chasing Vermeer.* Scholastic.

Bartolettei, S. C. (2005). *Hitler youth: Growing up in Hitler's shadow.* Scholastic.

Bat-Ami, M. (1999). *Two suns in the sky.* Front Street.

Berry, D., & Pearson, R. (2004). *Peter and the starcatchers.* Hyperion Books for Children.

Collins, S. (2003). *Gregor the overlander.* Scholastic.

Creech, S. (2004). *Heartbeat.* Joanna Cutler Books.

Cummings, P. (2004). *Red kayak.* Dutton Children's Books.

DiCamillo, K. (2003). *The tale of Despereaux.* Candlewick.

Farmer, N. (2004). *The sea of trolls.* Atheneum.

Funke, C. (2002). *The thief lord.* Translated by O. Latsch. Scholastic.

Hahn, M. D. (1991). *Stepping on the cracks.* Clarion.

Holub, J. (2005). *An innocent soldier.* Translated by M. Hoffmann. Scholastic.

Ibbotson, E. (2004). *The star of Kazan.* Dutton Children's Books.

McKernan, V. (2005). *Shackleton's stowaway.* Knopf.

Mochizuki, K. (1997). *Passage to freedom: The Sugihara story.* Lee & Low.

Oppel, K. (2004). *Airborn.* Eos.

Patneaude, D. (2004). *Thin wood walls.* Houghton Mifflin.

Ryan, P. M. (2004). *Becoming Naomi Leon.* Scholastic.

Weeks, S. (2004). *So B. it: A novel.* Laura Geringer Books.

Woodson, J. (2003). *Locomotion.* Putnam.

③ POETRY

The entire spectrum of students writing in today's grade 4–8 classrooms—from gifted to second-language learners to hard-to-motivate writers—can be encouraged to create poetry through the use of literacy scaffolds. **Scaffolding** is a support mechanism by which students are able to accomplish more difficult tasks than they could without assistance. The **literacy scaffold** is a kind of formula for writing a poem by imitating, to a greater or lesser degree, an existing poem. By simplifying the process of writing a poem—a process that can seem threatening and esoteric to many—students can see that once they are given the structure, they are freed to fill in their own creative thoughts and ideas. The following eight steps guide the teacher and students through the process (Cecil, 1994b).

scaffolding

literacy scaffold

ACTIVITY | *Writing Poetry Using a Literacy Scaffold*

1. Provide a literacy scaffold, or temporary writing framework, created from the work of a poet students admire, such as Shel Silverstein, Jack Prelutsky, or another selection (see Figure 6.9).

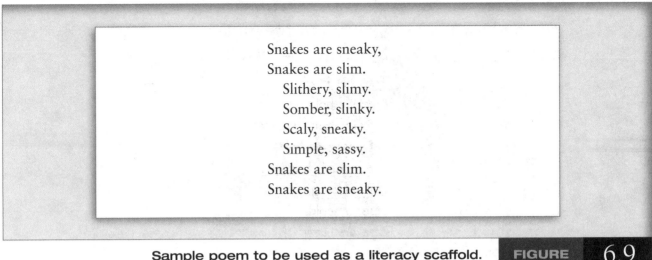

Snakes are sneaky,
Snakes are slim.
Slithery, slimy.
Somber, slinky.
Scaly, sneaky.
Simple, sassy.
Snakes are slim.
Snakes are sneaky.

Sample poem to be used as a literacy scaffold.   FIGURE   6.9

2. Read examples of other students' work, or your own, that contain the structure (save these from previous classes).

3. On an overhead projector, show students a poem using the structure and guide them to identify the structure, as well as the particular conventions (punctuation, spacing, capital letters, and so forth) that the poem employs.

4. As a group, brainstorm some topics for a poem that the whole class can contribute to using the scaffold.

5. Brainstorm some words or phrases that could be used in the poem.

6. Using the overhead, write a group poem on the chosen topic, using the scaffold and brainstormed words and phrases.

7. Individually, or in pairs for the reluctant, invite students to write their own poems using the literacy scaffold. (*Note:* More "seasoned" poets should feel free to deviate from the literacy scaffold.)

8. Have students follow the remaining steps in the writing process to revise, edit, share, and publish their work.

An example of how this process can be used was demonstrated recently by a class of fourth-graders. To achieve the objective of having students write a group poem, they were first read a poem about words, using a particular pattern, or literacy scaffold. Then they were shown the poem on the overhead projector and were able to discover the pattern of adjectives used in the poem, all beginning with the same letter sound. The teacher added that the adjectives in the first and last two lines are called *predicate adjectives,* because they come after the verb *are* and describe the noun. On further investigation, the students pointed out that the first two lines and the last two lines are the same, but in reverse. Finally, the students observed that all lines begin with a capital letter and noted the use of commas and periods. After brainstorming some topics for their group poem, the students settled on "bees," and then, with help from student dictionaries, brainstormed some words and phrases that would be associated with bees that also started with the letter *b.* Figure 6.10 shows the students' final product. Figure 6.11 shows a sample poem and two poems created by older students using a different scaffold with this process.

Bees

Bees are _buzzy_,
Bees are _bold_.
   Boisterous, bashful.
   Belligerent, bold.
   Beautiful, bellicose,
   Bewildering, bright.
Bees are _bold_,
Bees are _buzzy_.

FIGURE 6.10 Poem created by fourth-grade students using the model provided.

FIGURE 6.11 Career poem.

DESCRIPTION: This is a three-stanza poem that extols the virtues of a particular career or trade. In it, the poet muses about the tools of that career or trade. The brief verses follow this format:

> The song of the [*tool used in the job*]
> Is [*adjective describing the tool*]
> As they [*action of the tool*]
> [*Rhyme with line two*].
>
> *Repeat twice.*
>
> —Adapted from *Busy Carpenters,* by James S. Tippett

THE FARMER (student's career poem #1)

The song of the pitchfork
Is fine
As they get the hay in
Just barely in time.

The song of the reaper
Is grand
As they grow food to eat
From the rich land.

The song of the tractor
Is loyal
As they plow the fields
And till the soil.

—*Sabrina, grade 7*

FIRE FIGHTER (student's career poem #2)

The song of the fire truck
Is speed
As they rush to the fire
And help people in need.

The song of the water hose
Is kind
As they put out the flames
And save people they find.

The song of the siren
Is caring
As they spend their whole lives
Doing deeds that are daring.

—*Jim, grade 8*

Cecil, N. L. (1997). *For the Love of Poetry: Literacy Scaffolds, Extension Ideas, and More.* Winnipeg, Manitoba: Portage & Main.

4 INFORMATIONAL TEXT

Informational writing, often called "expository writing," generally explains an idea, an object, or a process. The expository paragraph or essay presents a certain amount of information about a topic. The main purpose of this mode of discourse is to explain or inform, to tell readers something they may not know, and to tell them in a way that they will understand (see Figure 6.12).

● informational writing

Instead of having, loosely, a beginning, middle, and end as in narrative structure, the expository paragraph/essay has a somewhat more rigid organization and is organized according to one of the patterns discussed in Chapter 7. Essentially, all expository writing has four main parts that students can be taught to include when creating an expository piece. Each piece of expository writing must contain the following:

1. *Thesis statement.* In an essay, the thesis statement occurs at the beginning of the piece and indicates the author's attitude or position on a topic. It tells the reader why the piece is being written. *Example:* Spiders play an important role in controlling certain insect populations.

2. *Topic sentence.* In a paragraph, the topic sentence tells the reader what the paragraph is going to be about. *Example:* Insects differ from spiders in several ways.

Example passages for contrasting expository and narrative writing. **FIGURE** 6.12

GIVING INFORMATION
(Explaining)

The dolphin may look like a fish, but this friendly sea creature is really a mammal. First of all, dolphins have lungs just like we do. They must come to the surface of the water to breathe and get oxygen from the air. Fish can take oxygen from the water. Like other mammals, dolphins have backbones and are warm blooded. Finally, they nurse young dolphins on milk just like a cow might nurse a calf. The dolphin's streamlined body and its big, strong tail might resemble a fish, but don't be fooled; it's definitely a mammal.

TELLING A STORY
(Narrating)

I was excited to see the dolphins, my favorite animal.
"Go closer to the tank," my father said.
I looked into the water and saw the beautiful animals swimming together. Someone was feeding them fish.
"I wish I could swim with the dolphins," I said.
"Maybe someday you will," said my father.
Just then one of the dolphins swam close to us and suddenly we were as wet as could be! We laughed and laughed.

3. *Transition phrases.* Important words that signal new ideas are often called transition phrases. They are the "glue" that holds the paragraphs in the piece together. *Examples:* Words and phrases such as *first, second,* and *finally, on the other hand, nevertheless,* and *in a similar way* are all examples of phrases that help the reader to realize that a new idea is about to be introduced.

4. *Examples, evidence, and explanations.* The essence of any expository piece is in the details. After giving a topic sentence or thesis statement, the writer must elaborate and make a case for the claim by providing examples, reasons, and facts; by citing evidence; and by offering an explanation, depending upon the organizational structure being used. *Example:* First, insects have six legs, while a spider has eight.

5. *Conclusion.* The expository piece is usually tied together with a conclusion that reminds the reader of the topic sentence/thesis statement. Because information has been given via the examples, evidence, or explanations, the conclusion is stated slightly differently than the original statement. *Example:* People should be careful about killing off the spiders in their yards and gardens because spiders are useful in controlling the population of other bugs.

Given appropriate instruction in the structure of informational text and a topic they find interesting, students in grades 4–8 are fully capable of coping with the complex organizational problems that occur when writing informational text. Indeed, even students in first and second grade can be successful in writing informational text. As an example, Read (2005) found that when students were allowed to write on topics of their own choosing, and were invited to write collaboratively, they worked out content problems aloud and provided feedback to each other regarding the organization of the content as well as the conventions of print.

Choosing a topic about which to write is often easier for students when they do informational writing rather than narrative writing (Read, 2005). There is far less, "I don't know what to write about!" when there are so many different topics they can become interested in. Students in grades 4–8 enjoy researching and then writing about their discoveries on a wide variety of topics, including wild and domestic animals, cars, other cultures and ancient civilizations, volcanoes, and planets, just to name a few. See the box on page 212 for websites to spur interest in informational topics.

Preparing to write a report documenting the student's discoveries can be accomplished through the use of the I-Search strategy.

ACTIVITY *I-Search Process*

Planning to write a report is a unique mode of preparation that requires a student to search for information and relate the details of that search to others. Bay Area Writing project teachers (Olson, 1986) attest to the effectiveness of the I-Search Strategy, or "hunting story," for teaching the skills students will need throughout their academic lives for reading and writing research reports.

Freedman (1986) teaches the *I-Search process* in three stages: (1) identifying the topic to be studied, (2) searching for information, and (3) writing the report. She advises teachers who are introducing the I-Search technique in the classroom (usually starting in third grade) to use the following procedure:

1. Begin with a before-writing exercise in which students write statements about topics of interest to them and then generate a list of things they would like to know about the topic. For example, one topic might be dinosaurs. Students might pose questions such as,

> "When did dinosaurs live?"
>
> "Did they kill people?"
>
> "What caused them to become extinct?"
>
> "Where did they live and what did they eat?"

2. After several ideas have been generated, have students select one topic of special interest from their lists to explore. This brainstorming activity helps to stimulate thinking and ensures that all students will have a topic that they care enough about to spend time gathering information about it.

3. Show students how to obtain information through the use of various resources available to them, such as the Internet, encyclopedias and other reference materials, trade books, interviews, and resource people.

4. Give students a structure to help them plan and organize their information so that they can share it with others. The I-Search reporting format is shown in Figure 6.13.

The I-Search reporting format.   **FIGURE** **6.13**

1. *Statement of the problem:* What do I want to know? (establish key questions)

    When did dinosaurs live?

    Why did they die out?

2. *The hunting process:* Where will I find information about my topic? (list possible resources)

    The Internet

    Encyclopedias in the library

    Books in the classroom

3. *Summary of findings:* What did I learn about my topic? (compose written summary)

    Dinosaurs lived many millions of years before the first human being appeared on earth. Although many cartoons show humans and dinosaurs together, that never really happened. Most dinosaurs were plant eaters, although some others were meat-eaters and hunted other, smaller dinosaurs. No one really knows for sure why dinosaurs became extinct. Some scientists think it was because of disease, while others believe an ice age, which caused the world to become very cold, killed them. Though we often imagine that they were ferocious and that we would fear them, we will never know, because no human EVER saw a live dinosaur!

4. *Conclusion:* How can I best share my information? (create multimedia presentation)

    I will use a PowerPoint presentation of the information and include some clip art of dinosaurs.

Websites for Informational Text

Children's Book Council (CBC), www.cbcbooks.org/

Provides the social studies list and science list of outstanding children's trade books for young people.

Cleveland Rock & Roll Hall of Fame, http://rockhall.com/programs.asp

This site offers lesson plans that integrate music with history and literature. Older children can explore the site independently.

Defenders of Wildlife, www.defenders.org/

The programs addressed here focus on the extinction of animal species and the destruction of their environment. The website is committed to protecting endangered plants and wild animals.

Eisenhower National Clearinghouse, www.enc.org/

This clearinghouse is dedicated to identifying superior curriculum resources, creating high-quality professional development materials, and improving science and math learning in K–12 classrooms.

Endangered Species Coalition, www.stopextinction.org.

This group is the watchdog for the Endangered Species Act of 1973. The website disseminates information and provides discussions about environmental, scientific, and conservation issues related to the ESA.

Fish America Foundation, www.fishamerica.org/

This organization has assisted more than 700 grassroots organizations to enhance fish production and increase water quality throughout North America.

Global Exchange, http://globalexchange.org/

Founded in 1988, Global Exchange is a human rights organization focused on promoting environmental rights and political awareness around the world.

Greenpeace, www.greenpeace.org/

This activist organization is dedicated to achieving change in environmental and conservationist issues through direct action and international conferences.

The History Place, www.historyplace.com

This site provides information about history that can be used as background for any social studies unit; especially good for World War II.

Journey North, www.learner.org/jnorth/

This site includes information about an Internet project and resources for the study of seasonal change. Children from all 50 states and Canada have taken part in the project.

Kids Web Japan, http://web-jpn.org/kidsweb/index.html

Introduces children to Japan, including Japanese lifestyle, pictures, and legends. Managed by the Japan Center for Intercultural Communications.

Knowledge Adventure, http://knowledgeadventure.com/home

This site features lesson plans on all subjects for all ages. Young children can find games right on the site.

Magic School Bus, http://scholastic.com/MagicSchoolBus/index.htm

This site includes content area materials and activities for students and is a resource area for teachers.

My Hero Project, www.myhero.com/home.asp

This site allows students to read about many heroes and heroines around the world as they come to understand what it means to make a difference.

New York Philharmonic Kidzone, www.nyphilkids.org/main.phtml

Activities on this site include videos about instruments, composing music, games, and puzzles.

Rainforest, www.ran.org/rankids_action/index1.html

Many environmental ideas, especially about saving the rainforest, can be found here. Contains marvelous color and sound effects that will delight young readers, although it is mainly a teacher resource center.

Transportation, http://www.libsci.sc.edu/miller/transportation2.html

Action songs and finger plays about transportation. Activities can be read on screen or reproduced.

TROUBLESHOOTING

Nothing is more satisfying to most students than sharing a piece that they have successfully drafted, revised, edited, and illustrated with a trusted audience and then receiving celebratory comments. However, a variety of factors can make writing a dreaded chore for many students. Following are some suggestions for this common dilemma.

No Confidence

Reluctant writers with little or no confidence in their ability to write—especially English learners just coming to terms with a new language—may initially prefer to draw pictures of their ideas in the prewriting stage. They can be invited to share these pictures orally with trusted peers or the teacher. Additionally, after using the writing process as discussed in this chapter, such students can be shown specific sentences that illustrate the strengths and limitations in their own writing and be told how to correct or avoid specific problems. Diederich (1991) suggests that writers lacking confidence generally respond better to praise of what they have done well than to any specific type or amount of correction. Further, Johnston (1992) offers that instead of asking reluctant writers questions about a weak part of their writing, it is more helpful to give a specific reason for your confusion. For example, instead of asking, "Why was the boy so sad at the end of your story?" it might be more helpful to state, "I really liked the way you ended your story, but I was confused about why the boy would have been sad when it appeared he had gotten his wish."

No Ideas

Often in writer's workshop, when students are given free rein to choose their own topics, some will complain that they do not know what to write about. Providing specific prompts ("What would you do with a million dollars?") and story starters (see Figure 6.14), provocative lead-in sentences that pique a student's imagination, can sometimes be helpful. When a student is "stuck" on a piece of writing and complains that she doesn't know what comes next, a helpful technique is to read the student's work and then offer a snippet of an idea that can lead the student to a new set of possibilities. For example, a student writing about a mirror in an attic may imagine a picnic area on the other side of the mirror but be unable to come up with an idea about what could happen there. The teacher might suggest, "I see a little squirrel scurrying away in the woods and . . . ," and then walk away, promising to check back later to see how the student is doing. Often, a tiny nudge of this sort will remove the block. Finally, teachers should not hesitate to tell students an important truth about writing: More often than not, inspiration occurs during writing rather than before it. In other words, as they simply take the leap and begin to write something, most students find that the fear dissipates as the ideas generated beget more ideas.

Too Many Ideas

Though it may not seem like much of a problem, certain students will have so many ideas that they will become overwhelmed, or even paralyzed, by indecision. In this case, an early idea mental rehearsal conference with a peer editor or the teacher can be helpful in assisting the child in picking a topic. For example, the student would talk about some of his ideas and the peer editor or teacher might ask questions or encourage the student to write about a particular idea. Also of help can be a discussion with the student about his experiences and resources. Most writers suggest that the best topics to write about are those about which one has the most information and personal experience. Therefore, although a student may wish to write about wild Shetland ponies, space flight, or getting lost at the mall, the last may be the best suited topic.

1. It was the most hideous, monstrous thing I had ever seen.

2. Who would think a tree branch could let go so suddenly?

3. Bringing a Martian home for dinner was something I never thought I'd be doing.

4. I don't suppose you ever spied on someone, at least not for weeks at a time, but I did.

5. I had always hated school until that day when . . .

6. Haunted house stories are a dime a dozen but, I promise you, this one will top them all.

7. The best friend I ever had was not a human but a . . .

8. We had always made fun of her.

9. Moving to the ranch had seemed like such a good idea until that morning when we all had our assigned chores to do.

10. There was blood all over the doorstep that morning when I went out to start my paper route.

11. A helium-filled balloon—especially a very large one—is not an easy thing to carry on a very windy day.

12. He was the tiniest little man (horse, dog, etc.) you ever saw and he was sitting right on my desk.

13. It looked like a very ordinary lamp—a little crooked perhaps, and rather dirty.

14. It was way too big to be a hen's egg, so what was it doing in the chicken coop?

15. I always thought jumping rope was a silly thing to do until my little sister challenged me to try it.

16. Roller blades can get you places in a hurry, as I found out that day.

17. It had been raining for a week and now the road had disappeared.

18. Making someone come back to life after being dead for years is a very scary thing to do.

19. The map was very old, and the paper cracked as I opened it.

20. Stowing away on a cruise ship is not easy but well worth the hassle.

21. "There's no such thing as a werewolf," I said as I watched the hairs on my hands grow longer.

22. "Of course I'll be all right!" I told my parents as they went off on vacation.

23. Summer camp is not all it's cracked up to be. Especially Camp Gitchigumi . . .

24. The little puppy sat by the window looking in at the warm fire.

25. "Three wishes," said the strange old lady, "and use them with great care!"

26. "Zap!!!" There was that annoying sound again. What *was* it???

27. There was no one there when I answered the doorbell, but there sat a very large package with a huge bow.

28. I have always loved to play jokes on people.

29. It had arms like a monkey, fur like a leopard, and a very human face.

30. "Of course I'm not afraid!" I told my friends as we ventured into the rain forest.

FIGURE 6.14   Story starters.

Unfamiliar Organizational Patterns

Each writing discourse has its own organization and conventions. Each time a new genre of writing is introduced to students, it must be modeled by the teacher and then reinforced. Because writing is organized in culturally specific ways (Gibbons, 2002), English learners often have an especially difficult time with unfamiliar genres. They may organize their thoughts differently. They may be used to circular structures rather than the linear or hierarchical structure used most often in our culture. Minilessons about the writing strategies and genres can be helpful to all students, but English learners, in particular, may benefit from initial class collaborations before they are asked to write independently. This affords English learners the opportunity to review the new genre, practice using the writing process, become familiar with the necessary academic language, and balance their energy between their ideas and the correct conventions.

No Interest in Writing

Often students enter a classroom with a decided aversion to writing—especially those children who have not been through the confidence-building adventure of a writer's workshop. Such students need to be encouraged to write and to experience the rewards of writing. Very often the reluctance also emanates from a history of having received numerous discouraging corrections on the mechanics of writing, including the spelling, grammar, and punctuation, as well as marks for poor penmanship. If this is where the problem lies, the teacher can intervene by recording the student's ideas and first draft, emphasizing the difference between the mere physical act of writing and the actual composing, for which the student is still being held responsible. A similar strategy is to allow the student to dictate ideas into a tape recorder and then write the first draft on a word processor, utilizing the spell check and grammar aids, if available. Finally, pairing social students who prefer oral activities over solitary ones for brainstorming discussions and writing the initial draft is a collaborative way to lessen their feelings of isolation and spur interest in writing.

SUMMARY

In a balanced and comprehensive literacy program, writing is not seen as merely the prosaic sum of its parts. Writing, like reading, is viewed as a tool for considering the world, or as a vehicle for sorting out and clarifying one's thinking. The more students reformulate content, the more their thinking and writing abilities grow. In the process, students play with words, organize their ideas into sentences and paragraphs, and express their innermost thoughts to increase their personal significance and self-awareness. Moreover, through a well-constructed writing program, students learn to harness skills that will enable them to examine their ideas and determine whether they can stand up to analysis by their peers.

The writing process, employed in the self-directed setting of the writer's workshop, shifts the emphasis in students' writing from the finished product to the problem-solving stages all writers go through as they gather and organize their ideas, draft them, and refine and polish their pieces with the help of others. Because the teacher is not the only person evaluating the final product, the students, as peer editors, become astute at discerning what does and does not constitute good writing. Reading and writing become reciprocal partners as students write and then read their own writing and that of other students.

To further help students understand what good writing is, 6 + 1 Trait Writing frameworks are used in a balanced and comprehensive literacy program in grades 4–8. Students of this age are ready to explore the important components of ideas, organization, voice, word choice, sentence fluency, and conventions. Writing is chosen that either exemplifies the trait the teacher is focusing on or fails to be effective because it lacks the trait. In either case, students receive valuable information as to what makes writing *work*. They extend this information to their own writing and to that of their peers.

Arguably, a large majority of the problems experienced by writers can be alleviated by having them write often, because active young authors become increasingly more engaged in the desire to communicate their ideas more clearly. Daily dialogue journals and frequent writing of novelettes are but two means to supplement the ample writing practice offered by writer's workshop.

Finally, teachers utilizing a balanced and comprehensive literacy program must convey the fundamental axiom to students that was proffered by Robert Frost: *"There is no art to writing but having something to say."*

To be sure, the writing process takes much effort and concentration; therefore, students must be gently guided through the process and encouraged to continue when they become discouraged or frustrated with the many revisions that every writer encounters. With the assistance of a teacher who truly believes that everyone has something to say, a writing revolution can occur in every classroom. Eventually, all students will have the confidence to produce a worthwhile piece of writing that they are proud of and eager to share with the world.

Questions
FOR JOURNAL WRITING AND DISCUSSION

1. Write a specific piece of fiction, nonfiction, or poetry for a specific group of students in grades 4–8. Note the process you went through to arrive at the finished product. How might you use your piece of writing in a writer's workshop to teach writing more effectively?

2. Reflect on your own experiences with learning to write in school. Describe any positive experiences that helped you to become a better writer. Also describe any negative experiences that may have hindered your development and/or your motivation to write. How do your experiences relate in terms of the ideas presented in this chapter?

3. Observe writing instruction taking place in a grade 4–8 classroom and write down your observations. Was the teacher following the process approach to writing or a different approach? How did the students feel about the writing they were doing? What did you think about the quality of their writing? What long-term effects do you think the approach will have on their future as writers?

Suggestions
FOR PROJECTS AND FIELD ACTIVITIES

1. Arrange to visit a middle school classroom during writer's workshop. Listen to the conversation that accompanies the composing process. Take notes on what you hear. How did "talk" facilitate the writing process in the situation you observed?

2. Ask a small group of intermediate or middle school students what they prefer to read and what they prefer to write: fiction (stories, novels), nonfiction (informational texts, biographies, expository prose), or poetry. Is there a difference in form between what students choose to read and write? Why might this be so?

3. Survey a small group of middle school students about their knowledge of computers. Characterize the computer literacy of these students. How comfortable are they with using the computer's word-processing capabilities? How accessible are computers to these students when they are writing? How often do they actually publish their work on the computer? How many use Inspiration software or other tools to plan and organize before writing?

REFERENCES

Atwell, N. (1998). *In the middle: New understandings about reading and writing with adolescents* (2nd ed.). Upper Montclair, NJ: Boynton/Cook.

Avery, C., & Graves, D. (1993). *And with a light touch: Learning about reading, writing and teaching with first graders.* Portsmouth, NH: Heinemann.

Block, C. C. (2000). *Teaching the language arts: Expanding thinking through student-centered instruction* (3rd ed.). Needham Heights, MA: Allyn & Bacon.

Calkins, L., & Huron, S. (1987). *The writing workshop: A world of difference.* Portsmouth, NH: Heinemann.

Calkins, L. M. (1991). *Living between the lines.* Portsmouth, NH: Heinemann.

Calkins, L. M. (1994). *The art of teaching writing.* Portsmouth, NH: Heinemann.

Cecil, N. L. (1994a). *Freedom fighters: Affective teaching of the language arts.* Salem, WI: Sheffield.

Cecil, N. L. (1994b). *For the love of language: Poetry for ALL learners.* Winnipeg, Manitoba: Peguis.

Cecil, N. L. (1997). For the love of poetry: Literacy scaffolds, extension ideas, and more. Winnipeg, Manitoba: Portage & Main.

Cecil, N. L. (2007a). *Striking a balance: Best practices for early literacy* (3rd ed.). Scottsdale, AZ: Holcomb Hathaway.

Cecil, N. L. (2007b). *Focus on fluency: A meaning-based approach.* Scottsdale, AZ: Holcomb Hathaway.

Cohen, S., & Riel, B. (1989). The effect of distant audiences on students' writing. *American Educational Research Journal, 26,* 143–159.

Cohle, D. M., & Towle, W. (2001). *Connecting reading and writing in the intermediate grades.* Newark, DE: International Reading Association.

Diederich, P. (1991). *Writing inservice guide for English language arts and TAAS.* Austin: Texas Education Agency.

Freedman, A. (1986). Adapting the I-Search paper for the elementary classroom. In C. B. Olson (Ed.), *Practical ideas for teaching writing as a process.* Sacramento: California State Department of Education.

Gibbons, P. (2002). *Scaffolding language, scaffolding learning: Teaching second language learners in the mainstream classroom.* Portsmouth, NH: Heinemann.

Gillet, J. W., & Beverly, L. (2001). *Directing the writing workshop: An elementary teacher's handbook.* New York: Guilford Press.

Gipe, J. P. (2006). *Multiple paths to literacy: Assessment differentiated instruction for diverse learners, K–12.* Upper Saddle River, NJ: Merrill Prentice Hall.

Graves, D. H. (1983). *Writing: Teachers and children at work.* Exeter, NH: Heinemann.

Graves, D. H. (1994). *A fresh look at writing.* Portsmouth, NH: Heinemann.

Hansen, J. (1987). *When writers read.* Portsmouth, NH: Heinemann.

Johnston, P. (1992). *Constructive evaluation in literacy.* White Plains, NY: Longman.

Laib, N. K. (1989, July 5). Good writing cannot be taught effectively as an empty collection of rules. *The Chronicle of Higher Education, 36.*

Langer, J. A., & Applebee, A. N. (1987). *How writing shapes thinking: A study of teaching and learning.* Urbana, IL: National Council of Teachers of English.

Martinez, E. B. (1986). It works! In C. B. Olson (Ed.), *Practical ideas for teaching writing as a process.* Sacramento: California State Department of Education.

Muschla, G. R. (1998a). *Reading workshop survival kit.* Center for Applied Research in Education.

Muschla, G. R. (1998b). *Writing workshop survival kit.* Center for Applied Research in Education.

Northwest Regional Educational Laboratory. (1998/1999). *Assessment and accountability program.* Portland, OR.

Norton, D. (1993). *The effective teaching of the language arts* (4th ed.). New York: Merrill.

Olson, C. B. (Ed.). (1986). A sample prompt, scoring guide, and model paper for the I-Search. In *Practical ideas for teaching writing as a process.* Sacramento: California Department of Education.

Peha, S. (1996). *The compleat writing teacher.* Unpublished manuscript.

Peyton, J. K., & Reed, L. (1990). *Dialogue journal writing with nonnative English speakers: A handbook for teachers.* Alexandria, VA: Teachers of English to Speakers of Other Languages.

Rasinski, T., & Padak, N. (2000). *Effective reading strategies: Teaching children who find reading difficult.* Upper Saddle River, NJ: Merrill Prentice Hall.

Read, S. (2005). First and second graders writing informational text. *The Reading Teacher, 59,* 36–44.

Shanahan, T. (1988). The reading-writing relationship: Seven instructional principles. *The Reading Teacher, 41,* 636–647.

Silva, C., & Yarborough, B. (1990). Help for young writers with spelling difficulties. *Journal of Reading, 34,* 48–53.

Spandel, V. (2000). *Creating writers through 6-trait writing assessment and instruction.* New York: Addison-Wesley/Longman.

Stuart, V., & Graves, D. (1987). *How to teach writing.* Urbana, IL: National Council of Teachers of English.

Weaver, C. (1996). *Teaching grammar in context.* Upper Montclair, NJ: Boynton/Cook.

Literacy in the
Content Areas

LEARNING FROM INFORMATIONAL TEXT

Seven

- Why is it important to use expository material to teach content area literacy strategies?

- How is content area text different from narrative text?

- What are some effective techniques for teaching expository reading and writing?

- What do students need to know about researching in the content areas?

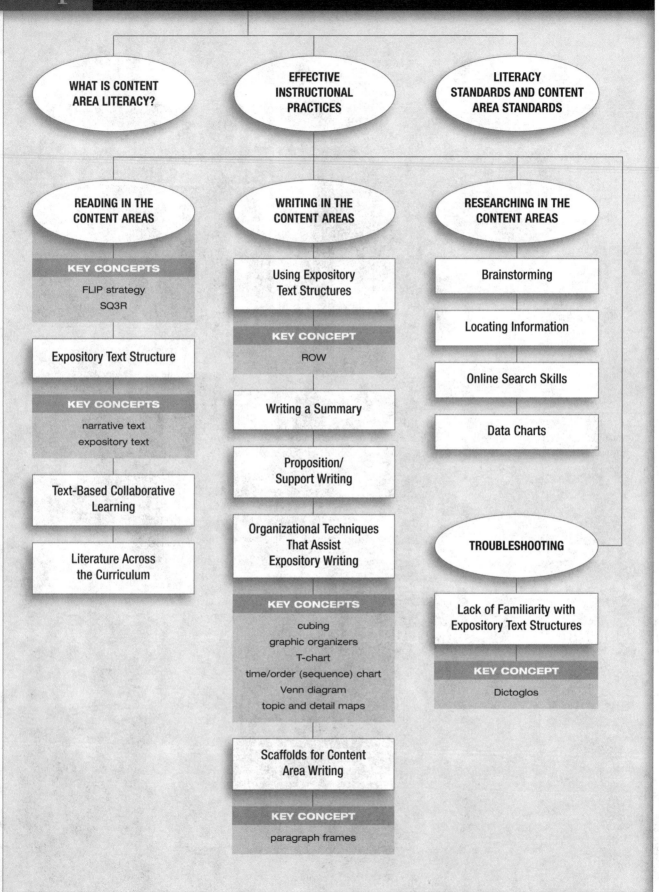

WHAT IS CONTENT AREA LITERACY?

EFFECTIVE INSTRUCTIONAL PRACTICES

LITERACY STANDARDS AND CONTENT AREA STANDARDS

READING IN THE CONTENT AREAS

KEY CONCEPTS

FLIP strategy
SQ3R

Expository Text Structure

KEY CONCEPTS

narrative text
expository text

Text-Based Collaborative Learning

Literature Across the Curriculum

WRITING IN THE CONTENT AREAS

Using Expository Text Structures

KEY CONCEPT

ROW

Writing a Summary

Proposition/ Support Writing

Organizational Techniques That Assist Expository Writing

KEY CONCEPTS

cubing
graphic organizers
T-chart
time/order (sequence) chart
Venn diagram
topic and detail maps

Scaffolds for Content Area Writing

KEY CONCEPT

paragraph frames

RESEARCHING IN THE CONTENT AREAS

Brainstorming

Locating Information

Online Search Skills

Data Charts

TROUBLESHOOTING

Lack of Familiarity with Expository Text Structures

KEY CONCEPT

Dictoglos

"Okay, now I will read the passage again, but this time I want you to write down some more key words or phrases to add to those you just wrote," Mrs. Martinez explains.

She then reads the same section of the seventh-grade social studies text that she had just read, this being the third time. The first time she read it, she directed students to just listen. The second time, she directed them to listen for key words or phrases—those words or phrases they thought were most important to the material. This time they will listen for some words or phrases they may have missed during the second reading. Mrs. Martinez is using a strategy called dictoglos (Wajnryb, 1990) to help her students, especially her English learners, both to understand the structure and language of expository text and to collaborate with others to learn specific content area knowledge.

After she finishes reading, Mrs. Martinez walks around the room looking at students' papers and asks, "Did everyone write more key words and phrases? All right. Now take your paper and pencil and get with your assigned partner." She waits while quietly counting to 30, knowing that it takes her students about 30 seconds to move their chairs in order to work with their partners. She continues, "Discuss your notes with your partner and try to re-create the text you just heard me read. Expand your notes and try to rewrite the text just as you heard me read it. You have 15 minutes to work on this."

Mrs. Martinez again moves around the classroom making sure each partnership is clear about what they are doing. After 15 minutes she says, "Okay, now join together with one other pair of students near you so that there are four of you working together."

After another quiet count of 30 seconds, Mrs. Martinez continues with her directions: "Combine all of your notes and try to re-create the text you heard me read. Try to make what you write as close to what I read as you can. After about 10 minutes I will ask you if you need an additional 5 minutes. If not, I will ask for volunteers to read what you have come up with and we will then discuss your work. Be thinking about what parts of the text are hard to re-create. We will analyze why some parts are harder than others to recall, and ways we might be able to remember those parts better."

WHAT IS CONTENT AREA LITERACY?

Content area literacy refers to the use of reading, writing, speaking, listening, viewing, and visually representing as tools for learning subject matter. Often students in grades 4–8 are expected to learn subject matter through reading, taking notes and outlining, listening to lectures, or perhaps viewing a documentary. But they are never taught *how* to learn in these ways. Learning informational material is different from reading or writing stories. A major part of the difference lies in the fact that stories are narrative material and informational text is expository material, and each type has its own distinctive structure. When teaching students to learn from informational, or content area, text, it is necessary to use expository material for modeling, demonstration, and practice to ensure students can identify the various text structures and apply appropriate strategies to other informational text. While most of the literacy strategies already introduced in this book are also applicable for use in the content areas—and should be integrated into content area instruction—these strategies need to be taught with expository material (Alfassi, 2004). In addition, there are strategies that are most effective for content area literacy. Before presenting these strategies, we provide an overview of the research for best practices in content area instruction in the box on the following page.

● content area literacy

Synopsis of Research on Best Practices

Before presenting strategies that are especially effective for literacy instruction in the content areas, we offer the following overview of research by Zemelman, Daniels, and Hyde (1998) on best practices in content area instruction.

BEST CLASSROOM STRUCTURES FOR CONTENT AREA INSTRUCTION

- Integrative units: multiweek chunks of curriculum organized around topics (e.g., whales) or themes (e.g., perseverance)

- Small group activities: less teacher talk; more active student involvement within continually shifting groupings (e.g., pairs, threes, study teams, group investigations) organized around skill needs, interests, or random assignment

- Representing-to-learn: a broadening of writing as a way to show what has been learned, including sketch books, maps, and other artistic and graphic representations

- Classroom workshop: a long, regularly scheduled chunk of time during which the focus is on doing the subject, such as doing writing, doing reading, doing math, doing history, doing science, rather than just hearing or reading about it. Student choice about what books to read, projects to complete, or topics to pursue, and frequent conferences between teacher and students are the two major elements of workshops. The typical time breakdown is 5 minutes for each student to share what will be worked on during the workshop; 30 minutes of workshop time, including conferences; and 10 minutes of each student sharing what was done that day.

- Authentic experiences: genuine real-world issues that are addressed similar to service-learning (see Chapter 10), beginning with student interest or natural curiosity for solving a problem or answering questions (e.g., homelessness—reasons for it and ways to help)

- Reflective assessment: use of observation, interviews, questionnaires, artifacts, portfolios, and rubrics with the goals of monitoring growth and helping students set goals, keep track of their own work, and evaluate their efforts (see Chapter 2)

BEST PRACTICES FOR MATH

use of manipulatives

cooperative groups

discussion

questioning

justification

writing about math

problem solving

word problems with everyday problems and applications

connecting to other subjects

understanding key concepts

estimation

spatial sense

collecting/organizing data

tables, graphs

use of multiple assessment techniques (written, oral, demonstration)

BEST PRACTICES FOR SOCIAL STUDIES

provision of choices about what to study in depth

inquiry and problem solving

student decision making

participation in community/school affairs

cooperative groups

integration of other curriculum areas

getting to know cultures

open expression of ideas (e.g., class meetings)

BEST PRACTICES FOR SCIENCE

hands-on activities

observation

hypothesizing

reflection

questioning

thinking

problem solving

in-depth study of a few important thematic topics

integration of reading, writing, and math

collaborative small group work

use of literature circles

LITERACY STANDARDS AND CONTENT AREA STANDARDS OVERLAP

All teachers are literacy teachers. In all the content areas, there are standards that incorporate and overlap with literacy standards. For example, note the terminology used in the following content area standards:

- National Social Studies Standards: "identify and give examples," "identify, research, and clarify," "document information from print or electronic sources," and "distinguish facts from opinions."
- National Science Education Standards for Science as Inquiry: "begin with a question, design an investigation, gather evidence, formulate answers, communicate the process and results . . . by producing oral and written reports, writing, labeling drawings, completing concept maps, designing computer graphics."
- National Council of Teachers of Mathematics (NCTM) Standards: "interpret and comprehend word problems," "develop, record, explain, critique strategies for solving computational problems," "understand patterns and describe verbally"; and for data analysis and probability, "formulate questions and collect data, organize and display relevant data to answer questions."

The same terminology is found in national literacy standards. The aspects of critical thinking, formulating questions, and communicating results are the same literacy tasks that are expected in all the content area standards (see NCTE/IRA Standards for the English Language Arts #1, 2, 4, 5, 6, 7, 8, 11, and 12 in Figure 2.4). Furthermore, as Kane (2007) notes, "Wide and varied opportunities for reading, writing, listening, speaking, and viewing can help students meet national content knowledge standards and benchmarks . . . a standards-based curriculum can use literacy strategies not as add-ons, but as integral to content teaching itself" (p. x).

Themed units are an effective way to integrate literacy instruction and to use the inquiry tools necessary for learning in the content areas. One possible set of inquiry tools for intermediate- and middle-grade students follows (Sierra-Perry et al., 1996, p. 37):

- identifying interesting and meaningful topics and questions to pursue;
- gathering quality source materials appropriate to their questions, interests, and abilities;
- gleaning information from these sources;
- organizing this information;
- responding to this information;
- sharing what they've learned; and
- pacing themselves for success.

READING IN THE CONTENT AREAS

We often assume that once students learn to read they can read just about anything. However, we must realize that not all reading tasks are alike. For example, the cognitive demands placed on readers by expository text differ from those placed by narrative text: they are not necessarily more difficult, but they are different. Readers must be taught how to recognize these differences and how to actively engage with expository text. Following is information about the texts that are used in content area classrooms and strategies for teaching students how to actively engage with them.

Content Area Materials

Reading in the content areas involves learning how to read a variety of discourse patterns and understanding the different text structures associated with a particular content area. When planning lessons, one strategy that might be helpful for teachers to use for examining content area texts is FLIP.

ACTIVITY   *The FLIP Strategy*

This strategy was originally developed as a before-reading strategy to determine the friendliness (F), language (L), interest (I), and prior knowledge (P) of a reading selection (Schumm & Mangrum, 1991). It can also be used effectively by teachers in preparing content area lessons. The steps for this strategy as presented by Sadler (2001) are based on the following questions:

Step 1 (F): To determine the friendliness, ask yourself the following questions:
- Which features of the content area material are easy to understand?
- Which features need further explanation (e.g., use of headings, sidebars, graphs)?

Step 2 (L): To determine the difficulty of the language, ask yourself:
- What terms might students have difficulty understanding?

Step 3 (I): To determine your students' likely interest, ask yourself:
- How much interest will my students have in this topic?
- How might their interest affect their level of involvement?
- How might I enhance their interest?

Step 4 (P): To determine students' prior knowledge about the text's topic, ask yourself:
- Do I know what my students already know about this topic?
- What methods will I use to find out?

For example, suppose your students are about to start a new science unit on light. The related chapter in their science textbook is "The Nature of Light." Examine this material and apply the FLIP strategy (Sadler, 2001, p. 38):

F The text is divided into sections with questions.

L Go over words such as *opaque, translucent,* and *transparent.*

I Think how fast light moves!

P Ask what students already know about light.

Note that you can also teach students to use the FLIP strategy before they attempt their content area reading. The following sections provide more information related to helping students deal with content area materials.

Types of texts used across the curriculum

Textbooks have traditionally been a central focus of most content area classes from elementary grades through college (Cuban, 1991; Gottfried & Kyle, 1992). They are certainly not the only materials appropriately used across the curriculum. Nonfiction trade books; nonfiction children's and young adult literature, including picture books (e.g., *Sweet Clara and the Freedom Quilt*, 1993) and certain graphic books/novels (e.g., *Fagin the Jew*, 2003); and electronic text provide useful tools for learning content and learning to read critically. They also can motivate and enrich content area teaching and learning. The nonfiction trade books available today are beautifully illustrative and cover a wide range of content area topics. Resources such as *Celebrating Children's Choices: 25 Years of Children's Favorite Books* (Post et al., 2000), *Nonfiction Matters: Reading, Writing, and Research in Grades 3–8* (Harvey, 1998), *Teaching with Picture Books in the Middle School* (Tiedt, 2000), *The Power of Picture Books in Teaching Math and Science* (Columba, Kim, & Moe, 2005), and *Using Literature in the Middle Grades: A Thematic Approach* (Moss, 1994) provide a wealth of information about specific book titles for use in the content areas.

As stated earlier, the genre of picture books and graphic books, including novels, must also be considered. For example, older students interested in social justice issues will find that picture books dealing with such subjects as homelessness (*Fly Away Home*, Bunting, 1991), the Holocaust (*Rose Blanche*, Gallaz & Innocenti, 2003), and the effects of the atom bomb (*Sadako*, Coerr & Young, 1993) make an impact not easily made through predominantly written accounts in history books. Likewise, graphic novels such as *Good-bye, Chunky Rice* (Thompson, 2006) and *Pedro and Me* (Winick, 2000) convey important messages in a way that is accessible to the most reluctant readers. (See Chapter 5 for more information about graphic novels and Appendix A for suggested picture books and graphic novels.)

Several valuable websites offer listings of materials, activities, supplies, and lesson plans, as well as links to extensive electronic text material for content area themes. Some of these websites are listed in the box on the following page.

Many content area teachers use both fiction and nonfiction literature as a way to introduce challenging subject area content. For example, historical fiction can be used to introduce and clarify a unit on World War II. A book such as *Friedrich* (Richter, 1970), a novel written from the perspective of a non-Jewish boy about the persecution and destruction of his Jewish neighbors and best friend in Nazi Germany, may be read aloud to students, and their responses to the characters and events may be written in journals and referred to at relevant points in the study of World War II.

Teachers may choose to use several books across a wide range of reading ability levels and genres on a particular topic (e.g., ocean life, rain forests, the Holocaust, the stars, shapes). These books are made available for students to search for answers to questions they have about the particular topic (see the discussion of data charts later in this chapter). The use of literature has the potential for enhancing the interest students have in a topic and also helps teachers address curriculum standards related to providing students with a variety of genres for individual content areas such as social studies, science, and mathematics. See Appendix A and Tables 5.1 and 5.2; see also Kane (2007, 2008) for extensive bibliographies of children's and young adult literature appropriate to the content areas.

WWW

Children's Picture Book Database
www.lib.muohio.edu/pictbks

Websites to Help Explore Content Area Themes

- **http://scholastic.com/MagicSchoolBus/theme/index.htm** lists materials, supplies, and activities related to popular science themes. For example, the Wetlands theme provides information and activities that are geared to help students persuade a town council to protect wetlands from being developed into a shopping mall—an all too real situation in many communities.

- **http://school.discoveryeducation.com/schrockguide** is one of the best sites for curriculum ideas in all content areas. This is a very thorough and well-maintained site. Visit the content-rich award-winning page for links to sites that are full of curriculum content organized by content areas. For example, under Science and Technology a

link to oceanography and "Secrets of the Ocean Realm" would relate to a thematic unit on oceans. This award-winning PBS-developed site provides extensive information, photos, and activities for a wide variety of ocean-related topics. It would also be a wonderful source for helping students locate the different structures found in expository text.

- **www.carolhurst.com** includes a collection of reviews of great books for kids; appropriate grade-level usages; ways to use these books in the classroom; and collections of books and activities on particular topics, curriculum areas, and themes.

Expository text structures

narrative text ●

expository text ●

The structure of expository text differs from the structure of narrative text. Stories represent the structure of **narrative text.** Stories have characters, settings, problems, key events, and resolutions. These elements work together to impart a message or theme, and sometimes to present a moral, or lesson. The purpose of **expository text** is to explain, describe, or persuade. Expository material has a content focus and provides information and ideas. Representative examples of expository writing include news stories, reports, case studies, comparison/contrast papers, and historical accounts. Expository writing is organized according to a variety of structures. The seven most common structures are: description, cause/effect, comparison/contrast, time/order, problem/solution, enumeration, and persuasion.

- *Description,* commonly found in informational text, provides characteristic features of the topic: "Eels are characterized by their snakelike shape, lack of spines in the fins, and the absence of ventral fins."

- *Cause/effect* tells of events and what happens as a result: "The Pilgrims were not used to such long, hard winters. Many Pilgrims became sick—so many that by spring about 50 percent of the population was dead."

- *Comparison/contrast* directly discusses two related topics, giving their essential characteristics, and often employs similes to help readers make connections to more familiar concepts: "Hurricanes usually form over warm, tropical water, whereas tornadoes usually form over land. When tornadoes approach, people often say the sound is like that of a fast-moving train."

- *Time/order* (also called sequence) presents a chronological, historical accounting of events: "Archaeologists have learned that the evolution of man began with . . . then . . . followed by . . ."

- *Problem/solution* presents real-life events that require research in seeking a solution: "Apples cost 99 cents per pound. Jack needed three pounds to make the applesauce. How much money will he need?" or "Wetlands are valuable nursery areas for aquatic and land animals. They can even filter out some kinds of pollution . . . but developers are planning to build on these wetlands."

- *Enumeration* (can also include sequence) presents listings, step-by-step directions, or stages of development: "Amphibians first lay their eggs in clumps in quiet water or on moist leaf mold. Then the eggs hatch into larvae, or tadpoles. The tadpoles develop legs and grow into frogs."

- *Persuasion* offers a statement that is a proposition—a statement that can be argued as accurate—and support for that proposition: "The school bond referendum should be passed, and this is why . . ." Examples of persuasive writing are reviews of books, plays, and films; editorials; letters to the editor; and position papers.

It is important to locate these structures within the expository materials that students will be using. The teacher should provide modeling and have small groups work together to find other examples within their classroom materials. Just as retellings are done for narrative comprehension, retellings of expository text can also be done by using the following guiding questions (Hoyt, 1999, p. 125):

The use of literature, including graphic texts, has the potential for enhancing the interest students have in a topic.

- What is the topic?
- What are the most important ideas to remember?
- What did you learn that you did not already know?
- What is the setting for this information?
- What did you notice about the organization and text structure?
- What did you notice about the visuals, such as graphs, charts, and pictures?
- Can you summarize what you learned?
- What do you think was the author's purpose for writing this [material]?

See Appendix D for a checklist based on these questions.

Content Area Strategies

After examining the content area material, you might plan for students to use one or more of the following content area reading strategies before, during, or after reading, as indicated.

The two-minute preview (before reading) (Stephens & Brown, 2000)

Time spent previewing a content area selection prior to reading it helps students prepare adequately for what might be difficult, complex, or technical material. Previewing the material places the student in an active role right from the start. A checklist such as the one in Figure 7.1 can be used to guide the previewing. The items might change depending on the purpose of reading and the nature of the

☐ **Introduction.** What is the selection about?

_____

_____

☐ **Headings.** What are the topics in this selection?

_____

_____

☐ **Graphics and other visuals.** Can I interpret this information?

_____

_____

☐ **Margin notes.** Are there notes in the margins? What kind of information do they contain?

_____

_____

☐ **Summary.** Is it a clear and concise overview of the selection? What is one key idea in the summary?

_____

_____

FIGURE 7.1   Two-minute preview checklist.

material. Students can work alone or in pairs for two minutes, jotting down their responses on the preview form. Following this, you might suggest a strategy for reading the selection, based on the structure of the material.

Anticipation guides (before reading, during reading, after reading)

A simple anticipation guide, a before-reading tool, may provide three to five statements and require students to indicate whether they agree or disagree with each statement. Students then read the text and either confirm or negate their choices.

1. There are about 1,500 active volcanoes. <u>disagree</u>
2. Mount St. Helens is a dormant volcano. <u>agree</u>
3. Mauna Loa is the world's most active volcano. <u>agree</u>
4. Once a volcano is dormant it can never erupt again. <u>agree</u>

Anticipation guides can be extended to include an additional part that is completed during or after the reading. In the extended anticipation guide (Duffelmeyer & Baum, 1992), students determine whether or not there is support in the text for their agree/disagree choices, indicating yes or no and stating why. For the preceding example, students asked to extend their thinking during or after reading might provide the following information:

1. No support. I disagreed, but the article says there are about 1,500 active volcanoes.

2. Support. I agreed, and the article says that when a volcano is between eruptions it is dormant. Since Mount St. Helens is not erupting now, it is dormant.

3. No support. I agreed that Mauna Loa is the most active volcano, but it is actually Kilauea, in Hawaii.

4. No support. I agreed that a dormant volcano never erupts again, but a volcano that never erupts again would be called extinct. Mount St. Helens erupted in 1980 after being dormant for about 120 years.

See Figure 7.2 for an anticipation guide for mathematics that goes beyond asking for agree/disagree responses. Students are asked to formulate/predict answers before reading.

Beyond Survey, Question, Read, Recite, Review (SQ3R)

Having a study system helps students develop an awareness of their own abilities to understand and learn information from expository material. Several systems are available to explore and perhaps modify to suit one's personal preferences. Most of these systems stem from, or are modifications of, the classic study strategy of **SQ3R—Survey, Question, Read, Recite, Review** (Robinson, 1946). Briefly, to *survey*, the student reads the title, introductory paragraph, main headings, and chapter summary and examines any illustrations. To *question*, the student

- SQ3R—Survey, Question, Read, Recite, Review

An anticipation guide for mathematics prepared by an education student. | FIGURE | 7.2

DIRECTIONS: Before reading Chapter One of *The Broken Dice: And Other Mathematical Tales of Chance*, by I. Ekeland, answer the following questions:

1. How many possible outcomes are there if two dice are rolled? How did you arrive at your answer?

2. To the best of your ability, draw a tree diagram that would represent the possible outcomes of rolling two dice, along with their probabilities. If you're not sure, draw something anyway to see if you discover anything.

3. What are some uses of dice?

4. For what purposes do you, personally, use dice?

5. What is meant by the phrase *loading the dice*? What is the effect of loading the dice?

6. What would happen if a die broke while in use? For example, if two faces of a die are facing up, should both numbers count?

Now you are ready to read the chapter. After the reading, we will have a class discussion of the story, and we will solve a problem that involves issues of the accuracy of the methods discussed in the story. Then, we will look at different ways to represent the use of dice to solve problems.

From S. Kane (2007). *Literacy and Learning in the Content Areas*, 2nd ed., p. 128. Scottsdale, AZ: Holcomb Hathaway,.

rephrases the main headings into questions to be answered during reading. The student then proceeds to *read*, with the purpose of answering the questions. To *recite*, the student simply recites the answers to the questions out loud. Finally, to *review*, the student tries to recall answers to questions as well as the general structure of the material, from memory. As students are introduced to a study strategy, they may find that a variation of that strategy works better for them. Students might be more willing to use a study system if they have participated in creating a personalized system. The many acronyms for study systems and brief descriptions of their characteristics follow:

SQ3R =	Survey, Question, Read, Recite, Review (Robinson, 1946)
PORPE =	Predict, Organize, Rehearse, Practice, Evaluate (Simpson, 1986)
STAR =	Skim and set purpose, Think, Anticipate and adjust, Review and retell (Stephens & Brown, 2000)
PLAE =	Preplan, List, Activate, Evaluate (Simpson & Nist, 1984)
PLAN =	Predict, Locate, Add, Note (Caverly et al., 1995)
PQRST =	Preview, Question, Read, Summarize, Test (Spache, 1963)
REAP =	Read, Encode, Annotate, Ponder (Eanet & Manzo, 1976)
SCAIT =	Select key words, Complete sentences, Accept final statements, Infer, Think (Wiesendanger & Bader, 1992)
SQRQCQ =	Survey, Question, Read, Question, Compute, Question (Fay, 1965)

ACTIVITY *Study Strategy Tryout*

The steps in this activity are as follows:

1. Model the use of several of the previously listed study systems.
2. Discuss with students what they seem to have in common, and invite students to use these strategies when reading informational text.
3. After students have had an opportunity to try various strategies, discuss which ones seemed most helpful.
4. Encourage students to create their own combinations of study systems that seem most helpful to them. Some systems created by students might look like the following (Stephens & Brown, 2000, p. 113):

    GOAL = Glance through, Order information, Adjust, Learn by retelling

    LAFF = Look over, Ask questions, Find answers, Follow through by reviewing and retelling

ACTIVITY *Find Someone Who . . .* (AFTER READING)

(Stephens & Brown, 2000, p. 60)

This strategy is a fun and motivating way for students to clarify their comprehension of expository material by interacting with classmates.

1. Explain to students that their goal is to locate a classmate who can respond to a particular prompt related to a specific content area topic.

Find someone who . . . (Use your math textbook if you need to.)

can tell the difference between a triangle and a quadrilateral. Page Number: Answer: Signature:	can give an example of a parallelogram. Page Number: Answer: Signature:
can define *polygon.* Page Number: Answer: Signature:	can list the kinds of quadrilaterals. Page Number: Answer: Signature:
knows what type of polygon has nine sides. Page Number: Answer: Signature:	can compare an equilateral triangle with an isosceles triangle. Page Number: Answer: Signature:

Find someone who . . .   **FIGURE 7.3**

2. Using a teacher-prepared form (see Figure 7.3), students should seek individuals who can provide the needed information. Give students sufficient time to interact with each other and find someone to sign each box.

3. Have students write comments about what they have learned.

4. Encourage students to use the material read as a resource if needed. This reminds students that their materials, as well as other people, are resources and that it is sometimes necessary to reread material that is complex or technical.

Important Words—The Top Five (AFTER READING)

To ensure that students come away from their expository reading with an awareness of important subject matter terminology, this strategy focuses on helping students connect particular vocabulary with a particular topic of study.

1. Following the reading of some informational text, ask students to look back over the material and choose about 10 words that they think are the most important words in the selection.

2. Have students work in pairs or small groups to develop a Top Five list of words for this material. (*Note:* The number of words to settle on can certainly be something other than five.) To do this, they will need to discuss the words' meanings and their relative importance to the topic, as well as learn to compromise.

3. Ask each pair, or group, to present their list and reasons to the whole class.

4. Follow with further discussion to develop a whole-class Top Five list of words for the selection.

5. Use a graphic organizer to show the relationship of certain words that could in turn help students see that some words are subsumed within others.

WRITING IN THE CONTENT AREAS

We often assume that if we teach students to write about their experiences or to write stories, they will then be able to transfer those abilities to writing in the content areas. But students must have opportunities to write in response to expository text, to use writing as a tool for learning, and to write in expository modes (i.e., to inform, describe, persuade, or explain) in order to develop these skills. As indicated by many states' content standards, we now expect students to be able to write in a variety of genres (see Chapter 2). The techniques described in the following sections can help guide teachers in planning instruction for writing in the content areas. In addition, scoring rubrics for assessing expository writing, like those found in Appendix D, are valuable tools.

Text-based Collaborative Learning

Text-based collaborative learning is an effective technique for helping all students (including those with learning disabilities in inclusive settings, and English learners) in grades 4–8 actively engage with expository material (Klingner et al., 2004; Langer, 2001). In **text-based collaborative learning,** students work with a partner or in a small group to discuss, question, clarify, and perform writing tasks involving expository text.

text-based collaborative ● learning

Text-Based Collaborative Learning

1. Introduce the subject of the text material and provide sufficient background information.

2. Have students work together to notice how the text information is organized (e.g., multiple sections and subheadings within chapters; a proposition with supporting paragraphs).

3. Ask them to determine questions (e.g., who, what, when, where, why, how).

4. Then, have them prepare general outlines using the headings and subheadings in the text material before even beginning the reading. In these ways students begin their reading with a purpose.

5. As students read silently, recommend that they write notes about unknown words, confusing parts, or answers to their questions, and start to fill in their general outlines.

6. Following the reading, have students return to the text with their partner or small group and discuss their notes in an effort to clarify the text.

Extension: Ash (2002) describes an extension, Reciprocal Teaching Plus, which engages students in critical evaluation of the text after reading. This strategy also uses peer support to clarify students' understanding of the text.

WWW

Reciprocal Teaching Plus
*www.readingonline.org/articles/
art_index.asp?HREF=ash*

Using Expository Text Structures

As students experience the variety of structures used in expository material through their reading (see earlier discussion of expository text structures), ask them to use these various structures in writing sessions. A strategy such as **ROW**, or Read/Organize/Write (Stephens & Brown, 2000), is useful as a framework for helping students move from locating each of the various text structures in their reading—one at a time—to identifying the characteristics of that structure, to writing their own selection for each of the text structures as they learn them.

● ROW

Read/Organize/Write (ROW)   ACTIVITY

The steps for using ROW are as follows:

1. Present a short, clear example of one of the expository text structures for the class to read. (**R**ead)

2. Guide students in developing a working definition of the text structure (see preceding definitions in the section "Expository Text Structures") and perhaps a graphic organizer that represents that structure (see the section "Organizational Techniques That Assist Expository Writing," below). (**O**rganize)

3. Using a current topic, have students write an expository piece using a particular expository text structure. (**W**rite)

Writing Summaries

It is quite common for students in grades 4–8 to be asked to write summaries of what they have read as a way of demonstrating comprehension of the content area material. It is expected that a summary will provide only the main points from the material without interpretation or commentary. Summaries are not retellings. In a retelling the student tries to include as much information as possible, whereas in a summary the goal is to be concise. These summaries may be kept in a notebook or used as a way to prepare for unit tests. Writing a summary is not an easy task for most students.

When asked to write a summary of what they have read, students often use personal criteria for deciding what is important to include, or they use a "copy and delete" method (Friend, 2000/2001), which means they copy or paraphrase some sentences and leave out others, again for personal reasons. Strategy instruction is needed to teach students how to determine the most important information and to summarize that information concisely. The best way to determine what is most important is to look for repeated information. When an argument is repeated often, or when reference is made to the same topic or idea even if different words or phrases are used, that is a clue that the information is important. Students should first ask themselves, "What does the author keep talking about?" A second question that will help lead students to a summary thesis statement is, "What is the author trying to say about [the idea identified in the first question]?"

Depending on the length of the material read, the summary might range from one sentence to a paragraph, or several paragraphs, but not more than about one-third of the length of the original piece. A good summary should be concise, with a minimum of details and with nothing repeated. Only the most central ideas are included, and these are written in the student's own words. For example, consider a lengthy section of a social studies text discussing Native Americans and how their life changed after Europeans arrived. This text provides detail about these people's differing views of the land, the clashes they had about land rights, the ensuing battles, and the emergence of reservations. It goes on to discuss joblessness among Native Americans and how several tribes (e.g., Choctaw, Navajo, Seminole, Cherokee, Passamaquoddy) began businesses to provide jobs for those living on the reservations. It continues with a discussion of powwows and what they mean to Native Americans. Friend (2000/2001) provides a model summary for this text:

> Native Americans are adjusting to mainstream American practices and strengthening tribal economies and culture. When the Europeans came to America, they took over most of the land and forced the Native Americans onto reservations. Recently many Native American tribes have opened businesses on their reservations to reduce unemployment. Their schools now teach their traditions along with modern American ideas. Powwows have become a social and cultural force to hold Native American people together. (p. 323)

ACTIVITY | *Writing a Summary*

Have students practice writing an effective summary using the sample passage below. Use the following steps:

1. Have students preview, think, and read. Ask students to preview the entire passage and think about what they expect to learn. Then have them read the passage.

2. Have students ask themselves, What does the author keep talking about? What is the author trying to say about this topic? This will be the main idea, or the thesis, of the material.

3. Have students ask the same two questions given in step 2 about each paragraph or group of paragraphs. Ask them to write that idea in their own words in one sentence but leave out details, examples, or stories, giving only the important idea.

4. Have students continue this process for the entire reading selection.

5. Have students check their sentences against the passage, ensuring that they tell the most important ideas, not the details. Have them make sure that nothing is repeated; that the sentences are their own words; and that their first sentence gives the overall main idea, or thesis, of the entire selection, with the following sentences supporting the meaning of the first sentence.

SAMPLE PASSAGE FOR "WRITING A SUMMARY" ACTIVITY

Animals' Body Coverings

Every animal's body covering is an adaptation that helps the animal survive. Feathers protect birds and help them fly. The fur or hair that covers most mammals helps keep them warm. Some mammals have sharp hairs that are used for protection. Others have whiskers that they use as sense organs. Many fish are covered with scales that protect them from disease and other animals that live in the water. A reptile's scales protect it from injury and from drying out.

Many animals have body coverings that are camouflage to help them hide. For example, a tiger's fur is striped. The stripes help the tiger blend in with the light and shadows of the tall grass in its environment. Toads—with their bumpy, brownish skin—look like pebbles on the forest floor. A chameleon's color changes to match its surroundings. The dark skin on an alligator's back makes it blend into the swamps where it lives. (Adapted from Lesson 2, "How Do Animals' Body Parts Help Them Meet Their Needs?" A16–A18 in *Science,* Grade 4.)

The following statements are intended as example student responses to the steps listed above for writing a summary.

1. I expect to learn about the different body coverings of animals.

2. The author keeps talking about the body coverings of animals, and how they help the animal survive.

3. The author is telling how body coverings can help animals blend in with their environment.

4. Animals have body coverings that help them survive by keeping them warm and protecting them from other animals, from injury, or from weather. Body coverings also help animals blend in with their environment so they can hide from their enemies.

Proposition/Support Writing

One of the purposes of expository writing is to persuade. Persuasive writing has its own style, one in which a proposal is made and then discussed and supported. There are many opportunities for authentic persuasive writing in the classroom. The school needs new playground equipment, or any number of other school needs; the neighborhood around the school faces environmental or safety issues that students recognize and want to do something about; state or federal budget discussions are threatening to cut education budgets—these are only a few examples of the types of issues that students can rally around and for which they can be taught to write persuasive essays or letters to the editor.

ACTIVITY *Proposition/Support Outline*

A strategy developed by Buehl (2001, p. 101) called Proposition/Support Outlines helps students to write persuasively and also to read more critically material of an editorial nature. Engaging in this strategy also helps build the analytical thinking skills so important for functioning in the world at large.

Five steps are involved in the strategy:

1. Discuss the difference between facts and opinions with students. Brainstorm examples of each and have students define the terms in their own words. Some examples might be the following:

   - The temperature today is 78 degrees. (Fact)
   - It feels warm today. (Opinion)
   - Everybody enjoys eating pizza. (Opinion)
   - There are 13 boys and 11 girls in our class. (Fact)
   - Dogs are the best pets. (Opinion)
   - Ten students in our room have a dog for a pet. (Fact)

2. For students, define the term *proposition* as "an opinion represented by a statement that is put forth as being true or accurate." Give an example, such as, "Wearing school uniforms increases student achievement." Have students brainstorm other examples of possible propositions. Then, in small groups, ask students to think of arguments they could make to support one of these propositions. Introduce the Proposition/Support Outline and model the five ways used to support propositions: facts, statistics, examples, expert authority, and logic and reasoning (see Figure 7.4).

3. Practice analyzing an author's persuasive piece using the outline. (Carefully choose a piece of writing that very clearly features the elements in the outline.) For example, students might work in pairs to analyze an editorial that details how the loss of a local wetland area will cause flooding in surrounding communities. They should be prepared to share the clues in the writing that helped them determine the facts, statistics, examples, expert authority, and logic and reasoning elements of the editorial.

4. Discuss the quality of the support presented in the material. Is it convincing? Is only one means of support (e.g., logic and reasoning) relied on? Are the statistics reliable? Are the examples far-fetched? Is more than one expert authority cited?

5. Use the outline to critique editorials, prepare for a class debate, guide independent research, or write a position paper.

Example of a proposition/support outline.   FIGURE   7.4

PROPOSITION/SUPPORT OUTLINE FOR RAIN FORESTS

PROPOSITION: The loss of rain forests will lead to an environmental disaster.

SUPPORT: 1. Facts

- Rain forests use carbon dioxide.
- There is increased carbon dioxide in the earth's atmosphere.
- The rain forests contain many endangered plant and animal species.
- Deforestation leads to widespread soil erosion in many areas.
- The burning of fossil fuels puts carbon dioxide into the environment.

2. Statistics

- The 1990s were the "hottest" decade in the last 100 years.
- One acre of rain forest disappears every second.
- Four million acres (larger than the state of Connecticut) disappear every year.
- Fifty to 100 species are destroyed with each acre of forest cleared.
- If present trends continue, half the rain forests of Honduras and Nicaragua were predicted to disappear by year 2000.

3. Examples

- India has almost no remaining rain forest.
- Current plans target eliminating much of the Congo's rain forest.
- Run-off from deforestation in Indonesia threatens their coral reefs and diminishes the fish population.
- Cutting of rain forests in Bangladesh and the Philippines has led to killer floods.

4. Expert Authority

- Computers predict doubling of carbon dioxide in the 21st century, raising temperatures by 3 to 9 degrees.
- The National Center for Atmospheric Research believes increased carbon dioxide results in the greenhouse effect and global warming.
- Environmentalist leader Al Gore calls the greenhouse effect our most serious threat ever.

5. Logic and Reasoning

- Warmer temperatures will harm crops and increase energy costs.
- More people will starve because of less food and increased population growth.
- The polar glaciers will melt and raise the sea level, flooding coastlines.
- Many species useful to humans will disappear.
- More sections of the world will become uninhabitable deserts due to soil loss, erosion, overgrazing, and overcultivation.

Source: From Buehl, D. (2001), *Classroom Strategies for Interactive Learning,* 2nd ed., p. 102. Reprinted with permission of Doug Buehl and the International Reading Association.

Organizational Techniques That Assist Expository Writing

Content standards usually include an expectation that students be able to write in a variety of genres and for a variety of purposes. In middle school, students are generally expected to be able to write research reports and persuasive letters or compositions. (See Figure 7.5 for some suggested resources for such writing.) Organizational techniques similar to those used to aid in reading comprehension (e.g., maps, webs, charts) also work for expository writing. Use of these techniques will result in better reports and research papers. The following are effective ways to assist students in expository writing.

FIGURE 7.5 "How-to" resources on writing and teaching writing in various genres.

Alber, M. (2001). Creative Writing and Chemistry. *Journal of Chemical Education, 78*(4), 478–480.

Bentley, N., & Guthrie, D. W. (1995). *The Young Producer's Video Book: How to Write, Direct and Shoot Your Own Video.* Brookfield, CT: Millbrook Press.

——. (1998). *The Young Journalist's Book: How to Write and Produce Your Own Newspaper.* Brookfield, CT: Millbrook Press.

Burkhardt, R. (2003). *Writing for Real: Strategies for Engaging Adolescent Writers.* Portland, ME: Stenhouse.

Chin, B. (Ed.). (2004). *How to Write a Great Research Paper.* Hoboken, NJ: J. Wiley & Sons.

Chinn, M. (2004). *Writing and Illustrating the Graphic Novel: Everything You Need to Know to Create Great Graphic Books.* Hauppauge, NY: Barron's.

Christinson, J., & Whited, A. (2005). *Nonfiction Writing Prompts for Math.* Englewood, CO: Advanced Learning Press.

Day, R. A. (1998). *How to Write and Publish a Scientific Paper.* Phoenix, AZ: Oryx Press.

Dragisic, P. (1998). *How to Write a Letter.* New York: Franklin Watts.

Fink, C. C. (2003). *Writing to Inform and Engage: The Essential Guide to Beginning News and Magazine Writing.* Boulder, CO: Westview.

Frey, N., Fisher, D., & Hernandez, T. (2003). "What's the Gist?": Summary Writing for Struggling Adolescent Writers. *Voices from the Middle, 11*(2), 43–49.

Geffner, A. B. (1995). *How to Write Better Business Letters* (2nd ed.). Hauppauge, NY: Barron's.

Gere, A. R., Christenbury, L., & Sassi, K. (2005). *Writing on Demand: Best Practices and Strategies for Success.* Portsmouth, NH: Heinemann.

Giblin, J. C. (1990). *Writing Books for Young People.* Boston: The Writer.

Goldberg, N. (1986). *Writing Down the Bones.* Boston: Shambhala Press.

Hand, B., Prain, V., Lawrence, C., & Yore, L. D. (1999). A Writing in Science Framework Designed to Enhance Science Literacy. *International Journal of Science Education, 21*(10), 1021–1035.

Ledoux, D. (1993). *Turning Memories into Memoirs: A Handbook for Writing Lifestories.* Lisbon Falls, ME: Soleil Press.

O'Neil, D. (2001). *The DC Guide to Writing Comics.* New York: Watson-Guptill Publications.

Phillips, E. H. (1999). *Shocked, Appalled, and Dismayed!: How to Write Letters of Complaint That Get Results.* New York: Vintage Books.

Sheffield, C. (1999). *Borderlands of Science: How to Think Like a Scientist and Write Science Fiction.* Riverdale, NY: Baen.

Wilson, E. O., & Bilger, B. (2001). *The Best American Science and Nature Writing 2001.* Boston: Houghton Mifflin.

Zinsser, W. (1998). *On Writing Well* (6th ed.). New York: HarperPerennial.

Adapted from S. Kane (2007). *Literacy and Learning in the Content Areas,* 2nd ed., p. 218. Scottsdale, AZ: Holcomb Hathaway.

Cubing

Cubing (Neeld, 1986) is a strategy that requires students to explore a topic from six viewpoints: describe, compare, associate, analyze, apply, and argue. Typically, cubes are created to show what has been learned about a topic or to review a topic being studied. However, they can also be used to help students respond in writing to expository text, and thus to learn forms of expository writing.

• cubing

For a content area topic the students have chosen or that the teacher has assigned, students answer key questions, some of which may represent the structure of expository text, using the six sides of a cube. They write their answers on each side of the cube, taking about three to five minutes. (See Figure 7.6 for a sample cube for writing about the topic of statistics.) Sample questions are as follows:

- What is it like [describe]?
- What is it similar to or different from [compare/contrast]?
- What does it make you think of [associate]?
- How is it made or what is it composed of [analysis]?
- How is it used [application]?
- What are arguments for or against it [persuasion].

Cubing for expository writing about statistics.   **FIGURE 7.6**

ASSOCIATE
doing research

APPLY
We did a bar graph. We can use our data to say dogs are the most popular pet.

DESCRIBE
Statistics—the collection and organizing of data

COMPARE
Portfolio—a collection of work organized to showcase abilities

ANALYZE
The data from our class show 10 people have dogs for pets, 5 have cats, 3 have fish, 1 has a bird.

ARGUE (FOR OR AGAINST)
Statistics: important b/c it helps us describe things we can use to persuade others.

Students can use these cubes as springboards for longer writing assignments. Small groups can also work together compiling their information into a group paper. Additionally, these cubes can be used to jigsaw (see Chapter 5) content area information and can be shared so all students have access to the information for review purposes.

Graphic organizers

As discussed in Chapter 5, graphic organizers are a visual aid for constructing meaning. As such, they help both reading comprehension if constructed during and after reading, and writing when used as a before-writing exercise to organize thoughts. Graphic organizers—maps, clusters, webs, Venn diagrams, T-charts, think-links, sequence charts, or outlines—provide a visible structure that can assist the writer with expository forms. With the appropriate use of symbols and/or arrows, graphic organizers can be constructed to correspond to the patterns found in expository text. As the examples in Figure 7.7 show, a student wishing to write about Abraham Lincoln's life might use a **time/order** or **sequence chart,** to indicate chronological order. Another student who is going to write about the causes of the Civil War would use a cause/effect web. Someone writing to compare or contrast two events or concepts could use a **T-chart** (a two-column chart that resembles a lower-case t) or a **Venn diagram** (two overlapping ovals to show both similarities and differences) to organize their thoughts. Simple **topic and details maps** are a way to organize paragraphs about a single topic. A student writing to describe a science concept might use a more web-like organizer to present characteristics of the concept with examples. A student explaining the steps to follow for solving a math problem could use a *listing (enumeration)* (an ordered category of elements) or a *flowchart* format (a visual description of a process).

time/order or sequence chart ●

T-chart ●
Venn diagram ●
topic and details map ●

K-W-L Plus

A widely used strategy called a K-W-L chart has been expanded to include developing a concept map that helps a student convert information learned through reading into an expository piece of writing. This expansion, the **K-W-L Plus strategy** (Carr & Ogle, 1987), which maintains the "Know," "Want to know," and "Learned" columns, has one added step: using the categories of information developed during the "know" phase to categorize (or organize) the information listed in the "Learned" column. That information is then arranged in a concept map that students can use for writing a summary of the information or an expository paper (see Figure 7.8).

K-W-L Plus strategy ●

Other variations of the original K-W-L chart include KNL (*N* = What do I *need* to know?), KWHL (*H* = *How* am I going to learn this, or research this, or investigate this, or report this?), KWLL (the second *L* = What do I *still* need to learn?), and KWLU (*U* = How can I *use* this information?) (Stephens & Brown, 2000).

Scaffolds for Content Area Writing

Even with teacher modeling and organizational frameworks, some students will experience difficulty with expository writing. **Paragraph frames** (Cudd & Roberts, 1989) can provide the kind of support needed for students who strug-

paragraph frames ●

Examples of graphic organizers for expository text patterns.   **FIGURE**   7.7

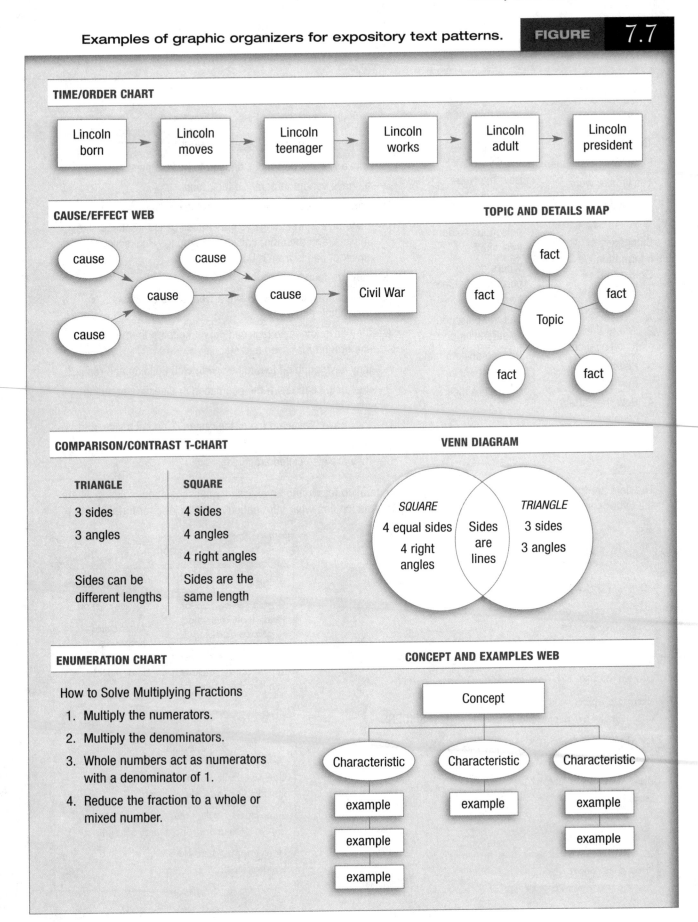

TIME/ORDER CHART

Lincoln born → Lincoln moves → Lincoln teenager → Lincoln works → Lincoln adult → Lincoln president

CAUSE/EFFECT WEB   **TOPIC AND DETAILS MAP**

cause, cause, cause, cause → Civil War

Topic: fact, fact, fact, fact, fact

COMPARISON/CONTRAST T-CHART   **VENN DIAGRAM**

TRIANGLE	SQUARE
3 sides	4 sides
3 angles	4 angles
	4 right angles
Sides can be different lengths	Sides are the same length

SQUARE: 4 equal sides, 4 right angles
Sides are lines
TRIANGLE: 3 sides, 3 angles

ENUMERATION CHART   **CONCEPT AND EXAMPLES WEB**

How to Solve Multiplying Fractions

1. Multiply the numerators.
2. Multiply the denominators.
3. Whole numbers act as numerators with a denominator of 1.
4. Reduce the fraction to a whole or mixed number.

Concept → Characteristic, Characteristic, Characteristic → example

FIGURE   7.8   K-W-L Plus for science writing, and the concept map generated.

TOPIC: SPIDERS

K (Know)	W (Want to know)	L (Learned)
They have 8 legs. Some are poisonous. They make webs. They eat insects. Categories of Information We Expect to Use: 1. What they are like (D = Description) 2. Where they live (L = Location) 3. How they live (A = Abilities) 4. How they affect people (P = People)	How many kinds are there? How many are poisonous? What do the poisonous spiders look like? Where do the poisonous spiders live? Can the poisonous spiders kill a person? How do spiders make their webs? Where are their eyes?	D—there are 30,000 species of spider. P—only a few are poisonous enough to harm a person. D—all have venom to paralyze their food. D—they eat insects, their 6-legged relatives. D—they have 2 breathing systems (tubes called tracheae, like insects, and the other called a book lung—looks like a stack of pages from a book). L—they are found everywhere. A—they can make silk to weave a web, or tie up insects, or wrap their eggs. A—they have knees so legs can curve, keeping them low to the ground for speed and stability. A—they have gripping feet to help with web building and repair. P—they help keep down the population of disease-spreading insects. D—they have 2 eyes on top of their head, 1 on each side, and 4 across their forehead—a total of 8 eyes. D—they are also called arachnids.

The data are then organized into a concept map in preparation for writing an expository passage about spiders, where the writer can indicate possible order of presenting information and what information is still lacking for further search.

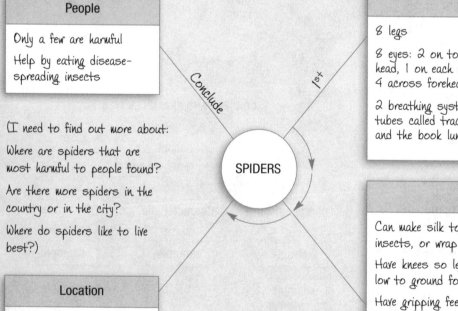

People

Only a few are harmful

Help by eating disease-spreading insects

(I need to find out more about:

Where are spiders that are most harmful to people found?

Are there more spiders in the country or in the city?

Where do spiders like to live best?)

Location

Found everywhere

SPIDERS

Conclude

1st

Description

8 legs

8 eyes: 2 on top of head, 1 on each side, 4 across forehead

2 breathing systems: tubes called tracheae and the book lung

30,000 species

All have venom

Also called arachnids

Eat insects

Abilities

Can make silk to weave webs, tie up insects, or wrap their eggs

Have knees so legs curve, keeping them low to ground for speed and stability

Have gripping feet that help with web building/repair

gle in this area. This instructional tool helps students write about what they learn in content area material following their reading. A modified cloze format is used that provides sentence starters concentrating on the various organizational structures for expository text; the sequence or time order structure is the easiest one to use to introduce this strategy. For example, the teacher writes a paragraph based on a content area topic currently being studied, being careful to use key words and phrases that will clearly reveal the expository structure. (See Figure 7.9 for examples of these key words.)

Next, the teacher puts the individual sentences on separate pieces of paper, or sentence strips. As a group, students are asked to think about the topic they are studying and then arrange the sentences into a paragraph. With practice students can learn to order these sentences on their own, and eventually to complete paragraph frames independently (see Figure 7.10). After working with paragraph frames, students will have many models for their own independent expository writing.

Example key words and phrases that indicate an expository structure.   **FIGURE 7.9**

EXPOSITORY STRUCTURE	KEY WORDS
Sequence or time/order	first, next, then, now, finally, before, after
Cause/effect	because, since, for, hence, so, as a result, if . . . then
Enumeration	one, two, three, another, more, to begin with, to continue, also
Comparison/contrast	but, however, although, yet, similar to, in contrast
Description	for example, in fact, characteristics are, for instance, like
Problem/solution	how, when, where, what, why, the problem is, one answer is
Persuasion	important, experts agree, percentage, statistics show, should

A completed paragraph frame for adding fractions (enumeration structure).   **FIGURE 7.10**

These are the directions for adding fractions. First, _look at the denominator of the fractions to see if they are the same._ Second, _change all the numbers, even the whole numbers, so they have the same denominator._ Third, _add the numerators. The denominator does not change._ Last, _if the fraction is more than a whole, change it to a mixed number._

ACTIVITY *Probable Passages*

An adaptation of probable passages (Wood, 1984), a strategy more commonly used to assist in the writing of narrative material, can also provide support for students who struggle when writing expository text. The steps in this adaptation are as follows:

1. Identify the most significant concepts or terms that appear in the content area material currently being studied. Place these terms on the board or an overhead transparency (see Figure 7.11).

FIGURE 7.11 Probable passage: sample terms/vocabulary, writing frame, and passage.

KEY CONCEPT: Blue Whale (terms/vocabulary)
Characteristics and Features:

breathing hole, or nostril	krill, a shrimplike creature	100 feet
up and down strokes	dorsal fin	arm bones
flukes	blowhole	flipper bones
mammal	blubber	two hours
largest creature	30 elephants	four-ton tongue
baleen	stringy plates of whalebone	few minutes

Probable Passage (writing frame)

This selection tells us about the blue whale. The blue whale is the _____ ever to live on Earth, weighing more than _____ and becoming _____ long. It is not a fish but a _____. It breathes through a _____, which is the same thing as a _____. The blue whale eats four tons of _____ every day in summer. When it eats, about 400 _____, called baleen, hang down from the upper lip. The _____ traps anything the blue whale catches. Then the whale's _____ forces water in and out of the mouth, making the food go down the throat. In winter the blue whale survives on its own body fat. A thick layer of _____ under the skin helps to keep in body heat.

   As the whale roams the oceans it uses its _____, the muscular tail flippers, in _____ to propel itself through the water at about 20 miles per hour. The whale also has a boneless _____, _____, and _____ to help it move and stay in an upright position. Because it is a mammal and needs air to breathe, the whale must come to the surface every _____, although it can hold its breath for up to _____.

The Blue Whale (actual passage)

This selection tells us about the blue whale. The blue whale is the largest creature ever to live on earth, weighing more than 30 elephants and becoming 100 feet long. It is not a fish but a mammal. It breathes through a blowhole, which is the same thing as a breathing hole, or nostril. The blue whale eats four tons of krill, a shrimplike creature, every day in summer. When it eats, about 400 stringy plates of whalebone, called baleen, hang down from the upper lip. The baleen traps anything the blue whale catches. Then the whale's four-ton tongue forces water in and out of the mouth, making the food go down the throat. In winter the blue whale survives on its own body fat. A thick layer of blubber under the skin helps to keep in body heat.

As the whale roams the oceans it uses its flukes, the muscular tail flippers, in up and down strokes to propel itself through the water at about 20 miles per hour. The whale also has a boneless dorsal fin, arm bones, and flipper bones to help it move and stay in an upright position. Because it is a mammal and needs air to breathe, the whale must come to the surface every few minutes, although it can hold its breath for up to two hours.

Continued.   **FIGURE**   7.11

2. Supply an incomplete writing frame, similar to a paragraph frame, representing one of the various expository writing structures. (Model use of this strategy with each of the structures over a series of days.) For example, see the writing frame in Figure 7.11.

3. Prior to their reading of the material, present to students the writing frame and the key vocabulary from the content area topic. Tell students this strategy is intended to help them learn the content area vocabulary and better comprehend the material they are about to read, as well as to help them write about the topic in the expository style.

4. Read and discuss the words with students. Invite students to think about where and how these words might be used in the writing frame. They may also use words not listed to complete the writing frame.

5. Work with students to develop a probable passage. They write in words and phrases to complete the writing frame.

6. Have students read a section of the related content area material.

7. After reading and discussing the material, have students look back at the probable passage and modify it to accurately reflect the information presented in the content area material (see the actual passage in Figure 7.11). After several teacher-directed sessions, students can work on their own, in pairs, or in small groups, to develop and share probable passages.

RESEARCHING IN THE CONTENT AREAS

Another important aspect of content area literacy is learning how to find out what you want to know. As all the content area standards indicate, students need to learn

- to be problem solvers.
- to ask questions.
- how to find out the answers.
- to communicate their findings.

In essence, this is what research is all about.

Brainstorming

Brainstorming is a structured way to activate learners' prior knowledge about and create interest in a topic. Students are asked to share their knowledge and experiences related to a set of words or concepts the teacher has identified from the content area materials. For example, before beginning a unit on Egypt, the teacher lists words such as *pyramids, mummies,* and *pharaohs* and asks students to share (either orally or in writing) what they know about these terms. As this information is shared, the teacher adds information that will assist the students in their understanding of these concepts (Sadler, 2001). Following this discussion, the teacher asks students what they want to find out about these concepts (see Figure 7.12). Questions from students are compiled and posted for all to see, providing purpose for upcoming readings. As stated by Koechlin and Zwaan (2006), "a good research question is one that guides the questioner through a quest to build personal meaning and understanding" (p. 47).

Locating Information

For students to locate information that helps to answer their questions about particular content area topics, they need several underlying skills. In addition to basic alphabetizing skills and knowledge of how to use book parts such as a table of contents, the index, glossaries, or appendices, students need to be able to categorize information in a variety of ways. For example, if students are trying to learn more about the habitat of the polar bear, they need to recognize that information about weather can also be found under the category heading of climate. Recognizing potentially useful category headings and "key words" is critical when using online resources such as www.google.com for Internet searches, or CD-ROM encyclopedias.

FIGURE 7.12   Inquiry question guide.

1. Regarding this unit, what are you really curious about?
2. Why do you want to explore this topic?
3. What do you already know about this topic?
4. What do you want or need to find out?
5. How will you make sense of the data you discover?
6. Who will you share your information with?
7. What do you want your audience to understand about your research?
8. How will you share your new learning?

Adapted from Koechlin & Zwaan (2006).

As a first step before beginning research, you can list possible sources of information for answering a research question. These sources, however, should only include the ones for which you have modeled the use. For example, part of novel studies (see Chapter 5) could include noting how much research the book's author needed to do in order to write the novel. Even though a novel may be considered narrative writing, you should point out that the novelist needs to do research in order to include accurate information—especially in the case of historical fiction. Some novels include features such as an Author's Note or a list of references describing the research the author did to write an accurate book. Both *Crossing the Wire* (Hobbs, 2006) and *Al Capone Does My Shirts* (Choldenko, 2004), mentioned in Table 5.2, provide an Author's Note discussing the research done related to illegal crossings from Mexico to the United States and the Alcatraz prison of the 1930s, respectively.

Possible sources for research are many, including almanacs, atlases, biographies, dictionaries, encyclopedias, magazines, maps, museum exhibits, newspapers, nonfiction books, photographs, published interviews, records, tapes, television programs, thesauri, and video productions. As online access has become common in classrooms, the Internet also has become a powerful research tool. You as a teacher, however, need to be aware that the amount of information available can be overwhelming to students. A single key word search can result in thousands of websites, which can vary substantially in the quality and accuracy of the information they provide. To help students better understand Internet sites, explain that the following domains indicate sites sponsored by the educational institutions, government, and the military: .edu, .gov, and .mil.

One of the best resources for classroom teachers using the Internet as part of their teaching is Kathy Schrock's website. She provides a wealth of information for educators, including suggested websites. She has also developed a set of relevant questions in both English and Spanish for elementary, middle, and secondary students to use in evaluating websites.

For a set of questions for use by the classroom teacher in evaluating websites, see Figure 7.13, a compilation of several checklists. In addition, a field trip to a public or university library can provide further instruction in using the Internet as well as the multitude of other resources available (Gipe, 2006).

WWW

Kathy Schrock
http://school.discoveryeducation.com/schrockguide/

Online Search Skills

As discussed in Chapter 5, reading online is a skill students need to develop as they use the Internet to research and write school assignments. One critical aspect of using the Internet is the ability to perform online searches that will lead to useful and high-quality information. And because there is so much information available on the Internet, students also need to carefully evaluate the websites they find. Appendix D provides students with a useful tool for evaluating websites.

Before beginning online searches, Henry (2006) recommends introducing students to the way search engines are organized (e.g., text matching, categories) and the way they work (e.g., word

Students must develop the ability to perform online searches that lead to useful and high-quality information.

FIGURE   7.13   Guidelines for evaluating websites.

The set of questions that follows is a compilation of several checklists developed for evaluating websites and is intended to be used by the classroom teacher.

AUTHOR CREDIBILITY

- Who is the author/source or producer?
- What is the authority or expertise of the individual or group that created this site? With what organization is the author of the website affiliated?
- Is there a way to contact the author or supply feedback?

  Tips: Check the header and footer information to determine the author and source.

  In the URL, a tilde (~) usually indicates a personal web directory rather than being part of the organization's official website.

  To verify an author's credentials, you may need to consult some printed sources such as *Who's Who in America* or the *Biography Index.*

ACCURACY AND RELIABILITY

- Is the information accurate?
- How current is the information? Is a date of publication provided? When was the website last revised? How frequently is the resource updated?
- Is the information presented in an objective, balanced manner?
- Is the information well written? Does the text follow basic rules of grammar, spelling, and composition?
- Are the sources of information stated? Can the information be verified?
- Does the information contradict something already known or learned from another source?
- Has the site been reviewed or ranked by an online reviewing agency?

SCOPE

- What is the primary purpose of the site (e.g., advertising, information)? Is the purpose of the resource clearly stated? Does it fulfill its purpose?
- Does the site contribute something unique on the subject?
- Is the material covered adequately?
- Is the site appropriate for the intended audience? Is it interactive enough to make students think?
- Are excerpts from texts provided or are entire texts available?

- Is the information available in other formats?
- Is the information factual or opinion?
- Does the site contain original information or simply links?
- Is a bibliography of print or web resources included?

FORMAT AND NAVIGATION

- Can you find your way around and easily locate a particular page from any other page?
- Is response time fast?
- How many links does it take to get to something useful?
- Is the arrangement of links uncluttered?
- If there are links to other sites, do they work? How up-to-date are the links?
- How many links lead to a dead end?
- How stable is the connection to the site?
- Do parts of it take too long to load?
- Does the site require additional software or hardware?
- Is the site open to everyone on the Internet, or do parts require fees?
- Can nonmembers still have access to part of the site?
- Must a name and password be registered before using the site?
- Is there a text alternative? Text only? Can the graphics be turned off?
- Do illustrations, video, or audio add value to the site?
- Is the site conceptually exciting? Does it do more than can be done with print?
- Do the multimedia, graphics, and art serve a function or are they decorative?
- What is the quality of the multimedia or graphic images? Do these images enhance the resource or distract from the content?
- Are the individual web pages concise, or does one have to scroll extensively?
- Does the site have its own search engine?
- Is the site easily browsable or searchable?

SOURCES

http://its.unc.edu/tl/guides/irg-49.php

www3.widener.edu/Academics/Libraries/Wolfram_Memorial_Library/Evaluate_Web_Pages/659/

http://library.usm.maine.edu/research/researchguides/webevaluating.html

frequency, sponsored links; see the NoodleTools site listed in the margin). She states, "once students have a good grasp of the organization of various search engines, they are much more successful in conducting searches and reading information" (p. 617). Henry goes on to describe an instructional framework, called SEARCH, which represents the research findings both for locating information in written text and for searching information on the Internet. The SEARCH acronym delineates the following skills:

1. Set a purpose for searching.
2. Employ effective search strategies.
3. Analyze search-engine results.
4. Read critically and synthesize information.
5. Cite your sources.
6. How successful was your search? (p. 618)

www

Search Engines by Category
*www.noodletools.com/debbie/literacies/information/
5locate/adviceengine.html*

Once the searching begins, students also need to learn how to decide which of the many links resulting from the search to follow. Coiro (2005) describes a critical thinking activity for helping students learn to predict which websites hold the most promise for providing answers to their questions. (An adaptation of this activity follows below, using the questions found in the data chart presented in Figure 7.14.)

Data Charts

A **data chart** serves as an organizational structure for keeping track of research questions, notes, and information from several sources. These charts can be kept by individual students or small cooperative study groups, or posted for whole-class contributions. They can also be used as listening or viewing guides for students who are gathering information from resources such as a television documentary or a taped interview. An example using the questions generated from brainstorming the topic of ocean life is presented in Figure 7.14. The completed

● data charts

Sample data chart for ocean features.   **FIGURE** 7.14

Research Group: <u>Ocean Features</u> (other groups are Ocean Plants and Ocean Animals)

Source	How many oceans are there?	How deep are the oceans?	What is on the ocean floor?	How much water is in the ocean?	Why is ocean water salty?	What causes waves?	What are tides?
1.							
2.							
3.							

data chart can reveal relationships among concepts and help students get an over-all picture of the topic being studied. These charts serve students well as study guides before exams or as guides for writing informational papers or project web pages, or preparing a speech or oral presentation.

ACTIVITY *Internet Search*

When working with students to help them improve Internet search skills, it is crucial to help them determine which Internet link(s) to follow when they are presented with a long list of possible choices. The following on-paper activi-ty for use with the data chart seen in Figure 7.14 "encourages students to stop, think, and make predictions about which Web sites to explore" (Coiro, 2005, p. 31).

1. Before presenting the activity to the class, you must conduct a search on the Internet for information relevant to your topic; in our example we'll use the study of Ocean Features, as in our data chart. Capture the first few entries from the search with a screen-capture program, and print them out. (See Figure 7.15.)

FIGURE **7.15** **Internet search results.**

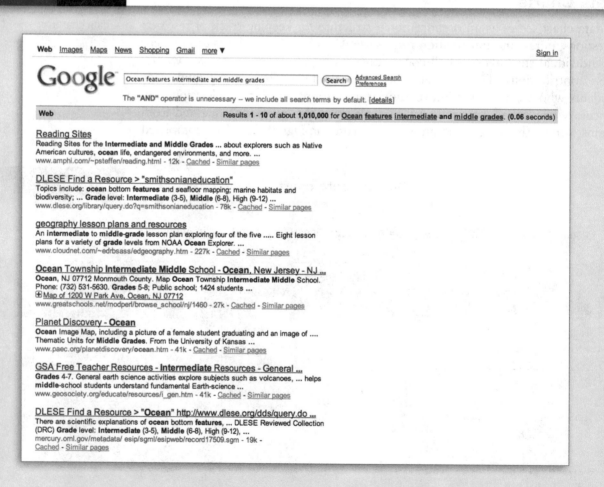

2. Provide small groups of students a handout that includes the first few results of the Internet search and a set of "questions that guide students to critically examine each entry on the list, noticing text and screen features embedded within the website addresses, website annotations, and file extensions after each hyperlinked resource" (Coiro, 2005, p. 31). See Figure 7.16.

3. Have small groups of students discuss their answers to each question and exchange strategies for deciding how to navigate the Internet. The website evaluation tool in Appendix D can be used to analyze the websites once they are opened.

Internet search activity: Use these questions to guide your small group discussion.   **FIGURE 7.16**

QUESTIONS AND ANSWERS	HOW DO YOU KNOW?	WHY IS THIS IMPORTANT TO KNOW?
1. How many websites were found using these search key words? Answer: 1,010,000	The line at the top of the page says, "Results 1-10 of about 1,010,000."	One million sites are too many to look at. Try using different key terms to make the results list shorter. Maybe try ocean features and resources as key terms.
2. Which website contains information about the topic you are studying? Answer: Site 2	The description says, "topics include ocean bottom features" as the first item listed. Site 1 includes the word "ocean" but it is not the main topic.	Reading the description saves time because it gives clues about what is in the website and what the website is mostly about.
3. Which site appears to be least helpful? Answer: Site 4	This is a link to a specific school in Ocean, New Jersey	Sometimes the results will include a site that might use only one of the words used in the key word search, like the word "ocean." This word might be used in the title, but the site has nothing to do with ocean features.
4. Which URL seems most likely to be available over the next several months? Answer: The URL for DLESE Find a Resource	The URL tells me it is an organization (.org), which is probably going to be around longer than a URL that includes ~ followed by someone's name, which indicates a personal site.	Looking carefully at the URL can give clues about who developed the site and whether it is a reliable source.

TROUBLESHOOTING

I t is very common for students who have made good progress in their literacy development up to the fourth grade to then start to show signs of difficulty. The increased attention to subject matter knowledge as opposed to narrative materials causes some students to struggle. Use of the content reading interview might help initially to identify students who need extra attention in this area (Figure 7.17). However, it is the lack of familiarity with expository text structure that is generally the basis for difficulty. The following section presents some ways to deal with this common difficulty.

FIGURE 7.17   **Content reading interview.**

1. How much do you read in _____(content area)_____
   What do you read? Why?

2. When you are reading in _____(content area)_____ and come to something you don't know, what do you do?
   Do you ever do anything else?

3. Who is the best reader you know in _____(content area)_____?
   What makes him or her a good reader in _____(content area)_____?

4. How good are you at reading your _____(content area)_____ book(s)?
   How do you know?

5. What is the hardest part about answering the questions in the book(s) used in _____(content area)_____?

6. If you needed to study a chapter in _____(content area)_____ so you could remember the information, how would you do it?

7. Have you ever tried _____(name a study strategy)_____?
   Tell about it.

8. What do you have to do to get a good grade in _____(content area)_____ class?

Source: Adapted from Wixson et al., 1984.

Lack of Familiarity with Expository Text Structures

Students who have sufficient abilities in reading narrative material need to recognize that these same abilities are applicable to the more unfamiliar structures of expository material. In some ways, developing these new skills in reading expository material is like learning a new language—the language of expository text. Providing opportunities to use the patterns of content area language through all the language arts areas will accelerate both learning the content knowledge and learning the structure of expository text language. Students need to become comfortable with the unfamiliar language patterns and structures associated with various subject areas.

Because we know that English-speaking students begin to have difficulty in their literacy development when content area material is the focus, it is no surprise that English learners might also experience difficulty. As the "In the Classroom" example of the dictoglos strategy demonstrates, it is especially valuable when working with English learners to integrate the language arts areas of reading, writing, listening, speaking, viewing, and visually representing toward the goal of achieving cognitive academic language proficiency (CALP); that is, the language of school. Learning the technical terms associated with each academic area is critical (Pilgreen, 2006).

Dictoglos

ACTIVITY

1. Select an expository passage from a textbook or nonfiction trade book and read aloud to class.
2. While reading, have students write down key words and phrases.
3. Have students work in pairs to rewrite the text as they heard it from their notes.
4. Have the pairs join together to form groups of four and repeat step 3.
5. Ask for volunteers to read their re-created passages.
6. Lead a discussion about the material in the passage that is hard to re-create and ways to make this material easier to remember.

As indicated earlier in this chapter, graphic organizers can be especially helpful to readers struggling in content area literacy. The use of such visuals can help English learners and native speakers alike understand expository text structures and comprehend organization patterns. When students are asked to read large quantities of material, some may have difficulty and feel they are overwhelmed with information. The visual format of a graphic organizer helps to make the information comprehensible, but it must also be used within a context where academic language (e.g., main idea, supporting details, "WH"—who, what, where, when, why, how—words) matches the academic concepts.

One example is the **herringbone strategy**, a graphic, structured outlining technique that helps readers organize the most important information from expository material. The herringbone structure (see Figure 7.18) reminds them of what information to look for while they are reading. Six basic questions are asked: Who? What? When? Where? How? and Why? In addition, readers are asked to determine the main idea. Students can easily reproduce the herringbone

● herringbone strategy

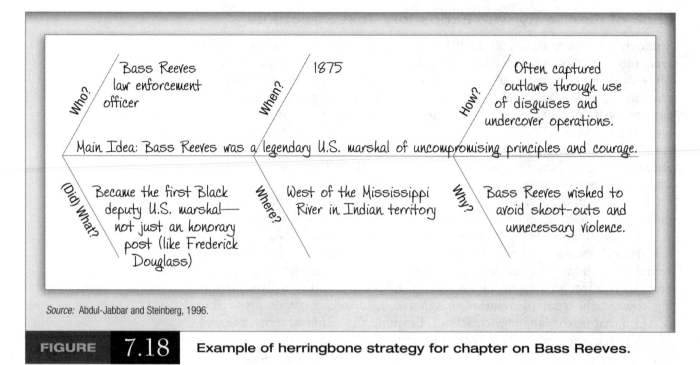

Source: Abdul-Jabbar and Steinberg, 1996.

FIGURE 7.18 Example of herringbone strategy for chapter on Bass Reeves.

form in their notebooks and record their answers there while they read informational texts. After several sessions involving teacher modeling, students are ready to begin completing their own herringbone forms. Students may notice that all the questions might not be answered within the selection they are reading. This situation leads to the recognition that a variety of sources is needed to learn as much about a topic as possible. Alvermann and Phelps (2005) report that students became more successful with using the herringbone technique over time, so teachers need to provide regular opportunities for its use.

SUMMARY

This chapter has presented a wealth of information about the nature of content area literacy and the relationship of literacy standards and content area standards, as well as many examples for instruction in content area reading, writing, and researching. The most important aspect of content area literacy instruction is to use expository material to teach the strategies that will help students most with informational text. Recognizing that expository text is different from narrative text, and how it is different, will help students understand that they will need to adjust their typical reading behaviors, such as reading fast, and do more stopping, thinking, and reviewing of informational material.

Questions
FOR JOURNAL WRITING AND DISCUSSION

1. Identify key concepts that students need to know in a math, science, or social studies text being used in a local school district. What kind of activities could you design that would enhance students' comprehension of these concepts?

2. Discuss the value of metacomprehension or comprehension monitoring abilities for reading in the content areas.

3. You have a friend whose child was given an open-ended homework assignment that requires the child to demonstrate his knowledge about the topic "ocean animals." Your friend and the child have no idea what to do or where to start. How could you help?

Suggestions FOR PROJECTS AND FIELD ACTIVITIES

1. Model the K-W-L Plus strategy with a small group of grade 4–8 students. Then, with new material, let the students try the technique. Question them regarding the effectiveness of the technique. Did they feel the strategy was helpful? Why or why not?

2. Prepare a paragraph frame based on a content area selection read by a student. Discuss the detail sentences with a student who typically has difficulty with expository text material. Have the student sequence the detail sentences and then complete the paragraph frame. Reflect with the student on the effectiveness of this technique. Did the student find this strategy helpful? Why or why not?

3. Choose a topic or theme that is widely used in your local school districts (e.g., rain forests, exploration, the planets, geometry in our daily lives), and prepare an annotated bibliography of fiction and nonfiction materials (not just text materials) that span a wide range of reading ability levels for this topic/theme.

REFERENCES

Abdul-Jabbar, K., & Steinberg, A. (1996). Bass Reeves. In *Black profiles in courage: A legacy of African American achievement* (pp. 112–139). New York: William Morrow and Company.

Alfassi, M. (2004). Reading to learn: Effects of combined strategy instruction on high school students. *Journal of Educational Research, 97,* 171–184.

Alvermann, D., & Phelps, S. (2005). *Content reading and literacy: Succeeding in today's diverse classrooms.* Boston: Pearson Education.

Ash, G. E. (2002). Teaching readers who struggle: A pragmatic middle school framework. *Reading Online, 5*(7). Available at www.readingonline.org/articles/art_index.asp?HREF=ash.

Buehl, D. (2001). *Classroom strategies for interactive learning* (2nd ed.). Newark, DE: International Reading Association.

Carr, E., & Ogle, D. (1987). K-W-L plus: A strategy for comprehension and summarization. *Journal of Reading, 30*(7), 626–631.

Carr, K. S., Buchanan, D. L., Wentz, J. B., Weiss, M. L., & Brant, K. J. (2001). Not just for the primary grades: A bibliography of picture books for secondary content teachers. *Journal of Adolescent & Adult Literacy, 45*(2), 146–153.

Caverly, D., Mandeville, T., & Nicholson, S. (1995). PLAN: A study-reading strategy for informational text. *Journal of Adolescent & Adult Literacy, 39,* 190–199.

Coiro, J. (2005). Making sense of online text. *Educational Leadership, 63*(2), 30–35.

Columba, L., Kim, C. Y., & Moe, A. J. (2005). *The power of picture books in teaching math and science, grades K–8.* Scottsdale, AZ: Holcomb Hathaway.

Cuban, L. (1991). History of teaching in social studies. In J. Shaver (Ed.), *Handbook of research on social studies teaching and learning* (pp. 197–209). New York: Macmillan.

Cudd, E. T., & Roberts, L. L. (1989). Using writing to enhance content area learning in the primary grades. *The Reading Teacher, 42,* 392–404.

Duffelmeyer, F. A., & Baum, D. D. (1992). The extended anticipation guide revisited. *Journal of Reading, 35,* 654–656.

Eanet, M. G., & Manzo, A. V. (1976). REAP—a strategy for improving reading/writing study skills. *Journal of Reading, 19,* 647–652.

Fay, L. (1965). Reading study skills: Math and science. In J. A. Figurel (Ed.), *Reading and inquiry.* Newark, DE: International Reading Association.

Friend, R. (2000/2001). Teaching summarization as a content area reading strategy. *Journal of Adolescent & Adult Literacy, 44*(4), 320–329.

Gipe, J. P. (2006). *Multiple paths to literacy: Assessment and differentiated instruction for diverse learners, K–12* (6th ed.). Upper Saddle River, NJ: Merrill/Prentice Hall.

Gottfried, S. S., & Kyle, W. C., Jr. (1992). Textbook use and the biology education desired state. *Journal of Research in Science Teaching, 29,* 35–49.

Harvey, S. (1998). *Nonfiction matters: Reading, writing, and research in grades 3–8.* York, ME: Stenhouse.

Henry, L. A. (2006). SEARCHing for an answer: The critical role of new literacies while reading on the Internet. *The Reading Teacher, 59,* 614–627.

Hoyt, L. (1999). *Revisit, reflect, retell: Strategies for improving reading comprehension.* Portsmouth, NH: Heinemann.

Kane, S. (2007). *Literacy and learning in the content areas* (2nd ed.). Scottsdale, AZ: Holcomb Hathaway.

Kane, S. (2008). *Integrating literature in the content areas: Enhancing adolescent learning and literacy.* Scottsdale, AZ: Holcomb Hathaway.

Klingner, J. K., Vaughn, S., Arguelles, M. E., Hughes, M. T., & Leftwich, S. A. (2004). Collaborative strategic reading: "Real world" lessons from classroom teachers. *Remedial and Special Education, 25,* 291–302.

Koechlin, C., & Zwaan, S. (2006). *Q tasks: How to empower students to ask questions and care about answers.* Portland, ME: Stenhouse.

Langer, J. A. (2001). Beating the odds: Teaching middle and high school students to read and write well. *American Educational Research Journal, 38,* 837–880.

Moss, J. G. (1994). *Using literature in the middle grades: A thematic approach.* Norwood, MA: Christopher-Gordon.

Neeld, E. C. (1986). *Writing* (2nd ed.). Glenview, IL: Scott Foresman.

Pilgreen, J. (2006). Supporting English learners: Developing academic language in the content area classroom. In T. A. Young & N. L. Hadaway (Eds.), *Supporting the literacy development of English learners* (pp. 41–60). Newark: DE: International Reading Association.

Post, A. D., with Scott, M., & Theberge, M. (2000). *Celebrating children's choices: 25 years of children's favorite books.* Newark, DE: International Reading Association.

Richter, H. P. (1970). *Friedrich.* Translated from the German by Edite Kroll. New York: Holt, Rinehart & Winston.

Robinson, F. P. (1946). *Effective study.* New York: Harper and Bros. (Also 1970, 4th ed. New York: Harper & Row.)

Sadler, C. R. (2001). *Comprehension strategies for middle grade learners: A handbook for content area teachers.* Newark, DE: International Reading Association.

Schumm, J. S., & Mangrum, C. T. (1991). FLIP: A framework for content area reading. *Journal of Reading, 35,* 120–124.

Sierra-Perry, M., with Ewing, J., Foertsch, D., & Sierra, S. (1996). *Standards in practice grades 3–5.* Urbana, IL: National Council of Teachers of English.

Simpson, M. L. (1986). PORPE: A writing strategy for studying and learning in the content areas. *Journal of Reading, 29,* 407–414.

Simpson, M. L., & Nist, S. L. (1984). PLAE: A model for planning successful independent learning. *Journal of Reading, 29,* 218–223.

Spache, G. (1963). *Toward better reading.* Champaign, IL: Garrard.

Stephens, E. C., & Brown, J. E. (2000). *A handbook of content literacy strategies: 75 practical reading and writing ideas.* Norwood, MA: Christopher-Gordon.

Tiedt, I. M. (2000). *Teaching with picture books in the middle school.* Newark, DE: International Reading Association.

Wajnryb, R. (1990). *Grammar dictation.* Oxford, England: Oxford University Press.

Wiesendanger, K. D., & Bader, L. (1992). SCAIT: A study technique to develop students' higher comprehension skills when reading content area material. *Journal of Reading, 35,* 399–400.

Wixson, K. K., Bosky, A. B., Yochum, M. N., & Alvermann, D. E. (1984). An interview for assessing students' perceptions of classroom reading tasks. *The Reading Teacher, 37*(4), 346–352.

Wood, K. D. (1984). Probable passages: A writing strategy. *The Reading Teacher, 37,* 496–499.

Wood, K. D. (2001). *Literacy strategies across the subject areas: Process-oriented blackline masters for the K–12 classroom.* Boston: Allyn & Bacon.

Zemelman, S., Daniels, H., & Hyde, A. (1998). *Best practice: New standards for teaching and learning in America's schools* (2nd ed.). Portsmouth, NH: Heinemann.

Fostering
Oral Language
in the Classroom

FOCUS QUESTIONS

- What should be the major objectives of an oral language program in grades 4–8?

- What are some evidence-based strategies to foster the development of both informal and formal oral language?

- How can drama be used to make language accessible for English learners?

257

FOSTERING ORAL LANGUAGE IN THE CLASSROOM

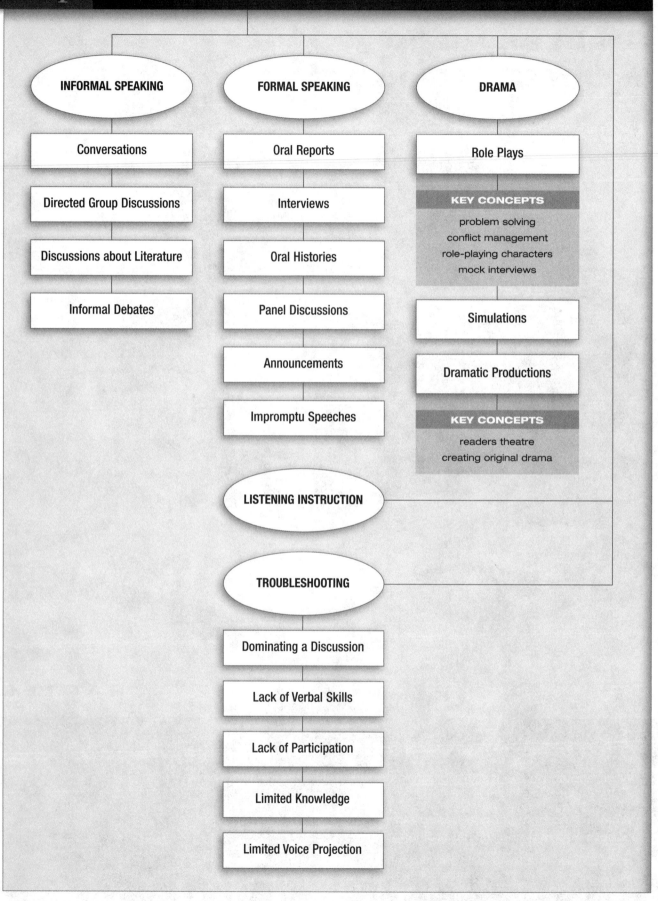

INFORMAL SPEAKING

Conversations

Directed Group Discussions

Discussions about Literature

Informal Debates

FORMAL SPEAKING

Oral Reports

Interviews

Oral Histories

Panel Discussions

Announcements

Impromptu Speeches

DRAMA

Role Plays

KEY CONCEPTS

problem solving
conflict management
role-playing characters
mock interviews

Simulations

Dramatic Productions

KEY CONCEPTS

readers theatre
creating original drama

LISTENING INSTRUCTION

TROUBLESHOOTING

Dominating a Discussion

Lack of Verbal Skills

Lack of Participation

Limited Knowledge

Limited Voice Projection

Mr. Pollard is preparing for a guided reading selection about tornadoes with his fourth-grade class. The school in which Mr. Pollard teaches is on the coast of North Carolina and, although most of the students have had firsthand experience with a hurricane, he wonders how much they know about tornadoes, another severe natural disaster. To prepare the students for the selection, Mr. Pollard leads a discussion:

Mr. Pollard: Many of our families have been affected by hurricanes, such as Katrina and Humberto, but how many of you have ever known anyone who was in a tornado? (Several students raise their hands.) So what do you know about tornadoes, Josh?

Joshua: We lived in Kansas when I was a baby. My mother told me there was a special kind of cellar you go into when a tornado is supposed to come. A tornado can pick a house right up in the air—or even a car—but a cellar is level, so you're safe there.

Mr. Pollard: Yes, tornadoes are very strong and can do a great deal of damage.

Patricia: Did you guys see the film *Twister*? A huge tornado threw a cow way up in the air and even a semi! Do you think that could really happen, Mr. Pollard?

Mr. Pollard: Well, it was certainly sensational, but if you recall from the movie, there are several degrees of severity for tornadoes and that may have been an especially fierce one.

Kendra: There was a fierce tornado in *The Wizard of Oz* that picked up their house.

Hoa: Oh, yeah, I saw that and my little sister has the book!

Mr. Pollard: You are exactly right, Hoa; a tornado was an important part in the book. Can anyone tell me how a tornado is different from a hurricane?

Joshua: From what I have seen on the news, it seems like you don't get much warning for a tornado. Like, there's this funnel cloud that rips through the town real quickly, smashing everything in its path. But when we had the hurricane here, they were telling us on the news to evacuate for a whole day.

Mandy: Yeah, the movie showed the tornado happening really fast, before the guys who were studying it had time to get out of the way! And they were in a car!

Mr. Pollard: So, you think the tornado comes on more suddenly?

Joshua: Oh, yeah—way more suddenly. I guess that would make 'em even scarier than a hurricane, and that was for sure

the most scared that I have ever been! (Others murmur in agreement.)

Raul: They're bigger and black, too. And I don't think you have to have any rain with them. At least what I've seen on the news.

Kendra: And is there an eye with them, the part that is the worst, like with a hurricane? I don't ever remember hearing about it if there is.

Hoa: Do we have tornadoes in North Carolina? I hope not!

Crystal: I'm pretty sure we do! My aunt lives in Greenville and there was one there a long time ago. My cousin told me about it. The roof of their trailer was torn off and a telephone wire came down on it. But it was weird because it was just in some parts of the town and not in others. My aunt was shopping when it happened, so she didn't get hurt.

Mr. Pollard: I am glad to hear your relatives were not hurt! You children seem to know quite a bit about tornadoes. From your comments, it seems that tornadoes have some similarities to and also some differences from a hurricane. Let's find out more. I brought in some photographs that I got from the Internet showing a recent tornado in Oklahoma. (He passes these around.)

Mr. Pollard explains that tornadoes are often called "twisters" because of their funnel shape. He adds that tornadoes usually occur in flat prairie land, so the chances of having one on the North Carolina coast, while not impossible, are not likely. He then asks students if they have any questions about tornadoes. Several students respond, and he writes their questions on the board:

What causes tornadoes? What kind of weather makes them happen?

Why do they twist and have a funnel shape?

Why are they found in flat prairie land but not on the coast?

How are they different from hurricanes?

Through discussion, Mr. Pollard has not only assessed the prior knowledge of the students in his class about the upcoming science selection, but he has allowed them to share their experience and knowledge with each other. While doing so, they have set purposes for their subsequent reading and will have a more personal involvement with the reading.

After the reading, Mr. Pollard leads a discussion based on the students' questions. They talk about the new information they have learned and compare the data from the selection with what they remembered from *Twister,* the movie many of them had seen, as well as their other previous associations with the topic. From their comments and questions, Mr. Pollard can evaluate how well the children read and understood the selection, and how they are able to synthesize the new information with their prior knowledge. The last question about how tornadoes are different from hurricanes was not addressed in the text, so Mr. Pollard breaks the class into discussion groups consisting of three or four members and invites them to use a Venn diagram to come up with a list of similarities and differences between tornadoes and hurricanes using information they find on the Internet and in trade books (see Figure 8.1). Finally, Mr. Pollard helps the groups to consolidate their lists into one, thus deepening their understanding of the two storms through reading and much rich oral discussion.

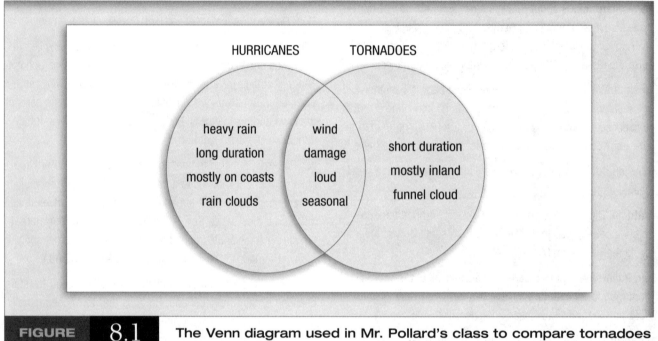

HURRICANES   TORNADOES

heavy rain

long duration

mostly on coasts

rain clouds

wind

damage

loud

seasonal

short duration

mostly inland

funnel cloud

FIGURE 8.1 **The Venn diagram used in Mr. Pollard's class to compare tornadoes and hurricanes.**

INTRODUCTION

The importance, academically, socially, and vocationally, of the ability to speak and listen with ease in contemporary society cannot be emphasized enough. Although we sometimes seem to believe that speaking and listening are learned automatically simply through contact with other people, we must remember that there are many forms of speaking and listening for which we need to reserve considerable classroom time for work at the oral level and, better yet, that we need to find ways to integrate the language arts of reading, writing, listening, speaking, viewing, and visually representing with other content areas. Additionally, with the influx of non–native English speakers into our schools, it becomes even more critical to create classrooms rich with the spoken word.

In particular, all students need a strong oral language base from which to develop other literacy skills. Through speaking and listening, students improve vocabulary, acquire new concepts, and become familiar with the structure of the English language—the essential building blocks of all learning (Smith, 2001). If students are going to learn speaking skills, it seems axiomatic they must have many opportunities to practice different types of speaking (Pinnell

260

& Jaggar, 2003). Students who possess strong oral language skills have a better chance of becoming proficient readers and greater potential for writing well than do students who lack such skills (Heath, 1983; Loban, 1976; Sampson, 1986). Moreover, some educators have discovered that peer talk increases motivation to read (Griffin, 2001).

The objectives of an oral language program around which most state standards are based include the following and are addressed at length in the remainder of this chapter. Students need to be taught to

- speak fluently and easily.
- use language as a way to communicate their ideas.
- perceive oral language as a way of learning.
- be familiar with specific skills of effective speaking.
- utilize different modes of expression.
- become strategic and skillful listeners.

To reach these objectives, a teacher in a balanced and comprehensive literacy program can expose students to informal speaking, including conversations, classroom discussions, and informal debates; formal speaking, including speeches, oral reports, and interviews; and drama, including role playing, readers theatre, and simulations. An excellent resource for additional activities that enhance oral communication skills is *Creating Competent Communicators: Activities for Teaching, Speaking, Listening, and Media Literacy in K–6 Classrooms* (Cooper & Morreale, 2003).

INFORMAL SPEAKING

nformal speaking, such as that contained in conversation and spontaneous or directed discussions, is the most frequently used expressive language mode. Most native English–speaking students are fluent users of oral language by the time they start school. Because most students have already acquired considerable competence using oral language, teachers often assume that oral language does not need to be emphasized in elementary classrooms, especially as students enter middle school. (In fact, some teachers expend considerable energy trying to *prevent* students from talking in class!) A significant body of research has shown, however, that students benefit greatly from participation in both formal and informal oral language activities (Strickland & Feeley, 2003). Moreover, it has become increasingly important to have a language-rich environment; such a classroom is the best source of language learning for the increasing numbers of students in today's schools who do not speak English or who are in the process of acquiring it (Peregoy & Boyle, 2005).

● informal speaking

Conversations

Oral language can and should be a natural and essential part of a balanced and comprehensive literacy program in grades 4–8. Older students can converse with peers as they plan and carry out collaborative projects or conduct writing conferences. Teachers, the primary models of standard English in any classroom, can also conduct informal conversations with students at various times during the day. Special time can be set aside for teachers to communicate with shy students, those who are experiencing difficulties in their lives, or those who need extra attention.

Oral language can and should be a natural and essential part of a comprehensive literacy program.

The rich context of a personally relevant conversation creates the *schema*, or background, necessary to store new word meanings. Moreover, the definitions students receive through conversations will probably be in terms they are developmentally able to understand. Then, in the context of that same conversation, students will often say the new word or words they have just learned. This immediate application further ensures that these terms will become part of students' permanent speaking, reading, and writing vocabulary.

Conversations, besides increasing vocabulary and helping students crystallize their thoughts on a variety of subjects, provide a way for teachers to make their students feel important and show respect for their ideas. Conversations can also provide teachers with important insights into the possible reading interests of their students as they discuss their likes and dislikes in the context of everyday discourse.

Students with similar interests can form self-initiated **conversation clubs,** to chat about an event, an idea, or an experience they have in common. During these sessions, teachers can learn much about the oral language prowess of students by taking anecdotal notes on which students

- extend the conversation without coaxing.
- hold listeners' attention.
- check for accuracy without being told to do so.
- ask questions for clarification.
- add interesting information.
- have adequate grammar and vocal habits.

conversation clubs

From these notes teachers can group students for minilessons on informative and interpersonal language uses.

Teachers may find it helpful to have at their command a list of provocative topics to which they can refer when they wish to plan a special conversation time (see Figure 8.2). Additionally, the following activities are sure to provoke even the quietest grade 4–8 student to contribute an oral response.

| FIGURE | 8.2 | Topics for informal conversations. |

What movies have you seen that you liked? Why?

What do you do on weekends?

What qualities do you value in a friend? Why?

What music groups do you enjoy? What do you like about them?

What is your favorite place to be? Why?

What is your favorite TV show? Why?

What is your favorite video game?

What would you do if you had a million dollars?

What things make you happy or sad?

What is your favorite Internet site? Why?

Do you have any pets? Describe your pet(s).

What is your favorite holiday? Why?

If you could go anywhere in the world, where would you go? Why?

Who is your favorite relative? Why?

What do you do to be kind to your brothers and sisters? How do they respond?

Just Suppose . . .

1. Develop a set of cards containing interesting suppositions (see suggestions).
2. Put students in pairs.
3. Give each pair a card with a printed Just Suppose . . . idea.
4. Allow students to talk about their idea for five minutes, weighing positives and negatives.
5. Encourage each pair to arrive at a consensus.
6. Invite pairs to share their ideas with the rest of the class.

SUGGESTIONS FOR "JUST SUPPOSE . . ." CARDS

. . . everyone looked exactly alike.

. . . you could talk to animals.

. . . you could become invisible.

. . . you could fly.

. . . you could learn by just taking pills.

. . . you were president of the United States.

. . . you could read people's minds.

. . . there was no money.

. . . you could "rewind" your life.

. . . there was only one kind of food.

Campfire

1. Change the seating arrangement for this activity to make it enjoyable and relaxing. One possibility might be to have students sit in a circle and pretend they are around a campfire. Be sure to audiotape or videotape the sharing period so that a tape will be available in a listening center designated for this purpose.
2. Select a topic (see Figure 8.2) or allow students to talk about a favorite object. Ask them to speak loudly enough so everyone can hear.
3. Instruct the class to listen politely as each student takes a turn speaking. Once each speaker has finished, invite students to ask a question of the speaker. The question must begin with one of the five Ws: Who, why, what, where, when. For example: "Where did you get that skateboard? Why is it so important to you?"
4. Correlate other subjects with this oral sharing time. For example, it might be combined with a current events lesson, where students can share something they have read in the newspaper or heard on the news.

Directed Group Discussions

Discussions are similar to conversations in several ways. Both involve the use of oral language in an informal setting. Both involve an exploration of an issue or a topic and offer students the opportunity to use a variety of speaking skills.

Suggestions for Teacher-Guided Discussions

Plan for the discussion by

- defining the issue to be discussed.
- preparing some leading questions.
- allowing students to research the topic.

Initiate the discussion by

- making a brief statement or offering a pertinent quotation.
- providing a handout with a summary of information about the topic.
- reminding students of guidelines for courteous behavior.

Keep the discussion running smoothly by

- having a recorder write responses on the board.
- discouraging domination of discussion by a vociferous few.
- inviting shy students to contribute.
- allowing gestures from and home language of English learners.

Bring out all sides of the topic by

- providing informative data from both sides of the issue.
- asking students to consider the opposing viewpoint.
- playing the role of "devil's advocate."

Help students to reach a consensus by

- summarizing points made by students on both sides.
- clarifying problematic issues as they arise.
- offering topics for subsequent

discussion ●

A **discussion** can be defined as "problem-solving by cooperative thinking." The goal of any discussion or problem resolution should be to consider a question from many angles, allowing all students a voice.

As students advance through the grades, teachers may begin to focus less on informal discussions and more on teacher-directed discussions, with a specific learning goal that the teacher has preidentified. Discussions are the principal means through which the conversational skills related to thinking patterns and to interpersonal functioning are developed. In the primary grades these skills are taught largely through teacher modeling. The teacher must contribute as well as solicit comments related to the topic under discussion; point out the connections among ideas being discussed; and demonstrate the processes of hypothesizing, summarizing, generalizing, and relating new information to one's own experience. Asking provocative questions that probe students' imagination helps these discussions become one of the richest sources of learning and processing information for students.

Gradually, as students progress through grades 4–8, they begin to incorporate these conversation skills into their own discussions. For example, in the vignette opening this chapter, the students in Mr. Pollard's class, typical of older students, were able to relate a new concept to their own experiences, make generalizations about hurricanes, and hypothesize about how they may be different from tornadoes.

Inquiry teaching, which is often used in social studies and science units, involves generating questions to be discussed with students. With inquiry teaching, learners are actively involved in deciding on topics to explore and directing their own discussions. This technique fosters rich oral language production for *all* students (Strickland & Feeley, 2003).

With inquiry learning, it is helpful to precede discussion periods with time for students to explore a specific content area topic to be addressed, such as "Why are the rain forests diminishing and what can we do about it?" Establishing this precedent helps students have a depth of information. One of the benefits of creating such informative and interactive discussions is that—provided the teacher has set up a safe, nonthreatening classroom environment, where no put-downs are allowed—students will appreciate their classmates' oral exchanges even more. They will actually learn from each other in a potent way not always possible from an adult.

For more formal discussions, and to foster a more student-centered classroom, it is sometimes helpful to appoint a discussion leader. The discussion leader has various specific responsibilities. The leader opens the discussion and establishes its goals. The leader may find it necessary to clarify participants' statements and to summarize progress as a basis for continuing productive discussion. Occasionally, the discussion leader will have to handle differences of opinion between participants. The leader also may need to learn to cope diplomatically, at times, with a talkative student who attempts to dominate the discussion and to draw in a shy student who needs to be invited to participate. Teachers will find it necessary to model discussion leader behavior for students initially, but then all students should have an opportunity to perform this role, which is so pivotal in developing leadership qualities.

The following guidelines may be helpful to share with students when initiating formal classroom discussions:

- Find out as much as you can about the topic ahead of time.
- Support your opinions with facts.
- Stay on the topic.
- Listen carefully to other speakers.
- Do not repeat what has already been said.
- Ask for clarification when you don't understand what has been said.
- At the end, help the leader summarize the most important points.

Discussions About Literature

Students need many opportunities to discuss books they have read or to hear discussions about books they may not yet be able to read. Smith (1998) cautions that simply asking students a list of questions about text to probe their thinking is rarely productive. Much as adults wish to share their feelings about a book they have recently read that touched them in some way, students' oral response to literature can deepen their appreciation for literature, and hearing their peers' perspectives on what they have read increases their critical and evaluative thinking about text (Gambrell & Almasi, 1996; Paratore & McCormack, 1998; Roser & Martinez, 1995).

grand conversations ●

These **grand conversations,** as they are sometimes called (Eeds & Wells, 1989), can follow a read-aloud or the independent reading of chapters in a novel. In small groups or in pairs, students can respond to story elements such as plot, illustrations, imagery, or specific characters. They can make connections between books, compare works by the same or another author, contrast other versions of the story, or compare some facet of the story to their own lives. These same ruminations about a text can follow the reading of a poem, listening to a story at a listening center, or guided reading of a difficult piece of literature with finely shaded meaning.

Literature circles (see Chapter 5) are also a wonderful means for encouraging intensive discussion and reflection about books students are reading. When students share their personal responses and interpretations of a book with their peers, they are able to gain a deeper understanding of themselves and their world. Moreover, the discussions lead to enhanced enjoyment of both literature and informational text (Straits & Nichols, 2006).

The most common approach to literature circles is for small groups or partners simply to sit together following the reading of a book or a portion of a book to talk about what they have read. They may discuss the same title or different books they have read on a similar theme, perhaps by the same author or illustrator, or from a particular literary genre. The teacher sets up a system that allows students to select books and schedules class time for students to meet. The partners or groups may have rotating, assigned roles, such as "discussion director" or "illustrator" or "vocabulary enhancer," or, in the case of informational text, "fact finder" or "science sleuth" (Straits & Nichols, 2006) to give individuals accountability for the reading and ensure that each student has a voice in the group discussion (refer back to Figure 5.5). This kind of rich, open-ended literature discussion offers literature experiences to all students regardless of current reading level.

Another, less structured form of literature discussion groups uses double entry journals (see Chapter 5). With this approach, students keep journal entries for every book they read. For each chapter or page assignment they are instructed to jot down quotes that strike them in some way. For example, the quote could remind them of something specific in their own life, or they could find the excerpt to be especially sad, humorous, interesting, or frightening.

Informal Debates

When a whole-class discussion has revolved around a controversial issue and the class has seemingly taken sides on it, an informal debate can be a perfect avenue for combining critical thinking with informal speaking. First, the teacher helps students to clarify what the issue is and what the opposing positions are. Then students are asked to move to opposite sides of the room, designated "opposers" and "supporters," depending on the position they have taken, and to appoint a spokesperson. If certain students have not made up their minds, they are asked to take a seat in the middle of the classroom. The opposing sides are then given 10 to 15 minutes to write down several arguments in support of their position. Next the teacher starts the debate by asking the spokesperson who is on the supporting side to make an opening statement. The opposition is then allowed to make a statement. After each of these statements has been made, both the neutral students and the opposing students may ask questions. After the debate, participants render an evaluation of the points made on both sides. No vote is required, but some kind of consensus may emerge.

Some possible topics for informal debate are as follows:

- Should there be homework on weekends?
- Should we explore outer space?
- Should scientists be allowed to clone human beings?
- Should animals be allowed in restaurants?
- Should 12-year-olds be allowed to drive? Vote?

FORMAL SPEAKING

Oral reports, interviews, panel discussions, announcements, and impromptu speeches are some of the formal ways students can learn to organize information and fluently express ideas and information. Through extensive classroom conversations and discussions, students gain confidence from their experience talking in groups, where the responsibility for communication is shared with others. Throughout grades 4–8, students will be introduced to more formal oral language experiences that require more preparation. Following are instructional practices and activities that provide formal speaking experiences.

Oral Reports

Oral reports are a way of sharing information and ideas before a group of people. Learning to prepare and deliver oral reports is an important part of the curriculum. It can be a positive, confidence-building event if authentic purposes are honored and adequate guidance in the process is provided. Teachers must remember (and convey to students) that research reports serve genuine language functions—to inform or (less frequently) persuade. When students give reports, they learn in-depth about the chosen topic and develop their communication abilities. Teachers must guide learners through the four steps in preparing a report:

● oral reports

1. choosing a topic
2. gathering information
3. organizing the information
4. making the presentation

Choosing a topic. Oral reports are most successful when students are involved in choosing their own topic. Choice allows them to feel ownership of the project, which will often motivate them to invest more time and energy in the preparation. In some cases, students can choose any topic that interests them, but in other cases the teacher may need to limit students to a broad topic within an area of class study. Within this broad area, they are then free to choose their specific topics. For example, the class may be studying the gold rush. Students could choose within that broad area a variety of topics such as cultural groups involved, how to pan for gold, people's reasons for going West, or hardships encountered there.

Gathering information. Students should be guided to gather information from a variety of sources, including the Internet, academic software, encyclopedias, almanacs, books, magazines, and primary sources such as interviews (discussed later). In addition to these print sources, students should learn to use video excerpts and to talk with experts in the area they are studying. For more information on researching, see Chapter 7. Notes in the form of key words or phrases may be recorded on note cards or diagrams.

Organizing the information. Students will need to cull the information they have gathered and decide in what sequence to present it. They should be encouraged and shown how to create visual aids such as posters, graphs, pictures, models, or PowerPoint presentations, which serve to enhance audience interest and understanding. They may also choose an unusual format for presentation if it lends itself to their specific topic. For example, a short skit might help an audience gain insight into the decision-making process a family had to go through in order to make the journey West in the 1840s in their quest for gold.

Making the presentation. The final step in the oral report is the actual presentation. Students should rehearse the presentation several times by reviewing key points and reading over the note cards or diagrams they have prepared. Before the presentations begin, the teacher should discuss the critical points that students need to remember. For example, speakers should speak slowly and loudly enough for all to hear, keep to the main points, refer to their note cards as prompts for important information but not read them, and weave in the visuals they have prepared. They should also make eye contact with the audience and speak with expression as opposed to speaking in a monotone.

Students may present their oral reports to the whole class or to small groups of students. For example, have students studying the gold rush give their reports to groups of five or six students at a time. Groups may be spread around the room, listening to each report and asking questions and giving comments, and then rotating on to a different speaker. In this way, students will be giving their first formal report to a small group, which is less intimidating than a large one, and they will each get a chance to give their report multiple times, affording practice and refinement. When students are more experienced, they can give their oral reports in front of the whole class and perhaps be videotaped. In response to the presentations, the class can offer constructive feedback on the content and effectiveness.

For information about assessing oral reports, see Chapter 2 and the scoring rubric for oral presentations in Appendix D.

Interviews

interview ● An **interview** is a form of oral information gathering. Interviewing is an important language tool that can be integrated effectively with almost any area of the curriculum. The interviewer may speak with one or two individuals or a small group of people. The interviewer may gather information regarding an individual's life history, a group he is involved in (e.g., sports, musical, political, or humanitarian), or a situation that concerns him (e.g., recycling, crime, terrorism, or climate change). Students may choose to interview local people, such as the principal, a local artist, a teacher, a spelling contest winner, or a person from a culture different from theirs. Students can also interview longtime area residents about local history, or even people who live far away—such as a favorite author or a professional athlete, using a long-distance telephone conference call.

The interviewer prepares a set of questions that will obtain the desired information. The questions should be written on note cards, one per question, and consist of open-ended queries, as opposed to questions that could be answered "yes" or "no." For example, "Why did your family emigrate from Russia?" The questions should be organized according to related topics and reviewed by the teacher to ensure that they will elicit the information the interviewer is seeking. As they become more experienced, students can ask follow-up questions, such as, "Could you tell me a little bit more about that?"

Interviewers should make an appointment with the person or persons in advance. They should also learn as much as they can about the person prior to the interview. Interviewers often tape interviews (video or audio), but permission should be obtained before taping. With the videocast feature on a recent release of the MacBook computer, students may even videocast their interviews. If, however, the interviewee does not permit taping or videocasting, then the interviewer should carefully write down all responses. When the interview is complete, the interviewer should thank the person for her time and follow up with a written note to that effect.

To share the results, the student should first carefully read over the notes or listen to the tape of the interview. Then the student should organize the information and decide on a format for presenting it (see Figure 8.3).

Following is an informal interview activity to use early in the year to help the class become acquainted and feel comfortable asking questions, an important precursor to a more formal interview.

Project presentation options.   **FIGURE 8.3**

PERFORMANCE	GRAPHICS/VISUALS
report	poster
review	collage
panel	PowerPoint slides
debate	video excerpt or iMovie
skit	time line
role play	map
simulation	mural
expert guest speaker	flow chart
	model
	overheads
	podcasts on PBS (using a podcast program, such as Apple's GarageBand)

ACTIVITY	*Getting to Know You*

1. Elicit a set of questions about things students may or may not have done. For example:

HAVE YOU EVER . . .	DO YOU . . .	WHO IS . . .
been in a country other than the United States?	have a brother or a sister?	the person you admire most?
flown in an airplane?	have a pet?	your favorite singing group?
had a part in a play?	like to read?	
planted a garden?	have a hobby?	your favorite TV star?
baby-sat?		your favorite movie star?
earned money?		

2. Write these questions on the board and ask students to copy them on a sheet of paper.
3. Divide the class in half. Designate half of the class as interviewers and the other half as interviewees.
4. For variety, allow each interviewer to ask a few "off-the-cuff" questions in addition to the listed ones. Instruct each interviewer to record all responses.
5. After the interviews are completed, have students switch roles and repeat the process.
6. Have the whole class compile the results in tallies, maps, or graphs, or use them in a bulletin board display entitled "Who Did What?"

Oral Histories

An interesting blend of the oral report and interview is the *oral history,* a way to connect history to students' own lives. One seventh-grade teacher in urban Los Angeles made history come alive using this approach. Mr. James Green had his middle school students discover their own histories (Cummins, Brown, & Sayers, 2007). He asked students to concentrate on two research questions: "Where does my family come from?" and "What history is contained in my family?" Then, Mr. Green introduced the approach that oral historians use to design interview questions, take notes, and organize information. He showed them how to use a tape recorder to record a conversation and later transcribe it. He also helped students prepare open-ended questions to invite conversation, such as "What was life like when . . .?" and "What do you remember about . . .?" Finally, he gave them time in the computer lab to look on the Internet at other oral history projects.

In addition to the interviews, students were given a choice of primary sources and other research tools they could use. Mr. Green showed them the various kinds of primary source material and historical documents on the Internet, explaining that all information viewed there must be evaluated critically for its accuracy and completeness, reinforcing visual and media literacy (see Chapter 10). He also asked students to consider the effectiveness of each technological tool for the task for which it would be used; for example, some

Internet Resources for Oral Histories

Digital Historical Inquiry Project, http://dhip.org

Digital historical inquiry uses current and emerging technologies to offer approaches to studying history that stress asking probing questions, examining differing perspectives, and constructing one's own meaning, as compared with the pervasive textbook-driven model to study history.

History Matters, http://historymatters.gmu.edu/mse/oral/

This website includes a guide to finding and using oral history online. It is a great first step for teachers and students to start using oral history interviews as historical evidence.

Step-by-step Guide to Oral History, www.dohistory.org/on_your_own/toolkit/oralHistory.html

This handy guide offers suggestions for collecting and organizing oral history. The website also deals with many issues to keep in mind when conducting and using oral histories.

Oral History Society, www.ohs.org.uk/

This comprehensive website explains what oral history is and how it can be used to bring a new dimension to the study of local and family history.

Oral History Websites, www.youthsource.ab.ca/teacher_resources/oral_websites.html

A clearinghouse, this website includes a host of links that demonstrate the uses of oral history, strategies for conducting oral histories, and accepted oral history practices such as interview techniques.

students found that the tape recorder hampered spontaneity when their family members were sharing personal recollections; others found that a family tree template they discovered on the Internet did not readily accommodate their nontraditional family. Additionally, some students were able to use a genealogical website that revealed much about distant relatives, while other students found nothing and had to rely on the oral history interviews.

Using the techniques introduced, students conducted individual investigations of their own families, wrote reports, and then presented their findings in oral presentations. As the students, who initially balked at the assignment, discovered the many fascinating details about the former lives of close and distant relatives, they became excited about the project and were eager to share their new insights at school. Their new information resulted, suddenly, in many student-generated history questions in class: "What was D Day, Mr. Green?" from a student whose grandfather had been a soldier in World War II, or "Why were so many people against the Vietnam War?" from a student whose uncle had fled to Canada rather than be drafted.

Mr. Green taught the students to use the digital video recorder to create an iMovie to capture the students' entire experience of researching and presenting their families' oral histories. The class iMovie was shown at Open House to a record number of eager parents, who had enjoyed participating in the oral history project. Many of the parents exclaimed how much communication with their youngster had been enriched through the project, with the students demonstrating a deeper pride and respect for their shared heritage. The project, while meeting a multitude of literacy and social studies goals, went far beyond the state standards as students were given the opportunity to connect with history in a deeply personal way.

Panel Discussions

A panel discussion is a favorite activity for formally sharing different kinds of information. The panel, usually consisting of three to eight members, conducts a discussion before the rest of the class. The topic, issue, or question is predetermined. The panel format is most effective when the presentation is thoughtful and informative rather than argumentative or spontaneous. When panelists conclude their presentations, class members are invited to ask them questions regarding a specific point that was made.

It is suggested that the teacher or panel members select a moderator. The moderator is responsible for organizing the panel to ensure that various points of view are represented and for monitoring the discussion so that all participants get an opportunity to be involved. A time limit should be placed on individual participation as well as the posing of questions by classmates. With practice, students will gain confidence in presenting information to their peers. Teachers are often surprised at how deeply student panelists will research a topic, given that it is a provocative subject.

The following is a variation on a panel discussion known as controlled participation, or CONPAR. The process was developed by General Motors for use with sales personnel in training sessions, but it is adapted here for use in grades 4–8. CONPAR is one of the best methods to guarantee the participation and involvement of all members of a group, regardless of group size or the age of the participants.

ACTIVITY *Controlled Participation (CONPAR)*

1. Decide on a problem to be solved or a topic to be discussed.
2. Select three to eight panel members.
3. Give the panel members and other class members the assignment to find out everything they can about the topic or problem (e.g., the diminishing rain forest).
4. Divide the other class members into groups, seat the groups together, and label each group.
5. Select a chairperson, to keep the discussion going, for each group, as well as a recorder.
6. Allow 10 minutes for discussion about the problem or topic. Instruct students in each group to come up with three questions and have the recorder write these on note cards.
7. Have the groups turn in the cards. Shuffle them and then read the first question aloud.
8. Invite one or more panel members to respond to the question. Limit each response to two minutes.

9. Read the second card aloud and ask different panel members to respond. Continue in this manner until all the questions have been answered.

10. At the end of the session take a few minutes to summarize key points that have been made.

Announcements

Announcements are common to all classroom situations and to all grade levels. Therefore, announcements are vehicles through which all students can learn how to deliver information clearly and concisely.

Some announcements are ineffectual because they do not express the ideas the speaker is trying to convey. Others are incomplete or simply fail to capture the listener's attention. As with most oral literacy activities, the teacher should first model how to make an effective announcement to offer learners an example worth imitating. When preparing an announcement, the speaker should create an introduction that will grab the listeners' attention. Then the essential information (what, where, why, when, who, and how) should be shared and restated. The message should be brief without sacrificing accuracy or clarity. Before the announcement is delivered, the speaker should practice saying it aloud in a clear, audible voice.

Students can practice making announcements by reading the lunch menu, participating in the morning routine of opening exercises, or explaining school activities on the public address system. See Figure 8.4 for an example of an effective announcement.

Impromptu Speeches

An **impromptu speech** can be defined as a talk that is prepared without extensive planning, thus requiring a modicum of creativity and "thinking on one's feet." The ability to give an impromptu speech is a very important formal oral language skill to develop because it is perhaps the one that will be used the most often in a person's later life.

● impromptu speech

Example of a fifth-grader's announcement.   FIGURE 8.4

Hey, kids! Did you hear about the awesome book fair coming to Arcadia Middle School? Well, this is your chance to buy all of the books you love in science fiction, romance, drama, historical fiction, poetry, and fantasy. Yes—there will even be all the Harry Potter books! And the best part is that they are all 20 percent cheaper than you can buy them in any bookstore! The book fair will be held in the cafeteria on Thursday, October 9, after school from 3 to 5:30. Hurry down there, because the first 30 book buyers will receive a free LeBron James poster. See you there!

To stimulate this type of formal speaking, prepare several 3 × 5 cards with provocative topics for students, such as "The strangest dream I ever had." Have each student select a card and then allow a few moments for the students to think about their topics. In a comfortable and safe small-group setting, invite each student to speak for three minutes on the topic on his or her card. Evaluations of this type of speaking should be supportive and positive. The following are additional examples of topics to use for impromptu speeches:

My favorite thing to do

If I were stranded on a desert island

Why conservation is important

The best movie I have ever seen

The person I most admire

Things that make me happy

Things I would like to change about the world

Things I do on weekends

A place I have been

If I were an animal

DRAMA

Drama is an integral part of a balanced and comprehensive literacy program. Classroom drama is an incomparable forum for language enjoyment, enriched comprehension, and community building. Additionally, drama can be a powerful way of learning and an alternative way of knowing—the actors become participants in the learning process and not merely passive bystanders (Wagner, 2003). Drama makes especially strong contributions to the growth of the speaking ability of English learners, because it provides natural comprehensible input: the words that are uttered are provided with an immediate context by the actions accompanying them. Furthermore, drama gives students opportunities to experiment with words, emotions, and social roles and encourages them to make sense out of their world in a multisensory way. Above all, through drama, students become more sensitive, confident communicators.

In this section, we explore three types of drama well suited to students in grades 4–8: role plays, simulations, and dramatic productions.

Role Plays

The term *role playing* is used to refer to a type of playacting in the classroom.

role playing ● By definition, **role playing** is a dramatic oral language activity in which students explore, in the most intimate way, the relationships of human living for the purpose of acquiring needed understandings and interpersonal communication skills. But unlike the dramatic play common to most primary classrooms, role playing can be structured for older students to be imbued with clear goals and desired outcomes. And unlike more formally structured theatrical presentations, in which set lines are read or memorized, role playing unfolds rather spontaneously, without a predetermined script. It uses the dramatic elements of characterization and dialogue. Empathy for another's point of view is usually heightened because the actor is attempting to take on the internal characteristics of the person who is being emulated.

Role plays can grow out of current daily situations, problems, past episodes, or dilemmas students may soon face, such as moving to a new grade. At times, the situation itself is the point of departure; at other times, the teacher sets the scene for the role play. Still another approach to role playing is to bring to life a favorite piece of children's literature in which there are complex relationships to be understood and rich opportunities for characterization, as will be discussed later. Lee Galda (1982) conducted a study in which a teacher read a familiar folktale to the class and then divided the students into three groups. The first group drew a picture about the story, the second group discussed the story, and the third group did a role play of the story. According to scores on a subsequent comprehension test and a retelling of the story, the dramatic activity was significantly more beneficial in deepening the students' understanding of the text.

Whether the situation enacted is a real-life experience that just took place, a story, an important concept, or a hypothetical event, the process through which language and literacy learning can evolve the most dynamically is through role play. Allow students to reflectively reenact an argument and they will develop insight and communication skills; let them simulate concepts through drama and what is unclear will be made clear and what is remote will become near and alive (Cecil, 1994).

Problem solving/conflict management through role plays

Consider the following scenario from a sixth-grade playground, typical of that which occurs daily on schoolyards all across the country, at recess:

Vlade: I'm getting tired of playing kickball every day. Today, why don't we play soccer instead?

Jason: Nah, let's not play soccer. I don't know how to. Besides, soccer's a sissy game. Let's just play kickball like we always do, or baseball.

Raúl: Uh uh. I like Vlade's idea. Let's play soccer for a change. I'll be the captain and Vlade can be the other captain. Let's choose up sides!

Jason: *No way!* I have the ball and you can't have it if you're going to play soccer.

Vlade: You are such a loser! I'm telling the teacher!

Jason: Go ahead! She'll take my side—she likes me!

Raúl: All right, Jason, just give me the ball right now or I'm gonna beat you up.

Jason: Oh, yeah? You and what army?

In the next few moments, of course, the argument escalates. Normally, this type of situation ends with angry feelings all around, as the teacher on recess duty reprimands all three boys and/or sends them to the principal's office.

Role playing is the vehicle through which such a commonplace scenario might be transformed into a dynamic oral language/social studies lesson, not only for the students directly involved but for the rest of the class as well. Because a variety of solutions are available for dealing with any conflict, role playing and discussing these options can provide insights into what causes conflicts and what effects can be expected with varying solutions.

ACTIVITY   *Role Play*

To help students gain insight from the previously mentioned scenario or another you create, guide students through the following activity:

1. Have a neutral observer from the class give his version of what took place.

2. Select students to play the roles of each person involved.

3. Ask the actors to take a few moments to prepare two role plays: the first a reenactment of the situation as it actually occurred, and a second that changes the outcome to a more positive solution to the conflict.

4. As the actors are preparing their role plays, instruct the other students as follows: "Watch what the actors do and say. Try to put yourself in their shoes and feel what they must be feeling. As you watch, be thinking of other ways the conflict could have been resolved."

5. Have the actors present their role plays in the center of the classroom, surrounded by other class members.

6. Discuss the differences in the outcomes of the two role plays. Invite other class members to contribute their alternative solutions to the problem. Write these on the board without evaluation.

7. Discuss the "cause" and "effect" patterns in the two role plays in terms of words or actions and resultant feelings and events.

For the particular actual playground scenario with Jason, Raúl, and Vlade, the three students might be asked to play themselves in the reenactment; or, to develop more insight into each other's point of view, they could be asked to switch roles. The three boys' alternative solution to the conflict might take the form of Vlade conceding that they will play kickball again as they always do. Other class members who have watched both role plays dispassionately may have some different suggestions for them; for example, since Jason has admitted that he doesn't know how to play soccer, might Vlade and Raúl teach him how to play? Could they set up a rotating schedule of playing soccer one day, kickball the next, and baseball the following day? What if they agreed to toss a coin each day to decide which game would be played?

Subsequently, through a teacher-guided reflective discussion, all the students in the class can begin to see exactly which turn of events caused the buildup of bad feelings that resulted in three friends arguing instead of communicating effectively to solve their conflict. Moreover, the entire class has orally problem solved ways for such an unfortunate event not to be repeated, while English learners have been provided with a rich context—the role play—for the ensuing discussion. To reinforce the concept of role play, a relevant children's literature selection could be read and discussed as a follow-up activity.

Role playing characters in literature

When you are reading a book that has many complex characters with a group of students, role playing can help make the characters come alive and enable students to discover the relationship between what they are reading and their own lives.

ideal vehicle through which to enhance oral language as well as include English learners.

Acting out an idea brings about a sense of discovery of the concept being introduced and also offers, in many cases, a visceral response that is not soon forgotten. Setting the stage for such discovery through simulation is often time consuming, and therefore not feasible for every concept that is addressed. Some concepts, however, such as the two prototypical activities described next, are worth the time and effort involved.

Haves and Have Nots

We hope that none of the students we teach will ever go to bed hungry, but it is important for them to understand the concept of "poverty" and all that it entails, in order for them to empathize fully with two-thirds of the world's population. Many students take it for granted that their basic needs will be met and therefore grow up quite insulated from, and apathetic to, the desperate concerns of those who are less fortunate. To launch a thematic unit featuring a novel set in the Holocaust or to give students a brief glimpse of how inequitable it is to have the world's wealth so unevenly distributed, do the following:

1. Arrange with the school cafeteria to provide lunch for only one-third of your students for one day. For another third, bring in small amounts of white rice and small bowls. The remaining third will receive no lunch. (Note: Letters must be sent to parents well in advance, explaining the educational objectives of this temporary change in routine.)

2. Explain to students that they will be taking part in a very important social experiment and that you will discuss the reasons later. Encourage them to write down all their questions, feelings, and complaints about the event, which will be addressed during the later discussion.

3. To begin the simulation, assign students to groups, at random, based on receipt of a blue (full lunch), red (bowl of rice), or yellow (no lunch) card that will determine what their lunch fare will be. There will, of course, be much moaning and groaning from those students who received only a bowl of rice, more from students who were given no lunch. Make it clear to these particular students that they may not buy any other food, but that they are free to ask the other students to share their food, although those students are not obligated to do so.

4. The next day, when hunger and anger have abated, encourage the three groups of students to vent their feelings and share their written records. As the yellow group complains that being given nothing to eat was unfair, they are now ready to hear that one-third of the people in the world have nothing to eat on a daily basis.

5. Poll the red and yellow groups to see how many received something to eat from the blue group. They are now ready to understand the concept of "charity" and how important it can be for those who are destitute.

6. Discuss the analogy of the simulation to the real world and conduct a brainstorming session so students can think of ways to ease world poverty.

Prejudice

Much has been written about some very intense simulations of prejudice that were carried to such an extreme that students were psychologically damaged when the teacher and students apparently began to lose touch with what was simulation and what was reality. Rest assured that a more reasoned simulation can have the desired effect without causing lasting harm.

The following simulation can enhance a multicultural unit in social studies. Because of the anger and frustration that this simulation quite naturally produces, the activity should not continue for more than a morning or afternoon, at most, and, of course, parents should be advised of the intentions of the simulation in advance.

1. Categorize students, artificially, as "good" or "bad" according to some trait over which they have no control, such as the color of their eyes or their gender. If eye color is chosen, for example, tell students that those with brown eyes will now have special privileges, such as being the first to go to lunch and extra computer time. Throughout the simulation period, they will receive many other special privileges, simply because of the color of their eyes.

2. When students question this favoritism, tell them that brown-eyed students are receiving special privileges because some people might believe that brown-eyed students are superior to students with other eye color.

3. When the time for the simulation is up, conduct an oral debriefing. Divide the chalkboard into two columns. Have the brown-eyed students share their feelings and reactions to the special treatment, and then the students with other eye color. Summarize the students' contributions on the board.

4. Explain that, although this was a rather unfair exercise, many people really do judge people merely on the basis of the color of their skin, their gender, or other traits they can do nothing about.

5. Lead a reflective discussion on how this activity might change the way participants behave toward others in the future.

Dramatic Productions

The ultimate goal of the drama component in a balanced and comprehensive literacy program for students in grades 4–8 is to have them eventually create and put on their own plays, thus bringing to life words, feelings, and ideas that have personal significance to them. Writing plays, however, demands some experience with the play as a unique form of expression, and many teachers today feel so pressured to teach skills that will be measured in annual testing that they tend to devalue this critical oral language activity, even though such language activities can actually help prepare students to do well on standardized tests.

It is often helpful to "work students up" to the goal of writing their own plays, especially if they have had little or no previous experience with formal drama. To minimize frustration, dramatic productions can be introduced in phases: First, stories and books shared in literature circles or through guided reading (see Chapter 5) are read dramatically in readers theatre, or are recalled, blocked, and turned into plays by students. Particular conventions of scripts are pointed out to students through minilessons. With this background of script reading and the creating of characters, settings, and actions, students are ready to write and take part in their own original plays.

Readers theatre: Turning stories into plays

Readers theatre is an oral interpretation strategy that provides an excellent opportunity for creative thinking, oral expression, practicing fluency skills, developing self-confidence, and teamwork to achieve common goals. It becomes a means to reinforce narrative structure through the language arts of reading, writing, listening, speaking, viewing, and visually representing. Perhaps the most important benefit of readers theatre, however, is the satisfying practice it affords of speaking informally before an audience and having an enjoyable experience with literature. See Chapter 3 for a detailed description of this activity.

Creating original drama

Many students will enjoy writing their own original scripts for puppet shows, skits, and formal productions. Such activities offer teachers an excellent opportunity to integrate the language arts because students will be discussing, writing, and then producing their work. Frequently, students enjoy working together to write the scripts, providing a remarkably natural vehicle for focused conversations.

Students can study existing play scripts to learn the layout and specific conventions used in preparing scripts. After students have read some plays in readers theatre format and looked at commercial scripts, and minilessons have reinforced the conventions used in script writing, the students can write an original script using their own creativity. Students have become sufficiently adept at utilizing commercial scripts when they can memorize or paraphrase their lines, speak them on cue, and create appropriate characterizations. As students go from reading and acting out the words of others to bringing their own words to life, they gain an enormous sense of pride and ownership from the cooperative undertaking. Figure 8.5 identifies a structure students can follow to create their own scripts.

To ensure the success of play writing, the most ambitious phase of the drama component in a balanced and comprehensive literacy program, the following suggestions may be helpful:

- Begin with simple one-act skits.
- Divide students into small, cooperative groups.
- Provide each group with a "plot" or structure from which to build.
- Eliminate makeup, which is distracting.
- Do not use prompters, thus encouraging students to learn each other's lines.
- Allow "spontaneous paraphrasing" of the script.

Although all dramatic enterprises fare best with an audience, the first skits do not necessarily require a stage or extensive props and scenery; in fact, a "propless playlet" has the advantages of increasing students' ability to imagine and being easily moved from classroom to classroom. This way, students are not overwhelmed by large crowds, nor must they shout to be heard for their first efforts.

To help students create an original script, ask them to consider the following four strands that constitute a complete drama:

(1) ROLES (OR IDENTITY)	(2) PLACE (OR SITUATION)	(3) FOCUS (OR ISSUE)	(4) CONFLICT (OR PROBLEM)
Who are you?	Where are you?	What is the play about?	What is the problem that needs solving?
Examples:	Examples:	Examples:	Examples:
a compassionate nurse	a hospital	saving lives and caring	nurse gets a disease
a sad soldier	a barracks	missing loved ones	soldier can't kill
a benevolent alien	a corn field	accepting differences	alien is feared

FIGURE 8.5 **Structure for creating original drama** (adapted from Block, 2000).

LISTENING INSTRUCTION

Research suggests that students who receive direct practice in listening comprehend better than students who have not received this instruction; listening plays a crucial, although often ignored, role in the literacy development of students, especially English learners (Opitz & Zbaracki, 2004). Research conducted by Pearson (1985) with students in the intermediate and middle grades produced especially positive results. This researcher reached the following conclusions based on this synthesis of research on comprehension and listening instruction:

1. Listening practice in the same skills typically taught in reading instruction (i.e., getting the main idea, comparing and contrasting) tends to improve comprehension in both listening and reading.

2. Listening comprehension is enhanced through students offering personal verbal reactions during and after listening.

3. Reading literature aloud to students tends to improve listening comprehension.

4. All the language arts tend to reinforce one another; in other words, instruction in one of the arts of reading, writing, listening, speaking, viewing, and visually representing is correlated with gains in the other language arts.

5. Direct teaching of listening strategies seems to help students become conscious of their listening habits better than less explicit approaches do.

Designing Listening Instruction

Listening instruction must be a major part of the curriculum if it is to improve students' listening ability. To increase listening comprehension, strive to integrate it into daily lesson plans rather than providing a "one-shot," infrequent activity. Five to 10 minutes a day of listening instruction or practice is generally more effective than longer, less frequent lessons.

Listening comprehension should focus on teaching students strategies they can use to listen, while listening activities can be included to give students an opportunity to practice these skills in various settings. Above all, listening instruction should provide for transfer of listening skills from practice situations

Effective Listening Skills

When attempting to list skills needed for effective listening, it is important to understand that the needed skills vary depending on the *purpose* for listening. We use different skills when we listen to learn than we do when we need to make critical decisions or when we are simply listening for enjoyment. Here are a few of the many purposes for listening and some of the related skills:

- *Listening for learning:* Skills include using memory techniques (e.g., rhyming, acronyms, and acrostics), listening for main ideas (have students paraphrase a message to assess their understanding of it), and taking notes.

- *Empathetic listening:* Skills include focusing attention on the speaker (including looking at the speaker and resisting distractions) and reacting with appropriate verbal and nonverbal clues (including nodding one's head and displaying appropriate facial expressions).

- *Critical listening:* Skills include learning to make informed decisions or judgments based on what is heard (such as when students must evaluate requests made of them by peers and adults) and learning to understand, judge, and evaluate information (such as when we question what we read and see and evaluate sources). Critical listening is very important in student interactions with media.

Teachers and their students must learn to distinguish among different types of listening so that the appropriate skills can be learned and applied.

From P. Cooper and S. Morreale (Eds.), 2003. *Creating competent communicators: Activities for teaching speaking, listening, and media literacy in K–6 classrooms* (p. 44). Scottsdale, AZ: Holcomb Hathaway.

to actual use in the classroom and beyond. Ideally, listening comprehension should be an integral piece of content area instruction through reading to students, modeling one's thinking, and asking thought-provoking questions; listening for the main idea in practice material should be quickly transferred to social studies or science content material.

Successful listening instruction encourages students to listen to meet their own needs, interests, and desires. For instance, students who are listening to complete an assignment, create an argument for escaping punishment, or find out how to build a project, or simply listening to a story for pleasure have differing purposes for attending, yet each situation is authentic and very important to them. The suggested teaching guidelines that follow develop both active listening and oral responses, because research shows that such responses result in optimal listening skill development:

1. Always set a purpose for listening by asking questions that will focus thought and encourage students to predict what will be included in the content.

2. Look for the structure of the content of informational material. Has the author organized the passage through comparison, contrast, sequential order, or simple enumeration? Brain researchers tell us that human beings naturally seek patterns in their experience. Use this tendency to point out to students the patterns in the text they are listening to.

3. When reading to students, categorize, relate, and associate new ideas with those that are already familiar to them. Give students guided practice, doing this as well by encouraging them to ask questions such as: How does this concern me? How does this relate to what I already know? What does this remind me of in my own life? How can I apply this information?

4. Summarize periodically as you are reading to students. In summarizing, the main ideas are identified and related briefly. Stop occasionally and encourage students to summarize also, in their minds, orally, or on paper.

5. Make oral or written responses to content and invite students to add their ideas to yours. This, as much as any other strategy, helps students to become active listeners and thinkers. Moreover, encourage students to listen with pencil in hand. This offers them a minimal structure for response, allows for physical involvement, and is a link to note taking.

6. Provide a structure for responding to a presentation, such as the following:
   - What was the speaker's purpose (persuading, informing, sharing, etc.)?
   - List five ideas the speaker had.
   - Write a three-sentence summary of the presentation.
   - Write down two things that you would now like to know more about.

ACTIVITY   *Listening Comprehension*   (Adapted from Block, 2000)

The following activity can be used to help students practice the skills of listening comprehension. (See Cooper & Morreale [2003] for additional activities that teach listening skills.) This activity can also be used to help teachers diagnose problems individual students have with listening comprehension.

1. Pair students and provide each pair with an unfamiliar short story on their instructional level.

2. For each pair, select one student to be the reader and the other to be the listener.

3. Have the reader read two pages silently and then "tell" the two pages to the listener.

4. Once the story has been read and retold in this way, have the listener summarize the entire story to the reader.

5. Have the reader write down everything the listener has said.

6. Have the pair look at the book together and compare it to the written retelling.

7. Have the pair discuss why certain parts were not included in the original retellings or the final summary (e.g., "not important," "didn't hear it," "didn't remember that part").

8. Have the pair note the parts omitted on the back of the story summary sheet, along with the listener's explanation for each part's absence.

9. Have partners switch roles and repeat the process.

10. Analyze each student's listening comprehension strengths and needs. Students can also be encouraged to assess their own listening skills by using the checklist provided in Appendix D.

TROUBLESHOOTING

The oral language skills—and confidence—of every learner can be enhanced through ample practice speaking and performing before a group of caring and supportive peers. However, there are several universal oral language concerns that may need to be addressed when they occur.

Dominating a Discussion

Students who tend to dominate conversations and discussions and do not listen to others can cause other students to withdraw entirely in any oral language situation. Teachers can help such students by providing them with specific listening purposes and then discussing these purposes with students after the oral language event. Another alternative is to advise such students that every student will have *one* turn to share ideas in the particular oral language event to ensure that everyone gets a chance to speak. Finally, a successful concentration strategy that some teachers use is to teach all students to stop, listen, and think before they hold up their hand. Making individual stop signs also helps them to remember the three steps of stop, listen, and think before participating in any discussion. After every student is cognizant of this strategy, students begin to monitor each other to be sure that everyone listens and thinks before speaking.

Teachers can help students who tend to dominate discussions by providing them with specific listening purposes.

Lack of Verbal Skills in English

If students are in the initial stages of learning to speak English, the best course of action is to allow those students the time they need to emerge from their "silent period," before they say their first words in the new language. Concentrate on building students' receptive language and allow gestures and other nonverbal cues to communicate with them. Make certain the classroom environment is supportive and safe to the degree that other classmates are rooting for these students to say their first English words. Additionally, in any oral or written language venture, encourage **code switching**, or having students speak some words in English and other words they do not know in their home language. Finally, totally disregard grammar and accent concerns whenever these students do speak. Concentrate only on understanding what they are attempting to communicate. Then, paraphrase their contribution in standard English while expressing appreciation for their participation.

● code switching

Limited Knowledge of Academic Language

Often, English learners who possess a moderate degree of skill in social or conversational language that is spoken informally lack a thorough understanding of the language that is used for instruction, or **academic language.** Teachers use this language when giving instruction about completing assignments and when teaching math, language arts, and the content areas. For

● academic language

example, when you ask the children to *compare and contrast* two civilizations, or invite students to *summarize* a story and then use a *Venn diagram* to compare it to another story they have just read, you are using academic language, often without explaining what is meant by these process words. Such terms (e.g., *compare, contrast, summarize*) usually are not new vocabulary for most students but are often unfamiliar concepts to English learners (Wong-Fillmore & Snow, 2002).

Although academic language is usually more decontextualized than social language and thus more demanding, it can be made easier for students. You can scaffold instruction to make academic language more accessible by doing the following:

- Have students work together in small cooperative groups, in which much conversation about the task at hand is encouraged.

- Involve students in creating projects to demonstrate and talk about their learning.

- Invite students to take part in much hands-on learning.

- Show instead of telling by using objects, photographs, and other realia to clarify meaning.

- Directly teach students how to listen to and read informational and content area texts.

- Connect lessons to students' prior experiences to build a background for new knowledge.

- Teach students to monitor their thinking so they know when they are confused, and demonstrate what they should do when this occurs. (Tompkins, 2006)

Lack of Participation

In many teacher-controlled classrooms, it appears that a student who rarely speaks is a blessing, but it seems axiomatic that students must be allowed plenty of opportunity to talk in order to process their ideas and learn on a deeper level; moreover, in our society the ability to speak fluently is arguably even more of an asset than the ability to read and write.

Some students who will not participate in large- or even small-group oral language events can practice speaking and become more comfortable doing it by conducting a series of speaking activities using a tape recorder. This has the added benefit of affording the teacher an opportunity to assess oral language development to determine whether there is an underlying language problem that is causing the student to refrain from speaking out, or if the student is simply shy. Additionally, some shy students will speak fluently with the aid of a prop, such as a puppet or a model that turns attention away from them; similarly, shy students can often be coaxed to take part in a dramatic activity, and many even seem to "bloom" when they are able to don a different persona. In addition to shyness, some students may experience higher levels of nervousness and anxiety than their peers when speaking in front of others. Communication specialists refer to this as **communication apprehension**. The Personal Report of Communication Fear (PRCF) provided in Appendix D will help you to

communication
apprehension ●

determine if a child is communication apprehensive. These students will benefit from the same type of oral activities as shy students and should be encouraged to speak as often as possible to reduce their fears.

Limited Voice Projection

A commonly reported problem with oral language activities is that many students speak so softly that they cannot be heard. This becomes a distinct problem when other classmates have been urged to listen politely. After a few minutes of straining their ears, even the most courteous of youngsters will begin to turn their attention elsewhere. Students must learn to lift their heads up and project their voice. One way to achieve this is to have them stand at their desks and project (not shout) the phrase, "How now brown cow!" and to tell them to "throw their words across the room and make them bounce off the opposite wall of the classroom." Additionally, choral reading, singing camp songs, and readers theatre provide opportunities to practice projecting one's voice.

SUMMARY

It is easy, but erroneous, to assume that students, especially if they are native English speakers, have already developed their oral language abilities. With such an assumption, we can often overlook the importance of helping students further their ability to speak confidently in many different situations. The basic curriculum cornerstones of reading and math take precedence over most other parts of the curriculum, and talk is not often interwoven effectively into content areas. However, oral language must be continually nurtured in a balanced and comprehensive literacy program, for speech is the most widely used of the expressive forms of discourse. Moreover, proficiency in speaking enhances ability in all the other language arts.

The foundation for a sound oral language program is the variety of spontaneous and planned speaking situations that occur every day in most classrooms. Opportunities for instruction in oral language occur frequently. They include informal speaking, as in casual conversations and discussions, and more formal speaking, as in oral reports, interviews, panel discussions, and debates.

Finally, there is no better avenue than drama to channel the boundless energy and emotions of students. Drama is a way of learning as well as a communication mode. Students thrive on a medium that allows them to create with their minds and bodies using expressive movements as well as their words. In addition, drama may be the prime vehicle to attach words with concepts in authentic context for the benefit of English learners. Finally, used on a routine basis, the recognition and community building afforded by drama can enhance the self-esteem of all learners. One budding sixth-grade actor summed it up this way: "I helped to write this play and put it on with my class. I got to be the biker dude and I also sang a song that had 'em rolling in the aisles. I also helped everybody else remember their lines. I usually hate writing and talking in front of the class, but this was more fun than summer camp!"

Questions
FOR JOURNAL WRITING AND DISCUSSION

1. Of the four interrelated literacy skills of reading, writing, listening, and speaking, which, if any, do you believe to be the most important? Why? Defend your answer.

2. Recall a time in grades 4–8 when you were in a skit or a play. What was your role and how did you prepare for it? What else do you remember about this event? How do you feel such activities can be conducive to confident oral speaking for native English speakers in a classroom? For English learners?

3. Respond to the following statement that an uninformed parent might make: "An oral language program in the intermediate grades is a waste of time, because children spend plenty of time talking on the playground and at home." How would your argument change if there were several English learners in your classroom?

Suggestions
FOR PROJECTS AND FIELD ACTIVITIES

1. Find a teacher in grades 4–8 who is currently preparing a dramatic production with students. Discuss with the teacher his reasons for using this instructional activity. Observe the students as they practice their roles. Are all the students involved? In what capacities? What are the major oral language goals that you believe are being achieved through this activity?

2. Observe a class giving oral reports. In what ways, if any, are students encouraged to use technology and multimedia to enhance their presentations? How has the delivery of oral presentations changed since you were in school?

3. After carefully reviewing the guidelines in "Suggestions for Teacher-Guided Discussions," earlier in this chapter, lead a discussion with a small group of students on a controversial topic, such as "Is homework a necessary evil?" Reflect afterward and share your reflections with the rest of the class. What went well? What was difficult? What would you do differently next time?

4. With a small group of other students, examine several curriculum guides to determine what provisions are made for the development of oral language from grade 4 through grade 8. Categorize your findings according to the types of purposeful speech activities presented in this chapter.

REFERENCES

Au, K. H. (1993). *Literacy instruction in multicultural settings.* Fort Worth, TX: Harcourt Brace Jovanovich.

Block, C. C. (2000). *Teaching the language arts: Expanding thinking through student-centered instruction* (3rd ed.). Needham Heights, MA: Allyn & Bacon.

Cazden, C. (1986). Classroom discourse. In M. C. Whitrock (Ed.), *Handbook of research on teaching* (3rd ed., pp. 432–463). New York: Macmillan.

Cecil, N. L. (1994). Role playing: Trying life on for size. In N. L. Cecil (Ed.), *Freedom fighters: Affective teaching of the language arts.* Salem, WI: Sheffield.

Cooper, P., & Morreale, S. (Eds.). *Creating competent communicators: Activities for teaching speaking, listening, and media literacy in K–6 classrooms* (p. 44). Scottsdale, AZ: Holcomb Hathaway.

Cummins, J., Brown, K., & Sayers, D. (2007). The oral history project: From a shrug to 'How much time do I have, Mr. Green?' In J. Cummins, K. Brown, & P. Sayers, *Literacy, technology, and diversity: Teaching for success in changing times.* Boston: Allyn & Bacon.

Daniels, H. (1994). *Literature circles: Voice and choice in the student-centered classroom.* York, ME: Stenhouse.

Devine, T. T. G. (1982). *Listening skills schoolwide: Activities and progress.* Urbana, IL: National Council of Teachers of English.

Eeds, M., & Wells, D. (1989). Grand conversations: An exploration of meaning construction in literature study groups. *Research in the Teaching of English, 23*(1), 4–29.

Galda, L. (1982). Playing about a story: Its impact on comprehension. *The Reading Teacher, 36,* 52–56.

Gambrell, L. B., & Almasi, J. F. (1996). *Lively discussions! Fostering engaged reading.* Newark, DE: International Reading Association.

Griffin, M. L. (2001). Social contexts of beginning reading. *Language Arts, 78,* 371–378.

Heath, S. (1983). *Ways with words.* London: Cambridge University Press.

Loban, W. (1976). *The complete book of language development: Kindergarten through grade twelve.* Urbana, IL: National Council of Teachers of English.

Martinez, M., Roser, N. L., & Strecker, S. (1998/1999). I never thought I could be a star: A reader's theatre ticket to fluency. *The Reading Teacher, 52,* 326–334.

McMahon, S. I., & Raphael, T. E. (Eds.). (1997). *The book club connection: Literacy learning and classroom talk.* Newark, DE: The International Reading Association.

Opitz, M. F., & Zbaracki, M. D. (2004). *Listen hear! 25 effective comprehension strategies.* Portsmouth, NH: Heinemann.

Paratore, J. R., & McCormack, R. L. (1998). *Peer talk in the classroom: Learning from research.* Newark, DE: International Reading Association.

Pearson, P. D. (1985). Changing the face of reading comprehension instruction. *The Reading Teacher, 38*(8), 724–738.

Peregoy, S. F., & Boyle, O. F. (2005). *Reading, writing, & learning in ESL* (4th ed.). White Plains, NY: Longman.

Pinnell, G. S., & Jaggar, A. M. (2003). Oral language: Speaking and listening in elementary classrooms. In J. Flood, D. Lapp, J. R. Squire, & J. M. Jensen (Eds.), *Handbook on teaching the English language arts* (2nd ed., pp. 881–913). Mahwah, NJ: Erlbaum.

Roser, N. L., & Martinez, M. G. (Eds.). (1995). *Book talk and beyond: Children and teachers respond to literature.* Newark, DE: International Reading Association.

Sampson, M. R. (1986). *The pursuit of literacy: Early reading and writing.* Dubuque, IA: Kendall/Hunt.

Samway, K. D., Whang, G., Cade, C., Gamil, M., Lubandina, M. A., & Phom Machanh, K. (1991). Reading the skeleton, the heart, and the brain of a book: Students' perspectives on literature study circles. *The Reading Teacher, 45,* 196–205.

Smith, K. (1998). Entertaining a text: A reciprocal process. In K. G. Short & K. M. Pierce (Eds.), *Talking about books: Literature discussion groups in K–8 classrooms* (pp. 17–31). Portsmouth, NH: Heinemann.

Smith, P. G. (2001). *Talking classrooms: Shaping children's learning through oral language instruction.* Newark, DE: International Reading Association.

Straits, W., & Nichols, S. (2006). Literature circles for science. *Science & Children, 44,* 52–55.

Strickland, D. S., & Feeley, J. T. (2003). Development in the elementary school years. In J. Flood, D. Lapp, J. R. Squire, & J. M. Jensen (Eds.), *Handbook of research on teaching the English language arts* (2nd ed., pp. 339–356). Mahwah, NJ: Erlbaum.

Tompkins, G. E. (2006). *Language arts essentials.* Boston: Allyn & Bacon.

Wagner, B. J. (1976). *Dorothy Heathcole: Drama as a learning medium.* Washington, DC: National Education Association.

Wagner, B. J. (2003). Imaginative expression. In J. Flood, D. Lapp, J. R. Squire, & J. M. Jensen (Eds.), *Handbook of research on teaching the English language arts* (2nd ed., pp. 1008–1025). Mahwah, NJ: Erlbaum.

Wong-Fillmore, L., & Snow, C. E. (2002). What teachers need to know about language. In C. T. Adger, C. E. Snow, & D. Christian (Eds.), *What teachers need to know about language* (pp. 7–54). Washington, DC: Center for Applied Linguistics.

Differentiating Instruction for Students with Special Needs

Nine

- What are the major groups of diverse learners for whom differentiated instruction is important?

- What are some specific adaptations for these diverse learner groups?

- When differentiating instruction to meet the needs of diverse learners, what curricular components can be modified?

291

DIFFERENTIATING INSTRUCTION FOR STUDENTS WITH SPECIAL NEEDS

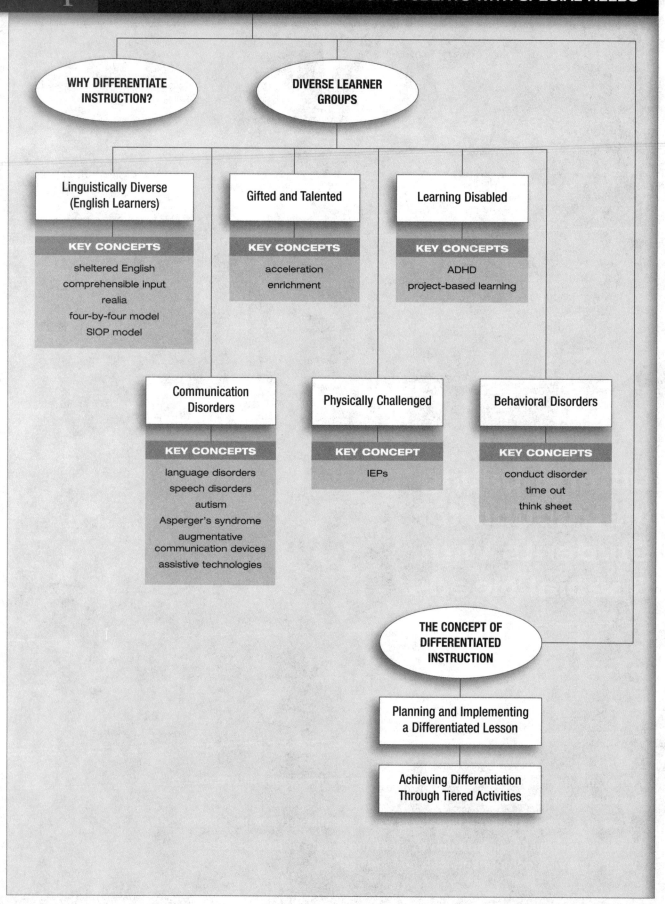

WHY DIFFERENTIATE INSTRUCTION?

DIVERSE LEARNER GROUPS

Linguistically Diverse (English Learners)

KEY CONCEPTS

sheltered English
comprehensible input
realia
four-by-four model
SIOP model

Gifted and Talented

KEY CONCEPTS

acceleration
enrichment

Learning Disabled

KEY CONCEPTS

ADHD
project-based learning

Communication Disorders

KEY CONCEPTS

language disorders
speech disorders
autism
Asperger's syndrome
augmentative communication devices
assistive technologies

Physically Challenged

KEY CONCEPT

IEPs

Behavioral Disorders

KEY CONCEPTS

conduct disorder
time out
think sheet

THE CONCEPT OF DIFFERENTIATED INSTRUCTION

Planning and Implementing a Differentiated Lesson

Achieving Differentiation Through Tiered Activities

Marcia, a special education student, and Jason, an advanced learner, both in fifth grade, are working together researching the Tasmanian devil—its habitat, eating habits, and physical characteristics. Their teacher, Mrs. Hooper, liked Mrs. Diaz's study of exotic animals so much (see Chapter 3) that she gave her fifth-grade students the choice of studying one particular animal that is real but also "exotic." Marcia and Jason both wished to study the Tasmanian devil, so they are working together on this research project, which will culminate with a creative presentation of the information they have learned. During computer searches for information, Jason does most of the reading. Marcia's strengths are more apparent in the creative areas of art and designing. She also likes cooking, so she suggests creating recipes for a pretend restaurant that caters to Tasmanian devils. She and Jason are working on the recipes and the restaurant for their presentation. During a brief sharing time, Marcia and Jason solicit feedback from their classmates on their ideas. Marcia shares some recipes she has created for Tas's Cave Café, which is only open for dinner since Tasmanian devils are nocturnal creatures. She tells classmates that she has created a poultry item for the menu that includes fried grubs as a side dish. She explains that Tasmanian devils eat grubs, small mammals, and birds. Jason tells how he realized their menu needed prices, and since Tasmanian devils live on Tasmania, an island south of Australia, he needed to figure out what the food costs would be in Tasmanian currency. He says he enjoyed converting American dollars and cents to Tasmanian money, giving as an example the poultry dish Marcia created, which is listed at $6.95 US or $7.48 AUD (Australian currency). Peer feedback comes in the form of both a compliment and a suggestion. Classmates say that they really like the idea of the restaurant and suggest that it will improve the presentation if they include on their menu more specific information about what Tasmanian devils look like.

WHY DIFFERENTIATE INSTRUCTION?

It is common knowledge that today's classrooms are places of great diversity. All classrooms are academically diverse, but classrooms are also diverse in other ways. Students come to school speaking a variety of first languages other than English. Some come with academic giftedness. Others experience a variety of physical and neurological challenges; examples of some of these are cerebral palsy; vision deficits; communication disorders affecting speech and hearing, including autism; and other cognitive learning disabilities, such as dyslexia and attention deficit hyperactivity disorder (ADHD). Still others demonstrate behavioral maladjustments or health and environmental issues associated with extreme poverty. Nearly all of these students will have academic, behavioral, physical, or social needs, or combinations of these, that will require instructional adaptations within the classroom setting (Lewis & Doorlag, 1999). Fortunately, many of the instructional adaptations recommended are effective for all learners—not just those with special needs.

Unfortunately, many teachers are not well prepared to recognize the needs of these diverse learners. The two main goals for this chapter are: (1) to provide information about the important characteristics and special adaptations for several diverse learner groups, and (2) to provide information about how to differentiate instruction in ways that help all students learn and grow. Recognition of who these diverse learners are and the importance of their perceptions of themselves as learners to their self-esteem is necessary for guiding their learning (Glazer, 1998). Therefore, it is important to explain to the entire class that we all learn differently, but that we are all capable of learning. Students may be doing different assignments on occasion, but these assignments are differentiated based on particular learning needs.

DIVERSE LEARNER GROUPS

In a sense, all learners are diverse, as each learner is unique, with his or her own set of learning needs. However, in this chapter the term *diverse learners* refers to those learners who, prior to the mandates of NCLB, often were removed from the regular classroom for instruction or were labeled in some way as needing special instruction. Typically these groups include students ➊ who speak a language other than English as their native language, ➋ who are identified as gifted ➌ or learning disabled, ➍ who demonstrate communication disorders, ➎ who are physically challenged in some way, or ➏ who demonstrate behavioral disorders. This chapter discusses each of these diverse learner groups.

➊ STUDENTS WHO ARE LINGUISTICALLY DIVERSE (ENGLISH LEARNERS)

Characteristics

Linguistic diversity is a reality in our public schools. According to Kindler (2002), more than 450 languages are spoken by students in our schools today. In addition, approximately 12 percent of preK–12 students are considered English learners (Gray & Fleischman, 2004/2005). Pearlman (as cited in Gray & Fleischman) projects that "by 2015, more than 50 percent of all students in K–12 public schools across the United States will not speak English as their first language" (p. 84).

Spanish speakers are currently the largest group of bilingual individuals in the United States, with other large groups being German, French, Chinese, and Italian speakers (U.S. Census Bureau, 2007). But there are many other languages represented in classrooms today: Arabic, Asian Indian, Filipino, Greek, Hmong, Hungarian, Japanese, Korean, Polish, Portuguese, Russian, Spanish, Ukranian, Vietnamese, Yiddish, and others, as well as a decreasing number of tribal languages of Native Americans. Linguistic diversity, moreover, is not limited to foreign languages. Dialects of English, such as African American Vernacular English (AAVE), are also represented in many classrooms.

When students acquire English as a second language, their speech may sound different from that of native English speakers. They may speak with an accent as a result of the nonequivalence of speech sounds between their native language and English. For example, a student whose native language is Spanish might say "chip" for "ship," or "sip" for "zip." A student who speaks AAVE might say "sick" for "six," or "birfday" for "birthday." Other sound differences for some of the many languages in today's schools are presented in Figure 9.1.

Adaptations

August and Shanahan (2006) point out that the research on acquiring literacy in a second language is limited. But they also state, "becoming literate in a second language depends on the quality of teaching, which is a function

LANGUAGE	SOUNDS EITHER NOT PART OF THE LANGUAGE OR PROBLEMATIC
Chinese	b ch d dg g oa sh s th v z f j l m n ng l-clusters r-clusters
French	ch ee j ng oo th a h oy s schwa
Greek	aw ee i oo schwa
Italian	a ar dg h i ng th schwa v l-clusters end clusters
Japanese	dg f i th oo v schwa h l r sh s w l-clusters r-clusters
Korean	b l oa ow p r sh t th l-clusters r-clusters
Spanish	dg j sh th z b d h m n ng r t v w y s-clusters

Problematic sounds for English learners. FIGURE 9.1

of the content coverage, intensity or thoroughness of instruction, methods used to support the special needs of second-language learners and to build on their strengths, how well learning is monitored, and teacher preparation" (p. 3). The professional literature does provide general principles, or best practices, that you should strive to keep in mind in order to be supportive of your English learners. As condensed from Barnitz (2006, pp. 55–58), these are as follows:

- Respect differences in languages and dialects as natural.
- Use methods that bridge cultural background knowledge and whatever texts are being read.
- Contextualize instruction on language structures and skills within the composing and comprehending process. Contextual supports include scaffolding in the form of simplified language, teacher modeling, visuals, graphic organizers, hands-on learning, and cooperative learning groups.
- Use authentic materials from the learner's community.
- Design literature-based instruction for developing language competence.
- Use technological and other communicative arts to facilitate oral and written language acquisition.
- Facilitate authentic, functional communication.
- Base literacy assessment on authentic language and literacy tasks and events: that is, a multidimensional approach to assessment that includes alternative assessments and modifications to traditional assessments (Lenski et al., 2006).
- In interpreting assessment data, be sensitive to cultural and linguistic variation.

These general principles serve as a basis for curriculum and lesson planning. In addition, Abate (2004) provides four specific recommendations for working with English learners.

1. *Know your students.* Find out something about their culture, first language, English proficiency levels for both oral and written language, educational experiences, learning styles, and interests. Communicate with their parents, with the ESL teacher if there is one, and with other classroom teachers. Examine their student records.

2. *Create lessons with clear goals and expectations.* The Sheltered Instruction Observation Protocol (SIOP) Model of sheltered instruction (Echevarria, Vogt, & Short, 2004) and the Four-by-Four Model (Mora, 2006) are both appropriate approaches for meeting the instructional needs of English learners (see further discussion later in this section).

3. *Group students by readiness levels and the complexity of the learning task.* Identify which aspects of learning tasks are imperative and which are negotiable. Learning tasks can also be categorized along continuums that include simple to complex, concrete to abstract, single-faceted to multi-faceted, highly structured to loosely structured, or fast-paced to slow-paced (Tomlinson, 2001). Considering the complexity level of the learning task allows for "planning that is tiered so as to allow students to experience success while being challenged to achieve higher levels of language mastery and content knowledge" (Mora, 2006, p. 33). (See guidelines for differentiated instruction later in this chapter.)

4. *Implement effective strategies.* These might include learning centers, graphic organizers, and supplemental texts.

General approaches for adapting instruction to better meet the needs of the English learner include cooperative learning and sheltered instruction.

Cooperative learning. This is an approach in which students work together to achieve a common goal. It is useful for English learners to work cooperatively with native English speakers because they will need to communicate orally with each other. Through cooperative learning, English learners can acquire competence in oral language because of the increased opportunities for "comprehensible input" from their peers (Krashen, 1987).

Comprehensible input refers to communicating with language learners (providing "input") in such a way that they are able to make connections between concepts known in their native language and those same concepts in the unknown language for the purpose of learning that new language, and involves making modifications to the new information that are both linguistic and nonlinguistic in nature. The use of such modifications is called scaffolding (see Chapters 6 and 7). Linguistic supports include use of less complex sentence structures, as well as "slower speech rates, clear articulation, less slang, fewer idioms, and a greater use of high-frequency vocabulary" (Krashen, as cited in Pilgreen, 2006, p. 43). Nonlinguistic supports are real objects (**realia**), visuals, videos, storyboarding, movement (total physical response, or TPR), role plays, and collaborative or cooperative learning. One teacher made the new vocabulary word *ecstatic* more comprehensible by happily shouting "hurray" and jumping in the air. This action would be an example of TPR. Another example using visuals and a concept organizer can be seen in Figure 9.2. Providing comprehensible input is critical when teaching content area material and is a major consideration in sheltered English instruction.

Sheltered instruction. The major approaches associated with sheltered instruction are SDAIE (Specially Designed Academic Instruction in English)

WWW

Differentiated Instruction
*www.betac.org/pdf/spring_
summer_04.pdf*

ESL Internet Meeting Place
www.eslcafe.com

comprehensible input ●

realia ●

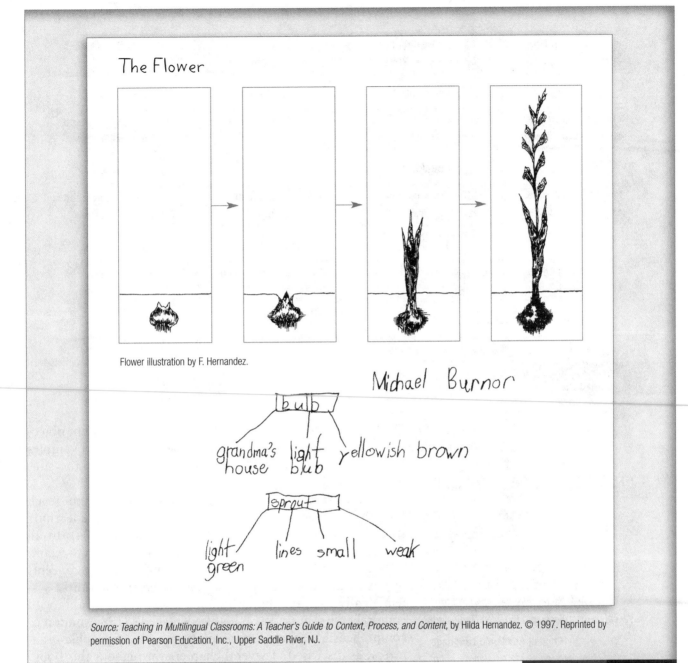

Flower illustration by F. Hernandez.

Example of a concept organizer for the concepts bulb and sprout. FIGURE 9.2

and ELD (English Language Development). SDAIE emphasizes *content learning* through modifications in instructional strategies, while ELD emphasizes English *language learning,* vocabulary development, and listening and speaking tasks using the content material as a vehicle. Two examples of instructional models employing sheltered English are the Four-by-Four Model and the SIOP (Sheltered Instruction Observation Protocol) Model.

The **Four-by-Four Model** uses content area themes and a matrix (see Figure 9.3) of four levels of language development skills (i.e., listening, speaking, reading, writing) and four levels of language proficiency (i.e., beginning, early intermediate, intermediate, early advanced) to provide an instructional framework for planning learning tasks and activities.

WWW
Four-by-Four Model
http://coe.sdsu.edu/people/ Jmora/Pages/4x4Guidelines.htm

● Four-by-Four Model

LEVEL 1: Beginning language proficiency	LEVEL 2: Early intermediate language proficiency	LEVEL 3: Intermediate language proficiency	LEVEL 4: Early advanced language proficiency
Listening	Listening	Listening	Listening
LEVEL 1: Beginning language proficiency	LEVEL 2: Early intermediate language proficiency	LEVEL 3: Intermediate language proficiency	LEVEL 4: Early advanced language proficiency
Speaking	Speaking	Speaking	Speaking
LEVEL 1: Beginning language proficiency	LEVEL 2: Early intermediate language proficiency	LEVEL 3: Intermediate language proficiency	LEVEL 4: Early advanced language proficiency
Reading	Reading	Reading	Reading
LEVEL 1: Beginning language proficiency	LEVEL 2: Early intermediate language proficiency	LEVEL 3: Intermediate language proficiency	LEVEL 4: Early advanced language proficiency
Writing	Writing	Writing	Writing

FIGURE 9.3 Matrix of the Four-by-Four thematic planning model.

SIOP Model •

In the **SIOP Model,** each lesson has separate language and content objectives that link to grade-level subject curriculum and standards. For examples of lesson plans adapted to the SIOP Model, visit the sites listed here.

The goal of sheltered English instruction is to teach English language skills at the same time students are learning specific subject matter knowledge (Echevarria, 2004). In all sheltered English instructional approaches, you need to examine the content of the lesson to identify and select key concepts or terms that are critical to the lesson. Then teach these systematically in ways that maximize your students' ability to comprehend: that is, ways that use Krashen's (1987) notion of comprehensible input. For example, the use of graphic organizers, as discussed in several chapters throughout this book, would be very appropriate. These structures provide visible and manipulable input that enables English learners to connect concepts and ideas to a new language for the purpose of learning that new language. In the case of grades 4–8, English academic language, or the language of school as discussed in Chapter 7 (e.g., *paragraph, caption, table, summarize, outline, compare and contrast, main ideas, details, implications*) is the *new* language. See Coxhead (2000) and Pilgreen (2006) for academic word lists, or visit the website listed in the margin.

Hernandez (1997) shares several types of organizers especially useful for English learners: realia, verb, noun, concept, and episodic. These organizers can be posted to provide a visual reference for students. Anything and everything should be used to create a context for the content information to make it understandable. In addition to realia, or real objects, pictures, sketches, gestures, body language, demonstrations, and dramatic enactments will all

WWW

SIOP Model Lesson Plans
www.cal.org/siop/lessons/
www.cal.org/siop/lessons/LPBB.html
www.cal.org/siop/lessons/LPAB.html
www.cal.org/siop/lessons/LPS.html
www.cal.org/siop/lessons/LPCI.html
www.cal.org/siop/lessons/LPRowlandTanios.pdf

English Academic Language
http://language.massey.ac.nz/staff/awl/index.shtml

provide for "comprehensible input." For example, for the sentence "Her facial expression was as sour as a lemon," students can be given a bit of lemon to taste as they look in a mirror. Examples from the students' own backgrounds should be included. Helping students personally identify with the topic will make the learning more meaningful to them.

 STUDENTS WHO ARE GIFTED AND TALENTED
Characteristics

Gifted and talented students have extraordinary intellectual abilities or they demonstrate exceptionally high achievement in particular academic areas or in the visual or performing arts compared with their peer group. These students represent all cultural, ethnic, and socioeconomic backgrounds. However, there is variability in the way individual states identify, classify, and implement programs for gifted and talented students. Frequently, intellectually gifted students are identified by very high scores on standardized tests and high achievement levels in school. Their linguistic abilities are usually highly developed compared with their peers. Hyperactivity may also be a sign of giftedness; students who are gifted often have high levels of activity in the classroom as a result of boredom or intense interest in an activity. See Figure 9.4 for characteristics of intellectually gifted children.

Characteristics of intellectually gifted learners.   FIGURE 9.4

Few students will display all of the characteristics in a given list; however, when clusters of these characteristics are present, they do serve as fairly reliable indicators. These characteristics are best used as signals to indicate that a particular student might warrant closer observation and could require specialized educational attention, pending a more comprehensive assessment by a qualified specialist.

GENERAL BEHAVIORAL CHARACTERISTICS

- Many typically learn to read earlier with a better comprehension of the nuances of the language. As many as half of the gifted and talented population have learned to read before entering school. They often read widely, quickly, and intensely and have large vocabularies.

- They commonly learn basic skills better, more quickly, and with less practice.

- They are frequently able to pick up and interpret nonverbal cues and can draw inferences which other children have to have spelled out for them.

- They take less for granted, seeking the "hows" and "whys."

- They display a better ability to work independently at an earlier age and for longer periods of time than other children.

- They can sustain longer periods of concentration and attention.

- Their interests are often both widely eclectic and intensely focused.

- They frequently have seemingly boundless energy, which sometimes leads to a misdiagnosis of "hyperactive."

- They are usually able to respond and relate well to parents, teachers, and other adults. They may prefer the company of older children and adults to that of their peers.

- They are willing to examine the unusual and are highly inquisitive.

- Their behavior is often well organized, goal directed, and efficient with respect to tasks and problems.

- They exhibit an intrinsic motivation to learn, find out, or explore and are often very persistent. "I'd rather do it myself" is a common attitude.

- They enjoy learning new things and new ways of doing things.

(continued)

LEARNING CHARACTERISTICS

- They may show keen powers of observation, exhibit a sense of the significant, and have an eye for important details.
- They may read a great deal on their own, preferring books and magazines written for youngsters older than themselves.
- They often take great pleasure in intellectual activity.
- They have well developed powers of abstraction, conceptualization, and synthesizing.
- They generally have rapid insight into cause–effect relationships.
- They often display a questioning attitude and seek information for the sake of having it as much as for its instrumental value.

- They are often skeptical, critical, and evaluative. They are quick to spot inconsistencies.
- They often have a large storehouse of information regarding a variety of topics which they can recall quickly.
- They show a ready grasp of underlying principles and can often make valid generalizations about events, people, and objects.
- They readily perceive similarities, differences, and anomalies.
- They often attack complicated material by separating it into its components and analyzing it systematically.

CREATIVE CHARACTERISTICS

- They are fluent thinkers, able to produce a large quantity of possibilities, consequences, or related ideas.
- They are flexible thinkers able to use many different alternatives and approaches to problem solving.
- They are original thinkers, seeking new, unusual, or unconventional associations and combinations among items of information. They also have an ability to see relationships among seemingly unrelated objects, ideas, or facts.
- They are elaborative thinkers, producing new steps, ideas, responses, or other embellishments to a basic idea, situation, or problem.
- They show a willingness to entertain complexity and seem to thrive in problem situations.

- They are good guessers and can construct hypotheses or "what if" questions readily.
- They are often aware of their own impulsiveness and the irrationality within themselves and show emotional sensitivity.
- They have a high level of curiosity about objects, ideas, situations, or events.
- They often display intellectual playfulness, fantasize, and imagine readily.
- They can be less intellectually inhibited than their peers in expressing opinions and ideas and often exhibit spirited disagreement.
- They have a sensitivity to beauty and are attracted to aesthetic dimensions.

Source: Whitmore, J. R. (1985). Characteristics of intellectually gifted children (Digest 344). *Digests on the gifted* (pp. 1–2). Reston, VA: The Council for Exceptional Children.

FIGURE 9.4   Continued.

www

National Organizations for Giftedness

www.nagc.org
www.gtworld.org
www.cec.sped.org

Students are also classified as creatively gifted and talented if they excel in the visual or performing arts. These talents usually become apparent when a student is relatively young. Davis (1995) lists 12 categories as representative of creative individuals: "original, independent, risk taking, aware of creativeness, energetic, curious, has a sense of humor, attracted to complexity, artistic, open-minded, needs time alone, and intuitive" (Mastropieri & Scruggs, 2000, p. 148). Further information about recognizing giftedness in students can be found on websites for national organizations.

Adaptations

Just because a student may have exceptional abilities does not mean he can realize his full potential without specially adapted educational programs. Gifted and talented students "often have special learning needs that are not fully met by the general education program" (Lewis & Doorlag, 1999, p. 394). The most common educational approaches for gifted and talented students are acceleration and enrichment. **Acceleration** simply means moving students through the curriculum at a faster pace than general education students. This could mean beginning school early, skipping grades, testing out of classes, or providing more ability-appropriate curriculum. Acceleration often means students do not remain with their age peers. **Enrichment** simply means expanding on the curriculum. The same subjects may be studied in greater depth, or after-school programs may provide instruction in additional subjects or content not typically found in the curriculum (e.g., chess, finance policies in state government). More often enrichment programs keep gifted students in their general education classrooms with their age peers. Both accelerated and enrichment programs can be provided within the regular classroom, in resource classes, in university classes, or through flexible scheduling or mentoring programs. General classroom teachers would do well to heed the advice of Kennedy (1995, pp. 233–234) when they find gifted students within their classrooms:

- acceleration

- enrichment

- Resist policies requiring more work of those who finish assignments quickly and easily. Instead, explore ways to assign different work.
- Seek out supplemental materials and ideas that extend, not merely reinforce, the curriculum.
- Deemphasize grades and other extrinsic rewards.
- Encourage intellectual and academic risk taking.
- Help all students develop social skills to relate well to one another.
- Take time to listen to responses that may at first appear to be off target.
- Provide opportunities for independent investigations in areas of interest.
- Be aware of the special needs of gifted girls (i.e., they can achieve high-level career goals and succeed in math and science).

③ STUDENTS WHO ARE LEARNING DISABLED
Characteristics

Students with a cognitive **learning disability** (LD) are typically average and bright learners who have difficulty processing information. These processing problems may be in the area of perception, attention, memory, or expressive language. Students who have a learning disability do not typically have hearing or visual impairments, physical or health issues, emotional disturbances, or environmental, cultural, or economic disadvantages, yet they perform poorly in school. They are often unfairly labeled and described in negative terms such as "neurologically impaired," "deficient," or "perceptually handicapped." They can be quite puzzling to their teachers. They often have poor strategies for learning because they learn differently and need to be taught alternative learning skills that take advantage of their individual strengths. As Mooney and Cole (2000) relate, it is important to remember that students with LD are bright and have many strengths, often in creativity, intuition, and emotional understanding. These particular strengths are recognized and addressed in Gardner's (1999) multiple intelligences (MI) theory within the spatial, intrapersonal, and interpersonal intelligences, respectively:

- learning disability

- Spatial: Ability to represent the visual world accurately in one's mind, or three-dimensional thinking.

- Intrapersonal: Ability to understand oneself.

- Interpersonal: Ability to interact with and understand others.

In addition to poor performance in school subjects, students with LD may lack the skill to communicate appropriate social messages, making group work difficult, and they often have a high activity level and difficulty paying attention. As a result, they are frequently diagnosed as having attention deficit hyperactivity disorder (ADHD), which can lead to a misplaced focus on behavioral issues rather than cognitive issues.

Resources Supporting Students with Special Needs
www.specialconnections.ku.edu

Adaptations

Because their difficulties are unique, students with learning disabilities present a special challenge to classroom teachers. You will need to use collaboration, creative thinking, and problem-solving strategies to best help these students. Mastropieri and Scruggs (2000, pp. 83–84) provide an extensive list of adaptations to consider when teaching students with cognitive learning disabilities; an abbreviated version follows:

- Adapt the physical environment to provide a distraction-free workplace that will help students focus their attention (e.g., rearrange seating positions, provide quiet space within the classroom, keep desks away from potentially troublesome stimulation).

- Model organization (e.g., a place for everything and everything in its place; show what an organized desk or notebook looks like).

- Structure daily routines and schedules (e.g., make a list of what to do first, second, etc.).

- Adapt instructional materials (e.g., make assignments more compatible with literacy skills and organizational abilities—see section on differentiated instruction later in this chapter).

- Teach study skills (e.g., how to schedule time, keep an assignment calendar, and use study strategies).

Higher Order Thinking Skills
www.hots.org

- Adapt instruction (e.g., use of SCREAM variables: structure, clarity, redundancy, enthusiasm, appropriate pace, maximized engagement; or HOTS, a creative instructional program that uses Socratic dialogue, technology, and dramatic techniques with students in grades 4–8).

- Vary presentation formats (e.g., verbal, visual aids, realia, field trips, computers, audio- and videotapes).

- Question students frequently (e.g., ask students to rephrase information in their own words, checking for understanding).

- Provide clear directions and accessible goals (e.g., use short, concise sentences, reminders for long-term assignments, regular monitoring).

- Teach students how to learn (e.g., model how to use learning strategies).

- Use peer tutors (e.g., classmates can provide assistance or additional practice).

- Conduct periodic reviews (e.g., recall previously taught content and relate to new information being learned).

- Adapt evaluation procedures (e.g., use alternatives to standard paper-and-pencil tests, such as drawings, sketches, or dramatic enactments).

The emerging awareness of ADHD as a cognitive learning disability rather than a behavioral disorder requires educators to address the learning needs of students diagnosed with ADHD (Tannock & Martinussen, 2001). In terms of designing lessons, Tannock and Martinussen suggest learning strategies that:

- include a system for remembering, such as a mnemonic device;
- are worded simply, which would also help English learners;
- begin with action words; and
- use words familiar to the students.

In addition, consider new forms of learning environments whenever possible. For example, project-based learning is a viable alternative for students with cognitive learning disabilities, and one that can enhance motivation levels for all learners.

Project-based learning. In **project-based learning,** students work collaboratively to engage in learning activities that are interdisciplinary, student-centered, and integrated with real-world issues. Students are usually asked to develop a product or creation to show what they learned. Because students with a cognitive learning disability find group work difficult, it is important to provide opportunities for developing this skill. Beginning with one simple task and a well-chosen partner and gradually moving toward tasks with small teams can ease these students comfortably into collaborative group work. Project-based learning provides the opportunity to develop collaborative group skills on a small scale with only two other students while engaged in a highly motivating and meaningful project.

- project-based learning

The fundamentals of project-based learning are:

1. Create teams of three or more students to work on an in-depth project for three to eight weeks.
2. Introduce a complex entry question that establishes a student's need to know, and scaffold the project with activities and new information that deepens the work.
3. Calendar the project through plans, drafts, timely benchmarks, and finally the team's presentation to an outside panel of experts drawn from parents and the community.
4. Provide timely assessments and/or feedback on the project for content, oral and written communication, teamwork, critical thinking, and other important skills. (Pearlman, 2006, p. 11)

The many benefits of project-based learning include the following:

- Deep understanding of subject matter
- Increased motivation and self-directedness
- Increased interpersonal skills
- More effective oral and written communication skills
- Improved research, problem-solving, and critical thinking skills.

WWW

Project-Based Learning Examples
http://pblmm.k12.ca.us/examples_main.htm

Project-Based Learning Benefits
http://pblmm.k12.ca.us/PBLGuide/WhyPBL.html

Problem-based learning. A term often used interchangeably with project-based learning is *problem*-based learning. While very similar approaches, project-based learning is more closely aligned with thematic teaching, while problem-based learning is more focused on suggesting solutions to real-world problems. Service learning projects are also recommended as alternative learning environments. For more information and examples of problem-based learning and service learning, see Chapter 10.

The majority of students with learning disabilities are not placed in special classes but remain in the regular classroom with some part-time help from a resource teacher. It is imperative that you strive to recognize these students' unique strengths and do your best to help them learn.

4 STUDENTS WHO HAVE COMMUNICATION DISORDERS
Characteristics

Communication disorders are those that affect a student's ability to interact with teachers and peers. Generally communication disorders involve language and speech disorders. **Language disorders** are characterized by the inability to use the oral and/or written symbols of language. Students have trouble expressing themselves either orally or in writing. Grammatical patterns are not used appropriately. Students' vocabulary is limited, and they have difficulty following directions. **Speech disorders** are characterized by frequent and severe difficulty in pronouncing certain sounds (articulation) or speaking fluently (stuttering). **Autism** is a condition that affects communication skills. It is defined in the 1990 Individuals with Disabilities Education Act (IDEA) as "a developmental disability significantly affecting verbal and nonverbal communication and social interaction, generally evident before age 3." Some children with autism do not speak at all, while others simply repeat back what they hear (echolalic speech). Students with **Asperger's syndrome,** a milder form of autism, have more developed communication ability and are often highly intelligent but have difficulty interacting socially. For obvious reasons, students with communication disorders will have difficulty becoming fully functioning members of the classroom community.

language disorders

speech disorders
autism

WWW

Communication Disorders
*www.comeunity.com/disability/
speech/communication.html*
www.asperger.org

Asperger's syndrome

Adaptations

Because they are able to participate in most aspects of the curriculum, students with communication disorders generally remain in regular classroom settings for their instructional needs. The possible exception is students with autism. For working with students with autism in the regular classroom setting, Wood, Lazzari, and Reeves (1993) provide some suggestions:

- Structure the learning environment so that it is predictable and consistent. This includes the physical structure of the classroom as well as routines, schedules, and teacher behavior.
- Design instructional programs to provide ways to help children learn to communicate. Remember that verbal communication is but one way to communicate; provide students with alternatives such as signing, writing, [or] using the computer.
- Since students with autism have difficulty managing their own behavior without structure, develop individual and group behavior plans that stress positive behavior management and set forth clear instructions, rules, and consequences.
- Work closely with the family to ensure consistency between school and home and other settings in approaches, methods of interaction, and response to students. (p. 115)

If literature circles are part of the classroom curriculum, one young adult novel that would help classmates better appreciate what it means to be autistic is *The Curious Incident of the Dog in the Night-time* (Haddon, 2003; see Table 5.2). Discussing this book can help students generate ideas for better engaging a student with autism in the regular classroom setting.

A specialist will help students with severe speech impairments develop speech skills. As the classroom teacher, you will need to reinforce the work of the specialist by providing opportunities for these students to practice their new skills in a safe, risk-free environment. Through modeling appropriate grammar, providing language models through quality children's literature, and emphasizing vocabulary development, you will be assisting the student with a communication disorder.

More specifically, teachers cannot allow peers to tease or ridicule students who make speech errors. Building a classroom atmosphere that is respectful of all learners, and recognizes that everyone has strengths and areas that need to be developed, is crucial not only for students with communication disorders but also for all members of the classroom community. When students with communication disorders do speak, they need to be listened to carefully. The teacher need not correct their speech but can model the appropriate articulation or word order in responding to the student. Attention to the content of what was said is most important.

For those students with more severe disorders, there are special devices, called **augmentative communication systems,** that may be used to help them communicate. One such device is the *communication board,* or *language board* (Johnston, Tulbert, & Sebastian, 2000). The board (which can be just a piece of paper with pictures pasted on) contains pictures of common objects or representative pictures for common activities that the student can simply point to in order to convey her ideas. Pictures could be faces that show the emotions of happiness or sadness; clothing items; food and beverage items; buildings such as school, home, or church, or rooms in the home; and the words *yes* and *no.* More sophisticated electronic devices, commonly referred to as **assistive technologies** (AT), are also available and are traditionally intended to provide students with severe communication disorders access to information (Boone & Higgins, 2007). These devices may have larger than normal keys, or keys with larger spaces between them so the desired keys are easier to locate and hit. Letter keys might appear in alphabetical order, or the keys may feature pictures or words rather than letters. The most sophisticated devices actually "talk" by using prerecorded speech when a particular key is pressed.

● augmentative communication systems

● assistive technologies

WWW

Assistive Technology Project
http://teacher.scholastic.com/products/read180/research/pdf/DesMoines_Study.pdf

Recently, accessibility to information and to learning through the capabilities of digital technologies is receiving attention in the research and development practices of assistive technology professionals. For example, one project focused on the use of text-reader software with computer-readable school texts for students with learning disabilities. Text-reader software "uses synthetic speech to read text aloud while the same text is highlighted on a computer screen" (Hasselbring & Bausch, 2005/2006, p. 73). Teachers found their students with disabilities more often reread the text passages for clarity using this software. But much more research is needed. Boone and Higgins (2007) state

> mere access to the content is inadequate as an AT unless that access is mediated with instructional design supports appropriate for the specific disability of the

user. This point is especially relevant for the large population of students who may have a combination of physical and cognitive disabilities. And although the traditional AT intervention of providing an alternate medium or format of the content for such an individual would be helpful, difficult vocabulary, poor organization, and distracting elements often remain. It still would not provide the access to learning that many educators have identified [is needed]. (p. 138)

5 STUDENTS WHO ARE PHYSICALLY CHALLENGED
Characteristics

Students with physical challenges represent a large group of students. In addition to the obvious challenges of a visual or hearing impairment, other physical challenges include AIDS, allergies, arthritis, asthma, cerebral palsy, congenital anomalies (e.g., albinism, cleft lip, spina bifida), diabetes, epilepsy, hemophilia, leukemia, muscular dystrophy, poliomyelitis, rheumatic fever, and Tourette's syndrome, as well as impairments resulting from a traumatic injury. (For more detailed explanations of these conditions, visit the websites listed here.) Because such a wide variety of conditions can cause physical challenges—the preceding list names only a few—there is not a concise list of characteristics; however, in general, these physical challenges are just that: physical. Students with one or some combination of physical disability are quite capable of performing well intellectually. For example, some individuals who have cerebral palsy with severe motor impairments are intellectually gifted. There is no relationship between the degree of physical impairment and intellectual ability. What can happen is that students may experience excessive absences or fatigue as a result of certain physical impairments, and learning problems can begin in this way. Students who are more "medically fragile"—that is, their participation in school requires heart monitors, oxygen tanks, suctioning units, or special medical support—are now being placed in regular classroom settings and **individualized education programs (IEPs)** are developed. IEPs help the teacher, support personnel, parents, and the student understand their respective responsibilities toward meeting educational and medical needs.

More about Physical Impairments

Visual impairment: www.navh.org

Hearing impairment: www.nad.org

Cerebral palsy: www.ucpa.org

Muscular dystrophy: www.mda.org

Spina bifida: www.sbaa.org

Brain injury: www.biausa.org

Epilepsy: www.epilepsyfoundation.org

Diabetes: www.diabetes.org

AIDS: www.aids.org

Easter Seals Disability Services: www.seals.com

American Academy of Pediatrics: www.aap.org

Others: http://education.qld.gov.au/curriculum/learning/ students/disabilities/resources/information/pi/pi.html

individualized education programs (IEPs)

Adaptations

For students with visual or hearing impairments, special arrangements within the learning environment can be made. For example, the use of technology, visuals, and special seating will allow maximum visual access to information for those with hearing impairments. And for those with visual impairments, three-dimensional models, oral presentations, and wide, clear aisles will be helpful. In addition, the structure of certain teaching procedures may need to be adapted, such as directly facing a student who is deaf to allow for lipreading or using American Sign Language, or for a student with a visual impairment, providing printed materials in a large print or Braille format and the extra time it will take to read these materials. Technological devices can also be used, such as amplification devices for those with hearing impairments and Braillewriters for students who are blind.

For most of the physical impairments that your students may have, you will first need to learn more about the particular condition. Again, as with visual and hearing impairments, the physical arrangement of the classroom may need to be adapted to provide students with mobility difficulties easy access to all classroom areas and activities. Other areas of the school also should be checked for accessibility (e.g., curb cuts in the sidewalks, handrails at the appropriate height, wide door openings, nonslip surfaces on the floors, toilet accessibility, and water fountains at a variety of heights). Students needing wheelchairs may also need a lapboard for writing. Crutch holders can be attached to the sides or backs of chairs. For students with muscular impairments, papers can be taped to their desk, or pencils attached to the desk by a string and thumbtacks. Some students may need to record their responses orally rather than write them. A plastic ruler serves the student with poor muscle control better than a paper bookmark (Glazzard, 1982). Sometimes simple modifications are all that is necessary.

STUDENTS WHO HAVE BEHAVIORAL DISORDERS
Characteristics

There is no one definition of behavioral disorder, nor does any single pattern of behavior identify a student as having a behavioral disorder. Behaviors range from extreme withdrawal to extreme aggression. It is common for classroom teachers, especially in grades 4–8, to be the first to recognize atypical behaviors and to begin the referral process (Lewis & Doorlag, 1999). A behavioral, or conduct, **disorder** is generally identified when a student's behavior deviates significantly from what is recognized as normal, occurs often and/or intensely, and occurs over time (Nelson, 1993). It is common for behavioral disorders to negatively impact the student's academic achievement, and there is the possibility that the student also has a learning disability. In fact, the behavioral disorder could be the result of poor academic performance brought about by the learning disability. Students with behavioral disorders are often described as hyperactive, distractible, or impulsive. Students with behavioral disorders experience difficulty because they do not have appropriate social and study skills. Instruction focused on these two areas should improve their chances of success in the classroom.

- behavioral disorder

Conduct Disorders
www.mentalhealthamerica.net/ go/information/get-info

Adaptations

Because study skills are discussed elsewhere in this book, suggestions for improving social skills (also called life skills) and classroom conduct are presented here. Enlist the school counselor or psychologist to help a student with a behavioral disorder. Additionally, inform the student's parents of the types of interventions being implemented at school so they can respond to their child in ways that are consistent with what the school is trying to achieve. General suggestions for helping students with behavioral disorders include:

- Establish an open, accepting classroom environment.
- Clearly state class rules and consequences.
- Stress positive behaviors and focus on student successes.
- Reward positive behaviors and state the behavior that is being rewarded.
- Provide extra opportunities for student success.
- Use good judgment, and be patient and tolerant.

- Teach self-control, self-monitoring, and conflict resolution using role playing and examples.
- Select activity partners carefully.
- Have alternative activities available.
- Allow groups of "one."
- Use behavioral contracts. (Mastropieri & Scruggs, 2000, p. 98)

WWW

Positive Behavioral Interventions and Support
www.pbis.org

It is important to have a consistent approach when reacting to students' inappropriate behavior. For example, rather than immediately reprimand negative behavior, say to the student in a normal tone of voice, "Stop and think about what you just did. What should you have done? Now, try to do this more appropriately." By using these same words each time students behave inappropriately, you will help students begin to take responsibility for their actions and to "learn that making good choices about their behavior is in their own best interest" (Mastropieri & Scruggs, 2000, p. 221).

time-out •

Some students will benefit from more formalized procedures. In potentially volatile situations, students may be asked to go to **time-out** so that they have a chance to cool down and think about their behavior. Time-out can be a location in the classroom, or a designated location within the school. Occasionally, the student may need to be escorted to a time-out location. Most schools have policies and procedures in place for such situations. A debriefing activity should occur after any cool-down periods. This can be a verbal conversation such as that in Figure 9.5, or the student can be asked to complete a **think**

think sheet •

sheet like the one in Figure 9.6, which can serve as a way of documenting behaviors and any positive changes that occur over time.

FIGURE 9.5 Debriefing following time-out.

Teacher:	Raúl, your time-out is over. But before you join the class, I want you to tell me what happened. Why were you sent to time-out?
Raúl:	[Raúl shrugs his shoulders, indicating he doesn't know.]
Teacher:	Okay, well, just tell me what happened.
Raúl:	Luis and Mike were pointing at me and laughing. I said, "What are you laughing at?" and they just kept laughing. So I threw my pencil at them and told them to stop it.
Teacher:	Did you have to go to time-out because Luis and Mike were laughing at you?
Raúl:	No.
Teacher:	No, you were sent to time-out because you threw the pencil.
Raúl:	Yes.
Teacher:	Do you know why it is not okay to throw pencils at other people?
Raúl:	The point could hit them in the eye and hurt them.
Teacher:	That's right. Our classroom needs to be a safe place for all of us, so we cannot throw things at other

people. Tell me what you can do the next time someone points at you or laughs at you.

Raúl:	Ignore them.
Teacher:	That's a good idea. If you ignore them they will probably just get bored and stop. What else could you do, if you think you will not be able to ignore them?
Raúl:	Tell you.
Teacher:	Okay, you could tell me and then I could try to help you not get into trouble, and also stop the people who are teasing you. Can you remember to try these ideas the next time something like this happens?
Raúl:	Yeah.
Teacher:	You don't have to throw things at people. Ignore them or come tell me if you are having a problem with somebody. You need to control your own behavior. I really like you, Raúl, and I want you to do well in school. Can you try these ideas?
Raúl:	Yeah.
Teacher:	Great! Okay, let's go back to class now. I know you will do better.

THINK SHEET

Name of student: _____

Teacher: _____   Date: _____

This is what I did:

_____

_____

This is the rule I broke:

_____

_____

I behaved this way because:

_____

_____

This is who I bothered when I behaved this way:

_____

_____

This is what I could have done instead:

_____

_____

Student signature: _____   Date: _____

Think sheet for use with students behaving inappropriately.   FIGURE   9.6

Students with behavioral disorders often lack basic knowledge of social skills. For example, they may not understand the components of a conversation—knowing how to join, interrupt, start, maintain, or end the conversation. Or they may not know how to ask for clarification, make a request, or exhibit politeness. "Play" skills are social skills that include being able to share with others, encourage and praise others, and invite others to join in the activity. Classroom skills include being on task, completing tasks, following directions, and trying to do the best one can. Self-help skills include good grooming (being clean and neat) and good table manners and eating behaviors. Commonly, students with behavior disorders lack knowledge of problem-solving, or coping, skills such as staying calm, thinking of possible solutions, choosing best solutions, taking responsibility for their actions, handling name calling and teasing, and avoiding trouble.

Social skills instruction begins with the teacher explaining and discussing the targeted social skill. Then the teacher needs to operationalize the targeted social skill (e.g., sharing, being a "good sport," handling name calling) by demonstrating both appropriate and inappropriate behavior while students observe and identify the skill.

Teacher: This is an example of how to get the markers you need to create your poster. "Please may I have the red and blue markers." This is *not* the way to get the markers. "Give me those markers!" or just grabbing the markers.

The teacher then describes a situation for students to role play, with the teacher's guidance, during which students can offer suggestions or give examples of appropriate behavior:

Teacher: Pretend you are on the playground and you kicked the soccer ball into a group of students by mistake, but they grab the ball and won't give it back to you. How should you act?

Students: We could say, "Please give the ball back to me" or "I'm sorry I kicked the ball too hard—it was my mistake. Could I please have the ball back?"

Teacher: Good suggestions! These ideas are examples of appropriate behavior.

As actual situations occur in the classroom, students can be reminded of the role plays and their behavior rewarded when they act in socially appropriate ways without being reminded.

THE CONCEPT OF DIFFERENTIATED INSTRUCTION

At the beginning of this chapter we asked, Why differentiate instruction? It should be very clear that there is no one approach or learning activity that will meet the needs of all the students in one classroom. Yet, the classroom teacher is responsible for providing a learning environment in which all students can achieve their full potential.

According to Tomlinson (1999, p. 12), a teacher who differentiates instruction embraces the following four principles:

- Respect the readiness level of each student.
- Expect all students to grow, and support their continual growth.
- Offer all students the opportunity to explore essential understandings and skills at degrees of difficulty that escalate consistently as they develop their understanding and skill.
- Offer all students tasks that look—and are—equally interesting, equally important, and equally engaging.

differentiated instruction

Figure 9.7 presents an overall look at the concept of **differentiated instruction,** in which the nature of all students' needs is taken into account. Notice that several of the strategies mentioned throughout this book are also strategies employed by teachers who use differentiated instruction. Most of the strategies presented throughout this book can be implemented with a wide variety of students.

Differentiated instruction is a way to meet the needs of all students, including those with special needs, because different tasks can take into account the nature of their needs. It is not necessary to differentiate every lesson; however, there are particular points within an instructional unit or topic of study that can be differentiated based on students' readiness for the topic, materials, or skills needed; their interests; and/or their learning profiles.

In any classroom there will be students who are capable of reading materials at or above their grade level and those who struggle with reading and need easier materials. There may also be a few nonreaders in the class. Likewise, not all students are interested in the same topics. Finally, students have different learning profiles. In addition to notations regarding particular special needs as

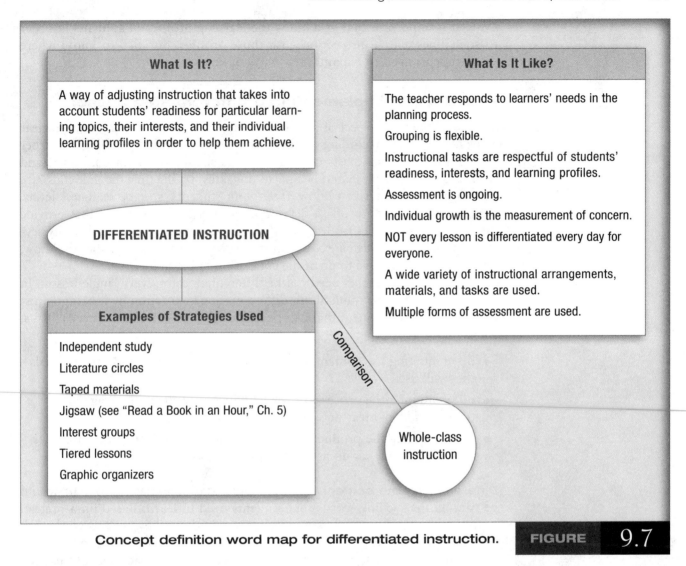

What Is It?

A way of adjusting instruction that takes into account students' readiness for particular learning topics, their interests, and their individual learning profiles in order to help them achieve.

DIFFERENTIATED INSTRUCTION

Examples of Strategies Used

Independent study

Literature circles

Taped materials

Jigsaw (see "Read a Book in an Hour," Ch. 5)

Interest groups

Tiered lessons

Graphic organizers

What Is It Like?

The teacher responds to learners' needs in the planning process.

Grouping is flexible.

Instructional tasks are respectful of students' readiness, interests, and learning profiles.

Assessment is ongoing.

Individual growth is the measurement of concern.

NOT every lesson is differentiated every day for everyone.

A wide variety of instructional arrangements, materials, and tasks are used.

Multiple forms of assessment are used.

Comparison

Whole-class instruction

Concept definition word map for differentiated instruction.   FIGURE **9.7**

described earlier in this chapter, these profiles include personality traits (e.g., shy, gregarious, sensitive); learning styles (visual learner, auditory learner, kinesthetic learner); and students' personal profiles of intelligences, or degrees to which they reflect linguistic, spatial, bodily-kinesthetic, logical-mathematical, musical, intrapersonal, interpersonal, or naturalist intelligences (Gardner, 1983, 1999). Attempts to match students' learning profiles with school tasks may help students initially with those tasks that are completely new and unfamiliar, but to match perfectly the learning environment on a regular basis to a student's developmental level will likely arrest the student at that level (Hunt, 1971). In other words, a certain amount of discomfort is a good thing and leads to growth. Joyce, Weil, and Calhoun (2000) make this point clear:

> For example, gregarious students are initially the most comfortable with social models and can profit from them quickly. However, the less-gregarious students were in the greatest need of the models least comfortable for them. Hence, the challenge is not to select the most comfortable models but to enable the students to develop the skills to relate to a wider variety of models, many of which appear, at least superficially, to be mismatched with their learning styles. . . . If environment and the student are too much in harmony, the student is permitted to operate at a level of comfort that does not require the challenge of growth. (p. 401)

WWW

Learning Styles Index
www.ncsu.edu/felder-public/ILSpage.html

Multiple Intelligences Inventory
http://surfaquarium.com/MI/inventory.htm

Thus, it is important that you know the learning profiles of students in order to sometimes match instruction with those profiles, but also to know where your students need to expand their ways of knowing.

Planning and Implementing a Differentiated Lesson

The most important aspect of planning a differentiated lesson is to establish clear goals for students. According to Tomlinson (1999) "During planning, a teacher should generate specific lists of what students should know (facts), understand (concepts and principles), and be able to do (skills) by the time the unit ends" (p. 40). Then, using what you know about your students' specific readiness levels, interests, and learning profiles, develop a set of engaging activities that provide the varied opportunities for learning that the students need. Finally, identify several options for students to demonstrate what they have come to know, understand, and be able to do at the conclusion of the unit.

All these components need not be differentiated for every single lesson. In fact, it may be best to think about differentiating instruction by looking at just one curricular component that can be modified to meet students' needs. Thus, we can look at

- differentiating the content, or what students will learn and the materials they will use.
- differentiating the process, or the activities students will engage in to understand key ideas and use essential skills.
- differentiating the product, or how students will demonstrate what they understand and can do as a result of the lesson.

Differentiating the content. One example of differentiating content would be varying the spelling words that students need to learn. Based on a pretest, some students may show they need to work with third-grade words, while others top out with a ninth-grade word list. The teacher could use the same procedures for presenting and practicing spelling words with all of the students, but the words themselves would be appropriate for their readiness levels. In other words, the students would not all be learning the same words, but they would be learning words appropriate to their needs, and they would be practicing and being tested on them in the same way.

Teachers may differentiate the content, the process, or the product to enhance learning for diverse student needs.

Differentiating the process. This same teacher could also differentiate the process, or the activities students use to learn the spelling of their words. For example, based on their learning profiles some students will best learn their words by writing each word with a crayon and then tracing it while spelling it out loud to get a sensory impression of the word. Other students may simply need to look at the whole word and then practice saying and writing it in order to learn the spelling.

Differentiating the product. Finally, the product could differ as well. In addition to the written spelling test, students with a particularly strong bodily-kinesthetic intelligence could literally use their bodies to spell out their words. Or they could perform a "cheerleader spelling" of the words, leading a small group of students in spelling out the words (Rogers, 1999).

Achieving Differentiation through Tiered Activities

A teacher can design and adapt a single lesson plan to meet the varied needs of the class as well as provide specific instructional aid to individual students through the use of **tiered activities;** that is, versions of activities that are designed to provide the same essential understandings but that address a variety of learning needs. "Tiered activities are very important when a teacher wants to ensure that students with different learning needs work with the same essential ideas and use the same key skills. For example, a student who struggles with reading or has a difficult time with abstract thinking nonetheless needs to make sense of the pivotal concepts and principles in a given chapter or story" (Tomlinson, 1999, p. 83). The following teacher guidelines are useful for developing tiered activities:

● tiered activities

- Identify the concept that will be the focus of the lesson.
- Think about your students. Know their talents, interests, and learning profiles.
- Create one activity that is interesting, requires high-level thought, and clearly focuses on elements that require students to use a key skill to understand a key idea.
- Draw a ladder, with the top rung representing a very high skill level and understanding and the bottom rung a low skill level and understanding. Decide where the activity you created fits on this ladder. Is it too challenging for the advanced students, or will it challenge the less advanced students? In this way you will see who needs another version of the activity.
- "Clone" the activity to provide versions that will work to meet the needs of all your students. This might mean varying the material students use, or varying the ways in which students will express their learning.
- Match a version of the activity to each student based on their needs.

In their companion books, *Differentiation in Practice: A Resource Guide for Differentiating Curriculum Grades K–5* and *Differentiation in Practice: A Resource Guide for Differentiating Curriculum Grades 5–9,* Tomlinson and Eidson (2003) provide models of differentiated units of study. The units include many examples of how teachers at all grade levels prepare tiered activities for lessons across the curriculum. For instance, one teacher shares tiered writing prompts based on the readiness levels of her students. The more detailed example that follows demonstrates a content area differentiated lesson in science with tiered activities at three different readiness levels.

Sixth-Grade Science Example: The Biosphere

Mr. Caday's sixth-grade students are studying the biosphere. They have read a text chapter and understand the meanings of words such as *organism* and *environment.* In the text chapter they were introduced to new vocabulary, including *atmosphere, energy, environmental factors,* and *biosphere.* The essential understanding that Mr. Caday wants his students to have is to be able to name and describe the four conditions necessary for most life on Earth—presence of water, an atmosphere, light, and temperature.

Mr. Caday knows his students well. Of the 28 students in his class, nine are reading at grade level, nine above grade level, seven are two years below grade level, and three read well below grade level. Of the three reading below grade level, two are English learners. One student in the class is learning disabled and has been diagnosed with ADHD. Another student has cerebral palsy, but he is in the group who reads above grade level. He uses a wheelchair and a special communication device for reading and writing. Through observation, Mr. Caday notes those students who learn better through visual means (the majority) and those who prefer auditory and kinesthetic activities. Mr. Caday also administers a survey to his students to help him identify their multiple intelligences profile. All of Mr. Caday's students can use context clues to determine word meanings, and they all enjoy word puzzles. They are a close group, and while there is the occasional misunderstanding, everyone gets along well.

Mr. Caday works at an urban school in a high-poverty location, so his students are unfamiliar with agricultural land uses. He has developed a small experiment as his "ladder" activity. On Friday, he plans to give each student four sandwich bags, some rye grass seed, four cotton balls—two wet and two dry—and some masking tape. He will then have each student "plant" the seeds inside the sandwich bag. Students will write their name on a piece of tape to identify their bags. Then Mr. Caday will collect one wet bag and one dry bag from each student and place these in a dark cabinet. The other bags will be taped to the windows in his classroom. Mr. Caday will ask the students to predict what will happen over the weekend to the seeds in both bags. Then, as some seeds sprout, Mr. Caday will ask students to predict what will happen to these sprouts under a variety of other conditions.

Mr. Caday places this activity in the middle of his ladder. He feels it is not challenging enough for his advanced students, but too physically challenging for the student with cerebral palsy (this student will not be able to plant his seeds). Mr. Caday likes the use of realia for his non-English speakers but will need to think about how he will help them understand the directions for planting and predicting. He will have his advanced students identify as many permutations of the experiment as they can to test the four conditions for life. He will create a poster that uses pictures and symbols to direct the English learners but will encourage them to give short oral explanations of what happened to the seeds. Finally, he will ask for a volunteer to help the student with cerebral palsy complete the physical aspects of the experiment.

Mr. Caday also wants to assess what his students learn from their tiered activity. Since he differentiated the process for his students with these tiered activities, Mr. Caday realizes that tiered assessment will also be needed, allowing students to adequately show their understanding of the four conditions necessary for life as demonstrated in the rye grass seed experiment. Therefore, Mr. Caday wants to differentiate the product, or how his students will demonstrate what they learned.

Mr. Caday will ask his advanced students to analyze their data on the permutations they set up, prepare charts to show the results of these permutations, and write a summary report on their findings. The majority of the students will prepare timelines showing each day the seeds were "planted" within the sandwich bags and what happened for each of the four bags. They will then write a summary report discussing their findings as related to the four conditions of life. The English learners will draw their results to share and orally explain

WWW

Multiple Intelligences Inventory
*www.surfaquarium.com/MI/
inventory.htm*

these results. The student with cerebral palsy will orally dictate the daily observations and explain these findings in writing using his assistive communication device for both oral dictation and writing.

Figure 9.8 shows the "ladder" of Mr. Caday's differentiated activity. Figure 9.9 shows the poster Mr. Caday used to represent the grass seed experiment.

Differentiated lessons portrayed as "ladder" activities.   FIGURE   9.8

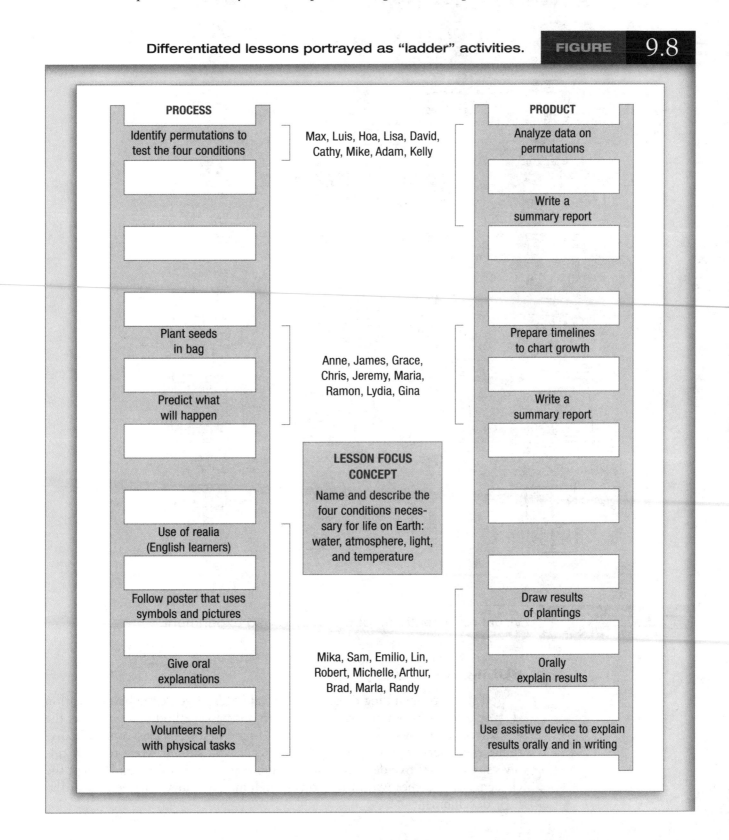

Grass Seed Experiment

FIGURE 9.9   Visual representation of the grass seed experiment.

SUMMARY

All students, including those with special needs, deserve the best education that teachers can provide. There is no one best method that will meet the needs of the wide variety of students found in today's classrooms. If anything, the diversity is increasing. As a teacher, you should strive to view this diversity as a positive development in the history of schooling, and accept the challenge that comes with it in terms of helping all students move forward in their development.

In this chapter, we provided brief descriptions of various categories of learners as they are classified by the educational system. We also presented information related to instructional adaptations appropriate to each learner type. Finally, we provided some guidelines for implementing instruction that is differentiated in an attempt to meet all learners' needs, along with an example to illustrate these guidelines.

WWW

Resources for Children with Special Needs
www.irsc.org

Questions
FOR JOURNAL WRITING AND DISCUSSION

1. Design an instructional program to address the needs of linguistically diverse students. What materials would be appropriate? What techniques would you use and why? How will your program help to meet the emotional needs of the students?

2. Divide a piece of paper into two columns. Label one column "Lead" and the other "Gold." Brainstorm a list of negative labels that are used to describe students who seem to learn differently from the norm (e.g., "dyslexic," "lazy") and list them in the "Lead" column. Then try to think of a positive word or phrase for each negative label and list these in the "Gold" column (e.g., "hyperactive" = a kinesthetic learner). Discuss your lists with your classmates.

3. Write about a time when you had difficulty learning something. What were your feelings? How were you finally able to learn? How might this experience impact your teaching?

Suggestions
FOR PROJECTS AND FIELD ACTIVITIES

1. Interview a student whose first language is not English. Ask the student how he came to speak English. Ask about the student's attitudes toward both English and his native language. Try to learn from the student some of the problems involved in translating from one language to another. Then use the information from this interview to identify the unique features of the student's language (phonology, syntax, structure, semantics, and lexical questions). What differences and similarities of language do you have with this student?

2. Over a period of three to five days, observe a student with one of the special needs discussed in this chapter. What can this student do well, and what seems to be difficult for this student? Summarize your observations, and make suggestions about how you could differentiate instruction to meet the needs of this particular student.

3. Begin to develop an annotated bibliography of books, poems, videos, or other materials that deal with students who have overcome adversity due to learning disabilities, physical challenges, language diversity, behavioral issues, or social problems caused by giftedness or by conditions of poverty. Sharing such materials with students in similar situations can be a form of bibliotherapy. (The article by Landrum [2001] can help you get started.)

REFERENCES

Abate, L. (2004, Spring/Summer). Differentiating instruction for limited English proficient students. *BETAC Interchange, 12*(2), 1, 3.

August, D., & Shanahan, T. (Eds.). (2006). Executive Summary: Developing literacy in second-language learners. *Report of the National Literacy Panel on Language Minority Children and Youth.* Mahwah, NJ: Erlbaum.

Barnitz, J. G. (2006). Linguistic diversity perspectives for literacy instruction. In J. P. Gipe, *Multiple paths to literacy: Assessment and differentiated instruction for diverse learners, K–12* (6th ed., pp. 44–64). Upper Saddle River, NJ: Merrill Prentice Hall.

Boone, R., & Higgins, K. (2007). The role of instructional design in assistive technology research and development. *Reading Research Quarterly, 42,* 135–140.

Coxhead, A. (2000). A new academic word list. *TESOL Quarterly, 34*(2), 213–238.

Davis, G. A. (1995). Identifying the creatively gifted. In J. L. Genshaft, M. Bireley, & C. L. Hollinger (Eds.), *Serving gifted and talented students: A resource for school personnel* (pp. 67–82). Austin, TX: Pro-Ed.

Echevarria, J. (2004). Improving comprehension of expository text for English language learners. PREL Focus on Comprehension Forum. Available online at www.prel.org/programs/rel/rel.asp with link to Focus on Comprehension, Topic 4.

Echevarria, J., Vogt, M. E., & Short, D. (2004). *Making content comprehensible to English language learners: The SIOP model* (2nd ed.). Boston: Allyn & Bacon.

Gardner, H. (1983). *Frames of mind: The theory of multiple intelligences.* New York: Basic Books.

Gardner, H. (1999). *Intelligence reframed: Multiple intelligences for the 21st century.* New York: Basic Books.

Glazer, S. M. (1998). *Assessment IS instruction: Reading, writing, spelling, and phonics for ALL learners.* Norwood, MA: Christopher-Gordon.

Glazzard, P. (1982). *Learning activities and teaching ideas for the special child in the regular classroom.* Englewood Cliffs, NJ: Prentice Hall.

Gray, T., & Fleischman, S. (2004/2005). Successful strategies for English language learners. *Educational Leadership, 62*(4), 84–85.

Hasselbring, T. S., & Bausch, M. E. (2005/2006). Assistive technologies for reading. *Educational Leadership, 63*(4), 72–75.

Hernandez, H. (1997). *Teaching in multilingual classrooms: A teacher's guide to context, process, and content.* Upper Saddle River, NJ: Merrill/Prentice Hall.

Hunt, D. E. (1971). *Matching models in education.* Toronto: Ontario Institute for Studies in Education.

Johnston, S. C., Tulbert, B. L., & Sebastian, J. P. (2000, May). Vocabulary development: A collaborative effort for teaching content vocabulary. *Intervention in School and Clinic, 35,* 311–315.

Joyce, B., Weil, M., with Calhoun, E. (2000). *Models of teaching* (6th ed.). Boston: Allyn & Bacon.

Kennedy, D. M. (1995). Plain talk about creating a gifted-friendly classroom. *Roeper Review, 17,* 232–234.

Kindler, A. L. (2002). *Survey of the states' limited English proficient students and available educational programs and services, 2000–2001 Summary Report.* Washington, DC: National Clearinghouse for English Language Acquisition and Language Instruction Educational Programs.

Krashen, S. D. (1987). *Principles and practices in second language acquisition.* Upper Saddle River, NJ: Prentice Hall.

Landrum, J. (2001). Selecting intermediate novels that feature characters with disabilities. *The Reading Teacher, 55*(3), 252–258.

Lenski, S. D., Ehlers-Zavala, F., Daniel, M. C., & Sun-Irminger, X. (2006). Assessing English-language learners in mainstream classrooms. *The Reading Teacher, 60,* 24–34.

Lewis, R. B., & Doorlag, D. H. (1999). *Teaching special students in general education classrooms* (5th ed.). Upper Saddle River, NJ: Merrill/Prentice Hall.

Mastropieri, M. A., & Scruggs, T. E. (2000). *The inclusive classroom: Strategies for effective instruction.* Upper Saddle River, NJ: Merrill/Prentice Hall.

Mooney, J., & Cole, D. (2000). *Learning outside the lines.* New York: Simon & Schuster.

Mora, J. K. (2006). Differentiating instruction for English learners: The four-by-four model. In T. Young and N. Hadaway (Eds.), *Supporting the literacy development of English learners* (pp. 24–40). Newark, DE: IRA.

Nelson, C. M. (1993). Students with behavioral disorders. In A. E. Blackhurst & W. H. Berdine (Eds.), *An introduction to special education* (3rd ed., pp. 528–561). New York: HarperCollins.

Pearlman, B. (2006, June). New skills [schools] for a new century. Edutopia. Available online: www.edutopia.org/magazine/ed1article.php?id=Art_1546&issue=jun_06.

Pilgreen, J. (2006). Supporting English learners: Developing academic language in the content area classroom. In T. Young & N. Hadaway (Eds.). *Supporting the literacy development of English learners* (pp. 41–60). Newark, DE: International Reading Association.

Rogers, L. K. (1999). Spelling cheerleading. *The Reading Teacher, 53,* 110–111.

Tannock, R., & Martinussen, R. (2001). Reconceptualizing ADHD. *Educational Leadership, 59*(3), 20–25.

Tomlinson, C. A. (1999). *The differentiated classroom: Responding to the needs of all learners.* Alexandria, VA: ASCD.

Tomlinson, C. A. (2001). *How to differentiate instruction in mixed-ability classrooms* (2nd ed.). Alexandria, VA: ASCD.

Tomlinson, C. A., & Eidson, C. C. (2003). *Differentiation in practice: A resource guide for differentiating curriculum, grades K–5.* Alexandria, VA: ASCD.

U.S. Census Bureau. (2007). The 2007 statistical abstract: The national data book, Table 222. Available online: www.census.gov/compendia/statab/education.

Wood, J. W., Lazzari, A., & Reeves, C. K. (1993). Educational characteristics and implications. In J. W. Wood (Ed.), *Mainstreaming* (2nd ed., pp. 78–120). New York: Merrill/Macmillan.

Young, T., & Hadaway, N. (Eds.). (2006). *Supporting the literacy development of English learners.* Newark, DE: IRA.

Fostering Literacy
Beyond the Classroom

FOCUS QUESTIONS

- What are some ways in which we engage in literacy outside the classroom?

- How can we develop motivation for engaging in the language arts?

- Why is service learning a valuable organizational/curricular element for grades 4–8?

- Why is it important to teach media literacy skills?

- What would some characteristics be of a school that emphasizes information literacy?

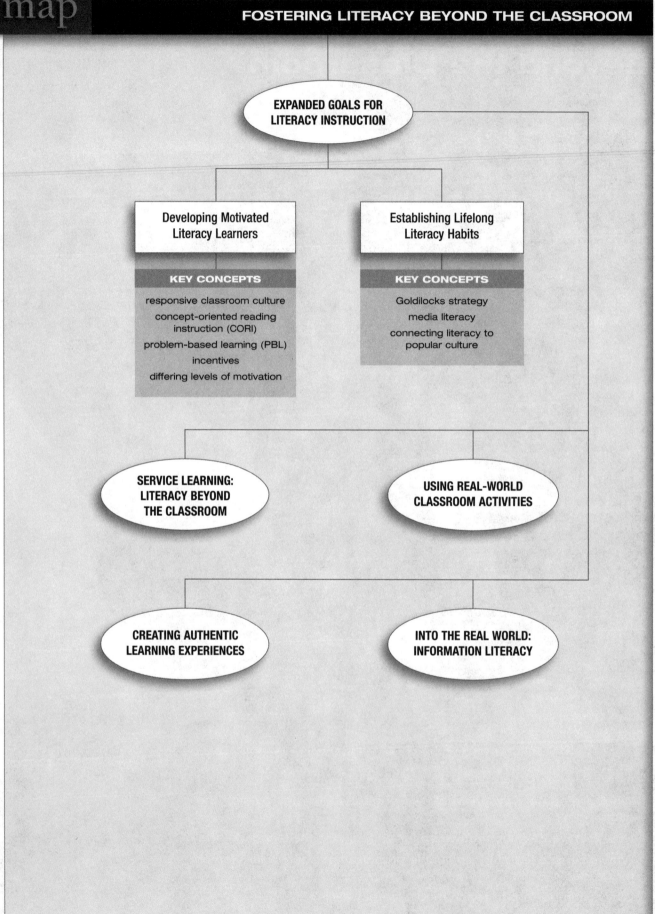

EXPANDED GOALS FOR LITERACY INSTRUCTION

Developing Motivated Literacy Learners

KEY CONCEPTS

responsive classroom culture

concept-oriented reading instruction (CORI)

problem-based learning (PBL)

incentives

differing levels of motivation

Establishing Lifelong Literacy Habits

KEY CONCEPTS

Goldilocks strategy

media literacy

connecting literacy to popular culture

SERVICE LEARNING: LITERACY BEYOND THE CLASSROOM

USING REAL-WORLD CLASSROOM ACTIVITIES

CREATING AUTHENTIC LEARNING EXPERIENCES

INTO THE REAL WORLD: INFORMATION LITERACY

"Let me share with you the ways I used literacy this weekend," Mr. Fortier begins. "Then I will ask you to think about your weekend and how you engaged in literacy outside the classroom." Mr. Fortier proceeds to give his eighth-graders a detailed account:

"I rose on Saturday morning and looked at the clock, which read 7:46. Then I read the newspaper while having breakfast. Later, I checked the TV listings to see if there was a sports program on that I wanted to watch. Seeing I had plenty of time before the game started, I decided to put together a chest of drawers I had purchased. The directions were clearly written, and I finished the project in about an hour. Next I made a grocery list for the week and went to the store. I am careful about what I eat, so I first checked the labels before buying several new items I have been wanting to try. When I returned home, I put the groceries away, and watched the Sacramento Kings basketball game on TV. After the game, I paid a few bills with checks. I then turned on my computer to check for e-mail and corresponded with some of my friends who live far away. While online, I searched for a website on kitchen appliances. I need to buy a new refrigerator, so I decided to gather information from the Internet so I can make a wise purchase. Before turning off my computer, I attempted the *New York Times* crossword puzzle online. For dinner, I wanted to try a new recipe, so I read the list of ingredients, gathered them, and began to prepare the meal. After dinner, I checked the TV listings again but didn't see anything appealing, so I decided to read a mystery novel instead. On Sunday, I attend religious services, so when I awoke I first looked at the clock to determine which service I would be able to attend and then got dressed. At the service I read through the weekly bulletin and used the hymnal to sing along with the choir. After services, I like to eat breakfast out, so I drove to one of my favorite breakfast places. At the restaurant I studied the menu and chose a pancake breakfast. On the way home, I bought the Sunday newspaper, which kept me busy for the next few hours. After a light lunch, I began to grade some papers and prepare lessons for Monday. I used Google to search for resources related to our upcoming WebQuest and explored some lesson plan sites for ideas to include in my own lessons. A new friend had invited me for Sunday dinner, so I checked my GPS to find the best route to my friend's house. On the way there, I watched the street signs closely so I would not miss my turns. After dinner, I returned home and read my mystery novel some more before watching the nightly news and going to bed."

Mr. Fortier then makes a four-column chart on the board. The headings are: Informational, Recreational, Occupational, and Environmental (Goodman, 1996). He and his students begin to classify the ways he used literacy during the weekend.

Mr. Fortier then directs his students to think back to their weekend, list all the literacy activities they can remember, and create a similar chart of their own, considering their current occupation as "student."

Language Art	Informational	Recreational	Occupational	Environmental
Reading	• Read newspaper • Read directions for chest of drawers • Read food labels • Found/read website for kitchen appliances • Read recipe • Read bulletin • Read menu	• Read TV listings • Read e-mail • Read mystery novel • Used hymnal	• Read and graded papers • Read information to help prepare WebQuest lesson	• Read clock • Read scores on TV • Read labels to gather ingredients for recipe • Read restaurant sign • Read street signs
Writing	• Wrote grocery list	• Wrote and sent e-mail • Attempted NY Times crossword puzzle	• Wrote checks to pay bills • Wrote lesson plan • Wrote comments and grades on student papers	*(continued)*

Language Art	Informational	Recreational	Occupational	Environmental
Listening	• Listened to TV news	• Sunday services • Listened to choir • Listened to the announcers for Kings' basketball game		
Speaking	• Ordered pancake breakfast	• Sang from hymnal • Visited with new friend over dinner		
Viewing	• Watched TV news	• NY Times Crossword puzzle online • Watched Kings play on TV	• Viewed Google sites to prepare WebQuest	• Interpreted GPS map
Visually Representing			• Developed graphic organizer for lesson	

EXPANDED GOALS FOR LITERACY INSTRUCTION

Literacy is a continuum of skills, including reading, writing, speaking, listening, viewing, visually representing, and critical thinking, applied in a social context to enable a person to function effectively in her group and community (Harris & Hodges, 1995). In this sense, literacy goes far beyond the classroom walls.

As students progress through the grades, the goals of literacy instruction change from ones that focus on learning to read, to ones that include reading to learn. But we not only want students to be able to read and to read to learn, we also want them to *want* to read and to recognize the value of literacy in their everyday lives. To continue developing their competencies in literacy, students must continue to engage in literate activities (reading, writing, speaking, listening, viewing, and visually representing) once they are beyond the classroom setting. Elsewhere in this book we have presented information on strategies for a variety of literacy competency areas, such as word recognition; vocabulary; comprehension of narrative, expository, and online text; and content area literacy. In this chapter, the emphasis is on two areas: the affective aspects of literacy, or developing positive attitudes toward and interests in the language arts; and the real-world (authentic) informational aspects of literacy, or establishing lifelong literacy habits. The goals of literacy instruction in grades 4–8 must expand to include

1 developing motivated literacy learners

2 establishing lifelong literacy habits

Each of these goals will be discussed in detail.

❶ DEVELOPING MOTIVATED LITERACY LEARNERS

Creating and enriching interests and positive attitudes will certainly go a long way in developing motivated literacy learners. As adults, we do not often engage in activities for which we have negative feelings or no interest. Attitudes toward reading and writing involve how an individual feels about reading and writing. These feelings can be positive or negative toward reading or writing in general, or they can vary depending on the subject area (Mathewson, 1985). In other words, an individual might really like reading about historical events but have very negative feelings about reading science material. This aspect of attitudes seems closely related to interests; in fact, Schiefele (1991) describes *individual interests* as relatively stable feelings (i.e., attitudes) about different areas such as reading. He distinguishes between individual interests (stable) and situational or text-based interests that are less stable because this type of interest might be sparked by a particular activity or text. There is support in the literature that individual feelings about reading relate to motivation and that reading interest positively affects comprehension (Alexander, Kulikowich, & Jetton, 1994; Mathewson, 1994; McKenna, 1994). Thus, it is important for teachers to help students develop both positive attitudes and reading interests in order for them to become motivated readers and writers.

Researchers have shown that reading motivation decreases as students advance in grade level (Eccles et al., 1993; Marsh, 1989). However, this same body of research also concludes that this decline results from changes in school and classroom environments. In reality, then, this is a hopeful finding because educators can control school and classroom environments. Next we consider several approaches for increasing student motivation.

Provide a responsive classroom culture

Oldfather (2001) suggests a responsive classroom culture as an effective environment for increasing motivation. A *responsive classroom culture* is one that honors student voices in the following ways:

1. It develops a community of learners that promotes the maintenance and enhancement of caring.
2. It gives teachers access to important insights for meeting students' educational needs.
3. It alleviates motivational struggles and promotes students' perceptions of self-determination and thus their ownership of their own learning agenda. (Oldfather, 2001, p. 14)

Common characteristics of responsive classrooms include the following:

- Teachers explain to their students reasons for particular activities or topics of study.
- The environment is one in which learning is more important than getting the right answer.
- Teachers discuss with students the value of what is being learned (e.g., How might this skill be useful to you in the future?).
- The atmosphere encourages risk taking.
- Each student's contribution of ideas is expected and responded to.
- Teacher and students participate together as learners.
- Desks are arranged to support group work.

- Samples of student work fill the room.
- The curriculum is developed thematically, incorporating students' interests and suggestions.
- Topics often relate to large issues, current events, or environmental concerns.
- Students read self-selected books as well as books from the core curriculum.
- Writing is a daily activity and often a favored activity.

www

Innovative Ideas
www.theteachersdesk.com

Several techniques already discussed in Chapter 5, such as literature circles, book clubs, and the use of graphic novels, would likely be found in a responsive classroom. These activities provide ways for teachers to lead students to read quality literature.

Employ concept-oriented reading instruction

concept-oriented reading
instruction (CORI) •

Guthrie and McCann (1997) researched an integrated curriculum plan they call **concept-oriented reading instruction (CORI)** with third- and fifth-grade classrooms as an instructional context to support the development of motivation. In this context, one containing many responsive classroom characteristics, students were encouraged to direct their own work, collaborate with classmates, develop new metacognitive strategies, and express their knowledge in innovative ways. After three years of CORI, Guthrie and McCann concluded that in this learning context, students exhibit strong intrinsic motivation and use effective strategies for finding books, managing time, locating places to read, and avoiding distractions to a greater extent than do students receiving traditionally organized curriculum.

www

CORI
www.cori.umd.edu

Use of problem-based learning

problem-based
learning (PBL) •

Authentic literacy projects can capture the interest of reluctant learners in ways not possible with the standard curriculum. Figure 10.1 presents a list of criteria for use to establish whether a learning activity is authentic. **Problem-based learning (PBL)**, one approach that provides students with authentic learning activities, organizes curriculum and instruction around real-world problems or carefully designed problems that mirror real-world problems. In small groups, students gather information and apply knowledge from multiple disciplines in their quest for solutions. Guided by the teacher acting as a facilitator, students develop critical thinking and decision-making, problem-solving, and collaborative skills as they identify problems, formulate questions and hypotheses, seek out resources and conduct data searches, perform experiments, propose solutions, and determine a "best fit" solution linked to the conditions of the problem. This process involves all six literacy components—reading, writing, speaking, listening, viewing, and visually representing. Problem-based learning enables students to embrace complexity, find relevance and joy in their learning, and enhance their capacity for creative and responsible real-world problem solving (Gordon, 1998).

www

PBL Examples
*www.edutopia.org/php/keyword.
php?is=037*
*www2.imsa.edu/programs/pbln/
problems/*

An example of a middle school science problem-based learning unit is related here. Elements of authentic learning as described in Figure 10.1 can readily be identified.

A seventh-grade science class is engaged in a unit on the environment. The entry question deals with the environmental health of a local stream. Working in groups of four or five, the students are directed to assess the health of this stream in order to prepare a formal PowerPoint presentation for the local

1. *Authentic learning activities have real-world relevance.* Activities match as nearly as possible the real-world tasks of professionals in practice.

2. *Authentic learning activities are purposely ill defined, requiring students to define the tasks needed to complete the activity.* Problems inherent in the activities are loosely structured and open to multiple interpretations, with solutions not readily apparent. Learners must make decisions about what tasks and subtasks are required to seek solutions to the problem.

3. *Authentic learning activities comprise complex tasks to be investigated by students over a sustained period of time.* Activities are completed in days, weeks, and months rather than minutes or hours. They require a significant investment of time and intellectual resources.

4. *Authentic learning activities provide the opportunity for students to examine the task from different perspectives, using a variety of resources.* The use of a variety of resources rather than a limited number of teacher-selected references requires students to examine the problem from several theoretical and practical perspectives, and to distinguish relevant from irrelevant information.

5. *Authentic learning activities provide the opportunity to collaborate.* Collaboration is integral to real world

tasks; seldom does an individual working alone solve real world problems.

6. *Authentic learning activities provide the opportunity to reflect.* Activities need to enable learners to make choices and reflect on their learning both individually and socially.

7. *Authentic learning activities can be integrated and applied across different subject areas and lead beyond domain-specific outcomes.* Activities encourage interdisciplinary perspectives and allow diverse roles and expertise rather than a single well-defined field or domain.

8. *Authentic learning activities are seamlessly integrated with assessment.* The manner of assessment for the major task reflects real world assessment, rather than separate, artificial assessment removed from the nature of the task.

9. *Authentic learning activities create polished products valuable in their own right rather than being preparation for something else.* Activities culminate in the creation of a whole product rather than being an exercise in preparation for something else.

10. *Authentic learning activities allow competing solutions and diversity of outcome.* A range of diverse and multiple solutions of an original nature are anticipated, rather than a single correct response obtained by the application of rules and procedures.

Source: Adapted from Reeves, T. C., Herrington, J., & Oliver, R. (2002). Authentic activities and online learning. p. 564. Available online at www.ecu.edu.au/conferences/herdsa/main/papers/ref/pdf/Reeves.pdf.

Criteria for authentic learning tasks. **FIGURE** **10.1**

Sewage and Water Board and the School Board, recommending ways to keep the stream healthy. The students work with local water experts and research ways to assess the health of the stream (W. U., personal communication, January 6, 2006).

WebQuests can also be good examples of problem-based learning and represent student-centered learning that utilizes the Internet. A **WebQuest** challenges students to explore the Internet for information related to a particular problem or inquiry. For information on learning to develop WebQuests and for intermediate and middle school examples, visit the websites provided here.

Offer incentives

Several studies demonstrate that the use of tangible incentives, such as prizes, under certain conditions can enhance intrinsic motivation. If a valued reward is offered (1) when the level of initial interest is low, (2) when the attractiveness of the activity will become apparent after engaging in it over time, or (3) when a certain level of mastery needs to be attained, then the reward will lead to

WWW

WebQuests

www.spa3.k12.sc.us/WebQuest Template/webquesttemp.htm

http://webquest.sdsu.edu/ webquestwebquest-ms.html

Authentic Learning Activities and Online Learning

www.ecu.edu.au/conferences/herdsa/ main/papers/ref/pdf/Reeves.pdf

intrinsic motivation (Lepper, Greene, & Nisbett, 1973; McLoyd, 1979). Thus, programs such as the All American Reading Challenge (sponsored by McDonald's, the American Library Association, and Scholastic), Book-It! (sponsored by Pizza Hut), Bucks for Books (sponsored by the Earning by Learning Foundation), Book Adventure (sponsored by Sylvan), and RUNNING START (sponsored by Reading Is Fundamental) can be effective for increasing intrinsic motivation. Verbal praise and positive feedback increase intrinsic motivation because of their informational value. Student choice is also a powerful incentive and is likely the reason that the sponsored reading programs and approaches such as book clubs and literature circles are successful. Students like to be in charge of choosing what they read. In fact, the research is most clear on the strong positive correlation between choice and the development of intrinsic motivation (Ivy & Broaddus, 2001; Oldfather, 1993; Paris & Oka, 1986; Pitcher et al., 2007; Rodin, Rennert, & Solomon, 1980; Turner, 1995).

Work with differing levels of motivation

Even within responsive classrooms there will be students who are not motivated intrinsically but who choose to be positive about the learning activity, maintain openmindedness, search for the worthwhileness of the activity, observe other classmates' interest in the activity, plunge ahead into the activity, and in doing so become motivated and fully participate. Then there are those who will do the activities but are only motivated by some type of reward system to complete their work. This lack of instrinsic motivation probably occurs for all students at some time or another. Finally, there are those students who are not motivated and who do not participate. This situation involves avoidance or perceived helplessness. Avoidance occurs when the student finds reasons for not getting around to the work, perhaps after several attempted starts. The more serious situation, perceived helplessness, often involves physical symptoms, such as feeling ill, or an excessive need to move. These students feel anxious and less than competent and need special accommodations for completing tasks, such as a choice of tasks, freedom to move in order to complete a task, or hands-on activities. Timed tests are usually a disaster for students in this category. Teachers who respond to these students with care and empathy and take actions to alleviate anxiety will best serve this group.

2 ESTABLISHING LIFELONG LITERACY HABITS

You can begin the effort to establish lifelong literacy habits by helping your students learn how to choose books, estimate the difficulty of reading material, and read and write for authentic reasons. Reading material that is at an appropriate level of difficulty is important for several reasons. First, students benefit from reading easy material in order to practice their reading skills. Second, by reading somewhat challenging material students will expand their reading skills. Finally, students should be able to independently recognize when text material is too easy, just right, or too hard for them, and then decide to stay with that material or look for something else. To promote lifelong literacy skills, provide your students with authentic reasons for literacy activities, help them develop media literacy skills, and connect literacy to popular culture.

Choosing books and estimating reading difficulty

Teachers must first locate material at a variety of readability levels to ensure that they will have sufficient examples for modeling appropriate difficulty levels with their students. Use of Fry's Readability Graph (see Appendix E) can assist the teacher in identifying the grade-level readability of text. Using a variety of genres, print media (e.g., books, magazines, newspapers), and topics, teachers can develop a series of activities that are designed to show students how to locate material on a particular topic and then how to look at this material to decide if it is "readable." For example, you might provide a list of titles that will actually be available to your students and another list of topics; then ask the students to match those titles with the topics they are likely to address. Once students complete this matching activity, the group can discuss their reasons for matching. Following this discussion, the actual materials should be made available so students can look at them to see if they indeed provide information on the topic they thought was a match.

WWW

Fry's Readability Graph
http://school.discoveryeducation.com/schrockguide/fry/fry.html

Using the "leveled" materials, teachers can model a process for locating material that is "too easy," "just right," or "too hard" for reading. Known as the **Goldilocks strategy** (Ohlhausen & Jepsen, 1992), this strategy is based on group discussion about what makes a book too easy, too hard, or just right. Easy books are books in which students can read every word and understand every idea. Hard books are books in which there are many words students cannot read and many ideas they cannot understand. Books that are just right are books in which students can read most of the words and can understand most of the ideas. Using actual examples, the teacher can think out loud about a "too easy" book using phrases such as "there are not many words on each page," or "I know all the words on the page," or "there are lots of illustrations in this book." A book that is "just right" represents material that is at a student's instructional reading level, or 95 percent word recognition accuracy. Thus, out of approximately 100 words, there should be no more than five words that are unknown. Keeping this in mind, the teacher might describe the book using phrases such as "there are a few words on each page that seem new to me," "there are no more than five words on a page that are new to me," "I think I will not have trouble with the number of words on each page," "I can figure out the words myself," "I know something about this topic already and that will help me read this," or "the pictures (or headings) look interesting." A "too hard" book is described using phrases such as "there are too many new words on each page," "the print is too small," "there are many words on each page," or "I would have to ask for lots of help reading this." Finally, the teacher needs to remind students that sometimes it is necessary to work with material that is really too hard in order to locate a particular piece of information, but most of the time, when the material seems too difficult, students and the teacher should look for something else, something that is "just right."

● Goldilocks strategy

The school library would be a great place for students to practice locating material on a particular topic and then deciding whether the material is appropriate for them. In this way students receive guided practice and also have access to a librarian who can assist them in finding something that is appropriate. This step will show students that they can independently seek information if they know what they are looking for. A field trip to the public library might also be arranged to further expand this practice.

The school library is a great place for students to practice locating material on a particular topic and then decide whether the material interests them and is appropriate for their reading level.

Authentic reasons for literacy activities

Once students can identify materials that are appropriate to their reading level, they are well on their way to becoming lifelong learners. An additional aspect of helping students develop lifelong literacy habits is to provide classroom experiences that relate to the types of real-world literacy activities they will engage in as adults and citizens living within a community. Shelley Harwayne (2000) shares a letter that she wrote to the families of students in the Manhattan New School. Relevant portions of that letter appear here:

> Dear families,
>
> . . . *[I responded by suggesting that literacy needs to be long lasting and making a promise:]* Your children will not only know how to read and write, but more importantly they will choose to read and write.
>
> *[I went on to explain this heartfelt promise.]* Your children will choose to read and write—has implications for classroom practice. It is no longer enough in the reading classroom for students to be able to answer questions at the end of a chapter or fill in the blanks on a worksheet. . . . Instead, we have much higher expectations. Students throughout the grades are being asked to read a wide range of beautifully crafted authentic materials and to read them deeply and critically, discovering new meanings, making personal interpretations, connecting one text to another, and even reading as a writer intent on borrowing techniques for their own writing.
>
> . . . Writing no longer means simply following a teacher's specific instructions. We are no longer asking for 250 words on "Your Summer Vacation." Instead, students throughout the grades are working much harder and learning a great deal more. Students are filling journals, discovering important and original ideas, shaping and revising those ideas into appropriate forms, and editing those drafts into publishable finished works that do real work in the real world. Students are sending letters, crafting picture books for younger students, performing original plays for their peers, publishing non-fiction texts for their class libraries, etc. . . . (pp. A-11–A-12)

Developing media literacy skills

media literacy ●

Lifelong literacy also includes developing the skills to be discriminating users of mass media. Teaching **media literacy** skills enables students to "access, analyze, evaluate, and create messages using media in various forms" (Hobbs, 2005, p. 58). Media literate individuals think critically about what they see, hear, and read in books, newspapers, magazines, advertisements, and music; on television, radio, movies, and the Internet; and through other emerging technologies (Hobbs, 2001). One way a teacher can foster critical literacy in relation to the media is to have students read reviews and critiques of films that they may typically watch without making judgments. For example, a teacher may show a clip from the Disney movie *Mulan* and have students think about its authenticity in terms of the Chinese culture and the values it portrays. The teacher can then have them read the article "A Mean Wink at Authenticity: Chinese Images in Disney's *Mulan*" (Mo & Shen, 2000). In this article the authors give details backing their claims that the film is culturally inauthentic, full of distortion and stereotypes, and guilty of using racially coded language. The students can then reconsider the movie based on the article's comments or those of another reviewer.

www

PBS Video Catalog
www.pbs.org/teachers/

The PBS Video website is an excellent resource for finding films for various grade levels and subject areas.

Figure 10.2 provides guiding questions to assist students to think critically about a feature or documentary film. The related activity encourages students to think about how people and cultures are portrayed in the media.

- What (or whose) point of view is represented in this film? How might the story be told differently using another's point of view?

- What content information did you learn from this movie? How does it connect with other things you've learned in this class or on your own?

- What do you see as a pervasive motif, or overall theme, to this movie? Is it well developed? How did the screenwriter or director convey this theme?

- Reflect on how you made sense of this film. Were there points of confusion for you? Did you combine what you were seeing and hearing with background information you already knew? What surprises did you become aware of as you watched?

- Which characters are well developed? Which were simple, and which were complex? Did any characters grow or change over the course of the story?

- What was the importance of the setting? What elements contributed to the successful portrayal of the setting?

- What symbols, archetypes, and/or motifs did you find? Were they effective for you?

- Discuss the use of special effects. Evaluate the film in terms of music, artistic quality, and crafting.

- What values are portrayed in this film? Did you feel it was preachy or manipulative? In what ways? What did you learn about people, human nature, or societies?

- If you also read the book (assuming there is one), which did you prefer? What differences did you notice? What characteristics were prominent or effective in each mode of presentation?

- What would you say to a friend who asked you about this movie?

Source: S. Kane, (2007). *Literacy & Learning in the Content Areas,* 2nd ed. Scottsdale, AZ: Holcomb Hathaway. Used with permission.

Guiding questions for viewing a documentary or feature film.   **FIGURE** 10.2

A media literate person can also create messages using print, audio, video, and multimedia. By learning to recognize how the mass media influence information and to analyze and think critically about the messages the creators of mass media send, students become savvy consumers and informed participants in a democratic society. For additional outcomes of increased media literacy skills, see Figure 10.3.

WWW

Media Literacy
www.medialit.org
www.acmecoalition.org

Potential outcomes of increased media literacy skills.   **FIGURE** 10.3

Media literacy . . .

1. empowers individuals to make independent judgments about media consumption.

2. focuses attention on the elements involved in the media communication process.

3. fosters an awareness of the impact of the media on the individual and society.

4. develops strategies with which to analyze and discuss media messages.

5. promotes awareness of interactive media content as a "text" that provides insight into our contemporary culture and ourselves.

6. cultivates enhanced enjoyment, understanding, and appreciation of media.

7. challenges interactive media communicators to produce effective and responsive media messages.

Source: Silverblatt, A. (2000, September). Media literacy in the digital age. *Reading Online, 4*(3). Available online at www.readingonline.org/newliteracies/lit_index.asp?HREF=/newliteracies/silverblatt/index.html.

ACTIVITY *Media Portrayals of People and Cultures*

(Cooper & Morreale, 2003)

This activity encourages students to think about how people and life in the United States are represented on television and in movies. It raises the issue of stereotypes, allowing students to begin to question media representations and images with regard to various stereotypes. They will learn to read physical and behavioral cues (clothing, hairstyles, interactive styles) to interpret characterizations.

1. Pose the following scenario and questions to students:

   Some students from another country are planning a visit to our city or town. These students have never been to the United States before and have decided to try to learn what they can through watching American television and movies. What might surprise them about our town if they are expecting it to be like the movies and TV?

   Prepare a tape to show a sampling of television content by channel surfing, spending several seconds on each channel, to help students think about questions involving stereotypes. The channel surfing tape should be made at a time when students are likely to be viewing—for example, right after school or in the evening.

2. List the students' impressions on the board as they respond to the following questions:

   a. Do you think the foreign students will get an accurate picture of what our town and people are like?

   b. What might surprise them about our town if they are expecting it to be like the movies and TV?

   c. What will they expect in terms of our quality of life? Rich, poor, or in between?

   d. What will they think about the way we look and dress?

   e. What will they expect our houses to be like?

   f. Do you think they will expect to find a lot of crime and violence?

   g. What will they think about how women and girls behave? Boys and men? People of different races and ethnic groups (stereotypes)?

   h. What will they think of how we solve problems?

   i. What will they think of the kind of humor we have and the jokes we make?

   j. Will they think we are polite or rude?

   k. What will they think about any extraordinary powers we might have?

3. Point out to the students the discrepancies between what they thought the visitor would expect based on media images and representations and what they think their town and its people are really like. Raise the question of whether these media characterizations might affect the way they think about themselves and their own lives in comparison to what they see through media.

4. Have students report on differences between real-life people and situations and those reflected through media. Ask them for explanations concerning the differences between media people and situations and real people and situations. Ask students to define and give examples of

stereotypes. Develop a chart on the board divided into the categories of TV and Reality. Have students generate ideas for characteristics and categorize them, noting which ones represent stereotypes.

Connecting literacy to popular culture

Students in grades 4–8 reject literacy tasks that lack purpose and interest (Pitcher et al., 2007). When limited to textbooks and whole-class activities, students miss opportunities to engage in authentic literacy tasks. Expanding our concept of "text" to include not only print material, such as newspapers and graphic novels, but also media text and electronic messaging as well as nonprint media, such as television shows, films, and songs, will increase engagement in literacy tasks (Phelps, 2006). "When we connect literacy to popular culture, our students can understand difficult content in new ways, as well as learn to question the media they are presented with on a daily basis" (Norton-Meier, 2005, p. 608). In addition, Fukunaga (2006) states, "we may be able to find students' potential literacy skills and their multiple identities by paying attention to their activities with popular culture texts and the Internet" (p. 219).

Instant messaging, as one example of an authentic literacy task used by today's youth, readily motivates learners "to engage in decoding, encoding, interpretation, and analysis, among other literacy processes" (Lewis & Fabos, 2005, p. 473). Lewis and Fabos found that students used font color, font size, and icons to communicate sarcasm and visually represent emotional content. Students also gave a great deal of thought to word choice during instant messaging. Students demonstrated themselves to be strategic language users in order to communicate their intended messages. Instructional strategies like dialogue journals and reading response logs can be easily adapted to make them candidates for use with instant messaging.

Song lyrics are an example of an artifact from popular culture that can be quite useful for literacy lessons. Using song lyrics of the performers they enjoy can help students connect their own experiences with the lesson objective. For example, instead of teaching students about poetry techniques in the usual ways, you might use the lyrics of some of their favorite songs and raps (Weinstein, 2007) to demonstrate the various poetry techniques. Using selected lyrics from "Where Is the Love?," sung by the Black Eyed Peas, and "Don't Laugh at Me," performed by Mark Wills, students could be introduced to the following techniques:

Hyperbole: a great exaggeration

Example: I feel the weight of the world on my shoulder. (*"Where Is the Love?"*)

Repetition: words or phrases are repeated

Example: Where is the love, where is the love, where is the love, the love, the love (*"Where Is the Love?"*)

Assonance: anywhere in the words there is repetition of the vowels without repetition of consonants, often used as an alternative to rhymes in verse

Example: It just ain't the same, always unchanged, new days are strange, is the world insane (*"Where Is the Love?"*)

Consonance: anywhere in words, there is repetition of consonant sounds

Example: Man you gotta have love just to set it [anger] straight, take control of your mind and meditate, let your soul gravitate to the love. (*"Where Is the Love?"*)

Rhyme: sound alike endings in words

End rhyme: words rhyme at the end of lines

Example: I'm the cripple on the corner you've passed me on the street,
and I wouldn't be out here beggin' if I had enough to eat. (*"Don't Laugh at Me"*)

Internal rhyme: words that rhyme are in the middle of the line

Example: People killin' people dyin' children hurt and you hear them cryin'
To discriminate only generates hate, and when you hate then you're bound
to get irate (*"Where Is the Love?"*)

Additional poetry techniques not represented in the two songs above include:

Simile: comparing two unlike things using like or as

Example: Her eyes are blue like the sky.

Metaphor: comparing two unlike things without using like or as

Example: Lies are a friend of some.

Personification: giving human-like characteristics to an inanimate object

Example: The stars winked at me.

Alliteration: there is a repetition of consonants at the beginning of words

Example: Bees are buzzy, bold, boisterous, and belligerent.

Onomatopoeia: words that sound like the actual word

Example: The burning wood snapped, crackled, and popped.

As seen in the examples above, song lyrics could also be used to develop vocabulary (e.g., synonyms, descriptive words, polysemantic words) and critical analysis skills (e.g., uncovering intended meanings or political meanings).

Another example from popular culture involves using visual images that permeate our lives. Identifying such images can help students understand difficult concepts or new content and learn to read critically and interpret meaning. Norton-Meier (2004) refers to the "bumper sticker curriculum," although any commonly found message signs could be used, such as highway billboards or even tagging and graffiti writing (MacGillivray & Curwen, 2007). Using a collection of bumper stickers (obtained from a bumper sticker company), students can first examine them for visual appeal. The ensuing discussion leads to questions that advertisers might ask: for example, "How big do letters need to be to be read by people in the car behind you?" (p. 262). Then the discussion can move to the message the bumper sticker conveys. Students can be observed discussing, questioning, and critiquing the use of print and visual images to comment on how the creators of the bumper stickers (or other signs) seek to influence or manipulate their thinking. Bumper sticker messages, such as those in the short list that follows, give some idea of the kinds of intellectually challenging lessons that could occur.

www

History Behind Song Lyrics
*www.readwritethink.org/lessons/
lesson_view.asp?id=812*

I Will Not Tolerate Intolerance

A Nation of Sheep Will Beget a Government of Wolves

I Think Therefore I Doubt

People Who Know the Least Always Seem to Know It the Loudest

Political Correctness Is a Disease

SERVICE LEARNING: TAKING LITERACY BEYOND THE CLASSROOM

It is the "real work in the real world" part of Shelley Harwayne's (2000) letter that brings us to the next focus of this chapter. More and more teachers and students are becoming involved in doing real literacy work within their communities, and this work is referred to as **service learning.** The term is generally defined as "a teaching strategy that combines classroom curriculum with community service, to enrich learning, teach civic responsibility, and strengthen communities" (National Commission on Service-Learning, 2002). Students of all ages, from all backgrounds, and from all over the world have become involved in service-learning projects. Of course, service-oriented organizations, such as Boy Scouts and Girl Scouts, have been doing this kind of community service work for many years. More recently, however, there has been a groundswell of interest in viewing service learning as part of what school is, or should be, about. Research also supports the inclusion of service learning by revealing many benefits for students, schools, and communities. Participation in effective service-learning programs is linked to such benefits as

● service learning

WWW

Service-Learning Projects
www.servicelearning.org

- higher scores on state achievement tests (Anderson et al., 1991)
- improved grades and increased attendance (Follman, 1998)
- increased classroom participation (Loesch-Griffin et al., 1995)
- improved problem-solving skills (Stephens, 1995)
- more positive and respectful relationships with peers and teachers (Weiler et al., 1998)
- fewer behavioral problems (Stephens, 1995; Switzer et al., 1995)
- greater acceptance of cultural differences (Berkas, 1997; Melchior, 1999)
- greater empathy and cognitive complexity than comparison groups (Courneya, 1994)

Especially relevant to the present chapter is service learning's potential to motivate disengaged students. For students who see little relevance between the school curriculum and their own lives, service learning highlights the relevance. Projects weave together such curricular areas as literacy, math, social studies, science, and health and nutrition. "Service learning puts academics into action because it puts learning into an authentic context. It engages young people in addressing real problems in their communities, not just fictitious problems in a textbook" (Glenn, 2002, p. 3). Some examples of service-learning projects are discussed below. They demonstrate the interweaving of several academic curricular areas, including literacy.

Garden project: Westfield Elementary School

Situated in an area of many Mexican and Southeast Asian families, Westfield Elementary School allocated a half acre of its property as a community garden. Forty families who were eager to receive a garden plot for family use were given their own plot in exchange for agreeing to help maintain the school garden. Students, teachers, student teachers, and parents all helped plant fruit trees and grapes around the perimeter of the garden and then planned an ornamental garden and flower beds. Mexican parents also planted corn and beans to share with the school. Gardening activities were connected to the curricular areas of science, language arts, math, and social studies. Writing became a

Gardens are popular service-learning projects and can be connected to many content area studies, including science, math, and social studies.

favorite tie-in to the garden project for language-building activities. Students wrote poetry and stories about the garden and kept field notes by recording and drawing what they saw happening in the garden. Sixth-graders connected to their social studies curriculum by planting ancient-world perennials, such as grapes, olives, and pomegranates. As vegetables were harvested from the garden, recipes were published in a multicultural cookbook. This activity reinforced lessons on fractions as well as other units of measurement (Hammond & Heredia, 2002).

Garden project: Chenowith Elementary School

Another garden project is tended by all students at Chenowith Elementary School, where 80 percent of the 370 students are on free or reduced-price lunch. To begin the project, parents, teachers, and students all worked together to create six raised flower beds. The art teacher and his fourth- and fifth-grade students painted over graffiti-filled walls to create beautiful, butterfly-filled murals surrounding the garden. The school secretary, a master gardener, shared how to take care of the soil and the plants with the students. The students are the ones who grow the plants from seeds, water and weed the garden, harvest the flowers and vegetables, and make compost to fertilize the soil. Keeping careful records of when things are planted, where, and how often they have been watered; counting days until plants are ready to harvest; and measuring for location of seeds and amount of fertilizer all involve doing literacy and math. The students harvest the vegetables and flowers and deliver them to senior citizens. They also lead tours of the garden and can describe the elements of the butterfly garden, an herb garden, and a garden of plants native to their area. The teachers note that this project is particularly beneficial for their English learners (Fredericks, Kaplan, & Zeisler, 2001).

Gardens are very popular service-learning projects. One such project led to the publication of *The Edible Schoolyard* (Learning in the Real World, 1999). This is a good resource for those who are interested in pursuing the curricular possibilities of such projects.

History of the community project: Horace Mann Academic Middle School

As the sixth-graders at Horace Mann began a language arts assignment to write a paper on the history of their community (the Mission District in San Francisco), they found there was little information available on a specific stage of development, called the "fifth stage" by historians. It was this stage of development that was most important to the students in understanding their community. The students and their teacher decided to address this shortage of information by talking with the people who were a part of the community's development. In so doing, they addressed an impressive list of academic skills. The students began by identifying the things they would need to do and the supplies they would need. They proceeded to write a project budget and develop a grant proposal to acquire what they needed. They then began to create a "living history" by talking with individuals identified as "community heroes." To prepare for this, students developed interview questions and interviewing skills. After hearing the stories of the heroes and compiling their biographies, the students created a mural to document the missing fifth stage and to celebrate the accomplishments of everyday heroes. Throughout the project, students needed to engage in multiple writing tasks, such as writing biographies of the heroes, letters to community members, and the grant proposal. They also learned good telephone skills through the numerous calls they made to invite speakers and gather information. The mural covers almost four city blocks, depicts 28 community heroes of the Mission District, and required much planning, measuring, and artistic designing (Learning In Deed, 2002).

REAL-WORLD CLASSROOM ACTIVITIES

Service learning is not the only way to add relevance to the curriculum in order to motivate and engage students. Other types of authentic, or real-world, activities can be used in the classroom to demonstrate that what students are learning in school has direct application in their own lives. A sampling of these activities follows.

Bike Repair

ACTIVITY

Most students either own or are familiar with bicycles. A number of bike-related activities can be accomplished within the classroom that allow students to practice the skills of reading comprehension, following directions, reasoning, and descriptive writing. Bike repair is one such activity.

1. Gather some bike repair manuals.
2. Ask a local bike dealer or a student if she has a used or broken bike she is willing to donate to the class for disassembling.
3. Gather a few simple tools: vise grips, adjustable wrench, screwdrivers, pliers, hammer, steel wool, oil can, Liquid Wrench, rags, oil.
4. Have students work on the bike during several class meetings and keep a log of what they did and why. This provides a record of the repair effort and requires students to write an explicit account.

Additional bike-related activities include obtaining bike registration (writing to local police or to the official trade association of the bicycle industry for information on how to set up a one-day bike registration drive); seeking information on local and national biking groups; and locating, reading, and sharing contents of bicycling magazines.

Job Market

ACTIVITY

The local business community is a great resource for materials that can provide relevant and exciting learning experiences for students.

1. Ask local businesses for sample job application forms and hints for interviewing. Fast-food restaurants, supermarkets, and discount stores will be the most likely businesses where students will find part-time jobs. Some businesses have application forms available online.

2. Invite managers to speak to classes about the importance of following directions when filling out job applications and interviewing techniques.

3. Have students fill out job application forms as neatly and accurately as possible.

4. Go over the forms with them as they work and then again when they finish to check spelling and accuracy.

ACTIVITY | *Developing Discriminating Consumers of Mass Media*

Food labels are an environmental artifact that can provide an authentic literacy task related to an important life skill. This activity on learning to read nutrition labels on food packages is a valuable and interesting critical literacy lesson that will help develop sophisticated consumers.

1. Have students examine the nutrition labels of popular food products.

2. Have them study the recommended serving size compared with the amount they might consume when eating the product. As an example of what to have students look for, a pint of "fat-free" sorbet shows the serving size to be one-half cup, with four servings per container and 130 calories per serving.

3. Using multiplication, have them determine if they are ingesting more calories than they realize. For example, if they decide to eat the entire pint of sorbet (4 servings) or six cookies instead of two (3 servings), they need to know to multiply the number of calories times the number of servings they are consuming (e.g., 4 x 130 = 520 calories).

Point out that how information is presented, in this case label design, impacts what they notice. Serving size information appears above a wide line (often solid black) separating it from information about the number of calories (e.g., 130) and other nutrition information contained in each serving. This important information is followed by another wide line (often solid black). The use of the two solid wide lines draws the eye to the nutritional information and away from the serving size recommendation.

Sometimes we purchase foods with fat-free labels thinking we will consume fewer calories. However, fat-free labeling can be misleading, as these foods often have more sugar and an even higher calorie count than the "regular" product might have.

Have students compare a variety of foods that have fat-free, sugar-free, and "regular" labels; this activity will prove quite enlightening to them. Such a lesson can lead to discussions of (1) how other types of information are presented and how the presentation influences our understanding of the message and (2) how we must be critical consumers of information.

ACTIVITY | *Reading Can Save You Money*

Students in grades 4–8 are already full participants in the consumer culture. It is a service to them to teach critical-reading and thinking skills as they relate to reading and responding to advertisements and making wise purchases. Constructing a lesson such as the following helps students to become smart consumers.

1. Browse for misleading advertisements in popular magazines. Depending on the student population, these could be related to weight reduction, skin problems, astrology, or hobbies.

2. Collect and laminate about 50 advertisements.

3. Choose from this group a few to be mounted on poster board for all to see.

4. As a readiness activity, have students share their own experiences related to misleading or deceptive mail-away offers, or other responses to advertisements that they, or family members, have personally experienced.

5. Using the mounted advertisements, discuss the misleading ads.

6. With students working in pairs, have each pair choose two additional ads from the 50 that were laminated. Have each pair read these aloud to each other, discuss them, and analyze them using a set of prepared questions (Figure 10.4).

7. Have students share their ad analyses in a whole-class discussion.

www

Media Smarts
http://pbskids.org/dontbuyit

Questions for analyzing misleading advertisements. **FIGURE** 10.4

1. What is the product being advertised?
2. What is the eye-catching line? Write it down exactly so you can read it to the class.
3. What does the advertiser want you to believe you will get?
4. What do you think you really will get for your money?
5. What is the total amount of money that this product will actually cost?
6. What do you think are the outright lies, if any, in this advertisement?

The World When You Were Born

ACTIVITY

An activity that integrates history with reading comprehension, skimming, and reference skills, The World When You Were Born fosters personal interest in a particular time period of history. The more general message of this activity is that history is being made each and every day. As students will learn from this activity, we are either making history or reacting to past history.

1. Find a resource such as *Our American Century* (Time Life) that provides excellent photographs and enough text to give an idea of what life was like during a particular decade.

2. Design a set of questions for students to answer that helps them understand what life was like when they were born and when they were growing up (see Figure 10.5).

3. To provide more depth, have students do further research on their decade or on what the world was like when their parents were born.

4. After the research, share memories with students and discuss the part of their lives that is already a part of history.

1. What significance did the Internet have?
2. Why was Colin Powell called the "Reluctant Warrior"?
3. What happened on April 19, 1995?
4. Who are Generation Xers?
5. Who is the sports idol known as "His Airness"?
6. What was the subculture "extreme sports"?
7. Who was Boris Yeltsin?
8. What is meant by "video game warfare"?
9. What happened on August 2, 1990?
10. What was the most successful sitcom of the 1990s?

ANSWER KEY:

1. The Internet has been a democratizing force giving ordinary people the same access to a wealth of information whether they live in a well-to-do suburb, a remote rural area, or the inner city. It has changed the way we communicate, learn, and work.

2. Because of his deliberate hesitation to use force until necessary in the Vietnam War.

3. A car bomb exploded at the Alfred P. Murrah Federal Building in Oklahoma City.

4. A label attached to upstart men and women in their 20s, who immersed themselves in retro fashion and grunge.

5. Michael Jordan.

6. A new breed of athlete on the lookout for novel, exciting, often dangerous physical challenges, e.g., snowboarding, street luge, sky surfing.

7. Russian president from 1991–1999.

8. Warfare that featured a new type of hi-tech weaponry, e.g., stealth bombers, night vision equipment.

9. Saddam Hussein's Iraqi army invaded Kuwait.

10. *Seinfeld.*

Source: The Digital Decade: The '90s, from the *Our American Century* series. Alexandria, VA: Time Life, 2000.

FIGURE 10.5   History questions for the 1990s.

Some of these activities only simulate real-world experiences. It is also important to give students assignments that are "real" in terms of interest, choice, doing what real workers do (e.g., scientists, teachers, or any other particular career), responsibility, and teamwork. For example, while on the playground a class of students noticed the earthworms living in the vacant lot next door. They were totally fascinated with these worms, so their teacher took advantage of this high level of interest and suggested that they find out more about the kind of habitat earthworms require. This led to an extended study of earthworms both within and outside the classroom walls. The experience was authentic scientific inquiry, and students acted as true researchers, asking questions, gathering data, manipulating variables, discovering answers, and asking more questions.

GUIDELINES FOR CREATING AUTHENTIC LEARNING EXPERIENCES

Zemelman, Daniels, and Hyde (1998) provide ideas for authentic learning that can occur both inside and outside the classroom.

INSIDE SCHOOL

- Let kids in on curriculum planning, choosing topics and readings, making schedules, keeping records.

- Develop broad, interdisciplinary, thematic units based on student concerns.
- Use tangible, tactile materials, artifacts, and live demonstrations where possible.
- Favor learn-by-doing over learn-by-sitting-there-quietly-and-listening.
- Follow news and current events, connecting them with curriculum.
- Include activities that connect with students' multiple intelligences and cognitive styles.
- Let students subdivide content, form groups, and conduct team projects.
- Use primary source documents, not just textbooks, to teach history, science, and other subjects.
- Invite to the classroom speakers, experts, and interview subjects from the community.
- Bring in parents to give presentations, conference with students, create materials.
- Mix children through multi-age grouping, cross-age projects, buddy programs, and mainstreamed special education.
- Schedule time in flexible blocks that match the curriculum.
- Stress student goal setting and self-assessment.

BEYOND SCHOOL

- Give homework assignments that require interaction with family and community.
- Share student work through parent and community newsletters, displays, and events.
- Display student artwork or research projects in off-campus settings.
- Plan regular field trips and attend arts performances that support the curriculum.
- Visit, study, and investigate local government, services, and businesses.
- Get involved in community issues: recycling, safety, programs for kids.
- Launch family and community history projects.
- Join in a community beautification or art project.
- Take students on outdoor education, wilderness, ecology, and adventure programs.
- In conjunction with integrative units, have fact-finding tours; students take notes, make observations, or conduct interviews.
- Conduct survey or opinion research, by mail or in person. (pp. 203–204)

Maehr (1976) discusses the concept of continuing motivation and describes this to mean "individuals' engagement in a learned activity outside the context in which it was learned" (p. 443). He argues that "schools focus too much on learning in school and not enough on promoting children's continuing motivation to learn outside the school setting" (Wigfield, 1997, p. 17). Perhaps by using the practices listed above, schools can promote continuing motivation. For example, using popular cultural texts, such as those found in music lyrics, as a way to explore multiple meanings can provide a way to engage students in school literacy practices and, at the same time, help you gain valuable insight into your students' lives (Alvermann & Hagood, 2000, p. 445). Similarly, using a readers workshop approach, Taylor and Nesheim (2000/2001) helped their students appreciate the value of reading aloud to young children, so as parents they would more likely engage in shared reading activities.

INTO THE REAL WORLD: INFORMATION LITERACY

www

Information Literacy Lessons
www.informationliteracy.org/
default.php

Book- and print-based literacies, and the industrial model of schooling built around book culture, are no longer wholly adequate in a changing information, social, and cultural environment" (Luke, 2000, p. 424). In our world today, information is expanding at an exponential rate along with enormous technological advancements. We are truly in the Information Age, and now knowledge, not agriculture or manufactured goods, is this country's most precious resource. Thus, people who are **information literate**—who know how to locate, acquire, and use information—are America's greatest resources.

The American Library Association Presidential Committee Report on Information Literacy (ALA, 1989) describes what we need to do as educators:

> To be information literate, a person must be able to recognize when information is needed and have the ability to locate, evaluate, and use effectively the needed information. Producing such a citizenry will require that schools and colleges appreciate and integrate the concept of information literacy into their learning programs and that they play a leadership role in equipping individuals and institutions to take advantage of the opportunities inherent within the information society. Ultimately, information literate people are those who have learned how to learn. They know how to learn because they know how knowledge is organized, how to find information, and how to use information in such a way that others can learn from them. They are people prepared for lifelong learning, because they can always find the information needed for any task or decision at hand. (p. 1 of 13)

Educators realize that the people who most need to be information literate, such as minority groups, at-risk students, illiterate adults, English learners, and those who are economically disadvantaged, are the least likely to have the learning experiences or the access to information that will enable them to improve their situation. For example, these individuals are most vulnerable when they need to make decisions about health care for their children; find affordable insurance; locate and select nursing care for an elderly parent; or purchase, finance, or insure a car. The emphasis placed in school on textbooks, workbooks, and lectures is not sufficient to provide the learning experiences needed for the Information Age. At the very least, providing students with a lifelong habit of library use should be an additional focus in grades 4–8. Such a focus would actively involve students in

- knowing when they have a need for information
- identifying information needed to address a given problem or issue
- finding needed information and evaluating the information (see the sections "Locating Information" and "Online Search Skills" in Chapter 7)
- organizing the information
- using the information effectively to address the problem or issue at hand (ALA, 1989, p. 6 of 13)

In addition to the activities already described in this chapter and the chapter on literacy in the content areas (see Chapter 7), the following items describe what education might be like if information literacy were a central focus, rather than a peripheral focus.

1. **The school would be more interactive in the following ways:**
   - Students interact with teachers, other students, multiple information resources, and their community in pursuit of questions that interest them personally.
   - Students engage in long-term quests for answers to at least one real and serious social, scientific, aesthetic, or political problem.
   - Quests involve searching print, electronic, and video information; interviewing people in and outside of school; reading original sources; and doing extended writing.
   - Learning is more self-initiated and more intellectually and emotionally demanding when asking important questions; gathering data; reducing and synthesizing data; and analyzing, interpreting, and reporting information in a variety of forms.
   - The results of student projects are prominently displayed.
   - Discussion and debate about substantive, relevant issues pervade the halls, playgrounds, and cafeteria, as well as the classroom.
   - Questions such as "How do you know that?" "What evidence do you have for saying that?" and "How can we find out?" are commonplace.

2. **Teachers would be team members, coaches, and guides:**
   - Not capable of being repositories of all information that is found in libraries and databases worldwide and that can be accessed by classroom computers, teachers focus on arousing curiosity, asking the right questions, leading serious debate and discussion, and modeling inquiry.
   - Together with librarians, media resource people, and instructional designers, teachers ensure that student projects are challenging, interesting, and productive learning experiences.
   - There is less lecturing and more coaching and guiding.

3. **Evaluation would reflect the interactive nature of the school:**
   - Interactive tutoring software provides useful diagnostic information to help teachers and students understand student needs.
   - A broad range of literacy indicators, including knowing appropriate information sources and the ability to perform information searches, are assessed.
   - Assessments would relate specifically to ways students use their minds and achieve success as information consumers, analyzers, interpreters, evaluators, and communicators of ideas.

In general, most schools are far from placing an emphasis on information literacy. Those who are engaging in the service-learning projects discussed earlier in this chapter probably come closest. However, as the strategies and activities presented throughout this book demonstrate, it is possible to develop literacy in ways that are compatible with the new demands of our world. Cooperative learning, comprehension skills, research skills, and writing in a variety of genres are all necessary skills in the Information Age.

SUMMARY

Motivation, lifelong literacy habits, involvement in real-world aspects of literacy, and information literacy were discussed in this chapter. There is no one way to develop motivation for literacy activities, and motivation can vary depending on the task. However, by engaging students in meaningful and relevant work, such as service-learning projects, or real-world applications that require the need for literate activity, chances improve of developing motivation and a lifelong habit of reading and writing—two major goals of literacy instruction in grades 4–8. Addressing the importance of becoming information literate will also motivate students to engage in literacy activities. Techniques for encouraging students to read quality literature, to select their own books, and to become involved in literate activities within their own communities serve to move students from needing extrinsic rewards for doing literate work, to being more intrinsically motivated. As a teacher you should strive to do whatever it takes to help your students become literate individuals, *especially* beyond the classroom.

Questions
FOR JOURNAL WRITING AND DISCUSSION

1. Recall a time when you were highly motivated to complete a task. Write about your feelings and try to explain why you were so motivated. Share your reasons with a small group of your classmates and compile a list of common characteristics for what motivates.

2. How do you choose a book to read for pleasure? How do you choose a book to read for information? How would you direct a student to locate a book to read for pleasure?

3. Develop a list of activities you could use in the classroom, or potential service-learning projects, that would involve students in doing real literacy work.

4. How would you explain to parents (or to a principal) your reasons for using artifacts of popular culture (e.g., television shows, song lyrics, films, magazines) in your classroom?

Suggestions
FOR PROJECTS AND FIELD ACTIVITIES

1. Interview a student who is in grades 4–8 and use one of the reading attitude or interest surveys found in Appendix D (or develop your own set of questions to ask). Analyze the results to draw some conclusions about the student's level of motivation. Then, if possible, observe this student within the classroom setting. Do the survey results match the student's actions?

2. Complete for yourself a chart similar to the one Mr. Fortier made with his students in the chapter's opening scenario. Then try to do the same with a group of students. Have a discussion with them on why it is important to be literate in today's world.

3. Choose several representative printed materials that students in grades 4–8 are expected to read. Determine the readability levels of these materials using the Fry Readability Graph (see Appendix E). Discuss this information with a classroom teacher. What other possible factors would make these materials more or less readable than the graph indicates?

4. View a sitcom that is popular with your students. Analyze the program for how different groups of people are portrayed. Identify any stereotypes presented. Then plan a lesson that will help your students critically analyze television's influence on personal and societal values.

REFERENCES

Alexander, P. A., Kulikowich, J. M., & Jetton, T. L. (1994). The role of subject-matter knowledge and interest in the processing of linear and nonlinear texts. *Review of Educational Research, 64,* 201–252.

Alvermann, D. E., & Hagood, M. C. (2000). Fandom and critical media literacy. *Journal of Adolescent & Adult Literacy, 43,* 436–446.

American Library Association. (1989). *Presidential Committee on Information Literacy Report* [Online]. Available at www.ala.org/acrl/nili/ilit1st.html.

Anderson, V., Kinsley, C., Negroni, P., & Price, C. (1991, June). Community service-learning and school improvement in Springfield, Massachusetts. *Phi Delta Kappan, 72,* 761–764.

Berkas, T. (1997). *Strategic review of the W. K. Kellogg Foundation's service-learning projects, 1990–1996.* Battle Creek, MI: W. K. Kellogg Foundation.

Cooper, P., & Morreale (2003). *Creating competent communicators: Activities for teaching, 7–12.* Scottsdale, AZ: Holcomb Hathaway.

Courneya, J. (1994). An evaluation of the Native American school's water quality testing program. In M. Neal, R. Shumer, & K. Gorak (Eds.), *Evaluation: The key to improving service-learning programs* (pp. 163–182). Minneapolis: Minnesota Department of Education and the University of Minnesota.

Eccles, J. S., Wigfield, A., Harold, R., & Blumenfeld, P. S. (1993). Age and gender differences in children's self- and task perceptions during elementary school. *Child Development, 64,* 830–847.

Follman, J. (1998). *Florida learn and serve: 1996–97 outcomes and correlations with 1994–95 and 1995–96.* Tallahassee: Florida State University, Center for Civic Education and Service.

Fredericks, L., Kaplan, F., & Zeisler, J. (2001). *Integrating youth voice in service-learning.* Learning In Deed issue paper produced by Education Commission of the States' Initiative and Learning in Deed, the W. K. Kellogg Foundation's Service Learning Initiative [Online]. Available at www.ecs.org.

Fukunaga, N. (2006). Those anime students: Foreign language literacy development through Japanese popular culture. *Journal of Adolescent & Adult Literacy, 50,* 206–222.

Glenn, J. (2002, June). Service-learning puts academics into action. *Education Update, 44*(4), 1, 3.

Goodman, K. S. (1996). *On reading.* Portsmouth, NH: Heinemann.

Gordon, R. (1998). Balancing real-world problems with real-world results. *Phi Delta Kappan, 79,* 390–393.

Guthrie, J. T., & McCann, A. D. (1997). Characteristics of classrooms that promote motivations and strategies for learning. In J. T. Guthrie & A. Wigfield (Eds.), *Reading engagement: Motivating readers through integrated instruction* (pp. 128–148). Newark, DE: International Reading Association.

Hammond, L., & Heredia, S. (2002, Spring). Fostering diversity through community service learning. *Service Learning Network, 9*(1), 2–4.

Harris, T. L., & Hodges, R. E. (Eds.) (1995). *The literacy dictionary: The vocabulary of reading and writing.* Newark, DE: International Reading Association.

Harwayne, S. (2000). *Lifetime guarantees: Toward ambitious literacy teaching.* Portsmouth, NH: Heinemann.

Hobbs, R. (2001, Spring). The great debates circa 2001: The promise and the potential of media literacy. *Community Media Review,* 25–27.

Hobbs, R. (2005). What's news? *Educational Leadership, 63*(2), 58–61.

Ivy, G., & Broaddus, K. (2001). Just plain reading: A survey of what makes students want to read in middle school classrooms. *Reading Research Quarterly, 36,* 350–377.

Learning In Deed. (2002). *Service-learning profiles* [Online]. Available at www.learningindeed.org/slcommission/horace.html.

Learning in the Real World. (1999). *The edible schoolyard.* Berkeley, CA: Center for Ecoliteracy.

Lepper, M. R., Greene, D., & Nisbett, R. E. (1973). Undermining children's intrinsic interest with extrinsic reward. *Journal of Personality and Social Psychology, 28,* 124–137.

Lewis, C., & Fabos, B. (2005). Instant messaging, literacies, and social identities. *Reading Research Quarterly, 40,* 470–501.

Loesch-Griffin, D., Petrides, L. A., & Pratt, C. (1995). *A comprehensive study of project YES—rethinking classrooms and communities: Service-learning as educational reform.* San Francisco: East Bay Conservation Corps.

Luke, C. (2000). New literacies in teacher education. *Journal of Adolescent & Adult Literacy, 43,* 424–435.

MacGillivray, L., & Curwen, M. S. (2007). Tagging as a social literacy practice. *Journal of Adolescent and Adult Literacy, 50*(5), 354–369.

Maehr, M. L. (1976). Continuing motivation: An analysis of a seldom considered educational outcome. *Review of Educational Research, 46,* 443–462.

Marsh, H. W. (1989). Age and sex effects in multiple dimensions of self-concept: Preadolescence to early adulthood. *Journal of Educational Psychology, 81,* 417–430.

Mathewson, G. C. (1985). Toward a comprehensive model of affect in the reading process. In H. Singer & R. B. Ruddell (Eds.), *Theoretical models and processes of reading* (3rd ed., pp. 841–856). Newark, DE: International Reading Association.

Mathewson, G. C. (1994). Model of attitude influence upon reading and learning to read. In R. B. Ruddell, M. R. Ruddell, & H. Singer (Eds.), *Theoretical models and processes of reading* (4th ed., pp. 1131–1161). Newark, DE: International Reading Association.

McKenna, M. C. (1994). Toward a model of reading attitude acquisition. In E. H. Cramer & M. Castle (Eds.), *Fostering the love of reading: The affective domain in reading education* (pp. 18–40). Newark, DE: International Reading Association.

McLoyd, V. C. (1979). The effects of extrinsic rewards of differential value on high and low intrinsic interest. *Child Development, 50,* 1010–1019.

Melchior, A. (1999). *Summary report: National evaluation of learn and serve America.* Waltham, MA: Center for Human Resources, Brandeis University.

Mo, W., & Shen, W. (2000, spring). A mean wink at authenticity: Chinese images in Disney's "Mulan." *New Advocate, 13*(2), 129–142.

National Commission on Service-Learning. (2002). *Learning in deed: The power of service-learning for American schools,* Final Report [Online]. Available at http://learningindeed.org/slcommission/report.html.

Norton-Meier, L. A. (2004). The bumper sticker curriculum: Learning from words on the backs of cars. *Journal of Adolescent & Adult Literacy, 48,* 260–263.

Norton-Meier, L. A. (2005). Trust the fungus: Lessons in media literacy learned from the movies. *Journal of Adolescent & Adult Literacy, 48,* 608–611.

Ohlhausen, M., & Jepsen, M. (1992). Lessons from Goldilocks: "Someone has been choosing my books but I can make my own choices now!" *The New Advocate, 5,* 31–46.

Oldfather, P. (1993). What students say about motivating experiences in a whole language classroom. *The Reading Teacher, 46,* 672–681.

Oldfather, P. (2001). *When students do not feel motivated for literacy learning: How a responsive classroom culture helps* [Online]. Available at http://curry.edschool.virginia.edu/go/clic/nrrc/respon_r8.html.

Paris, S. G., & Oka, E. R. (1986). Self-regulated learning among exceptional children. *Exceptional Children, 53,* 103–108.

Petrillo, L. (2002, January 4). *Grade school globe-trotters: Reading program has students 'crossing continents' for books* [Online]. Available at www.uniontrib.com/news/uniontrib/fri/metro/news_1mi4read.html.

Phelps, S. F. (2006). Introduction to Part I: Situating adolescents' literacies. In D. E. Alvermann, K. A. Hinchman, D. W. Moore, S. F. Phelps, & D. R. Waff (Eds.), *Reconceptualizing the literacies in adolescents' lives* (2nd ed., pp. 3–4). Mahwah, NJ: Erlbaum.

Pitcher, S. M., Albright, L. K., DeLaney, C. J., Walker, N. T., Seunarinesingh, K., Mogge, S., et al. (2007). Assessing adolescents' motivation to read. *Journal of Adolescent & Adult Literacy, 50,* 378–396.

Rodin, J., Rennert, K., & Solomon, S. (1980). Intrinsic motivation for control: Fact or fiction. In A. Baum, J. E. Singer, & S. Valios (Eds.), *Advances in environmental psychology II* (pp. 64–86). Hillsdale, NJ: Erlbaum.

Schiefele, U. (1991). Interest, learning, and motivation. *Educational Psychologist, 26,* 299–323.

Stephens, L. (1995). *The complete guide to learning through community-service, grades K–9.* Boston, MA: Allyn & Bacon.

Switzer, G., Simmons, R., Dew, M., Regalski, J., & Wang, C. (1995). The effect of a school-based helper program on adolescent self-image, attitudes, and behavior. *Journal of Early Adolescence, 15,* 429–455.

Taylor, S. V., & Nesheim, D. W. (2000/2001). Making literacy real for "high-risk" adolescent emerging readers: An innovative application of readers' workshop. *Journal of Adolescent & Adult Literacy, 44,* 308–318.

Turner, J. (1995). The influence of classroom contexts on young children's motivation for literacy. *Reading Research Quarterly, 30,* 410–441.

Weiler, D., LaGoy, A., Crane, E., & Rovner, A. (1998). *An evaluation of K–12 service-learning in California: Phase II final report.* Emeryville, CA: RPP International with the Search Institute.

Weinstein, S. (2007). A love for the thing: The pleasures of rap as a literacy practice. *Journal of Adolescent and Adult Literacy, 50*(4), 270–281.

Wigfield, A. (1997). Children's motivations for reading and reading engagement. In J. T. Guthrie & A. Wigfield (Eds.), *Reading engagement: Motivating readers through integrated instruction* (pp. 14–33). Newark, DE: International Reading Association.

Zemelman, S., Daniels, H., & Hyde, A. (1998). *Best practice: New standards for teaching and learning in America's schools* (2nd ed.). Portsmouth, NH: Heinemann.

Connecting Parents, Teachers, and Students

FOCUS QUESTIONS

- What should teachers know about the home backgrounds of their learners?

- How can teachers forge a relationship with parents or caregivers that facilitates the literacy development of their students?

- What should parents be told about literacy development in grades 4–8?

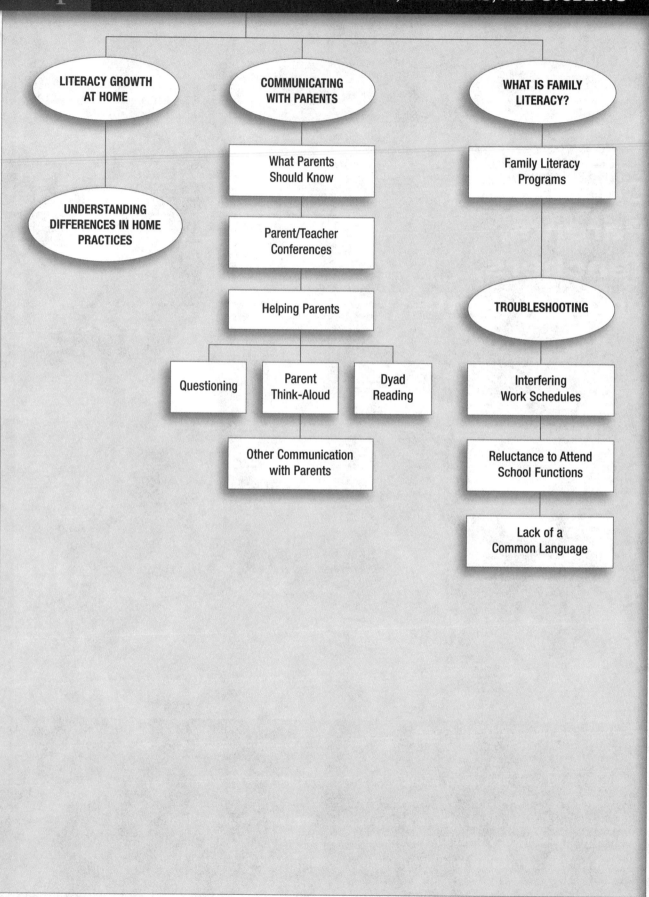

LITERACY GROWTH AT HOME

COMMUNICATING WITH PARENTS

WHAT IS FAMILY LITERACY?

What Parents Should Know

Family Literacy Programs

UNDERSTANDING DIFFERENCES IN HOME PRACTICES

Parent/Teacher Conferences

Helping Parents

TROUBLESHOOTING

Questioning

Parent Think-Aloud

Dyad Reading

Interfering Work Schedules

Other Communication with Parents

Reluctance to Attend School Functions

Lack of a Common Language

In the beginning of the school year, Ms. Janos has little success getting eleven-year-old Lydia's mother, a single parent from the Caribbean, to come to parent–teacher conferences. Mrs. Baptiste, a vivacious woman from St. Croix, U.S. Virgin Islands, who speaks a lilting Cruzan dialect, shares with Ms. Janos that she had to drop out of school at age 16 to care for younger siblings. She feels intimidated by the thought of going to an educational institution so different physically and culturally from that with which she is familiar. Mrs. Baptiste returns neither Ms. Janos's phone calls nor notes sent home with Lydia. Unperturbed, Ms. Janos quickly decides to make a home visit. She asks Lydia to arrange a time, at her mother's convenience, when she can pay a social visit. The two women meet one Friday afternoon and, over tea and Johnny cakes graciously offered by Lydia's mother, discuss nothing about school; instead, they chat about their shared affection for the little girl. The next time Mrs. Baptiste is summoned, she is less fearful, having fond memories of the respectful human connection that Ms. Janos has forged.

This evening, Ms. Janos smiles warmly as she greets Lydia's mother at the door of her classroom. She asks Mrs. Baptiste to sit down, and the two briefly exchange pleasantries. Then Ms. Janos shares Lydia's progress reports and discusses her improvement in reading and writing. She shows Mrs. Baptiste a portfolio of Lydia's writing at the beginning of the year, comparing it with a sample piece that she recently wrote and had asked to be included in her portfolio. Mrs. Baptiste is impressed. Ms. Janos explains, in simple terms, exactly what literacy skills Lydia has mastered thus far and explains her plans for continuing to meet Lydia's instructional needs.

The conference ends, as such conferences often do, with Mrs. Baptiste asking what she can do to help her child to become a successful student. However, she frowns and puts her head down as she reveals that she herself is barely able to read. Ms. Janos assures Mrs. Baptiste that there is much she can do to further her daughter's academic career. First, she acknowledges the fact that Mrs. Baptiste and her daughter have an enviable, close relationship and talk so easily together in such an animated fashion. She explains that such "talk" is crucial to literacy development. Second, she suggests that Mrs. Baptiste have Lydia read to *her* whenever it is convenient and that both of them discuss what was read in an enjoyable, pleasant atmosphere. Finally, she tells her that, in later meetings, she will offer a few specific "tips" of learning activities for selective objectives and instruct her in their use. But, for today, enough has been accomplished. Lydia's mother leaves the classroom beaming, reassured that her lack of a formal education will in no way impede her precious daughter's progress. Indeed, she has heard that she is already doing much "right," and she has been amazed to learn that simply by listening to Lydia read she will be furthering her growth. A true partnership has been formed.

LITERACY GROWTH AT HOME

Literacy was once defined as the ability to read and write. It was considered a set of neutral and objective skills independent of social context or ideology (Street, 1995; Verhoeven & Snow, 2001). Ethnographic research, however, has shed light on a wide range of culturally specific literacy practices among different communities. This research provides evidence that literacy involves much more than simply encoding and decoding symbols and is becoming much more complex and difficult to define (Bowman, 2002; Delgado-Gaitan, 2001; Heath, 1983; Valdés, 1996).

Moreover, literacy now extends beyond the acquisition of reading and writing skills to speaking, listening, viewing, and visually representing, and it entails the ability to use these skills in a socially appropriate context. The very notion of literacy is also evolving to include the wide array of skills required to function in a technological society. For example, *literacy* has come to refer to a wider domain of activities, from media literacy and computer literacy to citizenship literacy (Kinzer & Leander, 2003; Wilson, 2002). Are parents equipped to deal with all the basics of literacy, let alone the "new literacies" of the twenty-first century, at home?

Every teacher hopes for a class full of students whose parents or caretakers care about and support their literacy growth at home. Teachers know, intuitively and through research, that such students will have a much easier road to becoming readers and writers. Indeed, research from the 1970s on consistently identifies and reports strong correlations between parents reading to and with their children and the children's later success in literacy (Anderson et al., 1985; Chomsky, 1972; Laosa, 1982; National Center for Family Literacy, 2002; Teale & Sulzby, 1986). Other research has attempted to identify the essential nature of what transpires during parent–child reading interactions to make them so beneficial. Lancy and Bergin (1992) found that students who are more fluent and positive about reading came from parent–child pairs who viewed reading as fun, kept stories moving with a "meaning-seeking" rather than a purely "decoding" orientation, and encouraged questions and humor while reading together.

Teachers have long been telling parents simply to "read to your child!" but perhaps this exhortation has been misguided in the light of research findings. For example, Lancy, Draper, and Boyce (1989) describe the parents of good readers as using *expansionist strategies,* which include adding personal information and explanations, or scaffolding, as their children grapple to understand stories. For example, the parent might start reading a story with the child and then make guesses as to what will happen next, modeling the comprehension strategy of making predictions. Over time, the parent takes a less active role and encourages the child to utilize these strategies when reading. This is especially useful with a story that has been read multiple times. According to Lancy et al. (1989), when a child experiences difficulty, the parent of a good reader tends to make a mild joke of it, thus diffusing anxiety, whereas the parent of a poorer reader treats a decoding error as a serious infraction, sometimes even covering up an illustration in order to prevent "cheating."

UNDERSTANDING DIFFERENCES IN HOME PRACTICES

Although the statistics in the box accompanying this discussion may appear alarming, they are no reason to give up hope. An understanding of the literacy practices that DO occur in the homes of at-risk students can help teachers respect and build upon those practices.

Because many teachers come from middle-class backgrounds, there is often an unfortunate tendency to view effective home literacy practices to be only those that teachers recall experiencing in their own comfortable homes. The image that most often comes to mind, then, for most teachers is a young child sitting on the lap of a parent—usually a young female—while a large story book is being read. Such an image sets up the notion that parents who do not read books to their child in this manner are somehow to blame for their child's lack of progress in literacy. However, it is important to consider the wide range of literacy practices that may occur in the homes of a variety of diverse students. This approach allows us to build more effectively upon the literacy experiences that students from a host of backgrounds bring with them to school (Thomas, Fazio, & Stiefelmeyer, 1999).

Statistics on Today's Students and Their Home Environment

- Parental literacy is one of the single most important indicators of a child's success. The National Assessment of Education Progress (NAEP) has concluded that youngsters whose parents are functionally illiterate are twice as likely as other students to be functionally illiterate themselves.

- By age four, children who live in poor families will have heard 32 *million* fewer words than children living in professional families.

- One in five, or 20 percent, of America's children five years old and younger live in poverty.

- Some 30 million adults in the United States have extremely limited literacy skills. If one teacher could teach 100 adults to read, we would need 300,000 adult education teachers to meet this need.

- The Hispanic population is the largest minority in the United States and has the highest school dropout rate. More than two in five Hispanics living in America age 25 and older have not graduated from high school. (National Center for Family Literacy, 2007)

In fact, it appears that literacy in the home and community is very much a part of people's culture. Moreover, each community has its own special literate traditions. Shirley Brice Heath's (1983) seminal investigation of two different African American communities showed how literacy may vary widely depending on the cultural context of students' homes and communities. There were fewer reading materials in the first community she observed, but there seemed to be a collaborative approach to literacy. In the second community, a higher value was placed on literacy in terms of the people's statements, but not necessarily their actions. Both communities hold differing beliefs about how their children will learn to read and write; however, neither community's literacy concepts and practices match well with the concepts and practices of the formal literacy that is taught in school.

It is critical for teachers to keep in mind that most parents—regardless of income level or cultural or ethnic background—value education for their children. However, different parents may have differing perceptions of what it means to be literate, and they may not always be aware of the most effective tactics for them to take to foster literacy with their child. Several researchers have reported the high value placed on literacy by many low-income families. For example, Delgado-Gaitan (1987) found that the possibility of a better education for their children was cited as a major reason for Hispanics to immigrate to the United States. Taylor and Dorsey-Gaines (1988), studying low-income parents whose children succeed in school, noted extraordinary sacrifices and efforts being made by the parents in the interest of their children's education, despite the parents' limited educational levels. Fitzgerald, Spiegel, and Cunningham (1991), in a study of low- and high-income parents, reported that the low-income families rate the value of education even higher than the high-income families.

Perhaps a more important difference among parents concerns exactly what they view literacy to be. Baker et al. (1994) found that low-income Hispanic parents help their children acquire literacy mainly by emphasizing letter names and spelling–sound correspondences. Other studies on reading improvement with Latino students underscore the importance of parents reading aloud to and with their children. Ortiz and Ordonez-Jasis (2005) found that Latino parents like to choose books and enjoy sharing them with their children if they find the materials interesting, valuable, and relevant to their lives. Therefore, these researchers suggest that teachers include in their classroom libraries "multicultural literature that reflects the rich and diverse realities of Latino families" (p. 116). They recommend that middle-school teachers select books that reflect the Latino traditions, celebrate the richness of the culture, tell personal stories about people who share similar experiences and values, and address social issues and concerns (see box and Appendix A for some suggestions). Inviting students to discuss their readings with their families encourages strong home–school connections. If the students are then encouraged to share their parents' responses to the readings, children and their parents begin to believe that the teacher respects their culture and background. Though this study looked only at Latino families, the same principles certainly hold true for families from all diverse cultures.

Programs that model instructional strategies that parents of English learners can use with their own children are very helpful, such as the home literacy activities mentioned later in this chapter, and often prove to be successful in building connections between home and school.

In another study on parental literacy practices, Baker et al. (1994) reported that parents in low-income families spend much time explicitly instructing their children in the work and practice elements of reading, whereas middle-income parents use a more playful approach, through stories and play. Literacy is presented and modeled as an enjoyable pastime and an important avenue through which to understand the world. Knowing that this difference might occur, it seems that it would be helpful to emphasize to all parents that students who find literacy learning painful tend to avoid books and reading, whereas those who learn to enjoy reading for its own sake are more likely to ask for books and read recreationally, thus becoming more successful (Baker, Serpell, & Sonnenschein, 1995).

Teachers should be aware that all parents participate in some sort of literacy activities with their children. True, some parents may have problems reading and writing, or English may not be their first language, but nearly all still engage in a wide range of literacy activities in the course of their daily lives. In his research, Barton (1997) found many examples of parents experiencing difficulties with written communication who nonetheless kept diaries, maintained household accounts, wrote poetry, took phone messages, and sent letters. These parents dealt with shopping lists, bills, forms to fill out, recipes, junk mail, and TV schedules. Such parents should not be perceived as unintelligent people living in barren homes "waiting to be filled up by literacy," as the media would often lead us to believe. For the most part, adults who admit to problems with reading and writing are ordinary people leading ordinary lives and, if they have children, like other parents, they are deeply concerned about their children's education.

Educators are beginning to move beyond thinking of just the mother in a family as the key partner in literacy with the schools and are now including the father, siblings, and the cadre of relations and family friends whom children often cite as important in their literacy lives. Additionally, focusing

Multicultural Literature for Parents and Students to Read Together

NATIVE AMERICAN

Erdrich, L. (1999). *The Birchbark House.* Hyperion.

Sneve, V. D. H. (1989). *Dancing Teepees: Poems of American Indian Youth. Holiday.*

LATINO

Cisnero, S. (1983). *The House on Mango Street.* Art Publico.

Ryan, P. M. (2004). *Becoming Naomi Leon.* Scholastic.

ASIAN

Kadohata, C. (2004). *Kira-Kira.* Atheneum.

Whelan, G. (2000). *Homeless Bird.* HarperCollins.

AFRICAN AMERICAN

Freedman, R. (2004). *The Voice That Challenged a Nation: Marian Anderson and the Struggle for Equal Rights.* Clarion.

McWhorter, D. (2004). *A Dream of Freedom: The Civil Rights Movement from 1954–1968.* Scholastic.

exclusively on parent–child relations excludes important social agencies and community resources that may enhance literacy behaviors. Educators are also moving beyond the notion that parents should read only to young children, and recognizing that homes are significant places for a myriad of literacy practices to occur from infancy all the way up to the teenage years, and that parents can often learn from their children, too. Literacy learning can be a symbiotic event within families. Finally, rather then asking parents to replicate what teachers do in schools, teachers are now trying to support the practices parents are already doing, in their homes, to promote literacy (Barton, 1997).

COMMUNICATING WITH PARENTS

In this section, we first provide important information that should be communicated to parents about their child's literacy learning. Then we discuss the many ways teachers can communicate with the home.

What Parents Should Know about Literacy in Grades 4–8

There are certain basic understandings about the nature of literacy that, if understood by parents, will positively influence any assistance they offer their children at home. They must recognize that the simple naming of words, or "word calling," is not true reading and that until a meaningful communication is taking place between the author and the reader, there is no real reading by an acceptable definition of that process. Parents can be informed of the factors that influence that communication and lead to what we call reading comprehension.

First, comprehension is affected by decoding skills. Students who fail to obtain meaning from the printed page may fail to do so because their attention is so intently focused on trying to recognize individual words. It is difficult to maintain the gist of a passage while spending an inordinate amount of time struggling to identify its components. It is essential that students develop fluency in word recognition if maximum comprehension is to be attained. Parents need to be told, therefore, that both decoding and comprehension lead to proficient reading.

Second, comprehension is affected by experience. Essentially, what the reader will get from the printed page will only be in proportion to the experiences that the reader brings to it. Both comprehension and interpretation are based on past as well as present experiences, and the wider and deeper the past experiences the reader has had, the more basis that reader has for making judgments and, thus, the better will be the reader's comprehension and interpretation. No amount of teaching in school can offset a lack of experience, so it is important for parents to provide a wide range of experiences for their children and to discuss them at length, providing an expansion of vocabulary. A simple maxim can be shared with parents: *The more a child brings to a book, the more that child will take from it.*

Finally, comprehension is affected by fluency of language development in the language of instruction. Comprehension is dependent on the ease with which the reader decodes printed symbols into already mastered oral language patterns. If oral language is inadequate, there will be no fluency. Underlying reading is a spoken language in which written words must be translated. Inadequacy in language fluency in general, and in knowledge of the meaning of English words specifically, will limit comprehension. However, knowledge of reading strategies and meaning-getting techniques in one language transfers to another. Linguistically diverse parents who do not speak English but who are literate in their native language, therefore, can still help their children with reading comprehension through modeling and discussions of how they think through the reading process.

Parent–Teacher Conferences

Good communication right from the start of the new school year is essential between the home and the school in any balanced and comprehensive literacy program. This is particularly important in schools with diverse populations (Chavkin & Gonzalez, 1995). Because most educators are aware of the need, many schools provide several parent–teacher conference days when teachers are free to talk with the parents about the progress of their child. The parent–teacher conference can be a fruitful time for the teacher to explain to the parents or caregivers in clear terms the literacy program and how their child is progressing within the program. Moreover, it is the ideal time to let the parents know how much their partnership is needed to reinforce the notion upon which a balanced and comprehensive literacy program is based: that literacy activities are important in the world and enjoyable. After teachers have explained the literacy program, many parents will want to know how they can help their child at home. It is axiomatic that parents are concerned about their children. They often need reassurance that their concern is appropriate and that they possess the ability to take part in the partnership. The following points are helpful to consider in this regard:

1. Set up the conference with the comfort of the parents in mind. Rather than sitting behind a desk, as an authority figure, choose a setting in which all adults can sit side by side to create a friendlier tone.

2. Understand that parents have a right to their anxiety. It is quite normal for them to wonder how their child compares with her peers.

3. Inform parents about their child's strengths and instructional needs while sympathizing with their concerns. "Don't worry" is a phrase that has little value and should be avoided.

4. Refrain from being judgmental; instead, actively listen to parents, always seeking common ground. Instead of blaming them for what may not have occurred in the home, praise them for their concern and desire to help, engendering a feeling of true partnership.

5. Focus on specific constructive suggestions rather than vague generalities. "Your child needs help breaking down words into syllables" is much more helpful than "Your child is not reading well."

6. Discuss the student's progress using examples, such as actual progress forms, test results, or samples of the student's work.

7. Accept parents' questions and provide clear, honest responses.

8. Thank parents for attending and let them know that you are available for additional conferences if there are further concerns.

What brings parents to school? When both the school district and individual schools make a concerted effort to let parents and caregivers know that they want them, that they need them, and that they have valuable information to share with them about their child's literacy needs, they will come, if flexible scheduling makes attendance possible. Schools must also make clear that they respect and value information and insights parents might bring to bear about their children and their particular needs. Therefore, schools must take a positive approach and work with the strengths and needs of the families involved. Local radio and television stations as well as newspapers can help publicize the need for caring adults to meet with their children's teachers. In addition, the chamber of commerce can be asked to send letters to all area employers requesting that they release parents, and caregivers from work to attend partnership conferences.

Conference scheduling is vitally important. A variety of times should be scheduled for teachers to conduct the conferences because some parents cannot come to school during the regular school day. In order for this arrangement to be successful, the district's administrative unit must be fully committed to the partnership concept and arrange for teachers to receive compensation for their efforts.

Conferences can be productive and pleasant for both teachers and parents if teachers follow a few simple procedures. Begin the conference with a friendly and relaxed greeting. Adopt the tone of a friendly acquaintance with the parents, reinforcing the idea, in every way possible, that you are all on the same team. If the parents speak little or no English, arrange to have an aide or community member to translate or invite an older English-speaking sibling to perform this important task. In advance, ask the student to teach you a few polite phrases (e.g., "How are you?" or "I am very pleased to meet you.") in his home language to make the parents feel welcomed. Begin and end the conference on a positive note, addressing what is noteworthy and unique about the student. Focus on specific constructive suggestions (e.g., "Your child needs to concentrate on following written directions in sequence") rather than vague generalities ("Your child is not reading as well as her peers"). Discussing the student's progress using actual progress forms or work samples can help in this regard. Finally, offer the parents specific activities they can do at home, such as those offered in the next section, to help the child with any deficiencies or to enhance reading interest and proficiency.

Helping Parents Help Their Children

The most commonly heard query during parent conferences crosses all ethnic, cultural, and socioeconomic lines. It is, "What can I do to help my child become a better reader?" While this chapter offers a general idea of what kinds of practices are helpful, parents are also asking for some very specific activities that they can do with their children to help them succeed at literacy. Many teachers tell parents simply, "Turn off the TV and have your child read for 15 minutes every day." This is excellent advice, and if every parent did this there would no doubt be fewer reading failures; however, for parents capable and willing, several other activities may be undertaken with their children that will go even further to help the students comprehend well and enjoy reading. Many teachers have had great success conducting two or three workshops each academic year, each focusing on one activity. Three such activities are discussed next. Having refreshments or a parent potluck draws many parents, and a format of simple instructions for the activity followed by practicing the activity in small groups ensures that parents will have the confidence to try the activity at home with their own child.

Encourage parents to explore with their children the kinds of questions that provoke critical and creative thinking.

Home literacy activity: Questioning

Encourage parents to follow up the critical-thinking strategies introduced in class by exploring at home with their children the kinds of questions that extend and provoke critical and creative thinking. Instruct parents to follow every paragraph or so with a thought-provoking question that can *not* be answered by a simple yes or no. Tell them that questions such as "Why do you think . . . ?" and "What if . . . ?" almost always fulfill this purpose. Begin the workshop by brainstorming a list of questions that will be useful for expanding comprehension, and discuss the kind of responses they will likely generate. Then follow the instruction by giving every attendee a short story containing several paragraphs. Have parents contribute appropriate questions for each paragraph and praise all responses. If a contributed response is not appropriate, accept it and then rework it into a useful question. Example: A parent offers, "Did the boy go into the woods?" (the answer is given in the paragraph). This response can be accepted and then slightly modified into, "Why do you think the boy went into the woods?" The reader must then consider the information in the story, compare it with what he knows of the world, and create an answer.

Home literacy activity: Parent think-aloud

Parents who already read with their children can learn to extend the activity into a comprehension-modeling practice by utilizing think-alouds. Explain to parents that, as its name implies, this activity is one in which the parent shares aloud everything she is thinking as a paragraph is read, including these mental processes:

- *Making predictions:* "I bet Jerry will ask for his dog back."
- *Imaging:* "Ooh—that meadow reminds me of the field behind Mr. Darrow's farm where we used to hike, remember?"
- *Generalizing:* "So I guess these polar bears hibernate like the grizzlies we were reading about."
- *Using the context to figure out the meaning of unknown words:* "It says an Alaskan lifestyle is the *antithesis* of a Californian lifestyle. Since it seems they are way different, I'll bet *antithesis* means the opposite."

Using adult passages, model how parents might do a think-aloud by slowing their thinking way down and offering a window to the brain for the benefit of the child. Invite parents to add their observations about the passage to yours, praising comments that would be particularly helpful for children to have modeled. Pass out a passage to each attendee and have pairs of parents practice reading a paragraph out loud, sharing their meaning-gaining thought processes as they do so. Have them switch roles after each paragraph so that both parents get a chance to practice the technique. Finally, encourage parents to try this activity at home as they are doing shared reading. Explain that children can be invited to share their thoughts with their parents as they get the gist of the activity.

Home literacy activity: Dyad reading

A third activity for parents is one that is especially effective for informational text and, thus, will help parents be of assistance when their child has reading to do in the content areas of science and social studies. Explain to parents that dyad reading is a way to have their child read aloud and be sure the child is understanding what she is reading. Instruct them that if only one text is available, as is often the case with content area textbooks, the parent and child will sit side by side and take turns reading aloud, rotating after every paragraph. When the reader has finished the paragraph, the reader will summarize it for the listener, who will then add any material that may have been overlooked by the reader. They will then switch roles. To introduce this activity, explain the steps as you model them with a partner or attendee who has been briefed in advance. It is helpful to model the activity using one text, because this is the way it will be used at home, but for the purpose of the demonstration, the passage may be reproduced for the attendees. Additionally, explain to parents that an effective summary is a shortened version of the original—no more than a third in length—that contains the main idea as well as important details. Answer any questions parents may have about the steps of the procedure. Hand out new informational passages to pairs of parents and have them practice doing dyad reading, rotating roles after each paragraph. Encourage them to use this technique at home whenever their child has homework in the content areas that requires reading.

Other Communication with Parents

Besides conducting regularly scheduled conferences and workshops, teachers can keep parents informed in a variety of ways. One way is through a monthly newsletter. An attractive, simply written flyer sent to parents can help explain the child's literacy program and help avoid misunderstandings and confusion. The newsletter can also be a vehicle through which to convey or reiterate the suggestions for home reading previously discussed. Additionally, any questions that parents have been asking, or those that frequently come up every year, can be addressed in the letter.

Progress notes are a more personal way to keep parents informed about their child. At frequent intervals, short notes can be written about a child in a positive, congratulatory tone when the child has completed a book, asked an incisive question, or written an especially interesting piece. Such notes might also include a few open-ended questions for parents to ask their child about a story that has been read in class, or some vocabulary to discuss with their child. Parents might also be asked to listen to their child read a passage from a book recently finished so they can share in the enjoyable experience of completing a book and celebrating success.

A special idea to bring parents to the school for an occasion other than the formal parent–teacher conference is the reading festival. Any number of activities can be planned that have the parents, children, and invited community members coming together to share favorite books, articles, and stories. Parents can be asked to bring in their favorite children's book to read with the class, if they wish. Community members—especially those role models whom youngsters do not ordinarily associate with reading, such as firefighters, sports figures, and police officers—can be invited to read with small groups of children, or choral reading can be done with adults and children taking appropriate, or reverse, roles. Art activities can be planned, such as creating and playing reading games, or constructing dioramas or murals in connection with a favorite book. Such a festival works well in collaboration with a book fair or a book swap. The book fair can be organized with the help of a local bookstore or a children's paperback book company such as Scholastic. A book swap, on the other hand, requires less advance planning and can be arranged simply by asking students to bring in old books and magazines from home. They can then take turns reading the blurbs on the back covers and auction them, while teachers help parents match books to readers by interest and reading levels.

WHAT IS FAMILY LITERACY?

The term *family literacy* is used in several ways: (1) to describe the study of literacy in the family, (2) to describe a set of interventions related to literacy development of young children, and (3) to refer to a set of programs designed to enhance the literacy skills of more than one family member (Britto & Brooks-Gunn, 2001; Handel, 1999; Wasik et al., 2000).

Historically children were educated in the home, and parents were recognized as a child's first teacher. Children were able to see how literacy and numeracy skills were used for managing everyday domestic tasks, such as taking telephone messages, making shopping lists, following recipes, paying bills, and so forth. Reading stories in the lap of a family member, children learn to read for enjoyment. But children whose parents have low literacy

www

National Center for Family Literacy
www.famlit.org

levels or do not speak English at all may have few opportunities to grasp these benefits.

The ways in which parents interact with their child are paramount to the child's burgeoning literacy abilities, but some parents may require more assistance than teachers can offer in a traditional school-based workshop as we have discussed. Research is increasingly supporting the notion that parent–child interactions are often more complex than just reading to children and providing them with literacy materials. In fact, there is evidence that simply telling a parent to read to a child may even be counterproductive and lead to quite different behavior than the teacher intended, depending on the parent's background. Home-school programs need to be nonthreatening and the activities enjoyable. Easy-to-use materials should be introduced to students in school first (Morrow, Kuhn, & Schwanenflugel, 2007). To help families improve the literacy of all members, family literacy programs have evolved.

The ways in which parents interact with their children are paramount to their growing literacy.

Family Literacy Programs

For the past 20 years, educational policies have promoted family literacy programs in schools and community-based organizations. Family literacy appears in the Elementary and Secondary Education Act, Reading Excellence Act, Workforce Investment Act, Community Services Block Grant Act, and the Head Start Act (National Center for Family Literacy, 2002). The development of family literacy programs has drawn on multiple academic fields, among them adult literacy, English learning, child literacy education—in particular, the field of emergent literacy and special education—early childhood development, cognitive psychology, and parent education.

Family literacy programs were created to help adults develop literacy skills while promoting the learning success of their children. Reading together builds confidence for low-literacy parents who might be reluctant to read to other adults, provides a positive model of literacy for children, and fosters parent–child bonding. By supporting adult literacy, early childhood education, and parenting skills, family literacy programs aim to break the cycle of intergenerational illiteracy.

Family literacy programs generally address the following interrelated components:

- Adult literacy, basic skills, and life skills: To increase motivation, skills, and knowledge; to help parents find work or prepare for further training.
- Early childhood education: To help preschool children prepare for academic and social success in school.
- Parent education and support groups: To allow parents to share questions, concerns, and strategies with their peers and counselors.
- Parent–child interaction: To provide role models and structured situations for positive parent–child interactions.

Family Literacy Websites

The Home School Internet Resource Center, www.rsts.net

Provides an exciting, safe educational environment for the home schooling family. Free services include software, a used curriculum exchange, e-pals, a home school news magazine, curriculum reviews, and an inexhaustible list of subject reference links.

PBS It's My Life, http://pbskids.org/itsmylife/parents/resources/middleschool.html

It's My Life is funded by the Corporation for Public Broadcasting to create safe educational online media activities for children aged 9 to 12. Parents and children can read informative articles, share stories, play games, and get advice from experts.

International Reading Association, www.reading.org

An organization of teachers, librarians, researchers, parents, and others dedicated to promoting literacy for all.

National Center for Literacy, www.famlit.org

Parade Family Literacy InfoLine provides referrals for family literacy programs at a local level.

National Center for Literacy, www.nifl.gov

The NIFL site offers free copies of current publications on literacy.

Reading Is Fundamental, www.rif.org

Develops and delivers children's and family literacy programs that help prepare young children for reading and motivate school-aged children to read. Trains literacy providers, parents, and others to prepare all children to become lifelong readers.

See the box above for online resources for family literacy.

The federal government has set up a series of family literacy programs, such as Even Start, designed both to increase the literacy skills of the parents and to provide positive strategies and attitudes for enhancing their child's literacy at home. Projects are targeted for speakers of English as a first or second language and are located in a variety of settings, such as libraries, schools, universities, or family centers. A wide variety of activities take place in these programs, ranging from discussion groups to activities for parent–child interactions, as well as direct teaching of literacy skills for the parent leading to the attainment of a high school diploma.

In literacy programs aimed at both children and adults, there are various perspectives on what family literacy should be. Most initiatives act directly on the need most adult participants feel to help their children become literate, while many also stress the vital role of community in education. Additionally, family literacy, in general, provides the possibility of assisting adults in a way that need not be constrained by intimidating traditions of formal education but, instead, actually draws upon the knowledge that each family already possesses. Most educators working with families realize that there is no single road to becoming literate and that they must seek the help of the parents to ascertain what positive practices are already occurring in the home.

Mikulecky and Lloyd (1995) evaluated the impact of family literacy programs in five cities on parent–child literacy-related interactions. After approximately six months in such programs, significant gains were reported in such activities as parent–child home reading, visits to local libraries, quantity of literacy materials found in the home, and the children's independent literacy activities. For example, children's avowed reading of books and magazines increased by 60 percent, to more than once a day. Morrow, Tracey, and Maxwell (1995) summarized the results of more than 30 family literacy programs and found similar positive results. Their results supported a conclusion that such programs are correlated with more parental participation in school events and appear to help children not only have a more positive attitude toward school but actually experience more academic success.

It appears that long-term, community-based family literacy programs can be an important adjunct to the relationship the classroom teacher builds with the parent. The classroom teacher can support such programs by acknowledging that literacy is an issue whose domain is not exclusive to public schools.

TROUBLESHOOTING

Getting parents the help they need for general literacy interactions at home is the focus of family literacy programs. But what about parents with whom the teacher has been totally unable to communicate? Certainly, the value of the parent–teacher conference to discuss specific issues related to the literacy progress of students cannot be underestimated. Therefore, this section addresses several factors that preclude some parents' attendance at any school functions.

Interfering Work Schedules

Most schools have several parent–teacher days when teachers are free to talk with parents or caretakers about their child's progress. While this can be an ideal time to talk about the child's literacy, some parents work during the day and for various compelling reasons are not able to take time off to attend these important sessions. Because it is inappropriate—and impossible—for the teacher to evaluate the parents' priorities and work responsibilities, some schools try to rectify the problem with flexible scheduling. Having some conference slots later in the day or in the evening (with the teachers given the morning to prepare) has been helpful in many schools. Teachers who have adopted this flexible plan report being successful in reaching parents who had previously not attended conferences, citing job conflicts.

Reluctance to Attend School Functions

Some parents and caretakers may be reluctant to attend any school functions because they feel uncomfortable in the school environment. They themselves may not have done well in school, and for them anything related to school holds unpleasant memories—much as the dentist's office does for those who suffered painful experiences as a child. Furthermore, parents from certain other cultural groups may hold the teacher in such high esteem that they may feel ashamed of being unfamiliar with the language and customs and fear embarrassing themselves in the formal academic environment. These parents are most often the ones teachers usually wish to see in regard to their child's reading habits and attitudes. One suggestion to alleviate this problem is for the teacher to initially go to the family's home environment. A handwritten note or brief telephone call saying the teacher will be in the area on a particular day and requesting to visit for a chat is rarely refused. During this visit, nothing educational need be discussed, but the teacher should look for common ground with the parent; usually the adults' common care and concern for the child is sufficient. A warm and down-to-earth attitude by the teacher often forges an initial rapport that makes the parents' attempt to attend the next conference more likely.

Lack of a Common Language

A third barrier for parents is a tendency on the part of many teachers to use the technical "jargon" of literacy with the parents. Some parents refrain from attending meetings about their child because they hold the perception that they would not be astute enough to understand the teacher's "educated language," and, unfortunately, at times teachers are to blame for this concern. Perhaps in an effort to make the field of education appear as a true profession, educators have acquired a large vocabulary of very specific literacy terminology. *Dyslexia* is one such term (which, to our knowledge, no one has yet adequately defined) that might be better defined for parents more simply as "a problem with the child's reading," followed by a clear explanation of what the problem is, how it is being corrected in class, and how the parents might best help the child at home. Other literacy concepts can also be discussed in lay terms, with the outcome being that the parents feel they are capable of understanding what the teacher is talking about and able to help. To invite parents to be true partners in the education of their child is to convince them they can communicate as equals.

SUMMARY

To suggest that the relationship among the child, the parents or caretakers, and the school is a "triangle affair" is certainly nothing new. But it is not always appreciated just how much communication and sensitivity are required to make this relationship work optimally so that there is a true synergy between the student, the home, and the school. Teachers often need to be the prime movers, envisioning innovative ways to get the parents—from all cultural and linguistic backgrounds—to school, or in some cases, even visiting them in their homes. Teachers need to make parents or caregivers feel at ease by talking to them in clear terms about the progress of their son or daughter and finding ways to explain how parents or caregivers can reinforce the goals of a balanced and comprehensive literacy program at home. Teachers also must be aware of current research that supports the notion that parents, regardless of income level or educational background, care about their children's success in literacy and only need to be guided to the best practices to augment the school's literacy program. Finally, teachers need to be aware of new family literacy programs in their community that may offer possibilities for parents not only to help their children but also to further their own educational prowess. Such programs add another dimension to the triangle, letting parents and children know that the entire community sees reading as a positive and worthwhile activity, and providing a paraphrase for the popular statement: "It takes a village to *educate* a child."

Questions
FOR JOURNAL WRITING AND DISCUSSION

1. Recall from your childhood any literacy activities that took place in your family. How do you think these activities might have influenced your later academic success?

2. After reading this chapter, why do you think some educators object to labeling the children of poor parents "at risk"? How might you respond to a colleague who claims that "poor parents don't really care about their children's literacy development"?

3. What do you think parents should know about the literacy development of children in grades 4–8?

Suggestions
FOR PROJECTS AND FIELD ACTIVITIES

1. Arrange to sit in on a parent–teacher conference in a grade 4–8 class-room. To what extent were the suggestions in this chapter followed? What do you feel might have made the parents or caregivers more comfortable?

2. Read a short story to a small group of children in grades 4–8 using either the questioning or the think-aloud activity. Do you feel sharing such an activity with parents is preferable to telling them simply to "read to your child"? Why or why not?

3. Find out if there are any family literacy programs in your area. If there are, visit a center to determine what its programs offer and how often they are utilized by the parents of schoolchildren in your community. Share your findings with the other students in your class.

REFERENCES

Anderson, R. C., Hiebert, E. H., Scott, J. A., & Wilkinson, I. (1985). *Becoming a nation of readers: The report of the Commission on Reading.* Washington, DC: The National Institute of Education.

Baker, L., Serpell, R., & Sonnenschein, S. (1995). Opportunities for literacy learning in the homes of urban preschoolers. In L. Morrow (Ed.), *Family literacy: Connections in schools and communities* (pp. 236–252). Newark, DE: International Reading Association.

Baker, L., Sonnenschein, S., Serpell, R., Fernandez-Fein, S., & Scher, D. (1994). *Contexts of emergent literacy: Every-day home experiences of urban prekindergarten children* (Research report). Athens, GA: National Reading Research Center, University of Georgia and University of Maryland.

Barton, D. (1997). Family literacy programmes and home literacy practices. In D. Taylor (Ed.), *Many families, many literacies: An international declaration of principles.* Portsmouth, NH: Heinemann.

Bowman, B. (2002). Love to read: An introduction. In B. Bowman (Ed.), *Love to read: Essays in developing and enhancing early literacy skills of African American children* (pp. vii–ix). Washington, DC: National Black Child Development Institute.

Britto, P. R., & Brooks-Gunn, J. (2001). The role of family literacy environments in promoting young children's emerging literacy skills. Concluding comments. *New Directions for Child and Adolescent Development, 92*, 91–99.

Chavkin, N. F., & Gonzalez, D. L. (1995). *Forging partnerships between Mexican American parents and the schools.* Charleston, WV: ERIC Clearinghouse on Rural Education and Small Schools, No. ED 388489.

Chomsky, C. (1972). Stages in language development and reading exposure. *Harvard Educational Review, 42*, 1–33.

Delgado-Gaitan, C. (1987). Mexican adult literacy: New directions for immigrants. In S. R. Goldman & H. Trueba (Eds.), *Becoming literate in a second language* (pp. 9–32). Norwood, NJ: Ablex.

Delgado-Gaitan, C. (2001). *The power of community: Mobilizing for family and schooling.* New York: Rowman & Littlefield.

Fitzgerald, J., Spiegel, D. L., & Cunningham, J. W. (1991). The relationship between parental literacy level and perceptions of emergent literacy. *Journal of Reading Behavior, 13*(2), 191–212.

Handel, R. D. (1999). *Building family literacy in an urban community.* New York: Teachers College Press.

Heath, S. B. (1983). *Ways with words: Language, life, and work in communities and classrooms.* Cambridge, MA: Cambridge University Press.

Kinzer, C. K., & Leander, K. (2003). Technology and the language arts: Implications of an expanded definition of literacy. In J. Flood, D. Lapp, J. R. Squire, & J. M. Jensen (Eds.), *Handbook of research on teaching the English language arts* (2nd ed., pp. 534–545). Mahwah, NJ: Lawrence Erlbaum.

Lancy, D. F., & Bergin, C. (1992). *The role of parents in supporting beginning reading.* Paper presented at the annual meeting of the American Educational Research Association, San Francisco.

Lancy, D. F., Draper, K. D., & Boyce, G. (1989). Parental influence on children's acquisition of reading. *Contemporary Issues in Reading, 4*(1), 83–93.

Laosa, L. M. (1982). School, occupation, culture, and family: The impact of parental schooling on the parent–child relationship. *Journal of Educational Psychology, 74*(6), 791–827.

Mikulecky, L., & Lloyd, P. (1995). *Parent–child interactions in family literacy programs.* Paper presented at the National Center for Family Literacy conference, Louisville, KY.

Morrow, L. M. (1995). *Family literacy connections in schools and communities.* Newark, DE: International Reading Association.

Morrow, L. M., Kuhn, M. R., & Schwanenflugel, P. (2007). The family fluency program. *The Reading Teacher, 60*, 322–333.

Morrow, L. M., Tracey, D. H., & Maxwell, C. M. (Eds.). (1995). *A survey of family literacy.* Newark, DE: International Reading Association.

National Center for Family Literacy. (2002). *Family literacy: A strategy for educational improvement.* Louisville, KY: National Governors Association. Retrieved June 18, 2007, from www.nga.org/Files/pdf/110802LITERACY.pdf.

Ortiz, R. W., & Ordonez-Jasis, R. (October, 2005). Leyendo juntos (Reading together): New directions for Latino parents' literacy involvement. *The Reading Teacher, 59*, 110–121.

Street, B. V. (1995). *Social literacies: Critical approaches to literacy in development, ethnography and education.* New York: Longman.

Taylor, D. (Ed.). (1997). *Many families, many literacies: An international declaration of principles.* Portsmouth, NH: Heinemann.

Taylor, D., & Dorsey-Gaines, C. (1988). *Growing up literate: Learning from inner-city families.* Portsmouth, NH: Heinemann.

Teale, W. H., & Sulzby, E. (1986). Home background and young children's literacy development. In *Emergent literacy: Writing and reading.* Norwood, NJ: Ablex.

Thomas, A., Fazio, L., & Stiefelmeyer, B. L. (1999). *Families at school: A guide for educators.* Newark, DE: International Reading Association.

Valdés, G. (1996). *Con respeto: Bridging the distances between culturally diverse families and schools.* New York: Teachers College Press.

Verhoeven, L., & Snow, C. E. (2001). Literacy and motivation: Bridging cognitive and sociocultural viewpoints. In L. Verhoeven & C. Snow (Eds.), *Literacy and motivation: Reading engagement in individuals and groups* (pp. 1–23). Mahwah, NJ: Lawrence Erlbaum.

Wasik, B. H., Hermann, S., Berry, R. S., Dobbins, D. R., Schimizzi, A. M., Smith, T. K. et al. (2000). *Family literacy: An annotated bibliography.* Chapel Hill: University of North Carolina.

Wilson, K. K. (2002). *Promoting civic literacy.* (ERIC Document Reproduction Service No. ED 466924).

Literacy in Grades 4-8

ORCHESTRATING A BALANCED AND COMPREHENSIVE PROGRAM

FOCUS QUESTIONS

- How does a teacher's classroom practice emanate from a philosophy of teaching?

- How does a teacher effectively organize a classroom for literacy instruction?

- What does a typical day in an integrated classroom of grades 4-8 look like?

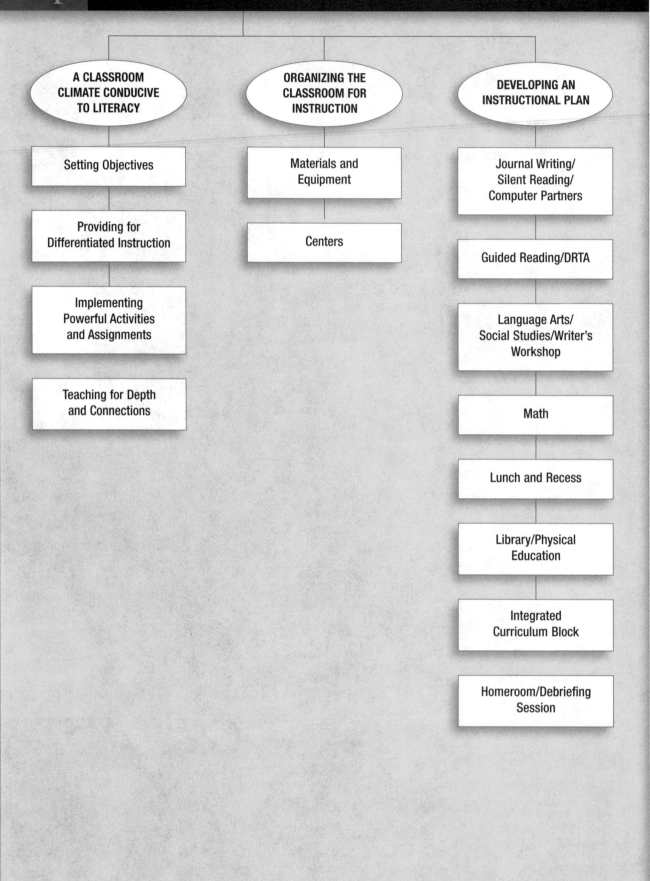

A CLASSROOM CLIMATE CONDUCIVE TO LITERACY

- Setting Objectives
- Providing for Differentiated Instruction
- Implementing Powerful Activities and Assignments
- Teaching for Depth and Connections

ORGANIZING THE CLASSROOM FOR INSTRUCTION

- Materials and Equipment
- Centers

DEVELOPING AN INSTRUCTIONAL PLAN

- Journal Writing/ Silent Reading/ Computer Partners
- Guided Reading/DRTA
- Language Arts/ Social Studies/Writer's Workshop
- Math
- Lunch and Recess
- Library/Physical Education
- Integrated Curriculum Block
- Homeroom/Debriefing Session

Mr. Fortney's fifth- and sixth-graders are studying the World War II era in their integrated language arts/social studies class. One group of students is reading and discussing Donna Jo Napoli's award-winning *Stones in Water* (1997), a novel about a young Italian boy who is torn from his family and taken to a Nazi work camp. It is an intense, gripping tale that engages students and allows the teacher to tie in the reading with all other subject areas.

Every day the students meet in small literature circles to discuss the book. Each student in each group reads the assigned chapter at home and is responsible for a specific role. Today, all of the students appear most eager to talk about the chapter they have just read. Dmitra, the summarizer in one of the groups, begins by offering an animated review of the major points in the chapter. Ezran, the investigator, uses a map to explain where in Germany the work camp is located and explains that Germany fought on the same side in the war as Italy. Leann, the vocabulary enricher, shows a set of 3 x 5 cards on which are written words with which she was unfamiliar in the chapter. She teaches the others the words *pummeled, squirmed, throbbed,* and *yelp* by acting them out; for the word *grotesque,* she draws a picture of a hideous monster, and for the word *wrath,* she tells a story of a time her uncle became very angry when someone stole his mail. Leann then adds these vocabulary words to a word wall that is posted in the classroom. The illustrator, a shy Pakistani girl who speaks little English, shows her picture of Roberto giving his food to the hungry little girl, a key incident in the chapter. The discussion director, Carlos, asks the group questions he has designed to get the group thinking and interacting, such as "Do you think you could have given up your food for a friend like Roberto did?" Finally, the literary luminary, Brett, shares his favorite part of the chapter aloud—the part where Enzo calls the guard names, knowing he does not understand his dialect—and tells the group how visualizing the scene made him laugh out loud.

Later, the students use their social studies books to learn more about the World War II era. They work in groups to read the three sections of the chapter. Then they report back to each other and Mr. Fortney helps to direct their focus to the main ideas in each section as he lists them on the overhead. Students in each group make a chart using the main ideas and adding details to their section of the chapter and later present their information to the class, wherever possible connecting this new information to ideas gleaned from the novel.

To exhibit their learning, the students in Mr. Fortney's class create an interactive museum about the Holocaust. Working in small groups, they create displays on the events leading up to World War II, the rise of Adolph Hitler, and what anti-Semitism meant and means today. Students work together to research their chosen topics using the classroom and school libraries as well as the Internet, compiling information on note cards. They engage museum visitors—which include parents, other classes, and community members—through the use of a PowerPoint presentation, a time-line mural, a skit based on the novel, and a panel discussion of religious intolerance and how it affects people.

To assess the students' learning, Mr. Fortney and his students developed a five-point rubric to evaluate their contribution to the museum display. By creating and discussing this rubric before initiating the reading and research, the students knew exactly what was expected of them. Knowing what is expected of them, and having many different ways to attain the desired goals, helps all the students in Mr. Fortney's class succeed.

INTRODUCTION

Many American grade 4–8 schools are departmentalized; that is, students receive daily instruction from several different teachers because each teacher specializes in a single subject. The rationale for such a structure is that the instructional content of each academic subject in grades 4–8 requires teachers who are experts in the area, and that instruction may be of higher quality when teachers can take special pride in their subject-matter discipline and can concentrate on preparing a limited number of outstanding lessons each day that are offered to several different classes.

In this text, we are not advocating for any particular grade structure or "label" (i.e., middle school, junior high, intermediate) for schools that educate students in the 10 to 14 age range. We agree with middle grades reformer Hayes Mizell (2002):

> It's not the sign in front of the building that matters, it's what is going on inside. Is the school focused on high achievement and success for all students? Have its leaders and supporters taken into account the unique developmental needs of this remarkable age group? All schools with middle grades should be judged by their academic excellence, their developmental responsiveness and their social equity. (p. 119)

We have chosen to present an outstanding classroom that we believe models all of these qualities. The class is for the most part self-contained, but with much team-teaching. This type of classroom, though certainly not the only possible model of excellence, exemplifies how literacy and the content areas can be artfully integrated.

Mr. Fortney has been teaching a fifth- and sixth-grade combination classroom at Oak Point Middle School for 13 years. Oak Point, which includes grades 4–8, is located in urban Sacramento, California. Most of the students at Oak Point come from low-income families, and more than 70 percent qualify for the free lunch program. Seven of the students in Mr. Fortney's class are English learners, and all speak some English. Nine different cultures are represented in the classroom.

Mr. Fortney works in a team with two other teachers, which is fairly typical of classrooms in grades 4–8. Before the school year begins, the team meets to make program decisions and to discuss matters such as scheduling and curricular responsibilities. The four classrooms in Mr. Fortney's team are made up of approximately 15 fifth-grade students and 15 sixth-grade students each. When the sixth-graders move on to seventh grade, 15 fifth-grade students take their place, so the students are with the same teachers for two years.

Mr. Fortney has read widely from the current literature on literacy, and in describing his program, he frequently refers to topics in that literature. When we asked him to describe the literacy program he and his colleagues have developed, this is what he had to say:

> The literacy program we have developed over the years reflects the unique challenge we encounter as middle school teachers. Our literacy goal for our students is to have them become actively engaged with text. Our students are required to analyze, identify, define, explain, and critique what they read rather than merely understand it, as was expected in earlier grades. But besides the cultural and linguistic differences in our students, the variability in reading ability is extreme in most students by grades 5 and 6. For example, one of my students, a 10-year-old, reads at an eleventh-grade level and typically reads an entire Harry Potter novel over several free reading periods, while another, 11 years old, struggles with anything higher than second-grade material. He finds it difficult to decode even short articles and displays very little interest at all in reading and writing; his only passion is basketball, so we build on that.
>
> This discrepancy in abilities and motivational levels presents a pressing obstacle for me and my colleagues: How do we meet the needs of all our students, given this formidable range of ability and interest? Given that current thinking in middle school instruction is to move away from traditional heterogeneous grouping of students toward whole-group and flexible group instruction, meeting the needs of the students becomes even more challenging. My colleagues and I are continually honing the methods and resources we use

to best address the literacy needs of each of our students while taking into account the state standards we are expected to address.

A CLASSROOM CLIMATE CONDUCIVE TO LITERACY

Despite the challenges facing Mr. Fortney and his colleagues, whatever "methods and resources" this team of teachers is currently using appear to be working. They have experienced success with their literacy program as measured by standardized test scores, which improve and exceed the state average every year, yet also evidenced by the fact that their students appear to have acquired a genuine love for reading and writing. Reading and writing attitude surveys these teachers administer at the beginning and end of every school year suggest that students' attitudes have strongly improved, and reading logs and book circulation attest to the fact that by the end of the school year, most of their students are choosing to read as a favorite free-time activity. How do they manage such success with students at an age when interest in literacy often declines?

The answer to that question lies, in part, in the way Mr. Fortney and his colleagues make decisions about classroom instruction. Any changes in the curriculum that the teachers have developed are usually precipitated by a combination of three factors:

1. Their ongoing assessment of their learners informs them that change is in order.

2. They have read about a strategy or observed an activity that they feel might be beneficial to help them reach their instructional goals.

3. They have reviewed research in a respected journal, such as *The Reading Teacher,* that provides compelling evidence that a literacy practice they have considered implementing is effective and should be tried.

As an example of their responsiveness to current research, Mr. Fortney explains to us that their philosophy of teaching draws upon four factors taken from current motivational theory (Brophy, 1998):

1. setting objectives and teaching to state standards
2. providing for differentiated instruction
3. implementing powerful activities and assignments
4. teaching for depth and connections

Setting Objectives

Mr. Fortney and his colleagues plan their curriculum based not on content, but on desired student knowledge and behaviors. When these teachers sit down at the end of a school year to decide what and how they will teach students in the coming year, they think first of how those students will think and behave differently at the end of the school year. Mr. Fortney confesses that when he first started teaching, he planned lessons and units based solely on the content included in the textbook and the activities he found helped students master this content. Essentially, he realized later, he was allowing the authors of the textbook to dictate what goals he would have. Over time, he began to see that his teaching must start with *his* goals—including the attitudes, knowledge, skills, and values he wants his students to come away with—and plan curriculum that will help students to operationalize these goals.

Today, Mr. Fortney and his colleagues plan their curriculum around the most important ideas they want their students to understand. Based on the State of California Content Standards (California Department of Education, 1999) and the District scope and sequence, they determine what their students should know, and then use a variety of resources to help students realize these goals.

Providing for Differentiated Instruction

Mr. Fortney and his colleagues organize instruction around the premise that all students can learn but that each student's needs are unique and, therefore, each will need a different amount of time and effort to complete assignments. They also offer multiple ways to access material and a variety of means by which students can complete an assignment. For example, students choose from a number of books to read to complete a book contract. The book contract is a self-contained set of information, through and beyond activities that relate to a particular book (see Chapter 5). The books for each book contract come in a range of reading and interest levels, and a variety of writing, art, and research activities can be chosen in order for students to respond personally to the text. In some cases, the books provided for this assignment all relate to a particular concept or era in the social sciences, such as a unit on China. Books chosen by Mr. Fortney for such a unit range from second- to eighth-grade reading level, yet each book covers the essential information about the Chinese culture and customs that will lead to later whole-class discussion. In addition to the book contract, students sometimes take part in literature circles, where each student assumes a role to help other classmates clarify and deepen their understanding of the chosen text (see Chapter 5).

All students can learn, but each student's needs are unique.

As another example of differentiated instruction, Mr. Fortney makes wide use of collaboration for research projects, with a variety of ways students can contribute to the final project, from a mural of rural Chinese life to a PowerPoint presentation to a ballad about working in the rice paddies (see Chapter 9). Such an approach not only ensures the engagement of all learners but taps into the wide range of learning styles and preferences and types of intelligences found in most classrooms.

Finally, Mr. Fortney forms many flexible groups so students who share the need for a reading skill or strategy will be taught as effectively as possible. Groups are deliberately impermanent and, because they exist for a specific purpose, will then be disbanded as soon as the teacher has completed the lessons planned for the group. At times, those students who are having particular difficulty receive individualized instruction—one-on-one sessions with the teacher—as soon as Mr. Fortney, through ongoing assessment (see Chapter 2), observes that a student is falling behind his classmates.

Implementing Powerful Activities and Assignments

Mr. Fortney and his colleagues understand that the most powerful activities and assignments are built around "powerful ideas," such as "freedom" or "oppression." Mr. Fortney shares with us his deep belief that the key to the effectiveness of any activities he chooses is that they get students actively thinking about and applying key ideas, preferably with conscious awareness of the preestablished learning goals mentioned earlier. Contrary to the practice of some teachers, Mr. Fortney believes that an appropriate activity is not one that merely has students all doing something quietly, but one that has them all thinking and talking about what they are doing as they move toward the attainment of an important goal.

Ultimately, Mr. Fortney also believes that the success of any activity depends not only on the quality of the activity itself, but also on the teacher–student debriefing that occurs into, through, and beyond the time period in which students are responding to the activity's demands. Mr. Fortney and his colleagues maximize the impact any activity has on their learners by introducing activities in ways that clarify their cognitive and affective goals and create in students the desire to accomplish those goals through constant student buy-in. Then, as students are working on the activity, Mr. Fortney monitors their progress and provides appropriate feedback. Throughout the days we visited, Mr. Fortney led students through many types of postsharing of and reflection on the insights that they had gained as a result of ongoing activities.

Finally, Mr. Fortney and his colleagues go to great lengths to involve parents in their children's instruction. When they found that few parents were coming to open houses and back-to-school night events, they began to think of more creative ways to reach parents. An early doughnuts-and-coffee social, for example, allowed parents to drop in before work to chat with the teachers and view the interactive museum and iMovie production their children had created. Additionally, the teachers in this team send home brief bulletins containing schedules of classroom activities and suggestions for books that can be read as a family that would complement current units.

Teaching for Depth and Connections

Mr. Fortney is aware that in recent years, both the findings of research on effective teaching and the instructional guidelines issued by national and state subject-matter specialists have stressed the importance of teaching for thorough understanding, or "mastery." Students who have learned content deeply not only have mastered the content itself but retain it in a form that will make it usable when it is needed. Mr. Fortney provides clear explanations and modeling of new ideas, so students can see how the new content is important, and then helps them see how the new ideas connect with ones with which they are already familiar. He encourages this connection through discussions and debates and helps students apply the new information in problem-solving or decision-making contexts. For example, when his students are studying about immigration in social studies, he makes sure that they have trade books on a variety of cultural groups who have immigrated to the United States from which to choose, in a range of reading levels, for literature circles (see Figure 12.1). Integrated math and social studies lessons center around bar graphs tracking groups of people, and Mr. Fortney finds songs that represent the travails of many of the immigrant groups to further integrate music. Finally, students are encouraged to bring in

YOUNG ADULT LITERATURE FOR IMMIGRATION

97 Orchard Street, New York: Stories of Immigrant Life, by Linda Granfield,
    Tundra Books, 2001 (varied cultures)

Becoming Mary Mehan: Two Novels, by Jennifer Armstrong, Laurelleaf, 2002
    (Irish immigrants)

Chantrea Conway's Story: A Voyage from Cambodia in 1975, by Clare Pastore,
    Berkeley, 2001 (Cambodian immigrants)

Coming to America, by Betsy Maestro, Scholastic, 1996 (varied cultures)

Dragonwings: Golden Mountain Memories, 1903, by Laurence Yep, HarperTrophy,
    1989 (Chinese immigrants)

The Gift, by Marcia S. Freeman, Maupin House, 2002 (Norwegian immigrants)

Grandfather's Journey, by Allen Say, Houghton Mifflin, 1993 (Japanese immigrants)

Habibi, by Naomi Shihab Nye, Pocket Books, 1999 (Israeli immigrants)

If Your Name Was Changed at Ellis Island, by Ellen Levine, Scholastic, 1994
    (varied cultures)

Immigrant Kids, by Russell Freedman, Scott Foresman, 1995 (varied cultures)

In the Year of the Boar and Jackie Robinson, by Bette Bao Lord, HarperTrophy,
    1986 (Chinese immigrants)

Letters from Rifka, by Karen Hesse, Puffin, 1993 (Russian immigrants)

FIGURE 12.1 Mr. Fortney's books for literature circles.

current newspaper articles concerning immigrants, which the class discusses;
students then individually write personal essays based on the discussion.

ORGANIZING THE CLASSROOM FOR INSTRUCTION

Another challenge facing Mr. Fortney and all other instructors in his overcrowded urban school is utilizing classroom space most effectively and
comfortably. Mr. Fortney takes time with students at the beginning of the
school year, gathering their input so that they feel ownership of the classroom.
They also offer suggestions concerning its organization. While all the ameni-
ties found in Mr. Fortney's classroom are not in all schools, certain
organizational features can be attained in most classrooms.

Materials and Equipment

Mr. Fortney is understandably proud of his extensive classroom library. Two
shelves line the periphery of the classroom, and the books from his personal collection are supplemented by books from the school or city library as the subjects
being studied necessitate more resources. He claims that he has amassed more
than a thousand trade books during his teaching career through commercial
book clubs, garage sales, auctions, library sales, and gifts from friends and family. These books range in readability level from low second grade all the way up

to high school and include every literary genre; they also reflect the various cultures found in the classroom, the community, and the world at large.

Desks, chairs, and tables are movable so that they can be reorganized based on the demands of a particular activity. The room also contains pillows, an old comfortable couch, and area rugs to further define space and indicate appropriate attitudes for particular projects, such as research, interviewing, illustrating a piece of writing, or simply skimming for information. Students' works are displayed on walls, bulletin boards, hanging mobiles, chart paper, and occasionally on easels. Additional materials and equipment are borrowed or purchased according to the needs of the subjects being studied and the realities of the limited school budget.

Centers

Besides bookshelves filled with books and reference materials, Mr. Fortney's classroom has centers (see Figure 12.2). Some centers are permanent, whereas others are temporary according to the unit being studied and are dismantled once the unit of study is finished. For example, a recent unit on the rain forest

Diagram of Mr. Fortney's classroom.   FIGURE 12.2

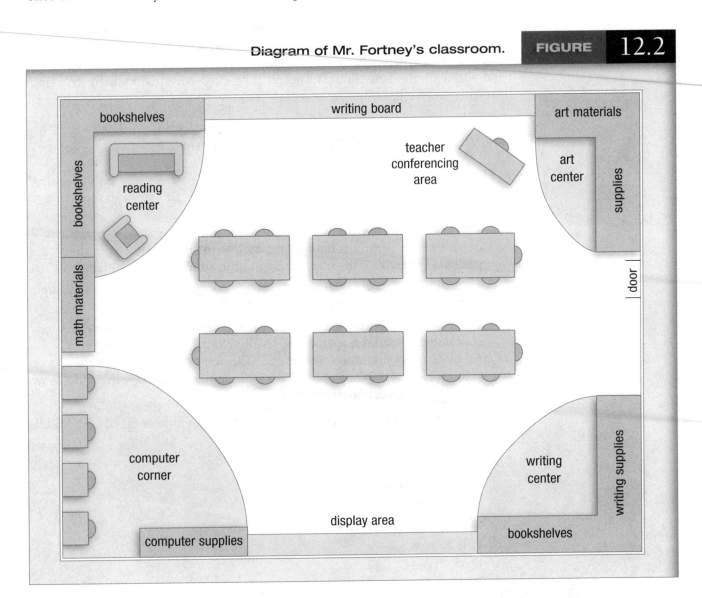

required that tables be moved to certain corners of the room so that students would have access to the science and social studies resources such as maps, globes, a terrarium, and examples of flora and fauna. Permanent centers include the classroom library, the reading area, the art center, the computer corner, and the writing center.

The writing center contains many items needed for writing and art activities, ranging from lined paper and perfumed stationery to elaborate computer paper and wallpaper samples. Writing utensils are similarly extensive to invite forays of fancy, including gel pens, ink pens, and even scented fine-line markers. The classroom library, located in a carpeted corner of the room containing the comfortable couch and pillows, is the focus of the classroom. The reading material on the shelves includes a variety of trade books, both narrative and informational, from different genres, on a wide range of topics, and at a variety of difficulty levels matching the learners in the class. Many cultures are represented in these books, and some are in languages of the English learners in the class. Magazines, catalogues, newspapers, and graphic novels find their way onto these shelves, and students can be seen browsing in the reading area during any free time in the day, as well as before and after school. The computer corner is another area where students can access information in a different way through e-mail correspondence and Internet searches. Finally, there is a well-stocked art center. Because the school does not have an art teacher, Mr. Fortney incorporates art activities with the students' language arts and social studies activities. The center is stocked with materials for coloring, painting, drawing, sculpting, and craft making.

DEVISING AN INSTRUCTIONAL PLAN

Three important attributes are evident in Mr. Fortney's and his colleagues' organization—curriculum content, space, time, and students:

- These teachers are committed to the idea of a homeroom, so that students feel one person is mainly responsible for them; moreover, the teachers appreciate this way of sharing the administrative duties.
- The team goes to great lengths to set aside large blocks of time so a topic can be covered in the depth it requires.
- These teachers center their instruction around broad unifying themes containing essential questions that will help drive the investigation. Additional essential questions for the theme in the chapter's opening vignette, for example, are: "Why did the Holocaust happen?" and "How can prejudices such as anti-Semitism be eliminated?"

A typical school day in Mr. Fortney's fifth/sixth grade at Oak Point Middle School looks like this:

[9:00–11:15 Homeroom]

9:00	Journal writing/silent reading/computer buddies
9:30	DRTA
10:15	Language arts/social studies/writer's workshop
11:15	Math
12:00	Lunch/recess

12:40   Physical education or library, alternating

1:20   Integrated curriculum block: science, art, music, and health, combined with reading, writing, listening, speaking, viewing, and visually representing

2:30   Homeroom: debriefing discussions

2:45   Dismissal

From this schedule, you can see that students remain with their homeroom teacher for more than two hours in the morning and then return in the afternoon. Mr. Fortney's fifth- and sixth-grade students stay with him from 9:00 until 11:15. The team teachers and the students like these large blocks in the schedule because they require fewer disruptive "downtimes" between classes and allow for more substantive relationships between teacher and student. The larger blocks also allow teachers to delve into a topic in greater depth, using extended time to make connections with other curricular areas. Finally, the blocks offer time for students to be in small groups in a self-directed manner, allowing the teacher to work closely with those students needing individual assistance.

Students split into grade-level groups for math and physical education. In the afternoon, the integrated curriculum blocks allow the team to teach in their area of greatest expertise; Mr. Fortney's undergraduate minor was in the physical sciences, and he has always enjoyed this field, while the other two teachers in the team prefer teaching health and art.

The large amount of time for the language arts and the integrated curriculum block provides an opportunity for the team to illustrate the interconnectedness of reading, writing, listening, speaking, viewing, and visually representing. The literature-based focus of both blocks of time allows for integration of content as well as flexibility in instruction; when more time is needed in science one day, for example, that subject can spill into the health and art time periods, or even the language arts period, without causing a problem. These team teachers are always looking for—and finding—unique opportunities to connect the reading to the other language arts, as well as to state standards and mandated content area material.

This team has found that the literature-based approach is highly motivational for students. Meeting to discuss what they have read, as described in the opening vignette, helps students develop rich schemata while responding enthusiastically to text in their own words. Mr. Fortney also finds that it is natural for him to model and talk about appropriate behavior with respect to literature, because he is able to share his own personal book club experiences with the students. Additionally, literature circles appear to have an advantage with students in the intermediate and middle grades because the students are unable to avoid being participants in the small group discussions, and other group members hold each other accountable for completing their assigned roles. Finally, a clear advantage to the literature circles approach is that students are able to select their own books. While the teacher usually selects all the texts that relate to the broad theme, such as immigration, the students have the freedom to choose which of the four trade books they would like to read, thus increasing the likelihood that they will choose a book that is of interest and at their level of reading ability. Novel study can also be effective (see Chapter 5).

Though unplanned events often interfere with Mr. Fortney's instructional plan (fire drills, assemblies, absences, parties, guest speakers, etc.), one would expect to see a day similar to the one described in the opening vignette. Following is a brief description of his fifth/sixth-grade students' daily routine.

9:00–9:30 Journal Writing/Silent Reading/ Computer Buddies

When students enter the classroom, they immediately take out their "dessert" (self-selected) books and their double-entry journals (see Chapter 5, p. 171). Because many of Oak Point's students have extremely chaotic home lives, these students appreciate the predictability of having a certain time of the day that rarely varies. As they read the books they have selected from the classroom library, they very often stop and write down in the first column of their journal a phrase or paragraph that catches their attention because they resonate with the character's feelings or actions. Then they explain, in the second column, how they personally relate to the particular excerpt. Some students have signed up to use the classroom computers to e-mail their computer buddy, a university preservice teacher. Mr. Fortney has set up this arrangement so that his students can have authentic electronic dialogues about the books they are currently reading. Both parties agree to read the same book, and then students enthusiastically "discuss" their reading with their university counterpart, who adds her own insights about the text.

9:30–10:15 DRTA

Mr. Fortney and his team are aware of the importance of direct instruction in reading and study strategies. Therefore, they set aside a time when reading comprehension, vocabulary skills, and comprehension strategies are modeled for students through many of the instructional strategies discussed in earlier chapters of this book. This day, Mr. Fortney prepares students to read a newspaper feature article about a Holocaust survivor who lives in Sacramento and has been reunited with a sister she had not seen since both were in Auschwitz. Mr. Fortney uses several paragraphs to show students how the meaning of the words *corroboration* and *universal* can be gleaned by using the context. The students pair off and use reciprocal questioning to read, summarize, predict, and clarify each paragraph. Then the pairs share their ideas with the whole class as the paragraph is displayed on the overhead projector.

10:15–11:15 Language Arts/Social Studies/ Writer's Workshop

Students get into their groups and quickly attend to the business of sharing their responses to the reading they did the night before. Besides *Stones in Water* (see the opening vignette), students are reading *The Diary of Anne Frank, The Upstairs Room,* and *Number the Stars.* After doing literature circles, students in one group devise a short readers theatre presentation to share with the rest of the class so that other groups will get a sense of the other books being read. Very often, Mr. Fortney states, students will opt to read all four books being utilized in the literature circles, for recreational reading outside of school. On this day, Mr. Fortney conducts a minilesson on the use of quotation marks in dialogue, the sixth of an ongoing set of lessons designed to teach students to become more effective writers through the use of the Six Traits. Students then incorporate this new learning in an essay about the importance of the Holocaust in today's world, which is assigned for homework. Tomorrow, students may peer edit these essays in writer's workshop, which occurs every other day at this time. At regular intervals, Mr. Fortney returns to the essential questions for a whole-class discussion on the Holocaust and how it has impacted recent events.

11:15–12:00 Math

Mr. Fortney and his team believe in adding an oral language component to all math activities by asking students to articulate their answers to word problems as well as computations and equations. Additionally, Mr. Fortney often checks for understanding by utilizing "quick writes," in which students are asked to paraphrase, in written form, their understanding of a math procedure that has just been taught, providing a check on how effectively the concept has been taught and understood.

12:00–12:40 Lunch and Recess

12:40–1:20 Library/Physical Education

Three days a week, students go to physical education with a specialist; the other two days, they are taken to the library, where the media specialist often provides a lesson on some aspect of study skills such as using a variety of reference materials to augment a report. Because students are allowed to borrow books during a portion of this time, Mr. Fortney is always available to "match books to readers," using his observations and the data from running records to determine reading levels, and the results of his reading interest inventory to get an idea of exactly what books might interest each student.

Integrated studies help students connect knowledge across content areas.

1:20–2:30 Integrated Curriculum Block

The integrated curriculum block time is an exciting time to channel the energy of middle school students through the implementation of cross-curricular thematic units, innovative teaching and learning, and a strong focus on the language arts. For the next four weeks the students in Mr. Fortney's class will be doing a unit called "Biomes of the World," studying the interactions between living things and their environment. Assessments are completed at the end of the group presentations using a teacher-made rubric and a self-evaluation rubric for the group and for individual students. The unit contains the following components that address the California science and language arts curriculum standards to which Mr. Fortney adheres:

- View and discuss videos on deserts, forest, marine, freshwater, grassland, and tundra habitats (*viewing; oral language*)
- Take a field trip to an environmental camp; summarize learning (*informational writing*)
- Use "Project Wild" conservation educational program materials (*science, reading, applying*)
- Participate in the "Oh Deer" game from Project Wild, allowing students to see and chart the cycle of deer populations in an ecosystem (*science, math*)

www

Project Wild
www.projectwild.org

- Explore NASA Earth Observatory websites and record information (*computer skills, media literacy, summarizing*)
- Create a PowerPoint presentation on symbiosis (*oral presentation, computer skills, visually representing*)
- Read and discuss *There's an Owl in the Shower,* by Jean Craighead George, using buddy reading (*reading, oral discussion*)
- Dissect owl pellets, label and classify them (*science, categorizing, classifying*)
- Create a "biome in a box" depicting characteristics of an assigned biome (*art, visually representing, science, describing*)
- Research their biome and present findings via posters, dioramas, skits, diagrams, and the "biome in a box" (*art, visually representing, summarizing, drama*)
- Adopt and research a zoo animal at the Sacramento Zoo (*research, technology, informational writing*)
- Using a word processing program, write a story about an imaginary creature and its habitat; create hypothetical adaptations for it (*science, creative writing, computer skills*)

2:30–2:45 Homeroom/Debriefing Session

Returning to their homerooms, students have a chance to reflect on what they have learned during the day, through either small-group discussion, quick writes, whole-group share, or question-and-answer sessions in which individual students ask for clarification concerning a concept or an assignment about which they feel unsure.

SUMMARY

Throughout this book we have explored ways to teach literacy in a comprehensive way that includes direct instruction in the skills of writing conventions, reading comprehension, decoding, and vocabulary enrichment while also focusing on personal response to literature in the most meaningful and joyous way. The skills of literacy, while absolutely necessary, are part and parcel of the more critical task—realizing what reading can mean and how it can make readers feel. To that end, many activities were included in this book that were designed for making text meaningful and using text as a springboard to substantive writing activities.

Yet learning about specific strategies—seeing only individual pieces of the big picture—is not totally satisfactory. Particularly if one has never taught, it is vital to see how a gifted teacher manages to orchestrate all of the elements into a total program. And this program must meet the required state standards while also meeting the needs of the heterogeneous garden of students, with various strengths and needs, who now face teachers in most classrooms.

Though there are many possible ways literacy instruction might be implemented, we chose to showcase one teacher in one team's approach. This team has had success despite major challenges of poverty in homes, limited home support, several home languages, and a wide range of ability levels. Based on the substantiation of test scores as well as an impartial observer's examination, the students appear to be learning the skills of literacy and to be able to apply them to the content areas in a rich and rewarding way.

Finally, Mr. Fortney's classroom, for us, stood out in another, more fundamental way: it was impossible to miss the zest for teaching and the love for all aspects of literacy, and learning in general, modeled in the classroom of this veteran teacher. He eagerly shared with us his involvement in reading and writing activities outside the classroom. With students, he often refers to books he is reading, or a poem or article he has recently written. Moreover, this teacher is integrally involved in his profession through conducting in-service workshops for colleagues; attending professional conferences; and, on occasion, discussing current journal articles in the teachers' lounge. His passion for learning is contagious and is clearly "caught" by the students with whom he works.

A balanced and comprehensive literacy program can be a reality in grades 4–8 when a competent and caring teacher puts forth the time and effort it takes to create a program that connects content areas with the language arts in deep and meaningful ways, and offers important ideas that students can wrap their minds around through engaging activities. Mr. Fortney's classroom truly embodies these goals.

Questions
FOR JOURNAL WRITING AND DISCUSSION

1. Reflect on a teacher you know who appears to be highly effective in teaching students in grades 4–8 to read for knowledge and enjoyment. In light of this chapter, what do you believe makes this teacher effective? What do you believe makes Mr. Fortney such an effective teacher of intermediate literacy? What are the similarities between the two teachers? Differences?

2. Brainstorm a list of ways you can ensure that the students in your class will read not only for knowledge but for enjoyment. Share and discuss this list with the others in your class. What do you consider the most effective methods?

3. Discuss the provisions that must be made so that linguistically and culturally diverse learners may succeed. How do you believe such provisions affect the native English speakers in the class?

Suggestions
FOR PROJECTS AND FIELD ACTIVITIES

1. Arrange to observe a fourth-, sixth-, or eighth-grade classroom. Make notes about the environment, the classroom climate, and the literacy activities in which the students engage. Your observation should be as objective as possible. Compare your experience with the other members of your class and include in your discussion your personal responses to the classroom you observed.

2. Interview a teacher in grades 4–8. Ask this teacher how decisions are made in his classroom about changing instruction. Which seems to be the most potent reason for changing a classroom practice for this teacher: (a) what research says, (b) what other teachers say, (c) what the district policy is, or (d) what assessment tells the teacher?

3. Make a sketch of what you consider to be an ideal classroom for grades 4–8, including furniture, materials, and storage space most suited to what you believe to be a balanced literacy environment. Compare your sketch to Figure 12.2. How is yours different? Why? Share your sketch with others in your class, discussing the benefits and drawbacks of each design.

REFERENCES

Brophy, J. (1998). *Motivating students to learn.* Boston: McGraw-Hill.

California Department of Education. (1999). *Reading/ language arts framework for California public schools.* Sacramento: California Department of Education.

Mizell, H. (2002). *Shooting for the sun: Middle school reform.* New York: Edna McConnell Clark Foundation.

Napoli, D. J. (1997). *Stones in water.* New York: Puffin Books.

Children's and Adolescent Literature References

MULTICULTURAL LITERATURE

The following books are suitable for introducing students to other cultures in a respectful and informative way.

Barrie, B. (1990). *Lone star.* New York: Delacorte. (Jewish American)

Bruchac, J. (1997). *Lasting echoes: An oral history of Native American people* (P. Morin, Ill.). San Diego: Harcourt. (Native American)

Delacre, L. (1996). *Golden tales: Myths, legends, and folktales from Latin America.* New York: Scholastic. (Latino American)

Dolphin, L. (1997). *Our journey from Tibet: Based on a true story.* New York: Dutton. (Asian American)

Ekoomiak, N. (1990). *Arctic memories.* New York: Holt. (Native American)

Filipovic, Z. (1993). *Zlata's diary: A child's life in Sarajevo.* New York: Viking. (European American)

Flora, J. (1994). *The fabulous fireworks family.* New York: McElderry. (Latino American)

Hest, A. (1997). *When Jessie came across the sea* (P. J. Lynch, Ill.). Cambridge, MA: Candlewick. (European American)

Hurmence, B. (1982). *A girl called boy.* New York: Clarion. (African American)

Jaffe, N. (1995). *Older brother, younger brother: A Korean folktale* (L. August, Ill.). New York: Penguin. (Asian American)

Jaffe, N. (1996). *The golden flower: A Taino myth from Puerto Rico* (E. O. Sanchez, Ill.). New York: Simon & Schuster. (Latino American)

Lee, M. (1997). *Nim and the war effort.* New York: Farrar, Straus & Giroux. (Asian American)

Mazer, A. (Ed.). (1993). *America street: A multicultural anthology of stories.* New York: Persea. (Many cultures)

Meltzer, M. (1988). *Rescue: The story of how Gentiles saved Jews in the Holocaust.* New York: Harper. (Jewish American)

Mochizuki, K. (1997). *Passage to freedom: The Sugihara story* (D. Lee, Ill.). New York: Lee and Low. (Asian American)

Myers, W. D. (1991). *Now is your time: The African-American struggle for freedom.* New York: Harper. (African American)

Myers, W. D. (1997). *Harlem* (C. Myers, Ill.). New York: Scholastic. (African American)

Napoli, D. J. (1997). *Stones in water.* New York: Puffin. (Jewish American)

Normandin, C. (Ed.). (1997). *Echoes of the elders: The stories and paintings of Chief Lalooska.* New York: DK. (Native American)

Nye, N. (1997). *Habibi.* New York: Simon & Schuster. (Jewish American)

Orlev, U. (1991). *The man from the other side.* New York: Houghton. (Jewish American)

Spivak, D. (1997). *Grass sandals: The travels of Basho* (Demi, Ill.). New York: Atheneum. (Asian American)

Turner, G. T. (1989). *Take a walk in their shoes.* New York: Cobblehill. (African American)

Vidal, B. (1991). *The legend of El Dorado: A Latin American tale.* New York: Knopf. (Latino American)

Wood, N. (Ed.). (1997). *The serpent's tongue: Prose, poetry, and art of the New Mexico pueblos.* New York: Dutton. (Native American)

LITERATURE ACROSS THE CURRICULUM

The following books can be used as a launching point or as an enhancement for a unit of study in a particular curriculum area.

Arnold, C. (2000). *Easter Island: Giant stone statues tell of a rich and tragic past.* New York: Clarion. (Archaeology)

Blackwood, G. (2000). *Shakespeare's scribe.* New York: Dutton. (Language Arts)

Buettner, D. (1997). *Africatrek: A journey by bicycle through Africa*. Minneapolis: Lerner. (Geography)

Carter, D. A., & Diaz, J. (1999). *The elements of pop-ups: A pop-up book for aspiring paper engineers*. New York: Simon & Schuster. (Art)

Cerullo, M. M. (2000). *The truth about great white sharks* (J. L. Rotman, Ill.). San Francisco: Chronicle. (Science)

Creech, S. (2000). *The wanderer* (D. Diaz, Ill.). New York: Cotler/HarperCollins. (Writing)

Demi. (1997). *One grain of rice: A mathematical folktale*. New York: Scholastic. (Math)

Fradin, D. B. (2000). *Bound for the North Star: True stories of fugitive slaves*. New York: Clarion. (History)

Jackson, D. M. (2000). *The wildlife detectives: How forensic scientists fight crimes against nature*. Boston: Houghton Mifflin. (Science)

Jones, C. F. (1999). *Yukon gold: The story of the Klondike goldrush*. New York: Holiday House. (History)

Matthews, T. L. (1999). *Always inventing: A photobiography of Alexander Graham Bell*. Washington, DC: National Geographic Society. (Science)

Monceau, M. (1994). *Jazz: My music, my people*. New York: Knopf. (Music)

Nagda, A. W., & Bickel, C. (2000). *Tiger math: Learning to graph from a baby tiger*. New York: Holt. (Math)

Rochelle, B. (Ed.). (2001). *Words with wings: A treasury of African-American poetry and art*. New York: HarperCollins. (Poetry/Art)

Stanley, D. (2000). *Roughing it on the Oregon Trail* (H. Berry, Ill.). New York: Cotler/HarperCollins. (History)

Vigna, G. (1999). *Jazz and its history*. New York: Baron's. (Music/History)

LITERATURE TO PROVOKE DISCUSSION

The following books concern relevant, provocative issues that would be useful for engaging students in grades 4–8 in lively discussions.

Aylette, J. (1990). *Families: A celebration of diversity, commitment, and love*. New York: Harper & Row. (Diverse family configurations)

Fenner, C. (1998). *The king of dragons*. New York: McElderry. (Homelessness)

Fleishman, P. (1991). *The borning room*. New York: HarperCollins. (Intergenerational relationships)

Krull, K. (1999). *They saw the future: Oracles, psychics, scientists, great thinkers, and pretty good guessers* (K. Brooker, Ill.). New York: Atheneum. (Parapsychology)

Macy, S., & Gottesman, J. (Eds.). (1999). *Play like a girl: A celebration of women in sports*. New York: Holt. (Sexism)

Pettit, J. (1993). *My name is San Ho*. New York: Scholastic. (Stepfamilies)

Rosen, M. J. (1995). *Bonesy and Isabel*. New York: Harcourt Brace. (Death of a pet)

Strachan, I. (1990). *Flawed glass*. Boston: Little, Brown. (Disabilities)

Woodson, J. (2001). *The other side* (E. B. Lewis, Ill.). New York: Putnam. (Racism)

LITERATURE FOR RECREATIONAL READING

The following books can form a foundation for a classroom library for the purpose of recreational reading in grades 4–8. These books were selected by teachers or students for their overall appeal to all readers.

Almond, D. (2000). *Kit's wilderness*. New York: Delacorte.

Ayres, K. (2000). *Silver dollar girl*. New York: Delacorte.

Baker, J. (1987). *Where the forest meets the sea*. New York: Greenwillow.

Blume, J. (1972). *Tales of a fourth-grade nothing*. New York: Dutton. (And other books by this author)

Buchanan, J. (2001). *Hank's story*. New York: Farrar, Straus & Giroux.

Curtis, C. P. (1999). *It's Bud, not Buddy*. New York: Delacorte.

Cushman, C. (1995). *Catherine called Birdy*. New York: Clarion.

Henkes, K. (1999). *The birthday room*. New York: Greenwillow.

Hesse, K. (1998). *Out of the dust*. New York: Scholastic.

Howe, D., & Howe, J. (1979). *Bunnicula: A rabbit-tale of mystery*. New York: Atheneum. (And other books in the series)

Kuhn, B. (1999). *The angels of mercy: The army nurses of World War II*. New York: Atheneum.

Lemieux, M. (1999). *Stormy night*. Buffalo, NY: Kids Can Press.

L'Engle, M. (1962). *A wrinkle in time*. New York: Farrar, Straus & Giroux. (And other books by this author)

Lowry, L. (1989). *Number the stars*. Boston: Houghton Mifflin.

Naylor, P. R. (1991). *Shiloh*. New York: Atheneum.

Patterson, K. (1977). *Bridge to Terabithia*. New York: Crowell.

Peck, R. (1999). *A long way from Chicago*. New York: Dial.

Rowling, J. K. (1997). *Harry Potter and the sorcerer's stone*. New York: Scholastic. (And other books in this series)

Spinelli, J. (1998). *Wringer*. New York: HarperCollins.

Wilder, L. I. (1953). *Little house in the big woods*. New York: Harper & Row. (And other books in this series)

Yep, L. (2000). *Dream soul*. New York: HarperCollins.

BOOKS TO PROMOTE VISUAL LITERACY

Picture books and graphic novels can promote not only visual literacy but also independent reading and content learning. Following are books that can be used for these purposes and are appropriate for grades 4–8.

Picture Books

Ambrose, S. (2001). *The good fight: How World War II was won*. New York: Atheneum.

Barasch, L. (2005). *Ask Albert Einstein*. New York: Farrar, Straus & Giroux.

Bunting, E. (1991). *Fly away home*. New York: Clarion.

Carey, C. (2000). *The Emancipation Proclamation*. Chanhassen, MN: Child's World.

Cherry, L. (1992). *A river ran wild: An environmental history*. New York: Dutton.

Coerr, E., & Young, E. (1993). *Sadako*. New York: Putnam.

Craats, R. (2000). *The science of sound*. Milwaukee, WI: Garth Stevens.

Hopkinson, D. (2003). *Sweet Clara and the freedom quilt*. New York: Knopf Books for Young Readers.

King, M. (1997). *I have a dream*. (Paintings by 15 Coretta Scott King Award and Honor Book Artists.) New York: Scholastic.

Lember, B. (1997). *The shell book*. Boston: Houghton Mifflin.

McEwan, I., & Innocenti, R. (2004). *Rose Blanche*. London: Red Fox.

Murphy, P. (2004). *Grace Hopper: Computer whiz*. Berkeley Heights, NJ: Enslow.

Jackson, D. (1996). *The bone detectives: How forensic anthropologists solve crimes and uncover mysteries of the dead*. Photos by C. Fellenbaum. Boston: Little, Brown.

Riley, J. (2005). *The nervous system*. Minneapolis, MN: Lerner.

Searle, B. *Inside a computer*. Danbury, CT: Grolier Educational.

Summer, L. (2001). *The march on Washington*. Chanhassen, MN: Child's World.

Tang, G., & Briggs, H. (2001). *The grapes of math: Mind-stretching math riddles*. New York: Scholastic.

Graphic Novels (list adapted from S. Kane, 2007)

Avi. (1993). *City of light, city of dark: A comic book novel*. Art by B. Floca. New York: Orchard Books.

Bradbury, R. (2003). *The best of Ray Bradbury: The graphic novel*. New York: ibooks.

Briggs, R. (1998). *Ethel & Ernest: A true story*. New York: Knopf.

Crane, S. (2005). *The red badge of courage*. New York: Puffin.

Curry, P., & Zarate, O. (1996). *Introducing Machiavelli*. New York: Totem Books.

Eisner, W. (1986). *Will Eisner's New York: The big city*. Northampton, MA: Kitchen Sink Press.

Eisner, W. (2003). *Fagin the Jew: A graphic novel*. New York: Doubleday.

Factoid Books. (1999). *The big book of Grimm, by the Brothers Grimm as channeled by J. Vankin and over 50 top comic artists!* New York: Paradox Press.

Giardino, V. (1997). *A Jew in Communist Prague: 1. Loss of innocence*. New York: NBM Comics Lit.

Gonick, L., & Outwater, A. (1996). *The cartoon guide to the environment*. New York: HarperCollins.

Harder, J. (2004). *Leviathan*. New York: Comics Lit/NBM.

Harris, S. (1989). *Einstein simplified: Cartoons on science*. New Brunswick, NJ: Rutgers University Press.

Martin, M. (2005). *Harriet Tubman and the underground railroad*. Mankato, MN: Capstone Press.

Martin, M. (2005). *The Salem witch trials*. Mankato, MN: Capstone Press.

Olson, K. M. (2005). *The assassination of Abraham Lincoln*. Mankato, MN: Capstone Press.

Pomplun, T. (Ed.). (2004). *Graphic classics: Edgar Allan Poe* (2nd ed.). Mount Horeb, WI: Eureka Productions.

Reed, G. (2005). *Mary Shelley's Frankenstein: The graphic novel*. New York: Penguin/Puffin.

Sartrapi, M. (2003). *Persepolis: The story of a childhood*. New York: Pantheon Books.

Shanower, E. (2004). *Sacrifice*. Berkeley, CA: Image Comics.

Spiegelman, A. (1997). *Maus: A survivor's tale*. New York: Pantheon.

Thompson, C. (2006). *Good-bye, Chunky Rice*. New York: Pantheon.

Winick, J. (2000). *Pedro & me: Friendship, loss, and what I learned*. New York: Henry Holt.

Literacy Websites

The following websites will be especially helpful for teachers of literacy. The sites include lesson plans in the language arts, as well as ideas for curriculum integration with other subject areas. Some of the sites can also be used by learners in the classroom and at home. Many of the sites have both teacher and student links.

www.ala.org/greatsites/ The American Library Association's Great Web Sites for Kids cyber-collection contains hundreds of worthwhile sites for learners of all ages. Topics include Animals, The Arts, Literature and Languages, History and Biography, Sciences, and Mathematics and Computers.

http://a4esl.org This site includes grammar quizzes, crossword puzzles, and Internet scavenger hunts designed especially for students who are English learners.

www.rockhall.com This is the Cleveland Rock & Roll Hall of Fame. It offers programs for teachers that integrate music with history and literature.

www.adventureonline.com AdventureOnline is an engaging way for students to practice their reading, writing, math, science, and social studies skills. Aligned with learning standards, it provides teachers and parents with meaningful feedback about students' performance.

www.awesomelibrary.org More than 33,000 carefully reviewed resources are organized by school subject for teachers, young children, teenagers, and parents. The top 5 percent education websites are included.

http://bookadventure.com This site provides a child-oriented reading program designed to encourage students in grades K–8 to read more often, for longer periods of time, and with greater understanding, offering stories, contests, quizzes, and awards.

www.ceismc.gatech.edu/busyt This easy-to-use, award-winning site provides busy K–12 teachers with annotated links to source material, lesson plans, and classroom activities.

www.education-world.com Found on this site are a variety of lesson plans, activities, and current news integrating the language arts with all disciplines.

www.pearsondigital.com A provider of digital learning solutions focused on the art and science of teaching and on helping all learners reach their potential.

http://english.unitecnology.ac.nz Originating in New Zealand, this site for K–12 English teachers is part of a professional development program comprising unit plans created by teachers throughout New Zealand and covering all grade levels.

www.free.ed.gov/ Sponsored by more than 30 federal agencies, this site provides a host of learning resources such as reading activities, famous paintings, historical documents, web-based tools, and ask-an-expert services.

www.scholastic.com Teacher lesson plans and classroom activities are provided here. Specific materials for current books, such as the *Harry Potter* series, address the books, the authors, and the stories.

www.kidsplanet.org This site provides a bibliography of books about specific species of animals, a large database of wolf-related curriculum designed for integrated language arts units, and much more.

www.rhlschool.com/reading.htm This site offers weekly worksheets, mostly for upper-elementary and middle school students, for teachers to copy and use at no charge.

http://falcon.jmu.edu/schoollibrary/biochildhome.htm Offered here is a plethora of information about children's and young adult's authors and illustrators.

www.eduplace.com This site provides classroom resources for teachers, including graphic organizers and links for using the web.

www.poetry.com On this site students can post their poems, enter poetry contests, use the world's most comprehensive rhyming dictionary, and read hundreds of poems by other students and accomplished poets.

http://www.ucalgary.ca/dkbrown/index.html The Children's Literature Web Guide is devoted entirely to young adult and children's literature.

www.artsconnected.org/classroom A database of educational materials for using the arts in the classroom.

http://ctell.uconn.edu/cases/newliteracies.htm Using 12 principles of effective literacy instruction, the Case Technologies to Enhance Literacy Learning (CTELL) group designs and assesses CTELL cases to inform preservice teacher education on best practices.

www.smithsonianeducation.org The Smithsonian Center for Education and Museum Studies links educators, families, and students to hundreds of online resources. Educators will find ideas for lesson plans and field trips in addition to websites and related publications.

www.readwritethink.org This IRA and NCTE sponsored site presents educators and students with the highest quality practices and resources in reading and language arts instruction.

www.loc.gov The Library of Congress website provides resources for kids and families as well as teachers.

FLUENCY

Coaching reading fluency
www.interdys.org/pdf/T38-Reading-Fluency.pdf#search=i_reading%20fluency

Readers Theatre
www.aaronshep.com/rt/RTE.html
www.teachingheart.net/readerstheater.htm
www.lisablau.com/freescripts.html
www.Humboldt.edu/~jmf2/floss/rt-eval.html

Peer tutor training manual
www.jimwrightonline.com/pdfdocs/prtutor_lessons3.pdf

Teaching fluency through poetry
www.poetry4kids.com/index.php

Fluency calculator
http://teacher.scholastic.com/reading/bestpractices/assessment/OFAcalc.htm

VOCABULARY

Vocabulary instruction
www.vocabulary.com

Chapter books to read aloud
www.kinderkorner.com/readalouds.html

Vocabulary lesson plans
http://lessonplancentral.com/lessons/Language_Arts/Vocabulary/index.htm

Vocabulary lists
www.tampareads.com/trial/vocabulary/index-vocab.htm

Other vocabulary development
www.techteachers.com/vocabulary.htm

TEXT COMPREHENSION

Children's Literature Web Guide
www.acs.ucalgary.ca/~dkbrown

Reading challenge
www.bookadventure.org

Literary lessons
http://home.att.net/~teaching/litlessons.htm

Reading strategies
http://curry.edschool.virginia.edu/go/readquest/links.html

Comprehension rubric
www.mrsmcgowan.com/reading/rubrics.htm#Comprehension

Commercial Assessment Tools

INFORMAL READING INVENTORIES

Analytical Reading Inventory (Woods, M. L., & Moe, A. J., 2007. Upper Saddle River, NJ: Merrill-Prentice Hall)

Basic Reading Inventory: Preprimer Through Grade Twelve & Early Literacy Assessments (Johns, J., 2007. Dubuque, IA: Kendall/Hunt)

Classroom Assessment of Reading Processes (Swearingen, R., & Allen, D., 1997. Boston: Houghton Mifflin)

Cooter/Flynt/Cooter Comprehensive Reading Inventory (Cooter, R. B., Flynt, E. S., & Cooter, K. S., 2007. Upper Saddle River, NJ: Merrill-Prentice Hall) Includes a Spanish reading inventory.

The Critical Reading Inventory: Assessing Students' Reading and Thinking (Applegate, M. D., Quinn, K. B., & Applegate, A. J., 2008. Upper Saddle River, NJ: Pearson Education)

Ekwall/Shanker Reading Inventory (Ekwall, E. E., & Shanker, J. L., 1999. Boston: Allyn & Bacon)

Informal Reading Inventory: Preprimer to Twelfth Grade (Burns, P. C., Roe, B. D., 2007. Boston: Houghton Mifflin)

Qualitative Reading Inventory (Leslie, L., & Caldwell, J., 2006. New York: Allyn & Bacon)

The Stieglitz Informal Reading Inventory: Assessing Reading Behaviors from Emergent to Advanced Levels (Stieglitz, E., 1997. Boston: Allyn & Bacon)

ATTITUDE SURVEYS

Valid and reliable attitude surveys for reading and writing are available for use or modification by teachers. Here is a partial listing:

Bottomley, D., Henk, W., & Melnick, S. (1997/1998). Assessing children's views about themselves as writers using the Writer Self-Perception Scale. *The Reading Teacher, 51,* 286–296.

Gambrell, L. G., Palmer, B. M., Codling, R. M., & Mazzoni, S. A. (1996). Assessing motivation to read. *The Reading Teacher, 49,* 518–533.

Henk, W. A., & Melnick, S. A. (1995). The Reader Self-Perception Scale (RSPS): A new tool for measuring how children feel about themselves as readers. *The Reading Teacher, 48,* 470–482.

Kear, D. J., Coffman, G. A., McKenna, M. C., & Ambrosio, A. L. (2000). Measuring attitude toward writing: A new tool for teachers. *The Reading Teacher, 54,* 10–23.

McKenna, M. C., & Kear, D. J. (1990). Measuring attitude toward reading: A new tool for teachers. *The Reading Teacher, 43,* 626–639.

Pitcher, S. M., Albright, L. K., DeLaney, C. J., Walker, N. T., Seunarinesingh, K., Mogge, S., et al. (2007). Assessing adolescents' motivation to read. *Journal of Adolescent & Adult Literacy, 50,* 378–396.

Tullock-Rhody, R., & Alexander, J. E. (1980). A scale for assessing attitudes toward reading in secondary schools. *Journal of Reading, 23,* 609–614.

STANDARDIZED TESTS

Stanford Diagnostic Reading Test (SDRT). This test provides six test levels for more specific information about reading skills. These skills are phonetic analysis, vocabulary, and comprehension at the red (grades 1.5–2.5), orange (grades 2.5–3.5), and green levels (grades 3.5–4.5), and the addition of scanning at the purple, brown, and blue levels. Comprehension is assessed using three types of reading material: recreational, textual, and functional. A review set of materials is available from Harcourt Brace Educational Measurement, 555 Academic Court, San Antonio, TX 78204-2498, 1-800-228-0752.

Estes Attitude Scales: Measures of Attitude Toward School Subjects (Estes, T. H., Estes, J. J., Richards, H. C., & Roettger, D. Austin, TX: Pro-Ed). This standardized instrument "is available in both elementary and secondary forms. As reviewed in the *Ninth Mental Measurements Yearbook* (Mitchell, 1985), the *Estes Attitude Scales* measure attitudes toward school subjects. The elementary form for grades 2–6 includes items for math, reading, and science; the secondary form for grades 6–12 includes items for English, math, reading, science, and social studies. The scales take 20–30 minutes to administer. Reliability is reported as .76–.88 for the elementary scale and .76–.93 for the secondary scale, which are quite respectable for measures of this sort. The *Estes Attitude Scales* would be useful for obtaining affective data for comparisons at local levels.

"This instrument is especially valuable in light of research that shows the importance of considering attitudes toward content areas at the middle and secondary levels (Alexander & Cobb, 1992). A positive attitude toward reading in a content area undeniably has an impact on achievement in that subject" (Gipe, 2002, p. 139).

OTHER ASSESSMENT RESOURCES

These handbooks contain a variety of assessment tools for both reading and writing.

Bader Reading and Language Inventory (Bader, L. A., 2002. Upper Saddle River, NJ: Merrill Prentice Hall). This instrument contains not only an abbreviated informal reading inventory, but also a test battery for student priorities and interests, English as a Second Language Quick Start, word recognition lists, spelling tests, visual and auditory discrimination tests, preliteracy assessments, phonics tests, cloze tests, oral and written language checklists, and an arithmetic test.

Literacy Assessment: A Handbook of Instruments (Rhodes, L. K., 1993. Portsmouth, NH: Heinemann). This handbook contains many examples of interest and attitude surveys for reading and writing, comprehension checklists, student self-assessment forms for reading and writing, observation checklists for teachers for reading and writing, emergent literacy assessments, interviews for parents, and assessment forms for evaluating the teaching of literacy.

Running Records for Classroom Teachers (Clay, M. M., 2000. Portsmouth, NH: Heinemann). This handbook describes the key ideas for using running records as an assessment tool. Directions and examples are given for how to take a running record and how to record, score, and interpret the results.

Literacy Assessment & Intervention for K–6 Classrooms (DeVries, B., 2007. Scottsdale, AZ: Holcomb Hathaway). This comprehensive resource covers both theory and practice and will help teachers recognize and assess reading and writing problems and provide effective interventions to help students succeed. It focuses on the major areas of literacy: phonemic awareness, phonics, word identification, comprehension of both narrative and expository text, vocabulary, fluency, and writing, including spelling. The author thoroughly explores each area, providing an overview of pertinent research, suggested methods for diagnosis and assessment, and intervention strategies and activities. Appendices include a wealth of assessment tools and visuals to accompany the intervention activities and strategies.

Informal Checklists and Assessment Devices

HOW THE TOOLS IN THIS APPENDIX ARE ORGANIZED:

Reading Interest/Attitude Devices

D.1   Reading Interest Inventory   388

D.2   Reading Attitude Survey—Interview Format   390

D.3   Reading Attitude Survey—Handout Format   391

D.4   Denver Reading Attitude Survey   392

D.5   Encuesta Sobre Lectura de Denver   395

Word Study

D.6   Spelling Inventory   397

D.7   Developmental Spelling Test (The "Monster Test")   400

D.8   Checklist for Assessing the Nifty-Thrifty-Fifty   401

Speaking and Listening

D.9   Personal Report of Communication Fear   403

D.10   Scoring Rubric for Oral Expression   404

D.11   Scoring Rubric for a Multimedia Presentation   405

D.12   Am I a Good Listener?   407

Writing

D.13   Editing Checklist   408

D.14   Student Self-Assessment Checklist for Effective Writing   409

D.15   Scoring Rubric for Expository Essay   410

Other

D.16   Expository Text Retelling Checklist   411

D.17   Website Evaluation Form   412

D.18   Checklist for Observations of Progress Toward Standards   413

D.19   Literacy Observation Checklist   415

D.20   Example of a Self-Assessment Scoring Rubric for a Specific Learning Target   416

D.21   A Teacher's Self-Evaluation for Literacy Instruction   417

APPENDIX **D.1** *Reading Interest Inventory*

Name _____ Grade _____ Date _____

1. What do you like to do most when you have spare time?

   _____

2. What do you usually do after school?

   _____

   . . . in the evenings?

   _____

   . . . on weekends?

   _____

   _____

   . . . on vacations?

   _____

   _____

3. Do you have brothers or sisters? If so, what activities do you like to do with them?

   _____

   _____

4. Are your parents/grandparents from a different country? Which one? What language do they speak?

   _____

5. What is the best movie/video you have ever seen? What did you like about it?

   _____

   _____

6. What is your favorite television show? What do you like about it?

   _____

   _____

7. Do you ever listen to the news on television?

   _____

8. What is your favorite sport/sports figure?

   _____

9. What songs/music do you like?

   _____

   _____

Reading Interest Inventory, CONTINUED

10. Do you take any special lessons? Describe them.

    _____

    _____

11. Do you have any pets? If not, what kind of animal(s) do you like or wish to own?

    _____

12. If you could meet anyone in the world, who would you choose?

    _____

13. What kind of job would you like to do to earn money?

    _____

14. Which of the following do you enjoy reading? (circle all that apply):

    magazines   newspapers   catalogs
    comic books/strips   books   manuals

15. What kinds of books appeal to you? (circle all that apply):

    fantasy   true stories   action/adventure
    biographies   mysteries   romance
    how to   humor   historical fiction
    autobiography   books in a series   poetry
    books based on TV characters   travel books

16. What book is your all-time favorite? Why?

    _____

    _____

17. Do you like to have someone read to you?

    _____

18. Do you prefer to read alone or with someone?

    _____

19. What books would you like to own?

    _____

20. Which of the following describe the kinds of books you most enjoy? (circle as many as apply):

    scary   sad   believable
    adventurous   informative   unbelievable
    insightful   humorous   characters like me
    helpful   historical   characters unlike me

Reading Attitude Survey—Interview Format

Attitude surveys address students' perceptions of reading and writing as processes and their perceptions of themselves as readers and writers. An interview format is appropriate for providing the teacher with this information. The interview might include some of the following key questions:

- ☐ Do you like to read (write)?
- ☐ What is your favorite book (or who is your favorite author)?
- ☐ When do you read (write)?
- ☐ Do you think you are a good reader (writer)? Why or why not?
- ☐ Who is the best reader (writer) you know? Why?
- ☐ When you do not understand what you read, what do you do?
- ☐ Would you rather read (write) or play sports?
- ☐ Would you rather read (write) or watch a movie?
- ☐ Would you rather read a story or write a story?
- ☐ Would you rather read (write) or do nothing?
- ☐ Would you rather read (write) or paint?
- ☐ Would you rather read (write) or do math homework?
- ☐ Would you rather read (write) or help with the chores?

Open-ended statements are also used to assess attitudes. For example, the student might be asked to complete the following sentences:

What I like most about reading is

_____

_____

I think writing

_____

_____

Most books

_____

_____

My writing

_____

_____

When my teacher reads

_____

_____

Adapted from Gipe, J. P. (2006). *Multiple Paths to Literacy: Assessment and Differentiated Instruction for Diverse Learners, K–12* (6th ed, p. 137). Upper Saddle River, NJ: Merrill-Prentice Hall. (See also Appendix C for commercial assessment tools for additional attitude surveys.)

Reading Attitude Survey—Handout Format

Name _____   Date _____

Directions: Make one check for each of your choices.

- ☐ I like reading a lot.
- ☐ Reading is O.K.
- ☐ I'd rather do other things.

What kinds of books do you like to read? Check as many as you like.

- ☐ realistic fiction
- ☐ poetry
- ☐ fantasy
- ☐ myths
- ☐ historical fiction
- ☐ biographies (about real people)
- ☐ (write any other kind you like here)

- ☐ picture books
- ☐ true facts
- ☐ folktales and fables
- ☐ mysteries
- ☐ plays
- ☐ science fiction

_____

_____

_____

How do you choose something to read?

- ☐ I listen to a friend
- ☐ I look at the front cover
- ☐ if it's part of a series I like
- ☐ I read the first few pages
- ☐ if I liked other books by that author

- ☐ I look to see if it's easy enough
- ☐ I look to see if it's hard enough
- ☐ I read the back cover or jacket flap
- ☐ I follow my teacher's suggestion

When do you prefer to read?

- ☐ in my spare time
- ☐ at home
- ☐ as part of my class work

How do you like to read?

- ☐ with friends
- ☐ with kids who read about the same as I do
- ☐ by myself
- ☐ with my teacher in the group

APPENDIX D.4 *Denver Reading Attitude Survey*

Description

The *Denver Reading Attitude Survey* provides an indication of students' engagement in reading activities, their perception of the importance and utility of reading, and their confidence in themselves as readers. The survey includes a few items from the National Assessment of Educational Progress.

Instructions for Administering

So that the results of the survey are not affected by variations in reading ability, read each item aloud. Students respond to each item by circling the letter of their response.

Spanish and English versions are available. Students should complete the survey in the language they are most confident using.

Explain that the purpose of the survey is to learn students' honest feelings about reading in and out of school. Emphasize that this is not a test; there are no right or wrong answers, and the results will have no effect on grades.

As you read the items, clarify them and answer questions as needed. Also draw attention to each change in the response format.

Denver Reading Attitude Survey, CONTINUED

Name _____   Grade _____

Teacher _____   Date _____

Make a circle around the answer that is most true for you.

How often do you do each of the following things?

	Almost every day	Once or twice a week	Once or twice a month	A few times a year	Never or hardly ever
1. Get so interested in something you're reading that you don't want to stop.	A	B	C	D	E
2. Read the newspaper.	A	B	C	D	E
3. Tell a friend about a good book.	A	B	C	D	E
4. Read on your own outside of school.	A	B	C	D	E
5. Read about something because you are curious about it.	A	B	C	D	E
6. Read more than one book by an author you like.	A	B	C	D	E

7. What kind of reader do you think you are?

    A. A very good reader.

    B. A good reader.

    C. An average reader.

    D. A poor reader.

    E. A very poor reader.

(continued)

Denver Reading Attitude Survey, CONTINUED

The following statements are true for some people. They may or may not be true for you, or they may be true for you only part of the time. How often is each of the following sentences true for you?

	Almost always	More than half the time	About half the time	Less than half the time	Never or hardly ever
8. Reading helps me learn about myself.	A	B	C	D	E
9. I feel good about how fast I can read.	A	B	C	D	E
10. Reading helps me understand why people feel or act the way they do.	A	B	C	D	E
11. I believe that reading will help me get ahead when I am no longer in school.	A	B	C	D	E
12. I feel proud about what I can read.	A	B	C	D	E
13. Reading helps me see what it might be like to live in a different place or in a different way.	A	B	C	D	E
14. Being able to read well is important to me.	A	B	C	D	E
15. I can understand what I read in school.	A	B	C	D	E
16. Other people think I read well.	A	B	C	D	E
17. I learn worthwhile things from reading books.	A	B	C	D	E

Encuesta Sobre Lectura de Denver

Nombre _____   Grado _____

Maestro/a _____   Feche _____

Encierre en un círculo la letra de la respuesta que sea mas cierta para usted.

¿Con que frecuencia hace cada una de las siguientes cosas?

	Casi cada día	Una o dos veces por semana	Una o dos veces por mes	Varias veces por año	Nunca o casi nunca
1. Se interesa tanto en la lectura que no puede dejar de leer.	A	B	C	D	E
2. Lee el periódico.	A	B	C	D	E
3. Le plactica a un(a) amigo(a) de un buen libro.	A	B	C	D	E
4. Lee libros de texto (como por ejemplo de ciencias sociales o naturales).	A	B	C	D	E
5. Lee algo por curiosidad.	A	B	C	D	E
6. Lee más de un libro de algún escritor que le guste.	A	B	C	D	E

7. ¿Qué tipo de lector se considera usted?

   A. Excelente lector.

   B. Buen lector.

   C. Lector regular.

   D. Lector con problemas.

   E. Lector con muchos problemas.

(continued)

Las siguientes declaraciones se refieren a ciertas personas. Estas declaraciones no necesariamente son aplicables a usted, o serán ciertas solo en algunas ocasiones. ¿Con qué frecuencia es cada una de las siguientes declaraciones cierta para usted?

	Casi siempre	Más de la mitad del tiempo	Como la mitad del tiempo	Menos de la mitad del tiempo	Nunca o casi nunca
8. La lectura me ayuda a aprender de mi mismo(a).	A	B	C	D	E
9. Me gusta la rapidez con la que leo.	A	B	C	D	E
10. La lectura me ayuda a entender por qué la gente se siente o actuá de la manera en que lo hace.	A	B	C	D	E
11. Pienso que la lectura me ayudará a salir adelante cuando ya no esté en la escuela.	A	B	C	D	E
12. Me siento orgulloso(a) de lo que puedo leer.	A	B	C	D	E
13. La lectura me ayuda a ver cómo sería vivir de otra manera o en otro lugar.	A	B	C	D	E
14. El poder leer bien es importante para mi.	A	B	C	D	E
15. Entiendo mi lectura escolar.	A	B	C	D	E
16. Otra gente piensa que yo leo bien.	A	B	C	D	E
17. Aprendo cosas que valen la pena a través de libros.	A	B	C	D	E

Spelling Inventory

Directions: Dictate the following words in groups of five. After saying each word, use it in a sentence. Then repeat the word. You may wish to stop your assessment at the end of a set if students seem frustrated with a particular group of words. Possible script: "I want you to spell some words. You have not had the chance to study these words, but I want you to spell them the best that you can. Some might be easy for you, and some might seem hard. If you think you don't know how to spell the word, just listen carefully to the word, say it to yourself, and then write down all the sounds you hear."

Set One

1. drawing   Joey was drawing a picture of a dog. *drawing*
2. trapped   The animals were trapped in their cages. *trapped*
3. waving   Mom was waving hello to us from the car. *waving*
4. powerful   The alligator's jaws are powerful. *powerful*
5. battle   The Battle of the Bands is this Saturday. *battle*

Set Two

6. sailor   Christopher Columbus was a sailor. *sailor*
7. lesson   Pat has a piano lesson every Tuesday. *lesson*
8. pennies   Save your pennies for a rainy day. *pennies*
9. fraction   One-fourth is a fraction. *fraction*
10. distance   The distance for the race is three miles. *distance*

Set Three

11. visible   The Big Dipper is visible without a telescope. *visible*
12. confusion   There was confusion over who was in charge. *confusion*
13. discovery   The scientists made a great discovery. *discovery*
14. resident   You are a resident of planet Earth. *resident*
15. fortunate   I was fortunate to win the grand prize. *fortunate*

Set Four

16. pleasure   Reading a good book brings me pleasure. *pleasure*
17. puncture   He used a sharp pencil to puncture a hole in the balloon. *puncture*
18. confidence   The speaker showed confidence when on stage. *confidence*
19. decorator   They hired a decorator to help them fix up their house. *decorator*
20. opposition   There was too much opposition to the idea and so most people voted against it. *opposition*

(continued)

APPENDIX   D.6   *Spelling Inventory,* CONTINUED

Student Record Sheet for Developmental Comparisons

Name _____   Name _____

Date _____ Spelling Level _____   Date _____ Spelling Level _____

	Stage		Stage
1. _____ _____		1. _____ _____	
2. _____ _____		2. _____ _____	
3. _____ _____		3. _____ _____	
4. _____ _____		4. _____ _____	
5. _____ _____		5. _____ _____	
6. _____ _____		6. _____ _____	
7. _____ _____		7. _____ _____	
8. _____ _____		8. _____ _____	
9. _____ _____		9. _____ _____	
10. _____ _____		10. _____ _____	
11. _____ _____		11. _____ _____	
12. _____ _____		12. _____ _____	
13. _____ _____		13. _____ _____	
14. _____ _____		14. _____ _____	
15. _____ _____		15. _____ _____	
16. _____ _____		16. _____ _____	
17. _____ _____		17. _____ _____	
18. _____ _____		18. _____ _____	
19. _____ _____		19. _____ _____	
20. _____ _____		20. _____ _____	

How to Analyze Students' Spellings

1. Look at the student's spelling for each word. Match the spelling with the spelling in the Scoring Chart, or find the spelling that comes closest.

2. Write an abbreviation of the matching spelling stage beside each of the words on the Student Record Sheet for Developmental Comparisons.

3. The stage that appears most often is the label that will be used as the spelling level for that administration date. Administer the same words again three to four months later for a comparison.

REFERENCES

Bear, D. R., Invernizzi, M., Templeton, S., & Johnston, F. (2000). *Words their way: Word study for phonics, vocabulary, and spelling instruction.* Upper Saddle River, NJ: Merrill.

Fiderer, A. (1995). *Practical assessments for literature-based reading classrooms.* New York: Scholastic Professional Books.

Spelling Inventory, CONTINUED

Scoring Chart for Spelling Inventory

Directions: Locate the spelling in the lists below that matches or comes closest to the student's spelling. Look straight up at the heading for the spelling stage represented by that spelling in the developmental continuum. Write that stage on the student record sheet.

Spelling Developmental Continuum for Intermediate Grades

TRANSITIONAL		SYLLABLES AND AFFIXES			DERIVATIONAL RELATIONS		
Middle	**Late**	**Early**	**Middle**	**Late**	**Early**	**Middle**	**Late**
draing	drauing	drawing					
trapt	traped	trappt	trapped				
waiving	weighving	waveing	waving				
pauerfle	pouerful	powerfle	powerfel	powerful			
batul	batil/batel	batle/battul	battle				
saler	sayler/saylor	sailer	sailor				
lisin	lesen/lesin/leson	lessin/lessen	lesson				
penes/penez	penknees/penees	penys/pennys	pennies				
	frakshun		frackshun	fracktion	fraction		
dizdance	disdance	distanz	distans	distance			
vizabull	vizabel	vizabul	vizable	visable	visible		
confushon	confushun/confution	confustion	conffusion	confusetion	confussion	confusion	
diskuverie	diskkuveree	discuveree	discovere	discoverie	discovery		
resatin	reserdent	rezudint	resadent/resedint	reseadent	resedent	residant	resident
	forhnat/frehnit	foohinit	forchenut/fochininte	fortunet	fortunate		
	plasr/plager/plejer	pleser	plesour	plesher	plesure/pleasur	pleasure	
	pucshr/pungchr/puncur	puncker/punksher	punchure	puncure	punture	puncsure	puncture
	confadents	confadence	confedense	confedence	confidince	confidense	confidence
	dector/decrater	decerator	decarator	decreator	decoratore	decorater	decorator
	opasishan/opozcison	opasitian	opasition	oppisition	oposision	oposition	opposition

Developmental Spelling Test (The "Monster Test")

An easily administered 10-word checklist, such as the following developmental test devised by Gentry (1985), makes it possible for teachers to assess children's developmental spelling level.

WORDS	PRECOMMUNICATIVE SPELLINGS	SEMI-PHONETIC SPELLINGS	PHONETIC SPELLINGS	TRANSITIONAL SPELLINGS	CORRECT SPELLINGS
1. monster	random letters	mtr	mostr	monstur	monster
2. united	random letters	u	unitid	younighted	united
3. dress	random letters	jrs	jras	dres	dress
4. bottom	random letters	bt	bodm	bottum	bottom
5. hiked	random letters	h	hikt	hicked	hiked
6. human	random letters	um	humm	humin	human
7. eagle	random letters	el	egl	egul	eagle
8. closed	random letters	kd	klosd	clossed	closed
9. bumped	random letters	b	bopt	bumpt	bumped
10. type	random letters	tp	tip	tipe	type

From Gentry, J. Richard (1985). You Can Analyze Developmental Spelling. *The Early Years* (9), 44–45. Reprinted with permission.

Checklist for Assessing the Nifty-Thrifty-Fifty

NIFTY-THRIFTY-FIFTY*	TRANSFERABLE	CHUNKS
1. ____ antifreeze	1. ____ anti	
2. ____ beautiful		2. ____ ful (y - i)
3. ____ classify		3. ____ ify
4. ____ communities	4. ____ com	4. ____ es (y - i)
5. ____ community	5. ____ com	5. ____ y
6. ____ composer	6. ____ com	6. ____ er
7. ____ continuous	7. ____ con	7. ____ ous (drop e)
8. ____ conversation	8. ____ con	8. ____ tion
9. ____ deodorize	9. ____ de	9. ____ ize
10. ____ different		10. ____ ent
11. ____ discovery	11. ____ dis	11. ____ y
12. ____ dishonest	12. ____ dis	
13. ____ electricity	13. ____ e	13. ____ ity
14. ____ employee	14. ____ em	14. ____ ee
15. ____ encouragement	15. ____ en	15. ____ ment
16. ____ expensive	16. ____ ex	16. ____ ive
17. ____ forecast	17. ____ fore	
18. ____ forgotten		18. ____ en (double t)
19. ____ governor		19. ____ or
20. ____ happiness		20. ____ ness (y - i)
21. ____ hopeless		21. ____ less
22. ____ illegal	22. ____ il	
23. ____ impossible	23. ____ im	23. ____ ible

(continued)

NIFTY-THRIFTY-FIFTY*		TRANSFERABLE		CHUNKS	
24. ____	impression	24. ____	im	24. ____	sion
25. ____	independence	25. ____	in	25. ____	ence
26. ____	international	26. ____	inter	26. ____	al
27. ____	invasion	27. ____	in	27. ____	sion
28. ____	irresponsible	28. ____	ir	28. ____	ible
29. ____	midnight	29. ____	mid		
30. ____	misunderstand	30. ____	mis		
31. ____	musician			31. ____	ian
32. ____	nonliving	32. ____	non	32. ____	ing (drop e)
33. ____	overpower	33. ____	over		
34. ____	performance	34. ____	per	34. ____	ance
35. ____	prehistoric	35. ____	pre	35. ____	ic
36. ____	prettier			36. ____	er (y - i)
37. ____	rearrange	37. ____	re		
38. ____	replacement	38. ____	re	38. ____	ment
39. ____	richest			39. ____	est
40. ____	semifinal	40. ____	semi		
41. ____	signature			41. ____	ture
42. ____	submarine	42. ____	sub		
43. ____	supermarkets	43. ____	super	43. ____	s
44. ____	swimming			44. ____	ing (double m)
45. ____	transportation	45. ____	trans	45. ____	tion
46. ____	underweight	46. ____	under		
47. ____	unfinished	47. ____	un	47. ____	ed
48. ____	unfriendly	48. ____	un	48. ____	ly
49. ____	unpleasant	49. ____	un	49. ____	ant (drop e)
50. ____	valuable			50. ____	able (drop e)

Personal Report of Communication Fear (PRCF)   APPENDIX   D.9

McCroskey & Richmond, 1991, pp. 41–43

Directions: The following 14 statements concern feelings about communicating with other people. Please indicate the degree to which each statement applies to you by circling your response. Mark "YES" if you strongly agree, "yes" if you agree, "?" if you are unsure, "no" if you disagree, or "NO" if you strongly disagree. There are no right or wrong answers. Answer quickly; record your first impression.

1. Talking with someone new scares me.

   YES   yes   ?   no   NO

2. I look forward to talking in class.

   YES   yes   ?   no   NO

3. I like standing up and talking to a group of people.

   YES   yes   ?   no   NO

4. I like to talk when the whole class listens.

   YES   yes   ?   no   NO

5. Standing up to talk in front of other people scares me.

   YES   yes   ?   no   NO

6. I like talking to teachers.

   YES   yes   ?   no   NO

7. I am scared to talk to people.

   YES   yes   ?   no   NO

8. I like it when it is my turn to talk in class.

   YES   yes   ?   no   NO

9. I like to talk to new people.

   YES   yes   ?   no   NO

10. When someone asks me a question, it scares me.

    YES   yes   ?   no   NO

11. There are a lot of people I am scared to talk to.

    YES   yes   ?   no   NO

12. I like to talk to people I haven't met before.

    YES   yes   ?   no   NO

13. I like it when I don't have to talk.

    YES   yes   ?   no   NO

14. Talking to teachers scares me.

    YES   yes   ?   no   NO

Scoring: YES = 1, yes = 2, ? = 3, no = 4, NO = 5.

To obtain the score for the PRCF, complete the following steps:

    Step 1. Add the scores for the following items: 2, 3, 4, 6, 8, 9, and 12.

    Step 2. Add the scores for the following items: 1, 5, 7, 10, 11, 13, and 14.

    Step 3. Compute the following: 42 (plus) total of Step 1 (minus) total of Step 2.

    Your score should be between 14 and 70.

The normal range of scores on the PRCF is between 28 and 47. Students who score above 47 are most likely communication-apprehensive. These are the children who need very careful, special attention. Those who score below 28, on the other hand, are very low in communication apprehension. These children are likely to be highly verbal, and they often will be the students who are most disruptive in the classroom. They are also those who most likely will do well in a traditional instructional system. In addition, they are frequently well liked by other students and, unless they are particularly disruptive, well liked by their teachers.

From J. McCroskey and V. Richmond, *Quiet Children and the Classroom Teacher* (Bloomington, IN: ERIC, 1991), 27–30. Used by permission of the National Communication Association.

APPENDIX	D.10	*Scoring Rubric for Oral Expression*

CRITERIA	NEEDS WORK (1)	MAKING PROGRESS (2)	DOING GREAT (3)	ABOVE AND BEYOND (4)	SCORE
Speaking	Monotone; speaker seemed uninterested in material.	Little eye contact; fast speaking rate, little expression, mumbling.	Clear articulation of ideas, but apparently lacks confidence with material.	Exceptional confidence with material displayed through poise, clear articulation, eye contact, and enthusiasm.	1 2 3 4
Creativity	Delivery is repetitive with little or no variety in presentation techniques; lacks visuals.	Material presented with little interpretation or originality; visual aid fails to grab attention and/or fails to communicate information.	Some apparent originality displayed through use of original interpretation of presented materials visually and/or orally.	Exceptional originality of presented material and interpretation both visually and orally.	1 2 3 4
Content	Results are unclear and information appears randomly chosen.	Results are clear, but supporting information is not available.	Results are very clear; many relevant points, but they are unaddressed.	Exceptional use of material that clearly relates to a focused thesis; abundance of varied supportive materials.	1 2 3 4
Clarity	No apparent logical order of presentation; unclear focus.	Content is loosely connected; transitions lack clarity.	Sequence of information is well organized for the most part, but more clarity with transitions is needed.	Development of thesis is clear through use of specific and appropriate examples; transitions are clear and create a succinct and even flow.	1 2 3 4
Presentation Length	Greatly exceeding or falling short of allotted time.	Exceeding or falling short of allotted time.	Remained close to the allotted time.	Presented within the allotted time.	1 2 3 4

Scoring Rubric for a Multimedia Presentation

Delivery (Total Possible: 36 points)

1 2 3 4   Student used a different form to communicate to the group other than simply screen reading.

1 2 3 4   Student used each slide as a lead into the wealth of additional information he or she found on the topic.

1 2 3 4   Student maintained eye contact with the audience, seldom returning to notes.

1 2 3 4   At conclusion of presentation, student checked for understanding via questions, oral quiz, written assessment, etc.

1 2 3 4   Student used allotted time effectively; the pacing of the presentation was appropriate.

1 2 3 4   Information was presented in a logical and interesting sequence that the audience could follow.

1 2 3 4   Student used a clear voice and correct, precise pronunciation of terms so all audience members could hear the presentation.

1 2 3 4   Each member of the audience was given a handout to accompany the presentation.

1 2 3 4   Audience was engaged throughout the presentation; if engagement waned, the presenting student managed to reengage the audience.

Graphics (Total Possible: 20 points)

1 2 3 4   The presentation included a minimum of 10 slides.

1 2 3 4   The presentation included a variety of text fields, graphics, sounds, and transitions.

1 2 3 4   The presentation had a professional look with an overall graphical theme appealing to the audience, with each slide visually neat and incorporating a variety of layouts.

1 2 3 4   Student's graphics explained and reinforced screen text and oral presentation.

1 2 3 4   Text fields were not overly crowded with text, and used a readable font and font size.

Content (Total Possible: 28 points)

1 2 3 4   All material was thoroughly proofread and without careless errors.

1 2 3 4   All information was well researched and well written, and reflects the student's own voice.

1 2 3 4   All flaws pointed out by the instructor and/or peer reviewers in drafts have been corrected.

1 2 3 4   Material showed strong understanding of major ideas and displayed evidence of critical thinking.

1 2 3 4   Presentation included a title page.

1 2 3 4   Presentation included a bibliography following APA citation rules.

1 2 3 4   Student demonstrated full knowledge of the topic by answering all class questions with explanations and elaborations.

Technical Skill (Total Possible: 16 points)

1 2 3 4   Student can access the server and has saved the presentation (website) in his or her personal folder, and has also made a backup copy of the presentation to assure against any disaster.

1 2 3 4   Student was facile at operating all equipment used during the presentation.

1 2 3 4   An electronic form of the presentation has been given to the instructor through a folder set up on the server by the instructor.

1 2 3 4   The handout each member of the audience received includes an area to take notes.

Total Points = _____ of 100

Delivery = 36   Graphics = 20   Content = 28   Technical Skill = 16

Am I a Good Listener?

Circle Y for "Yes" and N for "No" after each question about your listening habits and attitudes.

1. I like to listen to others.   Y   N

2. I listen even if I do not like the person who is talking.   Y   N

3. I listen even if I do not like the topic.   Y   N

4. I treat all people the same when I listen to them— whether or not they are friends, family, adults, children, male, female, or from a different country.   Y   N

5. I stop what I am doing so that I can give the speaker my full attention.   Y   N

6. I look at the speaker.   Y   N

7. I let the speaker finish what she/he is saying before I begin talking.   Y   N

8. I sometimes repeat back to the speaker what she/he said to see if I got it right.   Y   N

9. I ask questions if I don't understand an idea.   Y   N

10. I try to improve my listening.   Y   N

Source: Cooper, P. & Morreale, S. (Eds.) (2003). *Creating Competent Communicators*, p. 95. Scottsdale, AZ: Holcomb Hathaway.

APPENDIX D.13 *Editing Checklist*

	Author	Peer Editor	
	☐	☐	1. Did I read the piece backward, one sentence at a time, to check for spelling errors, sentence fragments, and run-on sentences?
	☐	☐	2. Did I use a dictionary, friend, spell checker, or other resource to find spelling errors?
	☐	☐	3. Did I check to make sure all proper nouns and the first words of each sentence are capitalized?
	☐	☐	4. Did I indent each paragraph?
	☐	☐	5. Did I make sure each sentence has the appropriate ending punctuation?
	☐	☐	6. Did I use commas appropriately? Are they only used for compound sentences, lists of items, introductory words or phrases, to set off interruptions, to separate adjectives, or in dates?
	☐	☐	7. Do I need to add commas? Have I made sure commas are not separating complete sentences?
	☐	☐	8. Have I used apostrophes only for contractions or to show ownership?
	☐	☐	9. Have I used more complex punctuation (dashes, semi-colons, hyphens, parentheses, etc.) correctly?
	☐	☐	10. Have I used common homonyms correctly, for example they're/their/there; your/you're; its/it's; too/two/to?
	☐	☐	11. Was I consistent in the use of either present or past tense in the entire piece?
	☐	☐	12. Was I consistent in my use of either first person or third person throughout the entire piece?

Student Self-Assessment Checklist for Effective Writing

Name: _____

Title of Work Assessed: _____

Did I . . . ?

- ☐ have a plan before I started writing?
- ☐ write complete sentences that are not run-on sentences?
- ☐ write some compound sentences that are connected with *and, or,* or *but?*
- ☐ write a good topic sentence for each paragraph?
- ☐ write supporting sentences that help support the topic sentence in each paragraph?
- ☐ write accurate nonfiction that is also interesting?
- ☐ provide good transitions between paragraphs?
- ☐ write a story that has a beginning, a middle, and an end?
- ☐ write a story with a problem and a solution?
- ☐ describe the main character well?
- ☐ include dialogue in my story?
- ☐ use correct punctuation in any dialogue?
- ☐ use interesting and vivid words?
- ☐ confer with others to revise?
- ☐ edit my drafts?

APPENDIX   D.15   *Scoring Rubric for Expository Essay*

CRITERIA	NEEDS WORK (1)	MAKING PROGRESS (2)	DOING GREAT (3)	ABOVE AND BEYOND (4)	SCORE
Understanding of Material	Apparent misunderstanding of material.	Limited understanding of material displayed by vague, unclear language.	Developing understanding of material.	Clear understanding of material displayed by clear, concrete language and complex ideas.	1 2 3 4
Structural Organization	Essay lacks logical progression of ideas.	Essay includes brief skeleton (introduction, body, conclusion) but lacks transitions.	Essay includes logical progression of ideas aided by clear transitions.	Essay is powerfully organized and fully developed.	1 2 3 4
Sentence Fluency (Flow)	Repetitive sentence patterns. There are no connecting words between sentences. Many sentences run into each other.	Sentence patterns are generally repetitive, with occasional variance. There are usually connecting words between sentences, where appropriate. Some sentences should be merged; others should be made into two or more sentences.	Sentence patterns are generally varied, but sometimes variations seem forced and inappropriate. There are connecting words between sentences, where appropriate. Each sentence contains a complete thought; there are no run-on sentences.	Varied and interesting sentence patterns. There are connecting words between sentences, where appropriate. Sentences are complete thoughts, with no run-ons.	1 2 3 4
Support	Few to no solid supporting ideas or evidence for the essay content.	Some supporting ideas and/or evidence for the essay content.	Support lacks specificity and is loosely developed.	Specific, developed details and superior support and evidence in the essay content.	1 2 3 4
Mechanics	Frequent errors in spelling, grammar, and punctuation.	Errors in grammar and punctuation, but spelling has been proofread.	Occasional grammatical errors. Spelling has been proofread.	Nearly error free. Reflects thorough proofreading for grammar and spelling.	1 2 3 4

Expository Text Retelling Checklist

Name: _____

Selection: _____

☐ What is the topic?

☐ What are the most important ideas to remember?

☐ What did you learn that you did not already know?

☐ What is the setting for the information?

☐ What did you notice about the organization and text structure?

☐ What new vocabulary did you learn?

☐ What did you notice about the visuals, such as graphs, charts, and pictures?

☐ Can you summarize what you have learned?

☐ What do you think was the author's purpose for writing this material?

Adapted from L. Hoyt (1999). *Revisit, reflect, retell: Strategies for improving reading comprehension.* Portsmouth, NH: Heinemann.

APPENDIX D.17 *Web Evaluation Form*

The Likert scale items that follow are intended for use by students.

Name of Website: Date:

URL:

Circle the number you think best reflects each item.   1 = Poor   5 = Excellent

Content

1. The title of the site is accurate.	1 2 3 4 5
2. Additional resource links are included.	1 2 3 4 5
3. The information is helpful.	1 2 3 4 5
4. There is much good content, and the site will be revisited.	1 2 3 4 5
5. This site ranks high compared with other sites having similar content.	1 2 3 4 5

Credibility

1. A contact person or e-mail address is given, as well as the host school, institution, or organization.	1 2 3 4 5
2. The site indicates when it was last updated.	1 2 3 4 5

Technical Elements

1. The links all work.	1 2 3 4 5
2. Graphics download quickly (within about 30 seconds).	1 2 3 4 5
3. A text alternative is offered when there are heavy graphics.	1 2 3 4 5

Design

1. The use of graphics and color makes the site visually appealing.	1 2 3 4 5
2. It is easy to move from page to page.	1 2 3 4 5
3. The links are clear and easy to find.	1 2 3 4 5
4. The text is easy to read with pages of appropriate length.	1 2 3 4 5

Add the total number of points for this website and write it in the blank below.

Total Score: _____ /70

Interpretation

If a website receives a score between 63 and 70, it is considered an excellent website.

If a website receives a score between 49 and 62, it is considered an above average website.

If a website receives a score between 35 and 48, it is considered an average website.

A website receiving a score below 35 is not well constructed and should not be used.

Checklist for Observations of Progress Toward Standards*   APPENDIX D.18

NAME: _____   GRADE: _____

STANDARDS	CONTEXT	DATE OBSERVED	CONTEXT	DATE OBSERVED	CONTEXT	DATE OBSERVED
1. Reads a wide range of print and nonprint texts						
2. Reads a wide range of literature (many time periods, many genres)						
3. Applies a wide range of strategies to comprehend, interpret, evaluate, and appreciate texts						
4. Adjusts use of spoken, written, and visual language to communicate effectively						
5. Employs a wide range of strategies for writing and different writing process elements to communicate effectively						
6. Applies knowledge of language structure, conventions, media techniques, figurative language, and genre to create, critique, and discuss print/nonprint texts						
7. Conducts research by generating ideas and questions, and by posing problems						
8. Uses a variety of technological and informational resources to gather/synthesize information and create/communicate knowledge						

*The standards used in this checklist are the NCTE/IRA Standards for the English Language Arts. Any state standards could be used, and the checklist can be made grade-level specific.

(continued)

Checklist for Observations of Progress, CONTINUED

STANDARDS	CONTEXT	DATE OBSERVED	CONTEXT	DATE OBSERVED	CONTEXT	DATE OBSERVED
9. Understands and respects diversity in language use, dialects, cultures						
10. If EL, makes use of native language to develop English competency						
11. Participates in a variety of literacy communities						
12. Uses spoken, written, and visual language to accomplish own purposes						

Literacy Observation Checklist

Name: _____   Grade level: _____   Teacher: _____

CONTENT STANDARDS	DATE						COMMENTS
Reads narrative text with fluency							
Reads expository text with fluency							
Identifies main events of the plot							
Makes inferences using text							
Makes inferences using illustrations							
Identifies structural patterns in expository text:							
—compare and contrast							
—cause and effect							
—order (enumeration or sequential)							
Asks questions							
Makes predictions							
Monitors own understanding							
Applies appropriate fix-up strategies							
Creates mental images while reading							
Retells to include salient points							
Makes text-to-self connections							
Uses clues to determine word meanings:							
—word clues							
—sentence or paragraph clues							
—background knowledge							

Example of a Self-Assessment Scoring Rubric

FOR A SPECIFIC LEARNING TARGET

TARGET:

STUDENT:

Requirements	FANTASTIC 4	NICE JOB! 3	OKAY 2	NEEDS IMPROVEMENT 1	SELF-ASSESSMENT	TEACHER'S ASSESSMENT
Cover Page	Includes title, author, and an appropriate illustration.	Includes two of the three required elements.	Includes one of the three required elements.	Does not include any of the three required elements, or is missing.		
Book Pages	Each page includes all required elements. Examples: (1) target word (2) word used in context (3) three facts about word (4) illustration for the word	Most pages include at least three required elements, and frequently four elements.	Many pages include two required elements, with several including three or four elements.	Many pages include only one or two required elements, or some pages are missing.		
Author Page	Includes author name, background information, an illustration or photo.	Includes two of the three required elements.	Includes one of the three required elements.	Does not include any of the three elements, or is missing.		

My strengths are:

What I need to work on:

A Teacher's Self-Evaluation for Literacy Instruction   APPENDIX   D.21

Name _____   Date _____

	Yes	Somewhat	No

1. I can recognize and describe the characteristics of emergent literacy.   ☐ ☐ ☐

2. I can list whole-group, small-group, and individual activities for the development of reading.   ☐ ☐ ☐

3. I can make a basic developmental reading lesson plan.   ☐ ☐ ☐

4. I know the components deemed necessary for a comprehensive, balanced reading program.   ☐ ☐ ☐

5. I can correctly write objectives (with three parts) for lessons.   ☐ ☐ ☐

6. I can describe and list at least 20 techniques for motivating students to read.   ☐ ☐ ☐

7. I can describe a variety of top-down and bottom-up approaches to teaching reading and the strengths and weaknesses of each.   ☐ ☐ ☐

8. I can explain how listening, speaking, reading, writing, viewing, and visually representing are related.   ☐ ☐ ☐

9. I understand the usage of authentic reading materials and how literature-based reading supports this.   ☐ ☐ ☐

10. I can develop and employ tools for diagnosing reading ability, including portfolios.   ☐ ☐ ☐

11. I am familiar with the reading material adopted by the State of _____ for use in grades 4–8 classrooms.   ☐ ☐ ☐

12. I know the terminology used by reading teachers (e.g., guided rdg., shared rdg.), including abbreviations (IRI, DRTA, IRA).   ☐ ☐ ☐

13. I can develop and analyze types of questions to get at various levels of comprehension and analyze students' answers.   ☐ ☐ ☐

14. I can identify and demonstrate techniques for teaching word analysis skills.   ☐ ☐ ☐

15. I can identify and demonstrate techniques for developing students' vocabulary.   ☐ ☐ ☐

16. I can list and develop techniques for teaching the various comprehension skills.   ☐ ☐ ☐

(continued)

APPENDIX   D.21   *A Teacher's Self-Evaluation,* CONTINUED

	Yes	Somewhat	No
17. I can plan and describe activities to aid special need students (e.g., gifted, physical handicap, special ed.).	☐	☐	☐
18. I can plan and describe activities to aid students with language differences.	☐	☐	☐
19. I can identify sources (places, journals, magazines) for instructional materials and teaching strategies.	☐	☐	☐
20. I understand the components of cooperative learning (and how it differs from group learning) and can incorporate it into my reading lessons.	☐	☐	☐
21. I can list activities for *meaningful* seatwork or learning centers to supplement the basic reading program.	☐	☐	☐
22. I can define basic linguistic terminology and describe the contribution of phonics to reading acquisition.	☐	☐	☐
23. I can use diagnostic techniques to identify the strengths and weaknesses in reading of the students in a class and devise a differentiated lesson for identified areas of need.	☐	☐	☐
24. I can plan reading lessons that are interdisciplinary.	☐	☐	☐
25. I know the professional organizations and journals that have reading as their focus.	☐	☐	☐
26. I am familiar with the purpose of the state framework, district benchmarks, and social improvement plan.	☐	☐	☐
27. I know various methods of presenting a children's book to students whether one copy or multiple copies are available.	☐	☐	☐
28. I enjoy reading and can be a good role model for students.	☐	☐	☐
29. I know the components of writer's workshop and could incorporate it in my classroom.	☐	☐	☐
30. I can design a literature-based three-day reading unit plan that includes reinforcement and enrichment tasks.	☐	☐	☐

Fry Readability Graph

Randomly select three average passages of exactly 100 words each. For each passage, count the number of sentences in the 100 words, estimating the length of the fraction of the last sentence to the nearest one-tenth. Count the number of syllables in each passage. If no hand counter is available, put a mark over every syllable *over* one for each word (e.g., a two-syllable word gets one mark); then when you get to the end of the passage, count the number of marks and add 100.

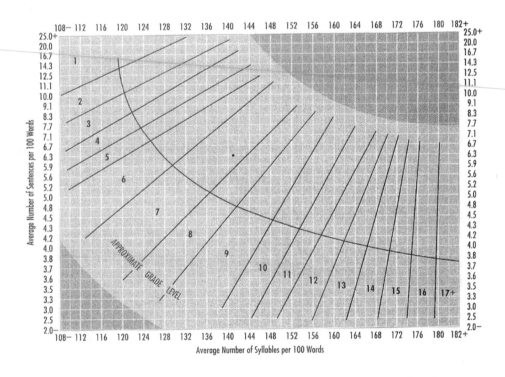

After you have completed these steps for all three passages, plot the *average* sentence length and *average* number of syllables on the graph. Where the two lines intersect, draw a dot. This point indicates the approximate grade level.

Choose additional passages if great variability is observed among the three original passages, recognizing that the book may have uneven readability.

Example:	Syllables	Sentences
1st Hundred Words	124	6.6
2nd Hundred Words	141	5.5
3rd Hundred Words	158	6.8
Average	141	6.3

Readability 7th Grade (see dot plotted on graph)

Word Lists

F.1   Nifty-Thrifty-Fifty Words

F.2   Transfer Words for the Nifty-Thrifty-Fifty

Nifty-Thrifty-Fifty Words

1. antifreeze
2. beautiful
3. classify
4. communities
5. community
6. composer
7. continuous
8. conversation
9. deodorize
10. different
11. discovery
12. dishonest
13. electricity
14. employee
15. encouragement
16. expensive
17. forecast
18. forgotten
19. governor
20. happiness
21. hopeless
22. illegal
23. impossible
24. impression
25. independence
26. international
27. invasion
28. irresponsible
29. midnight
30. misunderstand
31. musician
32. nonliving
33. overpower
34. performance
35. prehistoric
36. prettier
37. rearrange
38. replacement
39. richest
40. semifinal
41. signature
42. submarine
43. supermarkets
44. swimming
45. transportation
46. underweight
47. unfinished
48. unfriendly
49. unpleasant
50. valuable

From Cunningham, P.M. & R.L. Allington, *Classrooms That Work: They Can All Read and Write*, 3/e. Published by Allyn & Bacon, Boston, MA. Copyright © 2002 by Pearson Education. Adapted by permission of the publisher.

APPENDIX   F.2   *Transfer Words for the Nifty-Thrifty-Fifty*

Here are just some of the words students should be able to decode, spell, and discuss meanings for by using parts of all fifty words:

conform	relive	declassify	powerlessly
conformity	repose	decompose	powerlessness
inform	reclassify	deform	superpower
informer	revalue	deformity	finalize
informant	recover	prearrange	finalizing
information	rediscover	resign	finalization
misinform	electrical	resignation	weighty
uninformed	displease	designation	weightier
formation	discontinue	significant	weightiest
formal	disposal	significance	weightless
transform	musical	freezer	undervalue
transformation	continual	freezing	friendlier
performer	employer	freezable	friendliest
responsibility	employment	subfreezing	friendliness
responsive	unemployment	underclass	unfriendliness
responsiveness	unemployed	overexpose	unpleasantness
honesty	employable	underexpose	historical
dishonesty	unemployable	superimpose	historically
honestly	difference	undercover	expressive
legally	consignment	forecaster	impressive
illegally	nationality	forecasting	repressive
responsibly	nationalities	forecastable	invasive
irresponsibly	internationalize	miscast	noninvasive
arranging	interdependence	antidepressant	invasiveness
rearranging	depress	overture	hopefully
placing	depression	empower	hopelessly
replacing	depressive	empowerment	predispose
misplacing	deport	powerful	predisposition
report	deportation	powerfully	deodorant
reporter	deportee	powerfulness	beautician
refinish	devalue	powerless	electrician

Source: From Cunningham, P. M. & R. L. Allington. *Classrooms That Work: They Can All Read and Write,* 3/e. Published by Allyn & Bacon, Boston, MA. Copyright © 2002 by Pearson Education. Adapted by permission of the publisher.

A Typical Week's Word Study Plan

Monday. Display the five new words on a word wall large enough to be seen by students from their seats. **Word walls** are charts or bulletin boards on which important vocabulary words are placed, usually alphabetically, to be referred to during word study activities (see below). Use thick, bold permanent markers for printing the words. Model the decoding of these five words.

● word walls

Write a sentence using a new word on the board:

> If your pet licks the <u>antifreeze</u> off the garage floor, it could become very sick, and even die.
> Teacher: The underlined word contains a word you might already know and a prefix.
> A prefix is a word part that is added to the beginning of a word. Can anyone tell me the word without the prefix? (If not, draw a circle around freeze and ask again.)

Then discuss the meaning of the word, and other words that begin with "anti." Continue this process for the other four words of the day.

Tuesday. Come back to the five words introduced on Monday. Practice the five new words by saying the letters and syllables in these words as a rhythmic chant, almost like a song, or a cheer that a cheerleader might lead at a football game. For example, antifreeze might develop into

> a - n - t - i anti
> a - n - t - i anti
> a - n - t - i anti
> anti antifreeze

Again, the meanings of the affixes and the whole word should be discussed.

Wednesday. Return to the five words introduced on Monday. Examine the composition of each of the five new words. Focus on how the spelling of the root words may change when an affix is added. Have each student create a written chart such as the following:

WORD		PARTS	SPELLING CHANGES
antifreeze	=	anti + freeze	no changes
beautiful	=	beauty + ful	y changes to i
classify	=	class + ify	no changes
communities	=	com + unity + es	m doubles, y changes to i
community	=	com + unity	m doubles
		or com + unit + y	

Then ask questions about these words to focus on their meanings or other special characteristics:

1. Which word is the opposite of ugly?
2. Which word means the opposite of freezing?
3. Which two words have unity as their root?
4. How do you write the plural of community?
5. Which word tells what you do when you group things that are similar?

Students should check the spellings of the words they wrote using the word wall.

Thursday. Chant again (see Tuesday) the five new words introduced on Monday. Now help students see how knowing these words can help them recognize and spell other words they may not yet know. Using related forms of the words taught (see Appendix F.2), ask students to decode, spell, and discuss meanings for these words. For example, have students pronounce *declassify*, note its spelling (add "de" to "classify"), and talk about its meaning as undoing what had been done, or classified. Other words to use could be *classification, freezer, subfreezing, beautifully, powerful, hopeful, communication, mystify,* and *certify.*

Friday. Cover up the word wall. Administer a spelling test on the five new words, or include these in a weekly spelling test. The format might proceed as follows: Say the word, use the word in a sentence, and repeat the word. Then go on to the next word. Students can correct their own papers by writing the correct spelling from the word wall next to any misspelled words.

Word Study
www.sentex.net/~mmcadams/
spelling.html

After 10 weeks all of the words will have been learned. Because these 50 words contain morphological patterns for so many other words, they should be overlearned. The various elements will then be recognized and recalled automatically when needed during reading and writing. The transfer words in Appendix F.2 contain parts of the Nifty-Thrifty-Fifty words. Many other words can also be used as transfer words.

You can use this general pattern when teaching the morphology and etymology of words:

1. Begin with the known and move to the unknown.
2. Provide a means for making the transfer. Talk through the process. With practice and repetition, the process becomes internalized.
3. Discuss related words so that knowledge increases in an exponential way as opposed to just one word being studied at a time.
4. Value the content of particular disciplines by using the critical language in that discipline as a means of teaching a functional skill—word analysis.

academic language The language that teachers and students use for imparting information, acquiring new knowledge and skills, describing abstract ideas, and developing content area and conceptual understanding.

acceleration Progress through the curriculum at a faster rate.

accuracy The ability to recognize words correctly.

achievement test A formalized test that measures the extent to which a person has assimilated a body of information or possesses a certain skill after instruction has taken place.

affixes Bound morphemes that change the meaning or function of a root or stem to which they are attached, as the prefix *ad-* and the suffix *-ing* in *adjoining*.

alliteration A pattern in which all words begin with the same sound.

alphabetic principle The principle that there is a one-to-one correspondence between phonemes (or sounds) and graphemes (or letters); letters represent sounds.

analog A strategy of comparing patterns in words to ones already known.

anecdotal notes Written observations taken by the teacher—usually on a clipboard—of literacy-related behaviors in an authentic literacy context.

anticipation guide A prereading tool used to activate schemata and engage readers.

antonyms A pair of words that have opposite meanings.

Asperger's syndrome A mild form of autism.

assessment The process of gathering information about students' abilities using a variety of means and tools, both formal and informal.

assistive technologies Electronic devices, equipment, or products designed or modified specifically to improve the functional capabilities of individuals with severe communication disorders and other disabilities.

augmentative communication system Any system or device designed to enhance the communication abilities of individuals who are nonverbal or have speech too difficult to understand.

authentic assessment Assessment representing literacy behavior in the community and in the workplace.

autism A disability characterized by extreme withdrawal and underdeveloped communication or language skills.

automaticity Fluent performance without the conscious deployment of attention.

basal reader series A coordinated, graded set of textbooks, teacher's guides, and supplementary materials from which to teach reading.

basic words Commonplace words that are the building blocks of everyday language.

behavioral disorder A disability in which students are characterized by inappropriate school behavior.

big book An enlarged version of a book used by the teacher for mediated reading instruction so that students can track the print and attention can be focused on particular phonemic elements.

blend A consonant sequence before or after a vowel within a syllable, such as *cl*, *st*, or *br*; the written language equivalent of a consonant cluster.

book clubs Another term for (see) literature circles.

book contract An individual contract of literacy activities based upon a self-selected book.

book talk Brief teaser that teacher presents to interest students in a particular book.

CALP An acronym for cognitive academic language proficiency, or the language of school.

camouflage A vocabulary-enriching activity in which learners must try to disguise a chosen word by creating an oral story using several words above their normal speaking vocabulary. The other students must try to guess the hidden word.

clarifying table A graphic organizer used to help children understand the meaning of complex terms.

closed sorts Word sorts that classify words into predetermined categories.

cloze test An assessment device in which certain words are deleted from a passage by the teacher, with blanks left in their places for students to fill in by using the context of the sentence or paragraph.

code switching The use of English for known words and the home language for words not yet acquired in English.

cognitive academic language proficiency (CALP) Skill in academic language, or the language of school.

compound words A word composed of two separate words that have meaning on their own, such as *baseball* and *lipstick*.

comprehensible input New information that is modified to enable an English learner to make connections to already known information.

comprehension The interpretation of print on a page into a meaningful message that is dependent on the reader's decoding abilities, prior knowledge, cultural and social background, and monitoring strategies—the "essence of reading."

concept-oriented reading instruction (CORI) An integrated curriculum approach.

concepts about print Concepts about the way print works, including directionality, spacing, identification of words and letters, connection between written and spoken language, and the function of punctuation.

construct validity When test items assess the skills, knowledge, and understandings that most experts agree comprise the area being tested.

constructivist model of learning A learning theory suggesting that students are active learners who organize and relate new information to their prior knowledge.

content area literacy Reading, writing, speaking, listening, viewing, and visually representing with a focus on the bodies of knowledge in the academic curriculum; e.g., English, science, social studies, mathematics.

content standards Stated expectations of what students should know and be able to do in particular subjects and grade levels.

content validity When test items assess the ability needed to perform the behaviors expected in the course or curriculum.

context clues The syntactic and semantic information in the surrounding words, phrases, sentences, and paragraphs in a text.

context–relationship procedure A strategy utilized to help students integrate new words into their meaning vocabularies.

contract spelling Children have a written agreement with the teacher each week to learn specific words.

controlled vocabulary A system of introducing only a certain number of grade-level appropriate words before the reading of each basal story, with periodic review.

conventional spelling stage The final stage of spelling development, in which the student has mastered the basic principles of English orthography and spells most words correctly.

conversation clubs Small, student-led groups established to enhance oral language in an informal, enjoyable setting.

cooperative learning An instructional model in which students work together as a team to complete activities or assignments.

correct spelling stage See conventional spelling stage.

criterion-referenced assessment An assessment designed to reveal what a student knows, understands, or can do in relation to specific objectives or standards.

criterion-referenced test A test for which scores are interpreted by comparing the test taker's score to a specified performance level rather than to the scores of other students.

critical reading Reading to evaluate the material being read.

cubing A writing scaffold used for students to model how to organize a six-paragraph essay.

cuing systems The four language systems that readers rely upon for cues as they seek meaning from text: graphophonic (based on letter–sound relationships), syntactic (based on grammar or structure), semantic (based on meaning), and pragmatic (based on social and cultural norms).

curriculum-based assessment The process of matching the curriculum to the content standards assessed in a testing program to ensure that teachers will cover the material assessed.

data chart A table or grid for recording answers to specific research questions (columns) gathered from a variety of sources (rows).

decodable text Beginner-oriented books that contain the same letters or word patterns currently being studied, or those previously taught.

decoding The translation of written words into verbal speech for oral reading or mental speech for silent reading.

deduction The process of helping students construct meaning by going from the general to the particular, through explanation.

derivational relations stage A spelling stage characterized by the ability to recognize and spell bases and roots correctly. Correlates to an advanced stage of reading and writing.

developmental spelling stages Stage-like progressions through which students advance when learning to spell, characterized by increasingly complex understandings about the organizational patterns of words, including precommunicative, prephonetic, phonetic, transitional, and conventional spelling stages.

diagnosis The act, process, or result of identifying the nature of a disorder or disability through observation and examination, often including the planning of instruction and the assessment of the strengths and needs of the student.

diagnostic test Age-related, norm-referenced assessment of specific skills and behaviors students have acquired compared with other students of the same chronological age.

dialogue journals Journals that provide a means of two-way written communication between learners and their teachers, in which learners share their thoughts with teachers (including personal comments and descriptions of life experiences), and the teachers, in turn, write reactions to the learners' messages. Also called interactive journals.

differentiated instruction Instruction designed to meet the needs of all students by adjusting content, process, or product.

direct instruction Teacher control of the learning environment through structured, systematic lessons; goal setting; choice of activities; and feedback.

directed reading thinking activity (DRTA) A time-honored format for guiding students as they read selections, usually from basal reading programs.

directionality of print The concept that, in English, writing goes from left to right and from top to bottom. Directionality of print varies among languages.

directive context Text that provides helpful clues for figuring out word meanings.

discussion Oral communication in an informal setting, involving an exploration of an issue or topic; problem solving by cooperative thinking.

double entry journal This journal uses a two-column format for entries of two types of student response to text.

dramatic play Play that simulates real experiences with no set plot or goal.

dyad reading A paired reading activity in which students alternately read aloud or listen and summarize what their partner has read.

dyslexia A developmental reading disability, presumably congenital and often hereditary, that may vary in degree from mild to severe.

echo reading A strategy where a lead reader reads aloud a section of text and others follow immediately after it, or echo the leader's reading.

editing The process of reviewing text in draft form to check for correctness of the mechanics and conventions in writing.

emergent literacy A person's developing awareness of the interrelatedness of oral and written language that occurs from birth to beginning reading.

encoding Transferring oral language into written language.

engagement A process involving a complex set of ongoing activities that occur in the classroom.

English learner A person who is in the process of acquiring English as a second language.

enrichment Strategies designed to deepen appreciation for reading selections.

environmental print Print that is encountered outside of books and that is a pervasive part of everyday living.

ESL (English as a second language) A program for teaching English language skills to those whose native language is not English.

etymology The study of the history of words.

evaluation Making a judgment about assessment data or assigning a score or grade to assessment data.

experience–text relationship A lesson format for narrative text that helps students develop prior knowledge and relate it to what they read.

experiential background The fund of total experiences that aid a reader in finding meaning in printed symbols.

experimental spellings Unconventional spellings, or approximations, resulting from an emergent writer's initial attempts to associate sounds with letters.

expository frame A basic structure for expository text designed to help students organize their thoughts for writing or responding to text.

expository structure Content organized around a main idea and supporting details.

expository text A text written in a precise, factual writing style.

expressive writing Personal writing that expresses emotion, such as diaries or letters.

FLIP strategy A strategy readers use to examine a text for reader-friendliness, language, interest, and degree of prior knowledge needed to understand the text.

fluency Achieving speed and accuracy in recognizing words and comprehending text, and coordinating the two.

fluent reader A reader whose reading accuracy and rate meet or exceed normal expectations with respect to age, ability, and grade level; an independent reader.

formal assessments Commercially designed and produced tests given on single occasions.

formal (standardized) test A testing instrument for which readability and validity can be verified; the results of these tests are based on right or wrong answers, and individual scores are interpreted against national norms.

formative assessment Classroom-based measures intended to provide feedback to learners on areas needing improvement.

Four-by-Four Model A "sheltered English" (see below) instructional model that addresses four developmental levels of language proficiency (beginning, early intermediate, intermediate, early advanced) and four literacy skills (reading, writing, speaking, listening) through the use of content themes.

frustration level A level of reading difficulty at which a reader is unable to cope; when reading is on the frustration level, the reader recognizes approximately 90 percent or fewer of the words encountered and comprehends 50 percent or fewer.

general-utility words More complex words that are used often by proficient readers and speakers but tend not to be specific to any particular subject.

GIST (generating interactions between schemata and text) A strategy used by readers to summarize text.

Goldilocks strategy Students examine a book to determine if it is "too easy," "too hard," or "just right" for them to read.

grade-level equivalency score A conversion of a score on a test into one that tells how a student compares with others in the same grade; e.g., a grade equivalent score of 4.5 on a reading test would suggest that the student is reading as well as students in the normative sample who are in the fifth month of fourth grade.

graded word list A list of words at successive reading levels.

grand conversation A response to text strategy whereby students share personal connections to the text, make predictions, ask questions, and show individual appreciation.

grapheme A written symbol that represents a phoneme.

graphic novels Book-length comic books.

graphic organizer A visual representation of facts and concepts from a text and their relationships within an organized frame.

graphophonic cues Cues based on sound or visual similarities.

group profile A listing of scores on a specific reading or writing skill that allows the teacher to view the strengths and weaknesses of the whole class for purposes of reteaching and reporting to parents and others.

guided reading A teacher-mediated instructional method designed to help readers improve skills, comprehension, recall, and appreciation of text.

herringbone strategy A graphic organizer used with expository text to show who, what, when, where, why, and the main idea for a passage.

heterogeneous literature groups Literature circles based not upon reading ability level, but on self-selection of a particular book.

high-frequency words Words common in reading material that are often difficult to learn because they cannot be easily decoded.

high-stakes assessments Assessment tools mandated by the state or district in which the teachers work that are often used to determine how well students are doing compared with other students in the area, state, or nation and to help decide whether certain programs will be funded.

holistic approach A whole-to-parts approach in which meaning is considered to be more critical than the underlying skills of reading.

holographic stage The earliest language acquisition stage, in which one word is used to represent a concept or idea.

impromptu speech A short speech given on a topic with little or no preparation.

independent level A level of reading difficulty low enough that the reader can progress without noticeable obstructions; the reader can recognize approximately 98 percent of the words and comprehend at least 90 percent of what is read.

individual dictation A strategy in which the student dictates a message while the teacher writes it down, sounding out the words in front of the student.

individualized education program (IEP) A written educational plan specifying a special student's annual goals, current levels of educational achievement, and short-term instructional objectives; prepared by a team that includes the student's parents, teachers, and often the student.

induction The process of helping students to construct meaning by going from the particular to the general, with the help of examples.

informal assessment A nonstandardized measurement in which a teacher seeks to learn about what a student is able to do in a certain area of literacy, interprets the results, and uses those results to plan instruction.

informal reading inventory An informal assessment instrument designed to help the teacher determine a student's independent, instructional, frustration, and reading capacity levels.

informal speaking Oral language of a nonacademic, conversational nature.

information literate Knowing how to locate, acquire, and use information.

informational books Nonfiction books that provide factual information about a topic; expository text.

instructional level A level of difficulty low enough that the reader can be instructed by the teacher during the process; in order for the material to be at this level, the reader should be able to read approximately 95 percent of the words in a passage and comprehend at least 75 percent.

interactive electronic books Computerized programs that allow learners to read books on a computer while responding to questions about the text, exploring various aspects or sidelines of the text, and often even adapting the text.

interactive oral reading A method for teaching vocabulary in which adults read aloud to learners, stopping on occasion to discuss individual words.

interactive (story) writing A mediated writing experience used to assist emergent readers in learning to read and write. With help from the teacher, students dictate sentences, and the teacher verbally stretches each word so the students can distinguish sounds and letters. Students use chart paper to write the letter while repeating the sound.

interest and attitude inventory An informal assessment device that allows teachers to discover how their students feel about reading and about themselves as readers.

interest groups Students are organized according to a common interest in a topic or book selection.

interest inventory A list of questions used to assess a student's preferences in a particular area.

intervention The corrective instructional program the teacher devises as a result of assessment.

interview An oral language activity consisting of asking another person a specific set of questions.

jigsaw grouping A collaborative learning technique in which individuals become "experts" on one portion of text and share their expertise with a small group, called their home group. Each member of the home group becomes an "expert" on a different part of the text and shares his new knowledge with the group so that each group member will get a sense of the whole text.

journals Journals are kept by students in the same way artists keep sketch books. Students write in them regularly to record life events of their choosing or, for very beginning writers, to complete sentence stems offered by the teacher. At the beginning reader stage, journals are often accompanied by illustrations and are rarely corrected.

K-W-L Plus strategy A process intended to help students organize learned information into a coherent paragraph or research report; typically involves a chart with column headings such as "What We Know," "What We Want to Know," and "What We Learned." The "Plus" refers to using additional categories of information, perhaps to write summaries or reports.

language arts The global term for reading, writing, listening, speaking, viewing, and visually representing.

language disorders Communication disorders that involve poor speech or language performance due to various factors, including voice quality, speech fluency, and sound production.

language experience approach (LEA) An approach in which reading and the other language arts are interrelated and the experiences of students are used as the basis for the material that is written and then used for reading.

learning center A location within the classroom in which students are presented with instructional materials, specific directions, clearly defined objectives, and/or provisions for self-evaluation.

learning disability A condition in which a person with average or above intelligence is substantially delayed in academic achievement because of a processing disorder, not because of an environmental, an economic, or a cultural disadvantage.

learning logs Journals students use to summarize a day's lesson and to react to what they have learned.

letter name/alphabetic stage Spelling characterized by literally matching letters to sounds in a linear sound-by-sound fashion.

letter name stage See phonetic stage.

listening vocabulary The words a person is able to understand aurally; also known as receptive vocabulary.

literacy The competence to carry out the complex reading and writing tasks in a functionally useful way necessary to the world of work and life outside the school.

literacy scaffold A temporary writing structure.

literal comprehension Understanding those ideas that are directly stated.

literary sociogram A diagram used to help students understand the complexity of the relationships among characters in a story or chapter.

literature circles Small, student-led book discussion groups that meet regularly in the classroom to read and discuss self-selected books.

literature double response journal A special type of reading log with quotes from a story or informational book in the left column and a personal reflection on the quote in the right column.

literature response groups Same as literature circles and analogous to writing response groups; in literature response groups, students discuss the work of published authors; in writing response groups, they discuss the work of their peers.

long vowels Vowels that represent the sounds in words that are heard in letter names, such as the /a/ in *ape*, /e/ in *feet*, /i/ in *ice*, /o/ in *road*, and /u/ in *mule*.

look-say method An early meaning-based method of reading instruction requiring students to use the context alone to figure out words they did not know.

low-utility words Less frequently encountered words that are usually found in particular content areas.

masking Using a sliding frame or other device to help students focus on a particular word or part of a word.

Matthew effect The phenomenon that suggests that skilled decoders get better at reading while poor decoders tend to fall further behind.

meaning vocabulary That body of words the meaning of which one understands and can use.

media literacy The skill of thinking critically about what one sees, hears, and reads when presented through a wide variety of media.

mediated reading Large or small group instruction in which the teacher guides the students in selected reading skills.

metacognition A person's awareness of her own thinking and her conscious efforts to monitor this awareness.

metacognitive strategies Techniques for monitoring one's own thinking.

metacomprehension Understanding what you know about how you comprehend; self-knowledge about your own comprehension processes.

metalinguistic ability The conscious awareness of sound, meaning, and the practical nuances of language.

minilesson A short lesson on procedures, concepts, strategies, or skills taught based on teacher observation of the need for it.

miscue An unexpected reading response (deviation from text).

miscue analysis A procedure that lets the teacher gather important instructional information by providing a framework for observing students' oral reading and their ability to construct meaning.

mock interviews Pretend discussions with deceased or fictional figures.

modeling Showing an instructional strategy through teacher demonstration.

morning message Students observe as the teacher writes a meaningful morning message on the board about a specific event that is planned for the day, or an interesting question. It is used as an instructional tool for discussing skills that the students are learning, such as conventions of writing or phonic elements.

morpheme The smallest meaning-bearing linguistic unit in a language.

morphology The aspects of language structure related to the ways words are formed from prefixes, roots, and suffixes (e.g., "re-heat-ing") and are related to each other.

motivation The incentive to do something; a stimulus to act.

multicultural Classrooms are multicultural settings when students from a variety of cultures learn together daily, making it necessary to know how students' perceptions, knowledge, and demeanor are shaped by their experiences at home and in their own community.

narrative text Text that contains the structural features of a story.

nondirective context Text that does not provide helpful context clues for determining a word's meaning.

nonstage theory A theory that suggests that unskilled and skilled readers use the same strategies to figure out unknown words.

norm-referenced test A test designed to yield results interpretable in terms of the average results of a sample population.

norm (normative) group A large number of students chosen to represent the kinds of students for whom an assessment device is designed.

norms Statistics or data that summarize the test performance of specified groups, such as test takers of various ages or grades.

novel study The in-depth reading and interpretation of a novel or a group of related novels or stories.

one-to-one correspondence The concept that letters or combinations of letters correspond directly with certain sounds in the English language.

ongoing assessment Assessment that occurs within daily lessons and over time, usually through observation and anecdotal notes.

onset All the sounds of a word that come before the first vowel.

open sort A type of picture or word sort in which the categories for sorting are left up to the student.

oral recitation lessons (ORL) Three-part lessons designed to increase oral reading fluency.

oral report A presentation (often using multimedia) of information for an audience of classmates.

oral synthesis Hearing sounds in sequence and blending them together to make a word; sounding out.

orthographic knowledge Understanding of the writing system of a language, specifically the correct sequence of letters, characters, or symbols.

parent packets Folders containing early reading and writing reinforcement activities that can be completed at home with a student's parents or caretakers.

paragraph frame A scaffold for helping students write paragraphs; transition words are provided, and students fill in the substantive content words.

partner reading Also known as buddy reading. Oral reading with another student.

peer editor A student assigned to help a classmate evaluate a piece of writing and to provide helpful questions and suggestions.

percentile scores Raw scores that are converted to percentiles so that comparisons can be made. Percentiles range from 1 to 99, with 1 being the lowest.

performance descriptors The criteria that help communicate to teachers and students the standards that will be used to evaluate students' work.

phoneme The smallest unit of sound in a language.

phoneme blending Blending individual sounds to form a word.

phoneme counting Counting the number of sounds in a word.

phoneme deletion Omitting the beginning, middle, or ending sounds of a word.

phoneme isolation Identifying the beginning, middle, and/or ending sounds in a word.

phoneme substitution Substituting beginning, middle, or ending sounds of a word.

phonemic awareness The ability to hear, identify, and manipulate individual sounds in spoken words.

phonemic segmentation The process of separating sounds within a word.

phonetic stage The third stage of spelling development, in which consonants and vowels are used for each spoken syllable.

phonics Instruction in the association of speech sounds with printed symbols.

phonics generalizations Rules that help clarify English spelling patterns.

phonology The study of the sound system of language.

picture walk An instructional strategy in which the teacher guides students through the text by looking at and discussing the pictures before reading the story.

play centers Areas of the classroom containing inviting props and set aside for spontaneous dramatic play.

polysemantic words Words that can have different meanings depending on the context in which they are used.

portfolio Place to collect evidence of a student's literacy development. It may include artifacts collected by the student, the teacher, or both.

portmanteau word Word created from a combination of two existing words (e.g., motel = motor + hotel).

precommunicative stage The initial stage of spelling development, in which the student scribbles random letters with little concept of which letter makes which sound.

predictable texts Books that use repetition, rhythmic language patterns, and familiar patterns; sometimes called pattern books.

predictive questions Questions designed to activate students' prior knowledge before they read in order to focus their attention on key ideas as they read.

prefixes Meaningful chunks attached to the beginnings of words, such as re + play = replay.

preliterate stage See prephonetic stage.

prephonetic stage The second stage of spelling development, in which the student becomes aware of the alphabetic principle.

prewriting The initial creative and planning stage of writing, prior to drafting, in which the writer formulates ideas, gathers information, and considers ways in which to organize a piece of writing.

primary language The first language a student learns to speak, or the student's home language.

problem-based learning Organizes curriculum and instruction around authentic real-world problems with a focus on solving these problems as if the students were working in the area being studied.

process-oriented assessment A teacher's direct observations of students' reading and writing abilities for the purpose of noting which specific behaviors or strategies students use.

productive questioning Involves the use of students' responses to carefully crafted questions in guiding the development of conceptual thinking.

professional teaching standards Standards related to how well the teacher performs.

project-based learning Provides an alternative learning environment in which students work collaboratively to explore real-world issues in depth and to create a project that represents their learning.

QARs (question–answer relationships) A strategy in which students become aware of their own comprehension processes, particularly the importance of the knowledge they bring to text and their role as active seekers rather than passive receivers of information through reading.

quick write An activity in which students rapidly write down ideas about a topic.

r-controlled vowels Vowels that occur in a syllable preceding an *r* and in which the vowel sound is modified, such as the /r/ in car.

readability An objective measure of the difficulty of written material.

readers theatre A form of drama in which participants read aloud from scripts adapted from stories and convey ideas and emotions through vocal expression. This oral interpretation strategy helps students see that reading is an active process of constructing meaning. Unlike a play, there is no costuming, movement, stage sets, or memorizing of lines.

reading The construction of meaning from coded messages through symbol decoding, vocabulary awareness, comprehension, and reflection.

reading buddies A social reading activity in which students read and reread books with a partner who may help them with unfamiliar words and encourage them to continue reading.

reading capacity level The highest level of material that students can understand when the passage is read to them.

reading interest inventory An informal assessment device used to determine a student's interests so that the teacher can match appropriate reading material to the student.

reading process The steps a reader goes through to construct meaning from what the author has written.

reading product Some form of communication that results from the reading process.

reading rate Speed of reading, often reported in words per minute.

reading readiness The level of preparedness for formal reading instruction.

reading response journal A journal in which readers record their first reactions to something they have read.

reading vocabulary The words a person is able to understand in written form; part of receptive vocabulary.

realia Concrete pictures and other items used to show the meaning of words and concepts.

reciprocal teaching A technique to develop comprehension and metacognition in which the teacher and students take turns predicting, generating questions, summarizing, and clarifying ideas in a passage.

recreational reading An independent reading activity for motivating voluntary reading interest and appreciation rather than instruction.

reliability When a test consistently measures the same behavior with each administration of the test.

repeated readings The process of students rereading a selection for a different purpose and thinking again about what they have read. Rereading helps improve a young reader's speed, accuracy, expression, comprehension, and linguistic growth.

response guide A set of suggestions designed to help peer editors provide helpful feedback to student writers.

retelling The process of teachers analyzing students' retellings of text to gauge their level of comprehension and use of language. In examining the retellings, teachers look for the number of events recalled, how students interpret the message, and how students use details or make inferences to substantiate ideas.

revising The process of changing a piece of writing to improve clarity for its intended audience and to make certain that it accomplishes its intended purpose.

rime The first vowel in a word and all the sounds that follow.

role playing A form of dramatic play that involves having students act the part of another student or a fictional character.

root word A word to which prefixes and/or suffixes are added to create new, but related, words.

roots Base words.

ROW Read, organize, write: a strategy used to help students write summaries.

rubber-banding The process in which the teacher stretches out all the sounds in a word so learners can pay attention to each phoneme or sound.

running records A procedure for analyzing students' oral reading and noting their strengths and weaknesses when using various reading strategies.

scaffolding A support mechanism by which students are able to accomplish more difficult tasks than they could without assistance.

schema A preexisting knowledge structure developed about a thing, a place, or an idea; a framework of expectations based on previous knowledge.

scoring rubric A tool describing the levels of performance a student must demonstrate related to a particular achievement goal, whether it is written or oral.

self-monitoring The mental act of knowing when one does and does not understand what one is reading.

semantic cues Meaning clues.

semantic feature analysis An instructional activity in which students select a group of related words and then create a chart to classify them according to distinguishing characteristics.

semantic field A range of similarity among words.

semantic gradient A vocabulary-enriching activity that allows students to discuss the many shades of meaning of words, beginning with a word and ending with its opposite.

semantic map A graphic representation of the relationship among words and phrases in written material.

sentence fluency The careful crafting of sentences so that paragraphs flow smoothly and effortlessly.

sentence stems The first two or three words of a sentence followed by blank spaces offered to students to support initial attempts at writing.

sentence strips Rectangular pieces of tag board or construction paper upon which are written individual sentences from a story students have read.

service learning Curriculum projects that involve and enhance the surrounding community.

shared reading A mediated technique whereby the teacher reads aloud while students follow along using individual copies of the book, a class chart, or a big book.

sheltered English Lessons taught in a multisensory, multi-intelligence way to ensure understanding by English learners.

short vowels Vowels that represent the sound of /a/ in *apple*, /e/ in *end*, /i/ in *igloo*, /o/ in *octopus*, and /u/ in *bus*.

showcase portfolio A collection of artifacts taken from the working portfolio that demonstrates excellence in achievement.

sight vocabulary Words that the reader recognizes immediately, without having to resort to decoding.

sight word A word that is immediately recognized as a whole and does not require word analysis for identification.

SIOP Model SIOP (Sheltered Instruction Observation Protocol) is a "sheltered English" instructional model that delineates both language and content lesson objectives linked to subject area and curriculum standards.

6 + 1 Trait writing The important aspects of writing, including ideas, organization, voice, word choice, sentence fluency, conventions, and presentation.

speech disorders Disabilities characterized by deficits in speech, receptive language, and/or expressive language.

SQ3R (Survey, Question, Read, Recite, Review) A study strategy that asks readers first to survey the material and form questions based on that survey, then to read, restate in their own words, and review or rehearse what was read to help their comprehension and memory of the material.

Squire's model The notion that reading and writing are related because they place similar demands on one's thinking.

stage theory A theory that suggests that students go through three stages in acquiring literacy: the "selective cue stage," the "spelling-sound stage," and the "automatic stage."

standard deviation A number describing the variability in scores as indicated by their distance from the mean, or average.

standard error of measurement A number representing the error associated with a test.

standardized reading tests Achievement tests that are published; norm-referenced, group-administered, survey tests of reading ability.

standardized testing The use of norm-referenced tests to measure reading and writing skills as well as their subskills.

standards Broad curricular goals containing specific grade-level targets or benchmarks. They represent systematic ways for educators to ask themselves, What is it that we want our students to be able to know? and What do we want them to be able to do?

standards-based performance assessment Assessment tasks designed to show what has been learned as it relates to a particular content standard.

stanine scores Scores that have been converted into nine equally spaced groups, with 1 being the lowest.

story frame A basic outline for a story designed to help students organize their ideas about what they have read.

story grammar A set of rules that defines story structures.

strategic reader model A view of reading instruction that focuses on teaching readers a wide variety of strategies to use before, during, and after reading.

structural analysis Examination of words for meaningful parts (affixes, contractions, endings, compound words).

structured listening activity An activity in which students listen to a story accompanied by visuals that support the action in the story, and then retell the story with the help of the visuals.

suffix A meaningful chunk attached to the end of words, such as play + ing = playing.

summative assessment A compilation of summary data provided at the end of a program, units of study, or other intervals to report progress.

sustained silent reading (SSR) A program for setting aside a certain period of time daily for self-selected, silent reading. During SSR time, each student chooses material to read for a designated period of time, typically 10–15 minutes for beginning readers. Everyone, including the teacher, reads without interruption.

syllabication Breaking words into syllables; "chunking."

syllable juncture stage *See* syllables and affixes stage.

syllables The units of pronunciation that include a vowel sound.

syllables and affixes stage Spelling stage characterized by considering the conventions of preserving pattern-to-sound relationships at the place where syllables meet.

synonyms Groups of words that have the same, or very similar, meanings.

syntactic cues Clues derived from the word order, or grammar, of the sentence.

T-chart A two-column list used to compare the information in the column heads.

talk-to-yourself chart A chart to help students self-assess their ability to read and spell new words.

teachable moments Opportunities for spontaneous, indirect teaching that occur when teachers respond to students' questions or when students otherwise demonstrate the need to know something.

teacher observational portfolio A progress file containing observations and informal assessments of students' reading and writing behaviors and accomplishments.

telegraphic stage The language acquisition stage in which an idea or concept is represented by two words.

text-based collaborative learning A process in which students work with a partner or small group to clarify expository text.

think-aloud A strategy in which the teacher models aloud for students the thinking processes used when reading or writing.

think, pair, and share A cooperative learning strategy in which students listen to a question, think of a response, pair to discuss with a partner, and then share their collaboration with the whole class.

think sheet A written format used to help students with behavioral disorders devise better choices for ways to behave.

tiered activities Activities that are modified to meet the differentiated needs of learners.

time/order chart Sequencing to show chronological order.

time-out Removing a student who is acting disruptively from the immediate vicinity of instruction for a specified period of time, or until she can return and behave appropriately.

topic and details maps Charts showing relationships of details to main topic.

tracking Indicating understanding of the one-to-one correspondence of spoken and written words by finger-pointing.

trade book Any book that can be purchased by the general public in bookstores, through mail-order houses, or at book fairs.

transactional model A perspective of early reading instruction from cognitive psychology and psycholinguistic learning that views students as bringing a rich prior knowledge background to literacy learning.

transfer words Words containing elements that are also found in many other words.

transitional reader A reader who is aware of letter pattern units, or word families, and frequently occurring rimes.

transitional stage The fourth stage of spelling development, in which the student is able to approx- imate the spelling of various English words.

transmission model A perspective of early reading instruction from behavioral psychology that views children as empty vessels into which knowledge is poured.

validity The degree to which a test measures what it purports to measure.

Venn diagram A set of overlapping circles used to graphically illustrate the similarities and differences of two concepts, ideas, stories, or other items.

vicarious experiences Indirect experiences, not involving the senses.

viewing The interpretation and analysis of visual media.

visual literacy The ability to interpret the meaning of visual images as well as to construct effective visuals in order to convey ideas to others.

visually representing The process of communicating through visual images such as photographs, drawings, video presentations, cartoons, and other image types.

vocabulary The words that a person knows and uses.

voice The writer's personality emerging through words.

web A graphic organizer used to involve students in thinking about and planning what they will study, learn, read about, or write about within a larger topic.

WebQuest An inquiry-based and student-centered technique that challenges students to explore the Internet for information related to a particular topic or problem.

within word stage See transitional stage.

word attack An aspect of reading instruction that includes intentional strategies for learning to decode, sight read, and recognize written words.

word bank A collection of sight words that have been mastered, usually recorded on index cards.

word building An activity in which students arrange letter cards to spell words, practicing phonics and spelling concepts.

word choice The element of writing that involves using fresh and colorful language to make certain passages memorable and worthy of reading aloud.

word consciousness Students' awareness of new words and their desire to learn them and then to use them when speaking and writing.

word families Set of words formed from common rimes by onset substitution.

word hunt An activity in which students search for words that correspond to a certain pattern that has been identified by them or by the teacher.

word map A visual illustration of a word showing its meaning by offering examples, explaining what it is and what it is not.

word play The manipulation of sounds and words for purposes of language exploration, practice, and pleasure.

word sort An activity in which students sort a collection of words into two or more categories.

word study Analyzing words to discover the regularities, patterns, and rules of English orthography needed to read and spell.

word wall A chart or bulletin board on which are placed, alphabetically, important vocabulary to be referred to during word study activities.

wordless books Picture story books without words.

working portfolio A collection of completed work samples or works in progress that may be chosen for placement in a showcase portfolio.

writer's workshop A writing program that implements the writing process by having students write on topics that they choose themselves, assuming ownership of their writing and learning.

writing folder A folder where students keep rough drafts in various stages of the writing process and other daily compositions or reports, topics for future writing, and notes from minilessons.

writing process The process by which a piece of writing is completed for publication, involving prewriting, drafting, revising, editing, and publishing.

writing prompts Motivational ideas or structures that are offered by the teacher to inspire students to write.

Abate, L., 295
Abdul-Jabbar, K., 254
Adams, W., 85
Alber, S. R., 106
Alexander, P. A., 323
Allen, J., 114
Alliance for Excellent Education, 12
Allington, R. L., 82
Alvermann, D. E., 254, 340
American Library Association, 340
Anderson, R., 154
Anderson, R. C., 98, 102, 104, 348
Anderson, V., 333
Aronson, E., 160
Ash, G. E., 233
Atwell, N., 20, 189
August, D., 294
Azevedo, R., 167
Baker, L., 102, 350
Bandura, A., 17
Barnitz, J. G., 295
Barton, D., 350, 351
Baumann, J. F., 6, 98, 102, 107, 114
Bauer, S. W., 4
Beach, R., 154
Bear, D. R., 70, 74
Beck, I., 107
Beck, I. L., 98, 99, 100, 101, 102, 103, 112, 120, 135
Berkas, T., 333
Biancarosa, G., 139
Blachowicz, C. L. Z., 101, 103, 104
Block, C. C., 19, 181, 282, 284
Bloodgood, J. W., 76, 78
Bowman, B., 347
Britto, P. R., 356
Britton, B. K., 137
Bromley, K., 170
Brookhart, S. M., 31
Brooks, W., 138
Brophy, J., 367
Brown, R., 170
Bruchac, J., 170
Bruner, J., 14
Bryant, D. P., 90
Buehl, D., 7, 79, 236, 237
Burke, J., 165
California Department of Education, 368

Calkins, L., 19, 189
Cambourne, B., 50
Carlisle, J. F., 73, 106
Carlo, M. S., 103, 107, 125, 126
Carr, K. S., 240
Caverly, D., 230
Cecil, N. L., 11, 15, 120, 149, 156, 160, 187, 199, 201, 202, 204, 206, 208, 275
Chappuis, J., 61
Chavkin, N. F., 352
Childrey, J., 160
Chomsky, C., 348
Cisnero, S., 351
Clarke, L., 158
Clay, M., 46
Clemmons, J., 63
Cohle, D. M., 182
Coiro, J., 167, 249, 250, 251
Collins COBUILD Learner's Dictionary, 103, 115
Columba, L., 225
Cooper, J. D., 17, 29
Cooper, L. J., 44
Cooper, P., 261, 283
Cooter, R., 43, 385
Courneya, J., 333
Cousin, P. T., 31
Coxhead, A., 99, 126, 298
Coyne, M. D., 107, 125
Crawley, S. J., 124
Crichton, M., 69
Cuban, L., 225
Cudd, E. T., 240
Cummins, J., 270
Cunningham, A. E., 102, 125
Cunningham, J. W., 144
Cunningham, P. M., 14, 39, 59, 60, 76
Dale, E., 100
Daniels, H., 28, 64, 157, 158
Danielson, C., 63
Davey, B., 142
Davis, G. A., 300
DeFina, A. A., 63
Delgado-Gaitan, C., 347, 349
Diederich, P., 213
Dillon, S., 12
Duffelmeer, F. A., 170, 228
Duffy, G. G., 136

Durkin, D., 16
Eagleton, M. B., 8
Eanet, M. G., 230
Eccles, J. S., 323
Echevarria, J., 296, 298
Eeds, M., 266
Ellis, E., 99, 109, 110, 129
Englert, C. S., 136
Erdrich, L., 351
Falk, B., 38
Farnan, N., 9
Fay, L., 230
Feldman, K., 101, 103
Fiderer, A., 63
Fielding, L. G., 17
Fitzgerald, J., 349
Fletcher, J. M., 19, 20
Flynt, E. S., 43, 385
Follman, J., 333
Fountas, I. C., 143
Fox, B. J., 86
Fredericks, A. D., 85
Fredericks, L., 334
Freedman, A., 210
Freedman, R., 351
Friend, R., 234
Fry, E. B., 74, 327, 419
Fuchs, L. S., 46
Fukunaga, N., 331
Galda, L., 275
Gambrell, L. B., 9, 10, 143, 266
Gardner, H., 301, 311
Garland, S., 172
Garrison, J., 15
Gibbons, P., 214
Gillet, J. W., 182
Gipe, J., 44, 72, 73, 103, 112, 136, 200, 247
Glazer, S. M., 62, 293
Glazzard, P., 307
Glenn, J., 333
Goodman, K. S., 321
Goetze, S., 11
Gordon, R., 324
Gottfried, S. S., 225
Graves, D. H., 191, 192
Graves, M. F., 98, 99, 101, 102, 104, 107, 113, 114

Gray, T., 294
Greenwood, S. C., 121
Griffin, M. L., 261
Guskey, T. R., 29
Guthrie, J. T., 14, 55, 324
Hadaway, N., 156
Hammond, L., 334
Hancock, J., 16
Handel, R. D., 356
Hansen, J., 189
Harmon, J. M., 102, 126
Harp, B., 61
Harris, T. L., 3, 98, 138, 322
Harste, J., 164
Harvey, S., 137, 172, 225
Harwayne, S., 328, 333
Hasbrouck, J., 46
Hasselbring, T. S., 305
Haven, K., 85
Heath, S. B., 347, 349
Heath, S., 261
Henderson, E., 70
Henry, L. A., 168, 247, 249
Hernandez, H., 298
Herrell, A. L., 82, 171
Hickman, P., 125, 126
Hiebert, E. H., 99
Hill, B. C., 29
Hobbs, R., 328
Hoffman, J. V., 88
Hoyt, L., 227
Hunt, D. E., 311
Hyde, A. A., 5, 16
Invernezzi, M. A., 19
Isaacson, R. M., 168
Ivy, G., 326
Jenkins, C. B., 63, 102
Johnson, D. D., 69, 81, 108
Johnston, P., 31, 167, 213, 305
Jorm, A., 136
Joyce, B., 311
Kadohata, C., 351
Kane, S., 127, 222, 229, 238, 329
Kemper, L. W., 70
Kennedy, D. M., 301
Kennedy, E., 34
Kiefer, B. Z., 154
Kindler, A. L., 294
Kinzer, C. K., 348
Kirby, D., 59
Klinger, J. K., 141, 232
Koechlin, C., 246
Krashen, S. D., 296, 298
Kronowitz, E. L., 19
Kuhn, M. R., 83
Laib, N. K., 182
Lancy, D. F., 348
Langer, J. A., 182, 232
Lankshear, C., 167

Laosa, L. M., 348
Larsen-Blair, S. M., 11
Learning in Deed, 335
Learning in the Real World, 334
Lember, B. H., 127
Lenders, L., 9
Lenhart, A., 167
Lenski, S. D., 295
Lenz, B. K., 90
Lepper, M. R., 326
Leu, D. J., 10, 167, 168
Lewis, R. B., 293, 301, 307, 331
Liang, L. A., 141
Loban, W., 261
Locke, E. A., 55
Loesch-Griffin, D., 333
Luke, C., 340
MacGillivray, L., 332
Maehr, M. L., 339
Markle, S., 170
Marsh, H. W., 323
Martinez, E. B., 184
Mastropieri, M. A., 300, 302, 308
Mathewson, G. C., 323
McKenna, M. C., 323
McKeown, M. G., 103, 142
McLoyd, V. C., 326
McMahon, S. I., 156
McTaggert, 154
McVicker, C. J., 128
McWhorter, D., 351
Melchior, A., 333
Mikulecky, L., 359
Mizell, H., 366
Mooney, M. E., 14, 301
Moore, M. A., 18
Moravcsik, J. E., 137
Mora, J. K., 296
Morgan, B., 113
Morrow, L. M., 357, 359
Moss, J. G., 225
Muschla, G. R., 189
Myers, M., 63
Nagy, W. E., 98, 103, 110, 112
Napoli, D. J., 365
National Assessment of Education
    Progress, 349
National Center for Education Statistics,
    10, 139
National Center for Family Literacy, 348,
    349, 357
National Commission on Service-
    Learning, 333
National Endowment for the Arts, 10
National Institute of Child Health and
    Human Development, 19, 101, 104
National Reading Panel, 102, 125
NCTE/IRA, 35
Neeld, E. C., 239

Neill, D. M., 28
Nelson, C. M., 307
Nelson-Levitt, J., 15
Northwest Regional Educational
    Laboratory, 193
Norton, D., 199
Norton-Meier, L. A., 331, 332
O'Brien, D. G., 167
O'Sullivan, S., 27
Ohlhausen, M., 327
Oldfather, P., 323, 326
Olson, C. B., 210
Optiz, M. F., 282
Ortiz, R. W., 350
Palincsar, A., 148, 168
Paratore, J. R., 266
Paris, S. G., 326
Pearlman, B., 303
Pearson, P. D., 5, 12, 136, 282
Peha, S., 184, 189
Peregoy, S. F., 261
Peterson, R., 15
Phelps, S. F., 331
Pilgreen, J., 253, 296, 298
Pinnell, G. S., 8, 9, 261
Pintrich, P. R., 168
Pitcher, S. M., 326, 331
Pittelman, S. D., 110
Post, A. D., 225
Pressley, M., 135, 139
RAND Reading Study Group, 167
Raphael, T. E., 149, 150, 156, 157
Rasinski, T., 77, 199
Readence, J. E., 170
Reeves, T. C., 325
Reutzel, D. R., 89
Rhodes, L. K., 50
Richards, J. C., 170
Richardson, J. S., 82
Richter, H. P., 225
Robinson, F. P., 229, 230
Rodin, J., 326
Roe, B. D., 8, 10
Rosenblatt, L. M., 7, 15, 161
Rosenshine, B., 148, 168
Roser, N. L., 266
Ruddell, M. R., 74, 91
Rumelhart, D. E., 7
Ryan, P. M., 351
Sadler, C. R., 90, 224, 246
Samovar, L. A., 10
Sampson, M. R., 261
Schellenberg, S. J., 30
Schiefele, U., 323
Schmar-Dobler, E., 10
Schumm, J. S., 224
Schwanenflugel, P. J., 101
Scott, J. A., 103
Shanahan, T., 199

Shepard, A., 85
Shepard, L. A., 55
Sierra, J., 85
Sierra-Perry, M., 222
Silva, C., 200
Silverblatt, A., 329
Simpson, M. L., 230
Slavin, R. E., 15
Sloyer, S., 84, 85
Smith, K., 29, 265
Smith, P. G., 260
Sneve, V. D. H., 351
Spache, G., 230
Stahl, S. A., 11, 88, 104, 105, 119
Standards for the English Language
    Arts, 7
Stanovich, K., 7
Stauffer, R. G., 144
Stephens, E. C., 227, 230, 233, 240
Stephens, L., 333
Stiggins, R. J., 30
Straits, W., 266
Street, B. V., 324
Strickland, D. S., 261, 265

Stuart, V., 182, 189
Sunstein, B. S., 63
Sweet, A., 19
Switzer, G., 333
Tannock, R., 303
Taylor, D., 349
Taylor, S. V., 340
Taylor, W. L., 55
Teale, W. H., 348
Thomas, A., 348
Tierney, B., 92
Time Life, 338
Tomlinson, C. A., 296, 310, 312, 313
Tompkins, G. E., 286
Tower, C., 15
Turner, J., 326
Ulanoff, S. H., 126
U.S. Census Bureau, 294
U.S. Department of Commerce, 10
U.S. Department of Education, 27
Valdes, G., 347
Van den Broek, P. W., 137
Verhoevan, L., 347
Vogt, M. E., 10

Vygotsky, L. S., 3, 17, 161
Wagner, B. J., 9, 274
Wajnryb, R., 221
Wasik, B. H., 356
Weaver, C., 198
Weiler, D., 333
Weinstein, S., 331
Whelan, G., 351
Whitmore, J. R., 300
Wiesendanger, K. D., 230
Wigfield, A., 339
Wilcox, J., 29
Wilhelm, J. D., 35, 137
Wilson, K. K., 348
Wink, J., 11
Wixson, K. K., 252
Wong-Fillmore, L., 286
Wood, J. W., 304
Wood, K. D., 244
Woods, M. L., 46, 47, 48, 49
Worthy, J., 85
Yell, M. L., 135
Young, E., 172
Zemelman, S., 223, 338

Abstract words, 105
Academic language, 9, 99, 285–286
Academic Word List (AWL), 99
Acceleration, 301
Accountability, book contracts and, 155–156
Accuracy, of websites, 248
Achievement tests, 39 (see also Assessment)
  service learning and, 333
Activities (see also Strategies):
  content area reading, 230–245
  creative thinking–reading, 91–92
  for decoding words, 91, 92
  for increasing fluency, 84–86, 87, 88, 89
  for independent reading, 157–161
  for reading comprehension, 142–144, 147–151
  for vocabulary instruction, 108–109, 110–111, 113–114, 115–121, 122–124, 127
  for word study, 75–78, 79–80
  home literacy, 354–355
  implementing powerful, 369
  literacy beyond the classroom, 330–331, 335–338 (see also Literacy, beyond the classroom)
  oral language, 263, 270, 272, 276, 279, 280, 284 (see also Oral communication)
  reader response, 161, 164–166
  real-world, 335–340
  small group, 222
  tiered, 313–316
Adaptations:
  for English language learners, 294–299
  for gifted children, 301
  for students who are learning disabled, 301–304
  for students who are physically challenged, 306–307
  for students with behavioral disorders, 307–310
  for students with communication disorders, 304–306
Adequate Yearly Progress (AYP), 27
ADHD, 293, 302, 303, 314
Adolescence, characteristics of, 20–21
Adult literacy, 357 (see also Family literacy)

Advanced stage of reading/spelling, 71
Advertisements, analyzing, 336–337
Affective components, of balanced literacy program, 14–19
Affixes, 70, 73–74, 75, 423–424
  activity for, 78–79
  meaning-bearing, 74
African American culture, literature and, 351
African American Vernacular English (AAVE), 294
Aggression, 308
AIDS, 306
Al Capone Does My Shirts, 247
Albinism, 306
All American Reading Challenge, 326
Allergies, 306
Alliance for Excellent Education, 139
Alliteration, 197, 332
Almanacs, 247
Alphabetic principle, 70
American Library Association, 206, 326
  Presidential Committee Report on Information Literacy, 340
American Sign Language, 306
Analytic approach, to writing assessment, 59
Analytical Reading Inventory, 43, 385
Analyze, cubing and, 239
Anchor units, 151–153
Anecdotal notes, 41, 51–52
Anime, 155
Announcements, 273
Anticipation guides, 169–170, 228–229
Apply, cubing and, 239
Applying, part of integrated curriculum, 375
Apprehension, communication, 286–287
Argue, cubing and, 239
Art:
  center, 372
  part of integrated curriculum, 376
Artist, of literature circle/book club, 157
Asian culture:
  literature and, 351
  service learning and, 333
Asperger's syndrome, 304
Assessment:
  and focus on abilities, 30
  anecdotal notes, 51–52
  as a continuum, 31

authentic, 38, 43–61 (see also Informal assessment)
  authentic learning and, 325
  checklists and, 52–54
  cloze tests, 55, 57–58
  cultural bias in, 30
  current views of, 27–29
  curriculum-based, 35
  data managed in portfolios, 61–63
  defined, 28
  devices/tools, 387–418
  formative, 28, 31
  framework for, 32
  holistic/analytic approaches to, 59
  informal, 43–61 (see also Informal assessment)
  informal reading inventories, 43–46, 47–49, 61 (see also Informal reading inventories)
  interactivity and, 341
  list of commercial tools, 385–386
  listening, 407
  norm- and criterion-referenced tests, 34
  observation and, 29–30
  of a text's difficulty level, 327
  of integrated curriculum block, 375
  of progress in literacy, 27–63
  of websites, 387
  of word lists, 59–60
  ongoing, 28
  options for, 31–39
  principles of, 29–31
  process-oriented, 38–39
  reference list of tools, 385–386
  reflective, 222
  rubrics for scoring, 54–55, 56 (see also Rubrics)
  running records, 46, 50–51
  speaking, 403–406
  standardized procedures of, 39–43
  standards and, 28–29
  standards-based performance, 35–38
  student engagement in process, 30
  summative, 28, 31
  teaching and, 29–31 (see also Teaching)
  vs. evaluation, 28
Assignments, implementing powerful, 369
Assistive technology, 305
Associate, cubing and, 239
Assonance, music and, 331

Atlases, 247
At-risk students, 11 (*see also* Differentiating instruction; Diversity; English learners)
Attention deficit hyperactivity disorder (ADHD), 293, 302, 303, 314
Attention, to information in text, 137
Attitude surveys, 385, 390–395
Audience, writing and, 184
Augmentative communication systems, 305
Authentic assessment, 38, 43–61 (*see also* Informal assessment)
Authentic experiences, 222
Authentic learning, 324–341 (*see also* Real-world)
    guidelines for creating, 338–340
    information literacy and, 340–341
Authentic reading and writing experiences, 328
Authors:
    credibility of, 248
    questioning, 135, 168
    readers and, 9–10
Author's chair, 181
Autism, 304, 305
Automaticity, writing fluency and, 200–201

Background knowledge (*see also* Prior knowledge):
    anticipation guides and, 169–170
    reading comprehension and, 137
Background, respect for others', 18–19
Bader Reading and Language Inventory, 386
Balanced approach to literacy, 11–19 (*see also* Literacy)
Base words, 72
Basic Reading Inventory, 385
Basic Reading Inventory, Preprimer–12, 43
Basic words, 98
Becoming a Nation of Readers, 154
Before reading strategies:
    anticipation guides, 228–229
    two-minute preview, 227–228
Beginning stage of reading/spelling, 71
Behavior characteristics:
    of adolescent learners, 20–21
    of gifted learners, 299
Behavioral disorders, students with, 307–310
Behavioral problems, service learning and, 333
Benchmarks, *see* Standards
Best practices, synopsis of research on, 222
Bias, in assessment, 30
Bike Repair, activity, 335
Billboards, literacy lessons and, 332
Biographies, 247
Biosphere activity, 313–316

Black Profiles in Courage, 57–58
Black-eyed Peas, 331
Block, integrated curriculum, 375–376
Blocks, of instruction, 373
Blogging, reading comprehension and, 167
Bodily-kinesthetic learning style, 311
Body language, 298
Book Adventure, 326
Book clubs, 126, 373
    independent reading and, 156–161
    role descriptions for, 157, 365
Book contracts, 155–156, 368
    sample activities for, 163
Book talks, 105, 106
Book-It!, 326
Books (*see also* Literature):
    choosing, 326–327
    estimating difficulty, 327
    list of recommended, 158–159, 370
    nonfiction, 225 (*see also* Expository texts)
    references for children's/young adult, 379–382
    trade, 260
Boy Scouts, 333
Braille, 306
Brain injury, 306
Brainstorming, 204
    poetry and, 207
    research and, 246
    writing and, 184, 194
Bruner, Jerome, 14
Bucks for Books, 326
Buddy reading, 149
Building blocks, for balanced literacy program, 14–19
Bumper stickers, literacy lessons and, 332

C(2)QU, activity, 113–114
Camouflage, activity, 120–121
Campfire, activity, 263
Capitalization, 198
Career poem, 208
Cartoons, communication and, 11, 128 (*see also* Graphic novels)
Categorizing, 102, 376
Cause/effect:
    content area reading and, 226
    web, 241
CD-ROMs, as visual media, 10
Center on Education Policy, 12
Centers, classroom, 371–372
Cerebral palsy, 306, 314
Characters, novelettes and, 204–206
Charts, 240–241, 249–250
Checking back, on understanding, 140
Checklists, 52–54
    editing, 188
    for self-assessment, 54
    for the Nifty-Thrifty-Fifty, 60
    informal, 387, 401–402, 407, 408, 409, 411–415

two-minute preview, 228
Chenowith Elementary, 334
Children's literature, references, 379–382
Chinese, problematic sounds for, 295
Chunking, 72–73
    reading instruction and, 83
Cinque, Joseph, 57–58
Civil War, 240
Clarifying:
    table, 109–110
    vocabulary instruction and, 102
Class Dictionary, activity, 75
Classifying, part of integrated curriculum, 376
Classroom:
    assessment in, 35 (*see also* Assessment)
    centers for instruction, 371–372
    culture, 323–324
    fostering literacy beyond, 319–343
    fostering oral language in, 257–288 (*see also* Oral communication)
    ideal climate for literacy, 367–370
    materials/equipment for, 370–371
    organizing for instruction, 370–372
    real-world activities for, 335–340
    service learning beyond, 333–335
    student-centered, 265
    teacher-directed, 18
Classroom Assessment of Reading Processes, 385
Cleft lip, 306
Click and clunk, during reading, 141
Climate, for literacy, 367–370
Clip-art, 192
Cloze tests, 41, 55, 57–58
Clues, context, 111–114, 314
Clustering, 168, 184–185
Clusters, 240
Code switching, 285
Cognitive components, of literacy program, 14–19
Collaborative learning, 324–325
    text-based, 232–233
Collaborative Strategic Reading (CSR), 141–142
Collins COBUILD Learner's Dictionary, 103, 115
Comic strips, vocabulary and, 128 (*see also* Graphic novels)
Common language, lack of, 360
Communication:
    apprehension, 286–287
    board, 305
    disorders, 293, 304–306
    oral, 257–288 (*see also* Oral communication)
    through images, 11
    with parents, 351–356 (*see also* Parents)
Community, involvement in, 339
Community of learners, 14–15

Community Services Block Grant Act, 357
Compare, cubing and, 239
Comparison/contrast, 259–260
  academic language, 286
  content area reading and, 226, 239
  expository structure, 243
  t-chart, 241
Compliments, on writing, 186
Composing, 186 (see also Writing)
Compound words, 74
Comprehensible input, 296, 299
Comprehension, 6, 17
  context clues and, 111–114
  defined, 135–136
  listening, 282–284 (see also Listening)
  monitoring, 142, 168 (see also
    Assessment)
  questions, in IRIs, 44–45
  reading, 82–83 (see also Reading com-
    prehension)
  strategies for, 16–17
  troubleshooting, 89–92
  websites, 384
Computer (see also Internet):
  center, 372
  pal/buddy, 18, 374
  role in classroom, 10
  skills, 376
Concept and examples web, 241
Concept organizer, 296, 297
Concept-oriented reading instruction
  (CORI), 324
Conclusions, in writing, 210
Concrete words, 105
Conferences:
  about writing, 183, 190–191
  parent-teacher, 352–354
  state-of-the-class, 190–191
Confidence, writing and, 213
Conflict management, role playing and,
  275–276
Connecting, vocabulary and, 102
Connections:
  between text and self/other texts, 137
  reading and writing, 179–218
  teaching for, 369–370
  to text, 169–174
Connector, of literature circle/book club,
  157
Connotation, 100
CONPAR, 272–273
Consonance, music and, 331
Constructive process, reading as, 7
Constructivist model of learning, 4
Content, differentiating, 312 (see also
  Differentiated instruction)
Content, standards, 28–29
Content area literacy, 219–256
  best practices and, 222
  defined, 221
  expository structures and, 226–227,
    233

expository writing and, 232–245
  K-W-L chart and, 240, 242
  literature and, 225
  reading and, 222–232
  resources for various genres, 238
  scaffolds and, 240, 243–245
  websites regarding, 226
  writing and, 232–245
  writing summaries, 233–235
Content areas, 365–366
  Four-by-Four Model and, 297
  literacy and, 219–256 (see also
    Content area literacy)
  literature for, 379–380
  materials for, 224–227
  reading in, 222–232
  reading interview, 252
  researching in, 246–251
  standards, 223
  websites to explore, 226
  writing in, 232–245
Contents, table of, 246
Context:
  activity for, 113–114
  affect on reading comprehension, 136
  clues, 102–103, 111–114, 314
  using, 111–114, 355
  vocabulary, 102–103
Controlled Participation, activity,
  272–273
Conventions, writing, 198
Conversation clubs, 262
Conversational roundtable, 166
Conversations, 261–262
  grand, 15, 266
  social skills and, 309
  topics for informal, 262
Cooperative learning, 296, 341
Cooter/Flynt/Cooter Comprehensive
  Reading Inventory, 385
CORI, 324
Semantic Feature Analysis, activity,
  110–111
Creative questions, 150, 151
Creative reading, 6
Creative thinking–reading activities (CT-
  RAs), 91–92
Creative writing, part of integrated cur-
  riculum, 376
Creativity, of gifted learners, 300
Credibility, author, 248
Criterion-referenced tests, 34, 35
Critical:
  analysis, of text, 138
  listening, 283
  questions, 150, 151
  reading, 6
Critical thinking, 182
  as part of literacy, 3
  problem-based learning and, 324–325
Critical/evaluative questions, 45
Crossing the Wire, 126, 247

CT-RA, 91–92
Cubing, 239–240
Cultural bias, in assessment, 30
Culture:
  home environment and, 347–351
  literature and, 351
  literature references, 379
  media portrayals of, 330–331
  respect for others', 18–19
Curie, Marie, 277
Curious Incident of the Dog in the
  Night-time, 305
Curriculum (see also Content areas):
  and setting literacy objectives,
    367–368
  ideal elements of, 12
  instructional plan and, 372–376
  integrated block, 375–376
  literature across, 379–380 (see also
    Content area literacy)
  standards, 28–29
Curriculum-based assessment, 35

Data charts, 249–250
Debates, informal, 266–267
Debriefing, 308
Decision making, 324
Decoding, 352, 424
  CT-RAs for, 91–92
  multisyllabic words, 91
  reading comprehension and, 89–90
Deduction, 16
Denotation, 100
Denver Reading Attitude Survey,
  392–396
Depth, teaching for, 369–370
Derivational relations, 70, 71
Describe, cubing and, 239
Describing, part of integrated curriculum,
  376
Description:
  content area reading and, 226, 239
  expository structure, 243
Descriptors, of performance, 54
Detail map, 240
Developmental Spelling Test, 400
Diabetes, 306
Diagrams, as visual media, 10
Dialogue journals, 201–203, 331
Diary of a Young Girl, The, 173
Diary of Anne Frank, 374
Dictionaries, 6
  appropriate for classrooms, 115
  polysemantic words and, 118–119
  using, 103, 114–118
  word etymologies and, 76–77
Dictoglos, 221, 253
Differentiated instruction, 368 (see also
  Differentiating instruction)
Differentiating content, 312
Differentiating instruction:
  differentiating content, 312

differentiating process, 312
differentiating product, 313
for students who are English learners, 294–299
for students who are gifted/talented students, 299–301
for students who are learning disabled, 301–304
for students who are physically challenged, 306–307
for students with behavioral disorders, 307–310
for students with communication disorders, 304–306
planning/implementing a lesson, 312–316
problem-based learning, 303–304
project-based learning, 303
reasons for, 293–294, 310–312
sheltered instruction, 296–299
SIOP, 296, 298
tiered activities and, 313–316
Differentiation in Practice, 313
Differentiation, tiered activities and, 313–316
Digital disconnect, 167
Direct assessment, 43–61 (*see also* Informal assessment)
Direct instruction, in reading comprehension, 141–154
Directed Reading-Thinking Activity (DRTA), 144, 145–146, 374
Directive contexts, 103, 112
Disabilities, students with, 293 (*see also* Differentiating instruction; Learning disabilities)
Discovery.com, 226
Discussions:
    about literature, 265–266
    defined, 264
    directed group, 263–264
    dominating, 285
    leader, of literature circle/book club, 157, 365
    literature to provoke, 380
    panel, 272–273
    teacher-guided, 264–265
Disorders, communication, 304–306 (*see also* Communication)
Distributions, scoring, 42
Diverse learners, 291–318 (*see also* Differentiating instruction)
Diversity, 18–19 (*see also* Differentiating instruction)
    in home practices, 347–351
    lack of common language and, 360
    media portrayals of, 330–331
    multicultural literature references, 379
    views of literacy and, 350
Documentaries, evaluating, 329
Double entry journal, 170–171, 266
Drafting, 186 (*see also* Writing)

Drama, 274–282
    creating original, 281–282
    literary role plays, 276–277
    mock interviews, 277–278
    part of integrated curriculum, 376
    role plays, 274–278
    simulations, 278–280
Dramatic productions, 280–282 (*see also* Drama)
Drawings, as method of communication, 11
Drop Everything and Read (DEAR), 105, 126
DRTA, 144, 145–146, 374
Durkin, Delores, 16
DVD-ROMs, as visual media, 10
Dyad reading, 18, 149
    home literacy activity, 355
Dyslexia, 293, 360

Edible Schoolyard, The, 334
Editing, 188
    checklist, 188
    peer, 181, 187
    word processing and, 192
Ekwall/Shanker Reading Inventory, 385
Elaboration, vocabulary and, 102
Electronic portfolio, 63
Electronic text, 167–169
    impact on vocabulary, 103–104
Elementary and Secondary Education Act, 357
E-mail, 183
Emergent stage of reading/spelling, 71
Empathetic listening, 283
Encuesta Sobre Lectura de Denver, 395–396
Encyclopedias, 247
Engagement:
    in assessment process, 30
    in learning vocabulary, 103–104
    in reading/learning, 14–15
    with text, 137–138
English Language Development (ELD), 297
English learners, 294–299
    adaptations for, 294–299
    class collaboration and, 215
    clustering and, 184–186
    code switching and, 285
    content areas and, 253
    differentiated instruction and, 294–299, 314
    family literacy and, 347–351, 357
    information literacy and, 340
    journals and, 202
    lack of verbal skills and, 285
    learning vocabulary, 103
    listening and, 282, 285
    literature circles/book clubs and, 156
    parents of, 353
    polysemantic words and, 118–119

problematic sounds for, 295
    read-alouds and, 125–126
    relating new words to known, 107
    remembering new vocabulary, 126–128
    scaffolding and, 206
    shared reading and, 18
    speaking and, 260
    think-alouds and, 142–143
    troubleshooting vocabulary, 124–128
    using context clues, 113
English, sheltered, 296–299
Enrichment, 301
Enumeration, 240, 243
    chart, 241
    content area reading and, 227
    expository structure, 243
Environment:
    and reading comprehension, 136
    home, 349 (*see also* Home)
    unit on, 324–325
Environmental literacy, 321–322
Epilepsy, 306
Episodic novel, 204
Equipment, classroom, 370–371
Essay, expository, scoring rubric for, 410
Estes Attitude Scales, 385–386
Etymology, 72, 76–77, 424
    activity for, 79–81
Evaluation:
    by schools, 341
    scoring rubrics for, 54–55, 56
    vs. assessment, 28 (*see also* Assessment)
Even Start, 358
Evidence, in writing, 210
Examples:
    in writing, 210
    literacy instruction and, 16–17
Expansionist strategies, 348
Expectations, lessons with, 296
Experience, in reading, 124–126
Experiences, authentic, 222 (*see also* Authentic learning)
Explanations:
    in writing, 210
    literacy instruction and, 16–17
Explicit instruction, 105–107
Expository frames, 195
Expository text, 81–82, 224–227
    essay assessment, 410
    lack of familiarity with structures, 253–254
    literacy and, 219–256 (*see also* Content area literacy)
    preview of, 227–228
    retelling checklist, 411
    ROW activity, 233
    structures, 226–227, 233, 253–254
    writing summaries, 233–235
Expository writing, 209–212
    organizational techniques and, 238–243

Expression, improvement in, 86–87
    (*see also* Fluency)
Expressive vocabulary, 98

Fagin the Jew, 225
Family Circus, 128
Family literacy, 356–359
    activities, 354–355
    cultural differences, 347–351
    parental view of, 348
    programs, 357–359 (*see also* Parents)
    websites, 358
Feedback:
    for teachers, 29
    on writing, 183
Fifth stage, 334–335
Films, assessing, 328–329
Find Someone Who…, activity, 230–231
FLIP strategy, 224
Flowchart, 240
Fluency:
    activities for increasing, 84–86, 87,
        88, 89
    defined, 81
    increasing, 81–89
    intervention programs for, 87–89
    skimming/scanning and, 83–84
    troubleshooting, 89–92
    using phrase markings to increase,
        86–87
    websites, 384
    writing and, 197–198, 199–201
        (*see also* Writing fluency)
Fluency-oriented reading instruction
    (FORI), 87–88
Fly Away Home, 225
*Flynt-Cooter Reading Inventory for the
    Classroom,* 43
Fonts, word processing, 192
Formal speaking, 267–274
Format, of a website, 248
Formative assessment, 28, 31 (*see also*
    Assessment)
Four-by-Four Model, 296, 297–298
Fox Song, 170
Frames, paragraph, 240, 243
Framework, for literacy assessment
    process, 32
Frank, Anne, diary of, 173
Free association, 184
French, problematic sounds for, 295
Freud, Sigmund, 277
Friedrich, 225
Friendliness:
    as part of FLIP, 224
    reader, 136
Frodo's Notebook, 189
Frustration level, of reading, 45
Fry's Readability Graph, 327, 419
Functions, school, 359–360

Gandhi, Mahatma, 278

Garden projects, 333–334
Gardner, Howard, 301, 311
Garfield, 128
Generalizing, 355
General-utility words, 98, 99
Generating questions, 139–140, 141–142
Genres, writing and, 238
Getting to Know You, activity, 270
Gifted students, 293, 299–301
Girl Scouts, 333
GIST, 141, 144, 147–148
Giver, The, 171
Glossary, 114–115, 246
Goals:
    for expanded literacy, 322–332
    lessons and, 296
Going Beyond Visualizing, activity, 165
Goldilocks strategy, 327
Good-bye, Chunky Rice, 225
Google, 250
Government, family literacy and,
    357–358
GPS system, 321
Grades, service learning and, 333
Graffiti, literacy lessons and, 332
Grammar, 198
Grand conversations, 15, 266
Graphic novels, 154–155, 225, 331
    references for, 381–382
Graphic organizers, 107–110, 240–242
    activities using, 108–109, 110
    clarifying table, 109–110
    English learners and, 298
    herringbone strategy, 253–254
    reader response activity, 165–166
    semantic maps, 108–109
Graphics (*see also* Graphic organizers):
    oral presentation and, 268
    previewing, 228
Graphs, 10 (*see also* Graphic organizers)
Grass seed experiment, 314–316
Greek, problematic sounds for, 295
Gregarious students, 311
Group cloze test, 41
Group sharing, 192
Groups, small, 222
Guided reading, 17, 143, 259
    DRTA as, 144, 145–146

Hanna's Suitcase, 173
Harry Potter and the Sorcerer's Stone,
    166
Harry Potter role play, 277
Haves and Have Nots, activity, 279
Head Start Act, 357
Headings, preview of, 228
Hearing impairments, 306, 307
Heat, 126
Herringbone strategy, 253–254
Higher order thinking skills (HOTS), 302
Hinky Pinkies, activity, 122–123

Hispanic culture, views of literacy and,
    350
Historical fiction, 225
History:
    literature circle and, 365
    living, 334–335
    oral, 270–272
    personal, 337–338
    role plays and, 277–278
History Place, the, 212
Holistic approach, to writing assessment,
    59
Holistic process, reading as, 5–6
Holocaust, 173, 225
Home:
    literacy at, 345–361 (*see also* Family
        literacy)
    practices, 347–351
    schooling, website, 358
Horace Mann Academic Middle School,
    334–335
HOTS, 302
How Is It Used?, activity, 118–119
Hurricanes, 259–260
Hyperactivity, 299
Hyperbole, 331
Hyperstudio, creating portfolios and, 63

Ideas, writing and, 193–194, 213
IEPs, 306
Illustrations, 10, 266
Illustrator, literature circle and, 365
IM (instant messaging), 331
Imagery, of text, 140
Images, popular culture, 332
Imaging, 355
Immigration, literature about, 370
iMovie, 271
Implicit instruction, 154–166
Impromptu speeches, 273–274
Incentives, to read and write, 325–326
Incidental learning, 104–105
Independent level, for reading, 45
Independent reading, 154–161
Independent word-learning strategies,
    102–103
Indexes, 246
Indirect assessment, 39–43 (*see also*
    Assessment)
Individual interests, 323–324
Individualized education programs (IEPs),
    306
Individuals with Disabilities Education
    Act (IDEA), 304
Induction, 16
Inferential questions, 45, 150, 151
Inflections, 74
Informal assessment, 43–61
    anecdotal notes, 51–52
    attitude surveys, 61
    checklists, 52–54 (*see also* Checklists)
    cloze tests, 55–58

interest surveys, 61
IRI, *see* Informal reading inventories
running records, 46, 50–51
word lists, 59
writing folders, 59
Informal debates, 266–267
Informal reading inventories (IRIs), 38,
    41, 43–49, 61
    reference list of, 375
Informal Reading Inventory, 385
Informal speaking, 261–267
Information:
    attention to, 137
    gathering for oral report, 268
    locating, 246–251 (*see also* Research)
    organizing, 268
Information literacy, 321–322, 340–341
    English learners and, 340
Information literate, defined, 340
Informational texts, 212, 219–256 (*see*
    also Content area literacy;
    Expository text)
Informational writing, 209–212
    part of integrated curriculum, 375,
    376
Initiating an Oral Recitation Lesson,
    activity, 89
Input, comprehensible, 296, 299
Input, vocabulary and, 102
Inquiry teaching, 265
Inspiration software, 168
Inspiration, writing and, 201–212
Instant messaging, 331
Instruction:
    balanced and comprehensive, 11–19
    classroom centers for, 371–372
    classroom climate for, 367–370
    defined, 3
    devising a plan for, 372–376
    differentiating, 291–318, 368 (*see also*
      Differentiating instruction)
    direct, 374
    diversity and, 18–19 (*see also*
      Diversity)
    expanded literacy goals and, 322–332
    explanations/examples in, 16–17
    explicit, 105–107
    implicit, 154–166
    literature-based approach to, 373
    organizing the classroom for,
      370–372
    reading comprehension, 135–174
    sheltered, 296–299
    teacher's self-evaluation of, 417–418
    transmission/transactional models
      and, 15–16
    typical week's word study plan,
      423–424
    vocabulary, 97–128
    word study and, 71–81
    writing, 181–182 (*see also* Writing)
Instructional level, for reading, 45

Instructions:
    listening, 282–284
    problem-based learning and, 324–325
Integrated curriculum block, 375–376
Integrative units, 222
Intellectually gifted children, 299–301
Intelligences, multiple, 301–302, 311, 314
Interactive journal, 201–203
Interactive oral reading, 125
Interest:
    as part of FLIP, 224
    groups, 18
    in reading, 124–126
Interest and attitude inventories, 61,
    323–324
Intermediate stage of reading/spelling, 71
International Reading Association (IRA),
    7, 205
Internet:
    decline in reading and, 10
    reading comprehension and, 167–169
    research and, 247–248, 250–251
    visual literacy and, 10–11
Interpersonal intelligence, 302, 311
Interviews, 268–270
    content area, 252
    mock, 277–278
    taped, 247
Intolerance, 332
Intrapersonal intelligence, 302, 311
Introduction, preview of, 228
Inventories:
    informal reading, *see* Informal reading
      inventories
    interest and attitude, 61, 323–324
Investigator, literature circle and, 365
Iowa Test of Basic Skills, 34
IRI, *see* Informal reading inventories
I-Search process, 168, 210–211
Italian, problematic sounds for, 295

Japanese, problematic sounds for, 295
Jigsaw, activity, 160–161
Job Market, activity, 335–336
Journals:
    dialogue, 201–203, 331
    double-entry, 201–203, 266
    response, 4
    writing, 374
Journey North, website, 212
Jurassic Park, 69
Just Suppose, activity, 263

Key words, 243, 247
Kid's Online Magazine, 189
Knowledge, background, 137
Knowledge, prior, 224, 259
Korean, problematic sounds for, 295
K-W-L chart, 168
K-W-L Plus, 240, 242

Labeling, vocabulary instruction and, 102

Ladder, activities, 314–315
Language:
    academic, 9, 99, 285–286
    as part of FLIP, 224
    board, 305
    development, at home, 352
    disorders, 304–306
    lack of a common, 360
    love of, 122–124
    oral, 120–121
    word choice and, 196–197
Language arts, 260
    defined, 7
    everyday application of, 321–322,
      324–325
    integrated curriculum block, 375–376
Latino culture, literacy and, 350, 351
Learner as a Reader, The, 50
Learners (*see also* Students):
    characteristics of, 20–21, 300 (*see also*
      Diversity)
    diverse, 18–19, 291–318 (*see also*
      Differentiating instruction)
    English, *see* English learners
Learning:
    disabilities, 301–304
    authentic, 324–325, 338–340 (*see also*
      Authentic learning)
    collaborative, 232–233
    community, 14–15
    constructivist model of, 4
    cooperative, 296, 341
    engagement in, 14–15
    incidental, 104–105
    problem-based, 303–304, 324–325
    profiles, 311
    project-based, 303
    self-regulated, 168
    styles, 311
Legislation, literacy and, 19–20, 357–358
Lessons (*see also* Instruction):
    goals and, 296
    planning differentiated, 312–316 (*see*
      also Differentiating instruction)
    real-world, 332 (*see also* Real-world)
Letter name stage, 70–71
Library:
    classroom, 370–372
    school, 327, 375
Lincoln, Abraham, 145–147, 278
Linguistic diversity, 294–299 (*see also*
    English learners)
Linguistic learning style, 311
Linking, vocabulary instruction and, 102
Listening, 3, 282–284
    comprehension, 45, 282–284
    critical, 283
    empathetic, 283
    everyday examples of, 321–322
    purposes of, 283
    reading comprehension and, 8
    vocabulary, 73

Listing (enumeration), 240
Literacies:
    multiple, 3
    new, 167–169
Literacy:
    activity for home, 354–355
    adult, 357 (*see also* Family literacy)
    application of skills, 17
    assessment of progress in, 27–63 (*see also* Assessment)
    at home, 345–361 (*see also* Family literacy)
    balanced, comprehensive approach to, 11–19, 365–376
    beyond the classroom, 319–343
    classroom climate and, 367–370
    comparison of approaches to, 13
    components of balanced program, 14–19
    connecting to popular culture, 331–332, 336
    content areas and, 219–256 (*see also* Content area literacy)
    cultural differences, 347–351
    defined, 3
    differentiated instruction for, *see* Differentiating instruction
    emergent factors, 6
    establishing lifelong habits of, 326–332
    everyday examples of, 321–322
    explanations/examples in, 16–17
    factors in a successful program, 17–18
    family, 356–359 (*see also* Family literacy)
    framework for assessment in, 32 (*see also* Assessment)
    information, *see* Information literacy
    instructional goals, 322–332
    listening and, 8
    low-income families and, 350
    media, 328–331, 336
    national focus on, 19–20
    observation checklist, 53, 415
    oral communication and, 257–288 (*see also* Oral communication)
    parental view of, 348 (*see also* Parents)
    problem-based learning and, 324–325
    scaffold, 206–208
    self-evaluation for instruction, 417–418
    setting objectives for, 367–368
    standards, 223
    teacher/student roles in, 12–14
    traditional/skills based, 13
    transmission/transactional models and, 15–16
    views of Hispanic parents, 350
    views of Latino parents, 350
    visual, 10

    visual, books to promote, 381–382
    websites, 383–384
    what parents should know, 351–352
Literacy Assessment: A Handbook of Instruments, 386
Literal questions, 45, 149, 151
Literary luminary, literature circle and, 157, 365
Literature:
    across the curriculum, 225 (*see also* Content area literacy)
    circles, *see* Literature circles
    discussions about, 265–266, 380
    double entry journals, 168, 169
    instruction based on, 373
    multicultural, 138, 351, 379
    references for children's/young adult, 379–382
    role playing and, 276–277
    to provoke discussion, 380
Literature circles, 4, 126, 365, 373, 374
    activity, 157–160
    defined, 156
    independent reading and, 156–161
    sample book list for, 370
Literature response groups, 18
Living history, 334–335
Logical-mathematical intelligence, 311
Lon Po Po, 172
Lotus Seed, The, 172
Low-income families, literacy and, 350
Low-utility words, 98, 99
Lyrics, poetry techniques and, 331–332

Magazines, 247
Magic School Bus, 212, 226
Mainstreaming children, 339
Manga, 155
Manhattan New School, 328
Map, word, 311
Maps, 247
    as visual media, 10
    semantic, 108–109
Margin notes, preview of, 228
Mass media, informed consumers of, 336 (*see also* Media)
Mastery, 369
Materials, classroom, 370–371
Math:
    best practices for, 222
    enumeration and, 243
    oral language component to, 375
    part of integrated curriculum, 375
    real world use of, 336
    standards, 223
Maze test, 55
Meaning:
    of unknown words, 74
    reading and, 5 (*see also* Reading comprehension)
    vocabulary, 98
Media literacy, 328–331, 336

    part of integrated curriculum, 376
    Portrayals of People and Cultures, activity, 330–331
    informed consumers of, 336
    visual, *see* Visual media
Meeting of the Minds, 277
Mental representations, of text, 137
Merlyn's Pen, 189
Metacognition, 138
Metacomprehension, 138
Metaphor, music and, 332
Mexican culture, service learning and, 333
Minilesson, 17, 374
    writer's workshop, 189–190
Miscue analysis, 45–50
Miscues, of readers, 44
Mispronunciation, of words, 91–92
Mission District, 334–335
Mock interviews, 277–278
Modeling, 17
    automaticity, 200
    making connections with text and, 170, 172
    of a think-aloud 143
    oral communication, 265
    reading comprehension, 136
    reciprocal teaching and, 148–149
Monitoring, comprehension, 142, 168
Monster Test, The, 400
Morpheme, 103
Morphemic analysis, 103
Morphology, 72, 73–76, 424
Motivation, 339
    intrinsic, 326
    to read and write, 322–326
Mulan, 328
Multicultural literature, 138
    references, 379
Multiple intelligences theory, 301–302, 311, 314
Multisyllabic words, 72–73, 91
Muscular dystrophy, 306
Music, linking to literacy, 331–332, 339
Musical intelligence, 289, 311
My Hero Project, 212

Narrative text, writing, 204–206
Nation Online, A, 10
National Center for Education Statistics, 139
National Center for Literacy, 358
National Commission on Service-Learning, 333
National Council of Teachers of English (NCTE), 7
National Council of Teachers of Mathematics (NCTM) Standards, 223
National Institute of Child Health and Development (NICHD), 19
National Reading Panel (NRP), 20
National Science Education Standards for Science as Inquiry, 223

National Social Studies Standards, 223
Native American culture, 294
  literature and, 351
Naturalistic intelligence, 311
Navigation, of a website, 248
New literacies, 167–169
Newbery Medal, 205
Nifty-Thrifty-Fifty Words, 59–60, 421, 424
  transfer words, 422
  checklist, 401–402
  structural analysis of words and, 76
No Child Left Behind (NCLB) Act of 2001, 20, 27, 135, 294
Nondirective contexts, 103
Nonfiction books, 225, 247 (*see also* Content area literacy; Expository text)
Nonreaders, 310
Normal curve, scores and, 42
Norm-referenced tests, 33, 34, 39
Northwest Regional Educational Laboratory, 193
Notes, anecdotal, 51–52
Novel study, 151–154
Novelettes, 204–206
Novels, content areas and, 225 (*see also* Content area litearcy)
Novels, graphic, 154–155, 331
Number the Stars, 374

Objectives, setting literacy, 367–368
Observations:
  anecdotal notes and, 51–52
  assessment and, 29–30
  checklist for, 36–37, 52–54
  process-oriented assessment and, 38
Occupational literacy, 321–322
Ongoing assessment, 28
Online reading, 167–169
Online research, 247–248, 250–251
Onomatopoeia, music and, 332
Onset, 72
Open question stems, 140
Oral communication:
  announcements, 273
  assessment of, 404
  conversations, 261–262
  directed group discussions, 263–264
  drama, 274–282
  formal speaking, 267–274
  impromptu speeches, 273–274
  informal debates, 266–267
  informal speaking, 261–267
  interviews, 268–270
  listening and, 282–284 (*see also* Listening)
  literary role plays and, 276–277
  mock interviews and, 277–278
  oral reports, 267
  panel discussions, 272–273
  role playing, 274–278

simulations, 278–280
  troubleshooting regarding, 285–287
  voice projection and, 287
Oral histories, 270–272
Oral language, 257–288 (*see also* Oral communication)
  as component to math lesson, 375
  English learners and, 9
  expanding, 120–121
  home influence on, 352
  presentation, integrated curriculum and, 375, 376
  reading comprehension and, 8–9
Oral presentations, rubric for, 268
Oral reading skills, 6
Oral recitation lesson (ORL), 88–89
Oral reports, 267 (*see also* Oral communication)
Order:
  chronological, 240, 241
  sequential, 240, 241
  time sequence, 240, 241
Organization:
  expository writing and, 238–243
  formal speaking and, 268
  writing and, 195, 214–215
Organizational patterns, 214–215
Organizer, concept, 296, 297
Organizers, graphic, *see* Graphic organizers
Orthographic knowledge, 6
Our American Century, 337
Outlines, 240
  proposition and support, 235–237
Outside and Inside You, 170

Panel discussions, 272–273
Paragraph frames, 240, 243
Paragraphing, 198
Paraphrases, as assessment tool, 41
Paraphrastics, activity, 123–124
Parents:
  communicating with, 351–356
  connecting to schools, 345–361, 369
  helping them to help children, 354–355
  reluctance to attend school functions, 359–360
  view of literacy, 348 (*see also* Family literacy)
  what they should know about literacy, 351–352
  work schedules and, 359
Parent–teacher conferences, 352–354
  diversity and, 347
Parent Think-Aloud, 355
Participation, lack of, 286–287
Partner reading, 18, 149
Patterns, morphological, 76
Paulsen, Gary, 196
PBS Video website, 328
Pearson Assessments, 34
Pedro and Me, 225

Peer editing, 181, 187
Peer talk, 261
People, media portrayals of, 330–331
Percentile scores, 39, 41
Performance descriptors, 54
Personal Report of Communication Fear (PRCF), 286–287
Personal response, to reading, 18, 170–171
Personality traits, 311
Personification, music and, 332
Persuasion:
  content area reading and, 227
  expository structure, 243
Philosophy, of teaching, 367
Phonemic awareness, 71
Phonics, 71
Photographs, 10, 11, 247
Phrase marking, 86–87
Physical education, 375
Physical impairments, students with, 306–307
Picture books, 225
  learning vocabulary and, 127
  reference list of, 381
Pictures, communication and, 11
PLAE, 230
PLAN, 230
Planning, writing and, 183–186
Plays, *see* Drama; Readers theatre
Plot, 266
Poe, Edgar Allan, 152, 154
Poetry:
  music and, 331–332
  writing, 206–208
Poliomyelitis, 306
Polysemantic words, 118–120
Polysyllabic words, 72–73, 91
Popular culture, connecting literacy to, 331–332
PORPE, 230
Portfolios, 62–63
  assessment data and, 61–63
  writing, 41
Portmanteau words, 81
Possible Sentences, activity, 119–120
Poverty, role play and, 279
PowerPoint, 268, 324–325
  creating portfolios and, 63
PQP (praise, question, polish), 187
PQRST, 230
Practice, reading and writing, 17
Praise, question, polish, 187
Predicting, reading comprehension and, 139
Predictions, making, 355
Prefixes, 70, 73, 75, 103, 423–424
  word walls and, 77–81
Prejudice, activity, 280
Prereading strategies:
  anticipation guides, 228–229
  two-minute preview, 227–228

Presentation:
of oral report, 268–269 (see also Oral communication)
writing and, 199
Preview:
before reading, 141
of expository text, 227–228
Primary grades, word study instruction in, 71–72
Prior knowledge, 259, 352
as part of FLIP, 224
Probable Passages, activity, 244–245
Problem solving, 324
role playing and, 275–276
Problem/solution, content area reading and, 226–227, 243
Problem-based learning, 303–304, 324–325
Process, differentiating, 312 (see also Differentiated instruction)
Process-oriented assessment, 38–39
Product, differentiating, 313 (see also Differentiated instruction)
Productive questioning, 139–140
Productive vocabulary, 98
Professional teaching standards, 28–29
Progress notes, 356
Project-based learning, 303
Projection, voice, 287
Proposition writing, 235–237
Publishing, 189
Punctuation, 198

QARs, 149–151
Qualitative Reading Inventory, 43, 385
Question the Author, 135, 168
Question–answer relationships (QARs), 149–151
Questioning:
expository text, 229–230
vocabulary instruction and, 102
Questions:
comprehension, 44–45
creative, 150, 151
critical, 150, 151
for analyzing advertisements, 337
for viewing films, 329
generating, 139–140, 141–142
history activity, 338
home literacy activity, 354–355
in response guide, 186
inferential, 150, 151
inquiry, 246
literal, 149, 151
productive, 139–140
Quests, by students, 341
Quick write, 183–184
response to math lesson, 375

RAND Reading Study Group, 167
Rate, of reading, 82, 83

Read a Book in an Hour, example lesson, 162–163
Read/Organize/Write strategy, 233
Readability, assessing a book's, 327
Readability, Fry's Graph, 419
Read-alouds, 125–126
Reader response activities, 154, 161, 164–166
Reader, transitional, 70
Reader-friendliness of text, 136
Readers:
checking back, 140
comprehension factors within, 136–138
connection with authors, 9–10
developing motivated, 322–326
generating questions, 139–140, 141–142
level of word knowledge, 100–101
miscues of, 44
predicting what happens next, 139
reading comprehension and, see Reading comprehension
running records and, see Running records
visualizing text, 140
vocabulary knowledge and, 98 (see also Vocabulary)
writing and, 9 (see also Writing)
Readers theatre, 84, 164, 281, 374
activity, 84–86
resources/scripts for, 85–86
Readers workshop, 340
Readiness levels, 296
Reading (see also Readers; Reading comprehension; Reading process):
a book in an hour, 160–161, 162–163
and the other language arts, 7–11
and writing connections, 179–218
as a constructive process, 7
as a holistic process, 5–6
as a strategic process, 7
as an interactive process, 7
as part of literacy, 3
basic skills, 138
capacity level, 45
chunking and, 83
comparison of approaches to, 13
comprehension, see Reading comprehension
creative, 6
critical, 6
defined, 4–5
direct instruction in, 374
dyad, 149, 355
engagement in, 14–15
establishing lifelong habits of, 326–332
everyday examples of, 321–322
expression in, 86–87
festival, 356
fluency-oriented reading instruction, 87–88

for authentic reasons, 328
frustration level of, 45
guided, 143, 259
how to vs. how to read to learn, 12
in the content areas, 222–232 (see also Content area literacy)
incentives to, 325–326
independent, 154–161
independent level of, 45
instruction, 11–19, 82 (see also Instruction)
instructional level of, 45
interactive oral, 125
Internet use and, 10
limited interest/experience in, 124–126
making connections with text, 169–174
miscue analysis of, 45–50
modeling, 88–89
of expository text, 81–82 (see also Expository text)
online, 167–169
oral recitation lesson and, 89
part of integrated curriculum, 375, 376
personal response to, 18, 170–171
providing time for, 105
rate, 82, 83
receptive, 6
recreational, 380–381
saving money and, 336–337
shared, 18
silent, 82, 83, 105, 126, 374
skimming/scanning and, 83–84
stages of, 70–71
subskills, 6
suitability of, 55
summarizing text, 140
surveys, 388–296
time for, 126
transmission/transactional models and, 15–16
vocabulary, 97–98 (see also Vocabulary)
"Reading at Risk," 10
Reading Can Save You Money, activity, 336–337
Reading comprehension, 135–174
activities for, 142–144, 147–151
background knowledge and, 137, 224, 259, 352
click and clunk, 141
context and, 136 (see also Context)
defined, 167
effective direct instruction in, 141–154
engagement with text and, 137–138
external factors affecting, 136
factors affecting, 136–138
generating questions, 139–140, 141–142
getting the gist, 141

implicit instruction in, 154–166
internal factors affecting, 136–138
Internet and, 167–169
monitoring and, 142
parental knowledge of, 352
predicting, 139
previewing, 141
prior knowledge and, 137, 224, 259, 352
QARs and, 149–151
reader response activities and, 161, 164–166
reciprocal teaching and, 148–149, 168
strategies for, 138, 139–140
think-alouds, 142–143
troubleshooting, 169–174
wrap-up, 141–142
Reading Excellence Act, 357
Reading interest inventory, see Informal reading inventories
Reading Is Fundamental, 326, 358
Reading Next: A Vision for Action and Research in Middle and High School Literacy, 139
Reading process (see also Reading):
characteristics of, 5–7
listening and, 8
speaking and, 8–9
viewing and, 10–11
visually representing and, 11
writing and, 9–10
Reading Teacher's Book of Lists, The, 74
Real world:
classroom activities, 335–340
home literacy activities, 354–355
information literacy and, 340–341
learning, service learning, 333–335
problems, instruction and, 321–322, 324
Realia, 296, 298
REAP, 230
Receptive reading, 6
Receptive vocabulary, 98
Reciprocal teaching, 148–149
using the Internet and, 168
Recite, SQ3R and, 230
Recreational literacy, 321–322
Recreational reading, references for, 380–381
Reflection, on school day, 376
Reflective assessment, 222
Reflective statement, portfolios and, 61
Relating, vocabulary instruction and, 102
Reliability, of test results, 30
Reliability, website, 248
Repetition, music and, 331
Reports, oral, 267
Representing-to-learn, 222
Rereading, 140
Research:
in the content areas, 246–251
of best practices, 222

on reading comprehension, 136–138
online, 247–248, 250–251
oral histories, 271
part of integrated curriculum, 376
reports, 238
Respect, for others' backgrounds, 18–19
Response guide, 186–187
Response journals, 4
Response, to reading, 4, 18, 170–171, 186–187
Responsive classroom culture, 323–324
Retelling, 44–45
Review, SQ3R and, 230
Reviewing, after reading, 141–142
Revising, writing and, 186–187
Revision, 6 + 1Trait guide to, 193–194
(see also Six +1Trait approach)
Rewards, as motivation, 325–326
Rheumatic fever, 306
Rhyme, music and, 332
Rimes, 70
Role plays, 274–278
Roles, discussion group, 266
Roles, of literature circle/book club, 365
Roots, 72, 73, 75, 103
meaning-bearing, 74
word walls and, 77–81
Roots and Branches, activity, 78–79
Rose Blanche, 225
Rosenblatt, L., 161
ROW strategy, 233
Rubrics:
list of effective, 55
oral presentation, 268
scoring, 54–55, 56
scoring for expository essay, 410
scoring for oral expression, 404
Running records, 38, 41, 46, 50–51
Running Records for Classroom Teachers, 386
RUNNING START, 336
Rylant, Cynthia, 196

Sadako, 225
Scaffolding/scaffolds, 17, 206–208, 240, 243–245
SCAIT, 230
Scanning, 83–84
Schema, 7
for remembering new vocabulary, 126–128
GIST and, 144, 147–148
reading comprehension and, 137
Scholastic.com, 226
Schools, interactive, 341 (see also Service learning)
Schrock, Kathy, 247
Science:
best practices for, 222
differentiated lesson for, 313–316
garden projects and, 333–334
K-W-L Plus and, 240, 242

national standards regarding, 223
part of integrated curriculum, 375, 376
problem-based learning and, 324–325
Scope of a website, 248
Scores (see also Assessment):
distributions of, 42
graphic profile for examining, 40
interpretation of, 39, 41–43
normal curve of, 42
rubrics for, 54–55, 56
standard deviations of, 41–42
stanines, 41–42
SCREAM, 302
Scripts, for readers theatre, 85–86
Search, online, 247–248, 250–251
SEARCH strategy, 168, 249
Second-language learners, see English learners
Self-assessment (see also Assessment):
and levels of word knowledge, 100–101
checklist for, 54
scoring rubrics for, 55, 56
Self-regulated learning (SRL), 168
Semantic feature analysis, 110–111
Semantic Gradient, activity, 121
Semantic Map, activity, 108–109
Semantic maps, 108–109
Sensory impressions, 196
Sentence, fluency, 197–198
Sequence chart, 240, 241
Sequence, expository structure, 243
Service learning, 333–335
Shared reading, 18, 160–161
Sharing, writing, 192
Shell Book, The, 127
Sheltered English, 296–299
Sheltered Instruction Observation Protocol (SIOP), 296, 298
Showcase portfolio, 63
Sight vocabulary, 6, 15
Sight words, 6, 15
Silent reading, 82, 83, 374
Similes, 197, 332
Simulations, 278–280
SIOP, 296, 298
Six + 1 Trait approach, 183, 193–199, 201
conventions and, 198
fluency and, 197–198
ideas and, 193–194
organization and, 195
presentation and, 199
voice and, 195–196
word choice and, 196–197
Sketch to Sketch, activity, 164
Skills:
basic, 138
comprehension, 6 (see also Reading comprehension)
dictionary, see Dictionaries
English, 285 (see also English learners)

for reading, 6 (*see also* Reading;
Reading process)
listening, 282–284
oral communication, 6, 260–261 (*see
also* Oral communication)
social, 307–310
study, 6
word study, *see* Word study
Skimming, 83–84
Small group activities, 222
Social settings, instruction in, 18
Social skills, behavioral disorders and,
307–310
Social studies:
best practices for, 222
national standards regarding, 223
Socratic dialogue, 302
Software, text-reader, 305
Songs, linking to literacy, 331–332, 339
Sounds, problematic for ELL, 294–295
Spanish:
problematic sounds for, 295
reading assessment and, 395–396
Spatial intelligence, 302, 311
Speaking (*see also* Oral communication):
as part of literacy, 3
everyday examples of, 321–322
formal, 267–274
informal, 261–267
new vocabulary and, 120–121
reading comprehension and, 8–9
Special education, 293 (*see also*
Differentiating instruction)
Special needs, students with, 291–318
(*see also* Differentiating instruction)
Specialized vocabulary words, 41
Specially Designed Academic Instruction
in English (SDAIE), 296–297
Speech:
disorders, 304–306
impediments, 304–306
skills, 305 (*see also* Oral communication)
impromptu, 273–274 (*see also* Oral
communication)
Speed writing, 199–200
Spell-check, 200–201
Spelling, 198
automaticity and, 200–201
inventory, 397
stages of, 70–71
Spina bifida, 306
SQ3R, 229–230
SQRQCQ, 230
Standard deviation (SD), 41–42
Standard error of measurement (SEM),
42–43
Standardized tests, 33–35, 39–43 (*see
also* Assessment)
list of, 385–386
Standardized procedures for assessment,
39–43

Standards:
anchor units and, 151–153
assessment of progress toward,
413–414
checklist of progress toward, 36–37
content area, 223 (*see also* Content
area literacy)
curriculum/content, 28–29
integrated curriculum blocks and, 375
National Science Education, 223
National Social Studies, 223
NCTM, 223
planning curriculum around, 368
professional teaching, 28–29
Standards-based performance assessment,
35–38
Stanford Achievement Test (SAT), 34, 41
Stanford Diagnostic Reading Test
(SDRT), 34, 39, 385
Stanine scores, 41, 42
STAR, 230
Starters, story, 214
State-of-the-class conferences, 190–191
Stieglitz Informal Reading Inventory,
385
Stones in Water, 365
Story grammars, 195
Story starters, 214
Strategic process, reading as, 7
Strategic reader model, 136
Strategies:
content area, 224, 227–232
cubing, 238
FLIP, 224
for a comprehensive vocabulary program, 107–127
for decoding, 90
for improving fluency, 84–86
for learning new words, 102–103
for reading comprehension, 138,
139–140
ROW, 233
SEARCH, 249
study, 230
Structural analysis, 103
word list test, 41
of words, 72, 75–76
Structural overviews, *see* Graphic
organizers
Structures:
of texts, 81–82
writing and, 198
expository text and, 226–227, 233,
253–254
Student placement test, 43–46
Students:
anecdotal notes about, 51–52
at-risk, 11
books recommended for/by, 158–159
collaboration with teachers, 16
connecting to parents and teachers,
345–361

daily routine of, 374–376
different needs of, 368
engagement in assessment process, 30
engagement in learning vocabulary,
103–104
English learners, 294–299 (*see also*
English learners)
gifted and talented, 299–301
gregarious, 311
independent reading and, 154–161
inspiring to write, 201–212
literature circles, 156–161
portfolios and, *see* Portfolios
QARs and, 149–151
reader response activities and, 161,
164–166
reciprocal teaching and, 148–149
reflecting on what they've learned,
376
vocabulary instruction, 101–104
who are learning disabled, 301–304
with behavioral disorders, 307–310
word lists and, 59–60
Study, novel, 151–154
Study plan, word, 423–424
Study skills, 6
Study Strategy Tryout, activity, 230
Study systems, 230
Suffixes, 70, 74, 75, 103
word walls and, 77–81
Suitability, of texts, 55
Summaries:
as assessment tool, 41
writing, 233–235
Summarize, as academic language, 286
Summarizer, literature circle and, 157,
365
Summarizing, 140, 144, 145–146
part of integrated curriculum, 376
Summary, preview of, 228
Summative assessment, 28, 31
Summer of the Swans, The, 162–163
Support writing, 235–237
Surveys:
attitude, 385
of expository text, 229–230
reading, 388–396
Sustained Silent Reading (SSR), 105, 126
Sweet Clara and the Freedom Quilt, 225
Syllabication, 72–73
Syllables and affixes stage, 70, 71
Sylla-Search, activity, 91

Talented students, 299–301
Talk, reading comprehension and, 9
Talks, book, 105
Target organizer, 166
T-chart, 172, 173, 240
Teachers (*see also* Teaching):
as team members, 341
connecting to parents, 345–361
modeling, *see* Modeling

orchestrating a balance literacy program, 365–376
reciprocal teaching and, 148–149
role in balanced approach to literacy, 12–14
standards and, 28–29
standards-based performance assessment and, 38
Teaching (*see also* Instruction):
    for depth/connections, 369–370
    inquiry, 265
    philosophy of, 367
    reciprocal, 148–149, 168
    standards and, 28–29 (*see also* Standards)
Teams, project-based learning and, 303
Technological tools, 167–169
Technology:
    assistive, 305
    for responding to books, 18
    part of integrated curriculum, 376
    special needs and, 305, 306
    writing and, 192
Tests (*see also* Assessment):
    achievement, 39
    cloze, 41, 55, 57–58
    criterion-referenced, 35
    group cloze, 41
    interpretation of scores, 39, 41–43
    list of standardized, 385–386
    norm-referenced, 33
    reliability/validity of results, 30
    scores, *see* Scores
    standardized, 33–35, 39–43
Text:
    attention to information in, 137
    critical analysis of, 138
    electronic, 103–104, 167–169
    engagement with, 137–138, 169–174
    expository, *see* Expository text
    GIST and, 144, 147–148
    reader-friendliness of, 136
    summarizing, 140 (*see also* Summaries)
    visualizing, 140
Textbooks, 225–227 (*see also* Expository text)
Text patterns, expository, 240–241
Text-reader software, 305
Texts:
    complexity of, 81–82
    content area, 224–227
Thematic teaching, 303
Thematic units, 375–376
Thesaurus, 197
Thesis statement, 209
Think sheet, 308–309
Think-alouds, 142–143
Thinking, critical, *see* Critical thinking
Think-links, 240
Tiered activities, 313–316
Tiers, of vocabulary, 98–99
Tier Two words, 99, 100

Time, for reading, 82, 105, 126
Time/order sequence, 240, 241, 243
    content area reading and, 226
Time-out, 308
Tools, assessment, 31–39, 41 (*see also* Assessment)
Top Five, activity, 232
Topic:
    and details map, 240, 241
    choosing, 267–268
    modeling, 190
    sentence, 209
Tornadoes, 259–260
Total physical response (TPR), 296
Tourette's syndrome, 306
Trade books, 225, 260
Traditional/skills-based literacy program, 13
Transactional model, 15
Transactions, between teacher and student, 15–16
Transfer words, 76
    Nifty-Thrifty-Fifty, 422
Transition phrases, 195, 210
Transitional reader, 70
Transitional stage of reading/spelling, 71
Transitions, writing and, 195, 210
Transmission, of instruction, 15–16
Transmission model, 15
Troubleshooting:
    content area literacy and, 252–254
    oral language and, 285–287
    parental involvement and, 359–360
    reading comprehension, 169–174
    vocabulary instruction, 124–128
    word study/fluency and, 89–92
    writing and, 212–215
Tuck Everlasting, 97, 106
Tuned Out, 47–49
Tutoring, interactive, 341
Two-minute preview, 227–228

Understanding, checking back and, 140
Upstairs Room, The, 374

Validity, of test results, 30
Venn diagram, 240, 241, 260
    as academic language, 286
Very Important Term (VIT) Word Book, 115–118, 122
Video presentations, 10–11
Video recorder, 271
Vietnam War, 172
Viewing:
    as part of literacy, 3
    everyday examples of, 321–322
    part of integrated curriculum, 375
    reading comprehension and, 10–11
Virtual Field Trip, activity, 127
Visual arts, gifted students and, 300
Visual impairments, 306, 307
Visual learners, 311

Visual literacy, 10
    books to promote, 381
    Internet and, 10–11
Visual media:
    graphic novels and, 154–155
    Sketch to Sketch activity and, 164
    viewing and, 10
    visually representing and, 11
Visual organizers, *see* Graphic organizers
Visualizing:
    graphic organizers and, 107–110, 165–166
    modeling, 143
    text, 140
Visually representing:
    as part of literacy, 3
    everyday examples of, 321–322
    part of integrated curriculum, 376
    reading comprehension and, 11
Vocabulary, 6
    activities for increasing, 108–109, 110–111, 113–114, 115–121, 122–124, 127
    clarifiers, 109–110
    graphic organizers and, 107–110
    graphically illustrating, 106–107
    impact of reading on, 124–126
    Important Words activity, 232
    instruction in, 97–128
    integral to reading, 97–98
    learning new, 122–124
    listening, 73
    master, literature circle and, 157, 365
    meaning, 98
    principles of instruction, 101–104
    probable passages and, 244
    reading, 98
    schema for remembering, 126–128
    selecting which words to teach, 99–100
    semantic feature analysis and, 110–111
    sight, 15
    specialized, 41
    strategies for a comprehensive program, 107–127
    study plan, 423–424
    tiers of, 98–99
    troubleshooting, 124–128
    types of, 98–99
    using context clues, 111–114
    using resources, 114–118
    websites, 384
    writing/speaking and, 120–121
Voice projection, 287
Voice, writing and, 195–196
Vygotsky, L. S., 3–4, 161

WebQuests, 325
Webs, 240, 241
Websites:
    content area literacy and, 226
    criteria for evaluating, 247–248

evaluation form, 387
family literacy, 358
informational text and, 212
literacy, 383–384
oral history and, 271
Weschler Intelligence Scale, 42
Westfield Elementary, 333–334
Wheelchairs, 307
White Barn Press, 189
Woodcock Reading Mastery Test, 34
Word:
  choice, 196–197
  consciousness, 104
  families, 15
  knowledge, levels of, 100–101
  map, 311
  study, *see* Word study
  walls, 77–81, 423
Word Family Tree, activity, 79–81
Word lists, 41
  academic, 99
  assessing knowledge of, 59–60
Word meanings:
  graphically illustrating, 106–107
  grouping similar, 105–106
  polysemantic, 118–120
  resources for, 114–118
  teaching, 104–107
Word parts, 103
Word Power Challenge, 104
Word processing, 192
  spelling and, 200–201
Word study, 6, 70–92, 397–402
  activities, 75,78, 79–80
  advanced instruction in, 72–81
  defined, 70
Words:
  base, 72
  basic, 98
  compound, 74
  concrete vs. abstract, 105
  creating new, 81
  denotation/connotation of, 100
  encountered while reading, 125
  etymology of, 76–77
  general-utility, 98, 99
  important, 232
  key, 243
  knowledge of, 97–98 (*see also* Vocabulary)
  learning new, 101, 122–124 (*see also* Vocabulary)

lists, *see* Word lists
low-utility, 98, 99
mispronunciation of, 91–92
multisyllabic, 72–73
origins, *see* Etymology
parts of, 70, 73–74, 75
per minute, reading rate and, 82
play, 81
polysemantic, 118–120
portmanteau, 81
relating new to known, 107–111
structural analysis of, *see* Morphology
study, *see* Word study
tired, 122
transfer, 76
unknown meanings of, 74
using context to identify, 111–114
vocabulary, *see* Vocabulary
walls, *see* Word walls
Work Sampling Online, 38
Work schedules, parental, 359
Workforce Investment Act, 357
Working portfolio, 62–63
Workshop, 222
World War II, 225
World When You Were Born, activity, 337–338
World Wide Web, 260 (*see also* Internet)
Wrap-up, after reading, 141–142
Writers, developing motivated, 322–326
Writer's talk, 191
Writer's workshop, 17, 183, 184, 189–192, 201, 374
Writing:
  6 + 1 Trait approach, 193–199 (*see also* Six +1 Trait approach)
  and reading connections, 179–218
  as part of literacy, 3
  assessment, 408–410
  authentic purposes, 202
  automaticity and, 200–201
  brainstorming about, 184
  center, 372
  clustering and, 184–186
  composing/drafting, 186
  conclusions, 210
  conferences and, 190–191
  confidence and, 213
  conventions, 198
  critical thinking and, 182
  defined, 4
  dialogue journals and, 201–203

editing and, 188
establishing lifelong habits of, 326–332
everyday examples of, 321–322
expository, 232–245
extended narrative text, 204–206
feedback on, 183
fluency, 197–198, 199–201
folder, 59
for authentic reasons, 328
frame, 244–245
how instruction has changed, 181–182
ideas and, 213
in the content areas, 232–245
incentives to, 325–326
informational text, 209–212
inspiring students and, 201–212
lack of interest in, 215
new vocabulary and, 120–121
novelettes, 204–206
organization and, 195
peer editing and, 187
planning/prewriting, 183–186
poetry, 206–208
portfolios, 41
practice of new skills in, 17
probable passages, 244–245
process, 182–189
proposition/support, 235–237
publishing, 189
reading and, 9–10
response guide and, 186–187
scaffolds and, 240, 243–245
scheduling time for, 183
self-assessment checklist, 408–409
sharing, 181, 192
speed and, 199–200
story starters and, 214
summaries, 233–235
technology and, 192
tools, 198
transitions and, 195, 210
voice and, 195–196
word choice and, 196–197
Writer's workshop and, *see* Writer's workshop

Yen-Shen, target organizer for, 166
Young adult literature, references, 379–382
Young World, 189